DOCTRINES

AND

DISCIPLINE

OF

The Methodist Church

1960

[
THE METHODIST EPISCOPAL CHURCH
THE METHODIST EPISCOPAL CHURCH, SOUTH
THE METHODIST PROTESTANT CHURCH
]

THE METHODIST PUBLISHING HOUSE
NASHVILLE, TENNESSEE

The book editor, the secretary of the General Conference, and the publisher of The Methodist Church shall be charged with editing the Discipline. The editors in the exercise of their judgment shall have authority to make such changes in phraseology as may be necessary to harmonize legislation without changing its substance.

The editors are instructed to bring the 1960 Discipline to publication as soon as possible after the adjournment of the General Conference, and to that end they are authorized to omit the Directory. Instead, The Methodist Publishing House is authorized to compile and publish as a separate booklet a Methodist Directory containing the names and addresses of the bishops and other general officers of the church, and of the members and staff of all the general boards and other agencies. This Directory shall be published as soon as possible after the organization meetings of the boards, and a revised edition may be issued later in the quadrennium if desirable.

So that the 1960 Discipline may be published promptly, the editors are further authorized to omit Part IX, containing the Annual Conference boundaries, which under ¶ 29 of the Constitution must be determined, not by the General Conference, but by the several Jurisdictional and Central Conferences. For convenience in reference, however, they are requested to include in the Appendix unofficial condensed descriptions of the territories of the Annual Conferences as they exist at the time of adjournment of the General Conference; provided that these descriptions shall be introduced by a statement explaining that they are presented for information only, and that the official delineations of the boundaries are recorded in the archives of the respective Jurisdictional and Central Conferences.

—*Journal of the General Conference*, 1960

EMORY STEVENS BUCKE
BOOK EDITOR

LEON T. MOORE
SECRETARY OF THE GENERAL CONFERENCE

LOVICK PIERCE
PUBLISHER

GORDON B. DUNCAN
ASSISTANT BOOK EDITOR

PRINTED IN THE UNITED STATES OF AMERICA

Contents

Note: The basic unit in the Discipline is the paragraph (¶), rather than page, chapter, section, etc. The paragraphs are numbered in order through the entire volume, but with many numbers skipped, in order to allow for future enactments, and to fit into the following plan:

If a paragraph is divided into numbered parts, each is called a subsection (§). When a paragraph number is followed by a subsection number, the symbol § is replaced by a period, so that the two numbers appear in the form of a single decimal number. For example, ¶ 4.3 means paragraph 4, subsection 3.

CONTENTS

CONTENTS

CONTENTS

Episcopal Greetings

THE METHODIST DISCIPLINE is a growth rather than a purposive creation. The founders of Methodism did not work with a set plan, as to details. They dealt with conditions as these arose. The "class meeting," a distinctive feature of the movement, began as an instrument for the collection of funds. It soon revealed its fitness for religious nurture and took that work as its chief aim. The use of laymen as preachers came at first against Wesley's will, but it was continued because it seemed to be the one effective way of dealing with actual situations. Open-air preaching, always admitted as a "cross" by Mr. Wesley, came partly because the churches were closed to Methodist preachers, and partly because the people who most needed to be helped would not come to regular services in the sanctuaries. Even conferences gained their origin from the actual need of bringing workers together for consultation and inspiration.

This process of growth showed itself clearly as the church increased. Conference work was carried on by the asking of what were called "Minute Questions." These were not perfunctory and artificial. They dealt with the effective ways of presenting the deeper phases and duties of religious experience. As new forms of work were developed, new questions were added to the conference list.

In such a process of adjustment, the DISCIPLINE became a record of the successive stages of spiritual insight attained by Methodists under the grace of Christ. We have therefore expected that the DISCIPLINE would be administered, not merely as a legal document, but as a revelation of the Holy Spirit working in and through our people. We reverently insist that a fundamental aim of Methodism is to make her organization an instrument for the development of spiritual life. We do not regard the machinery as sacred in life itself, but we do regard as very sacred the souls for whom the church lives and works.

1

We do now express the faith and hope that the prayerful observance of the spiritual intent of the DISCIPLINE may be to the people called Methodists a veritable means of grace.

For this reason we wish that this publication might be found in every Methodist home, and the more so because it contains the Articles of Religion which are held more or less by all the Reformed churches of the world. Thus we remain your very affectionate brethren and pastors, who earnestly commend you to Christ.

THE COUNCIL OF BISHOPS
GERALD H. KENNEDY
President

PAUL E. MARTIN
Vice-President

ROY H. SHORT
Secretary

HISTORICAL STATEMENT

HISTORICAL STATEMENT

THE Methodist Church is a church of Christ in which
"the pure Word of God is preached, and the Sacraments
duly administered." This church is a great Protestant
body, though it did not come directly out of the Reformation but had its origin within the Church of England. Its
founder was John Wesley, a clergyman of that church, as
was his father before him. His mother, Susanna Wesley,
was a woman of zeal, devotion, and strength of character
who was perhaps the greatest single human influence in
Wesley's life.

Nurtured in this devout home, educated at Oxford University, the young John Wesley, like a second Paul,
sought in vain for religious satisfaction by the strict
observance of the rules of religion and the ordinances
of the church. The turning point in his life came when,
at a prayer meeting in Aldersgate Street, London, on
May 24, 1738, he learned what Paul had discovered, that
it is not by rules and laws, nor by our own efforts at
self-perfection, but by faith in God's mercy as it comes
to us in Christ, that man may enter upon life and peace.

The gospel which Wesley thus found for himself he began to proclaim to others, first to companions who sought
his counsel, including his brother Charles, then in widen-
ing circles that took him throughout the British Isles.
His message had a double emphasis, which has remained
with Methodism to this day. First was the gospel of God's
grace, offered to all men and equal to every human need.
Second was the moral ideal which this gospel presents to
men. The Bible, he declared, knows no salvation which
is not salvation from sin. He called men to holiness of
life, and this holiness, he insisted, is "social holiness,"
the love and service of their fellow men. Methodism meant
"Christianity in earnest." The General Rules which are
still found in our Discipline are the directions which
Wesley gave to his followers to enable them to test the

3

sincerity of their purpose and to guide them in this life.

Wesley did not plan to found a new church. In his work he simply followed, like Paul, the clear call of God, first to preach the gospel to the needy who were not being reached by the Established Church and its clergy, second to take care of those who were won to the Christian life. Step by step he was led on until Methodism became a great and transforming movement in the life of England. He gathered his people in groups, in classes and societies. He appointed leaders. He found men who were ready to carry the gospel to the masses, speaking on the streets, in the open fields, and in private homes. These men were not ordained ministers but lay preachers, or "local preachers," as they were called. He appointed these men, assigned them to various fields of labor, and supervised their work. Once a year he called them together for a conference, just as Methodist preachers meet in their Annual Conference sessions today.

Wesley thus united in extraordinary fashion three notable activities, in all of which he excelled. One was evangelism; "The world is my parish," he declared. His preachers went to the people; they did not wait for the people to come to them, and he himself knew the highways and byways of England as did no other man of his day. The second was organization and administration, by which he conserved the fruits of this preaching and extended its influence. The third was his appreciation of education and his use of the printed page. He made the press a servant of the Church and was the father of the mass circulation of inexpensive books, pamphlets, and periodicals.

From England Methodism spread to Ireland and then to America. In 1766 Philip Embury, a lay preacher from Ireland, began to preach in the city of New York. At about the same time Robert Strawbridge, another lay preacher from Ireland, settled in Frederick County, Maryland, and began the work there. In 1769 Wesley sent Richard Boardman and Joseph Pilmore to America, and two years later Francis Asbury, who became the great leader of American Methodism.

Methodism was especially adapted to American life.

4

These itinerant preachers served the people under conditions where a settled ministry was not feasible. They sought out the scattered homes, followed the tide of migration as it moved west, preached the gospel, organized societies, established "preaching places," and formed these into "circuits." Thus by the close of the American Revolution the Methodists numbered some fifteen thousand members and eighty preachers.

In the beginning Wesley had thought of his fellows not as constituting a church but simply as forming so many societies. The preachers were not ordained, and the members were supposed to receive the Sacraments in the Anglican Church. But the Anglican clergy in America were few and far between. The Revolution had severed America from England, and Methodism to all intents and purposes had become an independent church. Wesley responded to appeals for help from America by asking the Bishop of London to ordain some of his preachers. Failing in this, he himself ordained two men and set aside Dr. Thomas Coke, who was a presbyter of the Church of England, to be a superintendent, "to preside over the flock of Christ" in America. Coke was directed to ordain Francis Asbury as a second superintendent.

At the Christmas Conference, which met in Baltimore December 24, 1784, some sixty preachers, with Dr. Coke and his companions, organized the Methodist Episcopal Church in America. Wesley had sent over *The Sunday Service*, a simplified form of the English Book of Common Prayer, with the Articles of Religion reduced in number. This book they adopted, adding to the articles one which recognized the independence of the new nation.

Our present Articles of Religion come from this book and unite us with the historic faith of Christendom. Our Ritual, too, though it has been modified, has this as its source. However, the forms for public worship taken from the Book of Common Prayer were not adapted to the freer religious life of American Methodism and never entered into common use. Instead, Methodism created a book of its own, its Discipline. This contains today the Articles of Religion, Wesley's General Rules, the Ritual and other forms of worship, and a large section which deals with the ministry, the various church organizations, and the rules governing the life and work of the church.

In the history of Methodism two notable divisions occurred. In 1828 a group of earnest and godly persons, largely moved by an insistence on lay representation, separated and became the Methodist Protestant Church. In 1844 there was another division, the cause being construed by some as the question of slavery, by others as a constitutional issue over the powers of the General Conference versus the episcopacy. After years of negotiation a Plan of Union was agreed upon; and on May 10, 1939, The Methodist Episcopal Church, The Methodist Episcopal Church, South, and The Methodist Protestant Church united to form The Methodist Church.

The Methodist Church believes today, as Methodism has from the first, that the only infallible proof of a true church of Christ is its ability to seek and to save the lost, to disseminate the Pentecostal spirit and life, to spread scriptural holiness, and to transform all peoples and nations through the gospel of Christ. The sole object of the rules, regulations, and usages of The Methodist Church is to aid the church in fulfilling its divine commission. United Methodism thanks God for the new life and strength which have come with reunion, while realizing the new obligations which this brings. At the same time it rejoices in the fact that it is a part of the one Church of our Lord and shares in a common task. Its spirit is still expressed in Wesley's words: "I desire to have a league, offensive and defensive, with every soldier of Christ. We have not only one faith, one hope, one Lord, but are directly engaged in one warfare."

THE DECLARATION OF UNION

WHEREAS, The Methodist Episcopal Church, The Methodist Episcopal Church, South, and The Methodist Protestant Church did through their respective General Conferences appoint Commissions on Interdenominational Relations and Church Union; and

WHEREAS. These Commissions acting jointly did produce, propose, and present to the three Churches a Plan of Union; and

WHEREAS, These three Churches, each acting separately for and in its own behalf, did by more than the constitutional majorities endorse and adopt this Plan of Union, in accord with their respective constitutions and disciplines, and did effect the full consummation of union in accordance with the Plan of Union; and

WHEREAS, These three Churches in adopting this Plan of Union did authorize and provide for a Uniting Conference with certain powers and duties as therein set forth; and

WHEREAS, The Uniting Conference duly authorized and legally chosen in accordance with the Plan of Union is now in session in the city of Kansas City, Missouri:

Now, THEREFORE, We, the members of the Uniting Comference, the legal and authorized representatives of The Methodist Episcopal Church, The Methodist Episcopal Church, South, and The Methodist Protestant Church, in session here assembled on this the 10th day of May, 1939, do solemnly in the presence of God and before all the world make and publish the following Declarations of fact and principle:

I

The Methodist Episcopal Church, The Methodist Episcopal Church, South, and The Methodist Protestant Church are and shall be one United Church.

II

The Plan of Union as adopted is and shall be the constitution of this United Church, and of its three constituent bodies.

III

The Methodist Episcopal Church, The Methodist Episcopal Church, South, and The Methodist Protestant Church had their common origin in the organization of the Methodist Episcopal Church in America in 1784, A.D., and have ever held, adhered to and preserved a common belief, spirit and purpose, as expressed in their common Articles of Religion.

IV

The Methodist Episcopal Church, The Methodist Episcopal Church, South, and The Methodist Protestant Church, in adopting the name "The Methodist Church" for the United Church, do not and will not surrender any right, interest or title in and to these respective names, which, by long and honored use and association, have become dear to the ministry and membership of the three uniting Churches and have become enshrined in their history and records.

V

The Methodist Church is the ecclesiastical and lawful successor of the three uniting Churches, in and through which the three Churches as one United Church shall continue to live and have their existence, continue their institutions, and hold and enjoy their property, exercise and perform their several trusts under and in accord with the Plan of Union and Discipline of the United Church; and such trusts or corporate bodies as exist in the constituent Churches shall be continued as long as legally necessary.

VI

To The Methodist Church thus established we do now solemnly declare our allegiance, and upon all its life and service we do reverently invoke the blessing of Almighty God. Amen.

[Unanimously adopted by the Uniting Conference, Kansas City, Missouri, May 10, 1939.]

PART I

THE CONSTITUTION
THE ARTICLES OF RELIGION
THE GENERAL RULES

THE CONSTITUTION OF THE
METHODIST CHURCH

Plan of Union of The Methodist Episcopal Church, The Methodist Episcopal Church, South, The Methodist Protestant Church

TRANSMITTAL

WE, the Commissions on Interdenominational Relations and Church Union of The Methodist Episcopal Church, The Methodist Episcopal Church, South, and The Methodist Protestant Church, holding that these churches are essentially one in origin, in belief, in spirit, and in purpose, and desiring that this essential unity be made actual in organization and administration in the United States of America and throughout the world, do hereby propose and transmit to our respective General Conferences the following Plan of Union and recommend to the three churches its adoption by the processes which they respectively require.

DIVISION ONE

¶ 1. *Article I. Declaration of Union.*—The Methodist Episcopal Church, The Methodist Episcopal Church, South, and The Methodist Protestant Church shall be united in one church.

¶ 2. *Art. II. Name.*—The name of the church shall be The Methodist Church.

¶ **3.** *Art. III. Articles of Religion.*—The Articles of Religion shall be those historically held in common by the three uniting churches. (*See* ¶¶ 61-85.)

DIVISION TWO. CONFERENCES

¶ **4.** 1. There shall be a General Conference for the entire church with such powers, duties, and privileges as are hereinafter set forth.[1]

2. There shall be Jurisdictional Conferences for the church in the United States of America, with such powers, duties, and privileges as are hereinafter set forth.[2]

3. There shall be Central Conferences for the church outside the United States of America, with such powers, duties, and privileges as are hereinafter set forth.

4. There shall be Annual Conferences as the fundamental bodies in the church, with such powers, duties, and privileges as are hereinafter set forth.

Section I. General Conference

¶ **5.** *Article I.*—The General Conference shall be composed of not less than 600 nor more than 800 delegates, one half of whom shall be ministers and one half lay members, to be elected by the Annual Conferences.[3]

¶ **6.** *Art. II.*—The General Conference shall meet in the month of April or May once in four years, beginning with such year and at such place as shall be fixed by the Uniting Conference, and thereafter at such time and in such place as shall be determined by the General Conference or by its duly authorized committees.

¶ **7.** *Art. III.*—The General Conference shall fix the ratio of representation in the General, Jurisdictional, and Central Conferences from the Annual Conferences, with the total ministerial membership in the Annual Conference as a basis; provided that each Annual Conference shall be entitled to at least one ministerial and one lay delegate in the General Conference and also in the Jurisdictional or Central Conference.[4]

---

[1] *See* Judicial Council Decision 7.
[2] *See* Judicial Council Decision 128.
[3] *See* Amendment XI (¶ 45).
[4] *See* Amendment VII (¶ 45).

¶ 8. *Art. IV.*—The General Conference shall have full legislative power over all matters distinctively connectional,[5] and in the exercise of said powers shall have authority as follows:

1. To define and fix the conditions, privileges, and duties of church membership.

2. To define and fix the qualifications and duties of elders, deacons, supply preachers, local preachers, exhorters,[6] and deaconesses.[7]

3. To define and fix the powers and duties of Annual Conferences, Mission Conferences,[8] and Missions, and of District, Quarterly, and Church Conferences.[9]

4. To provide for the organization, promotion, and administration of the work of the church outside the United States of America.[10]

5. To define and fix the powers, duties, and privileges of the episcopacy, to adopt a plan for the support of the bishops, to provide a uniform rule for their superannuation, and to provide for the discontinuance of a bishop because of inefficiency or unacceptability.[11]

6. To provide and revise the Hymnal and Ritual of the church and to regulate all matters relating to the form and mode of worship, subject to the limitations of the first Restrictive Rule.

7. To provide a judicial system and a method of judicial procedure for the church, except as herein otherwise prescribed.

8. To initiate and to direct all connectional enterprises of the church, such as publishing, evangelistic, educational, missionary, and benevolent, and to provide boards for their promotion and administration.

9. To determine and provide for raising the funds

[5] *See* Judicial Council Decisions 7, 83-85, 96, 147.

[6] Exhorters in the legislative parts of the Discipline are called lay speakers.

[7] *See* Judicial Council Decisions 7, 58, 155.

[8] Mission Conferences beginning with Amendment IV of the Constitution and in the legislative parts of the Discipline are called Provisional Annual Conferences.

[9] *See* Judicial Council Decisions 7, 74, 105, 145, 146.

[10] *See* Judicial Council Decision 84.

[11] *See* Judicial Council Decisions 35, 68, 83, 84.

necessary to carry on the connectional work of the church.[12]

10. To fix a uniform basis upon which bishops shall be elected by the Jurisdictional Conferences and to determine the number of bishops that may be elected by Central Conferences.[13]

11. To select its presiding officers from the bishops, through a committee; provided that the bishops shall select from their own number the president of the opening session.[14]

12. To change the number and the boundaries of Jurisdictional Conferences upon the consent of a majority of the Annual Conferences in each Jurisdictional Conference involved.[15]

13. To establish such commissions for the general work of the church as may be deemed advisable.

14. To enact such other legislation as may be necessary, subject to the limitations and restrictions of the Constitution of the church.[16]

Sec. II. Restrictive Rules

¶ **9.** 1. The General Conference shall not revoke, alter, or change our Articles of Religion, or establish any new standards or rules of doctrine contrary to our present existing and established standards of doctrine.[17]

2. The General Conference shall not change or alter any part or rule of our government so as to do away episcopacy or destroy the plan of our itinerant general superintendency.

3. The General Conference shall not do away the privileges of our ministers or preachers of trial by a committee and of an appeal; neither shall it do away the privileges of our members of trial before the church, or by a committee, and of an appeal.

4. The General Conference shall not revoke or change the General Rules of the United Societies.

---

[12] *See* Judicial Council Decision 30.
[13] *See* Judicial Council Decision 84.
[14] *See* Judicial Council Decision 126.
[15] *See* Judicial Council Decisions 32, 56.
[16] *See* Judicial Council Decisions 58, 84, 147.
[17] *See* Judicial Council Decision 86, 142.

5. The General Conference shall not appropriate the produce of the Publishing House, the Book Concern, or the Chartered Fund to any purpose other than for the benefit of the traveling, supernumerary, superannuated, and worn-out preachers, their wives, widows, and children.

Sec. III. Amendments

¶ **10.** 1. Amendments to the Constitution may originate in either the General Conference or an Annual Conference.

2. Amendments to the Constitution shall be made upon a two-thirds majority of the General Conference present and voting and a two-thirds majority of all the members of the several Annual Conferences present and voting, except in the case of the first Restrictive Rule, which shall require a three-fourths majority of all the members of the Annual Conferences present and voting. The vote, after being completed, shall be canvassed by the Council of Bishops, and the amendment voted upon shall become effective upon their announcement of its having received the required majority.[18]

3. A Jurisdictional Conference may by a majority vote propose changes in the Constitution of the church, and such proposed changes shall be submitted to the next General Conference. If the General Conference adopt the measure by a two-thirds vote, it shall be submitted to the Annual Conferences according to the provision for amendments.

Sec. IV. Jurisdictional Conferences

¶ **11.** *Article I.*—The Jurisdictional Conferences shall be composed of as many representatives from the Annual Conferences as shall be determined by a uniform basis established by the General Conference.

¶ **12.** *Art. II.*—All Jurisdictional Conferences shall have the same status and the same privileges of action within the limits fixed by the Constitution. The ratio of representation of the Annual Conferences in the General Con-

---

[18] *See* Judicial Council Decisions 132, 154.

ference shall be the same for all Jurisdictional Conferences.

¶ **13.** *Art. III.*—The General Conference shall fix the basis of representation in the Jurisdictional Conferences; provided that the Jurisdictional Conferences shall be composed of an equal number of ministerial and lay delegates, the ministerial to be elected by the ministerial members of the Annual Conferences and the lay delegates by the lay members.[19]

¶ **14.** *Art. IV.*—Each Jurisdictional Conference shall meet within the twelve months succeeding the meeting of the General Conference at such time and place as shall have been determined by the preceding Jurisdictional Conference, or by its properly constituted committee. The first meeting of each Jurisdictional Conference after the General Conference shall be called by the Council of Bishops at a date fixed by them and at a place selected by a committee on entertainment appointed by them.

¶ **15.** *Art. V.*—The Jurisdictional Conferences shall have the following powers and duties and such others as may be conferred by the General Conference:[20]

1. To promote the evangelistic, educational, missionary, and benevolent interests of the church, and to provide for interests and institutions within their boundaries.[21]

2. To elect bishops and to co-operate in carrying out such plans for their support as may be determined by the General Conference.

3. To establish and constitute Jurisdictional Conference boards as auxiliary to the general boards of the church as the need may appear, and to choose their representatives on the general boards in such manner as the General Conference may determine.

4. To determine the boundaries of their Annual Conferences; provided that there shall be no Annual Conference with a membership of fewer than fifty ministers in full connection, except by the consent of the General Conference.[22]

---

[19] *See* Amendment IV (¶ 45), adopted following Judicial Council Decision 5.
[20] *See* Judicial Council Decision 84.
[21] *See* Judicial Council Decision 67.
[22] *See* Judicial Council Decisions 28, 85.

5. To make rules and regulations for the administration of the work of the church within the jurisdiction, subject to such powers as have been or shall be vested in the General Conference.[23]

6. To appoint a Committee on Appeals to hear and determine the appeal of a traveling preacher of that jurisdiction from the decision of a trial committee.

Sec. V. Central Conferences

¶ **16.** *Article I.*—There shall be Central Conferences for the work of the church outside the United States of America with such duties, powers, and privileges as are hereinafter set forth. The number and boundaries of the Central Conferences shall be determined by the Uniting Conference. Subsequently the General Conference shall have authority to change the number and boundaries of Central Conferences. The Central Conferences shall have the duties, powers, and privileges hereinafter set forth.

¶ **17.** *Art. II.*—The Central Conferences shall be composed of as many delegates as shall be determined by a basis established by the General Conference. The delegates shall be ministerial and lay in equal numbers, the ministerial delegates to be elected by the ministerial members and lay delegates to be elected by the lay members of the Annual Conferences.[24]

¶ **18.** *Art. III.*—The Central Conferences shall meet within the year succeeding the meeting of the General Conference at such times and places as shall have been determined by the preceding respective Central Conferences or by commissions appointed by them, or by the General Conference. The date and place of the first meeting succeeding the first General Conference shall be fixed by the bishops of the respective Central Conferences, or in such manner as shall be determined by the General Conference.

¶ **19.** *Art. IV.*—The Central Conferences shall have the following powers and duties and such others as may be conferred by the General Conference:

1. To promote the evangelistic, educational, missionary,

[23] *See* Judicial Council Decision 67.
[24] *See* Amendment II (¶ 45), adopted following Judicial Council Decision 6.

and benevolent interests and institutions of the church within their own boundaries.

2. To elect the bishops for the respective Central Conferences in number as may be determined from time to time, upon a basis fixed by the General Conference, and to co-operate in carrying out such plans for the support of their bishops as may be determined by the General Conference.

3. To establish and constitute such Central Conference boards as may be required and to elect their administrative officers.[25]

4. To determine the boundaries of the Annual Conferences within their respective areas.

5. To make such rules and regulations for the administration of the work within their boundaries as the conditions in the respective areas may require, subject to the powers that have been or shall be vested in the General Conference.[26]

6. To appoint a Committee on Appeals to hear and determine the appeal of a traveling preacher of that Central Conference from the decision of a Committee on Trial.

Sec. VI. Episcopal Administration in Central Conferences

¶ **20.** 1. The bishops of the Central Conferences shall be elected and inducted into office by their respective Central Conferences.

2. The bishops of the Central Conferences shall have membership in the Council of Bishops with vote limited to matters relating to their respective Central Conferences.[27]

3. The bishops of the Central Conferences shall preside in the sessions of their respective Central Conferences.

4. The bishops of each Central Conference shall arrange the plan of episcopal visitation within their Central Conference.

5. The Council of Bishops may assign one of their number to visit any Central Conference. When so assigned the bishop shall be recognized as an accredited representative of the general church; and when requested by a majority

---

[25] *See* Judicial Council Decision 69.
[26] *See* Judicial Council Decisions 69, 121, 142, 147, 155.
[27] *See* Amendment VI (¶ 45).

of the bishops of a Central Conference may exercise therein the functions of the episcopacy.

Sec. VII. Annual Conferences

¶ 21. *Article I.*—The Annual Conference shall be composed of all the traveling preachers in full connection with it, together with a lay member elected by each pastoral charge. The lay members shall be at least twenty-one (21) years of age and shall have been for the four years next preceding their election members of one of the constituent churches forming this union, or of The Methodist Church.[28]

¶ 22. *Art. II.*—The Annual Conference is the basic body in the church, and as such shall have reserved to it the right to vote on all constitutional amendments, on the election of ministerial and lay delegates to the General and the Jurisdictional or Central Conferences, on all matters relating to the character and conference relations of its ministerial members, and on the ordination of ministers, and such other rights as have not been delegated to the General Conference under the Constitution, with the exception that the lay members may not vote on matters of ordination, character, and conference relations of ministers. It shall discharge such duties and exercise such powers as the General Conference under the Constitution may determine.[29]

¶ 23. *Art. III.*—The Annual Conference shall elect ministerial and lay delegates to the General Conference and to its Jurisdictional or Central Conference in the manner provided in this section, Articles IV and V, at the session preceding the General Conference. The persons first elected up to the number determined by the ratio for representation in the General Conference shall be representatives in that body. Additional delegates shall be elected to complete the number determined by the ratio for representation in the Jurisdictional or Central Conference, who, together with those first elected as above, shall be delegates in the Jurisdictional or Central Con-

[28] *See* Amendment X (¶ 45) ; *see also* Judicial Council Decisions 24, 36, 42, 87, 112, 113, 129, 131, 136, 159.
[29] *See* Judicial Council Decisions 5-7, 38, 42, 43, 67, 72, 74-76, 78, 79, 98, 105. 115, 119, 123, 129, 132, 136.

ference. The additional delegates to the Jurisdictional or Central Conference shall in the order of their election be the reserve delegates to the General Conference. The Annual Conference shall also elect reserve ministerial and lay delegates to the Jurisdictional or Central Conference as it may deem desirable.[30]

¶ 24. *Art. IV.*—The ministerial delegates to the General Conference and to the Jurisdictional or Central Conference shall be elected by the ministerial members of the Annual Conference, provided that such delegates shall have been traveling preachers in the constituent churches forming this union, or in The Methodist Church, for at least four years next preceding their election and are in full connection with the Annual Conference[31] electing them when elected and at the time of holding the General and Jurisdictional or Central Conferences.

¶ 25. *Art. V.*—The lay delegates to the General Conference and to the Jurisdictional or Central Conference shall be elected by the lay members of the Annual Conference; provided that such delegates be at least twenty-five (25) years of age and shall have been members of the constituent churches forming this union, or of The Methodist Church, for at least four years next preceding their election, and are members thereof within the Annual Conference electing them at the time of holding the General and Jurisdictional or Central Conferences.[32]

Sec. VIII. Boundaries

¶ 26. *Article I.*—The Methodist Church in the United States of America shall have Jurisdictional Conferences made up as follows:

Northeastern—Maine, New Hampshire, Vermont, Massachusetts, Rhode Island, New York, Connecticut, Pennsylvania, New Jersey, Maryland, West Virginia, Delaware, District of Columbia, Puerto Rico.

Southeastern—Virginia, North Carolina, South Caro-

---

[30] *See* Judicial Council Decision 76.
[31] *See* Amendment VIII (¶ 45) ; *see also* Judicial Council Decisions 1, 76, 88, 124, 162.
[32] *See* Amendment III (¶ 45) ; *see also* Judicial Council Decisions 76, 124, 174.

lina, Georgia, Florida, Alabama, Tennessee, Kentucky, Mississippi, Cuba.

Central—The Negro Annual Conferences, the Negro Mission Conferences and Missions in the United States of America.[33]

North Central—Ohio, Indiana, Illinois, Michigan, Wisconsin, Minnesota, Iowa, North Dakota, South Dakota.

South Central—Missouri, Arkansas, Louisiana, Nebraska, Kansas, Oklahoma, Texas, New Mexico.

Western—Washington, Idaho, Oregon, California, Nevada, Utah, Arizona, Montana, Wyoming, Colorado, Alaska, Hawaiian Islands.[34]

¶ 27. *Art. II.*—The work of the church outside the United States of America may be formed into Central Conferences, the number and boundaries of which shall be determined by the Uniting Conference, the General Conference having authority subsequently to make changes in the number and boundaries.

¶ 28. *Art. III.*—Changes in the number, names, and boundaries of the Jurisdictional Conferences may be effected by the General Conference upon the consent of a majority of the Annual Conferences of each of the Jurisdictional Conferences involved.[35]

¶ 29. *Art. IV.*—Changes in the number, names, and boundaries of the Annual Conferences may be effected by the Jurisdictional Conferences in the United States of America and by the Central Conferences outside the United States of America, according to the provisions under the respective powers of the Jurisdictional and the Central Conferences.[36]

Sec. IX. District Conferences

¶ 30. *Article I.*—There may be organized in an Annual Conference, District Conferences composed of such persons and invested with such powers as the General Conference may determine.

---

[33] *See* Judicial Council Decision 128.
[34] *See* Amendment IX (¶ 45).
[35] *See* Amendment IX (¶ 45) ; *see also* Judicial Council Decisions 55, 56, 85.
[36] *See* Judicial Council Decisions 28, 85.

Sec. X. Quarterly Conferences

¶ **31.** *Article I.*—There shall be organized in each pastoral charge a Quarterly Conference composed of such persons and invested with such powers as the General Conference shall provide.[37]

¶ **32.** *Art. II.*—*Election of Church Officers.*—Unless the General Conference shall order otherwise, the officers of the church or churches constituting a pastoral charge shall be elected by the Quarterly Conference or by the members of said church or churches at a meeting called for that purpose, as may be arranged by the Quarterly Conference, unless the election is otherwise required by local church charters or state laws.

Sec. XI. Church Conferences

¶ **33.** There may be a Church Conference in each church, having such powers and duties as the General Conference may prescribe.

DIVISION THREE. EPISCOPACY

¶ **34.** *Article I.*—There shall be an episcopacy in The Methodist Church of like plan, powers, privileges, and duties as now exist in The Methodist Episcopal Church and The Methodist Episcopal Church, South.[38]

¶ **35.** *Art. II.*—The bishops shall be elected by the respective Jurisdictional and Central Conferences and ordained or consecrated in the historic manner of episcopal Methodism at such time and place as may be fixed by the General Conference.[39]

¶ **36.** *Art. III.*—There shall be a Council of Bishops composed of all the bishops of all the Jurisdictional and Central Conferences. The council shall meet at least once a year and plan for the general oversight and promotion of the temporal and spiritual interests of the entire church and for carrying into effect the rules, regulations, and responsibilities prescribed and enjoined by

---

[37] *See* Judicial Council Decision 93.
[38] *See* Judicial Council Decisions 4, 57, 127.
[39] *See* Amendment I (¶ 45) ; *see also* Judicial Council Decision 21.

the General Conference, and in accord with the provisions set forth in this Plan of Union.

¶ 37. *Art. IV.*—The bishops of each Jurisdictional and Central Conference shall arrange the plan of episcopal supervision of the Annual Conferences, Mission Conferences, and Missions within their respective territories.[40]

¶ 38. *Art. V.*—The bishops shall have residential and presidential supervision in the Jurisdictional Conferences in which they are elected. A bishop may be transferred from one jurisdiction to another jurisdiction for presidential and residential supervision by the Council of Bishops when such transfer is requested by the Jurisdictional Conference to which such proposed transfer is to be made.

A bishop may be assigned by the Council of Bishops for presidential service or other temporary service, not to exceed a year, in another jurisdiction than that which elected him, provided request is made by a majority of the bishops in the jurisdiction of the proposed service.

In the case of an emergency in any jurisdiction through the death or disability of its bishops the Council of Bishops may assign one or more bishops from other jurisdictions to the work of the said jurisdiction with the consent of a majority of the bishops of that jurisdiction.[41]

¶ 39. *Art. VI.*—The bishops of The Methodist Episcopal Church and of The Methodist Episcopal Church, South, at the time union is consummated, shall be bishops of The Methodist Church.[42]

The delegates from the Annual Conferences of The Methodist Protestant Church in the Uniting Conference shall have the authority and power to elect to the office of bishop two ministers of their church who, upon ordination or consecration at the Uniting Conference by the bishops of the other two churches, shall become effective bishops of The Methodist Church.

The effective bishops shall be assigned for service to the various Jurisdictional Conferences by the Uniting Conference.

---

[40] *See* Judicial Council Decisions 48. 57.
[41] *See* Judicial Council Decision 84.
[42] *See* Judicial Council Decision 84.

¶ **40.** *Art. VII.*—A bishop presiding over a District, Annual, or Jurisdictional Conference shall decide all questions of law coming before him in the regular business of a session; provided that such questions be presented in writing and that his decisions be recorded in the journal of the conference.

Such an episcopal decision shall not be authoritative except for the pending case until it shall have been passed upon by the Judicial Council. Each bishop shall report in writing annually all his decisions of law, with a syllabus of the same, to the Judicial Council, which shall affirm, modify, or reverse them.[43]

¶ **41.** *Art. VIII.*—The bishops of the several Jurisdictional Conferences shall preside in the sessions of their respective Jurisdictional Conferences.

DIVISION FOUR. THE JUDICIARY

¶ **42.** *Article I.*—There shall be a Judicial Council. The General Conference shall determine the number and qualifications of its members, their terms of office, and the method of election and the filling of vacancies.[44]

¶ **43.** *Art. II.*—The Judicial Council shall have authority:

1. To determine the constitutionality of any act of the General Conference upon an appeal of a majority of the Council of Bishops, or one fifth of the members of the General Conference; and to determine the constitutionality of any act of a Jurisdictional or Central Conference upon an appeal of a majority of the bishops of that Jurisdictional or Central Conference or upon the appeal of one fifth of the members of that Jurisdictional or Central Conference.

2. To hear and determine any appeal from a bishop's decision on a question of law made in the Annual or District Conference when said appeal has been made by one fifth of that conference present and voting.[45]

3. To pass upon decisions of law made by bishops in Annual or District Conferences.[46]

---

[43] *See* Judicial Council Decision 64.
[44] *See* Judicial Council Decision 62.
[45] *See* Judicial Council Decisions 66, 153.
[46] *See* Judicial Council Decision 153.

4. To hear and determine the legality of any action taken therein by any General Conference board or Jurisdictional or Central Conference board or body, upon appeal by one third of the members thereof, or upon request of the Council of Bishops or a majority of the bishops of a Jurisdictional or a Central Conference.

5. To have such other duties and powers as may be conferred upon it by the General Conference.

6. To provide its own methods of organization and procedure.

¶ **44.** *Art. III.*—All decisions of the Judicial Council shall be final. However, when the Judicial Council shall declare any act of the General Conference unconstitutional, that decision shall be reported back to that General Conference immediately.

¶ **45.** DIVISION FIVE. AMENDMENTS

[The date following each amendment is the date on which it became effective by announcement of the Council of Bishops (*see* ¶ 10.2).—EDITORS.]

Amendment I

Amend [Division Three, Article II (¶ 35), line 3] . . . *by striking out the words* ordained or, *so that the new paragraph will read:*

Art. II.—The bishops shall be elected by the respective Jurisdictional and Central Conferences and consecrated in the historic manner of episcopal Methodism at such time and place as may be fixed by the General Conference.[47] (December 15, 1943.)

Amendment II

Amend . . . *by adding* . . . *the words* or Mission Conferences, *so that* [Division Two, Section V, Article II (¶ 17)] *shall read:*

Art. II.—The Central Conferences shall be composed of as many delegates as shall be determined by a basis established by the General Conference. The delegates shall be ministerial and lay in equal numbers, the ministerial delegates to be elected by the ministerial members and the lay delegates to be elected by the lay members of the

---

[47] *See* Judicial Council Decision 21.

Annual Conferences or Mission Conferences.[48] (December 15, 1943.)

Amendment III

[Amend] *by changing the age to* twenty-one (21) *instead of* twenty-five (25) *as it now is* [in Division Two, Section VII, Article V (¶ 25), line 5], *so that the paragraph will read as follows:*

Art. V.—The lay delegates to the General Conference and to the Jurisdictional or Central Conferences shall be elected by the lay members of the Annual Conference; provided that such delegates be at least twenty-one (21) years of age and shall have been members of the constituent churches forming this union, or of The Methodist Church, for at least four years next preceding their election, and are members thereof within the Annual Conference electing them at the time of holding the General and Jurisdictional or Central Conferences.[49] (January 10, 1952.)

Amendment IV

[In Division Two, Section IV, Article III (¶ 13), line 6], *after the words* Annual Conferences *add the words* and the Provisional Annual Conferences. *The paragraph as amended will read:*

Art. III.—The General Conference shall fix the basis of representation in the Jurisdictional Conferences; provided that the Jurisdictional Conferences shall be composed of an equal number of ministerial and lay delegates, the ministerial to be elected by the ministerial members of the Annual Conferences and the Provisional Annual Conferences and the lay delegates by the lay members. (January 10, 1952.)

Amendment V

[This amendment was adopted by the General Conference of 1948 but failed of ratification by the requisite number of members of the several Annual Conferences. The same revision was adopted by the General Conference of 1952 as Amendment VI and, as indicated below, was ratified.—EDITORS.]

---

[48] Mission Conferences in later amendments to the Constitution and in the legislative parts of the Discipline are called Provisional Annual Conferences.

[49] *See* Judicial Council Decisions 76, 124, 174.

Amendment VI

Amend [Division Two, Section VI (¶ 20.2)] *by deleting the words* limited to matter relating to their respective Central Conferences, . . . *so that the paragraph when amended will read as follows:*

2. The bishops of the Central Conferences shall have membership in the Council of Bishops with vote.[50] (April 19, 1956.)

Amendment VII

Amend [Division Two, Section I, Article III (¶ 7)] . . . *so that the paragraph as amended will read as follows:*

Art. III.—The General Conference shall fix the ratio of representation in the General, Jurisdictional, and Central Conferences from the Annual Conferences and the Provisional Annual Conferences, with the total ministerial membership in the Annual Conference or the Provisional Annual Conference as a basis; provided that each Annual Conference or Provisional Annual Conference, except for the Provisional Annual Conferences of a Central Conference or a Provisional Central Conference, shall be entitled to at least one ministerial and one lay delegate in the General Conference and also in the Jurisdictional or Central Conference.[51] (April 19, 1956.)

Amendment VIII

Amend [Division Two, Section VII, Article IV (¶ 24)] . . . *so that the paragraph when amended will read as follows:*

Art. IV.—The ministerial delegates to the General Conference and to the Jurisdictional or Central Conference shall be elected by the ministerial members of the Annual Conference or Provisional Annual Conference; provided that such delegates shall have been traveling preachers in the constituent churches forming this union, or in The Methodist Church, for at least four years next preceding their election and are in full connection with the Annual Conference or Provisional Annual Conference electing them when elected and at the time of holding the General and Jurisdictional or Central Conferences.[52] (April 19, 1956.)

---

[50] *See* Judicial Council Decision 164.
[51] *See* Judicial Council Decision 154.
[52] *See* Judicial Council Decisions 1, 76, 88, 124, 154, 162.

Amendment IX

The Constitution of The Methodist Church shall be amended by adding a new article, to be known as Article V of Division Two, Section VIII, and to read as follows:

Art. V.—1. A local church may be transferred from one Annual Conference to another in which it is geographically located upon approval by a two-thirds vote of those present and voting in each of the following:

a) The Quarterly Conference of the local church.

b) A Church Conference of the local church.

c) Each of the two Annual Conferences involved.

The vote shall be certified by the secretaries of the specified conferences to the bishops having supervision of the Annual Conferences involved, and upon their announcement of the required majorities the transfer shall immediately be effective.

2. An Annual Conference may be transferred from one jurisdiction to another upon approval by:

a) The Annual Conference desiring transfer, by a two-thirds majority of those present and voting. The secretary of the conference shall certify the vote to the College of Bishops of the jurisdiction of which the conference has been a part.

b) The remainder of the jurisdiction from which transfer is to be made, by a two-thirds majority of the total of Annual Conference members present and voting. The vote shall be taken in the other Annual Conferences of the jurisdiction and certified by their secretaries to the College of Bishops, which shall determine whether two thirds of the total vote in the jurisdiction is favorable.

c) The jurisdiction to which transfer is to be made, by a two-thirds majority of the total of Annual Conference members present and voting. The vote shall be taken in the various Annual Conferences of the jurisdiction and certified by their secretaries to the College of Bishops, which shall determine whether two thirds of the total vote in the jurisdiction is favorable.

Upon announcement by the two Colleges of Bishops of the required majorities the transfer shall immediately be effective.

3. The vote on approval of transfer under either § 1 or

§ 2 shall be taken by each Annual Conference at its first session after the matter is submitted to it.

4. Transfers under the provisions of this article shall not be governed or restricted by other provisions of this Constitution relating to changes of boundaries of conferences.

5. Whenever twenty-five per cent of the local-church membership of the Central Jurisdiction have been transferred by this process to another jurisdiction or jurisdictions, the bishop of the area from which the largest number have been transferred shall be transferred to the jurisdiction which has received the largest number by such transfer, and the representation of the Central Jurisdiction on the boards and agencies of the church shall thereafter be proportionately reduced.

Article I of Division Two, Section VIII [¶ 26] of the Constitution of The Methodist Church shall be amended by adding at the end thereof a new paragraph as follows:

Abolition of the Central Jurisdiction.—The Central Jurisdiction shall be abolished when all of the Annual Conferences now comprising it have been transferred to other jurisdictions in accordance with the voluntary procedure of Article V of this section. Each remaining bishop of the Central Jurisdiction shall thereupon be transferred to the jurisdiction to which the majority of the membership of his area have been transferred, and the Central Jurisdiction shall then be dissolved.[53] (April 8, 1958.)

Amendment X

[Division Two, Section VII, Article I (¶ 21)] *shall be amended by inserting . . . after the first sentence* [a sentence as below, so that the paragraph] *as amended, will read:*

Article I.—The Annual Conference shall be composed of all the traveling preachers in full connection with it, together with a lay member elected by each pastoral charge. Each pastoral charge served by more than one minister in full connection shall be entitled to two lay members. The lay members shall be at least twenty-one

---

[53] *See* Judicial Council Decision 169.

(21) years of age and shall have been for the four years next preceding their election members of one of the constituent churches forming this union, or of The Methodist Church.[54] (April 8, 1958.)

Amendment XI

Amend [Division Two, Section I, Article I (¶ 5)] *by deleting the numeral* 800 *in line two, and substituting therefor the numeral* 900, *so that* [the paragraph], *as amended, will read:*

Article I.—The General Conference shall be composed of not less than 600 or more than 900 delegates, one half of whom shall be ministers and one half lay members, to be elected by the Annual Conferences. (April 8, 1958.)

¶ 46.   AMENDMENT PENDING RATIFICATION

[The General Conference of 1960 approved and referred to the members of the several Annual Conferences for ratification a constitutional amendment, to be known as Amendment XII, consisting of the six parts listed below.—EDITORS.]

1. [Division Two, Section I, Article I (¶ 5)] *shall be amended to read as follows:*

Article I.—The General Conference shall be composed of not fewer than 900 nor more than 1400 delegates, one half of whom shall be ministers and one half lay members, to be elected by the Annual Conferences.

2. [Division Two, Section IV, Article IV (¶ 14)] *shall be amended to read as follows:*

Art. IV.—Each Jurisdictional Conference shall convene (a) at the time and place of the General Conference, or (b) not more than sixty days prior to the date of the General Conference at such time and place as the preceding session of the Jurisdictional Conference, or its delegated committee, by a two-thirds vote, may determine.

3. [Division Two, Section V, Article III (¶ 18)] *shall be amended to read as follows:*

Art. III.—Each Central Conference shall meet within one year preceding or one year following the meeting of the General Conference at such times and places as shall have been determined by the preceding respective Central Conferences or by commissions appointed by them.

---

[54] *See* Judicial Council Decisions 24, 36, 42, 87, 112, 113, 129, 131, 136, 159.

4. [Division Two, Section VII, Article III (¶ 23)] *shall be amended to read as follows:*

Art. III.—The Annual Conference shall elect ministerial and lay delegates to the General Conference and to its Jurisdictional or Central Conference in the manner provided in this section, Articles IV and V, at the session preceding the Jurisdictional Conference. The persons elected, up to the number determined by the ratio of representation in the General Conference, shall be representatives in that body, and also in the Jurisdictional or Central Conference; provided that Annual and Provisional Annual Conferences of a Central Conference shall elect delegates for such Central Conference to complete the number determined by the General Conference for representation in the Central Conference. The Annual Conference shall also elect reserve ministerial and lay delegates to serve both at the General Conference and the Jurisdictional or Central Conference as it may deem desirable.

5. [Division Three, Article II (¶ 35)] *shall be amended to read as follows:*

Art. II.—The bishops shall be elected by the respective Jurisdictional and Central Conferences, and consecrated in the historic manner of episcopal Methodism. The bishops elected by the respective Jurisdictional Conferences shall be consecrated at the General Conference which meets concurrently or immediately following. The bishops elected by Central Conferences shall be consecrated at the electing Central Conference or at the next succeeding General Conference, as the Central Conference may determine.

6. [Division Three, Article V (¶ 38)] *shall be amended to read as follows:*

Art. V.—There shall be a General Conference Committee on Episcopacy composed of all the members of the Committees on Episcopacy of the several Jurisdictional Conferences, which:

1. May make proposals involving the transfer of bishops from one jurisdiction to another where said transfer (*a*) has been approved by a two-thirds majority of the members of the Committee on Episcopacy of the jurisdiction to which the transfer is to be made; (*b*) has not been disapproved by a two-thirds majority of the members of the Committee on Episcopacy of the jurisdiction out of which the transfer is to be made; and (*c*) has been consented to by the bishop involved.

2. Shall receive and accept the assignment of bishops as

made or finally approved by the several Jurisdictional Conferences after all transfers, if any, have been acted upon.

3. Shall announce to the General Conference the assignments made, or finally approved, by the respective Jurisdictional Conferences of all bishops, and no official announcement of the assignments of bishops shall be made prior thereto.

The General Conference upon receiving the announcement of its Committee on Episcopacy may not change the assignments within a jurisdiction. The General Conference upon receiving the announcement of its Committee on Episcopacy may not change transfers as announced by its committee or initiate proposals for transfer except (*a*) by a majority vote of the General Conference, and (*b*) by a majority vote of the Jurisdictional Conferences which are involved in the proposed transfer.

A bishop may be assigned by the Council of Bishops for presidential service or other temporary service, not to exceed a year, in another jurisdiction than that which elected him, provided request is made by a majority of the bishops in the jurisdiction of the proposed service.

In the case of an emergency in any jurisdiction through the death or disability of its bishops the Council of Bishops may assign one or more bishops from other jurisdictions to the work of the said jurisdiction with the consent of a majority of the bishops of that jurisdiction.

THE ARTICLES OF RELIGION

I. *Of Faith in the Holy Trinity*

¶ **61.** There is but one living and true God, everlasting, without body or parts, of infinite power, wisdom, and goodness; the maker and preserver of all things, visible and invisible. And in unity of this Godhead there are three persons, of one substance, power, and eternity—the Father, the Son, and the Holy Ghost.

II. *Of the Word, or Son of God, who was made very Man*

¶ **62.** The Son, who is the Word of the Father, the very and eternal God, of one substance with the Father, took man's nature in the womb of the blessed Virgin; so that two whole and perfect natures, that is to say, the Godhead and Manhood, were joined together in one person, never to be divided; whereof is one Christ, very God and very Man, who truly suffered, was crucified, dead, and buried, to reconcile his Father to us, and to be a sacrifice, not only for original guilt, but also for the actual sins of man.

III. *Of the Resurrection of Christ*

¶ **63.** Christ did truly rise again from the dead, and took again his body, with all things appertaining to the perfection of man's nature, wherewith he ascended into heaven, and there sitteth until he return to judge all men at the last day.

IV. *Of the Holy Ghost*

¶ **64.** The Holy Ghost, proceeding from the Father and the Son, is of one substance, majesty, and glory, with the Father and the Son, very and eternal God.

V. *Of the Sufficiency of the Holy Scriptures for Salvation*

¶ **65.** The Holy Scriptures contain all things necessary to salvation; so that whatsoever is not read therein, nor may be proved thereby, is not to be required of any man that it should be believed as an article of faith, or be thought requisite or necessary to salvation. In the name of the Holy Scriptures we do understand those canonical books of the Old and New Testament of whose authority was never any doubt in the Church. The names of the canonical books are:

Genesis, Exodus, Leviticus, Numbers, Deuteronomy, Joshua, Judges, Ruth, The First Book of Samuel, The Second Book of Samuel, The First Book of Kings, The Second Book of Kings, The First Book of Chronicles, The Second Book of Chronicles, The Book of Ezra, The Book of Nehemiah, The Book of Esther, The Book of Job, The Psalms, The Proverbs, Ecclesiastes or the Preacher, Cantica or Song of Solomon, Four Prophets the Greater, Twelve Prophets the Less.

All the books of the New Testament, as they are commonly received, we do receive and account canonical.

VI. *Of the Old Testament*

¶ **66.** The Old Testament is not contrary to the New; for both in the Old and New Testament everlasting life is offered to mankind by Christ, who is the only Mediator between God and man, being both God and Man. Wherefore they are not to be heard who feign that the old fathers did look only for transitory promises. Although the law given from God by Moses as touching ceremonies and rites doth not bind Christians, nor ought the civil precepts thereof of necessity be received in any commonwealth; yet notwithstanding, no Christian whatsoever is free from the obedience of the commandments which are called moral.

VII. *Of Original or Birth Sin*

¶ 67. Original sin standeth not in the following of Adam (as the Pelagians do vainly talk), but it is the corruption of the nature of every man, that naturally is engendered of the offspring of Adam, whereby man is very far gone from original righteousness, and of his own nature inclined to evil, and that continually.

VIII. *Of Free Will*

¶ 68. The condition of man after the fall of Adam is such that he cannot turn and prepare himself, by his own natural strength and works, to faith, and calling upon God; wherefore we have no power to do good works, pleasant and acceptable to God, without the grace of God by Christ preventing us, that we may have a good will, and working with us, when we have that good will.

IX. *Of the Justification of Man*

¶ 69. We are accounted righteous before God only for the merit of our Lord and Saviour Jesus Christ, by faith, and not for our own works or deservings. Wherefore, that we are justified by faith only is a most wholesome doctrine, and very full of comfort.

X. *Of Good Works*

¶ 70. Although good works, which are the fruits of faith, and follow after justification, cannot put away our sins, and endure the severity of God's judgment; yet are they pleasing and acceptable to God in Christ, and spring out of a true and lively faith, insomuch that by them a lively faith may be as evidently known as a tree is discerned by its fruit.

XI. *Of Works of Supererogation*

¶ 71. Voluntary works—besides, over and above God's commandments—which are called works of supererogation, cannot be taught without arrogancy and impiety. For by them men do declare that they do not only render unto God as much as they are bound to do, but that they do more for his sake than of bounden duty is required; whereas Christ saith plainly: When ye have done all that is commanded of you, say, We are unprofitable servants.

XII. *Of Sin after Justification*

¶ 72. Not every sin willingly committed after justification is the sin against the Holy Spirit, and unpardonable. Wherefore, the grant of repentance is not to be denied to such as fall into sin after justification: after we have received the Holy Spirit, we may depart from grace given, and fall into sin, and, by the grace of God, rise again and amend our lives. And therefore they are to be condemned who say they can no more sin as long as they live here; or deny the place of forgiveness to such as truly repent.

XIII. *Of the Church*

¶ 73. The visible Church of Christ is a congregation of faithful men in which the pure Word of God is preached, and the Sacraments duly administered according to Christ's ordinance, in all those things that of necessity are requisite to the same.

XIV. *Of Purgatory*

¶ 74. The Romish doctrine concerning purgatory, pardon, worshiping, and adoration, as well of images as of relics, and also invocation of saints, is a fond thing, vainly invented, and grounded upon no warrant of Scripture, but repugnant to the Word of God.

XV. *Of Speaking in the Congregation in such a Tongue as the People Understand*

¶ 75. It is a thing plainly repugnant to the Word of

God, and the custom of the primitive Church, to have public prayer in the church, or to administer the Sacrament_, in a tongue not understood by the people.

XVI. *Of the Sacraments*

¶ 76. Sacraments ordained of Christ are not only badges or tokens of Christian men's profession, but rather they are certain signs of grace, and God's good will toward us, by which he doth work invisibly in us, and doth not only quicken, but also strengthen and confirm, our faith in him.

There are two Sacraments ordained of Christ our Lord in the Gospel; that is to say, Baptism and the Supper of the Lord.

Those five commonly called sacraments, that is to say, confirmation, penance, orders, matrimony, and extreme unction, are not to be counted for Sacraments of the Gospel; being such as have partly grown out of the *corrupt* following of the apostles, and partly are states of life allowed in the Scriptures, but yet have not the like nature of Baptism and the Lord's Supper, because they have not any visible sign or ceremony ordained of God.

The Sacraments were not ordained of Christ to be gazed upon, or to be carried about; but that we should duly use them. And in such only as worthily receive the same they have a wholesome effect or operation; but they that receive them unworthily, purchase to themselves condemnation, as St. Paul saith, I Cor. 11:29.

XVII. *Of Baptism*

¶ 77. Baptism is not only a sign of profession and mark of difference whereby Christians are distinguished from others that are not baptized; but it is also a sign of regeneration or the new birth. The baptism of young children is to be retained in the church.[55]

XVIII. *Of the Lord's Supper*

¶ 78. The Supper of the Lord is not only a sign of the

---

[55] *See* Judicial Decision 142.

love that Christians ought to have among themselves one to another, but rather is a sacrament of our redemption by Christ's death; insomuch that, to such as rightly, worthily, and with faith receive the same, the bread which we break is a partaking of the body of Christ; and likewise the cup of blessing is a partaking of the blood of Christ.

Transubstantiation, or the change of the substance of bread and wine in the Supper of our Lord, cannot be proved by Holy Writ, but is repugnant to the plain words of Scripture, overthroweth the nature of a sacrament, and hath given occasion to many superstitions.

The body of Christ is given, taken, and eaten in the Supper, only after a heavenly and spiritual manner. And the means whereby the body of Christ is received and eaten in the Supper is faith.

The Sacrament of the Lord's Supper was not by Christ's ordinance reserved, carried about, lifted up, or worshiped.

XIX. *Of Both Kinds*

¶ 79. The cup of the Lord is not to be denied to the lay people; for both the parts of the Lord's Supper, by Christ's ordinance and commandment, ought to be administered to all Christians alike.

XX. *Of the One Oblation of Christ, finished upon the Cross*

¶ 80. The offering of Christ, once made, is that perfect redemption, propitiation, and satisfaction for all the sins of the whole world, both original and actual; and there is none other satisfaction for sin but that alone. Wherefore the sacrifice of masses, in the which it is commonly said that the priest doth offer Christ for the quick and the dead, to have remission of pain or guilt, is a blasphemous fable and dangerous deceit.

XXI. *Of the Marriage of Ministers*

¶ 81. The ministers of Christ are not commanded by God's law either to vow the estate of single life, or to abstain from marriage; therefore it is lawful for them, as for all other Christians, to marry at their own discretion, as they shall judge the same to serve best to godliness.

XXII. *Of the Rites and Ceremonies of Churches*

¶ **82.** It is not necessary that rites and ceremonies should in all places be the same, or exactly alike; for they have been always different, and may be changed according to the diversity of countries, times, and men's manners, so that nothing be ordained against God's Word. Whosoever, through his private judgment, willingly and purposely doth openly break the rites and ceremonies of the church to which he belongeth, which are not repugnant to the Word of God, and are ordained and approved by common authority, ought to be rebuked openly (that others may fear to do the like), as one that offendeth against the common order of the church, and woundeth the consciences of weak brethren.

Every particular church may ordain, change, or abolish rites and ceremonies, so that all things may be done to edification.

XXIII. *Of the Rulers of the United States of America*

¶ **83.** The President, the Congress, the general assemblies, the governers, and the councils of state *as the delegates of the people*, are the rulers of the United States of America, according to the division of power made to them by the Constitution of the United States and by the constitutions of their respective states. And the said states are a sovereign and independent nation, and ought not to be subject to any foreign jurisdiction.

XXIV. *Of Christian Men's Goods*

¶ **84.** The riches and goods of Christians are not common, as touching the right, title, and possession of the same, as some do falsely boast. Notwithstanding, every man ought, of such things as he possesseth, liberally to give alms to the poor, according to his ability.

XXV. *Of a Christian Man's Oath*

¶ **85.** As we confess that vain and rash swearing is

forbidden Christian men by our Lord Jesus Christ and James his apostle; so we judge that the Christian religion doth not prohibit, but that a man may swear when the magistrate requireth, in a cause of faith and charity, so it be done according to the prophet's teaching, in justice, judgment, and truth.

The following Article from the Methodist Protestant Discipline is placed here by the Uniting Conference. It was not one of the Articles of Religion voted upon by the three churches.

Of Sanctification

¶ 86. Sanctification is that renewal of our fallen nature by the Holy Ghost, received through faith in Jesus Christ, whose blood of atonement cleanseth from all sin; whereby we are not only delivered from the guilt of sin, but are washed from its pollution, saved from its power, and are enabled, through grace, to love God with all our hearts and to walk in his holy commandments blameless.

The following provision was adopted by the Uniting Conference. This statement seeks to interpret to our churches in foreign lands Article XXIII of the Articles of Religion. It is a legislative enactment but is not a part of the Constitution. (See Judicial Council Decision 41.)

Of the Duty of Christians to the Civil Authority

¶ 87. It is the duty of all Christians, and especially of all Christian ministers, to observe and obey the laws and commands of the governing or supreme authority of the country of which they are citizens or subjects or in which they reside, and to use all laudable means to encourage and enjoin obedience to the powers that be.

THE GENERAL RULES

The Nature, Design, and General Rules of Our United Societies

¶ 91. In the latter end of the year 1739 eight or ten persons who appeared to be deeply convicted of sin, and earnestly groaning for redemption, came to Mr. Wesley in London. They desired, as did two or three more the next day, that he would spend some time with them in prayer, and advise them how to flee from the wrath to come, which they saw continually hanging over their heads. That he might have more time for this great work, he appointed a day when they might all come together, which from thenceforward they did every week, namely, on Thursday in the evening. To these, and as many more as desired to join with them (for their number increased daily), he gave those advices from time to time which he judged most needful for them, and they always concluded their meeting with prayer suited to their several necessities.

¶ **92.** This was the rise of the **United Society,** first in Europe, and then in America. Such a society is no other than "*a company of men having the form and seeking the power of godliness, united in order to pray together, to receive the word of exhortation, and to watch over one another in love, that they may help each other to work out their salvation.*"

¶ **93.** That it may the more easily be discerned whether they are indeed working out their own salvation, each society is divided into smaller companies, called **classes,** according to their respective places of abode. There are about twelve persons in a class, one of whom is styled the **leader.** It is his duty,

1. To see each person in his class once a week at least, in order: (1) to inquire how his soul prospers; (2) to advise, reprove, comfort, or exhort, as occasion may require; (3) to receive what he is willing to give toward the relief of the preachers, church, and poor.

2. To meet the ministers and the stewards of the society once a week, in order: (1) to inform the minister of any that are sick, or of any that walk disorderly and will not be reproved; (2) to pay the stewards what he has received of his class in the week preceding.

¶ **94.** There is only one condition previously required of those who desire admission into these societies—"a desire to flee from the wrath to come, and to be saved from their sins." But wherever this is really fixed in the soul it will be shown by its fruits.

¶ **95.** It is therefore expected of all who continue therein that they shall continue to evidence their desire of salvation,

First: By doing no harm, by avoiding evil of every kind, especially that which is most generally practiced, such as:

The taking of the name of God in vain.

The profaning the day of the Lord, either by doing ordinary work therein or by buying or selling.

Drunkenness, buying or selling spirituous liquors, or drinking them, unless in cases of extreme necessity.

Slaveholding; buying or selling slaves.

Fighting, quarreling, brawling, brother going to law with brother; returning evil for evil, or railing for railing; the using of many words in buying or selling.

The buying or selling goods that have not paid the duty.

The giving or taking of things on usury—that is, unlawful interest.

Uncharitable or unprofitable conversation; particularly speaking evil of magistrates or ministers.

Doing to others as we would not they should do unto us.

Doing what we know is not for the glory of God, as:

The putting on of gold and costly apparel.

The taking of such diversions as cannot be used in the name of the Lord Jesus.

The singing those songs, or reading those books, which do not tend to the knowledge or love of God.

Softness and needless self-indulgence.

Laying up treasure upon earth.

Borrowing without a probability of paying; or taking up goods without a probability of paying for them.

¶ **96.** It is expected of all who continue in these societies that they shall continue to evidence their desire of salvation,

Second: By doing good; by being in every kind merciful after their power; as they have opportunity, doing good of every possible sort, and, as far as possible, to all men:

To their bodies, of the ability which God giveth, by giving food to the hungry, by clothing the naked, by visiting or helping them that are sick or in prison;

To their souls, by instructing, reproving, or exhorting all we have any intercourse with; trampling under foot that enthusiastic doctrine, that "we are not to do good unless *our hearts be free to it.*"

By doing good, especially to them that are of the household of faith or groaning so to be; employing them preferably to others; buying one of another; helping each other in business; and so much the more because the world will love its own and them *only.*

By all possible diligence and frugality, that the gospel be not blamed.

By running with patience the race which is set before them, denying themselves, and taking up their cross daily; submitting to bear the reproach of Christ, to be as the filth and offscouring of the world; and looking that men should say all manner of evil of them *falsely,* for the Lord's sake.

¶ **97.** It is expected of all who desire to continue in these societies that they shall continue to evidence their desire of salvation,

Third: By attending upon all the ordinances of God; such are:

The public worship of God.

The ministry of the Word, either read or expounded.

The Supper of the Lord.

Family and private prayer.

Searching the Scriptures.

Fasting or abstinence.

¶ **98.** These are the General Rules of our societies; all of which we are taught of God to observe, even in his written Word, which is the only rule, and the sufficient rule, both of our faith and practice. And all these we know his Spirit writes on truly awakened hearts. If there be any among us who observes them not, who habitually breaks any of them, let it be known unto them who watch over that soul as they who must give an account. We will admonish him of the error of his ways. We will bear with him for a season. But, if then he repent not, he hath no more place among us. We have delivered our own souls.

PART II

THE LOCAL CHURCH

CHAPTER I

THE PASTORAL CHARGE

¶ **101.** The visible Church of Christ is a congregation of faithful men in which the pure Word of God is preached, and the Sacraments duly administered according to Christ's ordinance, in all those things that of necessity are requisite to the same. (Article of Religion XIII, ¶ 73.)

¶ **102.** The **local church** is a connectional society of persons who have professed their faith in Christ, have been baptized, have assumed the vows of membership in The Methodist Church, and are associated in fellowship as a local Methodist church in order that they may hear the Word of God, receive the Sacraments, and carry forward the work which Christ has committed to his Church. Such a society of believers, being within The Methodist Church and subject to its Discipline, is also an inherent part of the Church Universal, which is composed of all who accept Jesus Christ as Lord and Saviour, and which in the Apostles' Creed we declare to be the holy catholic Church.[1]

¶ **103.** In order that each local church may be an effective connectional unit in The Methodist Church, it shall be the duty of all district superintendents and pastors to organize and administer the charges and churches committed to their care in accordance with the plan hereinafter set forth.

¶ **104.** A **pastoral charge** shall consist of one or more churches which are organized under, and subject to, the

---

[1] *See* Judicial Council Decision 86.

41

Discipline of The Methodist Church, with a single pastoral-charge Quarterly Conference, and to which a minister is or may be duly appointed or appointable as preacher in charge. A pastoral charge of two or more churches is a **circuit.**

CHAPTER II

CHURCH MEMBERSHIP

¶ 105. The membership of a local Methodist church shall consist of all persons who have been received into its fellowship on profession of their faith (¶¶ 107-9), by transfer from some other church (¶¶ 110-11), or by restoration (¶¶ 124, 127.5, 977), and whose membership has not been terminated by death, transfer (¶¶ 121-22), withdrawal (¶¶ 123-24), expulsion (¶ 974), or action of the Quarterly Conference (¶ 127.5). A member of a local Methodist church is a member of The Methodist Church.

SECTION I. **Admission into the Church**

¶ 107. All persons seeking to be saved from their sins and sincerely desiring to be Christian in faith and practice are proper candidates for membership in The Methodist Church. When such persons offer themselves for membership, it shall be the duty of the pastor, or of proper persons appointed by him, to instruct them in the meaning of the Christian faith and the history, organization, and teaching of The Methodist Church; to explain to them the baptismal and membership vows (¶¶ 1911-12, 1914-15) ; and to lead them to commit themselves to Jesus Christ as Lord and Saviour. When they shall have given proof of the genuineness of their faith in Christ and of their desire to assume the obligations and become faithful members of The Methodist Church, and after the rite of Baptism has been administered to those who have not been previously baptized, he shall bring them before the congregation, administer the vows (¶¶ 1914-15) and receive them into the fellowship of the Church, and duly enroll them as members.

¶ 108. A duly authorized minister of The Methodist Church while serving as chaplain of any organization, institution, or military unit, or while otherwise present where a local church is not available, may receive a person into the membership of The Methodist Church when such person shall have given proof of the genuineness of his faith in Christ and of his desire to assume the obligations and become a faithful member of the Church. After the vows of membership have been administered (¶¶ 1914-15), such minister shall issue a statement of membership to the local church of the choice of the person concerned, and the pastor thereof on receiving such statement shall duly enroll him as a member.

¶ 109. Any candidate for church membership who for good reason is unable to appear before the congregation may, at the discretion of the pastor and with the approval of the Official Board, be received elsewhere in accordance with the Ritual of The Methodist Church (¶¶ 1914-15); *provided* that in the event of a clear emergency the pastor may receive such person without the approval of the board, in which case he shall report his action to the board at its next meeting.

¶ 110. A person who is a member of The Methodist Church may have his membership transferred from one local church to another by a proper certificate of transfer.

¶ 111. A member in good standing in any Christian denomination who has been baptized and who desires to unite with The Methodist Church may be received into membership by a proper certificate of transfer from his former church, or by his own declaration of Christian faith, and upon affirming his willingness to be loyal to The Methodist Church, and after he and the members of the church have entered into solemn covenant with one another as provided in the Ritual (¶ 1916).

SEC. II.   **Children and the Church**

¶ 114. 1. Because the redeeming love of God, revealed in Jesus Christ, extends to all persons, and because Jesus explicitly included the children in his Kingdom, the pastor of each charge shall earnestly exhort all Christian parents or guardians to present their children to the Lord in Baptism at an early age.[2] Before Baptism is administered, he shall diligently instruct the parents or guardians regarding the meaning of this Sacrament and the vows which they assume. It is expected of parents or guardians who present their children for Baptism that they shall use all diligence in bringing them up in conformity to the Word of God. It is desired that one or both parents or guardians shall be members of a Christian church or that sponsors who are members shall assume the baptismal vows. They shall be admonished of this obligation and earnestly exhorted to faithfulness therein. At the time of Baptism they shall be informed that the church, with its church-school program, will aid them in the Christian nurture of their children.

2. The pastor of the church shall, at the time of administering the Sacrament of Baptism, furnish the parents or guardians of the child who is baptized with a **certificate of Baptism,** which shall also clearly state that the child is now enrolled as a preparatory member in The Methodist Church.

3. The pastor shall keep and transmit to his successor an accurate register of the names of all baptized children in his charge, including both those who have been baptized there and those who have been baptized elsewhere. This shall constitute the preparatory membership roll of the church (¶ 132). It shall give the full name of the child, the date of birth, the date and place of Baptism, and the names of the parents or guardians and their place of residence.

4. All baptized children under the care of a Methodist church shall be retained as preparatory members in the church until this status is terminated by: reception into full membership, after a proper course of training, both in the church school and in the pastor's class (see § 5 below); transfer to another Methodist church by the rules of ¶¶ 119-21; transfer to a church of another evangelical denomination (¶ 122); death; withdrawal (¶¶ 123-24); or transfer to the constituency roll of the church (¶ 132) at the age of sixteen.

---

[2] See Judicial Council Decision 142.

5. It shall be the duty of the pastor, the parents or guardians, and the officers and teachers of the church school to lead the children of the church to an understanding of the Christian faith, to an appreciation of the privileges and obligations of church membership, and to a personal commitment to Jesus Christ as Lord and Saviour, and to guide them in the use of the means of grace in living the Christian life. The pastor shall, at least annually, organize the children who have arrived at the age of decision into classes of instruction for church membership. Whenever children so trained in a course of study approved by The Methodist Church shall give evidence of their own Christian faith and purpose and of understanding the privileges and obligations of church membership, they may be received into full membership in the church according to the provisions of ¶ 107.

SEC. III. **Affiliate Membership**

¶ **116.** A member of The Methodist Church, residing for an extended period in a city or community at a distance from his home church, may on his request be enrolled as an affiliate member of a Methodist church located in the vicinity of his temporary residence (*see* ¶ 1916). His home pastor shall be notified of his affiliate membership. Such membership shall entitle him to the fellowship of that church, to its pastoral care and oversight, and to participation in its activities, including the holding of office, except as otherwise provided (*see* ¶¶ 138, 144, 207), but he shall be counted and reported only as a member of his home church. A member of another denomination may become an affiliate member under the same conditions.

SEC. IV. **Transfer and Termination of Membership**

¶ **118.** Membership in a local church may be terminated by death, transfer (¶¶ 121-22), withdrawal (¶¶ 123-24). expulsion (¶ 974), or action of the Quarterly Conference (¶ 127.5). It shall be the duty of the pastor of the charge or of the membership secretary to keep an accurate record of all terminations of membership and to report to each Quarterly Conference the names of all persons whose membership has been terminated since the conference preceding, in each instance indicating the reason for such termination.

¶ **119.** If a member of a Methodist church shall change his place of residence to another community, so far removed from his home church that he cannot participate regularly in its worship and activity, he shall be encouraged to transfer his membership to a Methodist church in the community of his newly established residence. As soon as his pastor is reliably informed of his change of residence, actual or contemplated, it shall be the pastor's duty and obligation to assist him to establish himself in the fellowship of a church in the community of his future home, and to send to a Methodist pastor in such community, or to the district superintendent, or (if neither is known) to the General Board of Evangelism, a letter of notification, giving the latest known address of the person or persons concerned and requesting local pastoral oversight. The above procedure is based on the recognition that absentee membership is not good for the individual or the church, and that it is essential that we recognize that the care of souls and the building up of the whole church is more important than retaining membership in a particular congregation, whether for sentiment or other reasons.

¶ **120.** When a pastor discovers a member of The Methodist Church residing in his community whose membership is in a church so far removed from his place of residence that he cannot participate regularly in its worship and activity, it shall be his duty and obligation to give pastoral oversight to such person, and to persuade him, if possible, to transfer his membership to a Methodist church in the community where he resides.

¶ **121.** When a pastor shall receive from another pastor of a Methodist church, or from the person concerned, a request for a **certificate of transfer** for a member of his church, he shall issue the same in the following form, and shall make proper entry on his church roll of the transfer of such person, and his membership shall thereby be transferred:

This is to certify that A.B. who resides at _____ *has*

been a member of the _____ Methodist Church in _____. On request his (her) membership is hereby transferred to the _____ Methodist Church in _____, and he (she) is affectionately commended to its care and fellowship. Notice of this certificate of transfer has been sent to the person above named.

_____, Pastor

Date _____   Address _____

The original certificate shall be accompanied by a blank for the acknowledgment of the same in the following form:

The certificate of transfer of the membership of A.B. from the _____ Methodist Church in _____ to the _____ Methodist Church is hereby acknowledged. He (she) has been duly received into our fellowship and recorded as a member in this church.

_____, Pastor

Date _____   Address _____

Notice shall be sent to the person whose membership is thus being transferred in the following form:

This day I have issued a certificate of transfer of your membership to the _____ Methodist Church in _____, commending you to its care and fellowship. In your new relationship we bid you Godspeed.

_____, Pastor

Date _____   Address _____

The certificate of transfer shall be sent directly to the pastor of the Methodist church to which the certificate is issued, or to the district superintendent if there is no pastor. On receipt of such certificate of transfer, the pastor or the district superintendent receiving the same shall record on the membership roll of the church the name of the person thus transferred, and the person shall be a member thereof; whereupon the pastor or district superintendent shall certify to the pastor issuing the certificate that the name appearing on said certificate has been duly entered on the membership roll of the receiving church.

¶ 122. A pastor upon receiving a request from a member of his church to transfer to a church of another denomination, or upon receiving such request from a pastor or duly authorized official of another denomination, shall (with the approval of the member) issue a certificate of transfer and shall properly record the transfer of such person on the membership roll of the local church; and his membership shall thereby be terminated. For the transfer of a member of The Methodist Church to a church of another denomination forms similar to those described in ¶ 121 shall be used, with the substitution of the name of the other denomination for the word "Methodist" in appropriate places in those forms.

¶ 123. If a pastor is informed that a member of his church has, without notice, united with a church of another denomination, he shall make diligent inquiry; and if the report is confirmed, he shall enter "Withdrawn" after the person's name on the membership roll, and shall report the same to the next Quarterly Conference.

¶ 124. If a member proposes to withdraw from The Methodist Church, he shall communicate his purpose in writing to the pastor of the local church in which his membership is held. On receiving such notice of withdrawal, the pastor shall properly record the fact of withdrawal on the membership roll. If requested, the pastor shall give a statement of withdrawal to such member. Such person, on his written request, may be restored to membership on recommendation of the pastor and by vote of the Quarterly Conference.

SEC. V.   Care of Church Members

¶ 126. The local church shall endeavor to enlist each member in activities for spiritual growth and in participation in the services of the church and its organizations. It shall be the duty of the pastor and of the Commission on Membership and Evangelism, by regular visitation, care, and spiritual oversight, to provide necessary activities and opportunities for spiritual growth through individual and family worship, and to aid continually the members to keep their vows to uphold the church by attendance, prayers, gifts, and service.

¶ 127. 1. If a member residing in the community is negligent of his vows or absents himself from the worship of the church, the pastor and the membership secretary shall report his name to the special committee created by the Commission on Membership and Evangelism for reclaiming the negligent (¶ 222.9), which committee shall do all in its power to re-enlist him in the active fellowship of the church. Only at his written request shall his name be removed from the membership roll; *provided,* however, that if after five years of serious cultivation by the committee he continues to absent himself from the worship of the church and refuses to support the church, his name may be removed by the procedure of § 5 below.

2. If a member whose address is known is residing outside the community and is not participating in the worship or activity of the church, the directives of ¶ 119 shall be followed each year until he joins another church or requests in writing that his name be removed from the membership roll; *provided,* however, that if after five years the committee has not been able to relate him to the church at his new place of residence, his name may be removed by the procedure of § 5 below.

3. If the address of a member is no longer known to the pastor, the membership secretary, and the Commission on Membership and Evangelism, they shall make every effort to locate him, including listing his name in the church bulletin, circularizing it throughout the parish, and reading it from the pulpit. If he can be located, the directives of either § 1 or § 2 above shall be followed; but if after two years of such efforts his address is still unknown, his name may be removed from the membership roll by the procedure of § 5 below.

4. The pastor, the membership secretary, and the Commission on Membership and Evangelism shall review annually the membership rolls of the church and shall see that they are complete and accurate. They shall report their findings to the fourth Quarterly Conference, including the names of the members whose addresses are unknown.

5. If the directives of § 1, § 2, or § 3 above have been followed for the specified number of years without suc-

cess, the member's name may be removed from the
membership roll by vote of the Quarterly Conference on
recommendation of the pastor and the Commission on
Membership and Evangelism, each name being considered
individually. On the roll there shall be entered after his
name: "Removed by order of the Quarterly Conference";
and if the action is on the basis of § 3, there shall be
added: "Reason: address unknown." The membership
of the person shall thereby be terminated, and the record
thereof shall be retained; *provided* that at his request he
may be restored to membership by recommendation of the
pastor; and *provided*, further, that should a transfer of
his membership be requested, the pastor may restore him
to membership for this purpose and issue the certificate of
transfer.

¶ 128. If a local church is discontinued, the pastor shall
transfer the members to such other local churches as they
may select. If any do not so seléct, the district superintendent shall select another Methodist church and transfer their membership thereto. (*See* ¶¶ 188, 354.)

Sec. VI.   **Membership Records and Reports**

¶ 130. The pastor shall report to each Quarterly Conference the names of persons received into the membership of the church or churches of the pastoral charge since
the Quarterly Conference preceding, and the names of
persons whose membership in the church or churches of
the pastoral charge has been terminated during the same
period, indicating in the case of each how he was received
or how his membership was terminated.

¶ 131. The basic membership records in each local
church shall consist of: (1) a permanent church register,
and (2) a card index or loose-leaf book.

1. The **permanent church register** shall be a bound
volume of durable material, prepared by The Methodist
Publishing House at a reasonable price, in the form approved by the Council on World Service and Finance
(¶ 1120.6). Space shall be provided for a record of members, showing the full name of each, how each was admitted into the church, the date, by whom received, and
how the membership of each was terminated, with the

date. Space shall also be provided for recording marriages, baptisms, deaths, pastoral terms, and such other matters as may be essential to a permanent record of the church's membership and ministry, as may be determined by the Council on World Service and Finance. The names shall be recorded chronologically as each person is received into the fellowship of that church, and without reference to alphabetical order. Each name shall be numbered, in regular numerical order, and the number of each shall appear on the corresponding card or page in the card index or loose-leaf membership roll. This provision is for the purpose of ensuring facility in locating any name on the permanent church register.

2. The **card index** or **loose-leaf membership record** shall be kept on a form approved by the Council on World Service and Finance (¶ 1120.6), or on other forms that include the items approved by the said council. Space shall be provided for the name and address, how and when received, and such other information as may be determined by the committee. This record of membership shall be filed in alphabetical order, and shall show the number appearing opposite each name on the permanent register so that such name may be promptly located. The pastor shall report annually to the Annual Conference the total membership of his charge as shown on his membership records.

¶ **132.** The pastor or membership secretary shall also keep a **constituency roll** containing the names and addresses of such persons as are not members of the church concerned, including unbaptized children and church-school members not yet members of the church, for whom the local church has pastoral responsibility; and a **preparatory membership roll** containing the names of all baptized children in the church who have not been received into full membership (¶ 114.3). Such other membership rolls, including an **affiliate membership roll** (¶ 116), shall be maintained as may be judged necessary for proper pastoral care and the general work of the church.

¶ **133.** The Quarterly Conference shall elect a **membership secretary,** whose duty shall be, under the direction of the pastor, to keep accurate records of all membership rolls as provided in ¶¶ 131-32.

Chapter III

THE QUARTERLY CONFERENCE

SECTION I.   General Provisions

¶ 137. Within the pastoral charge (¶ 104) the **Quarterly Conference** is the basic body of control uniting it to connectional Methodism, and through the Quarterly Conference the pastoral charge functions in its relationship thereto.[3] The Quarterly Conference shall therefore be organized in every pastoral charge, as provided in the Constitution (¶¶ 31-32). The membership thereof, and its authority, powers, duties, and responsibilities shall be as hereinafter set forth.

¶ 138. The following shall constitute the membership of the Quarterly Conference, in so far as the offices and relationships exist within the pastoral charge.

1. The pastor and the associate pastor or pastors; the retired and supernumerary ministers residing in that place who elect to hold membership therein; *provided* that each such person may be a member of one Quarterly Conference only; traveling preachers who, because they are assigned to special work, have been attached to the Quarterly Conference concerned by appointment of the bishop (¶ 432).

2. The local preachers holding their membership in the pastoral charge, and deaconesses appointed to labor therein or holding their membership in the charge while on leave of absence (¶ 1252.10).

3. The stewards, elective and ex officio (¶¶ 208-9), and the trustees of the church, or churches, in the pastoral charge (¶ 159); *provided*, however, that all lay members of the Quarterly Conference shall be members of a local church within the charge, and all except the president of the Methodist Youth Fellowship or the president of the

___
[3] *See* Judicial Council Decision 130.

Youth Council shall be not less than eighteen years of age.

¶ **139.** The district superintendent or an elder designated by him shall preside. The district superintendent shall fix the time for the meeting of the Quarterly Conference, but the conference may appoint the place; *provided* that should necessity arise the district superintendent and the pastor may change the place of meeting. A special session of the Quarterly Conference may be called by the district superintendent or by the pastor with the written consent of the district superintendent. Quarterly Conferences for two or more pastoral charges may be held at the same time and place, as the district superintendent may determine. (For provisions regarding notice of meetings *see* ¶¶ 154, 168, 170-72, 180.)

¶ **140.** There shall be held for each pastoral charge a first and fourth Quarterly Conference. The second and third Quarterly Conferences may be held at the discretion of the district superintendent. A **recording steward** shall be elected annually, who shall keep an accurate and permanent record of the proceedings and shall be the custodian of all records and reports, and who with the presiding officer shall sign the minutes.

¶ **141.** The Quarterly Conference, after a period of worship, shall transact the business committed to it by the Discipline,[4] following the order indicated on the form bearing the title "Minutes of the Quarterly Conference" approved by the Council on World Service and Finance (¶ 1120.6) and published by The Methodist Publishing House. The district superintendent is required in so far as possible to keep his record of each Quarterly Conference on this official form. It shall also be his duty to see that other Quarterly Conference and church records and reports are written on our approved forms. If the observance of the order of business as provided in these forms seems likely to protract a session beyond a reasonable limit, the presiding officer may, with the approval of the Quarterly Conference, select the more important matters and bring them forward.

---

[4] *See* Judicial Council Decision 102.

¶ **142.** To the Quarterly Conference are committed the following powers and duties:

1. To have general oversight of the Official Board, which is the administrative body of the Quarterly Conference in each local church. (*See* ¶¶ 206-16.)

2. To receive reports from the pastor (¶ 352.22), from church officers, and from the commissions, committees, and societies of the church or churches of the pastoral charge as the Quarterly Conference may require.

3. To elect the officers of the church or churches constituting the pastoral charge (¶ 32), unless otherwise provided, in harmony with the provisions of the Constitution of The Methodist Church, and to constitute the required and optional commissions for each local church (¶¶ 144, 219) and such committees as may be determined by the Quarterly Conference (¶ 145).

4. In cases where the Discipline permits more than one course of action in the administration and work of a pastoral charge, to determine what course shall be taken. (*See* ¶¶ 157, 176, 197-200.)

5. To recommend proper persons for license to preach and for the office of deaconess, and to certify lay speakers (¶ 146).

6. To fix the salary of the pastor or pastors (¶¶ 148, 215.2).

7. To determine annually the amount accepted by the charge for world service and conference benevolences (¶ 147).

8. Such other powers and duties as have been or may be duly committed to it.

Sec. II.   **Elections**

¶ **143.** The Quarterly Conference, preferably the fourth, shall elect annually, to serve from the beginning of the ensuing conference year, the following officers for the pastoral charge on nomination of the Committee on Nominations, or on nomination of the pastor if there is no such committee (¶¶ 142.3, 145.1), unless otherwise provided in the Discipline; or it shall authorize the Annual Church Conference to elect such officers, in which case it shall issue a call for an Annual Church Conference for that purpose (¶¶ 32, 197-200) ; *provided* that in no case shall the privilege of making nominations from the floor be denied.

1. The elective stewards of the church or churches of the pastoral charge (¶¶ 207-11).

2. The church lay leader or leaders (¶ 288).

3. The district steward and reserve district steward; *provided* that the Committee on Nominations or the pastor shall confer with the district superintendent before any nomination is made (¶¶ 796-97, **802**).

4. The lay member of the Annual Conference, annually or quadrennially, as the Annual Conference may direct, and one or more reserve members. If the charge's lay representative to the Annual Conference shall cease to be a member of the charge or shall for any reason fail to serve, a reserve member in the order of his election shall serve in his place.[5]

5. Elective members of the District Conference, if any (¶ 687).

6. The chairmen of the commissions (¶¶ 144, 219).

7. The church-school superintendent or superintendents (¶¶ 246.1, 248.3).

8. The membership cultivation superintendent and division superintendents of each church school, on nomination of its church-school superintendent-elect with the approval of the pastor in consultation with the minister or director of Christian education (¶ 246.1).

9. A director of Christian education, or educational assistant, if desired, on nomination of the pastor with the concurrence of the Commission on Education and the Committee on Pastoral Relations or the Committee on Lay Personnel (¶¶ 246-47). For appointment of a minister to such position *see* ¶ 247.1.

10. A director of music, if desired, on nomination of the pastor with the concurrence of the Music Committee (¶ 278.4), the Commission on Education, and the Committee on Lay Personnel (¶ 247.2). For appointment of a minister of music *see* ¶ 247.2.

11. A church business manager, if desired, on nomina-

---

[5] *See* Judicial Council Decision 109.

tion of the pastor with the concurrence of the Official Board (¶¶ 212.2, 269).

12. The secretary or secretaries of stewardship (¶¶ 262-63).

13. The communion steward or stewards, whose duty it shall be to provide the elements for Holy Communion, under the direction of the pastor, and properly to arrange the communion table.

14. The hospitals and homes steward or stewards, who shall be selected from among the elective stewards of § 1 above (¶ 278.3).

15. The membership secretary or secretaries (¶¶ 133, 221.1).

16. The recording steward (¶ 140).

17. Such other officers of the church, or churches, as may be called for by the General, Jurisdictional, Annual, or District Conference, or as shall be determined by the Quarterly Conference; *provided* that all such shall be in harmony with the provisions of the Discipline.

Note: For the election of trustees *see* ¶¶ 157-61, 183.

¶ **144.** The Quarterly Conference shall elect annually from the membership of the church or churches in the charge, on nomination of the Committee on Nominations, or of the pastor if there is no such committee, the commissions specified in ¶ 219; *provided* that in pastoral charges of more than one church the commissions shall be nominated by the Official Board of each church respectively with the concurrence of the pastor (or, if the board fails to make such nominations, they shall be made by the pastor); or it may authorize the Annual Church Conference to elect the commissions, in which case it shall authorize a call for an Annual Church Conference for that purpose (¶¶ 32, 197-200); *provided* that in no case shall the privilege of making nominations from the floor be denied. Unless otherwise provided (*see* ¶¶ 221, 274) the elected membership of each commission shall be not fewer than three, and as many additional members as the Quarterly Conference may determine; *provided* that in a small church, if the Quarterly Conference finds it necessary, each commission may be composed of the elected chairman (¶ 143.6) and the available ex officio members.

Each commission shall work under the authority and direction of the Official Board, the duties of each being hereinafter defined and set forth (¶¶ 220-76). Such commissions shall be elected at the fourth Quarterly Conference of the pastoral charge, and shall serve from the beginning of the ensuing conference year. Should the Quarterly Conference fail to elect the commissions, the Official Board shall elect them and report to the district superintendent. The chairmen of all commissions shall be nominated and elected in the same manner and at the same time as the members of the commissions (¶ 143.6).

¶ **145.** The Quarterly Conference shall select from the committees designated hereunder such committees as it determines to be necessary to the work of the Quarterly Conference, the same to be nominated by the Committee on Nominations (or by the pastor if there is no such committee), unless otherwise provided in the Discipline, and elected by the Quarterly Conference; or it may authorize the Annual Church Conference to elect such committees together with the commissions as provided in ¶ 144.

1. The **Committee on Nominations,** of which the pastor shall be chairman, which shall nominate to the Quarterly Conference or to the Annual Church Conference such officers and members of Quarterly Conference commissions and committees as the law of the church requires (¶ 144) or as the Quarterly Conference may determine as necessary to its work; *provided* that all the elective members of the Committee on Nominations shall be nominated from the floor.

2. The **Committee on Pastoral Relations,** which shall consist of not fewer than three nor more than nine persons; *provided* that in a circuit each church shall have at least one representative on the committee. The primary function of this committee is to aid the pastor in making his ministry most effective by being available for counsel, keeping him advised concerning conditions within the congregation as they affect relations between pastor and people, and keeping the people informed concerning the nature and function of the pastoral office. When the pastor is to be absent, the commitee shall co-operate with him to secure suitable supply ministers for preaching and other

pastoral service during his absence. Since a responsibility of the committee is to be at all times sensitive to the relationship between pastor and people, should it become evident to the committee that the best interests of the charge and pastor will be served by a change of pastors, the committee shall confer with the pastor and furnish him with this information. The committee shall co-operate with the pastor, the district superintendent, and the bishop in arranging for a change of pastors. The committee shall be amenable to the Quarterly Conference, and its relation to the district superintendent and bishop shall be advisory only.

3. The **Committee on Lay Personnel,** of which the pastor or a person designated by him shall be chairman, which shall be responsible for establishing and maintaining personnel policy for all lay employees, and other employees not within the jurisdiction of the Committee on Pastoral Relations, in keeping with highest standards of Christian practice. This committee shall make provision for range of compensation, working hours, vacation schedule, and sick leave. It shall, after study, recommend other lay employee benefits such as the retirement plan of the Lay Employees Pension Fund (¶ 1658) or other plans in addition to the Federal Social Security provisions; life insurance; health and hospitalization insurance; and disability insurance to compensate employees unable to work because of illness or injury. It should be the aim of this committee to insure for employees of the church rights and considerations at least no less than those representative of enlightened and Christian policies now commonly practiced by secular institutions. This committee shall be amenable to the Quarterly Conference.

4. The **Committee on Records and History,** which shall be responsible for assisting the pastor to see that all church and Quarterly Conference records are kept on the official record blanks provided by The Methodist Publishing House under the direction of the Council on World Service and Finance (¶ 1120.6). This committee shall examine the Quarterly Conference records annually after the fourth Quarterly Conference and shall report the results of its examination to the first Quarterly Conference

of the ensuing year. The committee, with the pastor, shall be responsible for preparing, where it does not already exist, and after the Quarterly Conference has approved such an undertaking, a history of the local church or churches from the time of organization, and provide for preserving the same in permanent form. At the close of each conference year it may add to this record facts concerning important activities and achievements of the church and its organizations. The committee shall see that any and all minute or record books no longer in current use are deposited with the recording steward. The committee shall co-operate with the recording steward in providing a permanent place for the safekeeping of the Quarterly Conference records and all other historical material belonging to the church.

5. The **Committee on Co-operation,** which shall be responsible for co-operation with other churches and constructive agencies and groups in the community; *provided* that in each instance such co-operation shall have been approved by the Quarterly Conference or the Official Board.

6. The **Committee on Policy,** which, after a careful survey of the work and needs of the pastoral charge, shall make recommendations concerning its improvement or extension; *provided* that the pastor shall nominate this committee and shall be its chairman. On charges of more than one church, each church shall have at least one member on this committee, and as far as practicable each of the commissions shall be represented thereon.

7. The **Parsonage Committee,** which, with the approval of the trustees, shall provide an adequate and comfortable residence for the pastor and maintain the proper upkeep and furnishing of the same; *provided* that on charges of only one church this committee shall be named by the Official Board, in which event it shall be responsible to the board (¶ 278.5).

8. The **Committee on Apportionments** (if the pastoral charge is a circuit), which shall recommend to the Quarterly Conference for its action and determination a proper schedule of apportionments among the churches of the pastoral charge for salaries, benevolences, and other items

properly apportioned to the charge, or assumed by it. Each church in the pastoral charge shall have representation on this committee.

9. The **Committee on Christian Vocations,** which shall be composed of the pastor, a layman elected by the Quarterly Conference, a representative of the Woman's Society of Christian Service, a representative of Methodist Men, the church-school superintendent, and the superintendents or representatives of the Youth and Adult Divisions. It shall co-operate with the Conference Commission on Christian Vocations. The duty of this committee shall be to see that the philosophy of Christian vocation and the opportunities and the challenge of church vocations are regularly presented to the youth and adults of the church, to advise interested young people and adults of the necessary qualifications for all church vocations, and to give encouragement and guidance to candidates for the pastoral ministry and other church-related vocations, working with and through the appropriate commissions of the local church. The committee may report regularly to the Official Board and to the Conference Commission on Christian Vocations.

10. The **Committee on Wills and Legacies,** which shall keep before Methodist people and any others, by such means as the committee may determine, the desirability of leaving bequests to the local church, or to other causes and institutions of The Methodist Church. The committee shall seek legal counsel to the end that bequests may be made in proper legal form. It shall report the name and address of its chairman to the Council on World Service and Finance so the council may provide suggested methods, materials, and procedures. In a small church the duty of this committee may be assigned to the Commission on Stewardship and Finance.

11. The **Farm and Home Committee,** composed of both men and women, which shall have the responsibility of assisting young couples to become established on the land and in small businesses inherent in the economy of the community, for the purpose of maintaining and strengthening the church community.

12. Any other committees which the Quarterly Con-

ference may determine to be necessary to its work, provided the same are in harmony with the provisions of the Discipline.

Sec. III. **Sundry Duties**

¶ **146.** The Quarterly Conference shall recommend or certify proper persons, as follows:

1. It shall, on application for issuance or renewal of a license to preach by a proper person, whose membership is within the charge, recommend such person to the District Committee on Ministerial Qualifications (¶ 695), if in the judgment of the Quarterly Conference his gifts, graces, and potential usefulness warrant such action. Such person shall conform with all the provisions of the Discipline (¶¶ 306-7). The vote to recommend shall be taken by written, secret ballot, and the recommendation shall be signed by the presiding officer.

2. It shall recommend and send to the Annual Conference Deaconess Board credentials for young women who may become candidates for the office of deaconess. (*See* ¶ 1252.1.)

3. It shall certify proper persons to serve as lay speakers, and inquire annually into the gifts, labors, and usefulness of lay speakers on the circuit, station, or mission, as specified in ¶ 293.

¶ **147.** The Quarterly Conference shall determine the amount accepted annually by the charge for world service and conference benevolences by the following procedure: As soon as practicable after the session of the Annual Conference, each district superintendent shall notify each pastoral charge in his district what amounts have been apportioned to it for world service and conference benevolences (¶¶ 795-96). It shall be the responsibility of the pastor and the respective church lay leaders to present to a meeting of each local church in the pastoral charge a statement of the apportionments for world service and conference benevolences, explaining the causes supported by each of these funds, and their place in the total program of the church. Such presentation to each local church shall be made before the Quarterly Conference of the pastoral charge shall set the amount of its acceptances. The first or second Quarterly Conference may accept, increase, or decrease the amount apportioned for world service and conference benevolences (¶ 142.7). The amount voted by the Quarterly Conference shall be the amount assumed by the pastoral charge for this cause. Should the amount contributed during the year for world service and conference benevolences exceed the charge's acceptance, the entire amount so contributed shall be remitted in regular order to the conference treasurer before the end of the conference year (¶ 267.6). The district superintendent shall also notify each pastoral charge of all other amounts properly apportioned to it. The apportionments to the pastoral charge for the General Administration Fund, for the Episcopal Fund, for district superintendents, for conference claimants, and for the minimum salary fund are not subject to change or alteration by the Quarterly Conference or by the local church.

¶ 148. The Quarterly Conference shall fix the salary and other remuneration of the pastor, or pastors, after the following procedure: At the session of the Quarterly Conference next preceding the regular annual session of the Annual Conference, on recommendation of the Official Board or Boards and after consultation with the pastor, the conference shall set the minimum salary of the pastor for the ensuing conference year. In pastoral charges of more than one church, the amount apportioned to each church shall be recorded in the minutes of the Quarterly Conference. The pastor's salary thus agreed upon shall not include the traveling and moving expenses of a new appointee to the pastoral charge. These expenses, when provided for, shall be classified as current expenses and so reported in the pastor's report to the Annual Conference. (*See also* ¶ 829.)

¶ 149. 1. Annually at the fall meeting of the Quarterly Conference the pastor shall answer the following questions, and the answers thereto shall be transmitted to the executive secretary of the Conference Board of Education, or, if there is no executive secretary, to the president thereof: (*a*) Who are the young people of this pastoral charge who are members of the senior class in high school? (*b*) Who are the young people of this pas-

toral charge who are members of the second year in junior
college? (c) Has a list of their names been sent to the ad-
missions officers of the Methodist college or colleges related to the Annual Conference for their information?
(d) Who are the young people now in colleges, universities, and schools of nursing? What is being done by
the local church to extend and maintain its ministry to
them? Who of these are recruits for life service in a
church vocation, and in what educational institutions are
they enrolled? (e) What young people from this pastoral
charge are now in theological schools, and in what school
is each enrolled? (f) What young people from this pastoral charge are in the armed services, and what is being
done to extend and maintain the church's ministry to
them?

2. Annually at the first Quarterly Conference the following questions shall be asked: (a) How many persons have been received into the fellowship of the church
on this pastoral charge during the past conference year?
(b) How many persons will this pastoral charge set as a
minimum number to be received on profession of faith this
conference year, and what means will it adopt to win
them? (c) What program has been adopted for assimilating new members into the life of the church, and
training them in Christian living and activity? (d) How
many persons signed Commitment Day cards, pledging
themselves to abstinence from the use of beverage alcohol?
(e) How many supplemental or renewal commitments?
(f) What are the plans for pressing the work in the area
of temperance this coming year?

3. At each Quarterly Conference the district superintendent shall ask the pastor to answer the following
questions: (a) What general Advance specials (¶ 758)
and conference Advance specials (¶ 759) have been assumed by the church or churches of this pastoral charge,
and in what amount? (b) What amounts have been collected on them during this conference year, and what
amounts have been remitted to the conference treasurer?
(c) What is the report concerning the observance of the
One Great Hour of Sharing (¶ 760)?

4. At each Quarterly Conference the following questions

shall be asked: Who are certified as lay speakers? Have their names and addresses been forwarded to the conference lay leader?

¶ 150. In addition to the duties and responsibilities hereinbefore mentioned, the Quarterly Conference shall be charged with the following:

1. Through the Official Board as its administrative agent to supervise and promote the financial interests of the charge, including the support of the ministry, the payment of world service and conference benevolences, and prompt discharge of financial obligations for the building, repair, and general physical maintenance of the church houses and parsonage of the charge.

2. To promote all the spiritual as well as temporal interests of the church—evangelistic, educational, missionary, and benevolent.

3. To receive reports of the work of the pastor, other officers, and all the organizations of the church or churches of the pastoral charge, as the Quarterly Conference may determine.

4. To fix the place of the next session of the Quarterly Conference. (See ¶ 139.)

5. Such duties and responsibilities as the General Conference may from time to time commit to it.

SEC. IV. Authority Regarding Church Property

¶ 151. In a pastoral charge (¶ 104) consisting of one local church, the Quarterly Conference as constituted in ¶ 138 shall be vested with authority and power in matters relative to the real and personal property of the local church concerned as set forth in ¶¶ 156-94.

¶ 152. In a pastoral charge (¶ 104) consisting of two or more local churches, a **Church Quarterly Conference** shall be organized in each local church therein, and such Church Quarterly Conference shall be vested with authority and power in matters relating to the real and personal property of the local church concerned as set forth in ¶¶ 156-94.

¶ 153. The following shall constitute the membership of the Church Quarterly Conference, in so far as the offices and relationships exist within the local church, these members being the same persons who are members of the pastoral-charge Quarterly Conference from the local church concerned:

1. The pastor and associate pastor or pastors; the retired and supernumerary preachers residing in that place who elect to hold membership therein; traveling preachers who, because they are assigned to special work, have been attached to the Quarterly Conference of the pastoral charge, and who are affiliated with the said local church.

2. The local preachers holding their membership in the local church and deaconesses appointed to labor therein.

3. The stewards of the local church, elective and ex officio, and the trustees of the local church; *provided*, however, that all lay members of the Church Quarterly Conference shall be members of the said local church, and all except the president of the Methodist Youth Fellowship or the president of the Youth Council shall be not less than eighteen years of age.

¶ 154. The district superintendent or an elder designated by him shall preside. The district superintendent shall fix the time and place of meeting. At his discretion he may call the respective Church Quarterly Conferences to meet at the same time and place as the Quarterly Conference of the pastoral charge to which the said local churches are attached; in which case he shall adjourn the Quarterly Conference of the pastoral charge, and shall call to order the respective Church Quarterly Conferences for the transaction of business specifically committed to them, each Church Quarterly Conference sitting as a separate and distinct entity. Or the district superintendent may call a Church Quarterly Conference to meet at such other time and place as he may designate; *provided* that at least ten days' notice shall be given of such meeting. The actions of all Church Quarterly Conferences shall be recorded in spaces included in the "Minutes of the Quarterly Conference" (¶ 141) of the pastoral charge. This is for the purpose of permanent record only, and the Quarterly Conference of the said pastoral charge shall have no voice in the decisions of the Church Quarterly Conference of any local church attached to it in matters specifically committed to the said Church Quarterly Conference.

Sec. V. The Method of Organizing a Local Church

¶ **155.** 1. When a local church is to be organized, the district superintendent shall, after a survey has been made and the need for a church is determined, recommend to the District Board of Church Location and Building (¶¶ 721-24) the site for the proposed new congregation. If there is a city or district missionary society (¶¶ 1218-20), that body shall also be asked to approve the site. (*See* ¶ 1227.)

2. The district superintendent shall call the persons interested in the proposed church to meet at an appointed time and place, or he may by written authorization designate any pastor in his district to call such a meeting.

3. The district superintendent, or the pastor holding authority from him, shall preside, and shall appoint a secretary to keep a record of the meeting. Following a period of worship (¶ 1930) opportunity shall be given those in attendance to present themselves for membership by proper certificates of transfer. Pastors issuing such certificates to a church not yet organized shall describe therein the proposed new church to which it is issued—as, for instance, "the proposed new church on Boston Avenue."

4. Opportunity shall also be given persons desiring to become members on profession of their faith in Christ to present themselves for membership. When the presiding minister is satisfied as to the genuineness of their faith and purpose (¶ 107), they shall be received into the membership of the church in accordance with the prescribed form (¶¶ 1914-15).

5. A list shall be made of all the persons received into the membership of the proposed church, by transfer and on profession. Those persons in the membership eighteen years of age and over shall be members of the constituting Church Conference, and each shall be entitled to vote.

6. The constituting Church Conference shall then be called to order, and it shall proceed to choose the elective stewards of the church (¶ 143.1), on nomination of a

committee on nominations. Such committee shall be appointed by the presiding minister or elected on nomination from the floor as the conference may determine. In either case the presiding minister shall be chairman. When the elective stewards have been chosen in proper number (¶ 208), the presiding minister shall declare the church properly constituted.

7. He shall then adjourn the Church Conference and call to order the Quarterly Conference of the pastoral charge. The membership of said Quarterly Conference shall be the newly elected stewards and any others entitled to membership under the provisions of the Discipline (¶ 138). The Quarterly Conference shall then elect such officers of the church as the Discipline requires, including trustees of church property (¶¶ 159-60), and shall set up commissions and committees as provided in the Discipline (¶¶ 144-45). When such officers have been duly elected and the proper commissions and committees constituted, the church is duly organized, and from this point its work shall proceed as described in the Discipline; *provided* that when a newly organized church is attached to a circuit, the pastoral-charge Quarterly Conference shall not be held until such time as representatives from all the churches of the charge can be properly assembled for that purpose.

8. The Quarterly Conference may take action, at its discretion, authorizing and directing the newly elected trustees to incorporate the newly organized church in accordance with local laws and the provisions of the Discipline.

9. For the presentation of a certificate of organization from the Annual Conference *see* ¶ 641.

Chapter IV

CHURCH PROPERTY

¶ **156.** All provisions of the Discipline relating to property, both real and personal, and relating to the formation and operation of any corporation, are conditioned upon their being in conformity with the local laws; and in the event of conflict therewith, the local laws shall prevail.[6]

SECTION I. Authority of the Quarterly Conference

¶ 157. In a pastoral charge consisting of one local church, the Quarterly Conference, constituted as set forth in ¶ 138, shall be vested with power and authority as hereinafter set forth in connection with the property, both real and personal, of the said local church, namely:

1. If it so elects, to direct the Board of Trustees to incorporate the local church, expressly subject, however, to the Discipline of The Methodist Church (¶¶ 176-78), and in accordance with the pertinent local laws, and in such manner as will fully protect and exempt from any and all legal liability the individual officials and members, jointly and severally, of the local church, and the Quarterly, Annual, Jurisdictional, and General Conferences of The Methodist Church, and each of them, for and on account of the debts and other obligations, of every kind and description, of the local church.

2. To direct the Board of Trustees with respect to the purchase, sale, mortgage, incumbrance, construction, repairing, remodeling, and maintenance of any and all property of the local church. (See ¶ 165.)

3. To direct the Board of Trustees with respect to the acceptance or rejection of any and all conveyances, grants, gifts, donations, legacies, bequests, or devises, absolute or in trust, for the use and benefit of the local church, and to require the administration of any such trust in accordance with the terms and provisions thereof and of the local laws appertaining thereto. (See ¶ 165.)

4. To elect the trustees of the local church, unless otherwise provided (¶ 32), in harmony with the provisions of the Discipline.[7]

5. To do any and all things necessary to exercise such other powers and duties relating to the property, real and personal, of the local church concerned as may be committed to it by the Discipline.[8]

---

[6] See Judicial Council Decision 93.
[7] See Judicial Council Decision 130.
[8] See Judicial Council Decision 103.

¶ **158.** In a pastoral charge consisting of two or more local churches, a Church Quarterly Conference, constituted and organized under the Discipline of The Methodist Church as set forth in ¶¶ 153-54, in each local church therein, shall be vested with authority and power in matters relating to the real and personal property of the local church concerned. Such Church Quarterly Conference shall elect the Board of Trustees of such local church in number and manner described in ¶¶ 159-61; and the duties of such trustees, duly elected, shall be the same as and identical with the duties described in ¶¶ 162-66. The duties, authority, and power vested in the Church Quarterly Conference, in so far as they relate to the property, real and personal, of the local church concerned, are the same as and identical with the authority and power vested in the Quarterly Conference of a pastoral charge of one local church as set forth in ¶¶ 157 and 167-94; and the authority, power, and limitations therein set forth shall be applicable to the Church Quarterly Conference as fully and to the same extent as if incorporated herein. The effect of the provisions for a Church Quarterly Conference is to give to each local church in a pastoral charge of two or more churches, rather than to the pastoral-charge Quarterly Conference, supervision over and control of its own property, subject to the limitations prescribed in the Discipline with regard to local-church property.

Sec. II.   **The Church Board of Trustees**

¶ **159.** In each local church there shall be a **Board of Trustees** consisting of not fewer than three nor more than nine persons, each of whom shall be not less than twenty-one years of age, and at least two thirds of whom shall be members of The Methodist Church.

¶ **160.** The members of the Board of Trustees shall be divided into three classes; and each class shall, as nearly as possible, consist of an equal number of members. At the fourth or final meeting of the Quarterly Conference for the Annual Conference year, upon nomination by the Committee on Nominations (¶ 145.1), of which the pastor shall be chairman (or if the committee fails to nominate, upon nomination of the pastor), or from the floor, it shall elect, to take office at the beginning of the ensuing conference year, to serve for a term of three years or until their successors have been duly elected and qualified, the required number of trustees to succeed those of the class whose terms then expire; *provided*, however, that nothing herein shall be construed to prevent the election of a trustee to succeed himself. Or the Quarterly Conference may determine that the Board of Trustees shall be elected by the members of the local church who are not less than eighteen years of age, at a meeting arranged and called for that purpose by the Quarterly Conference; *provided*, however, that at least ten days' notice of such meeting and the purpose thereof shall be given from the pulpit of the local church or in its weekly bulletin (¶ 32).[9]

¶ **161.** Any vacancy in the Board of Trustees may be filled until the next annual election, as hereinbefore provided, by the Quarterly Conference in any regular or special session upon nomination by the Committee on Nominations, or by the pastor; *provided* that the privilege of making nominations from the floor shall not be denied.

¶ **162.** 1. Within thirty days after the beginning of the ensuing conference year the Board of Trustees shall convene at a time and place designated by the president, or by the vice-president in the event that the president is not re-elected a trustee, or, because of his absence or disability, is unable to act, for the purpose of electing officers of the said board for the ensuing year and transacting any other business properly brought before it.

2. The Board of Trustees shall elect from the membership thereof, to hold office for a term of one year or until their successors shall be elected, a president, vice-president, secretary, and, if need requires, treasurer; *provided*, however, that the president and vice-president shall not be members of the same class; and *provided*, further, that the offices of secretary and treasurer may be held by the same person. The duties of each officer shall be the same as generally connected with the office held and which are usually and commonly discharged

---

[9] *See* Judicial Council Decisions 102, 130.

by the holder thereof. The Quarterly Conference may, if it is necessary to conform to the local laws, substitute the designations "chairman" and "vice-chairman" for and in place of "president" and "vice-president."

3. Where necessity requires, as a result of the incorporation of a local church, the corporation directors, in addition to electing officers as provided in this paragraph shall ratify and confirm, by appropriate action, and if necessary elect, as officers of the corporation the treasurer or treasurers, as the case may be, elected by the Official Board in accordance with the provisions of ¶¶ 212 and 268, whose duties and responsibilities shall be as therein set forth. If more than one account is maintained in the name of the corporation in any financial institution or institutions, each such account, and the treasurer thereof, shall be appropriately designated.

¶ 163. The Board of Trustees shall meet at the call of the pastor or of its president,[10] at such times and places as shall be designated in a notice which shall be mailed to each trustee at least five days prior to the appointed time of the meeting. Waiver of notice may be used as a means to validate meetings legally where the five-day notice is impracticable.

¶ 164. The Board of Trustees shall have such authority, powers, duties, and responsibilities as shall be vested in it by the provisions of the Dicipline, and it shall be subject to the directions of, and be responsible to, the Quarterly Conference,[11] and make a written report to the fourth or last Quarterly Conference, in which shall be included the following:

1. The legal description and the reasonable valuation of each parcel of real estate owned by the church.

2. The specific name of the grantee in each deed of conveyance of real estate to the local church.

3. An inventory and the reasonable valuation of all personal property owned by the local church.

4. The amount of income received from any income-producing property and a detailed list of expenditures in connection therewith.

---

[10] See Judicial Council Decision 102.
[11] See Judicial Council Decision 103.

5. The amount received during the year for building, rebuilding, remodeling, and improving real estate, and an itemized statement of expenditures.

6. Outstanding capital debts and how contracted.

7. Detailed statement of the insurance carried on each parcel of real estate, indicating whether restricted by co-insurance or other limiting conditions, and whether adequate insurance is carried.

8. The name of the custodian of all legal papers of the local church, and where they are kept.

9. A detailed list of all trusts in which the local church is the beneficiary, specifying where and how the funds are invested and in what manner the income therefrom is expended or applied.

¶ 165. Subject to the direction of the Quarterly Conference as hereinbefore provided, the Board of Trustees shall receive and administer all bequests made to the local church; shall receive and administer all trusts; shall invest all trust funds of the local church in conformity with law of the country, state, or like political unit in which the local church is located; and shall have the supervision, oversight, and care of all real property owned by the local church and of all property and equipment acquired directly by the local church or by any society, board, class, commission, or similar organization connected therewith; *provided* that the Board of Trustees shall not violate the rights of any local-church organization elsewhere granted in the Discipline; *provided*, further, that the Board of Trustees shall not prevent or interfere with the pastor in the use of any of the said property (¶ 174) for religious services or other proper meetings or purposes recognized by the law, usages, and customs of The Methodist Church, or permit the use of said property for religious or other meetings without the consent of the pastor, or in his absence the consent of the district superintendent; and *provided*, further, that the Quarterly Conference may assign certain of these duties to a Building Committee as set forth in ¶ 180. (*See also* ¶ 278.5, .6.)

¶ 166. 1. "Trustee," "trustees," and "Board of Trustees," as used herein or elsewhere in the Discipline, shall be construed to be synonymous with "director," "directors," and "Board of Directors" applied to corporations.

2. "Local laws" shall be construed to mean the laws of the country, state, or other like political unit within the geographical bounds of which the church property is located.

3. Trustees or other members of a local church shall not be required to guarantee personally any loan made to the church by any board created by or under the authority of the General Conference.

4. Should a trustee of a local church or a director of an incorporated local church refuse to execute properly a legal instrument relating to any property of the church, when duly directed so to do by the Quarterly Conference (¶¶ 157-58), and when all legal requirements have been satisfied with reference to such execution, the said Quarterly Conference may by majority vote declare his membership on the Board of Trustees or Board of Directors vacated, and elect his successor for the unexpired term.

SEC. III.   **Acquisition of Property**

¶ 167. If the local laws do not prescribe that title to property, both real and personal, shall be otherwise taken and held, in which event the provisions thereof shall take precedence and shall be observed and the provisions hereof subordinated thereto, the title to all **real property** now owned or hereafter acquired by an **unincorporated local church,** and any organization, board, commission, society, or similar body connected therewith, shall be held by and/or conveyed and transferred to its duly elected trustees, who shall be named in the written instrument conveying or transferring title, and their successors in office and their assigns, as the Board of Trustees of such local church (naming it and the individual trustees), in trust, nevertheless, for the use and benefit of such local church and of The Methodist Church. Every instrument of conveyance of real estate shall contain the appropriate trust clause, as hereinafter set forth in ¶ 174.

¶ 168. Prior to the purchase by an unincorporated local church of any real estate a resolution authorizing such action shall be passed at a meeting of the Quarterly

Conference, by a majority vote of its members present and voting, at a regular meeting or a special meeting of the Quarterly Conference called for that purpose; *provided*, however, that not less than ten days' notice of such meeting and the proposed action shall have been given from the pulpit or in the weekly bulletin of the church; and *provided*, further, that written consent to such action shall be given by the pastor and the district superintendent. (*See* ¶ 180.)

¶ **169.** If the local laws do not prescribe that title to real property of an **incorporated local church** shall be otherwise taken and held, in which event the provisions thereof shall take precedence and shall be observed, and the provisions hereof subordinated thereto, the title to all property, both real and personal, now owned or hereafter acquired by an incorporated local church, and any organization, board, commission, society, or similar body connected therewith, shall be held by and/or conveyed to the corporate body in its corporate name, in trust, nevertheless, for the use and benefit of such local church and of The Methodist Church. Every instrument of conveyance of real estate shall contain the appropriate trust clause, as hereinafter set forth in ¶ 174.

¶ **170.** Prior to the purchase by a local-church corporation of any real estate, a resolution authorizing such action shall be passed by the Quarterly Conference in corporate session, or such other corporate body as the local laws may require, with the members thereof acting in their capacity as members of the corporate body, by a majority vote of those present and voting, at any regular or special meeting called for that purpose; *provided* that not less than ten days' notice of such meeting and the proposed action shall have been given from the pulpit or in the weekly bulletin of the local church; and *provided*, further, that written consent to such action shall be given by the pastor and the district superintendent; and *provided*, further, that all such transactions shall have the approval of the Quarterly Conference. (*See* ¶ 180.)

SEC. IV.   **Sale, Transfer, and Mortgage of Property**

¶ **171.** Any real property owned by, or in which an **unincorporated local church** has any interest, may be sold, transferred, or mortgaged subject to the following procedure and conditions:

1. Notice of the proposed action and the date and time of the regular or special meeting of the Quarterly Conference at which it is to be considered shall be given at least ten days prior thereto (except as local laws may otherwise provide) from the pulpit of the church or in its weekly bulletin.

2. A resolution authorizing the proposed action shall be passed by a majority vote of the Quarterly Conference members present and voting and by a majority vote of the members of said church present and voting at a special meeting called to consider such action.

3. The written consent of the pastor of the local church and the district superintendent to the proposed action shall be necessary and shall be affixed to the instrument of sale, transfer, or mortgage.

4. The resolution authorizing such proposed action shall direct that any contract, deed, bill of sale, mortgage, or other necessary written instrument be executed by and on behalf of the local church by any two of the officers of its Board of Trustees, who thereupon shall be duly authorized to carry out the direction of the Quarterly Conference; and any written instrument so executed shall be binding and effective as the action of the local church. (*See* ¶ 173.)

¶ **172.** Any real property owned by, or in which an **incorporated local church** has any interest, may be sold, transferred, or mortgaged subject to the following procedure and conditions:

1. Notice of the proposed action and the date and time of the regular or special meeting of the members of the corporate body, i.e., members of the Quarterly Conference, at which it is to be considered, shall be given at least ten days prior thereto (except as local laws may otherwise provide) from the pulpit of the church or in its weekly bulletin.

2. A resolution authorizing the proposed action shall

be passed by a majority vote of the members of the corporate body present and voting at any regular or special meeting thereof called to consider such action, and by a majority vote of the members of said church present and voting at a special meeting called to consider such action; *provided* that for the sale of property which was conveyed to the church to be sold and its proceeds used for a specific purpose a vote of the members of said church shall not be required.

3. The written consent of the pastor of the local church and the district superintendent to the proposed action shall be necessary and shall be affixed to the instrument of sale, conveyance, transfer, or mortgage.

4. The resolution authorizing such proposed action shall direct and authorize the corporation's Board of Directors to take all necessary steps to carry out the action so authorized, and to cause to be executed, as hereinafter provided, any necessary contract, deed, bill of sale, mortgage, or other written instrument.

5. The Board of Directors at any regular or special meeting shall take such action and adopt such resolutions as may be necessary or required by the local laws.

6. Any required contract, deed, bill of sale, mortgage, or other written instrument necessary to carry out the action so authorized shall be executed in the name of the corporation by any two of its officers, and any written instrument so executed shall be binding and effective as the action of the corporation. (*See* ¶ 173.)

¶ 173. 1. No real property on which a church building or parsonage is located shall be mortgaged to provide for the current (or budget) expense of a local church, nor shall the principal proceeds of a sale of any such property be so used. This provision shall apply alike to unincorporated and incorporated local churches.

2. A local church, whether or not incorporated, on complying with the provisions of ¶ 171 or ¶ 172, may mortgage its unencumbered real property as security for a loan to be made to a Conference Board of Missions, or a city or district missionary society; *provided* that the proceeds of such loan shall be used only for aiding in the construction of a new church.

Sec. V. Trust Clauses and Release Therefrom

¶ **174.** 1. Except in conveyances from governmental agencies or subdivisions[12] which require that the real property so conveyed shall revert to the grantor if and when its use as a place of divine worship has been terminated, all written instruments of conveyance by which premises are held or hereafter acquired, for use as a place of divine worship for members of The Methodist Church or for other church activities, shall contain the following trust clause:

In trust, that said premises shall be used, kept, and maintained as a place of divine worship of the Methodist ministry and members of The Methodist Church; subject to the Discipline, usage, and ministerial appointments of said church as from time to time authorized and declared by the General Conference and by the Annual Conference within whose bounds the said premises are situated. This provision is solely for the benefit of the grantee, and the grantor reserves no right or interest in said premises.[13]

2. All written instruments by which premises are held or hereafter acquired as a parsonage for the use and occupancy of the ministers of The Methodist Church shall contain the following trust clause:

In trust, that such premises shall be held, kept, and maintained as a place of residence for the use and occupancy of the ministers of The Methodist Church who may from time to time be entitled to occupy the same by appointment; subject to the Discipline and usage of said church, as from time to time authorized and declared by the General Conference and by the Annual Conference within whose bounds the said premises are situated. This provision is solely for the benefit of the grantee, and the grantor reserves no right or interest in said premises.

3. However, the absence of the trust clause stipulated in § 1 or § 2 of this paragraph in deeds and conveyances

---

[12] *See* Judicial Council Decision 107.
[13] *See* Judicial Council Decision 135.

previously executed shall in no way exclude a local church from or relieve it of its Methodist connectional responsibilities. Nor shall it absolve a local congregation or Board of Trustees of its responsibility to The Methodist Church provided that the intent and desire of the founders and/or the later congregations and Boards of Trustees is shown by any or all of the following indications: (*a*) the conveyance of the property to the trustees of the local Methodist church or any of its predecessors; (*b*) the use of the name, customs, and polity of The Methodist Church in such a way as to be thus known to the community as a part of this denomination; (*c*) the acceptance of the pastorate of ministers appointed by a bishop of The Methodist Church or employed by the superintendent of the district in which it is located.

¶ 175. Real property acquired by a conveyance containing either or both of the foregoing trust clauses (¶ 174) may be sold in conformity with the provisions of the Discipline of The Methodist Church (¶¶ 171-73) when its use as a church building or parsonage, as the case may be, has been or is intended to be terminated; and when such real estate is sold or mortgaged in accordance with the provisions of the Discipline of The Methodist Church, the written acknowledged consent of the proper district superintendent representing The Methodist Church to the action taken shall constitute a release and discharge of the real property so sold and conveyed from either or both of the foregoing trust clauses; or, in the event of the execution of a mortgage, such consent of the district superintendent shall constitute a formal recognition of the priority of such mortgage lien and the subordination of the foregoing trust provisions thereof; and no bona fide purchaser or mortgagee relying upon the foregoing record shall be charged with any responsibility with respect to the disposition by such local church of the proceeds of any such sale or mortgage; but the Board of Trustees receiving such proceeds shall manage, control, disburse, and expend the same in conformity to the order and direction of the Quarterly Conference, subject to the provisions of the Discipline of The Methodist Church with respect thereto.

SEC. VI. **Incorporation of Local Churches**

¶ **176.** When so authorized and directed by its Quarterly Conference, the Board of Trustees of a local church shall immediately take and perform any and all necessary steps and actions to incorporate the local church under and in conformity with the laws of the country, state, or like political unit in which it is located. The necessary articles to be filed with the proper governmental officials to secure a charter, and any and all amendments thereto that at any time may be contemplated, shall be submitted to the district superintendent having jurisdiction for his written approval as to the conformity of the same with the provisions of the Discipline of The Methodist Church, and shall contain the following provisions:

1. The corporation shall support the doctrine, and it, and all its property, both real and personal, shall be subject to the laws, usages, and ministerial appointments of The Methodist Church as are now or shall be from time to time established, made, and declared by the lawful authority of the said church.

2. The Board of Directors of the corporation shall be the Board of Trustees of the local church, elected and organized as prescribed in the Discipline of The Methodist Church.

3. The corporation shall have the power to acquire and hold title in fee simple, in trust, or otherwise, to both real and personal property, and to improve, incumber, sell, convey, and dispose of all such property in conformity with the Discipline of The Methodist Church.

4. Subject to the provisions of the Discipline, the corporation shall have the power to erect and maintain buildings for the worship of God, for training in Christian faith and conduct, and for Christian social intercourse, and to acquire or build and maintain residences for the use and occupancy of its ministers.

5. The by-laws of the corporation shall include the Discipline of The Methodist Church as from time to time enacted, authorized, and declared by its General Conference; and no other by-law shall be adopted inconsistent with the provisions of the Discipline.

6. The members of the corporation shall be the mem-

bers of the Quarterly Conference, or such other body of the local church as the local laws may permit or require.

7. If, for any reason, the corporation shall cease to exist as a legal entity and its charter shall expire or be terminated, the title to all its property, both real and personal, shall be vested in the trustees of the Annual Conference, if the Annual Conference itself is unincorporated, in the same manner as it holds title to any other real estate, or in the Annual Conference in its corporate name if it is incorporated; and all such property shall be held in trust for the benefit of the local church.

8. Such provisions as may be required by the local laws.

¶ **177.** The provisions of ¶¶ 159-66 hereof, entitled "The Church Board of Trustees," shall be applicable to all corporations formed hereunder as fully and to the same extent as if set forth and incorporated herein; *provided*, however, that "trustee," "trustees," and "Board of Trustees" shall be construed to be synonymous with "director," "directors," and "Board of Directors," as applied to corporations.

¶ **178.** In the event that the title to any property, real or personal, of a local church shall vest in the trustees of the Annual Conference or in its corporate body as a result of the corporation ceasing to exist, then, and in that event, the Board of Trustees of the Annual Conference, if the Annual Conference itself is unincorporated, or the Board of Directors of its corporate body, shall be and is hereby authorized and directed, at the request of the Quarterly Conference of the local church and without any action by the Annual Conference, to reconvey the title to the local-church property in such manner as shall be requested by the Quarterly Conference with the approval of the district superintendent.

Sec. VII. Building, Purchasing, Remodeling

¶ **180.** Any local church planning to build or purchase a new church or educational building or a parsonage, or to remodel such a building if the cost will exceed ten per cent of its value, shall take the following steps:

1. It shall secure the written consent of the pastor and the district superintendent.

2. It shall secure approval of the proposed site by the District Board of Church Location and Building, as provided in ¶ 722.

3. Its Quarterly Conference (¶¶ 157-58) shall authorize the project at a regular or called meeting, not less than ten days' notice (except as local laws may otherwise provide) of such meeting and the proposed action having been given from the pulpit or in the weekly bulletin, and shall appoint a **Building Committee** of not fewer than three members of the local church to serve in the development of the project as hereinafter set forth; *provided* that the Quarterly Conference may commit to its Board of Trustees the duties of a Building Committee as here described.

4. The Building Committee shall:

a) Estimate carefully the building facilities needed to house the church's program of worship, education, and fellowship and/or to provide a residence for present and future pastors and their families.

b) Ascertain the cost of property to be purchased.

c) Develop preliminary sketches, complying with local building and fire codes, which shall clearly outline the location on the site of all proposed present and future construction. (For provisions for architectural advisory service *see* ¶¶ 1235.2, 1237, 1401.1.)

d) Secure an estimate of the cost of the proposed construction.

e) Develop a financial plan for defraying the total cost, including an estimate of the amount the membership can contribute in cash and pledges and the amount the local church can borrow if necessary.

5. The Building Committee shall submit to the District Board of Church Location and Building, for its consideration and approval, a statement of the need for the proposed facilities, and the sketches, estimates, and plans specified in § 4 above, as provided in ¶ 723.1.

6. The pastor, with the written consent of the district superintendent, shall call a Church Conference (¶ 196), giving not less than ten days' notice (except as local laws may otherwise provide) of the meeting and the proposed action from the pulpit or in the weekly bulletin.

At this conference the Building Committee shall submit, for approval by the membership, its recommendations for the proposed building project, including the data specified in §§ 4-5 above.

7. After approval of the preliminary sketches and estimates as provided in §§ 4-6 above, the Building Committee shall develop detailed plans and specifications and secure a reliable and detailed estimate of cost, and shall present these for approval to the Quarterly Conference and to the District Board of Church Location and Building, which shall study the data and report its conclusions as provided in ¶ 723.2.

8. The local church shall acquire a fee simple title to the lot or lots on which the building is to be erected, by deed of conveyance, executed as provided in this chapter (¶¶ 167-70, 174), and shall pay the purchase price thereof in full before beginning construction.

9. If a loan is needed, the local church shall comply with the provisions of ¶¶ 171-72.

10. The local church shall not enter into a building contract or, if using a plan for volunteer labor, incur obligations for materials until it has cash on hand, pledges payable during the construction period, and (if needed) a loan or written commitment therefor which will assure prompt payment of all contractual obligations and other accounts when due. (*See also* ¶ 271.)

¶ **181.** On acquisition or completion of any church building, parsonage, or other church unit a service of consecration may be held (¶ 1932). Before any church building, parsonage, or other church unit is formally dedicated (¶¶ 1933, 1936), all indebtedness against the same shall be discharged.

SEC. VIII. **Circuit and Joint Boards of Trustees**

¶ **183.** In the event that a circuit (¶ 104) shall own or acquire a parsonage for the use of the pastor appointed to serve the local churches comprising such circuit, or shall own or acquire any other real estate for any common use of its churches, the Quarterly Conference of the pastoral charge may elect a **Circuit Board of Trustees,** to be composed of not fewer than three nor more than nine members, all of whom shall be not less than twenty-one years of age; *provided*, however, that each local church in the circuit shall have at least one representative on the board. The members of the Circuit Board of Trustees shall be divided into three classes, and each class shall, as nearly as possible, consist of an equal number of members. Nominations shall be made by the Quarterly Conference Committee on Nominations (or, if the committee fails to nominate, by the pastor). At the first election under the provisions hereof, one class shall be elected for a term of one year, one class for a term of two years, and one class for a term of three years; and thereafter, at the fourth or final meeting of the circuit Quarterly Conference for the Annual Conference year, it shall elect, to take office at the beginning of the ensuing conference year to serve for a term of three years or until their successors have been elected and qualified, the required number of trustees to succeed those of the class whose terms then expire; *provided*, however, that nothing herein shall be construed to prevent the election of a trustee to succeed himself. The provisions of ¶¶ 157 and 161-64 shall be applicable to the Circuit Board of Trustees to the same extent as if incorporated herein.

¶ **184.** When two or more local churches compose a single pastoral charge having a parsonage, and one or more thereof is separated from such charge and established as a pastoral charge, or united with another pastoral charge which does not own a parsonage, each such local church shall be entitled to receive its just share of the then reasonable value of the parsonage in which it has invested funds; and the amount of such value and just share shall be determined by a committee of three persons, appointed by the district superintendent, who shall be members of The Methodist Church but not of any of the interested local churches. Such committee shall hear all interested parties, and shall take into account the investment of any church in any such property before arriving at a final determination. From any such determination there is reserved to each of the interested churches the right of appeal to the next succeeding Annual Conference, the decision of which shall be final and binding.

Any sum received as or from such share shall not be applied to current expense or current budget.

Sec. IX. **Sundry Provisions**

¶ **186.** Two or more local churches may merge and become a single church by pursuing the following procedure:

1. The merger must be proposed by the Quarterly Conference of each of the merging churches by a resolution stating the terms and conditions of the proposed merger.

2. The plan of the merger as proposed by the Quarterly Conference of each of the merging churches must be approved by a majority of the members of each of such churches, over the age of twenty-one years, present at a meeting thereof held in the usual place of public worship and called, for the purpose of considering such plan, by announcement made at a public service in such churches on two Sundays, the first not less than ten days next preceding the date of such meeting, and by written notice signed by the chairman and secretary of the Official Board of such churches, or otherwise, as the Quarterly Conference may direct (posted publicly in the usual places of worship of the churches contemplating merging), which announcement shall state the time and place of the meeting and the purpose thereof.

3. The merger must be approved by the superintendent or superintendents of the district or districts in which the merging churches are located.

4. The requirements of any and all laws of the state or states in which the merging churches are located affecting or relating to the merger of such churches must be complied with; and, in any case where there is a conflict between such laws and the procedure outlined in the Discipline, said laws shall prevail and the procedure outlined in the Discipline shall be modified to the extent necessary to eliminate such conflict.

¶ **187.** When two or more local churches are united, merged, or consolidated, the Quarterly Conferences of the constituent churches shall respectively take action to consummate legally the same, and direct the respective Boards of Trustees with respect to the transfer or disposition of the property, real and personal, as the local laws and the Discipline may require.

¶ **188.** 1. With the consent of the presiding bishop and of a majority of the district superintendents and of the District Board of Church Location and Building (¶¶ 721-24) of the district in which the action is contemplated, the Annual Conference may declare any local church within its bounds discontinued or abandoned. It shall be the duty of its Board of Trustees (¶ 190) to make such disposition of the property thereof as the Annual Conference shall direct; and if no such lawful trustees remain, or if for any reason said trustees fail to make such disposition, then it shall be the duty of the trustees of the Annual Conference to sell or dispose of said property in accordance with the direction of the Annual Conference; and it shall be the duty of the trustees thus effecting sale to remove, in so far as reasonably possible, all Christian and church insignia and symbols from such property. In the event of loss, damage to, or destruction of such local church property, the trustees of the Annual Conference are authorized to collect and receipt for any insurance payable on account thereof, as the duly and legally authorized representative of such local church.[14]

2. All the deeds, records, and other official and legal papers of a Methodist church that is declared to be abandoned or otherwise discontinued shall be collected by the district superintendent in whose district said church was located and shall be deposited for permanent safekeeping with the secretary of the Annual Conference.

3. Any gift, legacy, devise, annuity, or other benefit to a pastoral charge or local church that accrues or becomes available after said charge or church has been discontinued or abandoned shall become the property of the trustees of the Annual Conference within whose jurisdiction the said discontinued or abandoned church was located.

4. When a church property has been abandoned by its membership and no abandonment action has been taken by the Annual Conference, and circumstances make immediate action necessary, the Annual Conference trustees

---

[14] *See* Judicial Council Decision 138.

may take control of the property, with the consent of the presiding bishop and the District Board of Church Location and Building of the district in which the property is located. And in the event of the sale or lease of said property the trustees of the Annual Conference shall recommend to the Annual Conference at its next session the disposition of the proceeds derived from such sale or lease.[15]

¶ **189.** 1. With the consent of the presiding bishop and of a majority of the district superintendents and of the District Board of Church Location and Building, and at the request of the Quarterly Conference, or of a meeting of the membership of the church, where required by local law, and in accordance with the said law, the Annual Conference may instruct and direct the Board of Trustees of a local church to deed church property to a federated church.

2. With the consent of the presiding bishop and of a majority of the district superintendents and of the District Board of Church Location and Building, and at the request of the Quarterly Conference, or of a meeting of the membership of the church, where required by local law, and in accordance with said law, the Annual Conference may instruct and direct the Board of Trustees of a local church to deed church property to another evangelical denomination under an allocation, exchange of property, or comity agreement; *provided* that such agreement shall have been committed to writing and signed and approved by the duly qualified and authorized representatives of both parties concerned.

¶ **190.** The Quarterly Conference and the trustees or Board of Trustees of a local church shall fully comply with the instructions of the Annual Conference issued under the provisions of ¶¶ 188-89; and in the event of failure or refusal so to do, the trustees of the Annual Conference shall be vested with full power and authority to convey such property, and to carry out the instructions of the Annual Conference with regard to the disposal of the proceeds thereof.

¶ **194.** The provisions herein written concerning the

---

[15] *See* Judicial Council Decision 143.

organization and administration of the local church, including the procedure for acquiring, holding, and transferring real property, shall not be mandatory in Central Conferences, Provisional Central Conferences, Provisional Annual Conferences, or Missions; and in such instances the legislation in ¶¶ 541-616 shall apply.

CHAPTER V

THE CHURCH CONFERENCE

¶ **196.** There may be a **Church Conference** of any local church, composed of the members of such church who are eighteen years of age or over. It may be called by the pastor or the Quarterly Conference or the district superintendent; *provided* that not less than ten days' notice (except as local laws may otherwise provide) of such meeting and its main purpose shall be given to the members of the church in writing or from the pulpit or in the weekly bulletin. The pastor, district superintendent, or church lay leader may be its chairman. The conference shall elect a secretary, whose minutes shall be reviewed by the Committee on Records and made a part of the Quarterly Conference records. The conference may review the work of the church and adopt plans for the promotion of various phases of the church's work, subject to the limitations of the Discipline. (For special matters requiring action by a Church Conference *see* ¶¶ 45 ix, 155.5-.7, 171.2, 172.2, 180.6, 189, 532.)

¶ **197.** The Quarterly Conference may authorize and constitute in any pastoral charge an **Annual Church Conference,** composed of members of the church or churches of the charge who are eighteen years of age or older, in conjunction with the fourth Quarterly Conference. The district superintendent shall preside, or in his absence the pastor with the written consent of the district superintendent shall preside. The recording steward shall be the secretary of the meeting, or in his absence a secretary pro tem may be elected. The minutes shall be recorded in the records of the Quarterly Conference.

¶ **198.** An Annual Church Conference thus authorized by the Quarterly Conference may review the work of the year, and receive the reports of the officers, committees, and organizations of the charge as arranged in the order of business of the fourth Quarterly Conference. The Annual Church Conference may also, when such authority has been specifically granted it by the Quarterly Conference of the pastoral charge, elect such officers of the charge as would otherwise be elected by the Quarterly Conference (¶¶ 32, 143-45).

¶ **199.** The Quarterly Conference of a circuit, with the consent of the district superintendent, may authorize and constitute such an Annual Church Conference in any church of the circuit, subject to such additional qualifications as the district superintendent may specify.

¶ **200.** If matters presented in the Annual Church Conference are restricted to the action of the Quarterly Conference, only members of the Quarterly Conference may vote thereon.

CHAPTER VI

THE OFFICIAL BOARD

SECTION I.   **General Provisions**

¶ **206.** In every church of every pastoral charge there shall be an administrative body called the **Official Board,** hereinafter designated as the board; and it shall be the duty of the pastor and district superintendent to see that such organization is set up in every church as hereinafter set forth. The board shall be responsible to the Quarterly Conference, and shall report regularly to the sessions of the conference as its work and the occasion may require, and as the conference may request.[16]

¶ **207.** The board shall be constituted of the following persons:

1. The pastor of the local church and duly appointed associate pastor or pastors, if any, and deaconesses, if any.

---

[16] *See* Judicial Council Decision 103.

2. The stewards of the local church, duly elected (¶ 208).

3. The ex officio stewards of the local church (¶ 209).

4. The trustees of the local church (¶ 158), except such as may not be members of The Methodist Church.

All lay members of the board shall be members of the local Methodist church; and in nominating and electing persons to such membership the utmost care shall be taken that only morally disciplined persons shall be so nominated, with special reference to total abstinence from alcoholic beverages.[17]

¶ 208. Stewards shall be persons of genuine Christian character who love the church and are competent to administer its affairs. The **elective stewards** shall be not less than eighteen years of age and shall be elected annually by the Quarterly Conference at the regular session next preceding the regular session of the Annual Conference, on nomination of the Committee on Nominations (¶ 145.1), or of the pastor if the Quarterly Conference does not constitute such committee; or they may be elected by the members of the local church eighteen years of age and older at a Church Conference called for that purpose as may be arranged by the Quarterly Conference (¶ 198). Stewards-elect shall take office at the beginning of the conference year following their election; *provided* that in cases where a steward is elected to fill a vacancy in the board he shall take office immediately after election. Vacancies may be filled by the Quarterly Conference, in regular or special session; under no circumstances shall stewards be elected by the Official Board. Each local church shall be entitled to not fewer than three or more than thirty-five stewards, exclusive of ex officio and honorary stewards; *provided* that in churches of more than five hundred members one steward may be elected for each thirty additional members.

¶ 209. The following officers in the local church shall be **ex officio stewards** during their respective terms of office, and shall exercise all the rights and privileges which belong to a steward in The Methodist Church: the church lay leader, the church business manager if a member of the local church, the director of Christian education

---

[17] *See* Judicial Council Decision 147.

or the educational assistant, the church-school superintendent, the chairman of the Commission on Membership and Evangelism, the chairman of the Commission on Education, the chairman of the Commission on Missions, the chairman of the Commission on Stewardship and Finance, the secretary (formerly director) of stewardship, the lay member and the first reserve lay member of the Annual Conference if members of the local church, the president of the Woman's Society of Christian Service, the president of Methodist Men, the church treasurer or treasurers, the financial secretary if a member of the local church, the president of the Young Adult Fellowship, and the president of the Methodist Youth Fellowship, or the president of the Youth Council if more than one fellowship is organized.

¶ **210.** With the approval of the Quarterly Conference, any church or charge may provide for rotation in the office of elective stewards. In the event such rotation in office is proposed, a resolution shall be presented to the Quarterly Conference, for its action and determination, setting forth in detail the plan and the method proposed.

¶ **211.** In each church the Quarterly Conference may make provision for the recognition of the faithful service of those stewards on the board who have reached the age of seventy-two, or who may have become physically incapacitated, by electing them honorary stewards. An honorary steward shall be entitled to all the privileges of a steward, except the right to vote.

¶ **212.** 1. The board shall be organized annually by the election of a chairman, a vice-chairman, a recording secretary, a treasurer or treasurers (¶ 268), and, when deemed desirable, a financial secretary (¶ 269). These officers shall be elected by the members of the board on the nomination of a Committee on Nominations. (*See* ¶ 278.1.) Additional nominations may be made from the floor.

2. If a church business manager is desired, the board shall counsel with the pastor on his nomination to the Quarterly Conference. (*See* ¶¶ 143.11, 269.)

¶ **213.** To the board is committed the administration of the affairs of the local church, both spiritual and temporal, as hereinafter set forth, subject to the authority of the Quarterly Conference as set forth in ¶ 206. The board shall meet monthly at a time determined by the board. Special meetings may be ordered by the board, or called by the chairman or by the pastor or by a majority of the membership of the board.

¶ 214. The board shall not deny or take from any organization in the local church a right or power granted it by the Discipline.

¶ 215. It shall be the duty of the board:

1. As the administrative agency of the Quarterly Conference, to promote and to have general administrative oversight of the work of the local church, both spiritual and temporal, under the direction of the pastor, including the receiving of reports from all the organizations of the church.

2. After consultation with the pastor, and after careful consideration of all matters pertaining to his efficiency, to recommend to the Quarterly Conference, at the session next preceding the Annual Conference, the salary of the pastor, and of the associate pastor or pastors, if any (¶ 148); and to make ample provision for the other financial needs of the church (¶ 261).

3. To promote through an educational program interest in all the benevolent causes authorized by the General, Jurisdictional, Annual, and District Conferences, and to see that the fourth Sunday of each month is observed as **World Service Sunday,** for the purpose of supporting world service and conference benevolences, co-ordinating the same with the observance in the church school.

4. In co-operation with the pastor and the church lay leader, to promote the program of lay activities (¶¶ 286-93), in harmony with the plan and program of the General Board of Lay Activities.

5. To arrange for a program of visitation of the entire constituency of the church, particularly strangers in the community and members of the congregation who may be ill or in distress. (*See* ¶ 222.7-.8.)

6. Under the direction of the pastor, in co-operation with the commissions to plan and as needed to approve the program and work of the local church; to promote the spiritual and temporal interests of the local church; to

discharge faithfully any and all duties and responsibilities committed to it by the Quarterly Conference or by the law of the church; to take such action as it may determine to be for the well-being and progress of the local church; *provided* that all such actions shall be in harmony with the provisions of the Discipline.

¶ **216.** Before the close of the conference year the board shall devote at least one full meeting to the development of the total program of the local church for the succeeding year, based on the program elements provided by the commissions and other groups within the church. It shall be the responsibility of the pastor and the chairman to arrange for this meeting and to insure that the commissions and other groups make advance preparation for it. This planning shall be reviewed early in the new year and revised as needed, giving consideration to the goals and objectives adopted by the Annual Conference session in so far as they relate to the local church.

Sec. II   **Commissions**

¶ **219.** 1. No local church, however small, is adequately and effectively organized unless there is set up a minimum structure for participating in five of the major concerns of the Church Universal—evangelism, education, missions, stewardship, and Christian social concerns. To the Official Board, in co-operation with the pastor, is especially committed the promotion and administration of these phases of the church's life and ministry. It shall be the duty of the board to give continuous leadership and oversight therein, through five commissions, duly constituted, whose respective duties are hereinafter defined (¶¶ 220-75): (1) the Commission on Membership and Evangelism; (2) the Commission on Education; (3) the Commission on Missions; (4) the Commission on Stewardship and Finance; (5) the Commission on Christian Social Concerns; *provided* that, when desired, a Commission on Worship (¶ 276) may also be constituted for the promotion and supervision of this concern of the church. Each commission shall be elected by the Quarterly Conference (¶ 144), or by the board if the Quarterly Conference fails to do so, and shall be auxiliary to the board. The pastor and the church lay leader shall be ex officio members of each commission.

2. To develop a unified church program, each commission (except as provided for a small church in § 4 below) shall include a representative elected by each other commission not otherwise represented among its membership.

3. Interim vacancies in the commissions shall be filled in the same manner as those vacating office were chosen, except that vacancies in offices originally elected by the Quarterly Conference or Annual Church Conference may be filled by the Official Board.

4. In a small church, if the Quarterly Conference finds it necessary, each commission may be composed of the elected chairman (¶ 143.6) and the available ex officio members.

5. The Official Board may also organize such committees (¶ 278) as are needed to effect a broad coverage of the manifold interests of the church.

Sec. III.   **The Commission on Membership and Evangelism**

¶ 220. In each local church there shall be a **Commission on Membership and Evangelism** (¶¶ 144, 219), which shall be auxiliary to the General, Jurisdictional, and Annual Conference Boards of Evangelism, and the District Committee on Evangelism. It shall be the duty of this commission to seek out the unsaved and the unchurched in the community, and to exercise all diligence that they may be led into a saving knowledge of Jesus Christ and into the fellowship of the church. It shall also be the duty of the commission to seek out the inactive and negligent members of the local church, and to use all laudable means to restore them to active participation in the church's life and fellowship.

¶ 221. 1. The Commission on Membership and Evangelism shall be composed of the chairman, pastor, minister or director of evangelism if any, church lay leader, membership secretary (¶ 133), secretary of spiritual life of the Woman's Society of Christian Service, membership cultivation superintendent of the church school, a representative from Methodist Men, chairman of Christian witness of the Methodist Youth Fellowship, such members of the District Committee on Evangelism (¶¶ 1481-83) as have membership in the local church, <u>not fewer than six</u> and as many more members at large elected in accordance with ¶ 144 as the Quarterly Conference shall determine, and the representatives of other commissions specified in ¶ 219.2; *provided* that in a small church these provisions may be modified as stated in ¶ 219.4; and *provided*, further, that all members of the commission shall be members of The Methodist Church.

2. At the beginning of each conference year the chairman (¶ 143.6) shall call together the members for organization. The commission shall elect a vice-chairman, secretary, and such other officers and committees as it may determine.

3. The commission shall outline its program and estimate its anticipated financial needs, including evangelistic and devotional literature and materials essential to carrying on its total responsibilities as outlined in ¶ 222, and present, through its chairman and the representative from the Commission on Stewardship and Finance, a request for the necessary funds prior to the preparation of the annual budget (¶ 266).

4. The commission shall meet monthly in order to review and plan its work and receive reports. The chairman shall make a monthly report to the Official Board covering progress of the commission's work for the preceding month and plans for the future.

5. The pastor of a circuit may organize the several local-church commissions into a single commission, in which case its work shall be projected on a charge-wide basis.

¶ **222.** To the Commission on Membership and Evangelism in co-operation with the pastor are committed the following specific duties:

1. To promote the total program of evangelism (¶ 1464) within the church and its community.

2. In close co-operation with the pastor, and in line with the general program of The Methodist Church, to create and promote a local program and lead the local church in

the Period of Spiritual Enrichment, beginning the Sunday preceding Ash Wednesday, for the deepening of the spiritual life of all church members and for preparing and sending forth dedicated disciples to be witnesses for Christ and his Church. In this period, Ash Wednesday, the World Day of Prayer, and other high points of the pre-Easter season shall be used to the best advantage.

3. To take a religious census of the community periodically, if possible with the co-operation of the other churches in the community; and to seek the co-operation of the church school, the Woman's Society of Christian Service, and other church organizations in making a list of persons from these and other sources who should be won to Christ and his Church.

4. To recommend to the Quarterly Conference a minimum goal of persons to be received during the year on profession of faith, and to work diligently toward the attainment of the same.

5. To promote the use of the recommended special days, weeks, and seasons for evangelistic purposes.

6. To use all laudable means to create an evangelistic spirit within the membership, and under the leadership of the pastor to assist in planning and promoting special evangelistic preaching services at least annually.

7. To promote attendance upon the public worship of God (¶ 97) and through friendly visitation, distribution of literature, and other means to lead indifferent members to active participation in the life and work of the church.

8. To arrange for the visitation of strangers in the community and those members of the congregation who may be ill or in distress.

9. To create a special committee whose duty shall be to do all in its power to re-enlist in the active fellowship of the church all members who are negligent in attending worship or in participating in the church's life and work.

10. To initiate and develop prayer groups, missions, retreats, vigils, and prayer fellowships.

11. To distribute evangelistic and devotional literature, and to use all means for acquainting the community with the church and its program.

12. To encourage private and family worship, and to

promote the reading of the Holy Scriptures and the use of *The Upper Room* and other devotional literature.

13. To promote organized visitation evangelism during one or more periods each year, to secure new commitments to Christ, and the transfer of Methodists in the community whose memberships are elsewhere.

14. To encourage such groups as the Fisherman's Club, Fellowship of Evangelism, The Twelve, or kindred organizations, and to co-operate with them in their work.

15. To assist the pastor, when requested, in training classes for church membership.

16. To co-operate with the Commission on Education and the Commission on Missions in organizing new churches.

17. To develop an adequate program for assimilating new members into the life and work of the church and its organizations.

18. To review at least annually, preferably early in the year, the membership rolls of the church; to use these rolls as a basis for a program of spiritual visitation; to entreat and encourage all members to be faithful; to assist the pastor in urging those who have moved permanently from the community to join a Methodist church in their new community (¶ 119); and to make recommendations to the fourth Quarterly Conference after the provisions of ¶ 127 have been faithfully performed by the pastor and the commission. This commission shall regard its duty to be that of winning and saving members to the church.

¶ **223.** 1. If a **minister of evangelism** is desired, the Quarterly Conference shall request through the district superintendent that the bishop appoint one, and shall fix his salary (¶ 148).

2. If the employment of a layman as **director of evangelism** is desired, the pastor, with the concurrence of the commission, shall recommend a proper person to the Official Board, which shall have the power to employ him, fix his salary, and terminate his service.

3. The minister or director of evangelism shall be administratively responsible to the pastor and, in co-opera-

tion with the pastor and the chairman of the commission, shall guide the evangelistic program of the church.

Sec. IV.   **The Commission on Education**

¶ **231.** In order that a local church may be so organized and administered as to provide effectively for the Christian education of its entire constituency, there shall be a **Commission on Education** in each local church (¶ 144). It shall be auxiliary to the Annual Conference and Jurisdictional Boards of Education and to the Division of the Local Church of the General Board of Education. In a small church the Commission on Education and the Workers' Conference (¶ 249) may function as one body except in the election of the officers and teachers of the church school.

¶ **232.** 1. The persons holding the following offices are members of the Commission on Education: the chairman (¶ 143.6), pastor or pastors and church lay leader (¶ 219.1), church-school superintendent, division superintendents, membership cultivation superintendent, minister or director of Christian education (or educational assistant), minister or director of music, church-school secretary, and secretary of stewardship. The Woman's Society of Christian Service and Methodist Men shall each elect one representative to the commission, and the Methodist Youth Fellowship shall elect two. In addition there shall be not fewer than three and as many more members at large elected in accordance with ¶ 144 as the Quarterly Conference shall determine, chosen for special competency in the educational work of the church, and also the representatives of other commissions specified in ¶ 219.2. *Provided*, however, that in a small church the foregoing provisions may be modified as stated in ¶ 219.4.

2. At the beginning of each conference year the chairman shall call together the members for organization. The commission shall elect a vice-chairman, secretary, and such other officers and committees as are suggested in the commission manual or as the commission may determine.

¶ **233.** The functions and duties of the Commission on Education shall be as follows:

1. It shall determine the policies for the church school as a whole and its parts, and shall give general direction to all the educational work of the church. (*See* ¶ 1396.)

2. It shall study the educational needs of the church and shall provide for the organization, guidance, supervision, and, as needed, modification of the church school and of its three divisions with their departments, classes, and groups.

3. It shall be responsible for counseling with officers and teachers regarding the curriculum materials used by the classes and departments of the church school, and shall see that they are appropriate for each class and group, and that they are selected from the curriculum materials approved by the Curriculum Committee of the General Board of Education, and are ordered under the supervision of the commission. It shall be responsible for supervising the selection and use of music and hymnbooks in the church school, in harmony with the standards of the General Board of Education, and for the integration of children's and youth choirs into the Christian education program for children and youth. It shall also be responsible for supervising the selection and use of audio-visual materials in the church school and the training of officers, teachers, and other workers in their use, and shall see that all audio-visual materials used in the church school are in harmony with the standards of the General Board of Education.

4. In order that the statistical records of church schools in The Methodist Church may be reliable and uniform, it shall follow the standards of membership, attendance, and maintenance of the roll which are established by the General Board of Education, and shall use the forms and record books prepared by the board.

5. Along with other official bodies in the local church, it shall encourage and maintain opportunities for initiative and expression on the part of youth as well as opportunity for adult counsel.

6. It shall co-operate with the Official Board and the other commissions of the church in organizing and sponsoring new churches and church schools, as outlined in the commission manual. (*See* ¶¶ 155, 251.)

7. It shall perform the following other duties:

a) Enlist and train the necessary officers, counselors, teachers, and other leaders.

b) Elect certain officers and teachers as required by ¶ 246, fill vacancies in these positions, and, upon the recommendation of the pastor or the church-school superintendent, remove any officer or teacher for unsatisfactory service, habitual neglect, or improper conduct; *provided* that any officer elected or confirmed by the Quarterly Conference shall be removed from office only by the Quarterly Conference on recommendation of the pastor.

c) Plan the work of the church school by holding regular meetings of the commission and of all church-school workers, together and by divisions and departments. (*See* ¶ 249.)

d) Provide for the proper observance of the special days and occasions in the church year, giving particular attention to the special days that are authorized by the General Conference for observance in the church school. (*See* ¶¶ 250, 296.)

e) Provide study groups in marriage and Christian homemaking for parents and young people. (*See* ¶ 234.)

f) Provide education concerning the significance of Christian higher education and information about our church-related institutions of higher learning, Wesley Foundations, and other student activities; recommend support of these interests to the Commission on Stewardship and Finance; and encourage the observance of relevant special days in the church year. To further these interests the commission may have a Committee on Christian Higher Education.

g) Plan the financial program of the church school (including the requesting of funds, if needed, through the Commission on Stewardship and Finance), budgeting all church-school funds and giving careful supervision to expenditures.

h) Allocate space for departments and classes and control the equipment provided for the use of the church school.

i) Provide for the full utilization of the materials interpreting and leading up to church membership which are a part of the church-school curriculum of Methodism, and, when requested by the pastor, assist in training classes for church membership.

j) Provide guidance for local-church programs of camping. (*See* ¶ 1401.4.)

k) Be responsible for the guidance and supervision of all children- and youth-serving organizations meeting under the auspices of the church.

l) Co-operate in the development of the total church program as provided in ¶ 216.

¶ **234.** The Commission on Education may organize a **Committee on Family Life,** composed of the three division superintendents and two other members of the Commission on Education, one representative each of the Woman's Society of Christian Service, the Methodist Youth Fellowship, the Young Adult Fellowship, Methodist Men, and the Commission on Membership and Evangelism, and others chosen because of their special skill and concern for the Christian family, which shall recommend to the commission plans for the family life education program in the local church and assist in carrying out the recommendations of the General Conference concerning family life (¶ 2021). This committee shall be responsible to the commission and shall report to its regular meetings. In a small church the commission may elect an individual **director of the family life program** instead of a committee.

¶ **235.** The Commission on Education may, in co-operation with the other commissions, organize an **Intercommission Audio-Visual Committee,** composed of at least one representative from each commission and in addition one each from the Council of Children's Workers and the Woman's Society of Christian Service. This committee shall counsel all the commissions in the selection, purchase, and use of audio-visual materials and equipment, and in the evaluation and use of radio and television programs related to the program of the church; and it may serve as the contact group for the Television, Radio, and Film Commission. It shall report to the Commission on Education and the Official Board. When it is impractical to have a representative committee, an **audio-**

visual counselor may be appointed by the Commission on Education after consultation with the other interested commissions.

¶ **236.** The Commission on Education may elect a **Committee on Fellowship and Recreational Life,** composed of representatives of the Children's, Youth, and Adult Divisions and such other members as may be desired, which shall recommend to the commission plans for a comprehensive program of recreation. In a small church the commission may elect an individual **director of recreation** instead of a committee.

¶ **241.** In each local church there shall be a **church school** for the purpose of discharging the church's responsibility for instructing and guiding its entire constituency in Christian faith and living. The church school shall provide for education in the Holy Scriptures, the Christian religion, and the Christian Church (leading to commitment to Christ and to church membership) through worship, fellowship, study, and service. Its program shall include evangelism, stewardship, missions, social action, recreation, and other activities.

¶ **242.** The Commission on Education shall organize and administer the church school in harmony with the provisions of the Discipline and in accordance with standards and procedures as set forth in the manuals for church schools of various types and sizes, which manuals shall be prepared by the Division of the Local Church of the General Board of Education under the authority of the General Conference.

¶ **243.** The church school includes for all ages (1) Sunday school, (2) the Methodist Sunday Evening Fellowship, (3) weekday activities, and (4) home and extension service. Within these four parts of the church school there may be: classes and study groups; extended and additional sessions for children; Sunday evening and weekday meetings of children, youth, and adults; children's and youth choirs; nursery home roll; nursery schools and kindergartens (¶ 245); children, youth, and adult home members and extension members; vacation church school; camping for children, youth, and adults; leadership education agencies; parent study groups;

fellowship groups; and other activities appropriate to the Christian education of the people. When one becomes a member of any one of these groups in the church school, he thereby becomes a member of the church school. The membership roll of the church school shall be kept current in accordance with the suggested procedures of the General Board of Education. Records and reports to Quarterly and Annual Conferences shall be made in keeping with these provisions.

¶ **244.** 1. The church school shall be organized in three divisions: **Children's Division,** from birth through eleven years; **Youth Division** (Methodist Youth Fellowship), from twelve through twenty-one years; **Adult Division,** twenty-two years and over; *provided* that older young people approaching adulthood shall be grouped in either the Youth Division or the Adult Division on the basis of their maturity, interests, needs, and social grouping in the community; and *provided*, further, that the General Board of Education may, at its discretion, modify these age provisions. In small churches each division may be composed of one or more classes. In larger churches each division may be divided into departments with classes in each department.

2. In the organization of the church school there may be councils appropriate to each age group.

3. The Commission on Education shall follow the manual issued by the Division of the Local Church of the General Board of Education describing the organization of schools of various sizes. (*See* ¶ 242.)

4. Classes, departments, and divisions shall develop their work in harmony with the disciplinary provisions and with the standards established by the Conference and General Boards of Education. Each department and division shall include in its total program Sunday morning, Sunday evening, and such other meetings and activities as may be determined by the Commission on Education for the Christian education of the children, youth, and adults of the church; *provided* that the results shall be a unified or correlated program of work.

5. The youth of The Methodist Church between the ages of twelve and twenty-one inclusive who belong to any

group for, or organizational unit of, youth in the church, shall be members of the Youth Division and thereby members of the **Methodist Youth Fellowship.** These provisions shall include college students who are related to the local church through activities which the Commission on Education shall provide. In churches at college campuses these plans shall be worked out co-operatively with the campus-related Methodist student organization.

6. Children- and youth-serving agencies shall be included in the church school provided their program is a part of the program of the church school and is under the direction of the Commission on Education and the pastor. (*See* ¶ 233.7k.)

7. The Woman's Society of Christian Service and the Commission on Education shall co-operate in the missionary education of children and youth.

8. The secretaries of children's work and of youth work of the Woman's Society of Christian Service shall be members of the division councils for the age groups concerned.

9. The church lay leader, the presidents of the Woman's Society of Christian Service and of Methodist Men, the chairman of the Commission on Missions, and the leaders of such other adult groups as the Commission on Education may determine shall be members of the Adult Division Council.

¶ 245. When the needs of the children and the facilities and resources of the local church warrant it, the Commission on Education, on recommendation of the superintendent of the Children's Division and the pastor, and with the approval of the Official Board, may provide for a **through-the-week nursery school and/or kindergarten** as a part of the church school. In such case the commission shall be responsible for:

1. Determining the policies, program, and curriculum, and the conditions under which children may be enrolled.

2. Electing the teachers.

3. Providing for the physical safety of the children in accordance with local laws.

4. Recommending to the Commission on Stewardship

and Finance a budget of financial needs, including teachers' salaries, materials, and equipment.

5. Determining a schedule of payments by parents for such service to their children.

6. Receiving regular reports of the school from its director and keeping permanent records of its work, leadership, and finances.

¶ **246.** Great care shall be exercised in the selection of teachers, officers, and other workers in the church school. They shall be elected annually in the following manner:

1. The Quarterly Conference shall elect, to serve from the beginning of the ensuing conference or church-school year: (*a*) the church-school superintendent (¶¶ 143.7, 248.3); (*b*) a membership cultivation superintendent and three division superintendents (¶ 143.8); (*c*) a director of Christian education, or educational assistant, if desired (¶¶ 143.9, 247.1). Interim vacancies shall be filled by the Commission on Education, the pastor concurring, subject to confirmation by the next Quarterly Conference.

2. Each class or group concerned shall elect, prior to the beginning of the church-school year or as need may arise: (*a*) youth officers in the Youth Division; (*b*) officers in the Adult Division; and (*c*) the teachers of adult classes, after consultation with the church-school superintendent. Teachers of adult classes shall be subject to confirmation by the Commission on Education.

3. The Commission on Education shall elect, prior to the beginning of the church-school year, all teachers, officers, and workers not otherwise provided for, on nomination of the church-school superintendent with the approval of the pastor, the minister or director of Christian education, and the division superintendents. (*See* ¶ 233.7*b*.)

¶ **247.** 1. On nomination of the pastor, with the concurrence of the Commission on Education and the Committee on Pastoral Relations or the Committee on Lay Personnel, the Quarterly Conference may annually request the bishop to appoint, or may employ, a **minister or director of Christian education** or an educational assistant, who in co-operation with the pastor and the church-school superintendent shall guide the educational program of the local church in accordance with ¶ 233 and with the standards of the General Board of Education (¶ 1396). He shall be administratively responsible to the pastor. Provided he is certified as described in ¶ 1451, his title shall be minister of Christian education if he is an ordained ministerial member of an Annual Conference, or director of Christian education if he is a layman. In case he is not certified, his title shall be educational assistant. Two or more churches may join in using the services of such a person.

2. On nomination of the pastor, with the concurrence of the Music Committee (¶ 278.4), the Commission on Education, and the Committee on Pastoral Relations or the Committee on Lay Personnel, the Quarterly Conference may annually request the bishop to appoint, or may employ, a **minister or director of music,** who shall direct the total music program of the local church in accordance with the standards of the General Board of Education (¶ 1396) and of the General Commission on Worship (¶ 1569.2). He shall be administratively responsible to the pastor. Provided he is certified as described in ¶ 1451, his title shall be minister of music if he is an ordained ministerial member of an Annual Conference, or director of music if he is a layman.

¶ 248. In the educational work of the church the following relationships shall be observed:

1. The Christian education program of the local church school shall be the program set up and authorized by the Annual Conference Board of Education and the Division of the Local Church of the General Board of Education.

2. In the program of work herein outlined the pastor is, as elsewhere in all the work of the pastoral charge, the preacher in charge, and is responsible for the total educational program of the local church. Nothing in this plan is to be construed as interfering with his authority and responsibility.

3. The **church-school superintendent** is the administrative officer of the church school. It shall be his duty to co-operate with the pastor and with the minister or

director of Christian education, if any, to stimulate, encourage, and help the other officers and teachers and to plan with them for the work of the school as a whole and in all its parts. He shall carry out the policies of the Commission on Education.

4. Under the direction of the Commission on Education the church school shall engage in co-operative enterprises with other Methodist church schools in the same district, and with schools of other communions, looking toward community betterment and community service and other Christian activities.

5. The Christian education of church-school members calls for curriculums which are graded and adapted to the needs of the pupils. The curriculums shall be based on sound educational principles and the universal gospel of the living Christ. Methodist connectionalism requires curriculums which contain the present Methodist traditions, purposes, programs, and movements. Each church school shall provide instruction in the curriculums approved by the Curriculum Committee of the General Board of Education of The Methodist Church.

¶ 249. To provide opportunity for fellowship, study, and discussion of the educational work of the church, there shall be held quarterly a general meeting of all the officers, teachers, and leaders in the church school to be known as the **Workers' Conference.** The chairman shall be the church-school superintendent, who, with the pastor, and the minister or director of Christian education, if any, shall be responsible for planning the program of the Workers' Conference. There may also be meetings of the officers and teachers of departments in those church schools that are organized by departments.

¶ 250. The following special days shall be observed:

1. In order that the members of the church school may be informed concerning the world-wide service program of Methodism and share in its support, the fourth Sunday in each month shall be observed in the church school as **World Service Sunday.** An offering shall be taken in the school for world service and conference benevolences. This offering shall be sent with other offerings of the local church for this cause to the Annual Conference treasurer.

The amount raised annually in the church school for world service and conference benevolences shall be reported by the pastor and recorded in a column so designated in the statistical reports of the Annual Conference.

2. **Church School Rally Day** shall be observed in each school for the purpose of emphasizing the importance of Christian education and for receiving an offering for the Conference Board of Education for the program of its local church division. The funds raised on this day shall be remitted as may be determined by the Annual Conference. These funds shall be recorded in a column in the pastor's report to the Annual Conference, but shall not be charged to the share of the Conference Board of Education in the conference apportioned benevolences. The fixing of the date of this observance shall be the responsibility of the Division of the Local Church of the General Board of Education, which may delegate this responsibility to the Conference Boards of Education.

3. **Race Relations Sunday** shall be observed in every local church on the second Sunday in February each year. This shall be the occasion for reviewing the work of The Methodist Church in the founding and support of Negro schools. It shall also be an occasion for creating better relations among all races and particularly informing our people concerning the contributions and needs of Negro colleges. An offering shall be received for the benefit of Negro colleges related to the Board of Education, which may be a part of, or in addition to, such sums as may already be included in local-church or Annual Conference budgets. Due recognition shall be given to the historic responsibility of the former Methodist Episcopal Church, South, for aid to the Christian Methodist Episcopal Church.

4. **Methodist Student Day** shall be observed annually in every local church, preferably the second Sunday in June. If not on that date, it shall be observed on some other Sunday designated by the Annual Conference or the Commission on Education of the local church. On this day emphasis shall be given to the work of higher education in church-related institutions. An offering shall be re-

ceived for the support of National Methodist Scholarships and the Student Loan Fund for Methodist students.

5. Each local church shall observe **National Family Week** from the first to the second Sunday of May. It shall be the purpose of this week to focus attention on the importance of religious living. Ministers are urged to preach on the importance of Christian teaching in the home and the need for close co-operation between the church school and home and the use of religious literature in the home. Opportunity shall be given for parents to dedicate themselves to the teaching of religion in the home by precept and example. Because of the close relationship of the church school and the home in the teaching of children, youth, and adults, the promotion of the observance of National Family Week shall be the responsibility of the Division of the Local Church of the General Board of Education in co-operation with other boards and agencies of the church. The sole purpose of this observance shall be to strengthen family life in keeping with the resolution of the General Conference concerning the Christian family (¶ 2021). Therefore a special offering should not be taken in connection with National Family Week.

6. The first Sunday of National Family Week, or some other day selected by the Annual Conference, may be designated as **Children's Day,** for the purpose of emphasizing the responsibility of the church for our children, the same to be observed without a church-wide offering. The program for such a day shall be the concern of the Division of the Local Church of the General Board of Education and the Boards of Education of the various Annual Conferences.

¶ **251.** In a community where there is need of a Methodist church school, one may be organized with the written consent of the district superintendent. The church school, when organized, shall be under the direction of the Commission on Education of the church organizing it; or, if organized independent of a local church, it shall be under the direction and supervision of the district superintendent.

Sec. V.   **The Commission on Missions**

¶ **256.** There shall be organized in each local church a **Commission on Missions,** composed of not fewer than three and as many more members elected in accordance with ¶ 144 as the Quarterly Conference may determine, and in addition the following ex officio and representative members: the pastor or pastors; the church lay leader; the church-school superintendent; the hospitals and homes steward; two youth members, one of whom shall be the chairman of Christian outreach of the Methodist Youth Fellowship; the secretary of missionary education of the Woman's Society of Christian Service; and the representatives of other commissions specified in ¶ 219.2; *provided* that in a small church these provisions may be modified as stated in ¶ 219.4. It shall be auxiliary to the General Board of Missions and to the Jurisdictional and Annual Conference Boards of Missions and shall co-operate with these agencies in their plans and programs for missionary education and cultivation. At the beginning of each conference year the chairman (¶ 143.6) shall call together the members for organization. The commission shall elect a vice-chairman, secretary, and such other officers and committees as it may determine.

¶ **257.** It shall be the duty of the Commission on Missions as the central planning group for missionary education and cultivation:

1. To provide for the diffusion of missionary information, the distribution of missionary literature, the circulation of *World Outlook*, and the use of missionary audio-visual materials in the church.

2. To plan for a church-wide school of missions for children, youth, and adults in co-operation with the Woman's Society of Christian Service, the other commissions, and other agencies, using materials produced or approved by the Joint Section of Education and Cultivation. In the case of materials for children and youth, they shall also be approved by the Interboard Committee on Missionary Education.

3. To co-operate with other agencies in the survey and study of the needs of the community, and to recommend

to the Quarterly Conference plans whereby the local church may undertake missionary projects for the purpose of Christianizing the total life of its own community.

4. To study the program of the General Board of Missions and recommend to the Quarterly Conference and the Official Board such approved projects—district, conference, and world—as should be supported by the local church.

5. To co-operate with the pastor, Woman's Society of Christian Service, Commission on Education, and other organizations and agencies in the local church in all plans for the development of the missionary life and spirit of the local church, especially in programs and offerings for missions on fourth Sundays, plans for raising funds for world service and conference benevolences, and the support of missionary specials by individuals, organizations, and the whole church.

6. To confer with the Commission on Stewardship and Finance and recommend to it the projects and amounts to be included in the budget of the local church for benevolent causes; to co-operate with the pastor and the Commission on Stewardship and Finance in plans for raising the church's obligation for world service and conference benevolences; and to plan for proper observance of World Service Sunday (¶¶ 215.3, 250.1, 296.1a).

7. To co-operate with the pastor and the Commission on Stewardship and Finance in an effort to insure an effective every-member canvass each year, with emphasis on stewardship and missions.

8. To co-operate with the Official Board and the other commissions in organizing and sponsoring new churches and church schools. (See ¶¶ 155, 251.)

9. To represent the work of the Methodist Committee for Overseas Relief in the local church and encourage support of its projects.

10. To inform the whole local church, youth and adults alike, of the qualifications and current needs for missionary personnel, and to present the challenge of missionary service to the people.

11. To lead the local church in the observance of the One Great Hour of Sharing, and to interpret the Crusade scholarship program in the local church.

12. To prepare each year an operating budget for the commission and present it to the Commission on Stewardship and Finance, so that sufficient funds can be included in the annual budget (¶ 266) to enable it to do the work assigned by the Discipline.

13. To co-operate in the development of the total program of the church as provided in ¶ 216.

SEC. VI.   **The Commission on Stewardship and Finance**

¶ **261.** It shall be the responsibility of the Official Board to make proper and adequate provision for the financial needs of the church, including ministerial support (i.e., for the pastor or pastors, district superintendent, conference claimants, and bishops), approved items of local expense, world service and conference benevolences, other items apportioned the church by the proper authority, and all obligations assumed by the local church.

¶ **262.** 1. There shall be in every local church a **Commission on Stewardship and Finance,** which shall, under the authority and direction of the Official Board, promote and cultivate Christian stewardship and administer the financial program of the church. It shall be auxiliary to the General, Jurisdictional, Annual Conference, and District Boards of Lay Activities.

2. The commission shall be composed of the chairman (¶ 143.6), pastor or pastors and church lay leader (¶ 219.1), secretary of stewardship, chairman of the Official Board, financial secretary or church business manager, church treasurer or treasurers, one representative each of Methodist Men and the Methodist Youth Fellowship, not fewer than three and as many more members at large elected in accordance with ¶ 144 as the Quarterly Conference shall determine, and the representatives of other comissions specified in ¶ 219.2; *provided* that in a small church these provisions may be modified as stated in ¶ 219.4.

3. At the beginning of each conference year the chairman shall call together the members for organization. The commission shall elect a vice-chairman, a secretary, and such other officers and committees as are suggested

in the commission manual or as the commission may determine.

4. The commission shall co-operate in the development of the total church program as provided in ¶ 216.

5. It is recommended that there be two committees to function as part of the commission, the Committee on Finance and the Committee on Stewardship, and that the secretary of stewardship be chairman of the latter.

¶ **263.** In the cultivation and promotion of Christian stewardship the **secretary of stewardship** (¶ 143.12), formerly called director of stewardship, shall develop a program of stewardship education which in turn shall be presented to the total commission for review, revision, and adoption. After such adoption the secretary and the Committee on Stewardship shall carry out the program in harmony with the directives prepared by the General Board of Lay Activities in accordance with ¶ 1512.

¶ **264.** Inasmuch as the Discipline of our church clearly designates tithing as the minimum standard of giving for Methodists, it shall be the duty of every local church to carry on a program of education in the field of the stewardship of possessions with an emphasis on tithing. It shall be the duty of the secretary of stewardship, in consultation with the pastor and the chairman of the commission, to plan and recommend the details of this program of stewardship emphasis. This program should be implemented by an intensive emphasis in stewardship education and sustained by a year-round program of stewardship cultivation. It should be in the planning of every local church to give members an opportunity annually to make commitments to tithing. This program shall be auxiliary to the stewardship program as sponsored by the General Board of Lay Activities.

¶ **266.** 1. The commission shall each year set up a **budget** for the local church and submit it to the Official Board for review and final decision. The commissions and committees whose work is related to program and budget shall have opportunity to make recommendations, which shall be reviewed and co-ordinated by the program committee of the every-member canvass (¶ 267.1) and by the commission before presentation to the board.

2. In setting up the budget the commission shall confer each year with the Commission on Missions to the end that adequate provision shall be made for the benevolence causes of the church: world service and conference benevolences (through recommendation to the Quarterly Conference as described in ¶ 147), Advance specials, and conference and district projects of a missionary and church-extension nature.

3. It is recommended that the local-church expense and benevolence causes be set up separately, and that both causes be presented to the membership.

4. If a budget plan is used which combines local-church expense and benevolences in one system of pledging and contributing, the Commissions on Missions, Education, and Stewardship and Finance shall seriously study the ratio of the proposed acceptance for world service and conference benevolences to the amount appropriated for local-church expense and recommend a fair share for the benevolences. As there is a substantial increase in the pledging and giving of the people, conscientious care shall be taken that the benevolences receive an increase proportionate to the increase in local-church expense.

5. When causes are combined in the budget, the budgetary responsibilities of the Commission on Education and the church school, as stated in ¶ 233.7g, shall not be contravened.

¶ 267. When the program of the church has been developed as provided in ¶ 216 and the annual budget has been approved by the board, the commission shall, under the direction of the board, proceed to insure an income sufficient to cover the same, and shall administer the funds received according to the following plan, with such adaptations and adjustments as the board may determine:

1. There shall be an annual every-member canvass, by which all members of the local church shall be given an opportunity to make their individual pledges to the support of the church. Every member of a local church is obligated to support the entire program of the church. Pledges should be, as far as practicable, on a weekly basis, and in proportion to one's income.

2. Should the probable income appear insufficient to

meet the annual budget, steps shall be taken at the beginning of the year to provide for the deficit.

3. All payments on pledges shall be credited to the donors, and a proper account shall be kept of each subscriber and contributor.

4. Funds received shall be deposited promptly in a bank approved by the board, and the account therein shall be in the name of the local church.

5. Funds received shall be disbursed as the board directs, and to the objects for which they are contributed.

6. Contributions designated for specific causes and objects shall be promptly forwarded according to the intent of the donor, and shall not be used, even temporarily, for any other purpose.

7. When the budget of the local church has been approved, additional appropriations or items shall not be added thereto without the consent of the Official Board; and payments to no cause or item in the budget shall exceed the budget allowance except by order of the board.

8. As far as practicable, and under the direction of the commission, the treasurer shall prorate the income received each month among the respective items and causes represented in the budget, according to the proportional share of each; *provided* that the pastor's salary shall be excepted and given priority claim.

9. Report shall be made by the financial secretary and the treasurer or treasurers to the board each month, and to the Quarterly Conference when requested, of all receipts and disbursements, and of unpaid obligations against the budget.

10. It shall be the continuing duty of the commission to inform the congregation of the financial needs of the church.

¶ 268. The treasurer or treasurers elected by the board (¶ 212.1) shall receive and disburse all money contributed to causes represented in the local-church budget, and such other funds and contributions as the board may determine; or it may elect a treasurer to receive and disburse funds and contributions for local expense and a benevolence treasurer to receive and disburse funds and contributions for benevolences and similar causes, in every case under the supervision and direction of the board. The treasurer shall remit each month to the conference treasurer all world service and conference benevolence funds then on hand. (*See* ¶ 147.)

¶ 269. If a financial secretary is elected (¶ 212.1), he shall receive the contributions to the local church, keeping records of the contributors and their payments as provided in ¶ 267.3, and disburse them promptly to the treasurer or treasurers. If a financial secretary is not elected, the treasurer or treasurers shall assume these responsibilities; *provided*, however, that they may be assumed by a church business manager (¶¶ 143.11, 212.2) if deemed desirable by the pastor and the Official Board.

¶ 270. The commission shall make provision for an annual audit of the records of the financial officers of the local church and all its organizations, and shall report to the Quarterly Conference.

¶ 271. No local church shall engage as a fund-raising agent any person or organization not in the employ of the Board of Missions, or of some other General, Jurisdictional, or Annual Conference agency, without first obtaining the written consent of the district superintendent.

¶ 272. No lottery, raffle, or other game of chance shall be used in raising money for any purpose.

Sec. VII. The Commission on Christian Social Concerns

¶ 274. 1. A **Commission on Christian Social Concerns** shall be constituted by the Quarterly Conference, as provided in ¶¶ 144, 219, composed of four or more members elected by the Quarterly Conference. In addition the pastor, church lay leader, secretary of Christian social relations of the Woman's Society of Christian Service, chairman of Christian citizenship of the Methodist Youth Fellowship, and hospitals and homes steward shall be ex officio members; preferably no one of these shall serve as chairman. There shall also be representatives of other commissions as provided in ¶ 219.2. *Provided*, however, that in a small church the foregoing provisions may be modified as stated in ¶ 219.4.

2. In addition to the chairman elected by the Quarterly Conference (¶ 143.6) the commission may elect a vice-

chairman, a secretary, and such other officers as may be necessary.

3. The commission shall develop and promote programs and study and action projects in the following areas of Christian social concern: temperance, health, and welfare; peace and world order; and human relations and economic affairs. To this end, it may divide its membership into three committees of approximately equal size, patterned after the divisions of the general board (¶¶ 1535-41).

¶ **275.** 1. The commission shall provide for the observance of **World Order Sunday,** which shall be observed annually in each local church on the Sunday established by the proper department of the National Council of Churches (¶ 296.2*f*).

2. The commission shall, in co-operation with the pastor, promote in the local church the observance of **Commitment Day** on the first Sunday in December (¶¶ 296.2*g*, 1536).

SEC. VIII.   **The Commission on Worship**

¶ **276.** A **Commission on Worship** may be constituted by the Quarterly Conference, as provided in ¶ 219, composed of <u>not fewer than three</u> and as many more members elected in accordance with ¶ 144 as the Quarterly Conference may determine, and in addition the pastor and the church lay leader (¶ 219.1) and the representatives of other commissions specified in ¶ 219.2; *provided* that in a small church these provisions may be modified as stated in ¶ 219.4. (*See* ¶ 1569.11.)

SEC. IX.   **Committees**

¶ **278.** For the promoting of other interests and activities in the local church the Official Board shall create from its own membership and from the membership of the local church such committees as it may judge necessary, exercising care that these committees do not overlap or conflict with the committees of the Quarterly Conference. At least one member of each committee shall be a member of the board. Other members may be from the general membership of the church or from the board as the board may determine. Except where the Discipline provides otherwise, each committee shall elect its officers; *provided* that the chairman of each shall be a member of the Official Board. Each committee shall be responsible to the board, and shall report to the board regularly (and to the Quarterly Conference if requested). The board may create such committees as it may determine from the following list, and may add others as may appear advisable for the proper prosecution of its work:

1. The **Committee on Nominations,** elected by the board on nomination from the floor, or by ballot without nomination, which shall nominate to the board the officers thereof, and the members of its respective committees. The right of nomination from the floor for officers and committee members shall in no case be denied. The pastor shall be chairman of the Committee on Nominations. (*See* ¶ 212.)

2. The **Committee on Good Literature,** whose duty it shall be to call attention to the publication of new books of worth in forming and building the Christian life, arrange for exhibits of books and pamphlets relating to the work of The Methodist Church, promote the observance of Universal Bible Sunday, secure subscriptions to *Together*, *Christian Advocate*, *Central Christian Advocate*, and conference and area publications, and promote the use of approved publications in the church school.

3. The **Committee on Hospitals and Homes,** of which the hospitals and homes steward (¶ 143.14) shall be chairman, which shall promote in co-operation with the General, Jurisdictional, and Annual Conference Boards of Hospitals and Homes (¶¶ 1551-61) the interests of hospitals and homes of The Methodist Church and the particular hospitals and homes for whose support they are respectively responsible. This committee, on request of the pastor, shall have charge annually of the Golden Cross enrollment and the dissemination of literature to assist in relating the congregation not only to the greater philanthropy of the church but to the social welfare organizations represented in the local parish and community.

4. The **Music Committee,** which shall encourage the use of suitable music in the worship service of the local church and, with the approval of the board, make pro-

vision for proper music leadership; *provided* that if the responsibility of the music leader is to direct the total music program of the local church, including youth and children's choirs and assistance in the church school, his selection shall be as indicated in ¶ 247.2.

5. The **Parsonage Committee,** which shall take proper action in co-operation with the Board of Trustees (¶ 165) to provide an adequate and suitable residence for the pastor. (*See* ¶ 145.7.)

6. The **Committee on Church Property,** which, unless otherwise provided by the trustees, shall have supervision of the maintenance and upkeep of the sanctuary and other church units.

7. The **Committee on Men's Work,** which shall promote the training and active participation of men in the work of the local church, under the leadership of the General Board of Lay Activities.

8. Other committees as the board may determine.

SEC. X **The Woman's Society of Christian Service**

¶ **281.** In every local church there shall be a **Woman's Society of Christian Service.**[18] The following is the authorized constitution for such a society.

¶ **282.** *Article 1. Name.*—There shall be a Woman's Society of Christian Service in the local church, auxiliary to the Conference Woman's Society of Christian Service. A **Wesleyan Service Guild,** auxiliary to the Woman's Society of Christian Service, composed of employed women, may also be organized in a local church.

Art. 2. Purpose.—The purpose of the Woman's Society of Christian Service shall be to unite all the women of the church in Christian living and service; to help develop and support Christian work among women and children around the world; to develop the spiritual life; to study the needs of the world; to take part in such service activities as will strengthen the local church and improve civic, community, and world conditions. To this end this organization shall seek to enlist women, young people, and

---

[18] *See* Judicial Council Decision 138.

children in this Christian fellowship, and to secure funds
for the activities in the local church and the support of the
work undertaken at home and abroad for the establishment of a world Christian community.

Art. 3. Membership.—A woman may become a member
of this society by giving prayer, service, and an annual
contribution of money to the total budget through membership offerings, pledges, or gifts. She shall contribute
to, educate for, and promote the total program of the
women of Methodism. The pastor shall be a member of
the executive committee of the society.

*Art. 4. Officers, Secretaries of Lines of Work, and Com-
mittees.*—The local society shall elect a president, a vice-
president, a recording secretary, and a treasurer. Secretaries of lines of work and the Committee on Nominations
shall be elected, and other committees shall be appointed,
in accordance with the plans of the Woman's Division of
Christian Service as may be set forth in the by-laws for
the local society. Where a simpler form of organization is
necessary in a small church, there shall be five or more
officers and secretaries of lines of work as determined by
the local society.

Art. 5. Funds.—(1) All funds from whatsoever source
secured by this society belong to this organization and
shall be disbursed only in accordance with its constitution and by its order.[19]

(2) The total budget to be secured and administered
by a Woman's Society of Christian Service in the local
church shall include pledges to missions to be directed
through the regular channels of finance of the society and
also funds for local church and community activities.

(3) All undesignated funds channeled to the Woman's
Division of Christian Service shall be divided in the
office of the treasurer of the division on a basis
to be determined by the division. There shall be no division of such funds by the local society.

(4) Funds for local-church and community activities
shall be secured and administered by the Woman's Society of Christian Service in the local church.

(5) Each society in the local church shall make an an-

---

[19] *See* Judicial Council Decision 138.

nual pledge to the total budget adopted by the conference society.

(6) Each society in the local church shall include in its budget a definite amount for a cultivation fund.

Art. 6. Meetings.—The society shall hold one or more meetings during a month for the transaction of its business and for the study of the work.

Art. 7. Amendments.—Proposed amendments to this constitution may be sent to the recording secretary of the Woman's Division of Christian Service at least forty days before the last annual meeting of the division in the quadrennium. Proposed amendments may also be sent directly to the General Conference.

Note: For a description of the Woman's Division of Christian Service and its subsidiary organizations see ¶¶ 1240-58.

Sec. XI. **Lay Activities in the Local Church**

¶ **286.** The Official Board, in co-operation with the pastor, shall be responsible for the program of lay activities in the local church as outlined under the direction of the General, Jurisdictional, Annual Conference, and District Boards of Lay Activities (¶¶ 1490-1515). In the program of lay activities the pastor is, as in all the work of the pastoral charge, the preacher in charge, and is responsible for the total program of the church. Nothing in this plan is to be construed as interfering with his general authority and responsibility.

¶ **287.** The program of lay activities in the local church shall include the interests and causes that have been committed to the General Board of Lay Activities by the Discipline (¶ 1493).

¶ **288.** There shall be a **church lay leader** in each local church, elected by the Quarterly Conference (¶ 143.2), who shall promote, in co-operation with the pastor and the chairman of the Official Board, the program of lay activities of The Methodist Church. If the board chairman is a layman, he may also be elected the church lay leader. He shall be responsible for the presentation of the program to the board, for the adoption of plans necessary to carry on the work, and for continued leadership to make it effective. He shall make a report to each regular session of the board, and to the Quarterly Conference as requested. He shall also co-operate with the pastor in presenting benevolences to the congregation and in promoting the circulation of *The Methodist Layman.* There may be elected by the same procedure one or more associate church lay leaders, if desired.

¶ **289.** The pastor of a circuit, with the consent of the Official Boards of the charge, shall organize the several Official Boards into a single **Charge Board of Lay Activities,** of which one of the church lay leaders shall be elected chairman. This board shall promote the program of lay activities on a charge-wide basis and encourage harmony and Christian fellowship among the churches of the circuit, to the end that the charge may render a more effective service.

¶ **291.** The Official Board, in co-operation with the pastor and the lay leader, shall be responsible for organizing **Methodist Men** in the local church and encouraging them to secure a charter. The purpose shall be the development of the spiritual life of the men of the church and the attainment of the following objectives:

1. To seek daily Christ's way of life; to bear witness to this way in business dealings and in social contacts; to engage in some definite Christian service.

2. To study and become familiar with The Methodist Church, its organization, and its doctrines.

3. To promote personal evangelism, especially among men and boys.

4. To develop Christian fellowship in the church, especially among laymen, by promoting Christian understanding.

5. To co-operate with the pastor, district superintendent, and bishop in promoting the program of the church.

6. To co-operate with other units of Methodist Men in the promotion of district, conference, and church-wide projects under the leadership of the General Board of Lay Activities. (*See* ¶ 1511.)

¶ **292.** In order to achieve the six objectives enumerated in ¶ 291, Methodist Men, as an organized unit in the local church, shall plan a program of activities in which the following are given consideration:

1. Co-operation with the Commission on Membership and Evangelism in a program of personal evangelism, and in assuring that every adult male member of the congregation is visited at least once each year.

2. Co-operation with the Commission on Stewardship and Finance in the cultivation of Christian stewardship and assistance in the annual every-member canvass.

3. Co-operation with the Commission on Education in a program of youth activities, such as Scouting or 4-H Club work in those communities where this need is not otherwise met.

4. Co-operation with the Commission on Missions in some worthy project as an expression of Christian outreach.

5. Co-operation with other official bodies of the church in recruiting and assisting worthy young people in securing a Christian education.

6. Co-operation with the pastor to relieve him of some of the responsibilities demanding his time so as to release him for ministering more fully to the spiritual needs of the people.

7. Co-operation with the pastor and official bodies of the church in sponsoring a program of training in churchmanship, including the organization and doctrines of The Methodist Church.

8. Encouraging the reading of *The Methodist Layman* as the official organ of Methodist Men.

¶ **293.** 1. A **lay speaker** is a member of a local church certified by his Quarterly Conference as qualified to perform the following duties:

a) To conduct services of worship and hold meetings for prayer and exhortation whenever opportunity is afforded, subject to the consent and direction of the pastor; *provided*, however, that when no pastor is appointed to the circuit, station, or mission, such services or meetings shall be held subject to the approval and supervision of the district superintendent.

b) To serve as needed in other kinds of church or church-related meetings.

c) To attend and present a written report to all sessions of the District and Quarterly Conferences.

2. A candidate recommended for lay speaker shall be a person of evident Christian character, conduct, and concern; he shall have potential natural gifts and graces, a willingness to serve to improve himself in knowledge and understanding of the Bible, and a desire to grow in Christian grace.

3. To become a lay speaker the candidate shall:

a) Be recommended by the Official Board of his church.

b) Preferably be recommended by the District Committee on Lay Speaking (¶ 1509), on completion of the training course for lay speakers recommended by the General Board of Lay Activities.

c) Be certified by his Quarterly Conference, the certificate to be signed by the president thereof. It is recommended that a consecration service be held during the session of the Annual Conference, or in the district on an appropriate occasion with the bishop presiding.

4. A lay speaker shall be subject to an annual examination by the Quarterly Conference of his character, gifts, labors, and usefulness, and a renewal of certificate, to be signed by the president thereof.

SEC. XII.   **Special Days**

¶ **296.** The special days to be observed by local churches are as follows:

1. Days to be observed in the church or the church school with an offering:

a) World Service Sunday—the fourth Sunday of each month (¶¶ 215.3, 250.1).

b) Race Relations Sunday—the second Sunday in February (¶ 250.3).

c) One Great Hour of Sharing—on or about the fourth Sunday in Lent (¶ 760.1).

d) Methodist Student Day—the second Sunday in June (¶ 250.4).

e) World-wide Communion Sunday—the first Sunday in October (¶ 763).

f) Church School Rally Day—date set as provided in ¶ 250.2.

2. Days to be observed in the church or the church school without an offering:

   a) Period of Spiritual Enrichment—beginning the Sunday preceding Ash Wednesday (¶ 222.2).

   b) National Family Week—the first to the second Sunday of May (¶ 250.5).

   c) Children's Day—the first Sunday in National Family Week (¶ 250.6).

   d) Ministry Sunday—the Sunday of or preceding May 24 (Aldersgate Sunday).

   e) Laymen's Day—the third Sunday in October (¶ 1497).

   f) World Order Sunday—date set as provided in ¶ 275.1.

   g) Commitment Day—the first Sunday in December (¶¶ 275.2, 1536).

   h) Universal Bible Sunday—the second Sunday in December (¶ 278.2).

   i) Student Recognition Day—the Sunday after Christmas.

3. Days to be observed in the church or the church school as ordered by the Jurisdictional or Annual Conference:

   a) Hospitals and Homes Week, beginning with Golden Cross Enrollment Sunday (¶ 1559.1).

   b) Retired Ministers Day (¶ 1610.6).

   c) Rural Life Sunday—the fifth Sunday after Easter.

Part III

THE MINISTRY

Chapter I

THE CALL TO PREACH

¶ 301. When a member of a local church manifests a desire to preach, it shall be the duty of his pastor to counsel with him concerning the opportunities and requirements of the ministry; and if the pastor is persuaded that he possesses gifts, graces, and promise of usefulness, he shall guide him toward qualifying.

[The following questions were first asked by John Wesley at the third conference of Methodist preachers in 1746. They have been retained ever since, in substantially the same words, as the standards by which prospective Methodist preachers are to be judged.—Editors.]

¶ 302. In order that we may try those persons who profess to be moved by the Holy Spirit to preach, let the following questions be asked, namely:

1. Do they know God as a pardoning God? Have they the love of God abiding in them? Do they desire nothing but God? Are they holy in all manner of conversation?

2. Have they gifts, as well as grace, for the work? Have they a clear, sound understanding; a right judgment in the things of God; a just conception of salvation by faith? Do they speak justly, readily, clearly?

3. Have they fruit? Have any been truly convinced of sin and converted to God, and are believers edified by their preaching?

As long as these marks concur in anyone, we believe he is called of God to preach. These we receive as sufficient proof that he is moved by the Holy Spirit.

¶ **303.** Women are included in all provisions of the Discipline referring to the ministry.[1]

CHAPTER II

THE LOCAL MINISTRY

SECTION I.   **Local Preachers**

¶ **304.** 1. A **local preacher** is a lay member of The Methodist Church who has been granted a license to preach, or has been ordained, according to the laws of the church (¶¶ 306, 393, 403). He continues to be a lay member of a local church.[2] His license to preach must be renewed each year (¶¶ 307, 320) unless he has been ordained.

2. An unordained local preacher has authority to preach and to conduct divine worship; *provided*, however, that his authority shall be restricted to the charge in which his membership is held or to which he is appointed. For the authority conferred by ministerial orders *see* ¶¶ 392, 402.

3. A local preacher not serving a pastoral charge may assist his pastor, as requested by the pastor and under the pastor's supervision, subject to the laws of the church (¶¶ 308, 312).

4. A local preacher may serve a pastoral charge under the supervision of a district superintendent, either by temporary appointment (¶ 315.2), or by becoming an approved supply pastor (¶ 314).

5. A person must be a local preacher in order to become a candidate for the traveling ministry (¶ 321).

¶ **305.** No member is authorized to preach without a license.

¶ **306.** A license to preach may be issued as provided in ¶¶ 362.4, 690, 695 after the person has qualified by the following steps:

1. Secured the recommendation of his Quarterly Conference, as provided in ¶ 146.1.

---

[1] *See* Judicial Council Decision 155.
[2] *See* Judicial Council Decision 173.

2. Applied to the district superintendent in writing.

3. Appeared before the District Committee on Ministerial Qualifications and supplied such information as the committee may require for determining his gifts, graces, and potential usefulness.

4. Completed one fourth of the work required for the bachelor of divinity or equivalent degree in a school of theology accredited or approved by the University Senate, or passed the course of study prescribed for license to preach (¶ 1374.1), including Parts I, II, III, and IX of the Discipline. This course shall preferably be taken under the Department of Ministerial Education.

5. Agreed to make a complete dedication of himself to the highest ideals of the Christian ministry with respect to purity of life in body, in mind, and in spirit, and to bear witness thereto by abstinence from all indulgences, including tobacco, which may injure his influence.[3]

¶ 307. A license to preach shall be valid for one year. It may be renewed, as provided in ¶¶ 362.4, 690, 695, on recommendation of the person's Quarterly Conference, and on evidence that his gifts, graces, and usefulness continue to be satisfactory and that he is making regular progress in the required studies, as follows:

1. A local preacher who is enrolled as a pretheological or theological student in a school, college, university, or school of theology accredited or approved by the University Senate, or by the state accrediting agency, preparing for the traveling ministry shall present annually to the District Committee on Ministerial Qualifications a statement of his academic progress from the school he is attending. This statement shall take the place of any formal examination, provided his academic progress and character are satisfactory.

2. A local preacher who is not a student as defined in § 1 shall pursue the four-year ministerial course of study under the Department of Ministerial Education (¶ 1374; see also ¶ 327). The course must be completed within eight years after the date of issue of the first license to

---

[3] Amended in 1956 following Judicial Council Decision 100. Regarding § 5 see also Decisions 111, 157.

preach; *provided*, however, that this shall not apply to those licensed before May 1, 1956.[4]

Note: For special provisions regarding local preachers who are approved supply pastors *see* ¶¶ 317, 320.

¶ **308.** A local preacher, ordained or unordained, who is not serving a charge under a district superintendent, shall be a member of, and amenable to, the Quarterly Conference where he resides, except as hereinafter stated. When he changes his residence, he shall procure from his pastor or district superintendent a certificate of his official standing and dismissal and shall present it to the pastor of the charge to which he has moved. If he neglects to do this, he shall not be recognized or use his office as a local preacher in the charge to which he has moved; and he shall continue to be amenable to the Quarterly Conference of the charge from which he has moved, which, if the neglect is long continued, after due notice (thirty days) may try him for persistent disobedience to the order of the church, and upon conviction thereof deprive him of his ministerial office and credentials.

¶ **309.** 1. A local preacher, other than a student as defined in § 2 below, who is appointed to serve under a district superintendent as supply pastor shall procure from his pastor or district superintendent a certificate of his official standing and of dismissal, and shall present it to the Quarterly Conference of the charge to which he is appointed at its next session. His church membership shall be in that charge to which he is appointed; and he shall be a member of, and amenable to, its Quarterly Conference, subject to the jurisdiction of the Annual Conference.[5]

2. A local preacher who is serving as student supply pastor while attending a college or school of theology accredited or approved by the University Senate may retain his membership in his home church and Quarterly Conference, but in the discharge of his ministerial functions he shall be amenable to the district superintendent under whom he serves.

¶ **310.** When a full member of an Annual Conference is

---

[4] Amended in 1956 following Judicial Council Decision 100.
[5] *See* Judicial Council Decision 112.

located (¶¶ 374-79), or an ordained member on trial is discontinued (¶¶ 321, 328), he shall become a local preacher with membership in the Quarterly Conference of the pastoral charge where he resides.[6] When an unordained member on trial is discontinued, the District Committee on Ministerial Qualifications may issue him a license to preach for one year, which may be renewed as provided in ¶ 307. A preacher who has been located or discontinued shall be subject to the provisions of ¶¶ 308, 312, 362.3, and 432.8.

¶ **311.** Whenever a local preacher, ordained or unordained, severs his relation with The Methodist Church, the district superintendent shall require his license and credentials of him, and shall file them with the secretary of the Annual Conference.[7] (*See* ¶¶ 994-95.)

¶ **312.** A local preacher not serving a pastoral charge shall make to the Quarterly Conference and the District Committee on Ministerial Qualifications, and to the District Conference on request, a report of his labors, as follows: (1) number of sermons preached; (2) number of funerals conducted, with the names of the deceased; (3) evangelistic, educational, and missionary work done in co-operation with and under the direction of his pastor; (4) progress made in academic work or in the prescribed course of study; (5) miscellaneous items. If he is ordained, he shall include in his report the following: (6) number of marriages performed, with the names of persons married; (7) number of baptisms administered, with the names and birth dates of the persons baptized. He shall report items 2, 6, and 7 to the pastor for entry in the church records.

SEC. II.   **Approved Supply Pastors**

¶ **314.** An **approved supply pastor** is a local preacher, as defined in ¶ 304, who on recommendation of the Board of Ministerial Training and Qualifications has been approved by the Annual Conference as eligible for appointment during the ensuing year as a supply pastor of a charge. The approval shall be based on compliance with

---

[6] *See* Judicial Council Decisions 110. 173.
[7] *See* Judicial Council Decision 110.

¶¶ 306-7, 315-17 and shall expire unless renewed on the same basis at the next regular conference session. It does not guarantee an appointment but merely certifies eligibility. An appointment made thereunder may be terminated at any time during the conference year by a majority vote of the district superintendents.

¶ 315. 1. A local preacher desiring to become, or to continue as, an approved supply pastor must have his character, fitness, training, and effectiveness passed by a three-fourths majority of the District Committee on Ministerial Qualifications (¶ 695.3-.4), and by the Annual Conference after reference to and recommendation by its Board of Ministerial Training and Qualifications.

2. Between conference sessions a local preacher not on the approved supply pastors list may be appointed as a supply pastor. (*See* ¶¶ 362.3, 432.8.) If he fails to be approved at the following conference session, he cannot thereafter serve as a supply pastor until he is approved.

¶ 316. 1. On recommendation of the board the conference may approve annually students of other denominations enrolled in a school of theology accredited or approved by the University Senate to serve as supply pastors for the ensuing year under the supervision of a district superintendent.

2. On recommendation of the board the conference may also approve annually ministers in good standing in other evangelical denominations to serve as supply pastors while retaining their denominational affiliation; *provided* that they shall agree in writing to support and maintain the doctrine and polity of The Methodist Church while so serving. Their ordination credentials may be recognized as valid in The Methodist Church while they are serving therein.

¶ 317. In recommending to the conference those who have met the requirements to become approved supply pastors for the ensuing year the board shall classify them in three categories with educational requirements as hereinafter specified. Every approved supply pastor shall meet the educational requirements of his category. Any preacher who fails to meet these requirements shall not be appointed by a district superintendent. The categories shall be as follows:

1. *Student approved supply pastors.* These shall be enrolled as pretheological or theological students, under the definitions and requirements of ¶ 307.1 and ¶ 316.1.

2. *Full-time approved supply pastors.* A full-time approved supply pastor is a local preacher, ordained or unordained, (*a*) who meets the provisions of ¶¶ 306-7, 314-16; (*b*) who, unless ordained elder, has met the educational requirements by completing in the preceding year a full year's work in the ministerial course of study under the Department of Ministerial Education (¶ 1374), either in a school for courses of study or by correspondence; (*c*) who devotes his entire service to the church in the charge to which he is appointed; and (*d*) whose cash support per annum from all church sources is a sum equivalent to not less than the minimum salary established by the Annual Conference for full-time approved supply pastors.[8] (*See* ¶ 1631.1.)

3. *Part-time approved supply pastors.* A part-time approved supply pastor is one (*a*) who does not devote his entire service to the charge to which he is appointed, (*b*) who does not receive in cash support per annum from all church sources a sum equivalent to the minimum salary established by the Annual Conference for full-time approved supply pastors, and (*c*) who completes a minimum of two books a year in the course of study. A person who has met the qualifications for approval as a supply pastor may request to be classified as a part-time approved supply pastor for the ensuing year.

¶ 318. 1. An unordained approved supply pastor, only while serving as a regularly appointed pastor of a charge, may be permitted to administer the Sacraments of Baptism and the Lord's Supper and, if the laws of the state permit, to perform the marriage ceremony within the bounds of the charge to which he is assigned; *provided* that: (*a*) he shall have completed one fourth of the work required for the bachelor of divinity or equivalent degree in a school of theology accredited or approved by the Uni-

---

[8] Amended in 1956 following Judicial Council Decision 91, and in 1960 following Decision 156.

versity Senate, or shall have passed the introductory studies for the ministry (¶ 1374); and (*b*) each succeeding year he shall be enrolled as a regular full-time student in a pretheological or theological course in a college, university, or school of theology accredited or approved by the University Senate, or by the state accrediting agency, or shall have passed one full year of the ministerial course of study looking to full ordination. Failure to complete one full year annually shall cause suspension of this privilege. Authorization must be given in writing by the resident bishop under whom he serves after approval by the Annual Conference. In all missionary fields abroad the conferring of such authorization shall rest with the Central Conference in which the pastor serves.[9]

2. An unordained part-time approved supply pastor (¶ 317.3) who completes each year two books of the ministerial course of study, and continues until he is graduated from the course, shall be authorized, while serving as a regularly appointed pastor of a charge, to administer the Sacrament of Baptism and, if the laws of the state permit, to perform the marriage ceremony within the bounds of the charge to which he is assigned.

¶ **319.** An approved supply pastor who is in charge of a pastoral appointment shall attend the sessions of the Annual Conference. (*See* ¶¶ 622, 645.)

¶ **320.** When a local preacher is approved as a supply pastor, the Annual Conference alone has jurisdiction over his authority to preach. Continuance in this relation shall be equivalent to renewal of his license to preach. If at any time the conference declines to renew its approval of an unordained supply pastor, the District Committee on Ministerial Qualifications may renew his license to preach for one year; further renewal shall be subject to the provisions of ¶ 307. (*See* ¶¶ 362.3, 432.8.)

---

[9] Amended in 1956 following Judicial Council Decision 91.

CHAPTER III

TRAVELING PREACHERS

SECTION I. **Admission of Preachers on Trial**

¶ **321.** The first step into the traveling ministry of The Methodist Church is **admission on trial** into an Annual Conference. A member on trial is on probation as to his character, his preaching, and his competency as a pastor. During this period the church determines whether **he** is worthy of becoming a full member of the conference. A person on trial may be discontinued without any reflection on his character.[10]

¶ **322.** A candidate for the traveling ministry may be admitted on trial by vote of the ministerial members of an Annual Conference on recommendation of its Board of Ministerial Training and Qualifications after meeting the following conditions:

1. He must have a license to preach or have been ordained (¶ 304).

2. He must have been recommended in writing on the basis of a three-fourths majority vote of the District Conference or the District Committee on Ministerial Qualifications (¶¶ 690, 695.3-.4.)

3. He must have met the educational requirements (¶¶ 323-25).

4. He must present a satisfactory certificate of good health, on the prescribed form, from a physician approved by the board. The conference may require psychological tests to provide additional information on the candidate's fitness for the ministry.

5. He must file with the board, in triplicate, on the prescribed form, satisfactory written answers to such questions as the board may ask concerning his age, health, family, religious and church experience, call to the ministry, educational record, and plans for service in the church. The following questions shall be included:

(1) Are you convinced that you should enter the ministry of the church?

---

[10] *See* Judicial Conucil Decision 157.

(2) Are you willing to face any sacrifices that may be involved?

(3) Are you in debt so as to interfere with your work, or have you obligations to others which will make it difficult for you to live on the salary you are to receive?

(4) If you are married, is your wife or husband in sympathy with your ministerial calling and willing to share in the sacrifices of your vocation?

(5) Are you willing to make a complete dedication of yourself to the highest ideals of the Christian ministry with respect to purity of life in body, in mind, and in spirit, and to bear witness thereto by abstinence from all indulgences, including tobacco, which may injure your influence? [11]

(6) Will you keep before you as the one great objective of your life the advancement of God's Kingdom?

¶ 323. A candidate for admission on trial must (1) have been graduated with a bachelor of arts or equivalent degree in liberal education in a college or university accredited or approved by the University Senate, and (2) have completed at least one fourth of the work required for a bachelor of divinity or equivalent degree in a school of theology accredited or approved by the University Senate, except under the special conditions of ¶ 325.

¶ 324. Any Annual Conference may designate a bachelor of divinity or equivalent degree from a school of theology accredited or approved by the University Senate as the minimum educational requirement for admission on trial into that conference.

¶ 325. Under special conditions an Annual Conference may, by a three-fourths majority vote, admit on trial a candidate who exhibits exceptional promise for the ministry in the following cases:

1. If he is a graduate with a bachelor of arts or equivalent degree in liberal education from a college not accredited by the University Senate who has completed one fourth of the work required for the bachelor of divinity or equivalent degree in a school of theology accredited or approved by the University Senate. (See ¶¶ 330, 342.)

[11] See Judicial Council Decisions 111, 157.

2. If he is a graduate with a bachelor of arts or equivalent degree in liberal education from a college accredited or approved by the University Senate, and has completed satisfactorily the introductory studies for the ministry and the first year of the ministerial course of study (¶ 1374; *see also* ¶ 327).

3. If he is an approved supply pastor over thirty-five years of age who has (1) earned sixty semester hours of college credit, (2) completed the four-year ministerial course of study (¶ 1374), (3) served as an approved supply pastor in an Annual Conference for six consecutive years, and (4) been recommended by a three-fourths vote of the Cabinet and a three-fourths vote of the Board of Ministerial Training and Qualifications, written statements of such recommendations having been read to the conference before the vote is taken, setting forth the particular ways his ministry is exceptional and the special reasons he should be admitted on trial. (*See* ¶¶ 330, 343.2.)

¶ **326.** The Board of Ministerial Training and Qualifications shall require a transcript of credits from each applicant before recognizing any of his educational claims. In case of doubt the board may submit a transcript to the Department of Ministerial Education for evaluation.

¶ **327.** A preacher who discontinues his theological education may request that the Department of Ministerial Education evaluate his theological work for credit in the ministerial course of study. He shall be exempted from any portion of the introductory studies or the four-year course for which he has already completed equivalent work in a school of theology accredited or approved by the University Senate provided the department shall have examined an official transcript thereof and certified it as equivalent.

¶ **328.** While a member is on trial, the Annual Conference alone has jurisdiction over his authority to preach. His continuance on trial shall be equivalent to the renewal of his license to preach. If he be discontinued, he becomes a local preacher. (*See* ¶ 310.)

¶ **329.** An unordained member on trial who is regularly appointed to a pastoral charge without an ordained colleague is subject to the provisions of ¶ 318.1.

¶ **330.** To be continued as a member on trial, the candidate shall make regular progress in his ministerial studies. In case of failure or delay, the Board of Ministerial Training and Qualifications shall investigate the circumstances and judge whether to extend the time, within the following limits: (*a*) for completing the theological course for the bachelor of divinity or equivalent degree, a total of eight years; (*b*) for completing the first two years of the ministerial course of study, a total of four years; (*c*) for completing the entire course of study, a total of six years; (*d*) for completing the four courses of special study required of a candidate admitted under the conditions of ¶ 325.3 (*see* ¶ 343.2), a total of three years. In a case clearly recognized as exceptional the board by a three-fourths vote may recommend an extension beyond these limits, which may be approved by a three-fourths vote of the Annual Conference; *provided* that, in any case, a candidate admitted under the terms of ¶ 325.3 shall not be continued on trial beyond the fourth regular conference session following his admission, and any other candidate shall not be continued on trial beyond the eighth regular conference session following his admission. (*See* ¶ 635.)

¶ **331.** The educational standards and other requirements for admission shall be set by the Jurisdictional Conferences for the bilingual Annual and Provisional Annual Conferences within their territories, by the Central and Provisional Central Conferences for the Annual and Provisional Annual Conferences within their territories, and outside such territories by the Annual or Provisional Annual Conference itself.

Sec. II.   **Admission into Full Connection**

¶ **341.** A member on trial may be admitted into full connection in an Annual Conference by vote of its ministerial members, on recommendation of its Board of Ministerial Training and Qualifications,[12] provided he shall have: (*a*) served under regular appointment under the supervision of a district superintendent in one of the

---

[12] *See* Judicial Council Decision 157.

positions specified in ¶ 432.1-.6 for at least two years since being admitted on trial, or completed satisfactorily to the Board of Ministerial Training and Qualifications two years of supervised field work related to the polity and program of The Methodist Church in one of the Methodist schools of theology[13]; (b) been previously elected to deacon's orders (¶ 393); (c) fulfilled the educational requirements of ¶¶ 342-44; (d) satisfied the board regarding his physical, mental, and emotional health, by repeating the examination and tests described in ¶ 322.4 if so requested; (e) given satisfactory answers to the questions listed in ¶ 345.

¶ 342. A candidate for admission into full connection must have been graduated with a bachelor of divinity or equivalent degree in a school of theology accredited or approved by the University Senate, except under the special conditions of ¶ 343, and have completed the Methodist studies specified in ¶ 344. A candidate who was admitted on trial under the terms of ¶ 325.1 shall meet these requirements without exception.

¶ 343. 1. A candidate who was admitted on trial under the terms of ¶ 325.2 may meet the educational requirements for admission into full connection by completing the entire four-year ministerial course of study. (See ¶ 327.)

2. A candidate who was admitted on trial under the terms of ¶ 325.3 may meet the educational requirements for admission into full connection by completing four courses of special study by correspondence or in a school for courses of study under the direction of the Department of Ministerial Education.

3. Under conditions regarded as exceptional an Annual Conference may admit into full connection as provided in ¶ 341 a candidate otherwise qualified who, having discontinued his theological education subsequent to meeting the requirements of ¶ 323 for admission on trial, has completed all of the four-year ministerial course of study not covered by his theological work as provided in ¶ 327.

---

[13] Amended in 1956 following Judicial Council Decisions 49, 122, and in 1960 following Decision 152.

¶ **344.** Any candidate for admission into full connection
on the basis of a bachelor of divinity or equivalent degree
whose transcript does not show two semester hours of
credit in each of the following fields, Methodist history,
polity, and doctrine, or their equivalent, shall be required
to pass examinations in these subjects, administered by
the Board of Ministerial Training and Qualifications in
accordance with the standards established by the Department of Ministerial Education.

Examination for Admission into Full Connection

[Here follow the questions which every Methodist preacher
from the beginning has been required to answer upon becoming
a full member of a conference. These questions were formulated
by John Wesley and have been little changed throughout the
years.—EDITORS.]

¶ **345.** A preacher seeking admission into full connection in the conference shall, after solemn fasting and
prayer, be asked, before the conference, the following
questions, with any others which may be thought necessary, namely:

(1) Have you faith in Christ?

(2) Are you going on to perfection?

(3) Do you expect to be made perfect in love in this
life?

(4) Are you earnestly striving after it?

(5) Are you resolved to devote yourself wholly to God
and his work?

(6) Do you know the General Rules of our church?

(7) Will you keep them?

(8) Have you studied the doctrines of The Methodist
Church?

(9) After full examination do you believe that our
doctrines are in harmony with the Holy Scriptures?

(10) Will you preach and maintain them?

(11) Have you studied our form of church discipline
and polity?

(12) Do you approve our church government and
polity?

(13) Will you support and maintain them?

(14) Will you diligently instruct the children in every place?

(15) Will you visit from house to house?

(16) Will you recommend fasting or abstinence, both by precept and example?

(17) Are you determined to employ all your time in the work of God? [14]

(18) Are you in debt so as to embarrass you in your work?

(19) Will you observe the following directions?

(a) Be diligent. Never be unemployed. Never be triflingly employed. Never trifle away time; neither spend any more time at any one place than is strictly necessary.

(b) Be punctual. Do everything exactly at the time. And do not mend our rules, but keep them; not for wrath, but for conscience' sake.

SEC. III. **Pastors**

¶ 351. A pastor is a preacher who, by appointment of the bishop or the district superintendent, is in charge of a station or circuit.

¶ 352. The duties of a pastor are:

1. To preach the gospel.

2. To administer the Sacraments of Baptism and the Lord's Supper and to perform the marriage ceremony, if qualified to do so under ¶ 318, ¶ 329, ¶ 392, or ¶ 402, and to bury the dead.

3. To visit from house to house in order to give pastoral guidance and oversight to the members of the church and others in need of a pastor's help.

4. To instruct candidates for membership in the church in the doctrines, rules, and regulations of the church; to receive persons into membership; to receive and dismiss members by certificate.

5. To form classes of the children, youth, and adults for instruction in the Word of God, and to perform the duties prescribed for the training of children.

6. To instruct youth in Christian ideals for marriage

---

[14] *See* Judicial Council Decision 82.

and family living, with special reference to the problems involved in interfaith marriages.

7. To organize and maintain church schools, Methodist Youth Fellowships, Young Adult Fellowships, Woman's Societies of Christian Service, and Methodist Men clubs.

8. To hold or appoint prayer meetings, love feasts, and watch-night meetings, wherever advisable.

9. To have the oversight of the other preachers in his pastoral charge; and to arrange the appointments, wherever practicable, so as to give the local preachers regular employment on the Sabbath.

10. To see that class leaders are chosen, and to change them when necessary, and to examine each of them concerning his method of leading a class.

11. To administer all the provisions of the Discipline in his pastoral charge.

12. To see that the ordinances and regulations of the church are duly observed and that the General Rules are read and explained once a year in each congregation.

13. In the absence of the district superintendent and the bishop, to control the appointment of all services to be held in the churches in his charge.

14. To hold Quarterly Conferences, at the request of the district superintendent, and to serve as chairman of the Official Board, unless a chairman has been elected by the Official Board.

15. To explain the meaning and importance of the benevolences, and to urge their support by all the people in his charge.

16. To preach on the subject of missions and to nominate at the fourth Quarterly Conference, in case such nomination is not made by the Nominating Committee, a Commission on Missions and a chairman thereof for each congregation. (¶ 256.)

17. To preach on the subject of Christian education, and to urge upon parents the importance of educating their children, advising them to patronize the institutions of learning of our church.

18. To see that the people in the bounds of his charge are supplied with our church literature, including books,

church-school literature, and the periodicals *Together*, *Christian Advocate*, and *Central Christian Advocate*.

19. To teach and preach on Christian stewardship, temperance, and world peace, and to promote these causes within the bounds of his charge.

20. *a*) To preach on the meaning of Christian vocation and the call and challenge of the ministry and other types of full-time church work, and to advise with youth, students, and young adults about their educational and vocational plans. (*See* ¶ 149.1.)

b) To search out from among his membership and constituency young people for the ministry, to help them interpret the meaning of the call of God, to challenge them with the opportunities of the Christian ministry, to advise and assist them when they commit themselves thereto, to counsel with them and watch over them as their pastor through the course of their preparation, and to keep a careful record of all such decisions, reporting to the Annual Conference the number of such students enrolled in schools of theology accredited or approved by the University Senate.

21. To preach on the subject of the Bible and its circulation.

22. To make a written report to each Quarterly Conference on the following items:

a) The general state of the church in his charge.

b) The names of all who have been received into the church, with the method of reception indicated, and of all who have died, removed, withdrawn, or been expelled during the preceding quarter.

c) Number and condition of church schools, including Sunday-school meetings, weekday meetings of children, meetings of young people, fellowship meetings of adults, and vacation schools.

d) Number of sermons preached to children.

e) Other religious instruction conducted, with children and adults, including training classes.

f) Number of pastoral visits, and the use of the church-school roll in pastoral visitation.

g) Subscribers to our church periodicals.

h) Collections for benevolences.

i) Missions, including Woman's Societies of Christian Service, church extension, and missionary education in the church school.

j) Lay activities, including the financial system, lay speaking, training of the Official Board or Boards, Christian stewardship, and Methodist Men.

k) Other items worthy of record.

l) Plans for future work.

23. To keep a separate membership record for each local church of his charge in which shall be noted the name, with the time and manner of reception and disposal, of every member of the church, including the names of preparatory members in a separate list. (*See* ¶¶ 131-32.)

24. To enter in the permanent official records of the church accurate information concerning all baptisms and marriages.

25. To keep and transmit to his successor two directories, the one in which the residences of all the members shall be recorded, and the other a constituency roll with like information.

26. To furnish to every person uniting with the church on profession of faith, or from preparatory membership, a certificate of membership.

27. To leave to his successor an account of his charge, including a list of subscribers to the benevolences and to our periodicals.

28. To make report to the Annual Conference of all items required for the statistics of the conference, and to deliver to the conference treasurer all moneys raised for benevolent causes, or satisfactory vouchers for the same, using the forms supplied by The Methodist Publishing House.

¶ **353.** No pastor shall engage for an evangelist any person who is not a conference evangelist, a regular member of an Annual Conference, an approved supply pastor, a local preacher, or a lay speaker in good standing in The Methodist Church without first obtaining the written consent of his district superintendent. (*See* ¶¶ 363, 1474.2, 1480.)

¶ **354.** No pastor shall discontinue a preaching place in the interval between sessions of the Annual Conference without the consent of the Quarterly Conference and the district superintendent. (*See* ¶¶ 128, 188.)

¶ 355. The pastor is urged to study and prepare for increasingly adequate marriage and family counseling.

1. In planning to perform the rite of matrimony the minister shall have one or more unhurried premarital conferences with the parties to be married to emphasize the spiritual values in all phases of marital and parental life. It is recommended that he use the official manual of the church. It is strongly urged that these conferences be held as early as possible before the date of the wedding.

2. The minister shall make his counsel available to those under the threat of marriage breakdown in order to explore every possibility of reconstructing the marriage.

¶ 356. In view of the seriousness with which the Scriptures and the Church regard divorce, a minister may solemnize the marriage of a divorced person only when he has satisfied himself by careful counseling that: (*a*) the divorced person is sufficiently aware of the factors leading to the failure of the previous marriage, (*b*) the divorced person is sincerely preparing to make the proposed marriage truly Christian, and (*c*) sufficient time has elapsed for adequate preparation and counseling.

SEC. IV.   **District Superintendents**

¶ 361. **District superintendents** are to be chosen and appointed by the bishop. (*See* ¶ 432.3.)

¶ 362. The duties of a district superintendent are:

1. To travel through his district, in order to preach and to oversee the spiritual and temporal affairs of the church.

2. In the absence of a bishop to have charge of all the traveling and local preachers in his district.

3. To change, receive, or appoint preachers during the intervals between conferences and in the absence of the bishop, as the Discipline directs; *provided* that he shall not appoint any preacher who has been rejected as an applicant, or who has been discontinued or located, except at his own request, unless the conference at the time of such rejection, discontinuance, or location shall grant such authority; and he shall not appoint any preacher

who has previously been expelled from the ministry, or has surrendered his credentials to an Annual Conference, unless the conference to which he surrendered his credentials, or from which he was expelled, restores his credentials, or recommends him; and he shall not appoint any local preacher who is not listed as an approved supply pastor, except between sessions of the Annual Conference, and then only until its next session.

4. To issue and renew licenses for local preachers in accordance with the action of the District Conference or District Committee on Ministerial Qualifications; and to furnish certified lists of the persons licensed and their addresses to the Department of Ministerial Education and to the secretary of the Annual Conference for insertion in the conference journal.

5. To preside, or to designate elders to preside, in the Quarterly Conferences of each pastoral charge, and to preside at the District Conference.

6. To take care that every part of the Discipline is observed in his district.

7. To see that all charters, deeds, and other conveyances of church property in his district conform to the Discipline and to the laws, usages, and forms of the county, state, territory, or country within which such property is situated.

8. To counsel with the pastors in his district in regard to their pastoral responsibilities and other matters affecting their ministry.

9. To advise and encourage local preachers, candidates for the ministry, and conference undergraduates in their studies.

10. To report the names and addresses of the church lay leaders in his district to the secretary of the Annual Conference for insertion in the conference journal;[14] to report the names and addresses of all candidates for the ministry to the Department of Ministerial Education; and to report the names and addresses of commission and committee chairmen, church-school superintendents, and church lay leaders elected by each Quarterly Conference

---

[14] *See* Judicial Council Decision 146.

in his district as may be requested by any general agency supplying report forms therefor.

11. To prepare and deliver to his successor, and to the conference secretary, to be permanently recorded by him: (*a*) a list of all abandoned church properties and cemeteries within the bounds of his district; (*b*) a list of all church properties being permissively used by other religious organizations with the names of the local trustees thereof; (*c*) a list of all endowments, annuities, trust funds, investments, and unpaid legacies of which he has knowledge belonging to any pastoral charge or organization connected therewith in his district.

12. To report annually to the Annual Conference an accurate record of all financial transactions pertaining to abandoned properties.

13. To procure statistics from every charge and report them to the Annual Conference, in case the pastor should fail to make report; and to have the records of his District Conference at the Annual Conference for examination.

14. To decide all questions of law which may arise in the business of the Quarterly or District Conference, when submitted to him in writing, subject to an appeal to the president of the next Annual Conference.[15]

15. To promote all the interests of the church within the bounds of his district, in co-operation with the pastors and the Quarterly Conferences, giving particular attention to the following:

a) The cultivation of personal religion and the sharing of spiritual experience.

b) Evangelistic interest and activity among the churches and in behalf of the unevangelized.

c) Establishment of new preaching places and organization of new congregations wherever needed.

d) Missionary and social-service interests and activities, including the Woman's Societies of Christian Service, hospitals, homes, and orphanages.

e) Christian education, including the church schools, Methodist Youth Fellowships, church-related colleges,

---

[15] *See* Judicial Council Decisions 29, 52.

Wesley Foundations, and all other educational institutions and work. It shall be the duty of the district superintendent to bring the subject of Christian education before the Quarterly Conference of each pastoral charge. At least once a year he shall inquire into the character and effectiveness of the program of Christian education of every charge within his district. He shall co-operate with the Conference Board of Education and its executive secretary in promoting in all the churches of his district the plan of organization, the standards, and the literature provided or recommended by the General and Jurisdictional Boards of Education. He shall use the record and report forms provided by the General Board of Education for the use of district superintendents. He shall secure the names and addresses of the church-school superintendents of each charge and transmit them to the executive secretary of the Conference Board of Education on blanks furnished by the General Board of Education.

f) Christian literature, especially the circulation of our church papers and the distribution of literature and books issued by our Publishing House.

g) Lay activities, including personal evangelism, Christian stewardship, proper financial systems, temperance, social and economic justice, world peace, benevolences, and Christian life service.

h) Administration of the ordinances and Sacraments.

i) Formation of group ministries, larger parishes, or parish area plans to expedite the work of the church in larger areas.

16. To perform such other duties as the Discipline may direct. (*See Index*.)

¶ 363. No district superintendent shall engage for an evangelist any person who is not a conference evangelist, a regular member of an Annual Conference, an approved supply pastor, a local preacher, or a lay speaker in good standing in The Methodist Church without first obtaining the written consent of his bishop. (*See* ¶¶ 1474.2, 1480.)

SEC. V.   Sabbatical Leave

¶ 364. Any minister who has been in the effective relation in any Annual Conference or Conferences for ten consecutive years from the time of his admission on trial may be granted a **sabbatical leave** by a bishop for one year without losing his relationship as an effective minister. This sabbatical leave is to be allowed for travel, study, rest, or for other justifiable reasons. Sabbatical leave granted by the bishop holding the conference must be upon the vote of the Annual Conference to which the minister belongs, after said minister has given notice to his district superintendent, and after the district superintendent has given notice to the bishop of his intention to request such sabbatical leave. A sabbatical leave shall not be granted to the same man more frequently than one year in seven.

SEC. VI.   **Supernumerary Ministers**

¶ **365.** A **supernumerary minister** is one who, because of impaired health, or other equally sufficient reason, is temporarily unable to perform full work. This relation shall not be granted for more than five years in succession except by a two-thirds vote of the conference, upon recommendation of the Committee on Conference Relations,[16] and a statement of the reason for such recommendation. He may receive an appointment, or be left without one, according to the judgment of the Annual Conference of which he is a member; and he shall be subject to all limitations of the Discipline in respect to reappointment and continuance in the same charge that apply to effective ministers. In case he has no pastoral charge he shall have a seat in the Quarterly Conference, and all the privileges of membership, in the place where he resides. He shall report to the fourth Quarterly Conference, and to the pastor, all marriages performed and all baptisms administered. Should he reside outside the bounds of his Annual Conference, he shall forward to it annually a certificate similar to that required of a retired minister (¶ 370), and in case of failure to do so the Annual Conference may locate him without his consent. He shall have no claim on the conference funds except by vote of the conference.

---

[16] *See* Judicial Council Decision 105.

SEC. VII.   **Retired Ministers**

¶ **367.** A **retired minister** is one who, at his own request, or by action of the Annual Conference, on recommendation of the Committee on Conference Relations, has been placed in the retired relation.[17]

¶ **368.** Every clerical member of an Annual Conference whose seventy-second birthday precedes the first day of the regular session of his Annual Conference shall automatically be retired from the active ministry at said conference session.[18]

¶ **369.** If any member of an Annual Conference who has attained age sixty-five or has completed forty years of full-time approved service, as defined in ¶ 1618, prior to the date of the opening session of the conference so requests, the Annual Conference may place him in the retired relation with the privilege of making an annuity claim.[19] (*See* ¶ 1617.)

¶ **370.** Every retired minister who is not appointed as pastor of a charge shall have a seat in the Quarterly Conference, and all the privileges of membership in the church where he resides, except as set forth in ¶ 371. He shall report to the fourth Quarterly Conference and to the pastor all marriages performed and baptisms administered. If he resides outside the bounds of the conference, he shall forward annually to his conference a certificate of his Christian and his ministerial conduct, together with an account of the number and circumstances of his family, signed by the district superintendent or the pastor of the charge within the bounds of which he resides. Without this certificate the conference may, after due notice (thirty days), locate him without his consent.

¶ **371.** In the case of a Quarterly Conference in a mission among non-English-speaking people, retired ministers of different race shall have a vote in the Quarterly Conference only when they shall have been duly elected to the same.

---

[17] *See* Judicial Council Decisions 87, 165.
[18] *See* Judicial Council Decisions 7, 15.
[19] *See* Judicial Council Decision 133.

Sec. VIII. **Termination of Annual Conference Membership**

By Voluntary Location

¶ **374.** An Annual Conference may grant a member a certificate of location at his own request; *provided* that it shall first have examined his character at the conference session when the request is made and found him in good standing; and *provided*, further, that this relation shall be granted only to one who avowedly intends to discontinue regular ministerial or evangelistic work. This relation shall be certified by the president of the conference. The minister shall thereupon hold his membership, as local elder or deacon, in the Quarterly Conference of the charge where he resides, and shall be permitted to exercise ministerial functions only within the bounds of that charge, or of the charge to which he may be appointed. He shall report to the Quarterly Conference and the pastor all marriages performed, baptisms administered, and funerals conducted; and shall be held amenable for his conduct and the continuance of his ordination rights to the Annual Conference within which the Quarterly Conference membership is held.[20] (*See* ¶ 310.)

¶ **375.** Whenever a member of the Annual Conference applies for a location it shall be asked: Is he indebted to the Publishing House? If it be ascertained that he is so indebted, the conference shall require him to secure said debt, if judged necessary or proper, before a location is granted.

¶ **376.** A minister who has been located at his own request may be readmitted by an Annual Conference, at its discretion, upon presentation of his certificate of location and the recommendation of his District Committee on Ministerial Qualifications and of the Annual Conference from which he located. (*See* ¶¶ 379, 1630.15.)

By Involuntary Location

¶ **377.** Whenever it is determined by the Committee on Conference Relations that, in their judgment, a member of the Annual Conference is unacceptable, inefficient, or

---

[20] *See* Judicial Council Decision 110.

indifferent in the work of the ministry, or that his conduct is such as to impair seriously his usefulness as a
minister, or that his engagement in secular business,
except as required by the ill health of himself or of his
family, disqualifies him for pastoral work, they shall
notify him in writing, and ask him to request location
at the next session of the Annual Conference. If he refuses or neglects to locate as requested, the conference
may, by count vote, on recommendation of the Committee on Conference Relations, locate him without his
consent. In the case of involuntary location the authority
to exercise the ministerial office shall be suspended, and
the district superintendent shall require from him his
credentials to be deposited with the secretary of the
conference.

¶ 378. Whenever it is unanimously determined by the
district superintendents that a member of the Annual
Conference should be located for any of the reasons
cited in ¶ 377, they shall notify him in writing of their
judgment at least three months before the next session of
the Annual Conference, and ask him to request location
at such session under the provisions of ¶ 374. If he refuses or neglects to locate as requested, the district
superintendent shall certify the fact to the Committee
on Conference Relations, which committee shall proceed
to recommend his immediate location without his consent.
Upon such action his right to exercise the functions of the
ministry shall be suspended, and the district superintendent shall require from him his credentials to be
deposited with the secretary of the conference.

¶ 379. If a located person remains a member in good
standing of The Methodist Church until the age of voluntary retirement fixed by the General Conference, he shall
thereby retain the right to make an annuity claim, based
upon his years of approved service; *provided*, however,
that he shall have been readmitted by a two-thirds vote
of the Annual Conference which granted him location;
if it be nonexistent, then he shall apply for admission to
the Annual Conference within the boundaries of which
the major part of his service was rendered or its legal
successor. (*See* ¶¶ 376, 1630.15.)

By Surrender of the Ministerial Office

¶ 380. Any member of an Annual Conference in good standing who desires to surrender his ministerial office and withdraw from the conference may be allowed to do so by the conference at its session, in which case his credentials shall be filed with the official records of the Annual Conference of which he was a member, and his membership in the church shall be recorded in the society where he resides at the time of such surrender.

By Withdrawal

¶ 381. When a minister in good standing withdraws to unite with another church, his credentials should be surrendered to the conference, and, if he shall desire it, they may be returned to him with the following inscription written plainly across their face, namely:

A. B. *has this day been honorably dismissed by the* ———— *Annual Conference from the ministry of The Methodist Church.*

Dated ————   ————, *President*
                      ————, *Secretary*

¶ 382. When in the interval between sessions of an Annual Conference a member thereof shall deposit with a bishop or with his district superintendent a letter of withdrawal from our ministry, or his credentials, or both, the same shall be presented to the Annual Conference at its next session for its action thereon.

SEC. IX.   **Mission Traveling Preachers**

¶ 385. **A mission traveling preacher,** deacon, or elder, is one who is a member of a Mission without being a member of an Annual Conference. In the election of mission traveling deacons and elders the Mission shall require of all applicants the conditions and qualifications demanded of traveling deacons and elders by an Annual Conference. The duties, responsibilities, rights, and privileges of mission traveling deacons and elders shall be the same as those of traveling deacons and elders who are members of an Annual Conference; and such preachers may be transferred to an Annual Conference with the status attained in the Mission.

CHAPTER IV

MINISTERIAL ORDERS

SECTION I.   Deacons

¶ 391. A **deacon** is constituted by the election of the Annual Conference, on recommendation of the Board of Ministerial Training and Qualifications (¶ 671), and the laying on of the hands of a bishop.

¶ 392. A deacon has authority to preach, to conduct divine worship, to perform the marriage ceremony, to administer Baptism, and to assist an elder in administering the Lord's Supper; *provided* that, while serving as a regularly appointed pastor of a charge, he shall be authorized to administer the Lord's Supper under the conditions set forth in ¶ 318; and *provided*, further, that a local preacher who is ordained deacon shall be authorized to exercise ministerial functions only in the charge to which he is appointed or in which he resides.

¶ 393. Preachers of the following classes are eligible for the order of deacon:

1. *Theological students* who have been admitted on trial after having met the requirements of ¶ 323 or ¶ 325.1.

2. *Members on trial in the course of study* who, after being admitted under ¶ 325.2, have been on trial for two consecutive years and have completed two years of the ministerial course of study under the supervision of the Board of Ministerial Training and Qualifications.

3. *Approved supply pastors* who have been under appointment for two consecutive years, have completed the introductory studies for the ministry and two full years of the ministerial course of study under the supervision of the Board of Ministerial Training and Qualifications, and have been recommended in writing by their district superintendent and the District Committee on Ministerial Qualifications. (*See* ¶ 392.)

4. *Local preachers* who have been licensed for four consecutive years, who have completed two years of the ministerial course of study under the supervision of the Board of Ministerial Training and Qualifications, and who present to the Annual Conference a recommendation for deacon's orders from the District Committee on Ministerial Qualifications, duly attested by the chairman and secretary thereof. (*See* ¶ 392.)

5. *Missionaries* who have been admitted on trial and are to be appointed by a bishop to a foreign Mission, or to a remote field in any conference, or to a church in a foreign country outside the boundary of a Mission or Annual Conference; *provided* that the presiding bishop and a majority of the district superintendents shall have recommended election to the order of deacon.

6. *Chaplains* who have been admitted on trial and in time of urgent need are to be appointed by a bishop to serve on full-time duty with the Armed Forces or other agency related to the Commission on Chaplains; *provided* that the presiding bishop and a majority of the district superintendents shall have recommended election to the order of deacon.

SEC. II. **Elders**

¶ **401.** An **elder** is constituted by the election of the Annual Conference, on recommendation of the Board of Ministerial Training and Qualifications (¶ 671), and by the laying on of hands of a bishop and of elders.

¶ **402.** An elder has authority to preach, to conduct divine worship, to administer the Sacraments of Baptism and the Lord's Supper, and to perform the marriage ceremony; *provided*, however, that a local preacher who is ordained elder shall be authorized to exercise ministerial functions only in the charge to which he is appointed or in which he resides.

¶ **403.** Preachers of the following classes are eligible for the order of elder:

1. *Theological graduates* who have been deacons for at least one year and have been received into full connection after having met the requirements of ¶ 342.

2. *Course of study graduates* who have been deacons for at least two years and have been received into full connection after having met the requirements of ¶ 343.

3. *Approved supply pastors* who have been under appointment for two full consecutive years as deacons, who have completed the ministerial course of study under the supervision of the Board of Ministerial Training and Qualifications, and who have been recommended in writing by their district superintendent and the District Committee on Ministerial Qualifications. (*See* ¶ 402.)

4. *Local preachers* who have been deacons for four consecutive years, who have completed the entire ministerial course of study under the supervision of the Board of Ministerial Training and Qualifications, and who present a recommendation for elder's orders from the District Committee on Ministerial Qualifications, duly attested by the chairman and secretary thereof. (*See* ¶ 402.)

5. *Missionaries* who have served under appointment as deacons for one full year, have been admitted into full connection, and are to be appointed by a bishop to a foreign Mission, or to the pastorate of a church in a foreign country outside of a Mission or Annual Conference, or to a Mission among foreign people within an English-speaking conference.

6. *Chaplains* who have been admitted into full connection and in time of urgent need are to be appointed to serve on full-time duty with the Armed Forces or other agencies related to the Commission on Chaplains.

¶ 404. When a preacher has fulfilled the requirements for ordination and has been elected to the order of deacon, but fails to receive his ordination through the absence of the bishop, his eligibility to the order of elder shall count from the time of his election to the order of deacon.

¶ 405. No persons shall be elected to elder's orders except such as are of unquestionable moral character and genuine piety, sound in the fundamental doctrine of Christianity and faithful in the discharge of gospel duties.[21]

---

[21] *See* Judicial Council Decision 157.

CHAPTER V

MINISTERS FROM OTHER CHURCHES

¶ 411. Ministers coming from other evangelical churches, provided they present suitable testimonials of good standing through the Board of Ministerial Training and Qualifications, and give assurance of their faith, Christian experience, and other qualifications, and give evidence of their agreement with us in doctrine and discipline, and present a satisfactory certificate of good health on the prescribed form, from a physician approved by the Board of Ministerial Training and Qualifications, and meet the educational requirements, may be received into our ministry in the following manner:

1. The District Conference or District Committee on Ministerial Qualifications may receive them as local preachers not entitled to administer the Sacraments, pending the recognition of their orders by the Annual Conference.

2. The Annual Conference may recognize their orders as local deacons or elders provided their qualifications meet the educational and other requirements of the Discipline. (*See* ¶¶ 327, 393, 403.)

3. On recommendation of the District Committee on Ministerial Qualifications and the Board of Ministerial Training and Qualifications, the Annual Conference may recognize their orders and admit them into the membership of the conference, either on trial or in full connection, provided their qualifications meet the educational and other requirements of the Discipline, including the requirements in Methodist history, polity, and doctrine.[22] (*See* ¶¶ 321-45, 393, 403, 635.)

4. Ministers from other churches who can meet the educational standards required of Methodist ministers may apply through the Board of Ministerial Training and Qualifications to the Annual Conference, which may recognize their credentials and receive them on trial or into the full membership of the conference; *provided* that

---

[22] Amended in 1960 following Judicial Council Decision 31.

candidates for admission under this or the preceding item shall be required to answer satisfactorily the questions in ¶¶ 322, 345; and *provided*, further, that those from other than Methodist churches must take upon themselves our ordination vows, without the reimposition of hands.

5. The Annual Conference, on recommendation of the Conference Board of Ministerial Training and Qualifications, may also receive on equal standing preachers who are on trial in the ministry of another Methodist church, using, however, special care that before they are admitted to full membership, they shall meet all the educational and other requirements. (*See* ¶¶ 321-45, 635.)

¶ 412. The Board of Ministerial Training and Qualifications of an Annual Conference is required to ascertain from a minister seeking admission into its membership on credentials from another denomination whether or not membership in the effective relation was previously held in an Annual Conference of The Methodist Church, or one of its legal predecessors, and if so, when and under what circumstances his connection with such Annual Conference was severed.

¶ 413. A minister seeking admission into an Annual Conference on credentials from another denomination who has previously withdrawn from membership in the effective relation in an Annual Conference of The Methodist Church, or one of its legal predecessors, shall not be admitted or readmitted without the consent of the Annual Conference from which he withdrew, or its legal successor, or the Annual Conference of which the major portion of his former conference is a part.[23]

¶ 414. Whenever the orders of a minister are recognized according to the foregoing provisions, he shall be furnished with a certificate signed by the bishop according to the form:

This is to certify that the ——— Annual Conference of The Methodist Church, having examined the credentials of the Rev. A. B. as ——— [an elder or a deacon] of the ——— Church, and having received other testimonials of

---

[23] ¶¶ 412-13 were added in 1944 following Judicial Council Decision 16.

his graces, gifts, and usefulness, and being satisfied therewith, has this day accepted and recognized him in due form as —— [an elder or a deacon] in The Methodist Church, entitled to exercise under its authority all the functions pertaining to that ordination, so long as his life and doctrine become the gospel of Christ.

Given under my hand and seal at —— this —— day of —— in the year of our Lord ——.

——, President

¶ **415.** When the orders of a minister of another church shall have been duly recognized, his certificate of ordination by said church shall be returned to him with the following inscription written plainly across its face:

Accredited by the —— Annual Conference of The Methodist Church, this —— day of ——, 19——, as the basis of new credentials.

——, President
——, Secretary

Chapter VI

EPISCOPACY

Section I. **General Provisions**

¶ **421.** The general plan of episcopal supervision, including the **Council of Bishops,** is set forth in the Constitution (¶¶ 20, 34-41, 45 i, vi, 46.5-.6; *see also* ¶¶ 8.5, 9.2, 15.2, 19.2, 43.1-.4).

¶ **422.** The Jurisdictional and Central Conferences are authorized to fix the percentage of votes necessary to elect a bishop. It is recommended that at least three fifths of those present and voting be necessary to elect.

¶ **423.** The bishop or bishops elected by a Jurisdictional or Central Conference shall be consecrated at the session of the conference at which the election or elections take place, or at an adjourned session thereof, or at a time and place designated by the conference. At the consecration service the other Jurisdictional and Central Conferences and the church at large may be represented by one or more bishops appointed by the president of the Council of Bishops.[24]

¶ **424.** In the case of an emergency in a Central Conference through the death or expiration of term of service or any other disability of a bishop, the Council of Bishops may assign one of its number to furnish the necessary episcopal supervision for that field.

¶ **425.** The Council of Bishops shall promote the evangelistic activities of the church and shall appoint quadrennially one of their number who shall be the chairman of the General Board of Evangelism and furnish such inspirational leadership as the need and opportunity may demand.

Note: For other responsibilities of the Council of Bishops *see Index.*

¶ **427.** There shall be a **Conference of Methodist Bishops,** composed of all the bishops elected by the General, Jurisdictional, and Central Conferences, and bishops of affiliated autonomous Methodist churches, which shall meet in each quadrennium immediately prior to the General Conference, on call of the Council of Bishops. In case of an emergency a special meeting of the conference may be called by the Council of Bishops at any time during the quadrennium. The expense shall be charged to the Episcopal Fund. The travel expense of bishops from affiliated autonomous Methodist churches shall be paid on the same basis as that of the bishops of The Methodist Church.

Sec. II.   **Duties, Powers, and Limitations of Bishops**

¶ **431.** The duties of a bishop are:

1. To oversee the spiritual and temporal affairs of the church.

2. To preside in the General, Jurisdictional, Central, and Annual Conferences.

---

[24] *See* Judicial Council Decision 61. The General Conference of 1960 ordered that upon announcement by the Council of Bishops of the adoption of proposed Amendment XII to the Constitution (¶ 46) ¶ 423 should be repealed.

3. To form the districts according to his judgment, after consultation with the district superintendents, and after the number of the same has been determined by vote of the Annual Conference.

4. To fix the appointments of the preachers in the Annual Conferences, Provisional Annual Conferences, and Missions, as the Discipline may direct. He may appoint an associate pastor for a charge when in his judgment such an appointment is necessary.

5. To read the appointments of deaconesses.

6. To fix, either within their own conference or within the conference where they attend school, the Quarterly Conference membership of all ministers who are appointed to attend school.

7. To transfer, with the consent of the bishop of the receiving Annual Conference, a ministerial member of one Annual Conference to another, provided the ministerial member agrees to said transfer;[25] and to send immediately to the secretaries of both conferences involved, to the registrar of the conference in which the member is being received if he is on trial, and to the clearinghouse of the General Board of Pensions, written notices of the transfer of the member, and of his standing in the course of study if he is an undergraduate.

8. To organize such Missions as shall have been authorized by the General Conference.

9. To consecrate bishops, to ordain elders and deacons, to consecrate deaconesses, and to see that the names of the persons ordained and consecrated by him be entered on the journals of the conference, and that proper credentials be furnished to these persons.

10. To travel through the connection at large.

¶ 432. The following provisions and limitations shall be observed by the bishop when fixing the appointments:

1. He shall appoint preachers to pastoral charges annually after consultation with the district superintendents; *provided* that, before the official declaration of the assignments of the preachers, he shall announce openly to the Cabinet his appointments; and *provided*, further,

---

[25] *See* Judicial Council Decisions 114, 163.

that before the final announcement of appointments is made the district superintendents shall consult with the pastors except when the pastors involved have left the seat of the Annual Conference without the permission of the Annual Conference.[26]

2. He may make or change the appointments of preachers in the interval between sessions of the Annual Conference as necessity may require, after consultation with the district superintendents.

3. He shall choose and appoint the district superintendents annually; but within the Jurisdictional Conferences of the United States he shall not appoint any minister a district superintendent for more than six consecutive years nor for more than six years in any consecutive nine years.

4. He may make the following appointments annually: the publisher and his assistants; general and executive secretaries and their assistants, treasurers, and recording secretaries of the connectional benevolence boards and societies; editors, associate editors, and assistant editors of publications of The Methodist Church; chaplains in the Armed Forces, Veterans Administration, and other federal agencies and in state and local public and private institutions, including hospitals and charitable institutions; chaplains in industries and housing projects and to labor groups, whether organized or unorganized, within the episcopal area of the bishop making the appointment, *provided* that if the duties of such a chaplain carry him into another episcopal area his appointment must have the concurrence of the bishop or bishops o fthe areas concerned; preachers for seamen; ministers for community and federated churches; ministers in the service of the American Bible Society or of any state Bible society auxiliary thereto, or of the Sunday League of America; the presidents, principals, and teachers in institutions of learning under our auspices; secretaries and superintendents of city missions; executive and extension secretaries of Conference Boards of Education and confer-

---

[26] *See* Judicial Council Decision 101.

ence missionary secretaries; superintendents of Goodwill Industries affiliated with The Methodist Church; executive secretaries of preachers' aid societies and organizations of similar character; ministers of the Methodist Student Movement.[27]

5. On the recommendation of the district superintendents, confirmed by a two-thirds vote of the Annual Conference, he may appoint a person or persons: to travel throughout such conference to distribute tracts; to promote the cause of temperance; to promote or serve in our institutions of learning, hospitals and homes under our auspices, or other benevolence institutions; to serve in groups devoted to the promotion of peace and world order; to teach in institutions of learning not under our auspices; to be editors of unofficial papers or magazines published in the interests of The Methodist Church; *provided* that in no such case shall the church incur any financial responsibility.

6. On the recommendation of the Conference Board of Evangelism, confirmed by a two-thirds vote of the Annual Conference, he may appoint an effective member of the conference as conference evangelist; *provided* that the appointee shall meet the standards set up by the General and Conference Boards of Evangelism for conference evangelists. (*See* ¶¶ 1474.2, 1480.)

7. He may appoint a preacher on trial or a member of an Annual Conference who desires to attend school to any college or school of theology accredited or approved by the University Senate.[28]

8. He shall not appoint any preacher who has been rejected as an applicant, or who has been discontinued or located, except at his own request, unless the conference, at the time of such rejection, discontinuance, or location, shall give such liberty; and he shall not appoint as a supply any preacher who has previously been expelled from the ministry or has surrendered his credentials to an Annual Conference unless the conference to which he

---

[27] *See* Judicial Council Decisions 166, 167.
[28] *See* Judicial Council Decision 152.

surrendered his credentials, or from which he was expelled, restores his credentials or recommends it.

9. Every traveling preacher, unless retired, supernumerary, on sabbatical leave, or under arrest of character, must receive an appointment.

¶ **433.** When a bishop judges it necessary, he may divide a circuit, station, or mission into two or more charges and appoint the pastors thereto; and he may unite two or more circuits or stations and appoint one pastor for the united congregations.

¶ **434.** Bishops shall discharge such other duties as the Discipline may direct. (*See Index.*)

Sec. III.   **Retired Bishops**

¶ **435.** 1. If a bishop cease from traveling at large among the people without the consent of the Jurisdictional Conference, he shall not thereafter exercise in any degree the episcopal office in The Methodist Church.

2. A bishop may voluntarily resign from the episcopacy at any session of his Jurisdictional Conference. A bishop so resigning shall surrender to the secretary of his Jurisdictional Conference his consecration papers, and he shall be furnished with a certificate of his resignation which shall entitle him to membership as a traveling elder in the Annual Conference of which he was last a member, or its successor. When he or his surviving widow and dependent children become conference claimants, the Episcopal Fund shall pay a pension on account of his service as a bishop and his Annual Conference or Conferences on account of his approved service therein.

3. A bishop who by reason of impaired health is temporarily unable to perform full work may be released by the Jurisdictional Conference from the obligation to travel through the connection at large. He may choose the place of his residence, and the Council of Bishops shall be at liberty to assign him to such work as he may be able to perform. He shall receive his support as provided in ¶ 775.

¶ **436.** 1. A bishop whose seventieth birthday precedes the first day of the regular session of his Jurisdictional

Conference[29] shall be released at the close of that conference from the obligation to travel through the connection at large, and from residential supervision.

2. A bishop, at any age and for any reason deemed sufficient by his Jurisdictional Conference, may be released by that body from the obligation to travel through the connection at large, and from residential supervision.

3. A bishop who has reached the age of sixty-five years, or who will reach the age of sixty-five years during the calendar year in which his Jurisdictional Conference[29] is held, and who has given written notice that he so elects to the bishops of his jurisdiction, may be retired at the session of his Jurisdictional Conference[29] next following such notice.

4. A bishop who has been retired under § 1, § 2, or § 3 may, on vote of the Council of Bishops, be appointed to take charge of an episcopal area, or parts of an area, in case of the death, resignation, or disability of the resident bishop or because of judicial procedure (provided the request is made by a majority of the bishops in the jurisdiction of the proposed change). This appointment shall not continue beyond the next session of his Jurisdictional Conference.

¶ 437. 1. A bishop who has been released from the obligation to travel through the connection at large in accordance with any of the foregoing provisions shall not preside thereafter over any Annual Conference, Provisional Annual Conference, or Mission, or make appointments, or preside at the Jurisdictional or Central Conference, but may take the chair temporarily in any conference if requested to do so by the bishop presiding. He may participate in the Council of Bishops, but without vote.[30] In case, however, a retired bishop shall be appointed by the Council of Bishops to take charge of a

---

[29] The General Conference of 1960 ordered that upon announcement by the Council of Bishops of the adoption of proposed Amendment XII to the Constitution (¶ 46) ¶ 436.1, .3 should be amended by deleting the words "his Jurisdictional Conference" and substituting "the General Conference."

[30] See Judicial Council Decisions 35, 40.

vacant episcopal area, or parts of an area, under the provisions of ¶ 436.4, he may preside over sessions of an Annual Conference, Provisional Annual Conference, or Mission, make appointments, and participate and vote in the meetings of the bishops.

2. A bishop who has been released under any of the foregoing provisions may continue to exercise all the rights and privileges which pertain to the episcopal office, except as herein otherwise provided.

¶ **438.** Each Central Conference shall determine the rules for retirement of its bishops; *provided* that the age of retirement shall not exceed that fixed for bishops in the jurisdictions. In the event of retirement allowances' being paid from the Episcopal Fund, these rules shall be subject to the approval of the General Conference.[31]

SEC. IV.   **Bishops in Jurisdictions**

¶ **439.** Each jurisdiction having 500,000 church members or less shall be entitled to five bishops, and for each additional 500,000 church members or major fraction thereof shall be entitled to one additional bishop; *provided*, however, that in those jurisdictions where this requirement would result in there being an average of more than 70,000 square miles per episcopal area, such jurisdiction shall be entitled to five bishops for the first 400,000 church members or less, and for each additional 400,000 church members or two thirds thereof shall be entitled to one additional bishop; and *provided*, further, that the General Conference may authorize any Jurisdictional Conference to elect one or more bishops beyond the quota herein specified in order to provide episcopal supervision for mission fields outside the territory of a Jurisdictional Conference.[32]

¶ **440.** Each Jurisdictional Conference may fix the episcopal residences within its jurisdiction and assign the bishops to the same. (*See* ¶ 526.) The bishops of the jurisdiction shall fix the boundaries of the episcopal areas.[33]

---

[31] Amended in 1952 following Judicial Council Decision 83.
[32] *See* Judicial Council Decision 84.
[33] *See* Judicial Council Decisions 48, 57, 84.

SEC. V.   **Bishops in Central Conferences**

¶ **441.** The Central Conferences shall elect bishops in the number determined by the General Conference, whose episcopal supervision shall be within the territory included in the Central Conference by which they have been elected, subject to such other conditions as the General Conference shall prescribe; *provided*, however, that a bishop elected by one Central Conference may exercise episcopal supervision in another Central Conference when so requested by such other Central Conference.

¶ **442.** A bishop elected by a Central Conference shall be constituted by election in a Central Conference and consecrated by the laying on of hands of three bishops, or at least one bishop and two elders.[34]

¶ **443.** A bishop elected by a Central Conference shall have, within the bounds of the Central Conference by which he is elected or within which he is administering, authority similar to that exercised by bishops elected by or administering in a Jurisdictional Conference.

¶ **444.** A bishop elected by a Central Conference shall have the status, rights, and duties within his territory of a bishop elected by or functioning in a Jurisdictional Conference. A bishop elected by a Central Conference shall have membership in the Council of Bishops and shall have the privilege of full participation with vote. (*See* ¶ 45 vi.) Attendance on the annual meetings of the Council of Bishops by bishops elected by Central Conferences shall be left to the option of the bishops in each Central Conference.[35]

¶ **445.** In a Central Conference where term episcopacy prevails, a bishop whose term of office expires prior to the time of compulsory retirement because of age, and who is not re-elected by the Central Conference, shall be returned to membership as a traveling elder in the Annual Conference (or its successor) of which he ceased to be a member when elected bishop. His term of office shall expire at the close of the Central Conference at which his successor is elected, and he shall therefore be entitled to participate as

---

[34] *See* Judicial Council Decision 61.
[35] *See* Judicial Council Decisions 117, 164.

a bishop in the consecration of his successor. The credentials of his office as bishop shall be submitted to the secretary of the Central Conference, who shall make thereon the notation that he has honorably completed the term of service for which he was elected and has ceased to be a bishop of The Methodist Church. (*See* ¶ 559.2.)

SEC. VI.   **Missionary Bishops**

¶ **446.** 1. A **missionary bishop** is a bishop who has been elected for a specified foreign mission field with full episcopal powers, but with episcopal jurisdiction limited to the foreign mission field for which he was elected.[36]

2. Missionary bishops shall be included in all other provisions for the episcopacy, including relation to Jurisdictional Conferences, amenability, and provisions for support and retirement.

3. Notwithstanding the above definitions, in an emergency the Council of Bishops may assign a missionary bishop for specified service in any foreign field in consultation with the authorities, where such exist, of the Central Conference or the Provisional Central Conference concerned.

[36] *See* Judicial Council Decisions 21, 84, 127.

PART IV

THE CONFERENCES

CHAPTER I

THE GENERAL CONFERENCE

SECTION I.   Composition

¶ 501. The **General Conference** shall be composed of one ministerial member for every seventy ministerial members of each Annual Conference and one additional member for a major fraction thereof and an equal number of lay members, all of whom shall be elected by ballot and by a majority vote.[1] The term "ministerial members" as used above shall refer to effective members of the Annual Conference and also supernumerary and retired members. Every Annual Conference shall be entitled to at least one ministerial and one lay member. The secretaries of the several Annual Conferences shall furnish certificates of election to the delegates severally, and shall send a certificate of such election to the secretary

---

[1] The General Conference of 1960 ordered that upon announcement by the Council of Bishops of the adoption of proposed Amendment XII to the Constitution (¶ 46) the first sentence of ¶ 501 should be replaced by the following: "The General Conference shall be composed of an equal number of ministerial and lay members elected by the Annual Conferences. Not less than fourteen months prior to the General Conference the Council of Bishops shall announce the number of delegates to be elected by the respective Annual Conferences, which number shall be computed by taking the total number of delegates of which the General Conference is to be composed and allocating the same among the respective Annual Conferences on the basis of their relative ministerial membership, as shown by the General Minutes for the year two years prior to the General Conference." It further ordered that in such case the total number of delegates to the 1964 General Conference should be 1,400.

of the preceding General Conference immediately after the adjournment of said Annual Conference.

¶ 502. Members of the Council of Secretaries who are not elected members of the General Conference shall have the privilege of the floor on matters affecting the interests of their respective agencies, but without vote and at the expense of their respective agencies. If an agency by formal action shall so request, it may be represented by an associate secretary rather than by the regularly elected general or executive secretary.

¶ 503. Each Provisional Annual Conference and Mission outside the United States may designate a member to meet with the standing committees and have the privilege of the floor of the General Conference on matters affecting the interests of his conference, but without vote and without expense to the General Conference except for the per diem during its sessions.

¶ 504. 1. The ministerial and lay delegates and reserves to the General Conference shall be elected by ballot in accordance with the provisions of the Constitution (¶¶ 23, 45 iii, viii; *see also* ¶ 46.4).

2. The ministerial and lay members may meet separately to vote for the election of delegates to the General and Jurisdictional Conferences.[2]

3. The election of delegates, by ballot, shall be held at the session of the Annual Conference immediately preceding the General Conference.[2]

4. The General Conference recommends to the Annual Conferences that the delegates to the General Conference be first elected on a separate ballot, to be followed, after all the delegates to the General Conference have been elected, by balloting for delegates to the Jurisdictional Conference as reserves to the General Conference.[3]

Sec. II.   **Rules**

¶ 505. It is recommended that the meeting place of the

---

[2] *See* Judicial Council Decision 76.

[3] The General Conference of 1960 ordered that upon announcement by the Council of Bishops of the adoption of proposed Amendment XII to the Constitution (¶ 46) ¶ 504 should be amended by changing "General Conference" in § 3 to "Jurisdictional Conference," and by deleting all of § 4.

General Conference be rotated among the jurisdictions, provided satisfactory arrangements can be made for entertainment, with special reference to the requirement for equality of accommodations for all races, without discrimination or segregation.

¶ 506. When the General Conference is in session, it shall require the presence of a majority of the whole number of delegates to the General Conference to constitute a quorum for the transaction of business; but a smaller number may take a recess or adjourn from day to day in order to secure a quorum, and at the final session may approve the journal, order the record of the roll call, and adjourn *sine die*.

¶ 507. The ministerial and lay members shall deliberate as one body. They shall vote as one body, but a separate vote shall be taken on any question when requested by one third of either order of delegates present and voting. In all cases of separate voting it shall require the concurrence of a majority of each order to adopt the proposed measure. However, in the case of changes in the Constitution, a vote of two thirds of the General Conference, as provided in the Constitution, shall be required.

¶ 508. The plan of organization and rules of order of the General Conference shall be the plan of organization and rules of order as published in the journal of the preceding General Conference until they have been altered or modified by the action of the General Conference.

¶ 509. The Council of Bishops by two-thirds majority vote, or two thirds of all the Annual Conferences by a majority vote of each conference, shall have the power to call at any time an extra session of the General Conference to be held at such time as the Council of Bishops may choose and at such place as a committee chosen by the Council of Bishops may fix. The General Conference thus called shall be composed of the delegates elected to the preceding General Conference, except when an Annual Conference shall prefer to have a new election.

¶ 510. Any organization, minister, or lay member of The Methodist Church may petition the General Conference by sending to the secretary a memorial, which shall be signed and shall contain information indicating that the sender or senders are members of The Methodist Church. It is recommended that each memorial meet the following requirements: (*a*) Three copies of it should be supplied to the secretary in time to be received by him not later than the opening day of the conference session. (*b*) It should deal with only one subject, and should propose revisions within only one chapter of the Discipline. (*c*) If it is one of a series, each memorial should be written on a separate sheet.

SEC. III. **General Conference Powers**

¶ **511.** General Conference powers, and the restrictions thereon, are set forth in the Constitution (¶¶ 8-10; *see also* ¶¶ 11, 15-16, 18-19, 27, 30-33, 36, 42, 45 i, ii, iv, ix, 46.4, .6).

¶ **512.** No person, no paper, no organization has the authority to speak officially for The Methodist Church, except only the General Conference under the Constitution.

CHAPTER II

THE JURISDICTIONAL CONFERENCE

SECTION I. **General Provisions**

¶ **516.** All Jurisdictional Conferences shall have the same status and the same privileges of action within the limits fixed by the Constitution. (¶ 12.)

¶ **517.** The Jurisdictional Conference shall be composed of one ministerial delegate for every thirty ministerial members of each Annual Conference, or major fraction thereof, and an equal number of lay delegates; *provided* that no Annual Conference shall be denied the privilege of two delegates, one lay and one ministerial.[4]

---

[4] *See* Judicial Council Decision 125. The General Conference of 1960 ordered that upon announcement by the Council of Bishops of the adoption of proposed Amendment XII to the Constitution (¶ 46) ¶ 517 should be amended to read as follows: "The Jurisdictional Conference shall be composed of the ministerial and lay members who have been elected by the Annual Conferences within the jurisdiction to be delegates to the General Conference (¶¶ 45 iii, viii, 46.4)."

¶ **518.** The ministerial and lay delegates and reserves to the Jurisdictional Conferences shall be elected by ballot in accordance with the provisions of the Constitution. (¶¶ 23, 45 iii, viii; *see also* ¶ 46.4.)

¶ **519.** The ministers and lay delegates shall deliberate in one body.

¶ **520.** Each Jurisdictional Conference shall meet within the twelve months succeeding the meeting of the General Conference, but not earlier than six weeks after the convening of the General Conference, at such time and place as shall have been determined by the preceding Jurisdictional Conference or by its properly constituted committee.[5]

¶ **521.** The Jurisdictional Conference shall adopt its own procedure, rules, and plan of organization. It shall take a majority of the whole number of delegates elected to make a quorum for the transaction of business. But a smaller number may take a recess or adjourn from day to day, and at the final session may approve the journal, order the record of the roll call, and adjourn *sine die.*

¶ **522.** The Jurisdictional Conference shall provide for the expenses of its sessions.

¶ **523.** The bishops of a Jurisdictional Conference, by a two-thirds vote, shall have authority to call a special session of the conference when necessary. A called session cannot transact any other business than that indicated in the call.

¶ **524.** The Jurisdictional Conference shall be presided over by the bishops of the jurisdiction, except as provided in ¶ 38. In case no bishop of the jurisdiction is present, the conference may elect a president from the ministerial delegates.

¶ **525.** A bishop elected by or administering in a Jurisdictional Conference shall be amenable for his conduct to his Jurisdictional Conference. Any bishop shall have the right of appeal to the Judicial Council.

---

[5] The General Conference of 1960 ordered that upon announcement by the Council of Bishops of the adoption of proposed Amendment XII to the Constitution (¶ 46) ¶ 520 should be repealed (*see* ¶ 46.2), and it invited the Jurisdictional Conferences in such case to hold their 1964 sessions at the time and place of the 1964 General Conference.

¶ 526. The Jurisdictional Conference shall elect a standing **Committee on Episcopacy,** to consist of one ministerial and one lay delegate from each Annual Conference, on nomination of the Annual Conference delegation. The committee shall review the work of the bishops, pass on their character and official administration, and report to the Jurisdictional Conference its findings for such action as the conference may deem appropriate within its constitutional warrant of power. The committee shall recommend the assignments of the bishops to their respective residences, for final action by the Jurisdictional Conference; *provided* that no bishop shall be recommended for assignment to the same residence for more than twelve consecutive years, not counting years served before 1960. It may also make recommendations to the bishops of the jurisdiction concerning the formation of the episcopal areas within the jurisdiction. (*See* ¶ 440.) [6]

¶ 527. The Jurisdictional Conference shall have powers and duties as described in the Constitution (¶ 15), and such others as may be conferred by the General Conference. [7] It may adopt its own policies for promotion and administration by jurisdictional agencies.

¶ 528. In all elections in a Jurisdictional Conference which are based on the number of church members within that jurisdiction, the number counted shall include lay members, ministerial members, and bishops assigned to that jurisdiction. (*See* ¶¶ 439, 1101.)

¶ 529. The Jurisdictional Conference shall have authority to examine and acknowledge the journals of the Annual Conferences within its bounds, and shall make such rules for the drawing up of the journals as may seem necessary.

¶ 530. 1. The Jurisdictional Conference shall keep an official **journal** of its proceedings, duly signed by the

---

[6] The General Conference of 1960 ordered that upon announcement by the Council of Bishops of the adoption of proposed Amendment XII to the Constitution (¶ 46) the following sentence should be added to ¶ 526: "The committee shall report to the General Conference Committee on Episcopacy the assignments of bishops to the areas within the jurisdiction, in accordance with ¶ 46.6."

[7] *See* Judicial Council Decision 67.

secretary and president, the same to be sent for examination to the ensuing General Conference.

2. For the sake of convenience and uniformity, the journal when printed should conform in page size and formation to the General Conference journal; and the printing should be done at the expense of the jurisdiction by The Methodist Publishing House.

SEC. II.   **Jurisdictional Boundaries**

¶ **531.** The Methodist Church in the United States of America shall have Jurisdictional Conferences made up as described in the Constitution (¶ 26). For methods of changing the number, names, and boundaries of the Jurisdictional and Annual Conferences see ¶¶ 28, 29, 45 ix in the Constitution and also ¶ 532.

¶ **532.** Any local church shall be transferred from the jurisdiction of which it is part to another jurisdiction in which it is located geographically upon completion of all the following actions, regardless of the order in which taken: (*a*) approval by the membership and the Quarterly Conference of said church; (*b*) approval by both the Annual Conference of which the church has been a part and the Annual Conference to which transfer is desired; (*c*) approval by a majority of the Annual Conferences and also by the Jurisdictional Conference of both the jurisdiction of which the church has been a part and the jurisdiction to which transfer is desired; and (*d*) approval by the General Conference in the form of an enabling act. Such transfer shall be effected when all of the required actions have been certified to the Council of Bishops by the secretaries of all the conferences involved, whereupon the Council of Bishops shall issue a declaration that the transfer has been duly effected.[8]

SEC. III.   **Property**

¶ **533.** The Jurisdictional Conference shall not alienate any property or institution, or the proceeds derived from the sale or transfer of any property or institution, from The Methodist Church, nor shall the Jurisdictional Confer-

---

[8] Adopted in 1952 following Judicial Council Decisions 28, 32, 55, 56, 85.

ence or any of its boards involve the General Conference boards or any other organization of the church in any financial obligation without the official approval of said board or organization.

¶ **534.** When property rights are involved by the change of boundary lines of Annual Conferences within the jurisdiction, the Jurisdictional Conference shall constitute a committee of arbitration to adjust all claims and make final settlement of the same. In the case of interjurisdictional conflicts, the said committee shall act with a like committee from each of the other jurisdictions involved to reach a proper settlement.

¶ **535.** No invested funds, fiduciary trusts, or property acquired by bequest, donation, or otherwise for specific objects within the boundaries of an Annual Conference or Conferences may be diverted to other purposes except by the consent of the Annual Conference or Conferences involved and with the consent of the Jurisdictional Conference or Conferences concerned, and civil court approval when necessary; *provided* that local churches possessing such funds or property shall not be required to obtain the consent of the Jurisdictional Conferences. The same rule shall apply to similar funds or properties acquired by the Jurisdictional Conferences for work specifically jurisdictional in its scope. In such cases the Jurisdictional Conference shall determine the disposition of the interests involved, subject to an appeal to the Judicial Council.

Provided, moreover, that trust funds may not be divided or diverted to other purposes than for the specific objects for which donated, even with the consent of Annual Conferences or Jurisdictional Conferences, unless the said conferences are the beneficiaries of said trust funds or control them.[9]

Chapter III

THE CENTRAL CONFERENCE

Section I.　　　　　　　**Authorization**

¶ **541.** In territory outside the United States of Amer-

---

[9] *See* Judicial Council Decision 64.

ica, Annual Conferences, Provisional Annual Conferences, and Missions in such numbers as the General Conference by a two-thirds vote shall determine may be organized by the General Conference into Central Conferences or Provisional Central Conferences with such duties, privileges, and powers as are hereinafter set forth and as the General Conference by a two-thirds vote shall prescribe.

¶ **542.** There shall be such Central Conferences as have been authorized, or shall be hereafter authorized by the General Conference; *provided* that a Central Conference shall have at least a total of thirty ministerial and thirty lay delegates on the basis of representation as set forth in ¶ 543, except as the General Conference may fix a different number. A Central Conference now in existence may be continued with a lesser number of delegates for reasons deemed sufficient by the General Conference.

SEC. II. **Organization**

¶ **543.** The **Central Conference** shall be composed of ministerial and lay members in equal numbers, the ministerial elected by the ministerial members of the Annual Conference and the lay by the lay members thereof. For the first meeting their qualifications shall be the same as provided in ¶¶ 45 iii, viii, and the Annual Conference shall determine the manner of their choice. Thereafter, their qualifications and the manner of election shall be determined by the Central Conference itself.[10] Each Annual Conference and Provisional Annual Conference shall be entitled to at least two ministerial and two lay delegates, and no other selection of delegates shall be authorized which would provide for more than one ministerial delegate for every six ministerial members of an Annual Conference, except that a majority of the number fixed by a Central Conference as the ratio of representation shall entitle an Annual Conference to an additional ministerial delegate and to an additional lay delegate. A Mission is authorized to elect and send one of its members to the Central Conference concerned as the representative of the Mission, said representative to be accorded the

---

[10] *See* Judicial Council Decision 124.

privilege of sitting with the committees of the Central Conference, with the right to speak in the committees, and in the regular sessions of the Central Conference, but without the right to vote. The representative of the Mission shall have the same claim for payment of expenses as is allowed to members of the Central Conference.

¶ **544.** The first meeting of a Central Conference shall be called by the bishop or bishops in charge, at such time and place as he or they may select, to which members of the Annual Conferences, Provisional Annual Conferences, and Missions concerned shall be elected on the basis of representation in accordance with ¶ 543. The time and place of future meetings shall be determined by the Central Conference or its executive committee.

¶ **545.** Each Central Conference shall meet within the year succeeding the session of the General Conference, at such time and place as the Central Conference itself or its bishops may determine, with the right to hold such adjourned sessions as it may determine. The sessions of said conference shall be presided over by the bishops. In case no bishop be present, the conference shall elect a temporary president from among its own members. The bishops resident in a Central Conference, or a majority of them, with the concurrence of the executive committee or other authorized committee, shall have the authority to call an extra session of the Central Conference to be held at the time and place designated by them.

¶ **546.** The Council of Bishops may assign one or more of their number to visit any Central Conference or Provisional Central Conference. When so assigned, the bishop shall be an accredited representative of the general church and, when requested by a majority of the bishops resident in that conference, may exercise therein the functions of the episcopacy. (*See also* ¶¶ 593, 604.)

¶ **547.** The presiding officer of the Central Conference shall decide questions of order, subject to an appeal to the Central Conference, and he shall decide questions of law, subject to an appeal to the Judicial Council; but questions relating to the interpretation of the rules and regulations made by the Central Conference for the governing of its own session shall be decided by the Central Conference.

¶ **548.** Each Central Conference within the bounds of which the Board of Missions has work shall maintain a co-operative and consultative relationship with the said board through a duly constituted executive committee, executive board, or council of co-operation; but the legal distinction between the Board of Missions and the organized church on the field shall always be kept clear.

¶ **549.** The journal of the proceedings of a Central Conference, duly signed by the president and secretary, shall be sent for examination to the General Conference.

¶ **550.** A Provisional Central Conference may become a Central Conference upon the fulfillment of the necessary requirements and upon the authorization of the General Conference.

SEC. III.   **Central Conference Powers**

¶ **556.** To a Central Conference shall be committed for supervision and promotion, in harmony with the Discipline and interdenominational contractual agreements, the missionary, educational, evangelistic, industrial, publishing, medical, and other connectional interests of the Annual Conferences, Provisional Annual Conferences, and Missions within its territory, and such other matters as may be referred to it by said bodies, or by order of the General Conference; and it shall provide suitable organizations for such work and elect the necessary officers for the same.

¶ **557.** A Central Conference, when authorized by a specific enabling act of the General Conference, may elect one or more bishops from among the traveling elders of The Methodist Church. The number of bishops to be elected by each Central Conference shall be determined from time to time by the General Conference.

¶ **558.** When a Central Conference shall have been authorized to elect bishops, such elections shall be conducted under the same general procedure as prevails in the Jurisdictional Conferences for the election of bishops. A Central Conference shall have power to fix the tenure of bishops elected by the said Central Conference; *pro-*

vided that such tenure shall not be for a term longer than that in force at the time for bishops elected by the Jurisdictional Conferences.[11]

¶ **559.** 1. A Central Conference shall participate in the General Episcopal Fund on payment of its apportionment on the same basis as that fixed for Annual Conferences in Jurisdictional Conferences. When the total estimated support, including salaries and all allowances for the bishops elected by it, and the amount that it will be able to provide on apportionment, have been determined by a Central Conference, these amounts in itemized form shall be submitted to the Council on World Service and Finance. This council after consideration of the relative cost of living in various Central Conferences, shall determine the amount to be paid from the General Episcopal Fund in meeting this budget, after which the treasurer of the General Episcopal Fund shall pay the amount established to the bishop concerned, or as the Central Conference may determine.

2. A minister who has served a term, or part of a term, as a bishop in a Central Conference where term episcopacy has prevailed shall, upon his retirement from the effective relation in the ministry, be paid an allowance from the General Episcopal Fund in such sum as the Council on World Service and Finance shall determine for the years during which he served as a bishop. (*See* ¶ 445.)

¶ **560.** 1. A Central Conference, in consultation with the bishops of that Central Conference, shall fix the episcopal areas and residences and make assignments to them of the bishops who are to reside in that Central Conference. The bishops of a Central Conference shall arrange the plan of episcopal visitation within its bounds.

2. The secretary of a Central Conference in which one or more bishops have been chosen shall report to the secretary of the General Conference the names of the bishop or bishops and the residences to which they have been assigned by the Central Conference.

¶ **561.** A Central Conference shall have authority to

---

[11] *See* Judicial Council Decisions 4, 61, 80.

elect and support general officers in all departments of the work of the church within the boundaries of the Central Conferences, but may not determine the number of bishops.

¶ 562. A Central Conference shall have power to make such changes and adaptations as the peculiar conditions on the fields concerned require regarding the local church, ministry, special advices, worship, and temporal economy within its territory; *provided* that no action shall be taken which is contrary to the Constitution and the General Rules of The Methodist Church.[12]

¶ 563. A Central Conference shall have the authority to change the provisions for the ordination of ministers in such way that the ordination of an elder may follow immediately upon his ordination as a deacon, provided that other conditions are fully met.

¶ 564. A Central Conference shall fix the boundaries of the Annual Conferences, Provisional Annual Conferences, and Missions within its bounds, proposals for changes first having been submitted to the Annual Conferences concerned as prescribed in the Discipline of The Methodist Church; *provided*, however, that the number of Annual Conferences which may be organized within the bounds of a Central Conference shall first have been determined by the General Conference. No Annual Conference shall be organized with fewer than thirty-five ministerial members, except as provided by an enabling act for the quadrennium, which shall not reduce the number below twenty-five. Nor shall an Annual Conference be continued with fewer than twenty-five ministerial members, except as provided by an enabling act for the quadrennium.

¶ 565. A Central Conference may advise its Annual Conferences and Provisional Annual Conferences to set standards of character and other qualifications for admission of lay members.

¶ 566. A Central Conference shall have power to make changes and adaptations in procedure pertaining to the Annual, District, and Quarterly Conferences within its

---

[12] Amended in 1960 following Judicial Council Decisions 121, 142, 147, 155.

territory, and to add to the business of the Annual Conference supplementary questions considered desirable or necessary to meet its own needs.

¶ **567.** A Central Conference shall have authority to examine and acknowledge the journals of the Annual Conferences, Provisional Annual Conferences, and Missions located within its bounds, and to make rules for the drawing up of the journals as may seem necessary.

¶ **568.** A Central Conference may have a standing **Committee on Woman's Work.** This committee should preferably be composed of the women delegates and such other persons as the Central Conference may elect. The duty of this committee shall be to study the relation of women to the church and to devise ways and means of developing this portion of the church membership, to the end that it may assume its rightful responsibilities in the extension of the Kingdom. The committee shall make recommendations to the Central Conference regarding women's organizations within its areas. A Central Conference organization may become a member of the World Federation of Methodist Women and may elect a representative on the World Council of the federation.

¶ **569.** A Central Conference may organize a woman's unit, after consultation with the Committee on Woman's Work, in connection with any Annual Conference or Provisional Annual Conference within its bounds and provide a constitution and by-laws for it.

¶ **570.** A Central Conference shall have authority to adopt rules of procedure governing the investigation and trial of its ministers, including bishops, and lay members of the church and to provide the necessary means and methods of carrying them into effect; *provided*, however, that the ministers shall not be deprived of the right of trial by a ministerial committee, and lay members of the church of the right of trial by a duly constituted committee of church members; and *provided*, also, that the rights of appeal shall be adequately safeguarded. (*See* ¶ 930.)

¶ **571.** A Central Conference is authorized to prepare and translate simplified or adapted forms of such parts of the Ritual as it may deem necessary, such changes to require the approval of the resident bishop or bishops of the Central Conference.

¶ 572. A Central Conference shall have the power to conform the detailed rules, rites, and ceremonies for the solemnization of marriage to the statute laws of the country or countries within its jurisdiction.

¶ 573. Subject to the approval of the bishops resident therein, a Central Conference shall have the power to prescribe courses of study, including those in the vernaculars, for its ministry, both foreign and indigenous, including local preachers, lay speakers, Bible women, deaconesses, teachers both male and female, and all other workers whatsoever, ordained or lay. It shall also make rules and regulations for examinations in these courses.

¶ 574. A Central Conference shall have authority to edit and publish a Central Conference Discipline which shall contain, in addition to the Constitution of the church, such sections from the general Discipline of The Methodist Church as may be pertinent to the entire church; and also such revised, adapted, or new sections as shall have been enacted by the Central Conference concerned, under the powers given by the General Conference, with the understanding that legislation passed by the General Conference becomes effective immediately through the entire church, except as provided in ¶ 575.

¶ 575. In a Central Conference or Provisional Central Conference using a language other than English, legislation passed by a General Conference shall not take effect until six months after the close of that General Conference, in order to afford the necessary time to make adaptations and to publish a translation of the legislation which has been enacted, which translation shall be approved by the resident bishop or bishops of the Central Conference. This provision, however, shall not exclude the election of delegates to the General Conference by Annual Conferences within the territory of Central Conferences or Provisional Central Conferences.

¶ 576. A Central Conference is authorized to interpret Article XXIII of the Articles of Religion so as to recognize the government or governments of the country or countries within its territory.

¶ **577.** A Central Conference shall have power to authorize the congregations in a certain state or country to form special organizations in order to receive the acknowledgment of the state or country according to the laws of that state or country. These organizations shall be empowered to represent the interests of the church to the authorities of the state or country according to the rules and principles of The Methodist Church, and they shall be required to give regular reports of their activities to their respective Annual Conferences.

¶ **578.** A Central Conference may, with the consent of the bishops resident in that conference, enter into agreements with churches or missions of other denominations for the division of territory or of responsibility for Christian work within the territory of the Central Conference.

¶ **579.** A Central Conference shall have the right to negotiate with other Protestant bodies looking toward the possibility of church union; *provided* that any proposals for church union shall be submitted to the General Conference for approval before consummation.

¶ **580.** A Central Conference, where the laws of the land permit, shall have the power to organize and incorporate one or more executive committees, executive boards, or councils of co-operation, with such membership and such powers as may have been granted by the Central Conference, for the purpose of representing it in its property and legal interests and for transacting any necessary business that may arise in the interval between the sessions of the Central Conference, or that may be committed to said boards or committees by the Central Conferences.[13]

¶ **581.** 1. A Central Conference, through a duly incorporated property-holding body or bodies, shall have authority to purchase, own, hold, or transfer property for and on behalf of The Methodist Church, and of all the unincorporated organizations of The Methodist Church within the territory of that Central Conference, or on

---

[13] *See* Judicial Council Decision 69.

behalf of other organizations of The Methodist Church which have entrusted their property to that Central Conference.

2. A Central Conference shall have authority to make the necessary rules and regulations for the holding and management of such properties; *provided*, however, (*a*) that all procedure shall be subject to the laws of the country or countries concerned; (*b*) that no transfer of property shall be made from one Annual Conference to another without the consent of the conference holding title to such property; (*c*) that the status of properties held by local trustees or other holding bodies shall be recognized.

3. A Central Conference shall not, directly or indirectly through its incorporated property-holding body or bodies, alienate property or the proceeds of property without due consideration of its trusteeship for local churches, Annual Conferences, the Board of Missions, and other organizations, local or general, of the church.

4. A Central Conference, or any of its incorporated organizations, shall not involve the Board of Missions or any organization of the church in any financial obligation without the official approval of said board or organization. All invested funds, fiduciary trusts, or property belonging to an Annual Conference, a Provisional Annual Conference, or a Mission, or any of its institutions, acquired by bequests, donation, or otherwise, and designated for a specific use, shall be applied to the purpose for which they were designated. They shall not be diverted to any other purpose except by the consent of the conference or mission involved, and with the approval of the Central Conference concerned, and civil court action when necessary. The same rule shall apply to similar funds or properties acquired by a Central Conference for specific objects. In cases involving the diversion of trust funds and properties within the territory of a Central Conference, the Central Conference concerned shall determine the disposition of the interests involved subject to an appeal to the Judicial Court of the Central Conference.

Note: For description of the Commission on the Structure of Methodism Overseas *see* ¶ 2012.

Chapter IV

PROVISIONAL CENTRAL CONFERENCES

¶ **586.** Annual Conferences, Provisional Annual Conferences, and Missions outside the United States which are not included in Central Conferences or in the territory of affiliated autonomous churches, and which because of geographical, language, political, or other considerations have common interests that can best be served thereby, may be organized into **Provisional Central Conferences** as provided in ¶ 541.

¶ **587.** The organization of Provisional Central Conferences shall conform to the regulations prescribed for Central Conferences (¶¶ 543-49) in so far as they are considered applicable by the bishop in charge.

¶ **588.** The General Conference may grant to a Provisional Central Conference any of the powers of a Central Conference except that of electing bishops.

¶ **589.** In the interval between General Conferences the Board of Missions, upon the recommendation of the bishops in charge and after consultation with the Annual Conferences, Provisional Annual Conferences, and Missions concerned, may make changes in the boundaries of a Provisional Central Conference and may grant to a Provisional Central Conference or to any of its component parts any of the powers of a Central Conference except that of electing bishops. All changes in boundaries and all grants of powers authorized by the Board of Missions shall be reported to the ensuing session of the General Conference and shall expire at the close of that session unless renewed by the General Conference.

¶ **590.** An Annual Conference or a Provisional Annual Conference in the field of a Provisional Central Conference shall have the power to set standards of character and other qualifications for admission of its lay members.

¶ **591.** To Annual Conferences, Provisional Annual Conferences, and Missions which are outside the United States and are not included in Central Conferences or Provisional Central Conferences, the General Conference may grant any of the powers of Central Conferences except that of electing bishops; and in the interval between General Conferences the Board of Missions may grant such powers when requested to do so by the bishop in charge and by the Annual Conference, Provisional Annual Conference, or Mission concerned.

¶ 592. The General Conference shall make provision for the episcopal supervision of work in the territory outside the United States which is not now included in Central Conferences. (*See* ¶ 2005.)

¶ 593. The Council of Bishops may provide, if and when necessary, for episcopal visitation of mission fields not included in Central or Provisional Central Conferences. (*See* ¶ 546.)

Chapter V

AFFILIATED AUTONOMOUS CHURCHES

¶ 600. A self-governing church in whose establishment The Methodist Church has assisted and with which it is co-operating through its Board of Missions shall be known as an **affiliated autonomous church.** Relations between The Methodist Church and an affiliated autonomous church shall be such as may be mutually agreed on by the two churches. The Board of Missions shall serve as the agent of The Methodist Church in conferring with affiliated autonomous churches.

¶ 601. Contractual agreements with The Methodist Church of Mexico, The Methodist Church of Brazil, Korean Methodist Church, and United Church of Christ in Japan entered into by the former Methodist Episcopal Church and/or the former Methodist Episcopal Church, South, shall be continued until changed or modified by mutual agreement. The Board of Missions is authorized to harmonize and make uniform the present agreements and practices with respect to the four churches named above by extending to each of them any provision contained in the present agreement with any one of them, if such change is desired by the affiliated autonomous church concerned and judged to be advisable by the Board of Missions.

¶ **602.** The contractual agreements between The Methodist Church and The Methodist Church of Brazil, The Methodist Church of Mexico, and Korean Methodist Church include the following provisions:

1. Certificates of church membership given by ministers in one church shall be accepted by ministers in the others.

2. It shall be lawful for a minister to be transferred from an Annual or Provisional Annual Conference of The Methodist Church to an Annual or Provisional Annual Conference of the above-mentioned affiliated autonomous Methodist churches, and from an Annual or Provisional Annual Conference of any of the above-mentioned churches to an Annual or Provisional Annual Conference of The Methodist Church, with the approval and consent of the bishops involved in the transfer.

3. Each affiliated autonomous church shall be entitled to two delegates, a national and a missionary, elected by the Central Council or Council of Co-operation of the affiliated autonomous church, to the General Conference of The Methodist Church, with all the rights and privileges of delegates, including travel and per diem paid from the General Administration Fund, except the right to vote.

4. The Board of Missions of The Methodist Church may appoint two delegates to the General Conference of each of the above-mentioned affiliated autonomous Methodist churches, who shall be entitled to all the privileges of delegates except the right to vote.

¶ **603.** When an Annual Conference or a Provisional Annual Conference becomes a part of an affiliated autonomous Methodist church, the Council of Bishops may, at its discretion, transfer members of said conference, who desire transfer, to the conference from which they went to the mission field. If any have not previously had membership in another conference of The Methodist Church, the Council of Bishops may, at its discretion, transfer them to conferences as it may determine.

¶ **604.** The Council of Bishops may assign one or more of its members for episcopal visitation to the affiliated autonomous churches. (*See* ¶ 2005.3.)

¶ **605.** United or other non-Methodist autonomous

churches recognized by the Board of Missions as an area of its activity are authorized to send to the General Conference of The Methodist Church non-voting delegates, consisting of one national representative of the recognized church and one missionary of the Board of Missions of The Methodist Church, with travel and per diem allowance to be paid from the General Administration Fund.

CHAPTER VI

PROVISIONAL ANNUAL CONFERENCES

¶ 606. Any Mission established under the provisions of the Discipline may be constituted as a **Provisional Annual Conference** by the General Conference in consultation with the Central Conference, Provisional Central Conference, or Jurisdictional Conference within which the Mission is located; *provided* that no Provisional Annual Conference shall be organized with fewer than ten ministerial members, nor shall a Provisional Annual Conference be continued with fewer than six ministerial members.

¶ 607. A Provisional Annual Conference is authorized to exercise the powers of an Annual Conference subject to the approval of the presiding bishop;[14] and its members shall share *pro rata* in the produce of The Methodist Publishing House with members of the Annual Conferences. A Provisional Annual Conference within the territory of a Central Conference or of a Provisional Central Conference may elect delegates to a Central Conference or Provisional Central Conference on the same basis as an Annual Conference, but may not elect delegates to a General Conference.[15]

¶ 608. The bishop having episcopal supervision of a Provisional Annual Conference in a foreign or a home mission field may appoint a representative as **superintendent,** to whom may be committed specific responsi-

---

[14] *See* Judicial Council Decision 132.
[15] Amended in 1948 following Judicial Council Decision 60, but see subsequent Amendments IV, VII, VIII to the Constitution (¶ 45).

bility for the representation of the Board of Missions in its relation to the indigenous church and also in co-operation with other recognized evangelical missions. Such duties shall be exercised so as not to interfere with the work of the district superintendent. This superintendent may also be a district superintendent, provided he is a member of the said conference. He shall be responsible directly to the bishop appointed to administer the work in that episcopal area, and he shall make adequate reports of the work and needs of his field to the bishop and to the secretaries of the Board of Missions immediately concerned.

¶ 609. If there is no bishop present at an annual session of a Provisional Annual Conference, the superintendent shall preside; but if there is no superintendent present, the presidency shall be determined as in an Annual Conference.

¶ 610. Each Provisional Annual Conference or Mission at its annual session shall appoint a standing committee whose duty it shall be, with the concurrence of the president of the conference, to make an estimate of the amount necessary for the support of each pastoral charge, either in full or supplementary to the amount raised by the charge. Such estimates shall be subject to modification by the division of the Board of Missions immediately concerned.

¶ 611. A charge within a Provisional Annual Conference or Mission may receive aid from the Board of Missions without having been designated by the conference at its meeting.

¶ 612. In Provisional Annual Conferences in the home field there shall be a Conference Board of Missions constituted as in an Annual Conference, and having the same duties and powers. (*See* ¶¶ 1295-1307.)

CHAPTER VII

MISSIONS

SECTION I.　　　　　**In the Home Field**

¶ 615. 1. A Mission shall meet annually at the time

and place appointed by the bishop in charge, who shall preside. In the absence of the bishop the superintendent of the Mission shall preside. The presiding officer shall bring forward the regular business of the meeting, and arrange the work. For rules governing the administration of Missions in the home field *see* ¶ 1238, also ¶¶ 591-93, 610-11.

Sec. II. **In Foreign Fields**

¶ **616.** A foreign field outside of an Annual Conference, working under the care of the Board of Missions, not having met the requirements for the organization of a Provisional Annual Conference, may be organized into a Mission. For rules governing the administration of Missions in the foreign field *see* ¶ 1206, also ¶¶ 591-93, 610-11.

Chapter VIII

THE ANNUAL CONFERENCE

Section I. **Composition and Character**

¶ **621.** The composition and character of the **Annual Conference** are set forth in the Constitution (¶¶ 22-23, 45 iii, viii, x; *see also* ¶ 46.4).

¶ **622.** Approved supply pastors who are in charge of pastoral appointments shall be seated in the Annual Conference session and given the privilege of speaking on any question, but without vote.[16]

¶ **623.** Lay missionaries, both men and women, regularly appointed by the Board of Missions in fields outside the United States may be seated in the Annual Conference session and given the privileges of the floor without vote. By authorization of a Central Conference national lay workers may be given the same privileges.[17] (*See* ¶ 1187.2.)

¶ **624.** Deaconesses serving within the bounds of an

---

[16] *See* Judicial Council Decisions 112, 136.
[17] *See* Judicial Council Decisions 1, 24.

Annual Conference shall be seated in the Annual Conference session and given the privileges of the floor without vote.

Sec. II. Organization

¶ **625.** Annual Conferences may become severally bodies corporate, wherever practicable, under the law of the countries, states, and territories within whose bounds they are located.[18]

¶ **626.** The bishops shall appoint the times for holding the Annual Conferences.

¶ **627.** The Annual Conference or a committee thereof shall select the place for holding the conference; but should it become necessary for any reason to change the place of meeting, a majority of the district superintendents, with the consent of the bishop in charge, may change the place. The Annual Conference has the right and power to provide for an adjourned session. The bishop, with the concurrence of three fourths of the district superintendents, may call a special session of the Annual Conference. This special session shall be composed of the ministerial members of the Annual Conference and of the lay members elected for the previous session of the Annual Conference.

¶ **628.** A bishop shall preside over the Annual Conference. In the absence of a bishop, the conference shall by ballot, without nomination or debate, elect a president from among the traveling elders. The president thus elected shall discharge all the duties of a bishop except ordination.

¶ **629.** The Annual Conference at the first session following the General Conference or Jurisdictional or Central Conference (or, if it may desire, at the last session preceding the General Conference or Jurisdictional or Central Conference) shall elect a secretary and a statistician to serve for the succeeding quadrennium. (For the election and work of the treasurer of the Annual Conference *see* ¶¶ 792, 803-8.)

¶ **630.** All members of the Annual Conference, includ-

---

[18] *See* Judicial Council Decisions 38, 108, 143.

ing probationers, and all approved supply pastors shall attend the sessions of the Annual Conference, and they shall furnish to the Annual Conference such reports and in such form as the laws of the church may require.

SEC. III.   **Powers and Duties**

¶ **634.** The Annual Conference may make rules to govern its own procedure; *provided* that no Annual Conference shall make any rule contrary to the Constitution or to the powers granted it by the General Conference. An Annual Conference cannot financially obligate The Methodist Church or an organizational unit thereof except the Annual Conference itself.[19]

¶ **635.** An Annual Conference may admit into membership only those who have met all the Disciplinary requirements for membership and only in the manner prescribed in the Discipline.[20]

¶ **636.** The Annual Conference shall have power to hear complaints against its ministerial members and may try, reprove, suspend, deprive of ministerial office and credentials, expel, or acquit any against whom charges may have been preferred. The Annual Conference shall have power to locate a ministerial member for unacceptability or inefficiency.

¶ **637.** The relation of a ministerial member of the Annual Conference shall not be changed until he has had an opportunity to appear either in person or through a representative before the Committee on Conference Relations (¶ 668), except as provided in ¶¶ 377-78.

¶ **638.** Every transfer of a traveling preacher is conditioned on the passing of his character by the conference to which he is amenable up to the time of his transfer. The official announcement that a preacher is transferred changes his membership so that his rights and responsibilities in the conference to which he goes begin from the date of his transfer.

¶ **639.** The status of a ministerial member of the Annual Conference or of a probationer is further deter-

---

[19] *See* Judicial Council Decisions 43, 92, 115, 119, 141, 170.
[20] *See* Judicial Council Decision 170.

mined by those sections of the Discipline governing the ministry.

¶ **640.** The Annual Conference shall provide adequate surety bonds for all officers handling funds of the conference and shall have the books of said officers audited annually. (*See* ¶¶ 729, 803, 807.)

¶ **641.** The Annual Conference shall give recognition to any new churches that have been organized during the year and shall, through the presiding bishop and the secretary, send to each new church a **certificate of organization,** which the district superintendent shall on behalf of the conference present to the new church in an appropriate ceremony. (*See* ¶ 155.)

SEC. IV.　　**The Business of the Conference**

¶ **645.** After religious services the secretary of the previous Annual Conference shall call the roll, including the roll of approved supply pastors. (*See* ¶¶ 319, 622, 630.) The conference shall complete its organization and proceed with its business.

¶ **646.** Inquiries shall be made in the open conference as to whether all the ministerial members of the conference are blameless in their life and official administration. The district superintendent may answer for all the preachers in his district in one answer, if it be desired to call the name of each and every preacher in open session, or the Committee on Conference Relations (¶ 668) may make inquiry of each district superintendent about each man in his district and make one report to the bishop and the conference in open session; *provided* that the conference may order an executive session of the ministerial members to consider questions relating to matters of ordination, character, and conference relations.[21]

¶ **647.** The Committee on Conference Relations shall be prepared to answer at the call of the bishop the questions regarding the standing of all ministers in full connection in the conference: (*a*) all members of the Annual Conference whether effective, supernumerary, superannuated, on sabbatical leave, or students; (*b*) those transferred to

---

[21] *See* Judicial Council Decision 42.

other conferences during the year; (c) those transferred into the conference during the year.

¶ 648. At the conclusion of the examination of the standing of the ministers in the conference the presiding bishop may call to the bar of the conference the class to be admitted into full connection, and receive them into conference membership after asking the questions to be found in the Discipline. This examination of the ministers, and the passing of their characters, should be the business of one session.

¶ 649. Since the Annual Conference includes laymen and ministers, it is suggested that one single sitting of the conference should consider reports of the year's work. After the statistical questions have been answered, let the boards and committees of the conference make their reports for discussion and adoption.[22] The special interests of the conference may also present reports of their work, regard being given by the bishop to a proper allotment of time.

¶ 650. It is suggested that for one or more sittings the conference give due consideration to the work of the coming year. The representatives of connectional interests and church-wide movements, as well as those charged with the responsibility for conference work and programs, should present their challenge and their objectives.

¶ 651. The business of the Annual Conference shall be to inquire:

I. Organization and General Business

1. Who are elected for the quadrennium: secretary? statistician? treasurer? (¶¶ 629, 803.)

2. Is the Annual Conference incorporated? (¶ 625.)

3. a) What officers handling funds of the conference have been bonded, and in what amounts? (¶¶ 640, 729, 807.)

    b) Have the books of said officers or persons been audited? (¶¶ 640, 729, 803, 807.)

4. Have the conference boards, commissions, and committees (¶¶ 666-80) been appointed or elected:

---

[22] See Judicial Council Decision 123.

    a) Board of Ministerial Training and Qualifications?

    b) Committee on Conference Relations?

    c) District Committees on Ministerial Qualifications (¶ 695)?

    d) Committee of Investigation?

    e) District Boards of Church Location and Building (¶ 721)?

    f) Board of Trustees of the Annual Conference?

    g) Commission on World Service and Finance?

    h) Commission on Town and Country Work?

    i) Deaconess Board?

    j) Board of Missions?

    k) Board of Education?

    l) Board of Christian Social Concerns?

    m) Board of Lay Activities?

    n) Board of Hospitals and Homes?

    o) Board of Evangelism?

    p) Board of Pensions?

    q) Commission on Christian Vocations?

    r) Conference Woman's Society of Christian Service?

    s) Commission on Minimum Salaries?

    t) Commission on Promotion and Cultivation?

    u) Television, Radio, and Film Commission?

    v) Committee on Publishing Interests?

    w) Optional commissions and committees?

5. Have the secretaries, treasurers, and statisticians kept their respective records upon and according to the forms prescribed by The Methodist Church? (¶ 662.)

6. What is the report of the statistician?

7. What is the report of the treasurer?

8. What are the reports of the district superintendents as to the status of the work within their districts?

9. What is the schedule of minimum salaries for pastors? (¶ 826.)

10. What is the plan and what are the approved claims for the support of the district superintendents for the ensuing year? (¶¶ 801-2.)

11. What amount has been apportioned to the pastoral charges within the conference to be raised for the support of conference claimants? (¶¶ 1623, 1645.4.)

12. What are the apportionments to this conference:

 a) For the World Service Fund?

 b) For the Episcopal Fund?

 c) For the General Administration Fund?

 d) For the Interdenominational Co-operation Fund?

 e) For the Jurisdictional Administration Fund?

 f) For the maintenance of our institutions of higher learning?

13. What is the percentage division between world service and conference benevolences for the current year: world service? conference? (¶ 795.)

14. What are the reports, recommendations, and plans of the conference agencies:

 a) What is the report of the Board of Pensions, and what appropriations for conference claimants are reported and approved? (¶ 1623.)

 b) What is the report of the Board of Missions of disbursements of missionary aid within the conference? (¶ 1303.)

 c) What is the report of the Commission on World Service and Finance? (¶¶ 791-812.)

 d) What is the report of the Commission on Christian Vocations? (¶¶ 675-77.)

 e) What are the other reports?

15. What Methodist institutions or organizations are approved by the conference for annuity responsibility? (¶ 1618.2c, .9.)

16. What date is determined for Golden Cross Enrollment Sunday? (¶ 1559.)

17. a) Who is the conference lay leader? (¶ 1507.)

 b) What is his report?

 c) Who are the district and associate district lay leaders? (¶ 1510.)

18. What local churches have been:

 a) Organized? (¶ 155.)

 b) Merged? (¶¶ 186-87.)

 c) Discontinued? (¶¶ 128, 188, 354.)

 d) Relocated, and to what address?

 e) Transferred into this conference from the Central Jurisdiction, and with what membership: this year? previously? (¶ 532.)

II. Pertaining to Ministerial Relations

19. Are all the ministerial members of the conference blameless in their life and official administration?

20. Who constitute the Conference Committee of Investigation? (¶ 931.)

21. Who are the approved supply pastors:

a) Student approved supply pastors (¶¶ 317.1, 318), and in what schools are they enrolled?

b) Full-time approved supply pastors (¶¶ 317.2, 318), and what progress has each made in the course of study?

c) Part-time approved supply pastors (¶¶ 317.3, 318), and what progress has each made in the course of study?

22. What approved supply pastors are credited with annuity claim on account of full-time service during the past year? (To be answered after consultation of the Conference Board of Pensions with the district superintendents; ¶¶ 1631, 1632.10.)

23. What preachers, coming from other evangelical churches, have had their orders recognized (¶ 411.2): as local deacons? as local elders?

24. Who have been admitted from other evangelical churches as traveling preachers (¶ 411.3-.5):

a) As members on trial: deacons? elders?

b) As members in full connection: deacons? elders?

25. Who are admitted on trial:

a) With degrees from approved colleges and credits from approved schools of theology? (¶¶ 323-24.)

b) With degrees from colleges not accredited by the University Senate and credits from approved schools of theology? (¶ 325.1.)

c) With degrees from approved colleges and completion of the introductory studies for the ministry and the first year of the course of study? (¶ 325.2.)

d) With partial college credit, completion of the four-year course of study, and six years' service as approved supply pastors? (¶ 325.3.)

26. Who are continued on trial, and what progress have they made in their ministerial studies (¶ 330):

a) As students in approved schools of theology?

  b) As graduates of approved schools of theology?

  c) In the four-year course of study?

  d) In the four graduate courses of study? (¶ 343.2.)

27. Who on trial are discontinued?

28. Who are admitted into full connection?

29. Who have been elected deacons (¶ 393):

  a) Theological students?

  b) Members on trial in the course of study?

  c) Approved supply pastors?

  d) Other local preachers?

  e) Missionaries?

  f) Chaplains?

30. Who have been ordained deacons?

31. Who have been elected elders (¶ 403):

  a) Theological graduates?

  b) Course of study graduates?

  c) Approved supply pastors?

  d) Other local preachers?

  e) Missionaries?

  f) Chaplains?

32. Who have been ordained elders?

33. Who have been admitted or ordained to accommodate other conferences:

  a) Admitted: on trial? into full connection?

  b) Ordained after election by this conference: deacons? elders?

  c) Ordained after election by other conferences: deacons? elders?

34. Who are readmitted: as deacons? as elders?

35. What retired members have been made effective?

36. Who have been received by transfer?

37. Who have been transferred out?

38. Who have had their conference membership terminated:

  a) By voluntary location?

  b) By involuntary location?

  c) By withdrawal?

  d) By judicial procedure (expelled)?

39. a) What ministerial members have died during the year: while in effective relation? while inactive by retirement or otherwise?

b) What approved supply pastors have died during the year?

c) What deaconesses have died during the year?

40. Who are the supernumerary ministers, and for what number of years consecutively has each held this relation? (¶ 365.)

41. Who are granted sabbatical leave? (¶ 364.)

42. What ministerial members have been retired: this year? previously?

43. What approved supply pastors have been retired: this year? previously?

44. Who are appointed to attend school?

45. *a*) What is the number: of pastoral charges? of approved supply pastors? received on trial? received into full connection? transferred in? transferred out? received from other evangelical churches? readmitted? discontinued? withdrawn? expelled? located? deceased? of local preachers? of women under appointment? of retired ministers made effective? of retired ministers serving as supply pastors? of district parsonages, with their total value and indebtedness thereon?

b) What is the number of ministers:

(1) On trial: as pastors? under special appointment? appointed to attend school? total?

(2) In full connection: as pastors and district superintendents? under special appointment? appointed to attend school? on sabbatical leave? total effective? retired? supernumerary?

(3) Total of all ministers?

46. What other personal notation should be made?

III. Concluding Business

47. What are the detailed objectives of this conference for the coming year?

48. Where shall the next session of the conference be held?

49. Is there any other business?

50. What changes have been made in appointments since the last conference session?

51. Where are the preachers stationed for the ensuing year?

Note: For other directions about the program of Annual Conference sessions *see* ¶¶ 1301, 1441, 1504.5, 1571.3*b*, 1610.5.

SEC. V. **Records and Archives**

¶ **656.** The Annual Conference shall keep an exact record of its proceedings (¶ 658), according to the forms provided by the General, Jurisdictional, and Central Conferences. It shall send to its Jurisdictional Conference or Central Conference a bound copy of the minutes of the quadrennium for examination, said copy to be returned to the secretary of the Annual Conference to be placed in the archives (¶ 663) of the conference. If there be no archives of the Annual Conference, then the secretary shall keep the bound copy to be handed on to his successor in office.

¶ **657.** Each Annual Conference shall send to the Council on World Service and Finance two printed or written copies of its annual journal signed by its president and secretary, one copy being for the Department of Research and Statistics and the other for the File of Pastors and Church Officials.

¶ **658.** The General Conference recommends the following divisions, in the order named, for the Annual Conference journals:

    I. Officers of Annual Conference.
   II. Boards, Commissions, Committees. Rolls of Conference Members.
  III. Daily Proceedings.
  IV. Disciplinary Questions.
   V. Appointments.
  VI. Reports.
 VII. Memoirs.
VIII. Roll of Dead, Deceased Ministerial Members.
  IX. Historical.
   X. Miscellaneous.
  XI. Pastoral Record (including the records of accepted supply pastors in such manner as the conference may determine).
 XII. Index.

¶ **659.** An Annual Conference in the United States shall include in its journal a list of the missionaries, ministerial and lay, active and retired, who have gone from the conference into the active service of the church in fields outside the United States and its territories. The General Board of Missions shall furnish such lists to the secretaries of the Annual Conferences.

Note: For further directions on the content of Annual Conference journals *see* ¶¶ 362.4, .10, 431.9, 786, 806, 812, 829-30, 1223, 1254.4c, .7, 1296.1, 1451.2, 1612.7, 1618.4, .9, 1629, 1631.6.

¶ **661.** The secretary of each Annual Conference shall keep a service record, together with the dates of birth and marriage, of all ministerial members of the Annual Conference. This record shall be available for use by the Conference Board of Pensions of that conference and any other conference supplemental organization existing under ¶ 1611, and by the General Board of Pensions.

¶ **662.** All records of secretaries, statisticians, and treasurers shall be kept according to the forms prescribed by the laws of the church.

¶ **663.** In each Annual Conference there shall be a **Historical Society,** to be appointed or elected in whatever manner the conference may decide, whose duties it shall be to preserve the records of the conference, gather all data referring to its organization, its past history, its former members, and to collect all data of interest from elderly persons and to preserve these for future generations, together with a record of current items of importance, and to keep before the minds of our people the glorious deeds of the heroes of the past. (See ¶¶ 1591-92.)

SEC. VI.　　　　　　**Conference Agencies**

¶ **666.** The Annual Conference at the first session following the General Conference or Jurisdictional or Central Conference shall appoint or elect such quadrennial boards, commissions, or committees as shall be ordered by the General Conference or the Jurisdictional or the Central Conference of which the said Annual Conference is a part, or by the Annual Conference itself, for the purpose of promoting the work of The Methodist

Church within the bounds of the said Annual Conference. The powers and duties of said boards, commissions, and committees shall be prescribed by the conference authorizing them or as defined in certain paragraphs of this Discipline. Members of the above boards, commissions, and committees shall hold office until their successors are elected.[23]

¶ **667.** In the appointment of Annual Conference committees the provisions of the Discipline concerning membership requirements shall be held to be *minimum* requirements; each Annual Conference may make its committees of such size as its work may need.

¶ **668.** The Annual Conference shall elect a **Committee on Conference Relations.** This committee shall consist of not fewer than six traveling elders, arranged as far as practical in classes to serve three years each. It shall make recommendations to the Annual Conference concerning the relations of all elders in full connection seeking to become: superannuated or retired members, supernumeraries, ministers on sabbatical leave, students appointed to attend school.

¶ **669.** 1. Each Annual Conference at the first session following the General Conference shall elect for a term of four years a **Board of Ministerial Training and Qualifications,** consisting of not fewer than six nor more than twenty-five ministers in full connection in the conference, nominated by the presiding bishop after consultation with the chairman of the board of the previous quadrennium, or with a committee of the board, and with the Cabinet. It is recommended that the Conference Board of Education have due representation and that at least two thirds of the members be graduates of colleges and schools of theology accredited or approved by the University Senate. Vacancies shall be filled by the bishop after consultation with the chairman of the board.

2. The board shall organize by electing one of its members chairman and another registrar.

3. The board shall convene at the seat and time of the Annual Conference, preferably the day before the session

[23] *See* Judicial Council Decision 98.

opens, to review and complete the work of the past year and to plan for the future.

4. The board shall work in co-operation with the Department of Ministerial Education (¶¶ 1372-76).

¶ **670.** 1. The board shall seek, in co-operation with the Commission on Christian Vocations (¶¶ 675-77), with the bishop, district superintendents, pastors, and laymen of the conference, and with the Department of Ministerial Education and the Methodist schools of theology, to enlist suitable candidates for the Christian ministry. It shall seek in every way practicable to provide guidance and counsel to them in their training and preparation for the ministry, recommending colleges and schools of theology accredited or approved by the University Senate. It shall co-operate with our schools of theology by recommending from the Annual Conference students with definite ministerial promise.

2. For the purpose of making financial assistance available to students for the ministry, it is recommended that each Annual Conference and/or Jurisdictional Conference have a seminary loan fund or seminary student aid fund, under the direction of the Conference Board of Ministerial Training and Qualifications.

¶ **671.** The board shall examine (*a*) all applicants for employment as approved supply pastors and (*b*) for admission on trial as to their fitness for the ministry, as provided in ¶¶ 314-18, 321-30, and shall make full inquiry as to the fitness of (*c*) candidates for admission into full connection. This must include an examination as to character, habits of life, conversion, call to the ministry, Christian experience, evangelistic and missionary concern, age, educational qualifications, domestic situation, co-operation with others, ability to lead a service of worship, and understanding of the Church's mission. (*See* ¶¶ 341-45.) The answers to the examination questions may be submitted in writing. The board shall also report recommendations concerning: (*d*) candidates for ordination as deacons; (*e*) candidates for ordination as elders; (*f*) those to be received from other churches; (*g*) those transferred into the conference who are not elders in full connection; and (*h*) students, not yet elders in full connection, to be appointed to attend school and assigned to a Quarterly Conference (¶¶ 431.6, 432.7).[24]

¶ **672.** The board shall certify all information and recommendations concerning each candidate to the Annual Conference in duplicate. One copy of this record is to be kept by the registrar of the board, and one copy is to be mailed after each conference session to the Department of Ministerial Education.

¶ **673.** The board shall urge all members on trial to attend colleges and schools of theology related to The Methodist Church and accredited or approved by the University Senate, and shall encourage and assist them in every practicable way to complete the preparation recommended in ¶¶ 342, 344. It shall require and assist all who are not attending an approved school of theology to pursue promptly the courses of study (¶¶ 330, 343).

¶ **674.** 1. The **registrar** of the board shall keep a full personnel record, including transcripts of academic credit, for all ministerial candidates within the bounds of the conference.

2. He shall keep a permanent record of the standing of the students in the course of study, and report to the conference when required. This record shall include the credits allowed students for work done in accredited schools of theology (¶ 327), in approved schools in the courses of study, and by correspondence.

3. The registrar, or some other designated officer of the board, shall keep a record of the educational history and interests of each minister serving in the conference. This material shall be furnished to the board by active ministers. Such records are the property of the conference and shall be carefully preserved.

¶ **675.** In each Annual Conference there shall be a **Commission on Christian Vocations,** composed of: a representative of the Cabinet; the executive secretary of the Conference Board of Education; the conference director of youth work; the chairman (or registrar) of the Board of Ministerial Training and Qualifications; the secretary of missionary personnel of the Conference Woman's

[24] *See* Judicial Council Decision 157.

Society of Christian Service; one representative each
from the Conference Boards of Hospitals and Homes,
Missions, Lay Activities, Evangelism, and Christian Social
Concerns; one representative each from the Conference
Deaconess Board and the state or regional Methodist
Student Movement; and one youth not over twenty-one
years of age. The Cabinet or the commission may appoint
other members when advisable.

¶ **676.** It shall be the duty of this commission: (*a*) to
co-operate with the Interboard Committee on Christian
Vocations (¶ 1415), and with the Committee on Christian
Vocations in every local church (¶ 145.9); (*b*) to promote among youth and adults a philosophy of Christian
vocation that recognizes the potential sacredness of all useful work and all opportunities for Christian life service;
(*c*) to organize a program for presenting to youth and
adults the opportunities and claims of the pastoral ministry and other church vocations; (*d*) to take into account
the basic interests and aptitudes of interested youth and
adults and inform them of the necessary preparation for
specific church vocations; (*e*) to keep accurate and useful
records of each youth who has indicated an interest in
church vocations from the time of his first commitment
until he is appointed to full-time work in the church, or
until such time as responsibility for him is accepted by the
proper conference board or commission.

¶ **677.** Each Annual Conference, in whatever way it
may decide, shall make adequate provision for the financial support of the work of its Commission on Christian
Vocations so that the commission may be able to carry
forward an effective program of promotion and guidance
in the field of Christian vocations.

¶ **679.** There may be in any Annual Conference a **Conference** or **Interboard Council,** composed of representatives of all conference boards and commissions, the bishop
and his Cabinet, other administrative officers, and other
agencies as the conference may determine, for the purpose of correlating the planning and promotion of the
program of the church.[25]

---

[25] Adopted in 1956 following Judicial Council Decision 98.
See also Decision 148.

Note: For other Annual Conference agencies *see* as follows: Committee on Camps and Conferences, ¶ 1454; Committee or Commission on Christian Higher Education, ¶ 1452; Board of Christian Social Concerns, ¶¶ 1545-48; Commission on College and University Religious Work, ¶ 1371; Deaconess Board, ¶ 1254; Distributing Committee, ¶ 1609; Board of Education, ¶¶ 1441-58; Board of Evangelism, ¶¶ 1478-80; Committee on Family Life, ¶ 1453; Board of Hospitals and Homes, ¶ 1561; Committee of Investigation, ¶¶ 923, 931-36; Board of Lay Activities, ¶¶ 1503-5; Methodist Television-Radio Ministry Fund Committee, ¶ 762.2; Methodist Youth Fellowship, ¶ 1458; Commission on Minimum Salaries, ¶ 826; Board of Missions, ¶¶ 1295-1307; Board of Pensions, ¶¶ 1611, 1623-37; Committee on Proportional Payment of Ministerial Support, ¶ 1611; Commission on Promotion and Cultivation, ¶ 755; Committee on Public Relations and Methodist Information, ¶ 1590; Committee on Publishing Interests, ¶ 1158; Television, Radio, and Film Commission, ¶ 1583; Commission on Town and Country Work, ¶ 1231; Board of Trustees, ¶ 711; Committee on Urban Work, ¶ 1305; Woman's Society of Christian Service, ¶ 1256; Commission on World Service and Finance, ¶¶ 791-830; Commission on Worship, ¶ 1571.

Chapter IX

THE DISTRICT CONFERENCE

¶ **686.** A **District Conference** shall be held annually in each district if authorized by the Annual Conference. The district superintendent shall preside. If the district superintendent be absent, the District Conference is authorized to elect an elder to preside.

¶ **687.** A District Conference shall be composed of all the preachers—traveling, including retired and supernumerary, and local—the deaconesses, the church lay leader, church-school superintendent, and president of the Woman's Society of Christian Service from each local church in the district, the district stewards, the district trustees, the district lay leader and associate district lay leaders, the lay member of the Annual Conference from each charge, the president of the District Woman's Society of Christian Service, the district directors of children's, youth, adult, and general church-school work, and such other persons as the Annual Conference may determine.

¶ **688.** The district superintendent shall fix the date of the District Conference, but the District Conference shall fix the place. Should it become necessary to change the place, the district superintendent shall have authority to change it. The district superintendent may call special sessions when necessity requires.

¶ **689.** The District Conference shall inquire particularly into the condition of the several charges concerning: (1) their spiritual state (¶¶ 1481-82); (2) the missionary work of and in the district (¶¶ 1300, 1302.2); (3) the Christian education work through the church schools, including vacation schools and Methodist Youth Fellowships; (4) the women's work (¶ 1257); (5) the support of the church colleges and the attendance upon them; (6) the work done in and for the American Bible Society; (7) the lay activities, especially in behalf of benevolences and Christian stewardship, and in promoting worship in unserved sections and communities; (8) the work of and for our hospitals and homes; (9) the patronage of the church papers and our Publishing House; (10) the candidates for the ministry from the district and aid in their preparation; (11) the candidates for other forms of Christian service; (12) the support of the church, its ministry and its benevolences, and the financial systems that are being used. The District Conference shall receive for examination an annual report from the Committee on Records and History (¶ 145.4) of each Quarterly Conference.

¶ **690.** The District Conference shall vote on issuing or renewing licenses to preach, on recommendation of the District Committee on Ministerial Qualifications, and shall consider for approval the reports of this committee, as provided in ¶ 695.

¶ **691.** The District Conference may choose its own order of business, provided that all the business committed to it is transacted. The secretary duly elected shall keep an accurate record of the proceedings and submit it to the Annual Conference for examination.

¶ 695. 1. There shall be a **District Committee on Ministerial Qualifications,** composed of the district superintendent as chairman and five other traveling preachers of the district, nominated annually by him, and approved by the Annual Conference. Interim vacancies may be filled by the chairman.

2. The committee shall examine each person who applies in writing for a license to preach, or for a renewal of such license. Where there is evidence that his gifts, graces, and usefulness warrant and that he is qualified under ¶¶ 306-7, it may, on recommendation of his Quarterly Conference (¶ 146.1), recommend to the District Conference to issue or renew his license to preach; *provided,* however, that where no District Conference exists, final action may be taken by the committee; and *provided,* further, that before the ballot for licensing a person to preach is taken he shall have agreed to the condition set forth in ¶ 306.5. (*See* ¶ 362.4.)

3. The committee shall recommend to the Board of Ministerial Training and Qualifications of the Annual Conference suitable candidates for acceptance or continuance as approved supply pastors, for admission on trial, for local deacon's orders, for local elder's orders, and for restoration of credentials.

4. The vote of the committee in all such matters shall be by individual written ballot, and a three-fourths majority vote of the committee shall be required for license or approval.

5. The committee shall report its work to the District Conference for approval where such conference exists.

6. The chairman and another representative of the committee shall meet annually with the Board of Ministerial Training and Qualifications, on call of the chairman of the board, either separately or with representatives of all the districts.

7. The committee shall designate an official spokesman, other than the chairman, to confer with the board, when

so requested, about any candidate recommended to it by the committee.[26]

Note: For other district agencies *see* as follows: Committee on Camps and Conferences, ¶ 1461; staff of Christian education, ¶ 1460; Committee on Christian Social Concerns, ¶ 1549; Board of Church Location and Building, ¶¶ 721-24; Committee on Evangelism, ¶¶ 1481-83; Board of Lay Activities, ¶¶ 1506-8; Committee on Lay Speaking, ¶ 1509; Methodist Men, ¶ 1511; missionary society, ¶¶ 1218-27; Board of Stewards, ¶¶ 797, 802; Board of Trustees, ¶ 716.2; Woman's Society of Christian Service, ¶ 1257.

CHAPTER X

THE QUARTERLY CONFERENCE

The organization, powers, and duties of the Quarterly Conference are described in ¶¶ 137-55, under Part II, The Local Church.

---

[26] Amended in 1956 following Judicial Council Decision 100.

PART V

TEMPORAL ECONOMY

CHAPTER I

CHURCH PROPERTY

SECTION I. The Name "Methodist"

¶ **701.** The word "Methodist" is not by our approval or consent to be used as, or as a part of, a trade name or trade mark or as, or as a part of, the name of any business firm or organization except by corporations or other business units created for the administration of work undertaken directly by The Methodist Church.

SEC. II. **Incorporated Trustees of The Methodist Church**

¶ **703.** There shall be a board of trustees incorporated under the name of **The Board of Trustees of The Methodist Church.** This board shall be composed of three ministers and four lay persons. They shall be nominated, without reference to jurisdictional membership, by the Council of Bishops and be elected by the General Conference for a term of eight years, except as to the first such board, of which one clerical and two lay members shall be elected for a term of four years, and two clerical and two lay members shall be elected for a term of eight years, and they shall serve until their successors have been elected and qualified. Between General Conferences the Council of Bishops is designated to act on resignations and to fill vacancies in the membership of this board until the next session of the General Conference.

¶ **704.** This corporation shall receive and administer new trusts and funds, and so far as may be legal be the successor in trust of "The Trustees of The Methodist Episcopal Church," a corporation incorporated under the laws of the state of Ohio, and of "The Board of Trustees of The Methodist Episcopal Church, South," a corporation incorporated under the laws of the state of Tennessee, and of the "Board of Trustees of The Methodist Protestant Church," a corporation incorporated under the laws of the state of Maryland; and so far as is legal and as such successor in trust it shall be and is authorized and empowered to receive from its said predecessor corporations all trust funds and assets of every kind and character, real, personal, or mixed, held by them or any one of them; and it shall be and is authorized to administer such trusts and funds in accordance with the conditions under which they have been previously received and administered by said predecessor corporations. But nothing herein contained shall be construed to require the dissolution of the three corporations above mentioned, and they shall continue to administer such funds as may not be legally transferred to the new corporation. There shall be a correlating committee of nine members, of which three shall be appointed by each of the existing corporations. This committee shall have authority to secure a charter for the new corporation and to arrange the details for handling the trusts in accordance with their terms.[1]

¶ **705.** The object and duty of this board shall be to receive, collect, and hold in trust for the benefit of The Methodist Church any and all donations, bequests, and devises of any kind or character, real or personal, that may be given, devised, bequeathed, or conveyed unto said board or to The Methodist Church as such for any benevolent, charitable, or religious purpose, and to administer the same and the income therefrom in accordance with the directions of the donor, trustor, or testator, and in the interests of the church, society, institution, or agency contemplated by such donors, trustors, or testators under the direction of the General Conference. The board shall have power, in its discretion, and on the advice of compe-

---

[1] As provided in this paragraph. The Board of Trustees of The Methodist Church was incorporated under the laws of the state of Ohio in 1940.

tent investment counsel, to invest, reinvest, buy, sell, transfer, and convey any and all funds and properties which it may hold in trust, subject always to the terms of the legacy, devise, or donation. It shall have authority to determine the intent of the donor, trustor, or testator with respect to the use and disposition both of the corpus and of the income of each separate gift, bequest, or acquisition which it may receive; and if the terms of the gift, bequest, or other instrument involved are vague, uncertain, or impossible of literal fulfillment, it shall have authority, within its sound discretion, to determine the use or uses of each such fund which shall conform with the general purposes of the donor, trustor, or testator, provided such purposes can reasonably be determined from the terms of the gift, bequest, or other applicable instrument. If the specific or general purposes of the donor, trustor, or testator cannot be reasonably determined by the board with respect to any particular fund, such fund shall be held by the board as an undirected fund.

¶ 706. The board may intervene and take all necessary legal steps to safeguard and protect the interests and rights of The Methodist Church anywhere, in all matters relating to property and rights to property whether arising by gift, devise, or otherwise, or where held in trust or established for the benefit of The Methodist Church or its membership; or abandoned church property, where Annual Conference trustees neglect to take necessary steps to protect the interests of the members of The Methodist Church in such property.

¶ 707. It shall be the duty of the pastor within the bounds of whose charge any such gift, bequest, or devise is made to give prompt notice thereof to said board, which shall proceed to take such steps as are necessary and proper to conserve, protect, and administer the same. But the board may decline to receive or administer any such gift, devise, or bequest for any reason satisfactory to the board.

¶ 708. The board shall make to each General Conference a full, true, and faithful report of its doings, of all funds, moneys, securities, and property held in trust by it, and of its receipts and disbursements during the quadrennium.

The beneficiary of a fund held in trust by the board shall be entitled to a report at least annually on the condition of such fund and on the transactions affecting it. The amount of income accruing during a quadrennium from any undirected fund or funds held by the board shall be reported to the Council on World Service and Finance at least sixty days prior to the General Conference, for the recommendation prescribed in ¶ 737.13.

¶ 709. There shall be a fund known as **The Permanent Fund** to be held and administered by the board, the principal of which shall be kept intact forever, and the interest accumulating from said fund shall be used by the board as the General Conference shall direct.

Sec. III. Property in the District of Columbia

¶ 710. 1. There shall be a charitable corporation which shall hold title to certain property of The Methodist Church located in Washington, D.C., at Ward Circle at the intersection of Nebraska and Massachusetts Avenues. The Board of Directors of this corporation shall be elected for a four-year term by the General Conference, and shall consist of (a) one bishop, one minister, and one layman from each jurisdiction, nominated by the Council of Bishops, and (b) three representatives each from the Council of Bishops, Council on World Service and Finance, Co-ordinating Council, and Board of Christian Social Concerns, nominated by these respective bodies. The bishop resident in Washington, D.C., shall be ex officio chairman. Interim vacancies may be filled by the Board of Directors.

2. The corporation shall have complete authority to develop a program for the utilization of the property, and to implement it by the sale or lease of all or any part thereof to any agency of The Methodist Church, subject to compliance with ¶ 1107, on such terms as the Board of Directors may deem appropriate to over-all utilization of the property in the best interest of The Methodist Church and its program. The corporation is also authorized to liquidate the project in whole or in part if and when it concludes that it is not in the best interest of The Methodist Church to undertake a development or a further holding of the property. The corporation is author-

ized to receive and expend gifts and bequests for the development of this property.

3. The carrying charges of the property shall be paid from the General Administration Fund. The corporation shall not have authority to commit the General Conference to any other financial obligation without approval of the General Conference.

4. The corporation shall report to each succeeding General Conference as long as The Methodist Church holds an interest in the property.

SEC. IV. **Annual Conference Property**

¶ **711.** 1. Each Annual Conference shall have a **Board of Trustees,** which shall be incorporated unless the conference is incorporated in its own name (¶ 625).[2] In either case the board shall consist of twelve persons, who must be at least twenty-one years of age, and of whom six shall be ministers in the effective relation in the conference and six shall be members in good standing of local churches within the bounds of the conference, and such persons shall be the directors of the corporation. They shall be elected by the conference for a term of three years, except as to the first board, one third of whom shall be elected for a term of one year, one third for a term of two years, and one third for a term of three years, and shall serve until their successors have been elected; *provided,* however, that existing incorporated trustees of any Annual Conference may continue unaffected by this subsection unless and until such charter is amended.

2. The said corporation shall receive, collect, and hold in trust for the benefit of the Annual Conference any and all donations, bequests, and devises of any kind or character, real or personal, that may be given, devised, bequeathed, or conveyed to the said board or to the Annual Conference as such for any benevolent, charitable, or religious purpose, and shall administer the same and the income therefrom in accordance with the directions of the donor, trustor, or testator, and in the interest of the church, society, institution, or agency contemplated by

---

[2] Amended in 1960 following Judicial Council Decision 108.

such donor, trustor, or testator, under the direction of the Annual Conference. The board shall have power to invest, reinvest, buy, sell, transfer, and convey any and all funds and properties which it may hold in trust, subject always to the terms of the legacy, devise, or donation; *provided*, however, that the foregoing shall not apply to churches, colleges, camps, conference grounds, orphanages, or incorporated boards. When the use to be made of any such donation, bequest, or devise is not otherwise designated, the same shall be added to and become a part of the "Permanent Fund" of the Annual Conference. Funds committed to this board may be invested by it only in collateral that is amply secured and after such investments have been approved by the said board or its agency or committee charged with such investment, unless otherwise directed by the Annual Conference.[3]

3. The board may intervene and take all necessary legal steps to safeguard and protect the interests and rights of the Annual Conference anywhere, and in all matters relating to property and rights to property whether arising by gift, devise, or otherwise, or where held in trust or established for the benefit of the Annual Conference or its membership.

4. It shall be the duty of the pastor within the bounds of whose charge any such gift, bequest, or devise is made to give prompt notice thereof to said board, which shall proceed to take such steps as are necessary and proper to conserve, protect, and administer the same; *provided*, however, that the board may decline to receive or administer any such gift, devise, or bequest for any reason satisfactory to the board. It shall also be the duty of the pastor to report annually to the Board of Trustees of his Annual Conference a list of all property including real, personal, or mixed, within his charge belonging to or which should be under the control or jurisdiction of the said board.

5. The board shall make to each session of the Annual Conference a full, true, and faithful report of its doings, of all funds, moneys, securities, and property held in trust

[3] *See* Judicial Council Decisions 135, 160.

by it, and of its receipts and disbursements during the conference year. The beneficiary of a fund held in trust by the board shall also be entitled to a report at least annually on the condition of such fund and on the transactions affecting it.

¶ **712.** When authorized by two thirds of the Annual Conferences comprising an episcopal area, an **episcopal residence** for the resident bishop may be acquired, which shall be under the management and control of, and the title to which shall be held in trust by, the trustees of the Annual Conference within which the residence is located; and the purchase price and maintenance cost thereof shall be equitably distributed by the trustees among the several conferences in the area. Any such property so acquired and held shall not be sold or disposed of except with the consent of a majority of the conferences that participate in the ownership. Should an Annual Conference contribute to the purchase of an episcopal residence and later be transferred to an area not owning one, if it shall ask payment for its equity, such claim shall not be denied.

SEC. V.   **District Property**

¶ **716.** 1. A **district parsonage** for the district superintendent may be acquired, when authorized by the Quarterly Conferences of two thirds of the charges in the district, or when authorized by a two-thirds vote of the District Conference; *provided* that at least thirty days' notice of such proposed action shall have been given in writing by the district superintendent to the pastor and district steward of each charge.

2. The title of district property may be held in trust by a **District Board of Trustees** of not fewer than three nor more than nine persons of the same qualifications provided for trustees of local churches (¶ 159), who shall be nominated by the district superintendent and elected by the District Conference. Where there is no District Conference, they may be elected by the District Board of Stewards or by the Annual Conference on nomination of the district superintendent. They shall be elected for a term of one year and serve until their successors shall have been

elected, and shall report annually to the District Conference or Annual Conference. If the title to the district parsonage is not held by a District Board of Trustees, the same shall be held in trust by the trustees of the Annual Conference of which such district is a part, and such trustees shall report annually to the Annual Conference. Except as the laws of the state, territory, or country prescribe otherwise, district property held in trust by a District Board of Trustees may be mortgaged or sold and conveyed by them only by authority of the District Conference or Annual Conference; or, if such property is held in trust by the trustees of the Annual Conference, it may be mortgaged or sold and conveyed by such trustees only by authority of the Annual Conference. The purchase price and maintenance cost of a district parsonage shall be equitably distributed among the charges of the district by the District Board of Stewards.

3. When district boundaries are changed by division, rearrangement, or consolidation, so that a district parsonage purchased, owned, and maintained by one district is included within the bounds of another district, each such district shall be entitled to receive its just share of the then reasonable value of the parsonage in which it has invested funds; and the amount of such value and just share shall be determined by a committee of three persons, appointed by the bishop of the area, who shall not be residents of any of the said districts. The committee shall hear claims of each district regarding its interest therein before making decision. From any such determination there is reserved unto each of the interested districts the right of appeal to the next succeeding Annual Conference. Any sum received as or from such share shall be used for no other purpose than purchase or building of a parsonage in the district. The same procedure shall be followed in determining equities of a district in any other property which may be included in another district by changes in district boundaries.

SEC. VI.   District Board of Church Location and Building

¶ 721. There shall be in each district of an Annual

Conference a **District Board of Church Location and Building** consisting of the district superintendent, three ministers, and three laymen nominated by the district superintendent and elected annually by the Annual Conference; *provided* that in a district of great geographical extent an additional board may be so elected. The board shall file a report of any actions taken with the Quarterly Conference of each local church involved, and the report so filed shall become a part of the minutes of the said conference or conferences. The board shall also make a written report to the District Conference (or, if there is no District Conference, to the district superintendent), and this report shall become a part of the records of that conference.

¶ **722.** 1. The board shall investigate all proposed local-church building sites, ascertaining that such sites are properly located for the community to be served, and adequate in size to provide space for future expansion and parking facilities. (*See* ¶¶ 155.1, 180.2.)

2. If there is a Metropolitan Area Planning Commission (¶ 1220) in the district, the board shall consider its recommendations in planning a strategy for continuing the service of The Methodist Church in changing neighborhoods. If not, the board shall study the duties assigned to such a commission and seek ways to provide continuity of service in parishes where there is a change in the racial character of the residents, to the end that the resolutions of the General Conference involving such neighborhoods be given careful consideration.

¶ **723.** 1. The board shall require any local church in its district, before beginning or contracting for construction or purchase of a new church or educational building or a parsonage, or remodeling of such a building if the cost will exceed ten per cent of its value, to submit for consideration and approval a statement of the need for the proposed facilities, preliminary architectural sketches, an estimate of the cost, and a financial plan for defraying such cost, as provided in ¶ 180.4-.5. The board may submit the architectural sketches for review as provided in ¶¶ 1237 and 1401.1.

2. When the local church has secured final architectural

plans and specifications and a reliable and detailed estimate of the cost of the proposed undertaking as provided in ¶ 180.7, the board shall require their submission for consideration and approval. The board shall study carefully the feasibility and financial soundness of the undertaking, and ascertain whether the financial plan will provide funds necessary to assure prompt payment of all proposed contractual obligations; and it shall report its conclusions to the church in writing.

¶ 724. A decision of the board disapproving such purchase, building, or remodeling shall be final unless overruled by the Annual Conference, to which there is reserved unto the local church the right of appeal.

SEC. VII.   **Local-Church Property**

Regulations governing local-church property and the election and duties of trustees of local churches are set forth in ¶¶ 151-94 of Part II, The Local Church.

SEC. VIII.   **Sundry Provisions**

¶ 728. Trustees of schools, colleges, universities, hospitals, homes, orphanages, institutes, and other institutions owned or controlled by The Methodist Church shall be at least twenty-one years of age. At all times not less than three fourths of them shall be members of The Methodist Church; and all must be nominated, confirmed, or elected by some governing body of the church, or by some body or officer thereof to which or to whom this power has been delegated by the governing body of the church; *provided* that the number of trustees of any such institution owned or controlled by any Annual Conference or Conferences required to be members of The Methodist Church may be reduced to not less than the majority by a three-fourths vote of such Annual Conference or Conferences; and *provided*, further, that when an institution is owned and operated jointly with some other denomination or organization, said requirement that three fourths of the trustees shall be members of The Methodist Church shall apply only to the portion of the trustees representing The Methodist Church.

¶ **729.** All persons holding trust funds, securities, or moneys of any kind belonging to the General Conference or to Annual or Provisional Annual Conferences or to organizations under the control of the General, Annual, or Provisional Annual Conferences shall be bonded in a reliable company in such good and sufficient sum as the conference may direct. The accounts of such persons shall be audited at least annually by a recognized public or certified public accountant. (*See* ¶¶ 803, 807.) A report to an Annual Conference containing a financial statement which the Discipline requires to be audited shall not be approved until the audit is made and the financial statement is shown to be correct. Other parts of the report may be approved pending such audit.[4]

¶ **730.** Whenever the law of the state, territory, or country in which is located any property of The Methodist Church, its agencies or subdivisions, or the provisions of an existing charter of a corporation organized and holding property for such purposes, require otherwise than in this chapter prescribed, such law or charter shall apply and be substituted for such of the provisions of this chapter as are in conflict with such law or charter.[5]

CHAPTER II

CHURCH FINANCE

SECTION I. **General Statement**

¶ **731.** The work of the church requires the support of our people, and participation therein through service and gifts is a Christian duty and a means of grace. In order that all members of The Methodist Church may share in its manifold ministries at home and abroad and that the work committed to us may prosper, the financial plan which follows has been duly approved and adopted.

¶ **732.** The various causes, funds, and budgets of The Methodist Church shall be known and designated as fol-

---

[4] Amended in 1956 following Judicial Council Decision 77.
[5] *See* Judicial Council Decision 93.

lows: (1) **world service,** the general benevolences of
The Methodist Church, approved by the General Conference and included in the world service budget; (2)
conference benevolences, the Annual Conference benevolences and causes, approved by the conference and included in the conference benevolence budget; (3) the
world service budget, the **general administration budget,**
the **episcopal budget,** the **interdenominational co-operation budget,** the amounts approved or estimated by the
General Conference for these causes respectively; (4)
conference benevolence budget, the amounts approved
for Annual Conference causes respectively, and included
in one budget; (5) **world service and conference benevolence budget,** the world service apportionment to any
Annual Conference plus its conference benevolence budget,
included in one sum and distributed among the charges
of the conference; (6) the **World Service Fund** (¶¶ 740-
49), the **General Administration Fund** (¶¶ 765-68), the
Episcopal Fund (¶¶ 769-77), the **Interdenominational Co-
operation Fund** (¶ 778), the **Methodist Committee for
Overseas Relief Fund** (¶¶ 1311-15), the **Fellowship of
Suffering and Service Fund** (¶ 763), the **One Great Hour
of Sharing Fund** (¶ 760), the **Methodist Television-Radio
Ministry Fund** (¶ 762), funds received into the central
treasury for these causes respectively.

SEC. II. **Council on World Service and Finance**

¶ **735.** The General Conference at each quadrennial
session shall elect a **Council on World Service and
Finance** which shall through its central office receive and
disburse, in accordance with the directions hereinafter
set forth, all funds raised throughout the church for:
(1) the World Service Fund, including world service
special gifts and Advance special gifts, (2) the General
Administration Fund, (3) the Episcopal Fund, (4) the
Interdenominational Co-operation Fund, (5) the Methodist
Committee for Overseas Relief Fund, (6) the Fellowship
of Suffering and Service Fund, (7) the One Great Hour of
Sharing Fund, (8) the Methodist Television-Radio Ministry Fund, and (9) any other fund or funds as directed

by the proper authority. (For the authority and responsibility of the council in nonfiscal matters *see* ¶ 1120.)

¶ **736.** The council shall be elected and organized in accordance with the provisions of ¶¶ 1116-19.

¶ **737.** The council shall have the authority and responsibility to perform the following functions:

1. It shall submit to each quadrennial session of the General Conference, for its action and determination, a budget of annual expense for its own operation and for the world service agencies for the ensuing quadrennium. The expenses of the council, including the expense of the central office, shall be a first claim against the World Service Fund, the General Administration Fund, the Episcopal Fund, and the Interdenominational Co-operation Fund; and the total expense shall be prorated annually to each in proportion to the amount received on the account of each during the fiscal year. Out of funds thus provided the treasurer shall pay the expenses of the council, including the expense of the central office, and shall keep a true and accurate account thereof.

2. It shall require annually, one month in advance of its annual meeting, or as is deemed necessary, statements of proposed budgets of all agencies receiving general church funds. It shall also require certified public accountant audits annually of all treasuries receiving general church funds through the central treasury. (*See* ¶ 781). It shall review in each such agency budget the amount for administration, service, and promotion, with a view to maintaining a proper balance among the various parts of the budgets.

3. It shall withhold approval of any item or items for inclusion in the budget or budgets receiving general church funds which in its judgment represents unnecessary duplication of activities or programs within an agency or between two or more agencies. (*See* ¶¶ 784, 1113.1.)

4. It shall recommend to the General Conference, for its action and determination, a world service program outlining the general financial objectives of the church for the forthcoming quadrennium, and proposing the ratio

distribution of world service funds among the participating agencies. It shall indicate the proportion of world service funds to be used for administration, service, and promotion. It shall recommend apportionments to the Annual Conferences, subject to the approval of the General Conference.

5. It shall consult with the Co-ordinating Council and the Council of Bishops relative to the number and timing of all special days which are to be observed on a church-wide basis. After such consultation the Co-ordinating Council shall make appropriate recommendations to the General Conference. Between sessions of the General Conference the Council of Bishops and the Council on World Service and Finance may, in an emergency, authorize a financial appeal.

6. It shall have authority to employ a comptroller. It shall require all agencies receiving general church funds to follow uniform accounting classifications and procedures for reporting and to submit a yearly audit following such auditing procedures as it may specify. It shall have authority to pass on the acceptability of any auditing firm proposed by an agency for handling such yearly audit. All general agencies of the church shall observe a uniform fiscal year ending on May 31.

7. It shall review the investment policies of all agencies receiving general church funds with respect to permanent funds and shall require that Christian as well as sound economic principles in the handling of investment funds be observed.

8. After consultation with the agency, it shall perform or arrange facilities for handling the treasury functions for any general agency which is not large enough to have a full-time treasurer and the financial policies of which are not approved by the council. The cost of such service shall be charged to the agency.

9. On the request of a general agency, it shall hold and invest funds allocated to it when such funds are not intended for current expenditure by that agency. It shall also hold and invest funds for any general agency which does not have an investment program approved by the council.

10. It shall establish standardized annuity rates and formulate policies for the writing of annuities by institutions and agencies operating under the auspices of The Methodist Church.

11. It is authorized to set up a **Committee on Wills, Bequests, and Gifts.** This committee shall take such actions as may be deemed necessary to encourage Methodists to provide for their continued interest in world service, or in one or more of the world service agencies, through bequests and gifts. The income from these sources, where the recipient agency is not designated, shall be used as determined by the council. The expenses of this committee shall be a part of the prior claim for world service funds. The committee is authorized to cooperate with local-church Committees on Wills and Legacies (¶ 145.12) in such ways as may be deemed mutually helpful.

12. It shall administer the General Administration Fund (¶¶ 765-68), the Episcopal Fund (¶¶ 769-77), and the Interdenominational Co-operation Fund (¶ 778).

13. It shall receive from the Board of Trustees a report of the distributable income from undesignated funds held by the board (¶ 708), and shall recommend to the General Conference how such income should be distributed.

¶ **738.** The treasurer of the Council on World Service and Finance shall, not less than thirty days prior to the session of each Annual Conference, transmit to the presiding bishop thereof, to the president of the Conference Commission on World Service and Finance, and to the conference treasurer a statement of the apportionments to the conference for the World Service Fund, the General Administration Fund, the Episcopal Fund, the Interdenominational Co-operation Fund, and such other funds as may have been apportioned by the General Conference. (*See* ¶¶ 749, 767, 771, 778.) He shall keep an account of all amounts remitted to him by the conference treasurers and from other sources intended for: (1) the World Service Fund, including world service special gifts and Advance specials gifts, (2) the General Administration Fund, (3) the Episcopal Fund, (4) the Interdenominational Co-operation Fund, (5) the Methodist Committee for Overseas Relief Fund, (6) the Fellowship of Suffering and Service Fund, (7) the One Great Hour of Sharing Fund, (8) the Methodist Television-Radio Ministry Fund, and (9) any other fund so directed by the proper authority, and shall disburse the same as authorized by the General Conference and directed by the council. A separate account shall be kept of each such fund, and none of them shall be drawn on for the benefit of another. The fiscal year for the council and for the several funds, boards, and agencies related to it, shall be from June 1 to May 31 inclusive.

¶ **739.** The treasurer shall report annually to the council and to the respective conference commissions as to all amounts received and disbursed during the year. He shall also make to each quadrennial session of the General Conference a full report of the financial transactions of the council for the preceding quadrennium. The treasurer shall be bonded for such an amount as may be determined by the council. The books of the treasurer shall be audited annually by a certified public accountant approved by the executive committee.

SEC. III.　　　**The World Service Fund**

¶ **740.** The **World Service Fund** is basic in the financial program of The Methodist Church. World service on apportionment (¶¶ 749, 795) represents the minimum needs of the general agencies of the church. Payment in full of these apportionments by local churches and Annual Conferences is the first benevolent responsibility of the church. (*See* ¶ 804.)

¶ **741.** 1. Prior to each quadrennial session of the General Conference the Council on World Service and Finance shall make a diligent and detailed study of the needs of all the general causes or authorized agencies of the church asking to be included in the world service budget.

2. The general secretary or other duly authorized representative of each agency of The Methodist Church requesting support out of the World Service Fund, and the authorized representative of any other agency for which askings are authorized by the General Conference,

shall appear before the council at a designated time and place to represent the cause for which each is responsible.

¶ **742.** The Council on World Service and Finance shall make diligent effort to secure full information concerning the general benevolence and service causes of the church, in order that none may be neglected, jeopardized, or excluded. It shall study in relation to each other the proposed programs of the several agencies as presented to it (¶ 741.2) and shall withhold approval of any item or items for inclusion in the world service budget which in its judgment represents unnecessary duplication of activities or programs. Basing its judgment of needs upon the programs of the several agencies as approved by it, the council shall recommend to the General Conference for its action and determination the amount to be apportioned in the annual world service budget for each authorized agency of the church. The total amount thus designated by the council for the several agencies, when approved by the General Conference, shall be the annual world service budget for the ensuing quadrennium. The council shall recommend also to the General Conference for its action and determination a plan and schedule for the distribution of the receipts for the world service budget among the several agencies. During the quadrennium the council shall have full authority to correlate the work of the world service agencies in the interest of co-operation, economy, and effectiveness, as these relate to the financial interests of the church.

¶ **743.** Any general board, cause, agency, institution, or any organization, group, officer, or individual of The Methodist Church desiring or proposing to make a special church-wide financial appeal during the quadrennium, or at any time in the interim of the quadrennial sessions of the General Conference, shall present a request for authorization to make such appeal to the Council on World Service and Finance when the askings of the regular agencies are presented as provided in ¶ 741.2. The council shall then report such request to the General Conference with a recommendation for its action thereon. "Special appeal" shall be understood to mean any appeal other than the general appeal for support of the world service program as represented in the world service budget. (*See* ¶ 742.) "Church-wide appeal" shall be understood to mean any appeal to the church at large, except appeals to such special groups as alumni of an educational institution.

¶ **744.** The world service agencies shall not solicit additional or special gifts from individual donors or special groups, other than foundations, unless approval for such solicitation is first secured from the Council on World Service and Finance.

¶ **745.** Individual donors or local churches may make **special gifts** to the support of any cause or project which is a part of the work of any one of the world service agencies. Such gifts may be sent directly to the agency concerned, or to the central treasury of the Council on World Service and Finance. They shall not apply on the benevolence apportionment of any local church, and shall not be charged against the agency or agencies receiving them in the ratio distribution of the on-apportionment benevolences. Bequests, gifts on the annuity plan, gifts to permanent funds, and gifts of property shall be classified as special gifts. (*See* ¶ 746.5.)

¶ **746.** 1. All special gifts made to or administered by a general agency, except as provided in § 5, shall be acknowledged by **special-gift vouchers.**

2. The vouchers acknowledging such gifts to world service agencies shall be entitled "world service special-gift vouchers"; *provided*, however, that vouchers for such gifts to the Divisions of World Missions and of National Missions of the Board of Missions or the Methodist Committee for Overseas Relief (except as provided in ¶ 1314) shall be entitled "Advance special-gift vouchers" (¶ 758); and *provided*, further, that vouchers for the One Great Hour of Sharing offering (¶ 760), Fellowship of Suffering and Service offerings (¶ 763), and contributions to the Methodist Television-Radio Ministry Fund (¶ 762) shall bear the respective names of these appeals.

3. All special-gift vouchers shall be credited in their respective special columns in the Annual Conference minutes. The agency or office issuing each voucher shall

send at the same time a duplicate voucher to the central treasury for forwarding to the conference treasurer.

4. A world service agency or any individual or agency authorized to make a church-wide appeal for funds, not equipped to issue special-gift vouchers, shall channel all special gifts through the central treasury. Individuals soliciting such funds shall channel the money received through the central treasury or the treasurer of the appropriate agency, which shall issue the proper vouchers.

5. Bequests, gifts on the annuity plan at maturity, and gifts of real property shall be reported to the central treasury as **supplemental contributions,** and shall not be included among the promoted funds chargeable under ¶ 754.

¶ **747.** The Council on World Service and Finance shall also recommend to the General Conference the days in connection with the church-wide observance of which the taking of special offerings shall be authorized, and in the case of each shall recommend whether or not the receipts derived therefrom shall be credited to the contributing local church as a part of its world service apportionment, and charged against the claims of the agency receiving the same. All such recommendations are subject to the approval of the General Conference.

¶ **748.** The General Conference having determined the budgeted amounts and the plan and schedule of distribution to the participating boards and agencies as provided in ¶ 742, thereafter no benevolence interest shall be allowed to have a prior or preferred claim or increased ratio participation in the world service budget during the quadrennium except to meet an emergency, and then only by a three-fourths vote of those present and voting at a regular or called meeting of the Council on World Service and Finance, the Council of Bishops concurring in this action by a three-fourths vote of those present and voting; nor shall the total world service budget be changed in the interim between the quadrennial sessions of the General Conference except as required by unforeseen conditions, and then only by a three-fourths vote of those present and voting at a regular or called meeting of the council, the Council of Bishops concurring in this action by a three-fourths vote of those present and voting. No general board, cause, agency, institution, or any organization, group, officer, or individual employed by The Methodist Church or any of the authorized groups of The Methodist Church shall make a church-wide financial appeal in the interim of the quadrennial sessions of the General Conference, unless authorized as provided in ¶ 743, except with the approval of the Council on World Service and Finance and the Council of Bishops. In case of emergency the executive committee of either of these bodies may act in such matter for the body itself, but only by a three-fourths vote. (*See* ¶ 743.)

¶ **749.** The Council on World Service and Finance shall after careful study prepare an equitable schedule of apportionments by which the total world service budget (¶ 742) shall be distributed to the several Annual Conferences and shall present the same to the General Conference for its action and determination.[6] (*See* ¶ 740.)

Sec. IV.   **Commission on Promotion and Cultivation**

¶ **750.** 1. In order to co-ordinate the promotion of the general benevolence causes of The Methodist Church, to the end that our people may be informed about, and may adequately support, the work of the general agencies, there shall be a **Commission on Promotion and Cultivation,** which shall establish and maintain a central promotional office, operating under its authority and direction, for the purpose of promoting throughout the church the program of world service, Advance specials (¶ 758), One Great Hour of Sharing offerings (¶ 763), the Methodist Television-Radio Ministry Fund (¶ 762), the Interdenominational Co-operation Fund, and other general benevolence causes except as otherwise directed by the General Conference. The location of the central promotional office shall be subject to the approval of the Co-ordinating Council.

2. The commission shall be elected quadrennially and shall be constituted as follows: six bishops, one from each jurisdiction, elected by the Council of Bishops; one min-

---

[6] *See* Judicial Council Decision 30.

ister and one layman from each jurisdiction, and six members at large, at least three of whom shall be laymen, nominated by the Council of Bishops and elected by the General Conference. In addition the general secretaries of the several agencies of The Methodist Church which participate in funds promoted by the commission and the general secretary of the Woman's Division of Christian Service shall be ex officio members without vote.

3. The commission shall be constituted at the beginning of each quadrennium, and its members shall serve until their successors are duly elected and qualified. Interim vacancies among members at large shall be filled by the Council of Bishops and among jurisdictional representatives shall be filled by the College of Bishops of the jurisdiction concerned.

¶ 751. The commission shall elect quadrennially the following officers: a president, a vice-president, a recording secretary, and a **general secretary,** who shall be its administrative officer. The treasurer of the Council on World Service and Finance shall be its treasurer.

¶ 752. The general secretary, under the authority and direction of the commission, shall co-ordinate and promote on a church-wide basis world service and all other general benevolence causes except as otherwise directed by the General Conference. The commission shall set the general secretary's salary, and shall make provision for a staff and office facilities to carry on the work of the commission. The general secretary shall co-operate with the general secretary of the Council on World Service and Finance. He shall, by such plans as shall be authorized by the commission, promote the general benevolence causes of the church through the bishops, district superintendents, pastors, lay officials, and General, Jurisdictional, and Annual Conference boards and agencies.

¶ 753. 1. The commission shall have the responsibility of reviewing at least annually, and as often in addition as may be necessary, the several and combined plans of the general boards and agencies for the production and distribution of all free literature and promotional and resource periodicals (except church-school literature) for the purpose of co-ordinating the content, distribution, and timing of the release of such materials. In case of inability to work out adequate plans and procedures for co-ordinating the content, timing, and distribution, the matter shall be referred to the Co-ordinating Council.

2. The commission shall study the problems of co-ordinating and simplifying the methods and facilities for distribution of materials and may arrange for improved and more efficient distribution of literature.

3. The commission shall publish a **free local-church program journal** for pastors and local-church leaders. This journal shall present to the local church for its use the program and promotional materials of the general agencies in a correlated manner and shall be in lieu of general-agency promotional periodicals; *provided* that this shall not apply to *The Methodist Woman* and *The Methodist Layman.*

4. In view of the fact that there is an inseparable relationship between education in stewardship and giving, the commission shall co-operate with the Boards of Education and of Lay Activities in a church-wide program of stewardship education, with special emphasis on the stewardship of possessions, which shall be closely related to giving to the benevolence causes which Methodists are called on to support. Stewardship of possessions shall be interpreted to mean that the tithe is the minimum standard of giving for Methodist people, and shall be promoted by providing appropriate literature for the use of churches and pastors in enlisting Methodist people as tithers. To carry on this program there shall be an **Interboard Committee on Stewardship,** composed of representatives of the three agencies, which shall meet annually or oftener as it may determine. The chairmanship shall rotate annually among the agencies as the committee may determine.

5. The commission may commit to its central promotional office any other cause or undertaking, financial or otherwise, not herein mentioned, demanding church-wide promotion or publicity; *provided* that such action shall have been previously approved by the Council of Bishops and the Council on World Service and Finance, or by their respective executive committees.

6. The commission shall report to the General Conference.

¶ **754.** The expenses of the commission, including the editing, publishing, and distribution of the local-church program journal, fourth-Sunday world service leaflets, and other publications or visual aids for the promoting of general benevolences authorized by the General Conference, shall be paid out of world service receipts and quarterly prorated to the several promoted funds on the basis of receipts for each fund. The budget of the commission, as recommended by the Council on World Service and Finance and approved by the General Conference, shall be a prior charge against the promoted funds.

¶ **755.** 1. In each Annual Conference there shall be constituted a **Conference Commission on Promotion and Cultivation** to promote the program of world service and other general benevolence causes in the pastoral charges of the conference in co-operation with the central promotional office of the general commission; *provided*, however, that if a Conference Council or similar body (¶ 679) serves as the promotional agency for all general benevolences approved by the conference, it may function in lieu of a conference commission in co-operation with the central promotional office. This commission shall see that each agency provides for the proper presentation of the cause it represents to the Commission on World Service and Finance for consideration and recommendation to the conference in regular session. It shall also co-ordinate the promotion of all approved general and conference benevolence causes, and shall assign responsibility for the promotion of approved causes that do not clearly belong to an existing agency.

2. The commission shall be composed of the following members: the resident bishop and at least one member of his Cabinet chosen by the bishop; one minister and one layman from each district, nominated by the bishop and his Cabinet or by the conference nominating committee and elected by the conference; and any members of the general commission residing within the bounds of the conference. The chairmen of the Commission on

231

World Service and Finance and the Conference Board of Missions, the president of the Conference Woman's Society of Christian Service, and such additional officers as the bishop and Cabinet may name shall be ex officio members without vote.

3. In order to secure full participation in the support of the several benevolence causes the commission may organize under its authority and direction a World Service Committee, an Advance Committee, and such other committees as it may deem necessary.

4. The budget for the commission shall be provided by the conference through its Commission on World Service and Finance.

SEC. V.   **The Advance**

¶ **756.** For the more adequate support of the missionary program of the church, the **Advance** shall be organized and administered as hereinafter set forth, to the end that opportunity may be given each local church through its pastoral-charge Quarterly Conference to participate in such support, over and above its world service contributions, as each may determine. (*See* ¶ 149.3.) The Advance program shall include all special gifts (¶ 745) to missionary causes, which shall be designated as general Advance specials (¶ 758) or conference Advance specials (¶ 759), and One Great Hour of Sharing offerings (¶ 760).

¶ **757.** 1. There shall be a **General Advance Committee,** organized under the authority and direction of the General Commission on Promotion and Cultivation. It shall consist of twelve members, representing equally all six jurisdictions, and including at least two bishops, two ministers, and two laymen, named by the commission from its membership. In addition the general secretaries of the Division of World Missions, the Division of National Missions, and the Joint Section of Education and Cultivation of the Board of Missions; the Methodist Committee for Overseas Relief; the Council on World Service and Finance; and the General Commission on Promotion and Cultivation shall be ex officio members.

2. The committee shall have general oversight of the

Advance program in accordance with the plan and procedure hereinafter described.

¶ **758.** 1. The agencies participating in **general Advance specials** shall be the Division of World Missions and the Division of National Missions of the Board of Missions, and the Methodist Committee for Overseas Relief.

2. As far as practicable these specials shall be solicited for specific objects that may be visualized and described. Each such special object shall be approved by the Advance Committee (or by a committee on specials appointed by it) on recommendation of the agency concerned. An Annual Conference, local church, or individual may assume responsibility for an undesignated foreign, home, or overseas relief special, in which case the agency concerned shall determine where such special shall be allocated, shall inform the donor where his gift has been invested, and shall as far as practicable establish communication between donor and recipient. All specials authorized by the Advance Committee and solicited for special projects shall be reported in duplicate to the general secretary of the commission and to the treasurer of the Council on World Service and Finance.

3. Receipts for general Advance specials shall be remitted by the local-church treasurer to the conference treasurer, who shall make remittance each month to the general treasurer. The general treasurer shall remit monthly to the respective participating agencies the amount received for each; *provided*, however, that when a donor church or individual so elects, remittance may be made directly to the treasurer of the agency administering such special, whereupon the agency receiving such remittance shall send to the central treasury a voucher for the central treasurer and a voucher for the conference treasurer.

4. Each participating agency shall administer the general Advance specials received by it in harmony with procedures approved by the Advance Committee, and shall report them to the Advance Committee at such intervals and in such detail as the committee may request.

5. Each participating agency shall, on receipt of a gen-

eral Advance special, communicate with the donor, whether conference, local church, or individual, and as far as practicable establish communication between donor and recipient.

¶ **759.** Each Annual Conference is authorized to initiate and promote **conference Advance specials** for missionary and church-extension objects within the conference, as follows:

1. Proposed conference Advance specials shall be approved and promoted by the Conference Board of Missions.

2. Conference Advance specials may be administered by the Conference Board of Missions, or by the Division of National Missions on request of the Annual Conference concerned.

3. An Annual Conference may undertake a conference-wide campaign for a lump sum to be applied to its missionary and church-extension needs. The funds so received shall be designated as conference Advance specials, and shall be administered by the Conference Board of Missions. Local churches shall report their respective contributions as conference Advance specials.

4. Unless the Annual Conference directs otherwise, a district within the conference may authorize and promote Advance specials for church-extension and missionary needs within the district, such funds to be administered by a district missionary society organized for that purpose, or by a similar body set up by the District Conference. Such specials secured and administered on a district level shall be reported by each local church to the Annual Conference as conference Advance specials.

5. Annual Conference report forms shall include separate spaces designated as "Advance specials, general," and "Advance specials, conference"; and local churches shall report accordingly.

6. It is recommended that each Annual Conference or district administering conference Advance specials set aside each year ten per cent of the amount received for that purpose for aid to the weaker and more urgent situations outside the conference, and that such amount be remitted to the Division of National Missions, to be administered by it as a general Advance special.

¶ 760. The annual observance of the **One Great Hour of Sharing** (continuing the Week of Dedication offering) shall be under the general supervision of the Commission on Promotion and Cultivation, in accordance with the following directives:

1. The One Great Hour of Sharing shall be observed annually on or about the fourth Sunday in Lent. All local churches shall be fully informed and encouraged to contribute a freewill offering in behalf of the Crusade scholarship program (¶ 1290), the overseas relief program (¶¶ 1311-15), the ministry to servicemen overseas program of The Methodist Church, and such capital funds emergency projects of the Division of National Missions as may be authorized by the commission.

2. In connection with the One Great Hour of Sharing there shall be an emphasis on the spiritual implications of Christian stewardship.

3. The participating agencies shall administer the funds in accordance with the ratios determined by the commission: the Crusade Scholarship Committee for the Crusade Scholarship Fund (¶ 1290); the Methodist Committee for Overseas Relief for the Overseas Relief Fund (¶¶ 1311-15); the Division of World Missions for the Servicemen Overseas Fund in co-operation with the co-operative committee of the National Council of Churches; and the Division of National Missions for the capital funds emergency projects.

4. The One Great Hour of Sharing offering shall be promptly remitted by the local-church treasurer to the conference treasurer, who shall remit monthly to the general treasurer. The general treasurer shall distribute these funds to the participating agencies in accordance with the ratios determined by the commission.

5. A One Great Hour of Sharing special-gift voucher shall be issued (*see* ¶ 746), and a space for reporting the amount of the offering shall be included in the form for pastors' reports to the Annual Conference.

6. The expense budget for promoting the One Great Hour of sharing shall be subject to approval annually by the commission and shall be a prior charge against receipts from these offerings.

¶ **761.** The following general directives shall be observed in the promotion and administration of the Advance:

1. In the appeal and promotion of Advance specials and One Great Hour of Sharing offerings there shall be no goals or quotas, except as they may be set by the Annual Conferences for themselves.

2. The treasurer of the Council on World Service and Finance shall be treasurer of the Advance.

3. The expense of promotion for Advance specials shall be borne by the respective participating agencies in proportion to the amount received by each in Advance specials. The causes of the Advance shall be correlated with other financial appeals and shall be promoted by the central promotional office of the Commission on Promotion and Cultivation.

4. The appeal for Advance specials shall be channeled through bishops, district superintendents, and pastors, the details of the procedure to be determined by the Commission on Promotion and Cultivation in consultation with the Joint Section of Education and Cultivation of the Board of Missions and the Advance Committee.

5. In each Annual Conference the Conference Board of Missions, in co-operation with the General Board of Missions and the General and Conference Commissions on Promotion and Cultivation, shall promote Advance specials and One Great Hour of Sharing offerings through district missionary secretaries, conference and district missionary institutes, and other effective means as it may determine.

6. Should a clear emergency arise, any feature of the structure and administration of the Advance may be altered by the General Commission on Promotion and Cultivation on the approval of a majority of the Council of Bishops and of the Council on World Service and Finance.

SEC. VI.   **Other Special Appeals**

¶ **762.** There shall be a world service special-gift fund known as the **Methodist Television-Radio Ministry Fund,** which shall be raised as follows:

1. Promotion shall be by the central promotional office of the Commission on Promotion and Cultivation in consultation with the general secretary of the Television, Radio, and Film Commission or a special committee thereof as it may determine; and the appeal shall be channeled through the bishops, district superintendents, and pastors with the aid of the Conference Commissions on Promotion and Cultivation.

2. Each Annual Conference may appoint a **Methodist Television-Radio Ministry Fund Committee** to work on the conference and district level with the General and Conference Television, Radio, and Film Commissions in interpreting to the local churches the need for this fund.

3. No goals or quotas shall be given except as the Annual Conferences may determine for themselves.

4. A Methodist Television-Radio Ministry special-gift voucher shall be issued. (*See* ¶ 746.)

5. The Council on World Service and Finance is authorized to provide a space for recording contributions to this fund in the pastor's report to the Annual Conference.

6. All contributions for the fund shall be channeled through the conference treasurer to the treasurer of the Council on World Service and Finance.

7. If the Television, Radio, and Film Commission deems it desirable, the designation of special projects within the television-radio ministry program may be authorized.

¶ 763. The Fellowship of Suffering and Service appeal shall be continued until it is deemed no longer needed, either by the General Conference or, between its sessions, by three-fourths vote of the Council of Bishops and of the Council on World Service and Finance meeting separately. Each local church shall be requested to transmit, either through its conference treasurer or directly to the treasurer of the Council on World Service and Finance, under designation of the Fellowship of Suffering and Service, all the Communion offering received on Worldwide Communion Sunday (the first Sunday in October) and a portion of the Communion offerings received at subsequent observances of the Sacrament of the Lord's Supper. A Fellowship of Suffering and Service special-gift voucher shall be issued (*see* ¶ 746), and a space for reporting the amount of the offerings shall be included in the form for the pastor's report to the Annual Conference. The treasurer of the Council on World Service and Finance is authorized to distribute these receipts on the basis of fifty per cent to the Methodist Committee for Overseas Relief and twenty-five per cent each to the Commission on Chaplains and the Commission on Camp Activities.

¶ **764.** The General Commission on Promotion and Cultivation may organize special committees from its membership for the effective promotion of special days and other special appeals referred to it for promotion by the Council of Bishops and the Council on World Service and Finance.

SEC. VII. **The General Administration Fund**

¶ **765.** The General Administration Fund shall provide for the expenses of the sessions of the General Conference, the Judicial Council, the Co-ordinating Council (¶ 1112.4), the Department of Research and Statistics (¶ 1120.5), the Transportation Office (¶ 1120.7), the File of Pastors and Church Officials (¶ 1120.8), the Committee on Family Life (¶ 1417), the Commission on Worship (¶ 1568), the Commission on Church Union (¶ 1575), the Commission on Public Relations and Methodist Information (¶ 1588), the Association of Methodist Historical Societies (¶ 1591), the World Methodist Council (¶ 1594), the Commission on Ecumenical Consultation (¶ 1597), Religion in American Life (¶ 1599), such special commissions and committees as may be constituted by the General Conference (*see* ¶ 710), and such interchurch causes and other activities as may be authorized by the General Conference other than those provided for under the Interdenominational Co-operation Fund (¶ 778).[7] Any agency or institution requiring or desiring support from the General Administration Fund shall present its case for the same to the Council on World Service and Finance at a time and place which shall be indicated by the officers of the council. The council, having heard such requests, shall report the same to the General

---

[7] *See* Judicial Council Decision 17.

Conference with recommendations for its action and determination.

¶ **766.** The Council on World Service and Finance shall submit to each quadrennial session of the General Conference an annual general administration budget, including such items as in the judgment of the council should be provided for out of this fund for the ensuing quadrennium. The council shall likewise recommend to the General Conference what prior or preferred claims shall be allowed in the general administration budget, and by what plan or ratios the causes included in the budget shall share in the funds collected. The general administration budget thus submitted, including all recommendations, shall be subject to the action and determination of the General Conference.

¶ **767.** The Council on World Service and Finance shall apportion among the several Annual Conferences of the church the total general administration budget, as approved by the General Conference, by such ratio and percentage to the total giving (not including the payment of debts or for church buildings), as recorded in the General Minutes for the first three years of the quadrennium closing with the current session of the General Conference, as is necessary to raise the approved annual budget. The apportionments for the general administration budget shall not be subject to change or revision either by the Annual Conference or by the charge or local church.

¶ **768.** The treasurer of the Council on World Service and Finance shall disburse the funds received by him for the General Administration Fund as authorized by the General Conference and as directed by the council. Where the General Conference has not allocated definite sums to agencies receiving money from the General Administration Fund, the Council on World Service and Finance, or its executive committee, shall have authority to determine the amount to be allocated to each.

SEC. VIII.   **The Episcopal Fund**

¶ **769.** The Episcopal Fund, raised separately from all other funds, shall provide for the salary and expenses of effective bishops and for the support of retired bishops and of the widows and minor children of deceased bishops. Subject to the approval of the Council on World Service and Finance, the treasurer shall have authority to borrow for the benefit of the Episcopal Fund such amounts as may be necessary for the proper execution of the orders of the General Conference.

¶ **770.** The Council on World Service and Finance shall recommend to each quadrennial session of the General Conference for its action and determination: (1) the amounts to be fixed as salaries of the effective bishops; (2) a schedule of such amounts as may be judged adequate to provide for their expense of house, office, and travel; (3) the amounts to be fixed as annual pensions for the support of retired bishops; and (4) a schedule of allowance for the widows and for the support of minor children of deceased bishops. From the facts in hand the council shall estimate the approximate total amount required annually during the ensuing quadrennium to provide for the items of episcopal support above mentioned, and shall report the same to the General Conference. This amount as finally determined shall be the estimated episcopal budget.

¶ **771.** The Council on World Service and Finance shall estimate what percentage of the total salaries paid pastors and associate pastors by the entire church will yield an amount equal to the estimated episcopal budget, and shall make recommendations to the General Conference concerning the same for its action and determination. When such percentage has been approved by the General Conference, it shall be the basis of the annual apportionment to each Annual Conference for the Episcopal Fund. The apportionment to each Annual Conference shall be an amount equal to the approved percentage of the total cash salaries paid to the pastors and associate pastors serving charges under episcopal appointment or as supply pastors, as reported to the current session of the Annual Conference. This apportionment shall be distributed to the pastoral charges as the conference may determine. In every case the amount apportioned to a charge for the Episcopal Fund shall be paid in the same proportion as the charge pays its pastor.

¶ **772.** The treasurer of the Council on World Service and Finance shall remit monthly to each effective bishop one twelfth of his annual salary, and also one twelfth of his house rent or maintenance, and office expenses as approved by the council. Allowances for retired bishops and for the widows and minor children of deceased bishops shall be paid to them severally in equal monthly installments.

¶ **773.** The treasurer of the Council on World Service and Finance shall pay monthly the claim for the official travel of each bishop or missionary bishop, upon presentation of an itemized voucher.[8] "Official travel" of an effective bishop shall be interpreted to include all visitations to local churches within his area, and to institutions or enterprises of The Methodist Church where he is called in the performance of his official duties, and such journeys outside his area as are within the meaning of "travel through the connection at large" (¶ 431.10). No part of the expense and no honoraria for any such visitations shall be accepted from local Methodist churches or enterprises or institutions of The Methodist Church, such expense being a proper claim against the Episcopal Fund; *provided* that, when a bishop who is a member of an agency of the church is called to a meeting of the same or to a meeting of a committee thereof, the expense incident to such journey shall be paid by the said agency.

Nothing in this interpretation is intended to preclude special or nonofficial engagements of a bishop, other than the oversight of the temporal and spiritual affairs of the church (¶ 431.1), such as series of lectures in educational institutions, baccalaureate addresses, and preaching missions of several days' duration, when such engagements do not interfere with his official duties; nor does it preclude the acceptance of honoraria for such services.

¶ **774.** 1. The pensions for the support of retired bishops elected by General or Jurisdictional Conferences and the surviving widows and minor dependent children of such deceased bishops shall be provided by means of a contributory reserve pension fund to be held and ad-

[8] *See* Judicial Council Decisions 117, 164.

ministered by the Council on World Service and Finance in consultation with the General Board of Pensions.

2. The amounts of the annual pensions payable to such persons shall be determined by the General Conference, on recommendation of the council.

3. Each bishop in active service shall contribute annually to the fund an amount equal to three per cent of his cash salary. The treasurer of the Episcopal Fund is authorized and instructed to withhold from each bishop's salary the amount of his required contribution and pay it to the fund.

4. Any and all benefit derived from the contributions required of a bishop shall be regarded as a part of the total amount of the pension payable to said bishop upon his retirement and to his surviving widow and minor dependent children.

5. The remainder of the cost of the reserve funding of such pensions shall be provided from the Episcopal Fund in accordance with such program and procedure as may from time to time be determined by the council with the approval of the General Conference.

6. The council is directed to proceed as rapidly as possible to convert fully the present pension program to a program of reserve funding of the pensions of bishops and of the widows and dependent minor children of deceased bishops.

¶ 775. Should any effective bishop in the interim of the quadrennial sessions of his Jurisdictional Conference be relieved by the College of Bishops of his jurisdiction from the performance of regular episcopal duties (¶ 431), on account of ill health or for any other reason, the president of the said College of Bishops shall so notify the treasurer of the Episcopal Fund. Beginning ninety days after such notification, he shall receive the regular pension allowance of a retired bishop, and such pension allowance shall continue until he resumes the regular duties of an effective bishop or until his status shall have been determined by his Jurisdictional Conference. Assignment of another bishop or bishops to perform the regular episcopal duties of a bishop so disabled or otherwise incapacitated, for a period of sixty days or more shall be interpreted as a release of the said bishop from the performance of his regular episcopal duties.

¶ 776. Should any retired bishop, in the interim of the quadrennial sessions of his Jurisdictional Conference, be called into active service by the Council of Bishops and assigned to active episcopal duty (¶ 436.4), he shall be entitled to remuneration for such service out of the Episcopal Fund. In the event of such assignment of a retired bishop to active episcopal duty, the president of the Council of Bishops shall notify the treasurer of the Episcopal Fund, giving full information as to the nature and scope of the work assigned him. On the basis of this information the Council on World Service and Finance or its executive committee shall determine what salary remuneration and what expense allowance shall be allowed the bishop concerned during the period of his active service. The treasurer of the Episcopal Fund shall make remittance to him accordingly.

¶ 777. In determining the schedule of allowances for the widows of deceased bishops the following rule shall apply: Each beneficiary who prior to the death of her husband had been his wife for not less than fifteen years while he was engaged in the effective ministry of The Methodist Church, whether bishop or traveling preacher, shall receive the full allowance for the widow of a deceased bishop, as ordered by the General Conference. The allowance of the widow of a deceased bishop who prior to the death of her husband had been his wife for less than fifteen years while he was an effective minister of The Methodist Church shall be determined on the basis of that fraction of fifteen years during which she was his wife while he was an effective minister of The Methodist Church, whether bishop or traveling preacher; *provided* that the Council on World Service and Finance may at its discretion increase the said allowance if special need exists, but in no instance shall the allowance of the widow of a deceased bishop exceed the full allowance as hereinbefore set forth.

Sec. IX.   **The Interdenominational
                Co-operation Fund**

¶ **778.** The Council on World Service and Finance shall
recommend to the General Conference the sum which the
church shall undertake to provide as its share of the
budget of the National Council of Churches (¶ 1595) and
the World Council of Churches (¶ 1596). The sum approved by the General Conference for this purpose shall
be the interdenominational co-operation budget. The
Council on World Service and Finance shall recommend
to the General Conference, for its consideration and determination, appropriate measures to be employed in
order to provide the approved sum. The money contributed
by the local churches, boards, or other agencies for this
purpose shall be known as the Interdenominational Co-
operation Fund, and shall be received and held by the
treasurer of the Council on World Service and Finance
and disbursed as the General Conference shall direct.

Sec. X.   **Miscellaneous**

¶ **781.** All boards and other agencies receiving financial
support from the World Service Fund, the General Administration Fund, or any authorized church-wide appeal
shall make to the Council on World Service and Finance
audited reports of all receipts and disbursements in such
detail and at such times as the council may direct. (*See*
¶ 737.2, .6; *also* ¶ 729.)

¶ **782.** During the quadrennium these agencies shall
study their respective functions, programs, and internal
operations and institute such improvements and economies
in their work as they find to be feasible and practicable.
They shall co-operate with the council in working out, in
advance of these studies, the general areas to be included
and methods of carrying out this objective. They shall
report their accomplishments in improvements and economies at the close of each fiscal year to the council, which
shall prepare from this information a combined report for
the General Conference.

¶ **783.** 1. Each world service agency, so far as possible,
shall adopt the following levels in agency organization:

a) **Board** or **division**—the general organization of staff responsibility.

b) **Section**—a broad subdivision of responsibility in a board or division.

c) **Department**—a specific phase of service to the field.

d) **Bureau**—a subdivision of responsibility within a department.

2. Each world service agency shall adopt the following titles for staff executives:

a) **General secretary**—head of a council, board, division, commission, joint section, or the Methodist Committee for Overseas Relief.

b) **Associate secretary**—an executive second in authority to a general secretary, who may be assigned authority to speak for the general secretary in his absence; *provided* that the title **associate general secretary** may be used for an associate secretary who also has certain executive secretaries responsible to him, or who is administrative head of a division within a board which has one general secretary.

c) **Executive secretary**—head of a section or of an interboard committee.

d) **Director**—head of a department.

e) **Superintendent**—head of a bureau.

¶ 784. In the event of any interboard disagreement on matters of policy and program involving world service funds, the Council on World Service and Finance shall act as arbiter. It shall also consider any complaints from contributors, whether individuals or organizations. If it shall discover what in its judgment is unnecessary duplication of activities or lack of correlation in the programs of the several boards and agencies in relation to each other, it shall promptly direct the attention of the boards or agencies involved to the situation and shall co-operate with them in correcting the same and may decline to supply from the world service treasury money to continue activities which have been held by the council to duplicate each other unnecessarily or plainly violate the principle of correlation as applied to the total benevolence program of the church. (*See* ¶ 737.3.)

¶ 785. The Council on World Service and Finance may

receive, take title to, collect or hold, absolutely or in trust for the benefit of the World Service Fund, the General Administration Fund, the Episcopal Fund, the Interdenominational Co-operation Fund, the Methodist Committee for Overseas Relief Fund, the Fellowship of Suffering and Service Fund, the One Great Hour of Sharing Fund, or the Methodist Television-Radio Ministry Fund of The Methodist Church, or any other fund or funds properly committed to its care, or for proper distribution among the causes supported by these funds, any and all donations, bequests, and devises of any kind or character, real or personal, that may be given, devised, bequeathed, or conveyed unto said Council on World Service and Finance, and to administer the same and the income therefrom in accordance with the directions of the donor, trustor, or testator.

The Council on World Service and Finance shall also have power to invest, reinvest, buy, sell, transfer, and convey any and all funds and properties which it may hold absolutely or in trust, subject always to the terms of the legacy, devise, or donation.

¶ **786.** The Council on World Service and Finance shall recommend to each Conference Commission on World Service and Finance a uniform procedure for presenting its report to the Annual Conference and shall prepare a form for the guidance of the conference treasurer in making his annual statement in the conference journal. (*See* ¶ 806.)

SEC. XI. **The Conference Commission on World Service and Finance**

¶ **791.** Each Annual Conference shall elect, at its session next succeeding the General Conference, a **Commission on World Service and Finance,** nominated by the district superintendents or a nominating committee, as the conference may determine, and composed of five ministers and six lay persons; *provided* that in smaller conferences the number may be reduced to not less than two ministers and three lay persons. Their term of service shall begin with the adjournment of the said conference session, and they shall serve for the quadrennium and until their successors shall have been chosen. No member or employee of any conference board and no employee, trustee, or director of any agency or institution participating in the funds of the conference benevolence budget shall be eligible for membership on the commission. Any vacancy shall be filled by action of the commission until the next conference session, at which time the Annual Conference shall fill the vacancy.

¶ 792. The commission shall elect a president, a vice-president, and a secretary. The conference treasurer (¶ 803) shall be the treasurer of the commission. As an employee of the commission, he shall not be a member of it, but may sit with the commission and its executive committee at all sessions and have the privilege of the floor but without vote. He shall be bonded in a surety company approved by the commission, and for an amount which the commission judges to be adequate.

¶ 793. The chairman of each conference agency, or other duly authorized representative, shall have opportunity to represent the claims of his agency before the commission. The commission shall make diligent effort to secure full information regarding all conference benevolence and service causes, that none may be neglected, jeopardized, or excluded, and shall recommend to the Annual Conference for its action and determination the total amount to be apportioned for conference causes and included in the conference benevolence budget. All agencies receiving financial support from conference benevolences, or from any other authorized conference-wide appeal, shall make to the commission audited reports concerning all such receipts and the disbursements thereof in such detail and at such times as the commission may direct.[9]

¶ 794. The commission shall also recommend to the Annual Conference for its action and determination the amount or the percentage of the total sum of the conference benevolence budget which shall be apportioned to each cause included in the said budget.

¶ 795. The commission, on receiving from the treasurer

[9] *See* Judicial Council Decision 148.

of the Council on World Service and Finance a statement of the amount apportioned that Annual Conference for world service, shall combine the world service apportionment and the approved conference benevolence budget (¶ 793) in one total sum to be known as **world service and conference benevolences.** The total world service and conference benevolence budget thus established shall include a statement of the percentage for world service and the percentage for conference benevolences and shall be distributed annually among the districts or charges, by the method determined by the conference (¶ 796), and by such divisions and ratios as the conference may approve.[10] A like distribution shall be made of Jurisdictional Conference apportionments and any other apportionments that have been properly made to the Annual Conference. The distribution of all apportionments mentioned in this paragraph shall be subject to the approval of the Annual Conference.

¶ **796.** The commission shall recommend to the Annual Conference for its action and determination whether the apportionments referred to in ¶ 795 shall be made by the commission to the districts only, or to the charges of the conference. If the apportionments are made by the commission to the districts only, then the distribution to the charges of each district shall be made as provided in ¶ 797. The conference may order that the entire distribution to all the charges of the conference be made by the district superintendents.

¶ **797.** Should the Annual Conference make the apportionments to the districts only, the distribution to the charges of each district shall be made by its **District Board of Stewards,** composed of the district superintendent as chairman and the district stewards elected by the several Quarterly Conferences (¶ 143.3). In that case it shall be the duty of the district superintendent to call a meeting of the board as soon as practicable after the adjournment of the Annual Conference; and the board shall make the distribution to the charges of the district, using such methods as it may determine, unless

[10] *See* Judicial Council Decision 63.

the Annual Conference shall have determined the method of distribution to the charges.

¶ **798.** The commission shall include in its recommendations to the Annual Conference the amounts computed by the Conference Board of Pensions as necessary to meet the needs for annuity payments and relief. (*See* ¶ 1623.)

¶ **799.** The commission shall report to the Annual Conference at each session the standard percentage approved by the General Conference for the Episcopal Fund as an apportionment to the Annual Conference, as described in ¶ 771. This apportionment shall be distributed to the pastoral charges as the conference may determine.

¶ **800.** The commission, on receiving from the Council on World Service and Finance a statement of the amount apportioned to the Annual Conference for the General Administration Fund (¶ 767) and the Interdenominational Co-operation Fund (¶ 778), shall apportion the same to the several districts or charges as tne conference may direct.

¶ **801.** It shall be the duty of the commission, unless otherwise provided (¶ 802), to estimate the total amount necessary to furnish a sufficient and equitable support for the district superintendents of the conference, including salary and suitable provision for dwelling, travel, and office expense. The commission shall recommend to the Annual Conference for its action and determination the amount estimated, including the salary and other allowances specified above, for each of the several district superintendents. The commission shall also recommend to the Annual Conference for its action and determination the basis and method by which the total amount shall be apportioned to the districts or charges in harmony with ¶ 822. The conference treasurer shall, as far as practicable, remit monthly to the several district superintendents the amounts due them, respectively, and with the approval of the Annual Conference the commission, or the treasurer, as the conference may determine, may borrow the funds necessary to make this possible. If an Annual Conference adopts the basic salary plan (¶ 827) for ministerial support, the support for the several district superintendents thereof shall be included therein. The amounts necessary to provide for suitable dwelling, travel, and office expense may be included in the basic salary budget or apportioned separately as the conference may determine.[11]

¶ **802.** Annual Conferences which elect to do so may provide for the support of district superintendents through the District Board of Stewards in each of the several districts. In that case the board, under the chairmanship of the district superintendent (¶ 797), shall estimate the salary and expenses of the district superintendent and shall apportion the same among the several charges of the district by the plan it shall adopt. The amount apportioned for the support of the district superintendent shall be included in the items of ministerial support (¶ 821). The board may elect a **district treasurer,** to whom the treasurer of each local church shall make remittances, and who shall in turn make payment to the district superintendent. In the event that no such treasurer is elected, remittances shall be made directly to the district superintendent. There shall be a settlement at least once a quarter, when proportional payments for the various items of ministerial support shall be made. (*See* ¶ 823.)

¶ **803.** Each Annual Conference, on nomination of its Commission on World Service and Finance, shall, at the first session of the conference after the General Conference, elect a **conference treasurer.** He shall serve for the quadrennium or until his successor shall be elected and qualify. If a vacancy should occur during the quadrennium, the commission shall fill the vacancy until the next session of the Annual Conference. The commission shall have authority and supervision over the treasurer. After consultation with the bishop in charge, it may remove him from office for cause, and fill the vacancy until the next session of the conference. The commission shall have the accounts of the conference treasurer for the conference year preceding audited by a certified public accountant within ninety days after the close of each session of the Annual Conference. (*See* ¶ 729.)

¶ **804.** All amounts contributed in each local church

---

[11] *See* Judicial Council Decision 44.

for world service and conference benevolences shall be remitted monthly by the local-church treasurer to the conference treasurer, who shall each month divide the total amount thus received, setting aside the proper amount for world service and the proper amount for conference benevolences, according to the ratio of each established by the Annual Conference in the total world service and conference benevolence budget. He shall make monthly remittances of the share received by him for conference benevolences to the treasurers of the several agencies for conference work according to the rightful share and proportion of each. He shall remit monthly to the treasurer of the Council on World Service and Finance the total share received by him for world service. When the amount contributed during the year for world service and conference benevolences exceeds the amount apportioned to or accepted by the Annual Conference, the entire share contributed for world service shall be remitted in regular order to the treasurer of the Council on World Sevice and Finance before the end of the fiscal year. (See ¶ 267.6.)

¶ 805. The conference treasurer shall remit monthly to the treasurer of the Council on World Service and Finance the amounts received and payable for the General Administration Fund, the Episcopal Fund, and the Interdenominational Co-operation Fund. He shall also transmit all amounts received for world service special gifts, Advance special gifts, the Fellowship of Suffering and Service, the One Great Hour of Sharing, the Methodist Committee for Overseas Relief, the Methodist Television-Radio Ministry Fund, and all other general causes not otherwise directed.

¶ 806. The conference treasurer shall make each month a full report of all general funds handled by him to the treasurer of the Council on World Service and Finance, and annually a report of all receipts, disbursements, and balances of all funds under his direction, which report shall be printed in the conference journal. The reports shall be made on forms authorized by the council. (See ¶ 786.)

¶ **807.** The commission shall provide a suitable bond for the conference treasurer and shall designate a depository or depositories for conference funds. It shall require the treasurers of all conference boards and agencies to be properly bonded in companies approved by the commission, and shall require that their books be properly audited at least annually. The commission shall recommend to the Annual Conference the amount in which the treasurers of all unincorporated boards or commissions shall be protected by fidelity insurance, and application for such fidelity bonds shall be made by the corporate body of the Annual Conference, and the costs shall be provided for out of the funds held by the unincorporated board or commission so insured. Institutions and organizations that are incorporated under the laws of the state shall secure fidelity bonds for the treasurers of their funds and shall pay the cost of the premium required. (*See* ¶ 729.)

¶ **808.** For the sake of economy and efficiency the Annual Conference may constitute the conference treasury as a depository for funds designated for any or all conference boards and agencies participating in the conference benevolences, eliminating as far as possible the necessity of a treasurer for each. In this event the conference treasurer shall keep a separate account for each such conference board or agency, enter the proper credits in each at the end of each month's business, and disburse the same on proper order from each board or agency, respectively. None of the above-designated accounts shall be drawn on for the benefit of another.

¶ **809.** The commission shall co-operate with the Council on World Service and Finance and with the General Board of Lay Activities in promoting and standardizing the financial system in the local churches of the conference.

¶ **810.** No Annual Conference board or interest, such as a school, college, university, or hospital, shall make a special conference-wide appeal to the local churches for funds without the approval of the Annual Conference, except in case of an extreme emergency, when such approval may be given by a two-thirds vote of the district superintendents and of the commission, acting jointly.

¶ **811.** When application is made to the conference for the privilege of a special conference-wide financial appeal, whether by special collections, campaigns, or otherwise, the application shall be referred to the commission before final action is taken thereon. The commission shall investigate the application and its possible relation to other obligations of the conference, and in the light of the facts make recommendations to the conference for its action and determination. Such application for privilege of a special appeal may be made directly to the commission for recommendation to the Annual Conference.

¶ **812.** The various conference agencies shall report each year to their respective Annual Conferences the salaries and other expenses allowed each secretary in their employ, and the same shall be published in the conference journal.

SEC. XII.   **Ministerial Support**

¶ **821.** Assumption of the obligations of the itinerancy required to be made at the time of admission into the traveling connection puts upon the church the counter-obligation of providing support for the entire ministry of the church. In view of this, the claim for ministerial support in each pastoral charge shall include provision for the support of pastors, district superintendents, bishops, and conference claimants.

¶ **822.** Each Annual Conference shall determine what plan and method shall be used in distributing the apportionments to its several districts and charges for the Episcopal Fund (¶ 771), for the support of district superintendents and conference claimants, and for the minimum salary fund (¶ 826), whether by percentages based on the current cash salary paid to the ministers serving pastoral charges under episcopal appointment and to supply pastors, or by some other method.

¶ **823.** When the apportionments for bishops, district superintendents, conference claimants, and the minimum salary fund for the several districts and charges have been determined, payments made to the same in each pastoral charge shall be exactly proportional to the amount paid on the ministerial salary or salaries. (*See* ¶¶ 771,

1624.) The treasurer or treasurers of each pastoral charge shall accordingly make proportional distribution of the funds raised in that charge for the support of the ministry, and remit monthly, if practicable, and quarterly at the latest (¶ 802), the items for bishops, district superintendents, conference claimants, and the minimum salary fund to the proper treasurer or treasurers.

¶ **824.** The several Quarterly Conferences shall determine the pastors' salaries according to the provisions of ¶ 148.

¶ **825.** No pastor shall be entitled to any claim for unpaid salary against any church or charge he has served after his pastoral connection with the church or charge has ceased.

¶ **826.** *Minimum Salaries*—1. Each Annual Conference shall adopt a schedule of minimum salaries for pastors and shall create a **Commission on Minimum Salaries** composed of ministers and laymen to administer it. The commission shall carefully study the number and extent of the needs for additional ministerial support within the conference, and the sources of income, and with the approval of the Commission on World Service and Finance shall present to the conference for adoption a schedule of minimum salaries, subject to such rules and regulations as the conference may adopt, so long as the rules do not conflict with the provisions of this legislation. The schedule may allow for differences in living conditions, number of dependents in pastor's family, and any other variants the conference may direct.

2. In so far as practicable, this schedule of minimum salaries shall be observed by the bishops and district superintendents in arranging charges and making appointments.

3. The Commission on Minimum Salaries shall present its estimate of the amount required to comply with the schedule of minimum salaries for the pastors, as adopted by the conference, to the Conference Commission on World Service and Finance, which shall apportion the amount as

an item of ministerial support to the districts or the charges as the conference may direct.[12]

4. The minimum salary fund, secured as described in § 3, shall be used to provide each pastor who receives less than the minimum salary with an additional amount sufficient to make the salary approved by the pastoral charge plus the supplemental aid or income from other sources equal to the minimum salary approved by the conference; *provided* that nothing in this paragraph shall be construed as limiting the right of an Annual Conference to set a maximum amount to be used in attaining such minimum salary in any given case.

5. The Commission on Minimum Salaries shall see that the amounts for minimum salaries are collected and disbursed.

¶ **827.** *Basic Salary Plan.*—1. An Annual Conference may by a two-thirds majority vote at any regular session adopt a **basic salary plan** for the support of its active itinerants and supply pastors who are giving their full time to the ministry of the church; *provided*, however, that it shall not institute the basic salary plan until the plan has been approved and ratified by a majority vote of the members of the Quarterly Conferences present and voting in seventy-five per cent of the pastoral charges of such conference. The district superintendents shall certify to the conference secretary the results of the votes taken in the several Quarterly Conferences.

2. The basic salary plan shall provide an established salary schedule for the support of the regular active itinerants and supply pastors giving their full time to the ministry of the church, which may allow for differences of living conditions, number of dependents in the family, and other variants. On recommendation of the Commission on World Service and Finance the basic salary schedule may be changed from time to time by a majority vote of the Annual Conference.

3. The Commission on World Service and Finance shall estimate the amount necessary to provide such ministerial support as may be required by the schedule adopted,

---

[12] *See* Judicial Council Decision 90.

which amount shall be distributed as an apportionment to the districts or pastoral charges by a method to be determined by the conference.

4. The amounts due from the pastoral charges on apportionment shall be paid to a conference treasury established for that purpose, and all basic salaries due shall be paid from that treasury. The basic salary provided for each minister concerned shall constitute his entire salary except as hereinafter provided.

5. Any pastoral charge which has made adequate provision for paying its apportionments for all ministerial support items in full may augment the basic support of its pastor.

6. The Commission on World Service and Finance shall administer the basic salary plan and shall be responsible for collecting and disbursing the funds.[13]

¶ 828. *Sustentation Fund.*—An Annual Conference may establish a **sustentation fund,** which shall be administered by the Commission on World Service and Finance or some other agency created or designed for the purpose of providing emergency aid to the ministers of the conference who may be in special need. On recommendation of the commission the amount needed for this purpose may be apportioned to the pastoral charges as the conference may determine.

¶ 829. The total of all travel, automobile, and other expenses allowed and paid to a pastor in addition to his salary shall be reported for insertion in the journal of the Annual Conference, in a separate column from that of pastor's salary and adjacent thereto.[14] These expenses shall be distinguished from the moving expenses of a new appointee to a pastoral charge, which shall be reported as provided in ¶ 148.

¶ 830. Every ministerial member of an Annual Conference appointed to any other field than the pastorate or district superintendency shall furnish annually to the conference secretary, at the time of the conference session, a statement of his remuneration, and the salaries or

---

[13] *See* Judicial Council Decisions 65, 70.
[14] Adopted in 1952 following Judicial Council Decision 51; *see also* Decision 151.

remuneration of all men in special service shall be published in the journal of the Annual Conference.

Sec. XII. **The Local Church**

For description of the financial plan for the local church *see* ¶¶ 261-72 under Part II, The Local Church.

PART VI

JUDICIAL ADMINISTRATION

CHAPTER I

THE JUDICIAL COUNCIL

¶ **901.** *Article* 1. *Members.*—The **Judicial Council** shall be composed of nine members, five of whom shall be ministers and four shall be laymen. They shall be at least forty years of age, and members of The Methodist Church. Their terms of office shall be eight years; *provided*, however, that a member of the council whose seventieth birthday precedes the first day of the regular session of a General Conference shall be released at the close of that General Conference from membership or responsibility in the council regardless of the date of expiration of his term of office.

Members of the council shall be nominated and elected in the manner following: At each quadrennial session of the General Conference, the Council of Bishops shall nominate by majority vote six times the number of ministers and six times the number of laymen to be elected at such session of the General Conference. At the same daily session at which the above nominations are announced, nominations for each class may be made from the floor, but at no other time. The names of all such nominees shall be published in the *Daily Christian Advocate*, with the name of the conference to which each belongs, for two consecutive issues immediately prior to the day of election, which shall be set by action of the General Conference at the session at which the nominations are made;

258

and from these nominations the General Conference shall elect without discussion, by ballot and by majority vote, the necessary number of each class; *provided*, however, that as a result of the election each jurisdiction shall be represented on the council.[1]

Election of members shall be held at each session of the General Conference for only the number of members whose terms expire at such session.

Art. 2. *Alternates.*—There shall be eight alternates of each class, and their qualifications shall be the same as for membership on the Judicial Council. The term of the alternates shall be for eight years; *provided*, however, that an alternate whose seventieth birthday precedes the first day of the regular session of a General Conference shall be released at the close of that General Conference from membership or responsibility in the council regardless of the date of expiration of his term of office.

The alternates shall be elected in the manner following: From the nominees of each class remaining on the ballot after the election of the necessary number of members of the Judicial Council to be elected at sessions of the General Conference, the General Conference shall by separate ballot, without discussion and by majority vote, elect the number of alternates of each class to be elected at such session of the General Conference; *provided*, however, that as a result of the election each jurisdiction shall have at least one alternate of each class. An election shall be held at each session of the General Conference for only the number of each class whose terms expire at such session of the General Conference, or to fill vacancies. The above provisions shall apply as soon as expiration of the terms of the present alternates permits.

Art. 3. *Vacancies.*—If a vacancy in the membership of the Judicial Council occurs during the interim between sessions of the General Conference, it shall be filled by an alternate of the same class[2] and from the same jurisdiction as the member whom he succeeds, if there is such an alternate, and by the first elected if there is more than one. If there is no alternate of the same class and

---

[1] *See* Judicial Council Decision 62.
[2] *See* Judicial Council Decision 94.

jurisdiction, the vacancy shall be filled by an alternate of the same class in order of election. The alternate filling such vacancy shall hold office as a member of the Judicial Council for the unexpired term of the member whom he succeeds. In the event of any vacancy it shall be the duty of the president and secretary of the council to notify the alternate entitled to fill it.

In the event of the enforced absence of one or more members of the council at or during a session of the General Conference, such temporary vacancy may be filled for that session of the General Conference, or the remainder thereof, as provided above in this article; *provided*, however, that nothing in this provision shall affect the validity of any action of the council so long as a quorum is present.

Any permanent vacancy or vacancies among the alternates shall be filled by election at the next session of the General Conference to the class or respective classes in which such permanent vacancy or vacancies exist, and the person or persons so elected shall hold office during the unexpired term of the alternate whom each respectively succeeds.

If vacancies in the membership of the Judicial Council occur after exhaustion of the list of alternates, the council is authorized to fill such vacancies for the remainder of the quadrennium.

Art. 4. General.—The term of office of the members of the council and of the alternates shall expire upon the adjournment of the General Conference at which their successors are elected.

¶ **902.** Members of the council shall be ineligible for membership in the General Conference or Jurisdictional Conference or in any general or jurisdictional board or for administrative service in any connectional office.[3]

¶ **903.** The Judicial Council shall provide its own method of organization and procedure. It shall meet at the time and place of the meeting of the General Conference and shall continue in session until the adjournment of that body. It shall meet at such other times and places as it may deem necessary. Seven members shall constitute

---

[3] *See* Judicial Council Decision 120.

a quorum. An affirmative vote of at least six members of the council shall be necessary to declare any act of the General Conference unconstitutional. On other matters a majority vote of the entire council shall be sufficient.

¶ **904.** 1. The Judicial Council shall determine the constitutionality of any act of the General Conference upon an appeal of a majority of the Council of Bishops, or one fifth of the members of the General Conference.

2. The Judicial Council shall have jurisdiction to pass upon the constitutionality of any proposed legislation when such declaratory decision is requested by the General Conference or by the Council of Bishops.

¶ **905.** The Judicial Council shall determine the constitutionality of any act of a Jurisdictional or a Central Conference upon an appeal of a majority of the bishops of that Jurisdictional or Central Conference, or upon the appeal of one fifth of the members of that Jurisdictional or Central Conference.

¶ **906.** The Judicial Council shall hear and determine the legality of any action taken therein by any General Conference board, or Jurisdictional or Central Conference board or body, upon appeal by one third of the members thereof, or upon request of the Council of Bishops, or a majority of the bishops of the Jurisdictional or Central Conference.

¶ **907.** The Judicial Council shall hear and determine the legality of any action taken therein by a General Conference board, or Jurisdictional or Central Conference board or body, on a matter affecting an Annual or a Provisional Annual Conference, upon appeal by two thirds of the members of the Annual or Provisional Annual Conference present and voting.

¶ **908.** The Judicial Council shall hear and determine any appeal from a bishop's decision on a question of law made in the Annual or District Conference when said appeal has been made by one fifth of that conference present and voting.

¶ **909.** The Judicial Council shall meet at least once a year and pass upon the decisions of law made by the bishops in Annual and District Conferences upon questions submitted to them in writing, and reported in writing to the council with a syllabus of each case, and affirm, modify, or reverse them. Before affirmation no episcopal decision shall be authoritative except in the case pending. When the decisions are affirmed, they shall become the law of the church.

¶ 910. The Judicial Council shall hear and determine an appeal of a bishop when taken from the decision of the Trial Court in his case.

¶ 911. The Judicial Council shall have such other duties and powers as may be conferred upon it by the General Conference.

¶ 912. All decisions of the Judicial Council shall be final. However, when the Judicial Council shall declare any act of the General Conference unconstitutional, that decision shall be reported back to that General Conference immediately.

¶ 913. If it should occur that the opinion or decision of a Committee of Appeals of a Jurisdictional Conference should contravene a decision of the Committee of Appeals of another Jurisdictional Conference on a point or question of law, then:

a) Any person, conference, or organization interested therein may appeal the case to the Judicial Council on the ground of such conflict of decisions; or

b) The Committee on Appeals rendering the last of such opinions or decisions may certify the case to and file it with the Judicial Council on the ground of such conflict of decisions; or

c) The attention of the president of the Judicial Council being directed to such conflict, or alleged conflict of decisions, he may issue an order, in the nature of a writ of certiorari, directing the secretaries of the Committees of Appeals involved to certify a copy of a sufficient portion of the record to disclose the nature of the case, and the entire opinion and decision of the Committee of Appeals in each case, to the Judicial Council for its consideration at its next meeting.

The Judicial Council shall hear and determine the question of law involved, but shall not pass upon the facts in either case further than is necessary to decide the question of law involved. After deciding the question of law, the Judicial Council shall cause the same to be certified to each of the Committees of Appeals involved; and such Committees of Appeals shall take such action, if any, as may be necessary under the law as settled by the Judicial Council.

¶ **914.** When the General Conference shall have passed any act or legislation that appears to be unconstitutional or subject to more than one interpretation, or when any paragraph or paragraphs of the Discipline seem to be of doubtful meaning, or application, the Judicial Council, on petition as hereinafter provided, shall have jurisdiction to make a ruling in the nature of a **declaratory decision** as to the constitutionality, meaning, application, and effect of such act, legislation, or paragraph or paragraphs of the Discipline; and the decision of the Judicial Council thereon shall be as binding and effectual as a decision made by the Judicial Council on appeal under the law relating to appeals to the Judicial Council.

The following bodies in The Methodist Church are hereby authorized to make such petitions to the Judicial Council for declaratory decisions: (1) the Council of Bishops; (2) any General Conference board or body, on matters relating to or affecting the work of such board or body; (3) a majority of the bishops assigned to any jurisdiction on matters relating to or affecting jurisdictions or the work therein; (4) any Jurisdictional Conference, on matters relating to or affecting jurisdictions or Jurisdictional Conferences or the work therein; (5) any Jurisdictional Conference board or body, on matters relating to or affecting the work of such board or body;[4] (6) any Central Conference, on matters relating to or affecting Central Conferences, or the work therein; (7) any Central Conference board or body, on matters relating to or affecting the work of such board or body; (8) any Annual Conference, on matters relating to Annual Conferences or the work therein.

The Judicial Council shall determine from the facts in connection with each such petition whether or not it has jurisdiction to hear and determine the same.[5]

---

[4] *See* Judicial Council Decision 166.
[5] *See* Judicial Council Decision 23.

¶ **915.** When a declaratory decision is sought, all persons or bodies who have or claim any interest which would be affected by the declaration shall be parties to the proceeding, and the petition shall name such parties. If the council determines that other parties not named by the petition would be affected by such a decision, such additional parties shall also be added; and the petitioner or petitioners shall then be required to serve all parties so joined with a copy of the petition within fifteen days after the filing of the same with the Judicial Council. In like manner any interested party may on his or its own motion intervene and answer, plead, or interplead.

¶ **916.** All parties shall have the privilege of filing briefs and arguments, and presenting evidence, under such rules as the council may adopt from time to time. If the Judicial Council deems it necessary to a complete understanding of the facts, in any proceeding in the nature of a petition for a declaratory decision, it may hear evidence (either orally in session or by affidavits filed) or statements of facts agreed upon by adverse parties, or it may designate one or more of its members to hear evidence and report the same to the Judicial Council.

¶ **917.** In all other respects, except as provided herein, the proceedings before the Judicial Council in such matters shall be governed by the same rules and regulations as those under which appeals to the Judicial Council are heard.

¶ **918.** The decisions of the Judicial Council on questions of law, with a summary of the facts and of the opinion, shall be filed with the secretary of the General Conference, and shall be published in the following manner:

1. Following each session of the Judicial Council the official publications of the church shall publish an official summary, prepared by the secretary of the council, of the decisions arrived at during that session.

2. The decisions of the Judicial Council rendered during each year shall be published in the General Minutes (¶ 1120.5).

Chapter II

TRIAL OF A BISHOP OR TRAVELING PREACHER

Section I. Offenses for Which a Bishop or Traveling Preacher or Local Preacher May Be Tried

¶ 921. A bishop or traveling preacher or local preacher shall be liable to accusation and trial upon any of the following charges:

a) Unchristian tempers, words, or actions.

b) Disobedience to the order and discipline of the church.

c) Imprudent or unministerial conduct.

d) Habitual neglect of duties as a member or officer in the church.

e) Disseminating doctrines contrary to the Articles of Religion or other established standards of doctrine of the church.

f) Immorality or crime.

g) Maladministration in office in the church.

Sec. II. Investigation and Trial of a Bishop

¶ 922. A bishop is amenable for his conduct to the Jurisdictional or Central Conference in which he has residential or presidential supervision, or to the Jurisdictional or Central Conference to which he is related.

¶ 923. If a bishop shall be accused in writing of any of the offenses hereinbefore mentioned (¶ 921) in the interval between sessions of the Jurisdictional Conference, the district superintendent within whose district the offense is said to have been committed shall call the Committee of Investigation of that Annual Conference, who shall carefully inquire into the case; and if, in the judgment of the majority of them, there is reasonable ground for such accusation, they shall prepare and sign the proper charges and specifications, and send a copy of the same to the accused, and to the president of the College of Bishops of the jurisdiction in which the offense took place. The said president shall call together at some convenient place, in not less than ten nor more than fifteen days from the time he receives the charges, nine traveling elders of the said jurisdiction, and also the witnesses by whom the accusation is expected to be proved. The said president or some other bishop of the jurisdiction appointed by him shall preside at the investigation. If possible the accused shall have the right to make a statement in his own behalf and to interrogate witnesses, but shall not himself present any. If six or more of these traveling elders determine that a trial is justified, they shall order one, and they may suspend the bishop pending trial as hereinafter provided.

¶ **924.** In case a trial be ordered, the president of the College of Bishops of the said jurisdiction shall within seven days from the date on which a trial is ordered fix the time and place of it, which shall be in not less than thirty or more than sixty days from the date of such order. The **Trial Court** shall be constituted as follows:

1. The bishop shall arrange for a meeting of the accused and his counsel and the counsel for the church, as early as practicable after the trial is ordered, to select the members of the Trial Court.

2. The bishop shall nominate, as proposed members of the Trial Court, thirteen traveling elders from a list made up of the Committees of Investigation of not fewer than four Annual Conferences within the jurisdiction.

3. The church and the accused each shall have the right of peremptory challenge to the number of four and of unlimited challenge for cause.

4. For each name stricken from this list of thirteen through the exercise of the right of challenge, the bishop shall add another from the eligible group until the required number of thirteen is thus selected. If necessary to complete the panel, nominations may be made from other traveling elders in the jurisdiction.

5. By a continuation of this same process four alternates shall be chosen who shall be called in the order of their election to serve.

6. Should the accused be the president of the College of Bishops of the jurisdiction, then a copy of such charges and specifications shall be sent to the secretary of the College of Bishops of that jurisdiction, who shall per-

form the duties hereinabove prescribed for the president, or designate another bishop of the same juridiction.

¶ **925.** The court as thus constituted shall have full power to try the accused and by a vote of nine or more to suspend him from the exercise of the functions of his office; to depose him from his office or the ministry or both; to expel him from the church; or, in case of minor offenses, to fix a lesser penalty. Its findings shall be final, subject to appeal to the Judicial Council as hereinafter provided, and shall be reported to the Jurisdictional Conference for entry on its journal. The records of the trial, including the testimony, shall be signed by the president and secretary of the Trial Court and shall be placed in the custody of the secretary of the Jurisdictional Conference, together with all the documents in the case, for preservation with the papers of the Jurisdictional Conference, and shall be the basis of any appeal which may be taken.

¶ **926.** An accusation preferred during the session of a Jurisdictional Conference shall be made directly to the Committee on Episcopacy, which shall investigate the charge, and, if it consider a trial necessary, shall report to the Jurisdictional Conference. If the Committee on Episcopacy should decide a trial necessary, it shall formulate charges and specifications, conforming them to the grade of offense involved in the accusation, and it shall appoint one or more of its members to prosecute the case. The bill of charges and specifications shall be a part of the report of the committee to the Jurisdictional Conference.

¶ **927.** Every case to be tried under the process stated in the foregoing paragraph (¶ 926) shall be referred to a Trial Court which shall consist of thirteen traveling elders and a presiding officer, all of whom shall be appointed by the president in the chair or in such manner as the conference may determine. The church and the accused each shall have, in addition to the right of unlimited challenge for cause, the right of peremptory challenge to the number of four. The court as thus constituted shall have full power to try the accused and by a two-thirds vote to suspend him from his office; to depose him from his office or the ministry, or both; to expel him from the church; or, in case of minor offenses, to fix a lesser penalty. Its findings shall be final, subject to appeal to the Judicial Council as hereinafter provided.

¶ 928. A bishop suspended or deposed shall have no claim upon the Episcopal Fund for salary, dwelling, or any other expenses from the date of such suspension or deposition; but in case he is thereafter found not guilty of the charge or charges for which he was suspended or deposed, his claim upon the Episcopal Fund for the period during which he was deprived of the functions of his office shall be paid to him.

¶ 929. If an alleged offense has been committed beyond the bounds of any district, the district superintendent within the bounds of whose district the bishop resides shall proceed as hereinbefore provided.

¶ 930. The several Central Conferences shall make suitable rules for the investigation and trial of charges against bishops elected by them. In the absence of such rules the same procedure shall be followed as is provided for the investigation and trial of bishops in Jurisdictional Conferences; *provided*, however, that an appeal may be taken to the Judicial Council. If an accused bishop is the only bishop in his Central Conference, the Council of Bishops shall designate one of their number to conduct the trial.

SEC. III. Investigation and Trial of a Traveling Preacher

¶ 931. Each Annual Conference at each session, upon nomination of the presiding bishop, shall elect five elders, men of experience and sound judgment in the affairs of the church, who shall be known as the **Committee of Investigation,** and three reserves chosen in like manner, to serve in the absence or disqualification of the principals.

¶ 932. If a traveling preacher, whether on trial or in full connection, in the interval between sessions of his conference, shall be accused of any of the offenses enumerated in ¶ 921, his district superintendent, or the superintendent of the district within the bounds of which such acts are alleged to have taken place, shall call the Committee of Investigation to inquire into the same, and, if possible, bring the accused and accuser face to face. The accused

shall have the right to make a statement in his own behalf, but shall not present any witnesses. The district
superintendent shall preside throughout the proceedings,
and shall certify and declare the judgment of the committee.[6]

¶ 933. If the accused is a district superintendent, the
bishop in charge shall call in the superintendent of any
other district or a traveling elder of the Annual Conference, who shall summon the Committee of Investigation
of the Annual Conference of which the accused is a
member to investigate the case, and he shall preside at
the investigation.

¶ 934. If in the judgment of a majority of the Committee of Investigation there is reasonable ground for
such accusation, they shall prepare and sign the proper
charges and specifications, send a copy to the accused, to
the bishop in charge, to the district superintendent or
the traveling elder duly appointed by the bishop in
charge, and to the secretary of the Annual Conference.[7]
On recommendation of the Committee of Investigation
the bishop may suspend the accused from all ministerial
services pending the trial.

¶ 935. The bishop in charge, or the district superintendent or the traveling elder duly appointed by the
bishop in charge, within ten days after receipt of a copy
of such charges, shall appoint counsel for the church and
notify the accused in writing to appear at a fixed time
and place no less than seven days after service of such
notice and within a reasonable time thereafter to select
the members of the **Trial Court.** At the appointed time,
in the presence of the accused and his counsel, if requested, and counsel for the church, thirteen effective
elders shall be selected as a Trial Court. They shall be
selected from a panel of twenty-one effective elders of the
Annual Conference of which the accused is a member, who
have been nominated by the majority of the district superintendents of that conference. The counsel for the church
and the accused shall each have peremptory challenges to
the number of four and challenges for cause without limit.

---

[6] See Judicial Council Decision 89.
[7] See Judicial Council Decision 89.

If by reason of challenges for cause being sustained the number is reduced below thirteen, additional elders shall be nominated, in like manner as was the original panel, to take the places of the numbers challenged, who likewise shall be subject to challenge for cause. This method of procedure shall be followed until a Trial Court of thirteen members has been selected. The presiding officer in charge shall also fix the time and place for the trial, notice of which shall be given in writing to the accused by the counsel for the church seven days in advance of the time fixed; *provided* that, with the consent of the accused, the time of the trial may be fixed at an earlier date. The bishop in charge, or another bishop invited by him, or a traveling elder appointed by him, shall preside at the trial. The presiding officer shall appoint a secretary, who shall keep a record of the proceedings and of the testimony. The court thus constituted shall have full power to try the accused and upon his conviction by a vote of nine or more thereof shall have power to suspend him from the exercise of the functions of his office; to depose him from his office or the ministry or both; to expel him from the church; or, in case of conviction of minor offenses, to fix a lesser penalty. Its findings shall be final, subject to appeal to the Committee on Appeals of the Jurisdictional Conference or the Central Conference as the case may be. It shall make a faithful report in writing of all its proceedings, signed by the president and secretary of the committee, to the secretary of the Annual Conference for permanent record, and deliver to him therewith the bill of charges, the evidence taken, and the decision rendered, together with all documents brought into the trial.

¶ **936.** When accusation against a traveling preacher is preferred during the session of an Annual Conference, it shall be referred to the Annual Conference Committee of Investigation, which committee shall report to the conference whether or not a trial is deemed necessary. The Committee of Investigation, when reporting a case for trial, shall formulate a bill of charges and specifications. The presiding bishop shall appoint some traveling elder of the conference as counsel for the church.

¶ **937.** The conference may constitute a Trial Court of thirteen effective elders to try the accused in the same manner as in ¶ 935. The Trial Court in the presence of a bishop or of a chairman whom the president of the conference shall have appointed, and one of the secretaries of the conference, shall try the case. The Trial Court thus constituted shall have full power, upon conviction of the accused by two-thirds vote thereof, to expel him from the ministry and membership of the church; to depose him from the ministry of the church; to suspend him from his office in the ministry; or to fix a lesser penalty. Its findings shall be final, subject to appeal to the Committee on Appeals of the Jurisdictional Conference. It shall make a faithful report in writing of all its proceedings, duly signed by the president and secretary of the Trial Court, to the secretary of the Annual Conference for entry on its journal, and deliver to him therewith the bill of charges and specifications, the evidence taken, and the decision rendered, with all documents brought into the trial. The Annual Conference may order the completion of such trial before the final adjournment of the session.[8]

¶ **938.** When an accused is tried and the specific charge is not sustained by the evidence, but the accused has been found guilty of imprudent or of unministerial conduct, this fact may be so declared and suitable penalty imposed by the court.

¶ **939.** Any traveling preacher residing beyond the bounds of his own conference shall be subject to the investigation prescribed in ¶¶ 931-35, under the authority of the superintendent of the district within which he resides, or within which he is employed. The Committee of Investigation shall consist of the Committee of Investigation of that conference. If he resides or is employed within the bounds of a Mission, he shall be subject to investigation under the authority of the superintendent of the district within which he holds his Quarterly Conference membership or of the superintendent of the Mission and the Committee of Investigation of the same. If

[8] *See* Judicial Council Decision 116.

he is the superintendent of the Mission, the bishop in charge shall appoint an elder to act in the case.

¶ **940.** An Annual Conference may entertain and try charges against its ministerial members though no investigation of them has been held, or though the investigation has not resulted in suspension.

¶ **941.** In all the foregoing cases the papers, including the record, charges, evidence, and findings, shall be transmitted to the ensuing session of the Annual Conference of which the accused is a member; on which papers, and on such other evidence as may be admitted, and also upon such other charges or specifications as may be presented, due notice of the same having been given to the accused, the case shall be determined.

¶ **942.** In cases of unchristian temper, words, or actions, the traveling preacher so offending shall be admonished by his district superintendent. If he offends again, one or more ministers are to be taken as witnesses. If he continues to offend, the district superintendent shall proceed as directed in ¶¶ 931-35.

¶ **943.** Any traveling preacher who shall hold a religious service within the bounds of a pastoral charge not his own, when requested by the preacher in charge or the district superintendent not to hold such service, shall be deemed guilty of disobedience to the order and discipline of the church; and if he shall not refrain from such conduct, he shall be liable to investigation and trial.

¶ **944.** If a traveling preacher is charged with disseminating publicly or privately doctrines which are contrary to our Articles of Religion, or to other existing and established standards of doctrine, and the minister so offending shall solemnly promise the Committee of Investigation not to disseminate such erroneous doctrines in public or private, it may waive suspension in order that the case may be laid before the next Annual Conference, which shall determine the matter.

Sec. IV.　**Trial of an Approved Supply Pastor**

For the provisions regarding investigation and trial of an approved supply pastor *see* Chapter III, Section I,

"Investigation and Trial of a Local Preacher," ¶¶ 957-65, also ¶ 981.

SEC. V. **Preachers in Provisional Annual Conference**

¶ **946.** In all matters of judicial administration the rights, duties, and responsibilities of ministerial members of Missions and Provisional Annual Conferences are the same as those in Annual Conferences, and the procedure is the same.

SEC. VI. **Maladministration**

¶ **947.** Complaint against the administration of a bishop may be forwarded to the Jurisdictional or Central Conference and entertained there; *provided* that at least thirty days' notice in writing shall have been given to the accused and to the secretary of the conference. This shall not preclude earlier action as provided in ¶¶ 922-23.

¶ **948.** A traveling preacher shall be answerable to his conference on a charge of maladministration, but not for error in judgment.

¶ **949.** Errors of administration not connected with judicial proceedings may be presented in writing to the presiding bishop for his decision thereon; and the Annual Conference may order just and suitable remedies when the rights of ministers or members of the church have been injuriously affected by such errors.

SEC. VII. **Status of a Bishop or Traveling Preacher Deposed or Expelled**

¶ **950.** In case a bishop or a traveling preacher shall have been deposed from the ministry without being expelled from the church, he shall be given a **certificate of membership in the church** signed by the president and secretary of the conference.

¶ **951.** In case a bishop or a traveling preacher shall have been deposed from the ministry or expelled from the church for teaching publicly or privately doctrines contrary to our Articles of Religion, or our other established standards of doctrine, he shall not again be

273

licensed to preach until, if a traveling preacher, he shall have satisfied the Annual Conference from which he was deposed or expelled; or, if a bishop, he shall have satisfied the Annual Conference from which he was elected bishop, and shall have promised in writing to desist wholly from disseminating such doctrine.

Sec. VIII. Withdrawal Under Complaints or Charges

¶ **952.** When a bishop or a traveling preacher is accused of an offense under ¶ 921 and desires to withdraw from the church, the Jurisdictional or Central Conference in the case of a bishop, or the Annual Conference in the case of a traveling preacher, may permit him to withdraw; in which case the record shall be, "Withdrawn under complaints." If formal charges have been presented, he may be permitted to withdraw; in which case the record shall be "Withdrawn under charges." In either case his status shall be the same as if he had been expelled.[9]

Chapter III

INVESTIGATION AND TRIAL OF OTHER THAN TRAVELING PREACHERS

Section I. Investigation and Trial of a Local Preacher

¶ **957.** Each District Conference at each session, upon nomination of its president, shall elect three local preachers and two reserves, of experience and sound judgment in the affairs of the church, who shall be known as the **Committee of Investigation.** The reserves shall serve in the absence or disqualification of the principals. Where no District Conference exists, the Annual Conference Committee of Investigation shall act.

¶ **958.** When a local preacher, ordained or unordained, whether or not serving as an approved supply pastor, is accused of any of the offenses enumerated in ¶ 921, the district superintendent shall call the Committee of

---

[9] *See* Judicial Council Decision 104.

Investigation to meet, before which it shall be the duty of the accused to appear. If in the judgment of a majority of the Committee of Investigation there is reasonable ground for such accusation, they shall prepare and sign the proper charges and send a copy to the accused and to the district superintendent; and the accused may be suspended from all ministerial services pending trial. In all such cases at least seven days' notice shall be given the accused by the district superintendent. Such notice shall contain a full statement of the charges.

¶ 959. The district superintendent within ten days after giving notice of the charges shall select a **Trial Committee** of nine members and seven reserves, of experience and sound judgment in the affairs of the church, who shall be local preachers or, when necessary, members of the church. The reserves shall serve in the absence or disqualification of the principals. The church and the accused shall have three peremptory challenges and unlimited challenges for cause. The committee in the presence of the district superintendent or the traveling elder appointed by him, and a secretary appointed by the committee, shall have full power to consider and determine the case and by a two-thirds vote to convict the accused. They may suspend him from the functions of his office, or depose him from his office or the ministry or both, or expel him from the church. The secretary shall make a correct report in writing of all proceedings, evidence, and findings to the secretary of the District Conference and shall deliver to him all the papers in the case. Where there is no District Conference, then the Quarterly Conference of which the accused is a member shall act.

¶ 960. In case of unchristian temper, words, or actions, the local preacher so offending shall be admonished by his district superintendent. Should a second transgression take place, one or two members of the church are to be taken as witnesses. If he continues to offend, the case shall be investigated as provided in ¶¶ 958-59.

¶ 961. If on due trial a local preacher is found neglectful of his duties as a local preacher or unacceptable in his ministry, he may be deprived of his ministerial office; in which case, if he is ordained, the district superintendent shall require him to surrender his credentials that they may be returned to the Annual Conference.

¶ 962. If a local preacher shall disseminate, publicly or privately, doctrines which are contrary to our Articles of Religion, or to our other present existing and established standards of doctrine, the same procedure shall be observed as prescribed in ¶¶ 958-59.

¶ 963. A local preacher who shall hold religious services within the bounds of a pastoral charge not his own, when requested not to do so by the preacher in charge or district superintendent, shall be deemed guilty of disobedience to the order and discipline of the church and shall be brought to investigation or trial.

¶ 964. When a local elder or deacon is complained of as being so unacceptable or inefficient as to be no longer useful in his work, and the District or Quarterly Conference for that reason refuses to pass his character, the District or Quarterly Conference shall investigate the case; and if it appears that the complaint is well founded, and if he fails to give the conference satisfactory assurance that he will amend, or voluntarily surrender his credentials, the conference may depose him from the ministry. He may defend himself before the conference, in person or by representative. The president of the District or Quarterly Conference shall in this case comply with the requirements of ¶ 961.

¶ 965. In Provisional Annual Conferences or Missions in the United States, its territories, and insular possessions, the power to try local preachers shall remain with the respective District or Quarterly Conference; but local preachers so tried and convicted shall have the right of appeal to the annual session of the Provisional Annual Conference or the Mission.

SEC. II. **Investigation and Trial of a Deaconess**

¶ 966. When a deaconess is accused of any violation of a moral law, the district superintendent under whose supervision she works shall call a committee of three or more for investigation and preside at the investigation. This committee shall consist of one representative of the Commission on Deaconess Work and two or more members of the Annual Conference Deaconess Board of which the accused is a member. She shall appear before this committee, and, if charges are sustained, she shall be suspended from all deaconess services pending trial. This said district superintendent shall notify the bishop in charge, who within seven days of the receipt of such notice shall fix the time and date for the convening of the Trial Court. In this instance the Annual Conference Deaconess Board shall be the Trial Court. If the accused is found guilty, the Annual Conference Deaconess Board shall recommend to the Commission on Deaconess Work that she be suspended or deprived of office and credentials.

¶ 967. In case of improper temper, words, actions, or disloyalty to the rules and regulations of the administration or other organization with which she serves, the deaconess so offending shall be admonished by the president of the Annual Conference Deaconess Board. If she continues to offend, the case shall be investigated and tried as provided in ¶ 966.

¶ 968. If a deaconess shall contract debts which she is not able to pay, the president of the Annual Conference Deaconess Board shall appoint three judicious members of the Annual Conference Deaconess Board to consider her accounts, contracts, and circumstances. If, in their opinion, she has behaved dishonestly, or contracted debts without the probability of paying, the same procedure shall be followed as defined in ¶¶ 966-67.

Sec. III. Investigation and Trial of a Church Member

¶ 969. *Offenses for Which a Lay Member May Be Tried.*—A member shall be liable to accusation and trial upon any of the following charges:

a) Immorality or crime.

b) Disseminating doctrines contrary to the Articles of Religion or other established standards of doctrine of the church.

c) Disobedience to the order and discipline of the church.

d) Buying, selling, or manufacturing intoxicating liquor

277

as a beverage; renting his property for the manufacture or sale thereof; signing a petition in favor of granting a license for the sale thereof; procuring a license for the sale of such liquors; becoming surety on the bond of any person engaged in such traffic; or persisting in the use of intoxicating liquor after private reproof and admonition by the pastor or church lay leader.

¶ **970.** In cases of neglect of duties of any kind, indulging in sinful tempers or words, "taking such diversions as cannot be used in the name of the Lord Jesus," or disobedience to the order and discipline of the church, the pastor or church lay leader shall privately admonish a member; and if there is an acknowledgment of fault and proper repentance, the person may be borne with. Failing such, or on further offense, the pastor or lay leader may take with him one or two discreet members of the church and give further reproof. If the offense be continued, the member shall be brought to trial.

¶ **971.** If a member of the church shall be accused of endeavoring to sow dissension in the church by inveighing against its doctrines or discipline, its ministers or members, or in any other manner, he shall first be reproved by the pastor or church lay leader. If he shall persist in such practice, he shall be brought to trial.

¶ **972.** *Investigation.*—If charges are made in writing to the preacher in charge against a member of the church, the preacher in charge shall call a **Committee of Investigation** composed of seven members of the church in good standing, and shall preside at the investigation. The accused and the accuser shall be brought face to face if possible, and the accused shall have right of making a statement in his own behalf and of interrogating witnesses, but shall not have the right of presenting witnesses. If the Committee of Investigation determines that a trial is justified, it shall formulate the charges and specifications and order a trial.

¶ **973.** *Trial Court.*—If a member be brought to trial, it shall be before a **Trial Court** composed of not fewer than seven nor more than twelve members. They shall be chosen by the Quarterly Conference by ballot. The accused member and the person conducting the prosecution may each challenge anyone so chosen for cause of disqualification by reason of personal interest or having formed and expressed an opinion concerning the matter, and shall also have three peremptory challenges. If the pastor deem it advisable for obtaining a fair trial, the Quarterly Conference shall call a committee of like members from any part of the district. The same right of challenge shall be recognized. The district superintendent or a traveling elder appointed by him shall preside at the trial.

¶ **974.** *Penalties.*—If the accused shall be found guilty by the decision of at least two thirds of the Trial Court, they shall so declare, and the president of the Trial Court shall at once pronounce the member to be expelled from the church; *provided*, however, that the Trial Court may impose a lesser penalty because of mitigating circumstances or other grounds.

¶ **975.** *New Trial.*—If within sixty days after his conviction under the foregoing provisions the accused shall make application in writing to the district superintendent for a new trial on the ground of newly discovered evidence, and shall submit therewith a written statement of the same, and if it shall appear that such evidence is material to the issue involved, the district superintendent shall grant a new trial.

¶ **976.** In no case shall a new trial be granted upon newly discovered evidence which could have been obtained for the trial by the exercise of due diligence, or which is merely cumulative in its effect.

¶ **977.** *Restoration.*—An expelled member shall have no privileges of the society or of the Sacraments of the church without repentance, contrition, and satisfactory reformation according to the determination of the Quarterly Conference. In such case that body may restore the member into full membership.

SEC. IV. **Withdrawal Under Complaints or Charges**

¶ **981.** When a local preacher is accused of an offense under ¶ 921 and desires to withdraw from the church, the District Conference or, where there is no District Conference, the Quarterly Conference may permit him to withdraw; in which case the record shall be, "Withdrawn under complaints." If formal charges have been presented, he may be permitted to withdraw; in which case the record shall be, "Withdrawn under charges." In either case the status of the person withdrawn shall be the same as if expelled.

¶ 982. When a deaconess is accused of an offense and desires to withdraw from the church, the Annual Conference Deaconess Board may recommend to the Commission on Deaconess Work that she be permitted to withdraw, in which case the record shall be, "Withdrawn under complaints." If formal charges have been presented, such deaconess may be permitted to withdraw; in which case the record shall be, "Withdrawn under charges." In either case the status shall be the same as if the deaconess had been expelled.

¶ 983. When a member of the church is accused of an offense and desires to withdraw from the church, the Quarterly Conference may permit such member to withdraw; in which case the record shall be, "Withdrawn under complaints." If formal charges have been presented, such member may be permitted to withdraw; in which case the record shall be, "Withdrawn under charges." In either case the status shall be the same as if the member had been expelled.

Chapter IV

THE DEPRIVATION AND RESTORATION OF CREDENTIALS

Sec. I. Of the Credentials of Traveling Deacons or Elders

¶ 991. When a traveling deacon or elder is deprived of his credentials of ordination, by expulsion or otherwise, they shall be filed with the papers of his Annual Conference.

¶ 992. When a traveling deacon or elder desires to surrender his credentials and retain his membership in our church, he shall be permitted to do so, and to designate the local church in which he will hold membership. The secretary of the conference to which he surrenders his credentials shall issue to him a **certificate of membership** in the church; *provided* that no minister shall be permitted to take such action when charges involving his character have been made and sustained or are pending. When his character is involved in cases where the law permits final adjustment by the surrender of credentials, this shall be also the surrender of membership in the church.

¶ **993.** The Annual Conference to which credentials were surrendered as provided in ¶¶ 991-92 may restore the same at its discretion if no charges or complaints against the minister had been lodged or were impending at the time of his surrendering the said credentials; and if at the time of his request for the restoration of the said credentials he is a member in good standing of The Methodist Church and shall present from his Quarterly Conference a certificate of his character and a recommendation for the restoration of his credentials. In cases of surrender of credentials under situations involving the character of the minister the said credentials may be restored only after the lapse of a period of at least two years and upon the following conditions:

a) That the conference holding the credentials shall be assured that there has been a complete amendment of life upon the part of the former holder of the credentials.

b) That he shall have been readmitted on trial into the Annual Conference from which he withdrew or admitted to another Annual Conference on trial or been licensed as a local preacher by some District or Quarterly Conference.

c) That the Annual Conference which has admitted him on trial (if another than the one from which he withdrew) or the District or Quarterly Conference which licensed him shall present to the Annual Conference holding the credentials a certificate of his good character and a recommendation that his credentials be restored.[10]

SEC. II. **Of the Credentials of Local Deacons or Elders**

¶ **994.** When a local deacon or elder is deprived of his

---

[10] *See* Judicial Council Decisions 18, 104.

credentials of ordination, by expulsion or otherwise, the district superintendent shall require them of him, and file them with the Annual Conference in the bounds of which the local preacher resides.

¶ **995.** Should he later produce to the Annual Conference a recommendation from the District Conference for the restoration of his credentials, signed by its president and secretary, they may be restored to him.

Sec. III. **Of the Restoration of Lost Credentials**

¶ **996.** Should the credentials of any deacon or elder be destroyed or lost, the bishop who ordained him, or the bishop in whose territory he resides, upon ascertaining the necessary facts, may issue duplicate credentials.

Chapter V

GENERAL DIRECTIONS

Section I. Charges

¶ **1001.** No charge shall be entertained for any alleged offense which shall not have been committed within two years immediately preceding the filing of the complaint, except in cases where there is a conviction in a civil or criminal court, and in such cases the charges must be filed within one year after the entry of the final judgment.

¶ **1002.** A charge shall not allege more than one offense; several charges against the same person, however, with the specifications under each of them, may be presented at one and the same time and may be tried together. When several charges are tried at the same time, a vote on each specification and charge must be separately taken.

¶ **1003.** Amendments may be made to a bill of charges up to the time of the opening of the trial at the discretion of the presiding officer, *provided* they relate to the form of statement only and do not change the nature of the alleged offense and do not introduce new matter of which the accused has not had due notice.

¶ **1004.** In case of improper words, tempers, and actions, a charge of slander shall not be entertained unless signed by a person alleged to have been slandered.

¶ **1005.** Charges and specifications for the trial of a bishop, traveling preacher, local preacher, deaconess, or member shall define the offense by its generic term as set forth in ¶¶ 921 and 969 and shall state in substance the facts upon which said charges are based.

SEC. II.   **Counsel**

¶ **1006.** In all cases of trial the accused shall be entitled to appear and to be represented by counsel of his own selection and to be heard in oral or written argument. Such counsel shall be one traveling elder if the accused is a bishop or a traveling preacher, or one member in good standing in The Methodist Church if the accused is a lay member.

¶ **1007.** In all cases of trial where counsel has not been provided, such counsel shall be appointed by the presiding officer. The counsel for the church and for the accused each shall be entitled to one assistant counsel of his own choosing.[11]

SEC. III.   **Notice**

¶ **1008.** All notices required or provided for in this chapter shall be in writing, signed by or on behalf of the person or body giving or required to give such notice, and shall be addressed to the person or body to whom it is required to be given. Such notices shall be served at least seven days in advance by delivering a copy thereof to the party or chief officer of the body to whom it is addressed in person or by registered mail addressed to the last known residence or address of such party. The fact of the giving of the notice shall affirmatively appear over the signature of the party required to give such notice and become a part of the record of the case.

¶ **1009.** In all cases wherein it is provided that notice shall be given to a bishop or district superintendent and the charges or complaints are against that particular person, then such notice, in the case of a bishop,

---

[11] *See* Judicial Council Decision 116.

shall be given to another bishop within the same jurisdiction; in case of a district superintendent, to the bishop in charge.

Sec. IV.   Trials

¶ **1010.** In all cases of investigation or trial, notice to appear shall be given to such witnesses as either party may name, and shall be issued in the name of the church and be signed by the presiding officer of the trial court.

¶ **1011.** It shall be the duty of a minister or a member of the church to appear and testify when summoned.

¶ **1012.** As soon as the court has convened, the accused shall be called upon by the presiding officer to plead to the charge, and his pleas shall be duly recorded. On his neglect or refusal to plead, the plea of "not guilty" shall be entered for him, and the trial shall proceed; *provided* that for sufficient cause the court may adjourn from time to time as convenience or necessity may require; and *provided*, also, that the accused shall, at all times during the trial, have liberty to be present except as hereinafter mentioned and in due time and order to produce his testimony and to make his defense.

¶ **1013.** If in any case the accused person, after due notice (seven days) has been given him, shall refuse or neglect to appear at the time and place set forth for the hearing, the investigation or trial may proceed in his absence. In all cases, sufficient time shall be allowed for the person to appear at the given place and time, and for the accused to prepare for the investigation or trial. The president of the tribunal to investigate or try the case shall decide what constitutes "sufficient time."

¶ **1014.** The court shall be a continuing body until the final disposition of the charge. If any member of the court shall be unable to attend all of the sessions, he shall not vote upon the final determination of the case, but the rest of the court may proceed to judgment. It shall require a vote of two thirds or more of the original membership of the court to sustain the charges.

¶ **1015.** All objections to the regularity of the proceedings and the form and substance of charges and specifications shall be made at the first session of the trial. The presiding officer upon the filing of such objection shall, or on his own motion may, determine all such preliminary objection and may dismiss the case or in furtherance of truth and justice permit amendments to the specifications or charges not changing the general nature of the same.

¶ **1016.** Objections of any party to the proceedings shall be entered on the record.

¶ **1017.** No witness—afterward to be examined—shall be present during the examination of another witness if the opposing party objects. Witnesses shall be examined first by the party producing them, then cross-examined by the opposite party, after which any member of the court or either party may put additional questions. The presiding officer of the court shall determine all questions of relevancy and competency of evidence.

¶ **1018.** In case of investigation, trial, or appeal the presiding officer shall not deliver a charge reviewing or explaining the evidence or setting forth the merits of the case. He shall express no opinion on the law or the facts while the court is deliberating, unless the parties in interest be present. He shall remain and preside until the decision is rendered and the findings are completed, which he shall thereupon sign and certify.

Sec. V.   **Testimony**

¶ **1019.** The testimony shall be taken by a stenographer, if convenient, and reduced to writing and certified by the presiding officer and secretary. The record, including all exhibits, papers, and evidence in the case, shall be the basis of any appeal which may be taken.

¶ **1020.** A witness may not be disqualified because he is not a member of The Methodist Church.

¶ **1021.** The presiding officer of any court before which a case may be pending or the bishop in charge of an Annual Conference shall have power, whenever the necessity of the parties or of witnesses shall require, to appoint, on the application of either party, a commissioner or commissioners, either a minister or layman, or both, to examine the witnesses; *provided* that three days' notice of the time and place of taking such testimony shall have been given to the adverse party. Counsel for both parties shall be permitted to examine and cross-examine the witness or witnesses whose testimony is thus taken. The commissioners so appointed shall take such testimony in writing as may be offered by either party. The testimony properly certified by the signature of the commissioner or commissioners shall be transmitted to the presiding officer of the court before which the case is pending.

SEC. VI.   **Records**

¶ **1022.** In all investigations and trials the records shall be accurate and full; they shall include the proceedings in detail and all the evidence, taken stenographically if possible, the documents admitted, together with the charges, specifications, and findings, and shall be approved and attested by the presiding officer and secretary. In all investigations and trials the presiding officer shall appoint a secretary to keep a record of the proceedings and documents, of which records, when properly attested, the said presiding officer shall be the custodian. If no appeal is taken, the custodian shall deliver the entire record to the secretary of the conference concerned for record in its journal of the final disposition of the case.

¶ **1023.** If appeal be taken, the custodian shall deliver the entire record to the president of the proper appellate court, and after it has been used in the court it shall be returned to the secretary of the conference concerned for notation in its journal of the final disposition of the case.

¶ **1024.** The secretaries of Quarterly, District, Annual, and Jurisdictional Conferences shall be the custodians of the records of all trials occurring in their bodies respectively; and in case of appeal they shall deliver said records to the president or secretary of the proper appellate court. After the said appeal has been heard the records shall be returned to the conference from which they came.

Sec. VII.   **Appeals**

¶ **1025.** In all cases of appeal the appellant shall within thirty days give notice of appeal and at the same time shall furnish to the officer receiving such notice, and to the counsel for the church, a written statement of the grounds of his appeal, and the hearing in the appellate court shall be limited to the grounds set forth in such statement.[12]

¶ **1026.** When any appellate court shall reverse, in whole or in part, the findings of a trial court, or remand the case for a new trial, or change the penalty imposed by that court, it shall return to the Annual Conference or to the secretary of the trial court a statement of the grounds of its action.

¶ **1027.** An appeal shall not be allowed in any case in which the accused has failed or refused to be present in person or by counsel at his trial. Appeals, regularly taken, shall be heard by the proper appellate court, unless it shall appear to the said court that the appellant has forfeited his right to appeal by misconduct, such as refusal to abide by the findings of the committee of investigation or of the trial court; or by withdrawal from the church; or by failure to appear in person or by counsel to prosecute the appeal; or, prior to the final decision on appeal from his conviction, by resorting to suit in the civil courts against the complainant or any of the parties connected with the ecclesiastical court in which he was tried.[13]

¶ **1028.** The right of appeal, when once forfeited by neglect or otherwise, cannot be revived by any subsequent appellate court.

¶ **1029.** The right to take and to prosecute an appeal shall not be affected by the death of the person entitled to such right. His heirs or legal representatives may prosecute such appeal as he would be entitled to do if he were living.

¶ **1030.** The records and documents of the trial, including the evidence, and these only, shall be used in the hearing of any appeal, except as set forth in ¶¶ 947-49.

---

[12] *See* Judicial Council Decisions 3, 144.
[13] *See* Judicial Council Decision 3.

¶ **1031.** In no case shall an appeal operate as suspension of sentence. The finding of the trial court must stand until it is modified or reversed by the proper appellate court.

¶ **1032.** In all cases where an appeal is made, and admitted, by the appellate court, after the charges, findings, and evidence have been read and the arguments concluded, the parties shall withdraw, and the appellate court shall consider and decide the case. It may reverse, in whole or in part, the findings of the trial court, or it may remand the case for a new trial. It may determine what penalty, not higher than that affixed at the trial, may be imposed. If it neither reverses, in whole or in part, the judgment of the trial court, nor remands the case for a new trial, nor modifies the penalty, that judgment shall stand. The appellate court shall not reverse the judgment nor remand the case for a new trial on account of errors plainly not affecting the result.

¶ **1033.** In all cases the right to present evidence shall be exhausted when the case has been heard once on its merits in the proper court; but questions of law may be carried on appeal, step by step, to the Judicial Council.

¶ **1034.** The order of appeals on questions of law shall be as follows: From the decision of the district superintendent presiding in the Quarterly or District Conference to the bishop presiding in the Annual Conference, and from the decision of the bishop presiding in the Annual Conference to the Judicial Council; and from a Central Conference to the Judicial Council.

¶ **1035.** When an appeal is taken on a question of law, written notice of the same shall be served on the secretary of the body in which the decision has been rendered. It shall be his duty to see that an exact statement of the question submitted and the ruling of the chair thereon shall be entered on the journal. He shall then make and certify a copy of the question and ruling and transmit the same to the secretary of the body to which the appeal is taken. The secretary who thus receives said certified copy shall present the same in open conference and as soon as practicable lay it before the presiding officer for his ruling thereon; which ruling must be rendered before the final adjournment of that body, that said ruling together with the original question and ruling may be entered on the journal of that conference. The same course shall be followed in all subsequent appeals.

¶ **1036.** Errors or defects in judicial proceedings shall be duly considered when presented on appeal.

1. In regard to cases where there is an investigation under ¶¶ 931-35, but no trial is held as a result thereof, errors of law or administration committed by a district superintendent are to be corrected by the president of the next Annual Conference on request in open session, and in such event the conference may also order just and suitable remedies, if injury resulted from such errors.

2. Errors of law or defects in judicial proceedings which are discovered on appeal are to be corrected by the president of the next Annual Conference upon request in open session, and in such event the conference may also order just and suitable remedies, if injury has resulted from such errors.

SEC. VIII. **Appeal of a Bishop**

¶ **1041.** A bishop shall have the right of appeal to the Judicial Council in case of an adverse decision by the trial court; *provided* that within thirty days after his conviction he notify the secretary of the Jurisdictional Conference in writing of his intension to appeal, unless such decision shall be rendered within thirty days prior to the meeting of such conference, in which case notice shall be given within ten days after his conviction.

¶ **1042.** A bishop elected by a Central Conference shall have the right of appeal to the Judicial Council in case of an adverse decision by the Central Conference; *provided* that within thirty days after the decision of the Central Conference he shall notify the secretary of the Central Conference in writing of his intention to appeal unless such decision shall be rendered within thirty days prior to the meeting of such conference, in which case notice shall be given within ten days after his conviction.

¶ **1043.** It shall be the duty of the secretary of the Jurisdictional or the Central Conference, on receiving notice of such appeal, to notify the secretary of the

Judicial Council; and the council shall fix the time and place for the hearing of the appeal, and shall give due notice of the same to the appellant and to the secretary of the Jurisdictional or Central Conference, who in turn shall notify the counsel for the church.

SEC. IX.   Appeal of a Traveling Preacher

¶ 1045. Each Jurisdictional Conference, upon nomination of the College of Bishops, shall elect a **Court of Appeals** composed of nine traveling elders who have been at least six years successively members of The Methodist Church and an equal number of alternates. This court shall serve until its successors have been confirmed. This court shall have full power to hear and determine appeals of traveling preachers taken from any Annual Conference within the jurisdiction. The court shall elect its own president and secretary and shall adopt its own rules of procedure; and its decisions shall be final, except an appeal may be taken to the Judicial Council upon questions of law. (*See* ¶ 1033.)

¶ 1046. In case of conviction in a trial court, a traveling preacher shall have the right of appeal to the Jurisdictional Court of Appeals as above constituted; *provided* that within thirty days after his conviction he shall notify the president of the conference in writing of his intention to appeal.

¶ 1047. When notice of an appeal has been given to the president of the trial court, he shall give notice of the same to the secretary of the Court of Appeals of the Jurisdictional Conference and submit the documents in the case. The Jurisdictional Conference Court of Appeals shall give notice to the president of the conference from which the appeal is taken and to the appellant of the time and place where the appeal will be heard. Both the Annual Conference and the appellant may be represented by counsel. The president of the conference shall appoint counsel for the church.

¶ 1048. The Court of Appeals of the Jurisdictional Conference when acting as a court of appeals shall determine two questions only:

a) Does the evidence sustain the charge or charges?

b) Were there such errors of law as to vitiate the verdict?

These questions shall be determined by the records of the trial and the argument of counsel for the church and for the accused. The court shall in no case hear witnesses.

¶ 1049. All necessary traveling and sustenance expense incurred by the Court of Appeals, the counsel for the church, and the counsel for the defendant, in the hearing of an appeal case coming from an Annual Conference and appearing before any Jurisdictional Court of Appeals, shall be paid out of the administration fund of the Jurisdictional Conference in which the proceedings arise.

SEC. X.   **Appeal of a Local Preacher**

¶ 1051. In case of conviction, a local preacher shall be allowed to appeal to the Annual Conference; *provided* that within thirty days after his conviction he shall signify in writing to the superintendent of the district his determination to appeal.

¶ 1052. An appeal by a local preacher from a Quarterly Conference within the jurisdiction of a Mission shall be to the annual meeting of the said Mission.

SEC. XI.   **Appeal of a Deaconess**

¶ 1053. In case of conviction, a deaconess shall be allowed to appeal to the Commission on Deaconess Work; *provided* that within thirty days after her conviction she shall signify in writing to the district superintendent or president of the Annual Conference Deaconess Board by which she has been tried her determination to appeal to the Commission on Deaconess Work, which in full session, or by a special committee of not fewer than seven nor more than nine, shall hear the appeal; and its decision shall be the final determination of the case.

¶ 1054. An appeal by a deaconess from an Annual Conference Deaconess Board within the jurisdiction of a Provisional Annual Conference shall be to the Commission on Deaconess Work.

SEC. XII.   **Appeal of a Church Member**

¶ **1056.** The Quarterly Conference of each charge shall elect from among the members of the church a person of sound judgment and experience in the affairs of the church as a **trier of appeals for members.**

¶ **1057.** Any member of the church against whom judgment shall have been rendered by a Trial Court may appeal to a Court of Appeal, as hereinafter constituted, by giving written notice of his desire to the district superintendent within thirty days after judgment is rendered.

¶ **1058.** When thirty days' notice of appeal shall have been given, or sooner if agreed upon, the superintendent, having due regard for the wishes and rights of the appellant, shall convene a **Court of Appeal.** It shall be constituted of not fewer than seven nor more than nine triers of appeals in his district, but the trier of appeals of the charge to which the accused member belongs shall not be summoned. The district superintendent shall give not less than ten nor more than thirty days' notice to all persons concerned of the time and place at which the Court of Appeal shall assemble. The appellant shall have the right of challenge for cause of disqualification by reason of personal interest or other grounds deemed sufficient by the presiding officer, and he shall have the right of peremptory challenge of three of the panel summoned. The members of the court present and ready to proceed with the hearing shall not fall below seven, which number shall constitute a quorum. The district superintendent shall preside. The court may order a new trial or acquit the accused or impose any penalty prescribed in ¶ 974.

¶ **1059.** The findings of the Court of Appeal shall be certified by the district superintendent to the pastor of the church of which the accused is a member for consistent proceedings.

¶ **1060.** If the district superintendent shall find the convening of such a court to be impracticable or seriously inconvenient to the parties involved, he shall have the appeal heard by a Quarterly Conference within his district other than that of the local church. The proceedings shall be the same as provided in the foregoing paragraphs.

Sec. XIII. **Powers of Dismissal**

¶ **1065.** The various boards, committees, or commissions elected, authorized, or provided for by the General Conference shall have full power and authority to remove and dismiss in their discretion any member, officer, or employee thereof who shall be guilty of any immoral conduct or breach of trust, or who for any reason is unable to, or who fails to, perform the duties of his office, or for other misconduct which any of said boards, committees, or commissions may deem sufficient to warrant such dismissal and removal. In the event that any member, officer, or employee of such board, committee, or commission, including the Board of Publication, elected, authorized, or provided for by the General Conference, is found guilty of any crime involving moral turpitude by any federal, state, or county court or pleads guilty thereto, then and in that event, the board, committee, or commission of which he is a member, officer, or employee shall be and is hereby authorized to remove such officer, member, or employee so charged or convicted; and the place so vacated shall be filled as provided in the Discipline. The action of such board, committee, or commission in removing such member, officer, or employee in the circumstances above set forth shall be final; and such member, officer, or employee so removed shall have no further authority to participate in any way in the affairs of such board, committee, or commission.

Part VII

ADMINISTRATIVE AGENCIES

Chapter I

GENERAL PROVISIONS

¶ **1101.** If the membership of an agency is determined in part by the size of the church membership of the jurisdictions, the jurisdictional membership according to the latest official report preceding the General Conference, as shown in the General Minutes, shall be used to determine the size of the jurisdictional representation for the ensuing quadrennium. (*See* ¶ 528.)

¶ **1102.** No person other than a bishop shall serve at the same time on more than one agency, and no bishop shall serve at the same time on more than three agencies; *provided*, however, that this limitation shall not apply to a division of a board, to an interagency body, or to the Commission on Chaplains, the Methodist Committee for Overseas Relief, or the Commission on Camp Activities; and *provided*, further, that a bishop elected to the Council on World Service and Finance shall not serve on any other agency during his term on this council.

¶ **1103.** No person who receives compensation for services rendered or commissions of any kind from a board or other agency shall be eligible for voting membership on that board or agency.[1]

¶ **1104.** Tenure on any division, board, commission, or council, except the Council of Bishops and the Judicial Council, shall be limited to twelve consecutive years; *provided*, however, that this limitation shall take effect from

---

[1] *See* Judicial Council Decision 139.

the General Conference of 1952 and shall not be retro-active. To provide a continuing membership on these agencies, it is recommended that each nominating and electing body give special attention to rotation of its representatives.

¶ **1105.** Unless otherwise specified, vacancies on boards and other agencies occurring during the quadrennium shall be filled as follows: an episcopal vacancy shall be filled by the Council of Bishops; a vacancy in jurisdictional representation shall be filled by the College of Bishops of that jurisdiction; a vacancy in the membership at large shall be filled by the agency itself.

¶ **1106.** If a bishop is unable to attend a meeting of an agency of which he is a member, the Council of Bishops may name an alternate representative to attend that meeting with the privilege of vote.

¶ **1107.** An agency proposing to acquire real estate or erect a building or enter into a lease for a term in excess of five years (or with an option to extend or renew beyond such period or to purchase the property) to house its administrative activities or related operations in the continental United States shall present its plans in the formative stage to the Co-ordinating Council for approval. If the Co-ordinating Council disapproves, the agency shall delay the project until it can be considered by the next General Conference. *Provided*, however, that nothing in the foregoing shall include the operational requirements of the Board of Publication. (*See* ¶ 1113.6.)

¶ **1108.** An agency publishing or proposing to publish and circulate any magazine or periodical for promotional purposes shall secure the approval of the Co-ordinating Council. If the Co-ordinating Council disapproves, the agency shall delay such publication and circulation until its request can be submitted to the next General Conference for determination. *Provided*, however, that the foregoing shall not be deemed to apply to the periodicals exempted in ¶ 753.3, or to church-school curriculum materials. (*See* ¶ 1113.7.)

Note: For provisions regarding the finances of the administrative agencies *see* Part V, Chapter II, Church Finance, especially ¶¶ 737, 741-48, 765, 768, 781-84.

Chapter II

CO-ORDINATING COUNCIL

¶ **1111.** There shall be a **Co-ordinating Council,** responsible directly to the General Conference. It shall co-ordinate the work of the general administrative agencies of The Methodist Church. Its membership shall consist of one bishop, one minister, one lay man, and one lay woman from each jurisdiction, plus one minister and one lay person for each additional million members or major fraction thereof above the first million members in a jurisdiction, all nominated by the Council of Bishops and elected by the General Conference; and two additional persons appointed by the Council of Bishops from among members of the church overseas who are in the United States at the time of the meetings of the council; *provided* that the Council of Bishops shall replace the representatives of the church overseas when they leave the United States. The term of membership shall be four years. (*See* ¶ 1104.) Members shall serve until their successors are appointed or elected. Staff members of general agencies are not eligible to membership. (*See* ¶ 1102.) Vacancies which occur during the quadrennium shall be filled by the College of Bishops of the appropriate jurisdiction.

¶ **1112.** 1. The Co-ordinating Council shall elect a president, a vice-president, and a recording secretary, who shall keep a permanent record of its meetings and of any decisions reached. Certified copies of the minutes shall be filed with the secretary of the General Conference and with the Council on World Service and Finance.

2. It shall convene annually, and at such other times as are necessary on call of the president or on written request of one fifth of the members. Sixteen members shall constitute a quorum.

3. All decisions shall require a majority vote of the entire membership.

4. It may incur expense necessary to the performance of its functions, subject to such budgetary control as may be specified by the General Conference. Its annual expenses shall be paid from the General Administration Fund.

¶ **1113.** The Co-ordinating Council shall have the following responsibilities:

1. On request of a general board or other agency, or of an Annual Conference, it shall review questions involving overlapping in activity or lack of co-operation among or within general agencies, and shall make recommendations to the boards or agencies involved for resolving such issues; *provided* that in a review of any such question a bishop who is a member of an agency involved shall be disqualified. In the event of noncompliance, the recommendations shall be reported to the next General Conference. A record of all recommendations shall be kept, and a report of each shall be forwarded to the Council of Bishops, the Council on World Service and Finance, and the secretary of the General Conference.

2. It shall study the general organizational structure of The Methodist Church and recommend to the General Conference such changes as it considers essential to maintain effective and economical operation.

3. In consultation with the Council of Bishops and the Council of Secretaries it shall formulate and present to the General Conference, for its action and determination, plans for a unified, ongoing program for the church, including long-range objectives. The financial objectives shall be recommended by the Council on World Service and Finance to the General Conference for its action. In order to assure that such plans shall be effectively related to the life of the entire church, representatives of the Central Conferences shall participate in each phase of their development.

4. It shall recommend to the General Conference, after consultation with the Council of Bishops and the Council on World Service and Finance, the number and timing of all special days which are to be observed on a church-wide basis, except that the Council of Bishops and the Council on World Service and Finance may authorize a special financial appeal in an emergency.

5. It shall designate the agency which shall undertake any special study authorized by the General Conference when such agency has not been indicated by the General Conference.

6. It shall consider the plans of any general agency proposing to acquire real estate or erect a building or enter into a lease as described in ¶ 1107, and determine whether the proposed action is in the best interest of The Methodist Church. On the basis of that determination it shall approve or disapprove.

7. It shall consider the plans of any general agency to publish a promotional periodical, as provided in ¶ 1108.

¶ **1115.** There shall be an **Interagency Committee on Research,** organized as follows:

1. The Co-ordinating Council shall appoint one of its members as chairman of an organizing subcommittee, which shall consist of the director of the Department of Research and Statistics of the Council on World Service and Finance, the director of the Department of Research and Survey of the Division of National Missions of the Board of Missions, and two other persons, whom the above three shall name, one of whom shall be a professor engaged in social research in a Methodist school of theology.

2. The members of this subcommittee shall set the organizational meeting of the committee, and shall invite into membership with themselves persons engaged in research in the several agencies and schools of theology of The Methodist Church, and may in addition invite into membership non-agency research specialists up to a maximum of five persons.

3. The committee shall be convened by the representative of the Co-ordinating Council, and shall elect a chairman, vice-chairman, secretary, and such other officers as may be deemed necessary.

4. An annual written report of the committee shall be made to the Co-ordinating Council.

5. The necessary expense of the committee shall be subject to approval by the treasurer of, and be paid from, the General Administration Fund. The travel and other expenses of the members representing agencies and schools of theology shall be borne by the groups represented.

6. The committee shall meet annually for the purpose of: (*a*) establishing standards for conducting research; (*b*) reviewing and evaluating research projects in terms

of these standards; (c) serving in an advisory capacity to any general agency or official personnel on such matters as may properly come before such an interagency committee; (d) minimizing duplication and overlapping of research by two or more agencies.

7. The committee shall not itself conduct research projects but, if requested, may recommend appropriate agencies for specific research work.

CHAPTER III

COUNCIL ON WORLD SERVICE AND FINANCE

¶ **1116.** There shall be a **Council on World Service and Finance,** which shall be incorporated. Its members shall be elected quadrennially by the General Conference, as follows: two bishops, nominated by the Council of Bishops; two ministers and two lay persons from each jurisdiction, nominated by the bishops of that jurisdiction; and seven members at large, at least three of whom shall be women, nominated by the Council of Bishops without reference to jurisdictions. The members, including bishops (¶ 1102), shall not be eligible to membership on, or employment by, any other general agency except The Board of Trustees of The Methodist Church. They shall serve until their successors are elected and qualified. Vacancies occurring between sessions of the General Conference shall be filled by the council, on nomination of the bishops of the jurisdiction concerned or, in the event of a vacancy among the members at large, the Council of Bishops.

¶ **1117.** The officers of the Council on World Service and Finance shall be a president, a vice-president, a recording secretary, and a general secretary, who shall also be the treasurer of the council, all of whom shall be elected by the council. They shall serve until the adjournment of the next succeeding quadrennial session of the General Conference after their election and until their successors are duly elected and qualified. The president, vice-president, and recording secretary shall be elected from the membership of the council. The general secretary shall sit with the council and its executive committee at all sessions, and shall have right to the floor without the privilege of voting. (*See* ¶ 1103.) The employed personnel of the council shall be selected by and shall work under the direction of the general secretary.

¶ **1118.** The Council on World Service and Finance shall convene annually, and at such other times as are necessary on call of the president or on written request of one fifth of the members. Sixteen members shall constitute a quorum.

¶ **1119.** There shall be an executive committee of the Council on World Service and Finance consisting of the officers of the council and six members to be elected annually by the council. The executive committee shall meet on call of the president or of a majority of the membership thereof, and shall act for the council and exercise its powers in the interim of the meetings of the council; but it shall not take any action contrary to or in conflict with any action or policy of the council. A copy of the minutes of each meeting of the executive committee shall be sent from the central office to each member of the council as soon after the meeting as practicable.

¶ **1120.** The Council on World Service and Finance shall have the authority and responsibility to perform the following functions:

1. Receive and disburse, in accordance with budgets approved by the General Conference, or its properly authorized agency, the general funds of the church as set forth in ¶¶ 737-39.

2. Require each world service agency to follow uniform policies and practices in the employment and remuneration of personnel, recognizing differences in local employment conditions.

3. Establish titles for the employed executive staff of world service agencies, in the interest of uniformity and consistency. (*See* ¶ 783.)

4. Provide legal counsel where this is necessary in order to protect the interests of the church, and as the council deems advisable, at the request of a world service agency or of a bishop.

5. Maintain and supervise, under the direction of its general secretary, a **Department of Research and Statistics.** It shall be the duty of this department to: (a) prepare the important statistics relating to The Methodist Church for the General Minutes, the Fact Book, and such other publications and releases as may be authorized by the council; (b) initiate, on approval of the council or its executive committee, such research as may be deemed essential, provided due care is taken not to duplicate similar research being made by other general agencies; (c) analyze, interpret, and evaluate the facts gathered through research, making them available to the general agencies; (d) maintain a research library and an index, including a listing and cataloging of the past and current research made by or for the several agencies of the church; (e) maintain a roster of competent research persons who may be employed to do special research projects; (f) co-operate with specialized research personnel associated with other agencies of the church (see ¶ 1115). The services of the department shall be available to any other official agency of the church. The expense of the department, including the printing of the General Minutes and other approved publications, shall be borne by the General Administration Fund; *provided*, however, that where the research requested by an agency requires the employment of temporary additional staff, postage, supplies, or other necessary expense, an agreement as to the payment of this additional cost shall be entered into with the council before the research is undertaken. The number and qualifications of the regular employed staff shall be determined by the council.

6. Prepare and edit all official statistical blanks, record forms, and record books required for use in The Methodist Church, except official records for use in the local church school and forms used by the Woman's Division of Christian Service. In the preparation of these forms it shall consult with a committee appointed by the Council of Bishops from that body and with representatives of The Methodist Publishing House and of the general boards whose programs are directly involved. All

official statistical blanks, record forms, and record books required for use in The Methodist Church shall be printed and published by The Methodist Publishing House.

7. Maintain and supervise, under the direction of its general secretary, a department known as the **Transportation Office.** This department shall represent the church in its relation with the responsible persons or concerns operating the several modes of public transportation. The purchase of tickets and the securing of space reservations for travel shall be placed as nearly as possible on a self supporting basis. The costs of the Transportation Office shall be a charge against the General Administration Fund.

8. Operate, under the supervision of its general secretary, a department known as the **File of Pastors and Church Officials.** It shall be the function of this department to maintain an accurate record of the mail addresses of all bishops, ministers in the effective relation, supply pastors, including retired ministers serving charges, and conference lay leaders, and such lists of general, jurisdictional, conference, and district boards, commissions, and committees, and of officers of the same, and of local-church commission chairmen, as may be deemed necessary. The cost of maintaining such a service shall be a charge against the General Administration Fund. The general secretary is authorized and directed to make equitable charges for its use by various bodies. No use of the file shall be permitted for other than authorized bodies or officers of The Methodist Church.

9. Operate, under the supervision of its general secretary, a department known as the **Shipping and Service Department.** It shall be the function of this department to maintain such addressing, packaging, mailing, and duplicating service as may be deemed necessary to provide these services for the general agencies. The general secretary shall co-operate with the general secretary of the Commission on Promotion and Cultivation in scheduling the general mailings to pastors, in the interest of proper spacing. The general secretary is authorized and directed to make equitable charges to the agencies using these services.

Chapter IV

THE METHODIST PUBLISHING HOUSE

Section I. **Objects and Organization**

¶ **1121. The Methodist Publishing House** comprises the publishing interests of The Methodist Church.

¶ **1122.** The objects of The Methodist Publishing House shall be: the advancement of the cause of Christianity by disseminating religious knowledge and useful literary and scientific information in the form of books, tracts, and periodicals; the promotion of Christian education; the transaction of any and all business properly connected with the publishing, manufacturing, and distribution of books, tracts, periodicals, materials, and supplies for churches and church schools; and such other business as the General Conference may authorize and direct.

¶ **1123.** The Methodist Publishing House shall be under the direction and control of the **Board of Publication,** acting through an executive officer elected by the board, who shall be the **publisher of The Methodist Church,** and such other officers as the board may determine.

¶ **1124.** The net income from the operations of The Methodist Publishing House, after providing adequate reserves for the efficient operation of the business and allowing for reasonable growth and expansion, shall be appropriated by the Board of Publication and distributed annually to the several Annual Conferences for the persons who are and shall be conference claimants.

¶ **1125.** The net income from the operations of The Methodist Publishing House shall be appropriated to no other purpose than its own operating requirements and the conference claimants, as provided in ¶ 9.5 and ¶ 1124.

¶ **1126.** The members of the Board of Publication, and their successors in office, are declared to be the successors of the incorporators named in the charters of The Methodist Book Concern issued by the states of New York and Ohio, and in the charter of The Board of Publication of The Methodist Protestant Church issued by the state of Pennsylvania. The executive officer elected from time to time under this or any subsequent Discipline is declared to be the successor in office of the Book Agents of the Methodist Episcopal Church, South, named in the charter issued to the corporation of that name by the state of Tennessee.

¶ **1127.** Subject to the provisions of ¶ 1123, and to the continuing control and direction of the General Conference of The Methodist Church as set forth from time to time in the Discipline, the Board of Publication is authorized, empowered, and directed to cause the operations of The Methodist Publishing House to be carried on, and the objects defined in ¶ 1122 to be achieved, in such manner, through or by means of such agencies or instrumentalities, and by use of such procedures as the board may from time to time determine to be necessary, advisable, or appropriate, with full power and authority in the premises to take all such action and to do all such other acts and things as may be required or found to be advisable. In particular, and without limiting the generality of the foregoing, the board is authorized and empowered, for the purposes of this chapter:

1. To use, manage, operate, and otherwise utilize all property and assets of every kind, character, and description of four corporations—namely, The Methodist Book Concern, a corporation existing under the laws of the state of New York; The Methodist Book Concern, a corporation existing under the laws of the state of Ohio; The Board of Publication of The Methodist Protestant Church, a corporation existing under the laws of the state of Pennsylvania; and Book Agents of the Methodist Episcopal Church, South, a corporation existing under the laws of the state of Tennessee—as well as all income from such property and assets and the avails thereof, all with liability or obligation to account for such property and assets, the use thereof, the income therefrom, and avails thereof, only to the General Conference of The Methodist Church or as it shall direct.

2. To cause each of the said corporations to take all such action and to do all such things as the board may deem necessary or advisable to carry out the intent and purposes of this ¶ 1127. The governing body of each of the said corporations from time to time shall take all

action which the board deems to be necessary or advisable to carry out the intent and purposes of this ¶ 1127. The board shall cause all legal obligations of said four corporations, now existing or hereafter incurred, to be met, fulfilled, and performed.

3. To continue to exercise the powers and administer the duties and responsibilities conferred on it as an agency of The Methodist Church through the corporation named **Board of Publication of The Methodist Church,** incorporated under the laws of the state of Illinois in accord with authority delegated to it by the General Conference of 1952, or through such other means and agencies as it may from time to time determine to be expedient and necessary in order to give full effect to the purposes expressed in this chapter.

¶ 1128. 1. Under the corporate structure of Board of Publication of The Methodist Church, incorporated in the state of Illinois, and subject to the provisions of the preceding paragraphs of this chapter, the board is authorized and empowered to conduct its general operations under the name of The Methodist Publishing House.

2. The property, assets, and income of the said Illinois corporation shall be held by it, under the direction of the board, as an agency of The Methodist Church and shall at all times be subject to the control and direction of the General Conference of The Methodist Church as set forth from time to time in the Discipline.

3. In carrying out and executing its operations and functions, the Illinois corporation shall be entitled to hold, use, manage, operate, and otherwise utilize all property and assets of every kind, character, and description of each of the four corporations identified in ¶ 1127.1 (other than its corporate powers and franchises) and all income therefrom, and avails thereof, for the purposes and objects defined in this chapter.

4. The governing body of each of the five existing corporations under the direction of the board shall from time to time take all such action as the board deems necessary or advisable to carry out the intent and purposes of this paragraph and chapter.

5. The Illinois corporation shall be liable for and shall

execute and satisfy all legal obligations of each of the four corporations named in ¶ 1127.1, but neither it nor the board shall have or be under any obligation to account for principal and income to any such other corporation or to otherwise report to any of them; *provided*, however, that the Illinois corporation shall return to each of the other four corporations custody and control of its real property and account to it for the net amount of any other assets received from such other corporation if and when such return or accounting shall be directed or required by the board or by any General Conference of The Methodist Church.

SEC. II.　　　　**Board of Publication**

¶ 1129. The Board of Publication shall consist of forty-five members, including two bishops selected by the Council of Bishops. The remaining members shall be elected by the Jurisdictional Conferences on a ratio which will provide for an equitable distribution among the various jurisdictions, based on the memberships thereof; *provided* that no jurisdiction shall be represented by fewer than two members. Membership on the board shall be equally divided, as far as practicable, between ministers and laymen. It shall be the duty of the secretary of the General Conference to inform the various jurisdictional secretaries of the number of members to be elected from their jurisdictions, the ratio of such representation being computed on the basis of the latest official membership statistics available. The tenure of office of any member shall be limited to twelve years. In the first election, as nearly as may be, one third of the members from each jurisdiction shall be elected for only four years, one third for eight years, and one third for twelve years, the Jurisdictional Conference determining the tenure of office of each member elected. In case a vacancy occurs between sessions of the Jurisdictional Conference for any cause, the board shall fill the vacancy, for the unexpired term, from that jurisdiction in the representation of which the vacancy occurs. The president of Board of Publication of The Methodist Church, Incorporated, shall be an ex officio member of the board, without vote.

¶ **1130.** The board shall meet annually. The place and time of all meetings shall be designated by the board; but if it fails to do so, then the time and place shall be designated by the chairman. Special meetings may be called by the chairman on his own initiative or by the board. Special meetings shall also be called by the chairman on written request of one third of the members of the board. At all meetings of the board a majority of the members shall constitute a quorum.

¶ **1131.** The board shall keep a correct record of its proceedings and shall examine carefully into the affairs of The Methodist Publishing House and make written report thereof to the church through the General Conference.

¶ **1132.** The board shall fix the salaries of the following officers: president (publisher), book editor, editors of the official church papers, editor of church-school publications, and other salaried officers provided for by this chapter.

¶ **1133.** The board, at its discretion, may continue the publication of the quarterly *Religion in Life*, with the book editor responsible for its editorial content.

¶ **1134.** The members of the board and all officers elected by it shall hold office until their successors are chosen.

¶ **1135.** The board shall elect from its membership an **executive committee,** of sixteen members, including the chairman, vice chairman, and secretary of the board, who shall serve respectively as chairman, vice chairman, and secretary of the executive committee. Not more than four members of the executive committee shall be from any one jurisdiction. In addition, the president shall be an ex officio member without vote. Any vacancy occurring in the membership of the executive committee shall be filled by it, subject to confirmation by the board at its next meeting.

¶ **1136.** The executive committee shall have and may exercise all the powers of the board except those expressly reserved for board action by the Discipline or by the corporate charter and by-laws. It shall meet quarterly to examine the affairs under its charge and shall keep and submit to the board correct records of its proceedings. Special meetings may be called by the chairman on his own initiative, and shall be called on the written request of five members of the executive committee. A majority of the members shall constitute a quorum.

Sec. III.   **Executives**

¶ **1137.** Officers of each corporation under the direction of the board shall be elected annually in accordance with its charter and by-laws.

¶ **1138.** The executive officer elected pursuant to ¶ 1123 shall also be elected the **president** of each corporation under the direction of the board.

¶ **1139.** The board shall require written quarterly reports to the executive commitee covering the current condition and operating status of the business.

¶ **1140.** The president (publisher) and the board shall have authority to extend the business of The Methodist Publishing House in such manner as they may judge to be for the best interests of the church.

¶ **1141.** The board shall require the president and other corporate executive officers to give bond conditioned on the faithful discharge of their respective duties. It also shall authorize the execution of a blanket bond covering all staff personnel whose responsibilities justify such coverage. The amount of the bonds shall be fixed by the board, and the bonds shall be subject to the approval of the board. The premiums shall be paid by the board, and the chairman of the board shall be the custodian of the bonds.

¶ **1142.** The board shall have power to suspend, after hearing, and to remove, after hearing, the president or any of the officers created by this chapter, for misconduct or failure to perform the duties of their office.

Sec. IV.   **Book Editor**

¶ **1143.** The board shall elect quadrennially a **book editor,** who shall have joint responsibility with the publisher for approving manuscripts considered for publication. He shall edit all the books of our publication, and the quarterly *Religion in Life*. In the case of materials authorized by the Curriculum Committee in the field of

Christian education which are to be edited by the editor of church-school publications he shall collaborate with that editor whenever such collaboration is necessary or desired. He shall perform such other editorial duties as may be required of him by the board. He shall not have responsibility for materials issued by other boards and agencies of the church for program or promotional purposes.

SEC. V.   **General Church Periodicals**

¶ **1144.** 1. The board is authorized to publish a periodical for pastors, and a periodical for the family which shall be a general magazine informative and vital to the religious life of all Methodists. The board may, at its discretion, issue such editions of the official periodicals as in its judgment may be deemed advisable.

2. The board shall elect quadrennially the **editors** of these general church periodicals and shall define their general responsibilities.

3. There shall be published *Central Christian Advocate,* for service in the Central Jurisdiction. Its **editor** shall be elected quadrennially from the Central Jurisdiction by the Board of Publication.

4. All other details relating to the publishing and distribution of these periodicals, not specifically delegated to the editors, shall be under the direction of the publisher.

5. The board shall have power to suspend or remove, after hearing, any editor or associate editor for misconduct or failure to perform the duties of his office.

SEC. VI.   **Church-School Publications**

¶ **1145.** There shall be an **editor of church-school publications,** elected as set forth in ¶ 1429.

¶ **1146.** The editor of church-school publications shall be responsible for the preparation of all curriculum materials, as set forth in ¶ 1431.

¶ **1147.** The curriculum of the church school shall be determined by the Curriculum Committee, which shall include in its membership the editor of church-school publications, the book editor, and the publisher, as set forth in ¶ 1433.

¶ **1148.** The Board of Publication shall fix and pay the salaries of the editor of church-school publications and his assistants and shall have full financial responsibility for all other expenses connected with his work.

¶ **1149.** The publications of the General Board of Education shall be manufactured, published, and distributed through The Methodist Publishing House. In matters involving financial responsibility the final determination in every case shall lie with the Board of Publication. After consultation with the publisher, the editor of church-school publications shall prepare a complete budget for his work, including salaries of assistants and office secretaries, and travel, to be effective when approved by the Board of Publication, and shall direct its operation from year to year.

¶ **1150.** There shall be one complete co-ordinated system of literature published by The Methodist Publishing House for the entire Methodist Church. This literature is to be of such type and variety as to meet the needs of all groups of our people.

¶ **1151.** The Board of Publication and the publisher shall have authority to decline to publish any item of literature when in their judgment the cost would be greater than should be borne by The Methodist Publishing House.

¶ **1152.** The editor of church-school publications and the chairman of the Editorial Division of the General Board of Education shall have the right to sit with the Board of Publication for the consideration of matters pertaining to the joint interests of the Board of Publication and the Board of Education and shall have the privilege of the floor, without vote. (*See also* ¶ 1436.)

¶ **1153.** The provisions of this section shall not apply to the promotional materials of the Division of Higher Education or of the Division of the Local Church.

Sec. VII.   **Printing for Church Agencies**

¶ **1154.** It is recommended that the general agencies and institutions of The Methodist Church have all their printing done by The Methodist Publishing House.

¶ **1155.** All official statistical blanks, record forms, and record books required for use in The Methodist Church shall be printed and published by The Methodist Publishing House. (*See* ¶ 1120.6.)

SEC. VIII. Real Estate and Buildings

¶ **1156.** The Methodist Publishing House shall not buy, sell, or exchange any real estate except by order of the General Conference, or, between sessions of the General Conference, by a two-thirds vote of all the members of the Board of Publication; nor shall the board authorize any new buildings or make any improvements, alterations, or repairs to existing buildings to cost in excess of $100,000, except by order of the General Conference, or, between sessions of the General Conference, by a two-thirds vote of all members of the board. In either case, such vote shall be taken at a regular or called meeting of the board; and, if at a called meeting, the purpose of this meeting shall have been stated in the call. (*See* ¶¶ 1107, 1113.6 for additional requirements and restrictions.)

¶ **1157.** The erection of a new building, or the improvement, alteration, or repair of an existing building, involving an expenditure of not more than $100,000, may be authorized by the vote of a majority of the executive committee. These provisions shall not prevent the making of investments on mortgage security or the protection of the same, or the collection of claims and adjustments. (*See* ¶¶ 1107, 1113.6, 1156 for additional requirements and restrictions.)

SEC. IX. Annual Conference Committee

¶ **1158.** 1. There shall be organized in each Annual Conference a **Conference Committee on Publishing Interests,** consisting of no fewer than three nor more than five members at large. The resident bishop and the conference or area director of public relations and Methodist information shall be members ex officio. There may also be one additional person from each district, to be designated **district secretary of publishing interests.**

2. The committee shall meet at least once before or during every regular conference session, and shall act in

co-operation with the Board of Publication in promoting the work of the board within the bounds of the conference.

CHAPTER V

INTERBOARD COMMISSION ON THE LOCAL CHURCH

¶ **1160.** There shall be an **Interboard Commission on the Local Church,** whose function shall be to act as the co-ordinator of the policies and activities of its boards, namely: the Board of Missions through the Joint Section of Education and Cultivation and the Division of National Missions, the Board of Education and its divisions, the Board of Evangelism, the Board of Lay Activities, the Board of Christian Social Concerns and its divisions, and any other general agency for which the General Conference may hereafter provide a mandatory commission in the local church.

¶ **1161.** The commission shall be composed of three members elected by each board from its executive committee.

¶ **1162.** The commission, in carrying out its function of co-ordinating the work of the boards which it represents, shall see that plans and programs relating to the local church and to higher education do not overlap or duplicate in activity and literature.

¶ **1163.** Implementing the work of the commission there shall be a **secretarial council** consisting of the general secretaries of the Joint Section of Education and Cultivation, the Division of National Missions, the Board of Education and its divisions, the Board of Evangelism, the Board of Lay Activities, and the Board of Christian Social Concerns and its divisions. It shall be the function of this council to facilitate co-operation among the boards in the creative planning of programs and in avoiding overlapping of function or duplication of activity. The chairmanship of the secretarial council shall rotate annually among the several secretaries.

¶ **1164.** 1. The commission shall set up an **Interboard**

Committee on Ministry to Neglected Areas, composed of at least one representative each from the Division of National Missions and the Woman's Division of Christian Service of the Board of Missions, the Division of the Local Church of the Board of Education, the Board of Lay Activities, and the Board of Evangelism. Under the direction of the commission it shall study neglected metropolitan and rural areas and shall develop and recommend plans for (*a*) organizing new churches and church schools, (*b*) organizing and seeking support for mission churches and missions, (*c*) reviving and supporting dying and abandoned churches, (*d*) enlisting local churches and lay men and women in support of the foregoing activities with their means and services, and (*e*) taking other steps deemed appropriate to provide for ministry to such neglected areas and peoples.

2. When in the judgment of the commission such action would facilitate co-ordination among its boards, it may authorize other interboard committees and joint staff committees.

¶ **1165.** Any question of overlapping or duplication among the constituent boards which cannot be resolved by the commission, or any overlapping of function or duplication of activity between one of the constituent boards and another agency of The Methodist Church, shall be referred to the Co-ordinating Council. (*See* ¶ 1113.1.)

CHAPTER VI
BOARD OF MISSIONS

SECTION I. The Aim of Missions

¶ **1166.** The supreme aim of missions is to make the Lord Jesus Christ known to all peoples in all lands as their divine Saviour, to persuade them to become his disciples, and to gather these disciples into Christian churches; to enlist them in the building of the Kingdom of God; to co-operate with these churches; to promote world Christian fellowship; and to bring to bear on all human life the spirit and principles of Christ.

SEC. II.   **Incorporation**

¶ **1167.** There shall be an incorporated **Board of Missions** of The Methodist Church, hereinafter called the board. It shall conduct its operations through three administrative divisions, each of which shall be incorporated. The board and its divisions shall be incorporated in such state or states as the board may select. Subject to the limitations hereinafter specified, each of the incorporated divisions shall be subject to the supervision and control of the board, and shall be under the direction and control of the General Conference of The Methodist Church in all things not inconsistent with the constitution and laws of the United States and of the states of incorporation.

¶ **1168.** The board shall have control of all the work formerly controlled and administered by the following: the Board of Missions and Church Extension of The Methodist Church; the Missionary Society, the Board of Foreign Missions, the Board of Home Missions and Church Extension, the Woman's Foreign Missionary Society, the Woman's Home Missionary Society, the Wesleyan Service Guild, and the Ladies' Aid Societies of the Methodist Episcopal Church; the Board of Missions, including the Woman's Missionary Society, the Woman's Board of Foreign Missions, the Woman's Board of Home Missions, and the Woman's Missionary Council, and the Board of Church Extension[2] of the Methodist Episcopal Church, South; and the Board of Missions of the Methodist Protestant Church, and such other corporations or agencies of the General Conference as do similar work; but this list shall not be construed as exclusive.

SEC. III.   **Constitution**

¶ **1169.** *Article* 1. *Name and Object.*—The name of this organization shall be the Board of Missions of The Methodist Church. Its objects are religious, philanthropic, and educational, designed to diffuse more generally the blessings of Christianity in every part of the world, by the promotion and support of all phases of missionary

---

[2] *See* Judicial Council Decision 99.

and church-extension activity in the United States and other countries; to promote missionary intelligence, interest, and zeal throughout The Methodist Church; and to aid in Christianizing personal life and the social order in all lands and among all peoples. Other agencies of The Methodist Church shall conduct work in foreign fields only with the consent of and in co-operation with the Board of Missions.

¶ 1170. *Art. 2. Authority.*—The board shall have authority to regulate its own proceedings in accordance with its constitution and charter; to buy, acquire, receive by gift, devise, or bequest, property, real, personal, and mixed, and to hold, sell, and dispose of property; to secure, appropriate, and administer funds for its work; to sue and be sued; to elect the necessary officers and members of its staff, remove them for cause, and fill vacancies; to make by-laws in harmony with the Discipline of The Methodist Church and the charter of the board; and to administer its affairs through its respective divisions; and shall be clothed with the power and shall have the right to do any and all things which shall be authorized by its charter.

¶ 1171. *Art. 3. Board of Managers.*—The management and disposition of the affairs of the board, the making and administration of appropriations, and all other activities shall be vested in a **Board of Managers.**

¶ 1172. The Board of Managers shall be composed as follows:

1. One half of the eligible effective bishops of The Methodist Church resident in the United States, elected by the Council of Bishops; and in addition six bishops serving overseas, designated by the Council of Bishops, who shall have the status of members of the board in meetings which they may be able to attend, subject to such travel regulations as are provided in the Discipline for overseas bishops.

2. Members elected quadrennially by the Jurisdictional Conferences as follows: one minister and three lay members, two of whom shall be women, from each jurisdiction for each 600,000 members, or major fraction thereof, in

the jurisdiction; *provided* that no jurisdiction, in addition to the bishops, shall have fewer than two ministers and six lay members, four of whom shall be women and two men. In nominating and electing such members, the Jurisdictional Conference shall have as a basis for choice the following: (*a*) one minister and one lay man designated by each Annual Conference of the jurisdiction, on nomination of its Conference Board of Missions; (*b*) six additional names nominated by the College of Bishops of the jurisdiction; (*c*) twice the necessary number of lay women, designated by the Jurisdiction Woman's Society of Christian Service from three members nominated by each Conference Woman's Society of Christian Service of the jurisdiction. Vacancies among these members shall be filled by the bishops of the jurisdiction in which the vacancies occur *ad interim*, having regard to the various classifications of members.

3. Twenty-eight lay men, at least four from each jurisdiction, elected quadrennially by the board on nomination of the Council of Bishops, to serve as members at large of the board, and to be assigned equally to the Divisions of World Missions and of National Missions.

4. Twelve women, two from each jurisdiction, elected quadrennially by the board on nomination of the Woman's Division of Christian Service, to serve as members at large of the board and of this division.

5. Six young people—four representing the Methodist Youth Fellowship, one of whom shall be the chairman of Christian outreach of the National Conference thereof, and two representing the Methodist Student Movement, one of whom shall be the national chairman of the Commission on World Missions of the Church—elected quadrennially by the board on nomination of the Joint Staff on Youth and Student Work, which shall have selected the nominees as provided in ¶ 1405.2. Vacancies among these members shall be filled by the board on nomination of the joint staff.

¶ **1173.** The term of office of all members whose election is provided for in ¶ 1172 shall begin, and the board shall organize, at a meeting to be held within ninety days after the adjournment of the last meeting of the several Jurisdictional Conferences held after the adjournment of the General Conference.

¶ **1174.** The board shall elect quadrennially a president, who shall be the presiding officer, four vice-presidents (the nominees being the presidents of the three divisions and the Joint Section of Education and Cultivation), a recording secretary, and such other officers as it may need. Their duties shall be those usually performed by such officers. The board shall elect quadrennially such standing committees as may be necessary to carry on its regular business. It may from time to time elect other committees as may be needed for special business.

¶ **1175.** The board shall elect quadrennially, on nomination of the respective divisions, a **general executive committee** of thirty-eight members: nine from the Division of World Missions, two of whom shall be women; nine from the Division of National Missions, two of whom shall be women; nine women from the Woman's Division of Christian Service; five women and five men from the Joint Section of Education and Cultivation; and the president of the board, who shall be chairman. A majority of the members shall constitute a quorum. This general executive committee shall exercise the powers of the board *ad interim.*

¶ **1176.** *Art. 4. Duties.*—The duties of the board shall be:

1. Consistent with its constitution and charter, to establish, develop, expand, and have general oversight of the missionary and church-extension programs of The Methodist Church in home and foreign fields.

2. To determine the broad lines of policy and program, and, through the respective divisions, to carry out the program.

3. To safeguard for each division the fullest measure of autonomy consistent with presenting a united front and a mutually supporting program.

4. To provide for and foster the correlation and harmonization of the work of its various units.

5. On recommendation of the divisions, to determine fields to be occupied and the nature of the work to be undertaken; to secure, appropriate, and expend money

for the support of all work under its care; to build and maintain churches, hospitals, homes, schools, parsonages, and other institutions of Christian service; and to enlist, train, and support the workers.

6. To elect, on nomination of the divisions, the staff of the respective divisions.

7. To receive and properly administer all properties and trust funds coming into the possession of the board as a board for missionary or other purposes, except as hereinafter provided.

8. To assist in the organization of and in the maintenance of co-operative relations with the boards, committees, and other agencies of the General Conference; also with the Jurisdictional, Central, and Annual Conference boards, committees, and agencies; likewise with interdenominational and other missionary agencies in the home and foreign fields.

9. To make a report of its activities during the quadrennium to the General Conference and the Jurisdictional Conferences.

¶ **1178.** *Art.* 5. *Divisions.*—1. The board shall conduct its activities through three administrative divisions—namely, a Division of World Missions, a Division of National Missions, and a Woman's Division of Christian Service—and a Joint Section of Education and Cultivation.

2. In contituting the membership of its divisions the board may elect from the membership of the Divisions of World Missions and National Missions, respectively, to the Woman's Division of Christian Service a number not to exceed the number of members which the Woman's Division of Christian Service has on the Division of World Missions and the Division of National Missions. (*See* ¶¶ 1195, 1210, 1240.3.)

¶ **1179.** *Art.* 6. *General Secretaries.*—1. The board shall elect quadrennially, on nomination of the respective divisions and joint section, one or more **general secretaries** for each of the three administrative divisions and two general secretaries, one man and one woman, for the Joint Section of Education and Cultivation.

2. The general secretaries shall be subject to the direc-

tion of the board and of their respective divisions and joint section. On recommendation of the divisions and joint section their salaries shall be fixed and paid as the board may determine. They shall be employed exclusively in the work of the board, promoting its activities as the board may approve.

3. One general secretary from each of the three administrative divisions and two general secretaries from the Joint Section of Education and Cultivation shall be members of the board and of their respective divisions and joint section, but without vote. (*See* ¶ 1103.)

¶ **1180.** *Art.* 7. *Treasurers.*—1. The board shall elect quadrennially a **treasurer** of the board, to be chosen from the treasurers of the three administrative divisions. He shall receive and handle general funds of the board not belonging to any one division and shall act as the legal financial representative of the board in matters affecting the board as a whole. It may also elect one or more assistant treasurers.

2. The treasurer of the board and the treasurers of the divisions shall be responsible for receiving the funds of the board and of the respective divisions, holding the same in a safe depository and disbursing them according to the regulation of the board or the respective divisions on proper order. The board, the divisions, and the joint section shall designate depositories for their funds. The treasurers shall also be charged with the responsibility of receiving all trust funds, endowments, and securities of the board and of the respective divisions and properly disbursing the returns therefrom according to the regulations of the board and the respective divisions, and shall further be responsible, under the direction of finance committees, for the investing of said trust funds, endowments, and other permanent funds, excepting such funds as shall be available for loans to churches to be administered by the Section of Church Extension.

3. The treasurers, associate and assistant treasurers, and all employees of the board, the divisions, and the joint section handling cash and securities shall be bonded by the employing board, division, or joint section in such sum and on such conditions as it may determine.

Their books shall be audited at least annually by certified public accountants chosen by the employing board, division, or joint section; and the reports of the treasurers and auditors shall be presented to the board at each annual meeting.

¶ **1181.** *Art.* 8. *Other Staff.*—1. The board shall elect, on nomination of the respective divisions and joint section, such other staff as the need may require.

2. All elected staff members shall be subject to the direction of the board and of their respective divisions and joint section. On recommendation of the divisions and joint section their salaries shall be fixed and paid as the board may determine.

¶ **1182.** *Art.* 9. *Retirement.*—All elected staff members shall retire on reaching the retirement age fixed by the board's pension plan.

¶ **1183.** *Art.* 10. *Financial Policies.*—1. All properties, trust funds, permanent funds, and other special funds and endowments now held and administered by the several organizations merging into the Board of Missions shall be carefully safeguarded and administered in the interest of those persons and causes for which said funds were established; *provided* that the properties, trust funds, and permanent and endowment funds shall be transferred to the Board of Missions or its respective divisions from merging boards and societies and departments of such boards and societies only when such transfers may be made in accordance with the laws of the states where the several boards and societies are chartered and on the recommendation of the respective divisions and on the approval of such boards and societies. Funds of the three administrative divisions, and their preceding corporations and societies, which are subject to appropriation shall be appropriated only on recommendation of the respective divisions and for the work for which the respective divisions are responsible.

2. The income of the divisions of the board, exclusive of the Woman's Division of Christian Service (*see* ¶ 1250), shall be derived from apportionments, assessments, or askings distributed to jurisdictions, Annual Conferences, and pastoral charges by the budget-making agency of the

General Conference in such manner as the General Conference may prescribe, and from church schools, gifts, donations, freewill offerings, annuities, bequests, specials, and other sources from which missionary and benevolence funds are usually derived, in harmony with the Discipline of The Methodist Church and actions of the General Conference.

3. Askings shall be received from the fields, and budgets shall be prepared by the Division of World Missions and the Division of National Missions in such manner as the board may prescribe, consistent with its constitution and charter; and this combined budget shall be presented to the budget-making agency of the General Conference. In the allocation of funds to the Division of World Missions and the Division of National Missions the board shall recognize the principle of equal distribution, but only in so far as this provides an equitable basis of division.

4. The board shall not appropriate for the regular maintenance of its work in any one year more money than was received by it for appropriation the previous fiscal year.

¶ 1184. *Art. 11. Joint Committee on Missionary Personnel.*—There shall be a **Joint Committee on Missionary Personnel** of the several divisions of the board, which shall be responsible for the enlistment, cultivation, training, and recommendation of candidates for missionary' service at home and abroad and deaconess service in the United States. This committee shall co-operate in the work of the Interboard Committee on Christian Vocations (¶ 1415).

¶ 1185. *Art. 12. Missionaries.*—Standards and qualifications of missionary candidates for home and foreign service, including deaconesses, shall be determined by the board on the recommendation of the Joint Committee on Missionary Personnel.

¶ 1186. A person shall be constituted a missionary and receive support as such from the funds of the board when such person has been commissioned by the board and has been assigned to some definite field. A person shall be constituted a deaconess when she has met the necessary requirements, including a period of probation,

321

and has been duly licensed, consecrated, and commissioned by a bishop. (*See* ¶ 1252.)

¶ **1187.** 1. All missionaries who serve in fields outside the United States should relate themselves as directly as possible to the organized church in these fields through membership in a local church or Annual Conference.

2. In fields outside the United States the Annual Conference may seat in its session regularly appointed lay missionaries of the Board of Missions, and national heads of major institutions in such numbers and with such qualifications as the Central Conference may prescribe, and give them the privileges of the floor. Special-term ordained missionaries who retain their conference relations in the United States may be granted similar privileges.[3] (*See* ¶ 623.)

SEC. IV.   **Division of World Missions**

¶ **1193.** *Article* 1. *Organization.*—Within the board there shall be a **Division of World Missions,** hereinafter called the division, which shall be one of the co-ordinate administrative divisions of the board.

¶ **1194.** The division shall be incorporated as hereinbefore provided.

¶ **1195.** The division shall be composed of board members as follows: one half of the bishops resident in the United States, one half of the bishops from overseas, one half of the ministers, one half of the lay men, one third of the lay women, and one third of the youth. (*See* ¶ 1178.2.) The division shall meet annually at the time of the meeting of the board, and at such other times as it may deem necessary.

¶ **1196.** *Art.* 2. *Authority.*—The division shall have authority to make by-laws in harmony with the charter and constitution of the board and of its divisions; to regulate its own proceedings in harmony with its by-laws; to elect such officers as are to be elected by the division, to remove any of them for cause, and to fill vacancies among the officers so elected; to nominate such staff as are to be elected by the board, to recommend

---

[3] Amended following Judicial Council Decisions 1, 24.

their removal for cause, and to present nominations to the board to fill vacancies; to recommend fields of labor; to accept, train, and maintain workers; to buy and sell property; to secure and administer funds for the support of all work under its charge; to solicit and accept contributions subject to annuity under the board's regulations; and to recommend to the board appropriations for its work.

¶ **1197.** The division shall administer and promote the work of missions outside the United States and its dependencies formerly administered by the Board of Foreign Missions of the Methodist Episcopal Church, and the work outside of the United States of the Board of Missions, General Section, of the Methodist Episcopal Church, South, and the Board of Missions of the Methodist Protestant Church, except such activities of the Woman's Convention of the Methodist Protestant Church, and shall have committed to it all the general foreign missionary activities of The Methodist Church in foreign fields.

¶ **1198.** This division shall: (1) estimate the needs of the work under its care and present the same to the board for consideration and approval; (2) present to the board for appointment for its various fields of service missionaries who have been approved by the Joint Committee on Missionary Personnel.

¶ **1199.** 1. The division, in co-operation with the Department of Work in Foreign Fields of the Woman's Division, shall formulate plans and policies for the administration of foreign missions, shall consider lines of work, fields to be occupied, and various enterprises, and make recommendations to the board for approval.

2. There shall be an **Interdivision Committee on Foreign Work** with equal representation from the Division of World Missions and the Department of Work in Foreign Fields of the Woman's Division of Christian Service, which shall consider policies, programs, and estimates which come from Committees on Co-ordination (¶ 1202). The committee shall make recommendations regarding correlation and co-ordination to the respective divisions.

¶ **1200.** The division shall recommend to the board for appropriation an emergency or contingent fund of not less than three per cent nor more than five per cent of the total amount appropriated for the division. It shall not recommend to the board for appropriation, including the emergency fund, for a fiscal year more than the total amount received for the division from all sources during the preceding fiscal year.

¶ **1201.** The division shall elect quadrennially a president, one or more vice-presidents, a treasurer, and a recording secretary, who together with a general secretary and an associate general secretary shall be elected by the division as officers of the corporation, and also additional treasurers as needed. Vacancies occurring during the quadrennium shall be filled by the division or its executive committee. Such other officers as the division may need it shall elect annually. The division shall also nominate for election by the board one or more general secretaries and such other secretaries and directors as the need may require. The division shall determine the powers and duties of its officers and staff and shall recommend remuneration of staff.

¶ **1202.** *Art. 3. Committees on Co-ordination.*—In a foreign mission field of the board each Annual or Provisional Annual Conference shall elect a **Committee on Co-ordination,** composed of the presiding bishop, who shall be chairman, and wherever possible an equal number of national and missionary members. The national membership shall be composed of an equal number of men and women, and the women shall be nominated by the woman's organization of the conference. The missionary membership, which should wherever possible be an equal number of men and women, shall be nominated by the missionaries within the bounds of the conference and approved by the Division of World Missions and the Woman's Division of Christian Service. On authorization by the Central Conference, the Annual or Provisional Annual Conference may add the district superintendents as ex officio members without vote. The duties of the committee shall be:

1. To elect its vice-chairman, who shall be authorized to call meetings in the absence of the bishop, and its secre-

tary; to forward its minutes promptly to the respective divisions of the board, and the report of its recommendations to the divisions for approval.

2. To study and co-ordinate the work of the Division of World Missions and the Woman's Division of Christian Service.

3. To consult with the board through the respective divisions on all matters of mutual concern.

4. To receive and transmit to the board reports from all the institutions and agencies of the church which receive aid from the board.

5. To prepare estimates of funds requested from the board for aid to work in the Annual or Provisional Annual Conference and for aid to institutions and other projects; except the financial requirement for missionary support, which is the direct responsibility of the board.

¶ 1203. In a mission field where there is a Central Conference in which there is an executive board or council of co-operation constituted, the estimates for the maintenance and development of the work, prepared by the various Committees on Co-ordination, may be presented to the Division of World Missions and to the Woman's Division of Christian Service after approval by said executive board or council of co-operation. The estimates shall be presented, conference by conference, and by projects within the conference. These estimates shall be prepared and submitted separately for the two divisions in such form as may be required.

¶ 1204. In a Central or Provisional Central Conference where there is no executive board or council of co-operation, the estimates shall be sent direct to the Division of World Missions and to the Woman's Division of Christian Service from the Committee on Co-ordination of each Annual or Provisional Annual Conference.

¶ 1205. Wherever desired by an affiliated autonomous Methodist church and the missionaries working in relation to such church, there shall be a joint council composed of members of the affiliated autonomous church and missionaries of the board working in that field, under a constitution approved by the board. This joint council shall be the agency through which the board shall cooperate with such affiliated autonomous church.

¶ **1206.** *Art. 4. Administration of a Mission.*—1. Foreign fields outside of an Annual Conference working under the care of the Board of Missions, not having met the requirements for the organization of a Provisional Annual Conference, may be organized into a **Mission.**

2. The Mission shall meet annually. It shall be composed of all regularly appointed missionaries, both lay and clerical, and mission traveling preachers, and other lay members. Each Mission shall determine the number of lay members and the mode of their appointment.

3. A bishop, or in his absence one of the superintendents chosen by ballot by the Mission, shall preside in the annual meeting. This meeting shall exercise in a general way the functions of a District Conference. It shall have power to license suitable persons to preach, and to pass on the character of preachers not members of an Annual Conference, to receive on trial mission traveling preachers, and to recommend to an Annual Conference proper persons for deacon's and elder's orders. The bishop or president shall at the annual meeting assign the missionaries and mission traveling preachers to the several charges for the ensuing year; *provided* that no missionary shall be transferred to or from a Mission without previous consultation with the board.

4. The work of a Mission shall be divided, when necessary, into districts, over each of which shall be placed a superintendent. It shall be the duty of the superintendent, in the absence of the bishop, to take general supervision of the work in his district with all its interests, and to report the state of that work and its needs to the bishop in charge and to the board.

5. For the consideration of financial and other matters relative to the policies of the board and the work of the missionaries, the missionaries of each Mission shall hold an annual **missionaries' meeting** and report their proceedings to the board. In the absence of a bishop one of the missionaries shall be elected by ballot to preside.

¶ **1207.** *Art. 5. Missionaries of The Methodist Church Serving Other Churches.*—1. Missionaries of The Methodist Church, on action of the Board of Missions, may be assigned to serve in affiliated autonomous churches, independent churches, churches resulting from the union of Methodist churches and other communions, or in other evangelical denominations.

2. Such missionaries, while retaining their membership in their home local churches and Annual Conferences, and without impairing their relationship to the Board of Missions, shall, while on service in such fields, be free to accept such rights and privileges as may be offered to them by such churches.

3. The missionaries in such mission fields may be organized into mission councils under constitutions approved by the Board of Missions.

Sec. V.   **Division of National Missions**

¶ 1208. *Article* 1. *Organization.*—Within the board there shall be a **Division of National Missions,** hereinafter called the division, which shall be one of the coordinate administrative divisions of the board.

¶ 1209. The division shall be incorporated as hereinbefore provided.

¶ 1210. The division shall be composed of board members as follows: one half of the bishops resident in the United States, one half of the ministers, one half of the lay men, one third of the lay women, and one third of the youth. (*See* ¶ 1178.2.) The division shall meet annually at the time of the meeting of the board and at such other times as it may deem necessary.

¶ 1211. *Art* 2. *Authority.*—The division shall have authority to make by-laws in harmony with the charter and constitution of the board and of its divisions; to regulate its own proceedings in harmony with its by-laws; to elect such officers as are to be elected by the division, to remove any of them for cause, and to fill vacancies among the officers so elected; to nominate such staff as are to be elected by the board, to recommend their removal for cause, and to present nominations to the board to fill vacancies; to recommend fields of labor; to accept, train, and maintain missionaries and special workers; to buy and sell property; to own and operate radio stations; to secure and administer funds for the support of all work under its charge; to solicit and accept contributions subject to annuity under the board's regulations; and to recommend to the board appropriations for its work.

¶ **1212.** *Art. 3. Officers.*—The division shall elect quadrennially a president, one or more vice-presidents, a treasurer, and a recording secretary, who together with a general secretary shall be elected by the division as officers of the corporation, and also additional treasurers as needed. Vacancies occurring during the quadrennium shall be filled by the division or its executive committee. Such other officers as the division may need it shall elect annually. The division shall also nominate for election by the board one or more general secretaries and such other secretaries and directors as the need may require. The division shall determine the powers and duties of its officers and staff and shall recommend remuneration of staff.

¶ **1213.** *Art. 4. Functions.*—The division shall have general supervision and administration of the work of missions and church extension in the United States of America and the Dominican Republic; and administration of all donation aid, loan funds, and endowment contributed and established for the work of church extension, except such as may be administered by the Jurisdictional and Annual Conferences.

¶ **1214.** The division shall have two sections: Section of Home Missions and Section of Church Extension.

¶ **1215.** 1. The **Section of Home Missions** shall have the following departments, or such departments and administrative units as the board, on recommendation of the division, may determine:

    a) Department of City Work.

    b) Department of Town and Country Work.

    c) Department of Goodwill Industries.

    d) Department of Research and Survey.

All administrative units shall work in close co-operation with one another, particularly in any overlapping work.

  2. The section shall give special study and promotion

to mission work among minority language and ethnic groups and conduct such activities as the development of the work may require. It shall assign staff members to serve these special groups, who shall administer such appropriations as are committed to them for the work of the field to which they are assigned. They shall co-operate with other boards and agencies as their work may affect the group involved.

3. The division shall appoint, on nomination of the director concerned, not more than fifteen members for each department or administrative unit, who shall be chosen from among the members of the division and others who are actively engaged in the work or administration of projects within the fields of the respective departments or administrative units.

4. Bilingual work in the United States, except in organized bilingual Provisional Annual Conferences and Missions, shall be administered through English-speaking Annual Conferences, under the joint supervision of the Division of National Missions and the district superintendents.

¶ 1216. The general secretary or secretaries shall communicate to the bishops such information as he or they may possess concerning missions in their respective areas. He or they, or their representative, shall counsel with the bishops relative to missionary activities and needs; also, relative to the appointment of mission superintendents and special workers who are maintained by appropriations from missionary funds.

¶ 1217. The **Department of City Work** shall promote missionary work in cities with a population of ten thousand or more. It shall aid in making studies in cities with special reference to the religious conditions of urban populations; the necessary location and adaptation of church buildings; and the programs required for needy and congested communities. It shall also aid in the organization and development of adequate religious centers in city territory, and may aid wherever possible in the development of co-operative procedures among the church and other agencies for the betterment of the community life of the people of the cities. It shall administer such appropriations as may be committed to it by the division. All askings for missionary work in cities of ten thousand population or more shall require the review and recommendation of the department or its director.

¶ **1218.** The department shall promote the organization of **city (metropolitan) or district missionary societies** wherever possible and practicable.

¶ **1219.** 1. A city (metropolitan) or district missionary society may be organized in the interest of missions and church extension, under such name and control as it may determine, wherever, in the judgment of the bishop or bishops and district superintendent or superintendents concerned, it is deemed advisable. When two or more districts, conferences, episcopal areas, or jurisdictions have churches in the same city or metropolitan area, it is recommended that the society be so organized as to include all these churches. The bishops involved shall initiate the effort to develop the society.

2. The purpose of such a society is to promote evangelization and to co-ordinate the work of the church in cities and contiguous communities. Charges in communities adjacent to a city but not attached to the city may be included in the society. All bishops, district superintendents, and superintendents of Missions or Provisional Annual Conferences having jurisdiction within the geographical territory covered by the society, and all pastors therein shall be ex officio members of the society or its board of managers. Each Quarterly Conference in the territory shall be entitled to at least one lay representative in the society or board.

¶ **1220.** In a metropolitan area included within the bounds of two or more Annual Conferences the Department of City Work may promote, with the approval of the bishops and the conferences, the organization of a **Metropolitan Area Planning Commission,** which shall be composed of the bishops, the district superintendents involved, and a selected group of ministers and laymen, representing Conference Boards of Missions, Committees on Urban Work, city missionary societies, and local churches, who have skills and experience enabling them to do creative planning for Methodism in the metropolitan area. The commission shall serve in an advisory capacity to Methodist leaders and organizations in the metropolitan area and shall make recommendations regarding immediate and long-term planning and strategy.

¶ **1221.** The city (metropolitan) or district missionary society·may include in its work the organization of church schools and the organization (but not the constituting) of churches, the aid of weak churches, the acquisition of real estate and the erection of buildings, the adaptation of downtown churches to their altered environment, the securing and holding of endowments for the society and for dependent churches, the conducting of missions among foreign-speaking and other needy peoples, the development of well-organized open-air evangelism, the maintenance of kindergartens and industrial schools, the promotion of social and settlement work, including services rendered in connection with juvenile court cases, and the support of rescue missions and of institutions for the relief of the sick and the destitute.

¶ **1222.** In order to receive financial assistance from the division, the society shall meet the following conditions:

a) It shall be organized according to the *Discipline*.

b) It shall have an executive committee meeting at least once each quarter.

c) It shall be actively at work.

d) It shall have made a report to the division including: (1) number of ministers or missionaries supported in whole or in part, amount paid to each, and kind of work in which each is engaged; (2) expenses of administration; (3) total amount raised by the society and how expended; (4) such other items as the division shall require.

e) It shall endeavor to raise annually by collections or otherwise an amount at least equal to that appropriated to it by the board, exclusive of appropriations made for work among foreign-speaking people.

¶ **1223.** Each Annual Conference is directed to take such friendly interest in the societies which are wholly or partially within its bounds as shall promote their efficiency and facilitate their work, to arrange for the publication of their reports in the conference journal, and to provide a separate column in connection with the statement of the benevolence collections for the itemized report of the offerings for this work.

¶ 1224. If the society has an executive officer giving his entire time to the work, it is recommended that he be invited into consultation with the bishop and district superintendents in the consideration of the appointments that affect missions or churches administered or aided by the society.

¶ 1225. The society shall have authority, in the territory covered by its constitution or charter, to make apportionments to the pastoral charges, and to collect and disburse moneys for all the objects contemplated in its organization.

¶ 1226. It shall be the duty of each pastor whose charge lies within the territory of the society once each year to present its interests to his congregation, take a collection for it, or provide for the amount apportioned in the benevolence budget, and report the amount received to the Annual Conference.

¶ 1227. It is recommended that any local church within its territory expecting to receive aid from the society for buildings or improvement be required to secure, as a condition to receiving such aid, the approval of the society with respect to location, plans, and methods of financing.

¶ 1228. The Department of City Work, in co-operation with the Council of Bishops and other interested groups, shall promote a quadrennial **Convocation on Urban Work,** which shall be called by the Council of Bishops at such time as the council and the department may determine.

¶ 1229. 1. The **Department of Town and Country Work** shall promote, in co-operation with other boards and agencies, all phases of the work of the church in rural territory and in places of less than ten thousand population; conduct surveys and research studies, and use the findings for more effective church work; administer funds committed to it by the division; develop a co-operative procedure among church and other agencies that seek to improve the economic, social, educational, and religious life of people in town and country areas; seek to develop co-operative procedures between Methodist churches and those of other denominations; and promote among ministers and in colleges and schools of theology a study of town and country life and effective ways and means of church and community work.

2. It shall give encouragement and support to Conference Boards of Missions, to Commissions on Town and Country Work, and to Jurisdictional Boards of Missions in their efforts to develop more effective and constructive work in town and country communities.

3. It shall administer such appropriations as may be committed to it by the division. All askings for missionary work in town or country (communities of less than ten thousand population) shall require the review and recommendation of the department or its director.

4. It shall assist the district superintendents and Commissions on Town and Country Work in making surveys and developing plans for local parish and charge reorganization in town and country areas. This shall include recommendation of the type of multiple parish which seems most appropriate to the area under consideration.

5. It shall seek to aid Annual Conferences and local churches in establishing Methodist families on the land and in town and country communities through making available information concerning procedures and resources for this purpose from private, governmental, and religious agencies.

6. It shall promote the organization of district missionary societies (¶¶ 1218-27) wherever possible and practicable.

7. In co-operation with the Council of Bishops and the Interboard Committee on Town and Country Work, it shall promote and administer a quadrennial **National Conference on Town and Country Work,** which shall be called by the Council of Bishops at such time as the council, the department, and the committee may determine.

¶ 1230. 1. There shall be an **Interboard Committee on Town and Country Work,** composed of six bishops composing a Committee on Town and Country Work of the Council of Bishops, whose chairman shall convene this committee early in the quadrennium, and representatives elected by agencies as follows: three from the Board of

Missions, one of whom shall be from the Woman's Division of Christian Service; three from the General Board of Education; and one each from the Board of Evangelism, the Board of Lay Activities, and the Division of Human Relations and Economic Affairs of the Board of Christian Social Concerns. In addition, staff members of the participating agencies whose specific function is town and country work shall be ex officio members. The committee may invite other persons to meet with it as consultants. Expenses of members attending meetings shall be borne by the agencies which they represent. Expenses of the consultants shall be borne by the agency extending the invitation.

2. The members shall hold office for the quadrennium and/or until their successors are chosen.

3. The functions of the committee shall be: (*a*) to provide a means of co-operative planning among the participating agencies for the strengthening of town and country work in The Methodist Church; (*b*) to plan the quadrennial National Conference on Town and Country Work as provided in ¶ 1229.7; (*c*) to ascertain the phases of rural work the participating agencies propose to carry on and to give assistance in correlating the programs for a full service to town and country churches; (*d*) to prepare a clear statement on interdenominational co-operation with regard to allocation of new fields of work and to disposition of properties through federations, union churches, exchange of fields, withdrawals, and similar forms of co-operative work.

4. The committee shall organize by electing such officers and subcommittees as may be needed, and shall determine its frequency of meetings. It shall report annually to the participating agencies and may make suggestions concerning work in town and country churches.

¶ **1231.** 1. Each Annual Conference shall set up quadrennially, under the direction of the bishop and his Cabinet, a **Commission on Town and Country Work.** The members shall be the bishop and the district superintendents; the conference missionary secretary; the conference secretary of evangelism; the executive secretary of the Board of Education; the president or vice-president of the

Conference Woman's Society of Christian Service; a representative elected by each of the following conference agencies: the Board of Missions, the Board of Education, the Woman's Society of Christian Service, the Board of Lay Activities, the Board of Evangelism, the Methodist Youth Fellowship, and the Methodist Rural Fellowship; the members of the Interboard Committee on Town and Country Work and of the corresponding jurisdictional agency who reside within the conference; and one rural layman and one rural pastor to represent each district, nominated by the district superintendents or the nominating committee of the conference, and elected by the conference. The conference may add to the commission membership, in accordance with ¶ 667 and its usual nominating procedures, such additional ministers and laymen especially interested in town and country work as are recommended by the commission. All special workers in the conference employed by The Methodist Church in rural communities shall be members of the commission. If a district ceases to be represented by its resident lay or ministerial member, the vacancy may be filled by the executive committee of the commission until the next conference session.

2. The commission shall work with the conference agencies and the conference in program areas of town and country responsibility. It shall conduct surveys and research studies of town and country areas within the bounds of the conference; develop co-operative procedures between the church and social and governmental agencies, and with the town and country departments of state councils of churches and with the churches of other denominations in local communities; work to improve the effectiveness of the town and country churches and pastors; recommend a program to co-ordinate the work of the participating boards and agencies in this program area; and outline a program of town and country work to be presented to the participating agencies and to the conference. In program areas of town and country work the conference agencies shall consult with the commission or its executive committee.

3. At the beginning of the quadrennium a convener

designated by the bishop shall call the commission together at the first conference session, or within ninety
days after the Jurisdictional Conference, for the purpose of
organizing and determining its initial activities, procedures, and time of meeting. Reports of all meetings
shall be furnished to the secretaries of the co-operating
agencies, and an annual report of findings and recommendations shall be presented to these agencies and to the
conference.

4. The officers of the commission shall be a chairman,
vice chairman, recording secretary, and treasurer, all
elected quadrennially. There shall be an **executive secretary,** or a promotional secretary, elected by the commission after consultation with the bishop and his Cabinet
and confirmed by the conference. The executive or promotional secretary shall have responsibility for the general
oversight and promotion of the work of the commission.

¶ 1232. The **Department of Goodwill Industries** shall
provide for the religious, educational, social, and industrial welfare of the handicapped and unfortunate.
It shall promote and establish Goodwill Industries in
various centers; shall review missionary askings and
administer appropriations for Goodwill Industries; shall
endorse and assist only those local Goodwill Industries
which are organized and conducted according to its
standards, rules, and regulations; and shall urge them to
co-operate with the departments, sections, divisions, and
boards of The Methodist Church, and other organizations
serving the handicapped and unfortunate. The department may conduct national and regional institutes, and
such other special training activities as will help to develop the specialized leadership required for the direction
of Goodwill Industries.

¶ 1233. The **Department of Research and Survey** shall
conduct surveys and research studies in both cities and
rural territories, giving attention to migrations of population, new and growing communities, changed neighborhoods, and religious conditions of racial and other groups.
It shall co-operate with conference boards in making
surveys. It may promote kindred activities on college and
seminary campuses and within various areas of The

Methodist Church. It may produce and circulate materials designed to aid administrators and pastors in conducting community self-studies and surveys. (*See also* ¶ 1115.)

¶ **1235.** The **Section of Church Extension** shall conduct its work under the following provisions and regulations:

1. It shall encourage the erection of churches in communities not already adequately supplied, and shall assist in the building of churches, parsonages, and other mission buildings where assistance is most needed.

2. It shall give special attention to church architecture. Local churches seeking financial aid from the section shall submit preliminary sketches of their architectural plans and specifications to the section for approval before final working drawings are started. (*See* ¶ 1237.)

3. The division shall appropriate money for the various types of work in the field and the conduct of the work of the office. The section or such committee as it may designate shall recommend to the executive committee of the division what should be donated or loaned to each applicant and shall administer all donation aid, loan funds, and endowments contributed and established for the work of church extension except such as may be administered by the Annual Conferences; and do such other business as may be legitimate and proper for it to do.

4. Aid in the form of donations in the erection, remodeling, and repairing of churches and parsonages shall be made available primarily to clearly missionary projects. Assistance in the development of other types of church property, if and when granted, shall be provided as loans. Priority shall be given to applications to provide churches for new communities.

5. All applications for aid from the section shall be made through the Conference Board of Missions. Grants shall be made by the division, its executive committee, or such other committee as the division may designate, on recommendation of the section and the secretary or secretaries.

6. In granting donations to churches and parsonages the division shall require from the trustees of each aided local church an obligation which shall be a lien on the property involved for the return of the amount donated

in the event that the work shall cease or the property shall be alienated from The Methodist Church; *provided* that these provisions may be waived in cases involving donations of one thousand dollars or less. Said lien may be subordinated to enable the trustees of the church involved to give a first mortgage for a loan. In case of relocation the division's investment and lien may be transferred to the new property.

7. When a donation is granted by the division where the property involved is held in trust by the Board of Trustees of the Annual Conference or by a board of trustees elected by and responsible to the General Conference, no lien shall be required by the division, provided the trustees agree, with the approval of the Annual Conference or the General Conference, that the property shall not be conveyed without protecting the claim of the division.

8. The division or its constituent corporations shall raise and administer a loan fund and a revolving loan fund which shall be held separate from funds secured for general distribution. They shall consist of all money or other properties especially donated or bequeathed to the board or division or its constituent corporations as permanent funds, subject to annuity or otherwise, where the gift is intended to assist in the building and financing of churches and parsonages in the field of the Division of National Missions. These funds shall be used only as loans on adequate security or upon such terms as may be determined by the section.

9. It shall be lawful for the division to accept contributions to its funds from any person or persons capable of making the same, subject to annuity, payable to the persons making such donations, or other contractual beneficiaries; *provided* that in all cases the division or any of its constituent corporations shall conform to the laws of the state or states in which they are incorporated.

10. The section shall have a Department of Finance and Field Service and a Department of Architecture as set forth in ¶¶ 1236-37.

¶ **1236.** The section shall have a **Department of Finance and Field Service.** A fund may be set up by the section to be secured from gifts and legacies, and the income shall be used in supporting the work of this department. The purposes of this department shall be:

1. Raising funds for church, parsonage, and Christian educational buildings and equipment; for renovating, remodeling, and repair projects; and for other institutions and causes, such as conference pensions, schools of theology, Wesley Foundations, colleges, hospitals, and homes.

2. Raising funds for the retirement of church and other institution obligations. A nominal charge shall be made for fund-raising services.

3. Assisting and guiding churches in developing effective budget and other financial plans.

4. Providing counsel and suggesting plans for church building enterprises.

5. Providing construction supervision of mission church, parsonage, and school building projects.

¶ **1237.** The section shall have a **Department of Architecture.** The purposes of the department shall be:

1. To prepare up-to-date church plans of a general nature in order to guide local churches in formulating a building program.

2. To distribute leaflets, folders, and booklets giving illustrations and descriptive material as a guide in development of wise, constructive programs for remodeling and enlarging existing buildings and planning for the erection of new ones.

3. To confer in the section offices with representatives from throughout the church concerning architectural problems and building procedures.

4. To review and criticize sketches which are submitted by local churches and District Boards of Church Location and Building, and assist them in avoiding architectural blunders, as to both design and floor plans. (*See* ¶¶ 180, 723.)

5. To visit local churches, on request and as the department is able, in order to furnish architectural counsel at the building site.

6. To consult with local architects who have been retained by local churches.

7. To furnish counsel in the preparation of plans for

missionary projects which are constructed or supervised by the church builders on the staff of the Department of Finance and Field Service.

¶ **1238.** *Administration of a Mission.*—1. In home fields outside of an Annual Conference, or among racial groups, work under the care of the Board of Missions not having met the requirements for the organization of a Provisional Annual Conference shall be administered by the board as a **Mission.**

2. The Mission shall meet annually, and shall be composed of all regularly appointed missionaries, both lay and clerical, and mission traveling preachers, and other lay members, the number of whom and the mode of their appointment each Mission shall determine for itself.

3. The bishop in charge of a Mission may appoint a superintendent of the Mission, or as many superintendents as may appear to him necessary or wise, for whom support has been provided. He shall determine the groups or charges over which the respective superintendents shall have supervision.

4. A bishop, or in his absence one of the superintendents chosen by ballot by the Mission, shall preside in the annual meeting. This meeting shall exercise in a general way the functions of a District Conference. It shall have power to license suitable persons to preach, and to pass on the character of preachers not members of an Annual Conference, to receive on trial mission traveling preachers, and to recommend to an Annual Conference proper persons for deacon's and elder's orders. The bishop or president shall at the annual meeting assign the missionaries and mission traveling preachers to the several charges for the ensuing year; *provided* that no missionary shall be transferred to or from a Mission without previous consultation with the board.

5. In case of a Mission using more than one language besides English, and extending over a wide geographical territory, the bishop may assemble in annual meetings the members of the Mission on a racial or geographical basis. The Mission may delegate to such subgroups the work of examining and recommending to an Annual Conference

candidates for admission on trial, under such limitations as the Discipline provides.

6. In Missions, examinations of local and traveling preachers shall be held by the Mission, and certified to an Annual Conference. The Missions also shall make recommendations for reception on trial in an Annual Conference.

¶ 1239. There shall be an **Interdivision Committee on Work in Home Fields** with equal representation from the Division of National Missions and the Department of Work in Home Fields of the Woman's Division of Christian Service, which shall co-ordinate and correlate plans and policies for home missions and arrange for such co-operative activities and joint projects as may be mutually acceptable. The committee shall make recommendations regarding correlation and co-ordination to the respective divisions.

SEC. VI. Woman's Division of Christian Service

¶ 1240. *Article* 1. *Organization.*—1. Within the board there shall be a **Woman's Division of Christian Service,** hereinafter called the division, which shall be one of the co-ordinate administrative divisions of the board.

2. The division shall be incorporated as hereinbefore provided.

3. The division shall be composed of board members as follows: all the women (¶ 1172.2, .4), one bishop from each jurisdiction, one half of the bishops from overseas, and one third of the youth. Additional members may be elected by the board from the Divisions of World Missions and of National Missions as provided in ¶ 1178.2. The division shall hold a regular annual meeting and such other meetings as shall be called by the division or the executive committee.

4. The division shall include in its scope the interests and activities formerly promoted and administered by the Woman's Foreign Missionary Society, the Woman's Home Missionary Society, the Wesleyan Service Guild, and the Ladies' Aid Societies of the Methodist Episcopal Church; the types of work and interests included in the Board of Missions, Section of Woman's Work, the Woman's Mission-

ary Council, and former boards and societies (the Woman's Missionary Society, the Woman's Board of Foreign Missions, and the Woman's Board of Home Missions) of the Methodist Episcopal Church, South; such activities of the Woman's Convention of the Methodist Protestant Church as logically fall within the organization; and all deaconess work of the uniting churches within the United States. All other organizations of women of similar purpose operating in the charges of the uniting churches may come under the scope of this division.

¶ **1241.** *Art. 2. Authority.*—1. The division shall have authority to make by-laws in harmony with the charter and constitution of the board and of its divisions; to regulate its own proceedings in harmony with its by-laws; to elect such officers as are to be elected by the division, to remove any of them for cause, and to fill vacancies among the officers so elected; to nominate such staff as are to be elected by the board, to recommend their removal for cause, and to present nominations to the board to fill vacancies; to recommend fields of labor; to train and present to the board for appointment in its various fields of service missionaries and deaconesses who have been approved by the Joint Committee on Missionary Personnel, and to maintain workers; to buy and sell property; to secure and administer funds for the support of all work under its charge; to solicit and accept contributions subject to annuity under the board's regulations; to recommend to the board appropriations for its work; to organize jurisdiction, conference, district, and local-church societies for adults, youth, and children as auxiliary to the division; and to recommend constitutions and by-laws for the same.

2. The division shall be empowered to create such standing and special committees as the work may demand.

3. There shall be an **executive committee,** which shall exercise the powers of the division *ad interim.*

¶ **1242.** *Art. 3. Purpose.*—The purpose of the division shall be to develop and maintain Christian work among women and children at home and abroad; to cultivate Christian family life; to enlist and organize the efforts of Christian women, youth, and children in behalf of native and foreign groups, needy childhood, and community welfare; to assist in the promotion of a missionary spirit throughout the church; to select, train, and maintain Christian workers; to co-operate with the local church in its responsibilities; and to seek fellowship with Christian women of this and other lands in establishing a Christian social order around the world.

¶ **1243.** *Art.* 4. *Officers.*—The division shall elect quadrenially a president, one or more vice-presidents, a treasurer, and a recording secretary, who together with a general secretary shall be elected by the division as officers of the corporation, and also additional treasurers as needed. Vacancies occurring during the quadrennium shall be filled by the division or its executive committee. Such other officers as the division may need it shall elect annually. The division shall also nominate for election by the board a general secretary, one or more executive secretaries, and such other secretaries and staff as the need may require. The division shall determine the powers and duties of its officers and staff and shall recommend remuneration of staff.

¶ **1244.** 1. The division shall be organized into three departments:

a) Department of Work in Foreign Fields.

b) Department of Work in Home Fields.

c) Department of Christian Social Relations.

2. There shall be such committees and other organizational units as shall best promote its interests. The functions of these, other than as hereinafter determined, shall be defined by the division.

3. The division shall elect chairmen for the respective departments, who shall be vice-presidents of the division.

4. There shall be an executive secretary or secretaries in each department. The number and duties of such secretaries shall be determined and defined by the division.

¶ **1245.** The **Department of Work in Foreign Fields** shall administer and promote the work of missions outside the United States of America and the Dominican Republic.

1. There shall be a **standing committee** composed of the chairman and executive, associate, and assistant

secretaries of the department and such members of the division as may be appointed by the department.

2. There shall be an Interdivision Committee on Foreign Work. (*See* ¶ 1199.2.)

¶ **1246.** The legislation included under ¶¶ 1202-7 applies also to the work of the Woman's Division of Christian Service: (*a*) Committees on Co-ordination (¶¶ 1202-5); (*b*) administration of a Mission (¶ 1206); (*c*) missionaries of The Methodist Church serving other churches (¶ 1207).

¶ **1247.** The **Department of Work in Home Fields** shall administer and promote the work of missions within the United States of America and the Dominican Republic.

1. There shall be a **standing committee** composed of the chairman and executive, associate, and assistant secretaries of the department and such members of the division as may be appointed by the department.

2. There shall be an Interdivision Committee on Work in Home Fields. (*See* ¶ 1239.)

3. There shall be a consultive interboard staff committee with the Board of Hospitals and Homes. (*See* ¶ 1567.)

4. There shall be a Committee on Co-operation and Counsel with the Board of Education. (*See* ¶ 1360.)

5. In the Department of Work in Home Fields there shall be a Commission on Deaconess Work. (*See* ¶ 1252.)

¶ **1248.** The **Department of Christian Social Relations** shall promote the work of the division along the lines of community service and social relations.

1. It shall seek to make real and effective the teachings of Jesus as applied to individual, group, racial, and world relationships. It shall endeavor to enlist the participation of church women in such questions as have a moral or religious significance or an important bearing on public welfare.

2. It shall seek to co-operate with other agencies of the church having similar purposes, endeavoring to develop Christian fellowship and to deepen concern for the total responsibility of the church.

3. There shall be a **standing committee** composed of the chairman and secretaries of the department, the chairmen of the committees, and such other persons as the

division may provide on recommendation of the department.

¶ **1249.** 1. The **Section of Education and Cultivation** shall promote the work of the division and its auxiliary organizations. The plans and policies for such promotion shall be carried out by the Woman's Section of the Joint Section of Education and Cultivation.

2. The division, through the Woman's Section of the Joint Section of Education and Cultivation, is authorized to co-operate with the Interboard Committee on Missionary Education in the missionary education of adults, youth, and children in accordance with plans to be determined by the Board of Missions and the Board of Education.

¶ **1250.** The funds for the maintenance of the work of the Woman's Division of Christian Service shall be derived from annual pledges, special memberships, devises, bequests, annuities, special offerings, gifts, and moneys raised by special projects or collected in meetings held in the interest of the work of the division; *provided* that the funds thus raised shall be appropriated to the work established by the several uniting organizations composing the division, or work hereafter to be entered on by the division. All funds, except those designated for local purposes, shall be forwarded through the regular channels of the Woman's Societies of Christian Service to the treasurer of the division. All undesignated funds shall be allocated by the division on recommendation of its Committee on Finance and Estimates on a definite percentage basis to the work of the several departments of the division.

¶ **1251.** There shall be a delegated body termed the **Assembly,** which shall meet at such time and place as the division may determine. The purpose of the Assembly shall be to promote and deepen interest in the work of the division. The division shall determine the composition, functions, and power of the Assembly.

¶ **1252.** 1. The office of **deaconess** is hereby authorized in The Methodist Church. A deaconess is a woman who has been led by the Holy Spirit to devote herself to Christlike service under the direction of the Church, and who, having met the requirements prescribed by the Joint Committee on Missionary Personnel of the Board of Missions, including a period of not less than one year of probation, has been duly licensed, consecrated, and commissioned by a bishop. (*See* ¶¶ 1184-86.) This office entitles a woman to serve The Methodist Church through any of its agencies in any capacity not requiring full clergy rights.

a) All deaconess work in the United States and its dependencies shall be under the supervision of the **Commission on Deaconess Work** of the Woman's Division of Christian Service.

b) All deaconess work outside of the United States and its dependencies shall be under the supervision of the Central Conferences or Provisional Central Conferences concerned, or the Annual Conferences where there is not a Central Conference.

c) There shall be an **executive secretary,** who shall be nominated by the commission in consultation with the Woman's Division of Christian Service and elected by the Board of Missions.

2. All properties, trust funds, permanent funds, other special funds, and endowments now held and administered by or for the several forms of administration of deaconess work under the uniting churches shall be carefully safeguarded and administered by the several forms of administration in the interest of those persons and causes for which said funds were established.

3. The commission shall be composed of one bishop chosen by the Council of Bishops; four persons from each jurisdiction chosen by the Jurisdiction Deaconess Association, two of whom shall be deaconess members of the association, one a minister of the jurisdiction, and one the president of the Jurisdiction Woman's Society of Christian Service; three representatives of the Woman's Division of Christian Service chosen by the division; one representative of the Board of Pensions; one representative of the Board of Hospitals and Homes; one representative of the Board of Education; the executive secretary of the Interboard Committee on Christian Vocations; and one staff representative of the Joint Committee on Missionary Personnel. The executive secretary

of the Commission on Deaconesss Work shall be a member without vote. (*See* ¶ 1103.)

4. The duties of the commission shall be:

a) To recommend to the Joint Committee on Missionary Personnel standards and procedures for enlisting and training young women for deaconess work in The Methodist Church.

b) To establish minimum salary standards for deaconesses.

c) To receive and act on recommendations from Conference Deaconess Boards, Jurisdiction Deaconess Associations, and other agencies.

d) Other duties in harmony with the constitution, as may be set forth in the by-laws of the commission.

5. The commission shall meet annually. Its officers shall be elected quadrennially.

6. There shall be an **executive committee.** Such other committees may be constituted as are necessary for carrying out the duties of the commission.

7. A deaconess shall receive her appointment through the regular channels of the Commission on Deaconess Work and the Conference Deaconess Board.

8. A sabbatical leave for a definite period of time, not exceeding a year, to be spent in special study, may be granted with full or part salary on recommendation of the executive secretary of the Commission on Deaconess Work and the Conference Deaconess Board. Pension credit shall be granted for such sabbatical leave. All agencies employing deaconesses shall be encouraged to make an annual payment into the commission fund for sabbatical leave.

9. *a*) There shall be a contributory pension plan for all deaconesses commissioned on or after July 24, 1940.

b) For deaconesses commissioned or consecrated previous to July, 1940, former agreements are continued, and the administrations with which they were connected are responsible for the pensions.

c) A deaconess employed by an agency having its own pension plan shall participate in that plan during her term of service with that agency.

10. A deaconess may be granted a leave of absence,

not to exceed three years, for health reasons, study, or necessary home duties, with the privilege of continuing her participation in the pension plan. If an extension of leave is granted by the Commission on Deaconess Work, participation in the pension plan for additional years on leave shall not be permitted. A deaconess on leave of absence shall be a member of the Quarterly Conference (¶ 138) and the Conference Deaconess Board where she places her church membership while on leave.

11. A deaconess shall surrender her credentials when she is no longer available for an appointment in The Methodist Church.

12. A person may be reinstated as a deaconess on recommendation of the Conference Deaconess Board and the Commission on Deaconess Work and approval by the Joint Committee on Missionary Personnel.

¶ **1253.** 1. In each jurisdiction there shall be a **Jurisdiction Deaconess Association.**

2. *a*) All active deaconesses working within the bounds of the jurisdiction shall be members of the association.

b) All deaconesses in the retired relation shall be honorary members of the association.

c) Other members shall be the president of the Jurisdiction Woman's Society of Christian Service, the jurisdiction secretary of missionary service in home fields, and the president of each Conference Woman's Society of Christian Service within the jurisdiction.

3. There shall be a meeting of the association held annually or biennially in connection with the Jurisdiction Woman's Society of Christian Service.

4. The association shall elect its officers.

5. There shall be an executive committee in the association.

6. The duties of the association shall be:

a) To promote deaconess work as authorized by the Commission on Deaconess Work.

b) To arrange workers' conferences.

c) To provide opportunities for fellowship among workers in the jurisdiction.

d) Other duties in harmony with the constitution, as may be set forth in by-laws.

¶ **1254.** 1. In each Annual Conference there shall be a **Conference Deaconess Board.**

2. The purpose of the board shall be to create and maintain interest in deaconess work, to establish and interpret deaconess relationships to the Annual Conference, and to co-operate with the Commission on Deaconess Work in forming policies and making recommendations regarding deaconess work.

3. The board shall be composed of all active deaconesses serving within the bounds of the conference; the members of the Cabinet; pastors of local churches employing deaconesses; four representatives of the Conference Woman's Society of Christian Service; one representative from the Commission on Christian Vocations; and one representative, not a deaconess, from the local board of managers or committee of each project within the conference where deaconesses live or are employed. Retired deaconesses living within the bounds of the conference shall be honorary members, having the privilege of the floor without vote.

4. The duties of the board shall be:

a) To review, evaluate, and report annually to the Commission on Deaconess Work the standing of all deaconesses within the conference.

b) To study credentials received from Quarterly Conferences (¶ 146.2) and recommend to the Joint Committee on Missionary Personnel possible candidates for the office of deaconess.

c) To co-operate with the Commission on Deaconess Work in the annual appointments of deaconesses. It shall submit the list of appointments to be read by the bishop presiding at the Annual Conference, and to be printed in the journal.

d) To arrange for the licensing and the consecration service of those deaconesses assigned to the conference for these purposes.

e) In co-operation with the Conference Woman's Society of Christian Service and other agencies of the church, to initiate and develop plans for the promotion of deaconess work, including an annual program on deaconess work.

f) To consider complaints and charges against deaconesses; to act as a trial court in case of trial; and to make recommendations to the Commission on Deaconess Work.

5. The board shall meet annually and elect its officers.

6. There shall be an executive committee and other committees as are necessary for carrying out the duties of the board.

7. The board shall report annually to the Annual Conference, the Jurisdiction Deaconess Association, and the Commission on Deaconess Work. Its report shall be printed in the journal of the Annual Conference.

¶ **1255.** Constitution of the **Jurisdiction Woman's Society of Christian Service:**

Article 1. *Name.*—There shall be in each jurisdiction a Jurisdiction Woman's Society of Christian Service auxiliary to the Woman's Division of Christian Service of the Board of Missions. This shall include the Wesleyan Service Guild for employed women.

Art. 2. *Function or Authority.*—Each jurisdiction society shall have authority to promote its work in accordance with the program and policy of the division. It shall also recommend to the division such plans and policies as will make the work within the jurisdiction more effective.

Art. 3. *Membership.*—The jurisdiction society shall be composed of its officers and secretaries of lines of work; six delegates from each Conference Woman's Society of Christian Service within the jurisdiction, three of whom shall be conference officers or secretaries of lines of work; all the women members of the Jurisdictional Board of Missions and any members of the Woman's Division of Christian Service living within the jurisdiction; a representative of the Jurisdiction Deaconess Association; all the bishops of the jurisdiction; and such other persons as the society may determine.

Art. 4. *Officers, Secretaries of Lines of Work, and Committees.*—Each jurisdiction society shall elect a president, a vice-president, a recording secretary, and a treasurer. Secretaries of lines of work and the Committee on Nominations shall be elected, and the other committees appointed, in accordance with the plans of the Woman's Division of Christian Service as may be set forth in the by-laws for the jurisdiction society. The jurisdiction society shall confirm the election of the jurisdiction secretary of the Wesleyan Service Guild.

Art. 5. Elections.—Officers, secretaries of lines of work, and the Committee on Nominations shall be elected at the first meeting of the society following the meeting of the Jurisdictional Conference, for a term of four years, with the privilege of re-election for one additional term in the same office. This term of office applies to all officers and secretaries of lines of work. For an officer or secretary elected during a quadrennium the period to be served shall be considered the first term, thus giving the privilege of re-election for one additional term in the same office.

Art. 6. Meetings.—Each jurisdiction society shall meet annually at such time and place as it may determine; *provided* that in the year of the Assembly the annual meeting may take the form of an enlarged executive committee meeting. A majority shall constitute a quorum.

Art. 7. Amendments.—Proposed amendments to this constitution shall be sent to the recording secretary of the Woman's Division of Christian Service at least forty days before the last annual meeting of the division in the quadrennium.

¶ **1256.** Constitution of the **Conference Woman's Society of Christian Service:**

Article 1. Name.—In each Annual Conference there shall be organized a Conference Woman's Society of Christian Service auxiliary to the Jurisdiction Woman's Society of Christian Service and to the Woman's Division of Christian Service of the Board of Missions. This shall include the Wesleyan Service Guild for employed women.

Art. 2. Purpose.—The purpose of the conference society shall be to plan and direct the work of the society within the conference in accordance with the constitution and by-laws of the division.

Art. 3. Membership.—The conference society shall be composed of representatives from societies in the local churches, the number to be determined by each conference society according to its requirements; such district of-

351

ficers and secretaries of lines of work as the conference society may determine; the conference officers and secretaries of lines of work and chairmen of standing committees; and any members of the Woman's Division of Christian Service and of the Jurisdiction Woman's Society of Christian Service residing within the bounds of the conference. The resident bishop shall be a member of the executive committee.

Art. 4. Officers, Secretaries of Lines of Work, and Committees.—The conference society shall elect a president, a vice-president, a recording secretary, and a treasurer. Secretaries of lines of work and the Committee on Nominations shall be elected, and the other conference committees appointed, in accordance with the plans of the Woman's Division of Christian Service as may be set forth in the by-laws for the conference society. The conference society shall confirm the election of the conference secretary of the Wesleyan Service Guild.

Art. 5. Annual Conference Relationships.—The president of the conference society shall be seated in the Annual Conference, but without the right to vote unless she is otherwise a member of the conference.

Art. 6. Meetings.—There shall be an annual meeting of the society when reports shall be received from the conference officers and secretaries of lines of work, and from the districts. Officers and secretaries of lines of work shall be elected, the necessary business transacted, and pledges made for the year. There shall be a program of inspiration and information in harmony with the plans and projects of the Jurisdiction Woman's Society of Christian Service and the Woman's Division of Christian Service.

Art. 7. Elections.—1. At the last annual meeting of the quadrennium the society shall elect, according to the instructions in ¶ 1255.3, six women from the conference, three of whom shall be conference officers or secretaries of lines of work, for membership in the Jurisdiction Woman's Society of Christian Service.

2. At the annual meeting preceding the jurisdiction society's last annual meeting of the quadrennium the conference society shall nominate three women for member-

ship on the General Board of Missions, the names to be sent to the jurisdiction society, according to the instructions in ¶ 1172.2.

Art. 8. Amendments.—Proposed amendments to this constitution shall be sent to the recording secretary of the Woman's Division of Christian Service at least forty days before the last annual meeting of the division in the quadrennium.

¶ **1257.** Constitution of the **District Woman's Society of Christian Service:**

Article 1. Name.—There shall be a District Woman's Society of Christian Service auxiliary to the Conference Woman's Society of Christian Service. This shall include the Wesleyan Service Guild for employed women.

Art. 2. Purpose.—The purpose of the district society shall be to unite all the societies within the district in an earnest effort for the promotion of the work of the Conference Woman's Society of Christian Service.

Art. 3. Membership.—All members of Woman's Societies of Christian Service in the local churches of the district shall be considered members of the district society. The district superintendent shall be a member of the executive committee.

Art. 4. Officers, Secretaries of Lines of Work, and Committees.—The district society shall elect a president, a vice president, a recording secretary, and a treasurer. Secretaries of lines of work and the Committee on Nominations shall be elected, and the other committees appointed, in accordance with the plans of the Woman's Division of Christian Service as may be set forth in the by-laws for the district society. The district society shall confirm the election of the district secretary of the Wesleyan Service Guild. The district president shall be the only district representative with vote on the conference executive committee.

Art. 5. Meetings.—There shall be an annual meeting of the district society, when reports shall be received from the societies in the district. Officers, secretaries of lines of work, and the Committee on Nominations shall be elected, necessary business transacted, pledges made by the societies, and a program of inspiration and information given along the lines of work of the Woman's Society of Christian Service.

Art. 6. Amendments.—Proposed amendments to this constitution shall be sent to the recording secretary of the Woman's Division of Christian Service at least forty days before the last annual meeting of the division in the quadrennium.

¶ **1258.** There shall be a Woman's Society of Christian Service in the local church, auxiliary to the Conference Woman's Society of Christian Service. *See* ¶ 282 under Part II, The Local Church.

Sec. VII. Joint Section of Education and Cultivation

¶ **1268.** The Joint Section of Education and Cultivation shall undergird with education and cultivation the total program of the Board of Missions. It shall be composed of six bishops, one from each jurisdiction; six men and two women from the Division of World Missions, elected by that division; six men and two women from the Division of National Missions, elected by that division; eight women from the Woman's Division of Christian Service, one of whom shall be the president of the division, elected by that division. In all these selections there must be due regard to equitable representation from the jurisdictions. The general secretaries of the joint section shall be ex officio members without vote.

¶ **1269.** The joint section shall elect quadrennially a president, one or more vice-presidents, one of whom shall be chairman of the Woman's Section, and a recording secretary. It shall also nominate, for election by the board, two general secretaries (one man and one woman) and other secretaries, directors, a treasurer, who shall be the director of one of its departments, and such other staff as it may determine. The treasurer of the Woman's Division of Christian Service shall be treasurer of the Woman's Section. Vacancies shall be filled by the same procedure. The joint section shall determine the powers and duties of its officers and staff and shall recommend remuneration of staff.

354

¶ **1270.** There shall be an annual meeting of the joint section, and it may meet at such other times as the chairman may designate.

¶ **1271.** The joint section shall edit, publish, sell, and circulate books, literature, and periodicals for the work of the board and shall be responsible for editing and preparing the same. It shall co-operate with the Board of Education and all agencies of The Methodist Church and with interdenominational agencies in the preparation and distribution of missionary literature.

¶ **1272.** The joint section shall promote missionary councils, conventions, institutes, an annual **Week of Prayer,** and other meetings throughout the church for the purpose of developing a missionary spirit, spreading missionary information, and acquainting the church with the plans and policies of the board. It shall seek the co-operation of Jurisdictional and Annual Conferences, district superintendents, pastors, missionary societies, and other agencies of the church.

¶ **1273.** The joint section shall be responsible for promoting the missionary program of the church and, in consultation with the respective administrative divisions of the Board of Missions, and in co-operation with the Commission on Promotion and Cultivation, shall have charge of plans for cultivating missionary giving; *provided*, however, that all such plans shall be subject to and in harmony with the general financial system of The Methodist Church as adopted by the General Conference.

¶ **1274.** The joint section shall co-operate with the Interboard Committee on Missionary Education.

¶ **1275.** The joint section shall co-operate with schools of theology and departments of missions in the conduct of missionary institutes in such institutions, and shall develop other plans for affording missionary information and inspiration to students.

¶ **1276.** 1. The secretaries, directors, and editors of the General Section of the joint section shall carry out the plans and policies of the Division of World Missions and the Division of National Missions in the promotion of missionary education in all the age groups of the church school, in co-operation with the Board of Education, and in creating, editing, and publishing such periodicals, books, and leaflets for the local congregations, the districts, and the Annual Conferences as the work of the general divisions may necessitate.

2. The secretaries and editors of the Woman's Section of the joint section shall carry out the plans and policies of the Woman's Division of Christian Service for the various age groups, including the promotion of organizations for women in local churches, districts, conferences, and jurisdictions; in providing missionary education for children, youth, students, and women; in creating, editing, and publishing such periodicals, books, and leaflets as the work may necessitate. The joint section shall give guidance in those local-church activities that will strengthen the total life and work of the local church, and shall co-operate in all plans necessary for the efficiency of the Woman's Societies of Christian Service in the jurisdictions, conferences, districts, and local churches.

¶ **1277.** The funds for the Joint Section of Education and Cultivation shall be appropriated by the board.

SEC. VIII.   **Councils**

¶ **1280.** *Article* 1. *Secretarial Council.*—There shall be a **secretarial council,** composed of one general secretary and the treasurer from each of the three administrative divisions and two general secretaries from the Joint Section of Education and Cultivation, the persons to be designated quadrennially by the divisions. The council shall elect its own chairman annually from the divisions in rotation, and shall have regular meetings at such time and place as the council or the board may determine. It shall be the duty of this council to make recommendations to the board or to the divisions on matters which concern the board as a whole, to have general supervision of joint services of the board and the several divisions, and to prepare items of business and to carry out such arrangements for board and committee meetings as may be required.

¶ **1281.** *Art.* 2. *Missionary Councils.*—1. There may be a **General Missionary Council,** composed of the members of the board and the secretaries, associate and assistant secretaries, treasurers, directors, superintendents, and other members of the full-time employed staff of the Board of Missions, Jurisdictional Boards of Missions, and Conference Boards of Missions, and conference missionary secretaries, presidents, and other representatives of the Conference Boards of Missions. Meetings of this council may be held, at such times and places as the Joint Section of Education and Cultivation or the council itself may determine, for the consideration of any or all matters relating to missions and church extension and for the dissemination of missionary information and inspiration throughout the church.

2. There may be a **Jurisdictional Missionary Council** held within each jurisdiction at such times and places as the Jurisdictional Board of Missions may determine in consultation with the Joint Section of Education and Cultivation and in harmony with its plans.

Sec. IX. **Co-operation with Other Boards and Agencies**

¶ 1283. For the purpose of more effectively promoting Christian education outside the United States there shall be a **Joint Committee on Christian Education in Foreign Fields,** composed of twenty-two members. Ten shall be from the Board of Education: the general secretary and five other staff members of the Division of the Local Church, the general secretary and one other staff member of the Editorial Division, and two members of the board. Ten shall be from the Board of Missions: the staff chairman, treasurer, two area secretaries, and one member of the Division of World Missions, and the staff chairman, three area secretaries, and one member of the Department of Work in Foreign Fields of the Woman's Division of Christian Service. The other two shall be the executive secretary of the Interboard Committee on Missionary Education and the staff member responsible for promotion of the Methodist Youth Fund.

¶ 1284. The committee, as its work requires, may nominate staff for election by the Board of Missions and confirmation by the Board of Education. The staff shall be administratively related to the Board of Missions.

¶ **1285.** 1. The committee shall meet annually and at such other times as it shall determine, and shall report its actions to the Boards of Education and of Missions at their annual meetings.

2. It shall have a budget for its work provided by the two boards. The major responsibility for the budget rests on the Board of Missions, supplemented by support from the Board of Education, in which the Methodist Youth Fund shall have a part.

¶ **1286.** For the purpose of promoting effective co-operation between the Board of Missions and the Board of Education in missionary education there shall be an **Interboard Committee on Missionary Education,** composed of the general secretaries of the three divisions of the Board of Education and five other persons appointed by that board; and an equal number from the Board of Missions, which shall consist of two secretaries each from the Joint Section of Education and Cultivation and the three administrative divisions. The committee shall provide for age-group subcommittees and such other subcommittees as may be needed. This committee and its subcommittees shall be advisory and creative in character. The promotion of plans and materials created by this committee shall be a responsibility of the Board of Education and of the Board of Missions.

¶ **1287.** The duties of this committee shall be: (*a*) to develop a unified program of missionary education for all age groups in the local church and in the colleges, universities, and schools of theology; (*b*) to co-operate with the Curriculum Committee of the Board of Education in providing missionary information for church-school literature and in the planning and preparation of curriculum materials on missions; (*c*) to co-operate in the publication of books for missionary education in the church; (*d*) to develop co-operative plans for the missionary education and missionary giving of children, youth (*see* ¶ 1414 for relationships to the Methodist Youth Fund and its advisory committee), and adults; and (*e*) to report annually to the Board of Missions and to the Board of Education. The committee shall meet annually, and at such other times as it may determine.

¶ **1288.** There shall be an **executive secretary** of the committee, who shall be elected quadrennially by the Board of Education, on nomination of the committee, and shall be confirmed by the Board of Missions. He shall be the secretary for missionary education of the Board of Education with staff relationship to the Division of the Local Church. He shall likewise be the secretary for missionary education of the Board of Missions, having staff relationship to the Joint Section of Education and Cultivation. The committee shall have a budget provided for its work by the two boards on such ratio as they may decide. In missionary education the executive secretary and the members of the staff shall be the representatives equally of the Board of Missions and of the Board of Education. During the period between the General Conference and the organization of the new committee for the coming quadrennium, the staff and those members who have served on the committee during the past quadrennium shall continue to function until the new committee is organized.

¶ **1289.** There shall be a **Joint Committee on Architecture,** composed of staff personnel as follows: the executive secretary of the Section of Church Extension, the director of the Department of Architecture, and two others elected by the Division of National Missions of the Board of Missions; the general secretary and three others elected by the Division of the Local Church of the Board of Education. It shall have authority to prepare standards for the architecture of churches, parsonages, and religious educational buildings and to recommend them to the co-operating boards, and is authorized, under such provisions as the boards may agree on, to offer counsel in the erection of such buildings. It shall meet annually and at such other times as its work may require.

¶ **1290.** 1. There shall be a program of **Crusade scholarships** to give financial assistance in the training of future leadership of the churches in the mission fields.

2. There shall be a **Crusade Scholarship Committee,** composed of fifteen members elected quadrennially as follows: from the Board of Missions three each elected by the Division of World Missions, the Division of Na-

tional Missions, and the Woman's Division of Christian Service from its Department of Work in Foreign Fields; from the Board of Education three elected by the Division of Higher Education; from the Commission on Promotion and Cultivation three elected by the commission. Vacancies shall be filled by the agency in which they occur.

3. The committee shall elect its own officers quadrennially.

4. The committee shall be responsible for the selection of students recommended for the scholarships provided by the One Great Hour of Sharing offering (¶ 760) and other grants made specifically for Crusade scholarships by any of the agencies represented thereon.

5. The committee shall provide for the administration of the Crusade scholarship program, including provision of an office, approval of a budget for administration, and election of a director, who together with office staff shall be related to the Board of Missions and be included in the board's staff pension plan.

¶ **1291.** The Board of Missions and the Board of Christian Social Concerns shall co-operate in developing service projects for Methodist young people on a non-missionary basis which will meet United States Selective Service standards for alternative service for conscientious objectors. The financing shall be the responsibility of the Board of Missions.

¶ **1292.** The Board of Missions is authorized to appoint not more than fifteen representatives to a **Joint Commission on Co-operation and Counsel,** with like representation from the Christian Methodist Episcopal Church, for study and consideration of the problems involved. This committee shall include co-opted members from other boards having co-operative relations with the Christian Methodist Episcopal Church.

SEC. X.   **Jurisdictional Boards**

¶ **1294.** In each jurisdiction there may be a **Jurisdictional Board of Missions,** auxiliary to the general board, as the Jurisdictional Conference may determine. (*See* ¶¶ 15.3, 527.)

Sec. XI.   **Annual Conference Boards**

¶ **1295.** The **Conference Board of Missions** shall be auxiliary to the general and jurisdictional boards and shall be composed of the following members, elected quadrennially: one or more lay members and an equal number of ministers from each district, and five members at large, nominated by the conference nominating committee and elected quadrennially by the Annual Conference; the chairman of Christian outreach and one other representative, eighteen years of age or younger, elected by the Conference Methodist Youth Fellowship; one student elected by the state or regional unit of the Methodist Student Movement; the conference and district missionary secretaries, the conference lay leader, the conference secretary of evangelism, the president of the Conference Woman's Society of Christian Service, the chairman of the Commission on Town and Country Work the presidents and full-time executives of city (metropolitan) and district missionary societies, the chairman of the Committee on Urban Work, the chairman of the Commission on Minimum Salaries, and any members of the general board residing within the bounds of the conference. The district superintendents may be members of the board, at the discretion of the Annual Conference.

¶ **1296.** 1. The board shall elect its own officers, and hold its annual meeting at the call of the president, or any three members, on due notice. The transactions of the year shall be reported by the president to the Annual Conference, and a detailed statement of all disbursements of missionary and church-extension aid within the conference shall be printed in the conference journal.

2. It may hold a midyear meeting, at which time necessary business may be transacted and open meetings planned for a general and public discussion of all matters pertaining to home and foreign missions and church extension.

¶ **1297.** The officers and three additional members elected by the board shall constitute an **executive committee.** The executive committee shall exercise the powers of the board *ad interim.*

¶ **1298.** The board shall make nominations in accordance with ¶ 1172 for membership on the general board.

¶ **1299.** The board shall co-operate with the general board in carrying out the policies and promoting all phases of the work of missions and church extension. It shall also represent the interests of the Methodist Committee for Overseas Relief and promote its projects in the conference. It shall co-operate with the Joint Section of Education and Cultivation in developing an effective program of education and cultivation within the conference. To expedite this program there shall be created a Committee on Education and Cultivation of which the conference missionary secretary shall be chairman and all district missionary secretaries shall be members. There shall also be on the committee at least one lay man and one lay woman elected by the board, and one district superintendent selected by the Cabinet.

¶ **1300.** There shall be held annually in each district a training program which may be a **district missionary institute,** workshop, missionary festival, or rally. It shall be for the purposes of informing, training, and motivating the pastors, members of Commissions on Missions, and other laymen of local churches within the whole district. The board, through its Committee on Education and Cultivation, shall project conference-wide plans for education and cultivation. The district superintendents and district missionary secretaries shall promote and conduct the program in their respective districts. They shall consult with the secretary of missionary education and the secretary of promotion of the District Woman's Society of Christian Service. The Joint Section of Education and Cultivation shall co-operate with them in furnishing recommendations and resources for the program, including current study books, literature, audio-visual aids, speakers, and methods. Plans should include adequate time and numbers of meetings to reach all churches effectively.

¶ **1301.** The board shall co-operate with the Annual Conference program committee in arranging for a **missions anniversary** at each conference session, in which the work of the General Board of Missions shall be presented.

The president of the conference board shall have charge of such anniversary.

¶ **1302.** 1. The Annual Conference, on nomination of the board in consultation with the Cabinet, may elect annually an **executive secretary** of the board, who, if he is a ministerial member of the conference, shall be appointed by the bishop. He shall be a member of the board without vote and shall perform such duties in the field of missions and church extension as may be assigned by the board. The expenses of his salary and of his office shall be included in the budget of the board.

2. The Annual Conference, on nomination of the board, shall elect annually a **conference missionary secretary,** to be publicly assigned by the bishop. A vacancy in this office during the conference year may be filled by the executive committee. This secretary shall promote the policies and plans of the Board of Missions, and be its representative in the conference.

3. There shall be a **district missionary secretary** in each district, appointed by the district superintendent after consultation with the conference missionary secretary, and publicly assigned by the bishop. A vacancy in this office during the conference year may be filled by appointment by the district superintendent. This secretary shall work in co-operation with the district superintendent and conference missionary secretary.

¶ **1303.** In the program of home missions and church extension within the bounds of the Annual Conference the board shall act as follows:

1. It shall review, approve, or adjust the askings of the district superintendents for the maintenance program before they are presented to the general board, keeping in mind that, in making final decisions on all askings from the several conferences, the Division of National Missions must take into account the comparative missionary needs of each project and its permanent value of service to the entire church.

2. It may estimate annually the amount necessary for the support of conference missionary work and also the amount necessary for conference church extension, and shall report both estimates to the Commission on World

Service and Finance of the conference. The amount raised on these apportionments shall be administered by the board and applied respectively to missions and to church extension. The work of the board shall be subject to the approval of the Annual Conference. The board shall seek to cover all unoccupied territory in the conference by the establishment and support of missions, but missions shall be established only with the consent of the bishop in charge and his Cabinet, and with due consideration to the board's quadrennial plan of survey and strategy.

3. At least quadrennially, in consultation with the Cabinet and, where advisable, with city (metropolitan) or district missionary boards or societies, it shall provide for a survey of the missionary and church-extension needs of the several districts, placing special emphasis on the unchurched areas, and the population and other community, changes, with a view to determining in each what should be the over-all financial objective. Due consideration shall be given to the responsibility of the Division of National Missions for areas requiring missionary and church-extension aid beyond that which the conference is able to provide. From this study an adequate conference-initiated financial program shall be formulated with a view to meeting these needs. A priority list of projects to be developed shall be prepared. The list and all revisions shall be filed with the Division of National Missions.

4. Through its executive committee, or its Section of Church Extension, composed of not less than one third of its members, it shall administer such funds as come into its possession for church extension within the conference; *provided* that it may turn over all its church-extension funds to the Section of Church Extension of the Division of National Missions, which shall expend them within the bounds of the conference under the direction of the conference board. It shall provide for consultation between city (metropolitan) and district missionary societies and District Boards of Church Location and Building and the Division of National Missions in the development of standards and procedures for local-church building

projects in the fields of site selection, study and approval of architectural plans, and financial programs.

5. In the administration of such funds as come into its possession for church-extension purposes within the conference it shall have authority to lend or donate any part thereof, whichever in its judgment will better accomplish the desired end. When funds lent or donated are returned, it shall administer them as a portion of the total church-extension funds at its disposal. The foregoing shall not apply to conference board loan funds administered prior to the General Conference of 1948 by the Section of Church Extension of the Division of National Missions. If, however, an Annual Conference so elects, funds lent may become a part of the conference board loan fund, to be administered by the Section of Church Extension of the Division of National Missions on the same terms, conditions, and policies used by the Section of Church Extension.

¶ **1304.** The board may appoint a **Committee on Research and Survey,** which shall conduct surveys and make research studies within the bounds of the conference, and shall co-operate with the Department of Research and Survey of the Division of National Missions.

¶ **1305.** 1. The board shall appoint, in consultation with the Cabinet, a **Committee on Urban Work,** composed of pastors; district superintendents; laity experienced in the fields of city church work, urban planning and renewal, health, welfare, recreation, education, industry, and labor; and representatives of such church agencies as church-extension and research committees, city (metropolitan) and district missionary societies, Boards of Lay Activities, Woman's Societies of Christian Service, and Commissions on Town and Country Work.

2. The function of the committee shall be in the area of consultation and recommendation to the board, to which it shall be amenable. It shall inform itself, the board, the Cabinet, the Annual Conference, and the Department of City Work of the Division of National Missions relative to effectiveness of urban churches and an urban church strategy needed in keeping with city planning and urban renewal. It shall co-operate with committees on research

and church extension, city (metropolitan) and district missionary societies, and councils of churches in initiating studies of city churches and the needs or urban regions and in establishing mutually acceptable standards for serving urban residents.

3. The committee shall help the Department of City Work plan and promote the quadrennial Convocation on Urban Work (¶ 1228) by: (*a*) sharing areas of concern, successful experiences, and resource persons; (*b*) nominating delegates from the conference and promoting attendance; and (*c*) planning and helping execute follow-up workshops and institutes within the conference.

¶ **1306.** The board may appoint a **Committee on Town and Country Work,** composed of the executive committee of the Commission on Town and Country Work and others as may be determined. (*See* ¶ 1231.)

¶ **1307.** The promotional work of the Conference Board of Missions shall be included in the conference benevolence budget.

SEC. XII.   **Local-Church Commissions**

For description of the organization and duties of the Commission on Missions *see* ¶¶ 256-57 under Part II, The Local Church.

CHAPTER VII

METHODIST COMMITTEE FOR OVERSEAS RELIEF

¶ **1311.** There shall be a **Methodist Committee for Overseas Relief,** composed of twelve members as follows: one person from each jurisdiction, nominated by the College of Bishops and elected by the Jurisdictional Conference, and three persons each elected by the Department of Work in Foreign Fields of the Woman's Division of Christian Service and by the Division of World Missions of the Board of Missions. The committee shall be empowered to co-opt not more than seven members at large. Vacancies shall be filled by the body concerned: by the College of Bishops of the jurisdiction, or by the department or division, or, in the case of the co-opted members, by the committee itself. The committee is authorized to elect its own officers, to appoint sub-committees if desired, to employ such assistance as may be needed (*see* ¶ 783.2*a*), and to provide for its necessary expense of administration and promotion out of un-designated receipts. Its financial officers shall be bonded.

¶ **1312.** The committee is authorized and empowered:

1. To be the representative of The Methodist Church in the field of overseas relief; also in the field of rehabilita-tion, in conference with the units of the Board of Missions named in ¶ 1311.

2. To transmit to the church the appeals for help from recognized agencies, and to receive and allocate the funds contributed for relief and rehabilitation purposes by churches, groups, or individuals; *provided* that no church-wide appeal for funds shall be made without the approval of the Council of Bishops and the Council on World Service and Finance.

3. To give special attention and assistance to the na-tional workers and the people of our Methodist churches overseas who are in need because of war or other disasters. In countries where the Board of Missions is at work, it is expected that the administration of specifically Meth-odist relief be through the board and the bishops in charge and, where possible, the indigenous church.

4. To co-operate with Church World Service and other interdenominational relief agencies, as the committee may deem wise from time to time.

5. When considered desirable, to supplement the work of other agencies ministering to the relief of human suffering in the spirit of Christ.

¶ **1313.** In order to provide adequate means for the prosecution of this work, the committee, in addition to its receipts by voluntary gifts and by participation in the Fellowship of Suffering and Service offerings (¶ 763), shall be included in any general church-wide appeal for war emergencies or postwar work. (*See* ¶¶ 758, 760.)

¶ **1314.** Authorization is given to the committee to acknowledge gifts by its own vouchers. Such gifts, how-

ever, cannot receive credit on world service apportionments. (See ¶ 746.)

¶ 1315. If at any time during the quadrennium the
Council of Bishops, the Council on World Service and
Finance, and the Board of Missions decide that the
specific work of the committee is no longer needed, the
committee shall be discharged and its responsibilities and
assets shall be assigned to such agency as those three
bodies may determine.

CHAPTER VIII

BOARD OF EDUCATION

SECTION I.   **Purpose**

¶ 1324. Christian education has its roots in the nature
of the Christian gospel itself. Jesus is frequently called
Master or Teacher, and he is the authority in our church's
program of Christian nurture. His Great Commission is:
"Go therefore and make disciples of all nations, . . .
teaching them to observe all that I have commanded you;
and lo, I am with you always." The purpose of Christian
education is to learn, to teach, and to use his way by which
persons of all ages are related through Jesus Christ to
God as Father and to all men as brothers. The divisions of
the Board of Education shall develop standards consistent
with this purpose and support their attainment through
appropriate program and curriculum materials in Methodism's local churches, colleges, universities, and schools
of theology.

SEC. II   **Organization**

¶ 1325. 1.   There shall be a **Board of Education** of
The Methodist Church, hereinafter referred to as the
General Board of Education, for the promotion of Christian education. The board shall have general oversight of
the educational interests of the church in the United
States. It may co-operate with the Board of Missions for
the advancement of Christian education in other lands.

2. The General Board of Education shall be incorporated under the laws of whatever state the board may determine.

3. The board shall meet annually at such time and place as it may determine, subject to the provisions of the act of incorporation, and may hold such special meetings as may be necessary. A majority of the members of the board shall constitute a quorum.

4. The board shall appoint such committees as may be necessary for the proper discharge of its business. It may adopt such by-laws for the regulation of the affairs of the board and its divisions and committees as are not inconsistent with the act of incorporation or with General Conference legislation.

¶ 1326. 1. The board shall be constituted quadrennially, and its members and all officers elected by it shall hold office until their successors have been chosen.

2. Membership of the board shall consist of one half of the eligible effective bishops of The Methodist Church resident in the United States, selected by the Council of Bishops, together with additional members selected as follows: each Jurisdictional Conference shall elect to the membership of the Board of Education on nomination of its Committee on Education one minister and one layman without regard to the number of members within the jurisdiction, and in addition one minister and one layman for each 400,000 members or major fraction thereof within the jurisdiction; *provided* that not more than two thereof shall be from any one Annual Conference.

3. The board shall elect, from nominations made by the Council of Bishops, sufficient members at large without respect to jurisdictions or Annual Conferences to bring the membership to a total of ninety-one.

4. There shall be six young people—four representing the Methodist Youth Fellowship, one of whom shall be the president of the National Conference thereof, and two representing the Methodist Student Movement— elected quadrennially by the board on nomination of the Joint Staff on Youth and Student Work, which shall have selected the nominees as provided in ¶ 1405.2.

¶ 1327. 1. Within three months after the adjournment of the last Jurisdictional Conference to meet in that year, the elected members of the board shall be assembled by a convener, designated by the Council of Bishops, to organize in the following manner.

2. A nominating committee shall be elected, which shall be composed of one member chosen by the members from each jurisdiction and one bishop chosen by the bishops who are members of the board.

3. The nominating committee shall nominate for election by the board: (a) members at large from the list submitted by the Council of Bishops (¶ 1326.3); (b) members of the three constituent divisions of the board—the Division of Higher Education, the Division of the Local Church, and the Editorial Division—in ratio of five, five and two; (c) a president and a recording secretary for the board.

4. The members of the divisions and the president and recording secretary of the board shall be elected from the membership of the board. The president, who shall be a presiding, not an administrative, officer, shall preside over the meetings of the board and of the executive committee. Each division shall elect a chairman, and these chairmen shall be vice-presidents of the board. The officers of the board and members of the divisions, together with the officers of each division, shall hold office for the quadrennium.

5. The general secretaries of the Division of Higher Education and the Division of the Local Church shall be elected for the quadrennium by the board from nominations made by the respective divisions. A vacancy in either office shall be filled by election by the board. The general secretary of the Editorial Division shall be elected as provided in ¶ 1429.

6. The treasurer shall be elected by the board on nomination of the executive committee.

7. No member of the board shall be a salaried officer of the board.

8. The salaries and duties of all employees of the board except in the Editorial Division shall be fixed by the board.

¶ **1328.** The board is authorized to solicit and create special funds, to receive gifts and bequests, to hold properties and securities in trust, and to administer all these financial affairs in accordance with its own rules and the provisions of the Discipline.

¶ **1329.** 1. The board shall conduct its work through the three administrative divisions hereinbefore named (¶ 1327.3*b*), each of which shall be responsible for the specific areas assigned to it by the board.

2. Each of the divisions shall elect from its members an **advisory committee,** consisting of its chairman, recording secretary, and other members to the following totals: Division of Higher Education, seven; Division of the Local Church, seven; Editorial Division, four. In addition the president of the board shall be ex officio a member of each advisory committee.

These committees shall assist in the conduct of the work and serve as members of the executive committee of the board. (*See* ¶ 1330.1.)

3. The **general secretaries** of the divisions shall be the administrative officers of their respective divisions under such regulations as the board may make. Reports of the work of the respective divisions, including organization and budget, except the budget of the Editorial Division, shall be presented annually by them to the board. Assistants to the general secretaries of the Division of Higher Education and the Division of the Local Church shall be elected annually by the divisions on nomination of the respective general secretaries. Assistants to the general secretary of the Editorial Division shall be appointed by him and reported to the board.

4. Each of the divisions shall provide for a review of its work, pass upon recommendations of its general secretary and staff, and make recommendations to the board concerning its needs and programs.

5. The general secretaries shall attend the meetings of the board, the executive committee, and their respective divisions, participating in their deliberations, but without vote.

6. The three general secretaries shall form a **secretarial council,** which shall choose annually in rotation from its members a presiding officer, and shall meet as necessary to correlate the work of the three divisions.

¶ **1330.** 1. The **executive committee** of the board shall be composed of the president and recording secretary of the board and the members of the advisory committees of the three divisions as provided in ¶ 1329.2. A majority of the members shall constitute a quorum.

2. The executive committee shall manage the funds of the board under such regulations as the board may adopt; appoint finance and investment committees, which shall render to it detailed reports at each meeting; fix the official bond of the treasurer and of any other officers entrusted with the handling of funds; consider and approve the administrative budgets of the board and its divisions, except the Editorial Division.

3. The **treasurer** of the board shall be the custodian of all the funds of the board. He shall keep the accounts of the assets, liabilities, receipts, and disbursements of the board and of the Division of Higher Education and the Division of the Local Church. He shall pay out funds on order of the general secretaries of these divisions. He shall report annually to the board and to the executive committee as requested by it. An associate treasurer may be elected by the board on nomination of the executive committee.

4. The board may commit to the executive committee such other powers and duties as it may determine. Minutes of the executive committee shall be sent to the members of the board and submitted to the annual meeting of the board for approval. Meetings of the Committee shall be held at least once each year, not including meetings held in connection with the annual meetings of the board.

¶ **1331.** All assets and liabilities existing at the time of union in the funds of the Boards of Education of the three uniting churches shall be the assets and liabilities of the corresponding divisions in the new Board of Education.

¶ **1332.** The Division of Higher Education and the Division of the Local Church shall present quadrennially to the Council on World Service and Finance a statement of the amounts required for their general expenses and for the support of their work, and the appropriations of the council shall be made to each division. The Editorial Division shall be financed as provided in ¶¶ 1148-49. In all cases the purposes for which funds are committed to the board shall be strictly observed.

¶ **1333.** The board shall have authority to make provision for co-operation with any of the general boards or other agencies of the church, or with other agencies, in matters within its field. Each Annual Conference shall determine for itself to what extent it will undertake to co-operate with other denominations or agencies in its own territory.

¶ **1334.** The Board of Education shall be the legal successor and successor in trust of the General Board of Christian Education of the Methodist Episcopal Church, South, the Board of Education of the Methodist Episcopal Church, the Board of Education of the Methodist Protestant Church, the Board of Education for Negroes of the Methodist Episcopal Church, the Board of Sunday Schools of the Methodist Episcopal Church, and the Epworth League of the Methodist Episcopal Church; and it is authorized and empowered at any time it may deem such action to be desirable or convenient to take corporate action in the name of said corporations to surrender the charter or charters of one or several or all of said corporations (including a transfer of all of the properties of said corporations to the Board of Education if necessary or desirable), or to merge, consolidate, or affiliate such corporations, or any of them, with the Board of Education in compliance with appropriate state corporation laws, so as to accomplish as nearly as may legally be possible the end result that the Board of Education shall be the one legal entity authorized to act on behalf of the interests heretofore or hereafter in the name of one of the other of said corporations.

¶ **1335.** As a means of educating the church in regard to better race relations and the needs of Negro schools, **Race Relations Sunday** shall be observed in all the congregations. (*See* ¶ 250.3.)

SEC. III   **Division of Higher Education**

¶ **1351.** 1. Higher education is part of both our Methodist heritage and our present task. In establishing and maintaining educational institutions and in ministering to students the church continues its historic work of uniting knowledge and vital piety.

2. There shall be a **Division of Higher Education,** which shall represent The Methodist Church in all activities connected with secondary, higher, and ministerial education. The division shall have an advisory relationship to all educational institutions in the United States affiliated with The Methodist Church: universities, colleges, secondary schools, schools of theology, and Wesley Foundations and similar organizations. On request it may serve in an advisory capacity to the several agencies of the church owning or administering educational institutions.

3. Its principal objectives shall be: (*a*) to develop an educational plan and purpose which shall definitely relate the educational institutions of the church to the church; (*b*) to foster within them the highest educational standards and soundest business practices; (*c*) to interpret to them their place and function in the life and work of the church; (*d*) to encourage them in their commitment to Christian standards and ideals in their teaching, policies, and practices; (*e*) to create and maintain within them an atmosphere conducive to a knowledge and understanding of the Christian message and mission; (*f*) to interpret to the membership of the church the distinctive services rendered by these educational institutions and their functions in the church and society; and (*g*) to lead the church in a program designed to assure their permanence, efficiency, academic excellence, and Christian commitment.

4. It shall operate through three constituent departments: Educational Institutions, College and University Religious Life, and Ministerial Education.

5. It shall elect, on nomination of the general secretary, directors for each of the departments, and such other staff members as are needed for the operation of the division.

6. It shall engage personnel, appoint such commissions and committees and adopt such regulations as necessary for the discharge of its responsibilities.

¶ **1352.** The specific responsibilities of the division are:

1. To devise ways and means to interpret and aid the higher education program of the church. (*See* ¶ 1356.2.)

2. To co-operate with Annual Conferences in establishing and conducting institutions of higher education in the United States in areas in which facilities for Christian higher education are not adequately provided. (*See* 1391.)

3. To maintain an advisory relationship to the schools of theology in the planning of their educational programs and in the development of their financial support, and in developing and conducting in-service programs of education for preachers, including approved supply pastors and other local preachers.

4. To promote Christian instruction, afford opportunities for Christian service, and offer guidance in Christian vocations for students at educational institutions of The Methodist Church and for Methodist students at tax-supported and other institutions not related to The Methodist Church.[4]

5. To make use, in so far as is practicable, of the existing church organization and publications for carrying out its work of interpretation, setting up such conferences and producing such materials as will strengthen the interrelation of the church and its educational institutions.

6. To study the financial status of Methodist educational institutions, encourage the church to give them continuing and conscientious support, provide guidance and leadership in their special financial campaigns, and formulate procedures by which they can approach Methodist members and constituents for gifts and bequests.

7. To direct attention to the work and needs of educational institutions which stand in special relationship to the church at large, and to request support for them, with due recognition of the needs of schools and colleges historically operated for Negroes.

8. To furnish guidance, plans of procedure, personal leadership, and plans for special gifts to be known as **educational specials** in the promotion of the work of higher education in the Annual Conferences and in the local churches.

---

[4] *See* Judicial Council Decision 175.

9. To devise methods of credit for local-church giving to educational institutions related to the division, including the listing of all such giving in appropriate columns in the statistical reports of the Annual Conference minutes.

¶ 1353. The **Department of Educational Institutions,** which term shall include universities, colleges, and secondary schools, shall have primary responsibility for the work of the division as outlined in ¶¶ 1351-52 and hereafter described more specifically in ¶¶ 1354-59 in so far as the provisions thereof relate to the universities, colleges, secondary, and other schools of The Methodist Church.

¶ 1354. 1. The division shall appropriate the funds available for the support of educational institutions related to The Methodist Church, under such rules as it may adopt.

2. In making appropriations for the support of educational institutions, the division shall give due consideration to their current financial needs as shown in carefully prepared reports presented by them on forms provided. Appropriations to institutions from funds at the disposal of the division shall not debar those institutions from soliciting aid from their supporting conferences or from other sources. (*See* ¶ 1391.)

3. The division shall co-operate with the General and Annual Conferences in their efforts to provide the institutions related to them adequate financial income for the operation of accredited educational programs.

4. The division shall recommend to Jurisdictional and Annual Conference Boards of Education concerned with the appropriation of conference funds those institutions whose educational and religious aims and programs are in active accord with the policies of the church as expressed in the Discipline and through special General Conference enactments. (*See* ¶¶ 1367, 1385.)

5. The division shall have power to administer under the rules and regulations of the board any and all funds, gifts, and bequests which have been or may be committed to it; and, subject to the approval of the board, it may solicit or create special funds for its projects. The purposes

for which the funds are given and accepted shall be sacredly observed.

6. The division shall take such action as is necessary to protect or recover the investment which it or an Annual Conference has made in capital funds to any institution founded, organized, developed, or assisted under the direction or with the co-operation of The Methodist Church, should any such institution discontinue operation or move to sever or to modify its connection with the church or violate the terms of any such grant of new capital funds made by The Methodist Church.

¶ 1355. 1. The division shall, in co-operation with the University Senate, study population growth and trends and make recommendations to the Annual Conferences concerning the needs for new institutions of learning and the discontinuance, relocation, and merger of existing institutions.

2. No educational institution hereafter established or acquired shall be qualified for classification as a Methodist institution or be aided by the division unless the division shall have been consulted and shall have approved the expenditures involved in the establishment or acquisition of such institution. (*See* ¶¶ 1367, 1391.)

3. An institution receiving appropriations from the division which incurs debt obligations, bonded or otherwise, for expansion programs without first submitting its proposed plans to the division for consideration and counsel relinquishes its right to appropriations until the debt so incurred is liquidated.

¶ 1356. 1. The division, through such officers, committees, and commissions as it may deem necessary, shall provide for the co-operative study of plans for maximum correlation of the work of our educational institutions with the church's entire program of Christian education.

2. In co-operation with the Annual Conferences and the pastors and Commissions on Education of local churches, the division shall bring to the attention of our members the contribution of our educational institutions to the life and character of youth, and the place the institutions

have in the preservation and propagation of Christianity. (*See* ¶¶ 233.7*f*, 352.17, 1352.1.)

¶ **1357.** 1. The division shall be the agency of the board in administering institutions for **Christian education among Negroes,** except those institutions now owned by other agencies. It shall have authority to institute plans by which schools sponsored by the division may co-operate with or may unite with schools of other denominations or under independent control, provided the interests of The Methodist Church are adequately protected.

2. The division shall encourage such schools to secure adequate endowments for their support and maintenance. Whenever the division is assured that their support will be adequate and the property will be conserved and perpetuated for Christian education under the auspices and control of The Methodist Church, it may transfer the schools to boards of trustees under such conditions as the General Board of Education may prescribe, including right of reversion to the General Board of Education.

3. The division shall be responsible for promoting Race Relations Sunday. (*See* ¶¶ 250.3, 1335.)

¶ **1358.** 1. The division shall promote and administer the **Student Loan Fund,** the **National Methodist Scholarship Fund,** and other grants and bequests made to the division for the aid of students in accordance with regulations recommended by the division and adopted by the board.

2. The division shall be responsible for promoting Methodist Student Day. (*See* ¶ 250.4.)

Note: For the participation of the division in the Crusade scholarship program *see* ¶ 1290.

¶ **1359. Educational societies** or **foundations** created by Annual Conferences for the promotion of work in Christian higher education may be recognized as auxiliaries to the Division of Higher Education when their objects and purposes, their articles of incorporation, and their methods of administration shall have been approved by the Annual Conference within whose bounds they are incorporated. All auxiliaries thus approved may be required to make an annual report of their fiscal and administrative affairs to the division.

¶ 1360. There shall be a **Committee on Co-operation and Counsel** of ten members, five to be appointed by the Division of Higher Education and five by the Board of Missions, nominated by the Department of Work in Home Fields of the Woman's Division of Christian Service, to take under consideration all matters involving educational work in institutions in which agencies of both boards may have responsibility.

¶ 1363. The **Department of College and University Religious Life** shall have primary responsibility for the work of the division with college and university students as outlined in ¶¶ 1351-52 and hereafter described more specifically in ¶¶ 1364-71.

¶ 1364. In its work with students the division, in co-operation with Annual Conferences, shall have the following responsibilities:

1. To organize and maintain Wesley Foundations at tax-supported and independent institutions.

2. To assist Methodist institutions of higher education in their religious activities.[5]

3. To study the religious needs of students, provide for evangelistic work among students, and enlist suitable candidates for full-time religious vocations.

¶ 1365. There shall be a governing body for the student work in every college community where The Methodist Church is at work, as follows:

1. For each Wesley Foundation there shall be a Board of Directors as described in ¶ 1366.

2. The division shall encourage each Methodist-related college or university to establish a **Committee on Campus Religious Life**, which may serve also as a Campus-Church Relations Committee, and to state qualifications and define duties of the committee in consultation with the division.

3. For each other institution there shall be a **Campus-Church Relations Committee** nominated by a local Methodist body and elected by the Conference Board of Education.[6]

---

[5] *See* Judicial Council Decision 175.
[6] *See* Judicial Council Decision 175.

¶ 1366. 1. A **Wesley Foundation** is the organized educational ministry through which The Methodist Church makes a unified approach to the tax-supported or independent college or university. The nature of its work shall be defined by the division.

2. A Wesley Foundation shall have a **Board of Directors** composed of members from the local campus-church community and members at large representing the interests of the Annual Conference or Conferences. They shall be elected by the Annual Conference or Conferences on nomination of the Conference Board or Boards of Education.

3. The Board of Directors shall be responsible for the direction and administration of the foundation in accordance with the policies and standards established by the conference board or boards and the division. The foundation shall be related functionally and co-operatively, through its Board of Directors, to the Methodist local church or churches in the immediate vicinity of the college or university. The Board of Directors, when incorporated, may hold property, according to the laws of The Methodist Church and the state in which the foundation is located.[7]

¶ 1367. The division shall appoint a **Commission on Standards for Wesley Foundations,** which shall be the accrediting agency for all Wesley Foundations and interdenominational student work related to The Methodist Church at tax-supported and independent colleges and universities in the United States. It shall be composed of six members of the division and five persons, not members of the General Board of Education, who are actively engaged in Wesley Foundation work, and who are fitted by training and experience to establish standards and evaluate the educational, religious, and financial program of Wesley Foundations. It shall report annually to the division and to the Annual Conferences those Wesley Foundations which meet the standards it has established.[8]

¶ 1368. To fulfill its responsibility for the religious

---

[7] Amended in 1960 concurrently with Judicial Council Decision 175.

[8] *See* Judicial Council Decisions 137, 175.

training and activities of Methodist students the division may make appropriations to approved Wesley Foundations and for the support and development of other organizations in the United States with similar purposes. In making financial appropriations, the approval or other evaluation of the Commission on Standards for Wesley Foundations shall be given careful consideration by the division and by the Conference Boards of Education. A Wesley Foundation at a non-Methodist institution or other similar organization in a Methodist institution receiving financial aid shall submit annually reports of its work and financial operations on forms provided by the division. Appropriations made by the division toward the maintenance of religious work at any given institution shall not preclude the solicitation of additional funds from supporting conferences.

¶ **1369.** 1. In carrying out its responsibility for the operation and maintenance of religious work among Methodist students enrolled in institutions of higher education, the division through the Department of College and University Religious Life shall relate campus Christian organizations on Methodist campuses, Wesley Foundations at tax-supported and independent colleges and universities, and such other organizations as may be developed, to the intercollegiate Christian movement known as the **Methodist Student Movement.** There shall be such state or similar area units, regional and national, as the division shall see fit to maintain. The department shall publish such materials as are necessary to develop this work.

2. Some of the purposes of the Methodist Student Movement shall be:

a) To lead all members of the college and university community to accept the Christian faith in God according to the Scriptures, to live as true disciples of Jesus Christ, and to become members of Christ's Church.

b) To deepen, enrich, and mature the Christian faith of college and university men and women through commitment to Jesus Christ and his Church, and to prepare them for active lives of service and leadership in and through the Church during and after their student years.

c) To witness in the campus community to the mission, message, and life of the Church.

¶ **1370.** 1. There shall be a **National Conference of the Methodist Student Movement** for the purpose of fellowship, evaluation, and program planning in areas that relate to student work. It shall be composed of the presidents of Methodist student organizations of state or similar geographical regions, the Methodist Student Movement delegates to the National Student Christian Federation, eight representative students at large, seven state or similar area directors of student work, the staff of the Department of College and University Religious Life, student members of the general boards and other agencies, and the staff responsible for student work of other general agencies.

2. Through this conference the students shall have free opportunity to participate creatively in planning the church's program by making recommendations to all the agencies of the church and by proposing student members for nomination to the general boards as provided in ¶ 1405. The conference shall report to the division annually on its meetings and activities.

¶ **1371.** The Boards of Education of the Annual Conferences of a given state or similar geographical region shall create or provide for continuing at the beginning of each quadrennium a Conference or an **Interconference Commission on College and University Religious Work,** which shall co-ordinate all intercollegiate work of the Methodist Student Movement and give general oversight to student work at the institutions of higher learning in that region. It shall co-operate with the Department of College and University Religious Life in the general program of the Methodist Student Movement. The duties of the commission shall be: (*a*) to evaluate the student work within its region; (*b*) to report its evaluation to the Conference Board or Boards of Education; (*c*) to recommend improvements in facilities, program, finance, and personnel; and (*d*) to co-operate in the interpretation of the Methodist Student Movement. This commission may elect a state or regional **director of student work,** whose duties and responsibilities shall be determined by the commission in co-operation with the executive secretaries of the conference boards involved.

Note: For provisions for correlating youth and student work *see* ¶ 1405.

¶ **1372.** 1. The **Department of Ministerial Education** shall have primary responsibility for the work of the division in relation to the schools of theology and the preparation of the ministry of the church, and shall be responsible for promoting theological education in the church. It shall be composed of twelve persons, six bishops and six ministers, selected from the membership of the division. In addition the division shall select six administrators from the Methodist schools of theology to serve as advisory members of the department; *provided* that these representatives shall not participate in the allocation of appropriations for schools of theology. The division shall also select from the faculties of the schools of theology six advisory members to assist in preparing the courses of study described in ¶ 1374.

2. The division shall elect, on nomination of the general secretary, a **director of ministerial education,** who shall be responsible for that part of the program of the division concerned with the enlistment and educational preparation of candidates for the ministry. In matters pertaining to ministerial education he shall serve as liaison officer between the boards and other agencies and the schools of theology of the church.

3. The division shall elect, on nomination of the general secretary, such associate directors as are deemed necessary to assist in the program of the department.

4. The department shall be responsible for: maintenance of the educational standards for the ministry (see Part III, The Ministry, Chapters II-V, ¶¶ 304-415); development and promotion of a program of ministerial enlistment and guidance (in co-operative relationship with the Interboard Committee on Christian Vocations); the educational preparation of candidates for the ministry; relationships with the Annual Conference Boards of Ministerial Training and Qualifications (¶¶ 669-74); schools and programs of continuing education and inspiration for ministers; supervision of the courses of

study as described in ¶ 1374; and interdenominational relationships that relate to the ministry, such as with the Department of the Ministry of the National Council of Churches.

¶ **1373.** The work of the department shall be supported from the general benevolences of the church. The division shall recommend to the Council on World Service and Finance, as items apart from its own budget, the amounts of financial support which should be allocated for ministerial education. (*See* ¶ 1378.)

¶ **1374.** 1. The department shall prescribe the courses of study required for license to preach and for admission on trial; also a four-year **ministerial course of study** for candidates qualifying for the traveling ministry under ¶¶ 325.3, 343, for approved supply pastors (¶ 317.2, .3), and for candidates for orders as local preachers (¶¶ 393, 403; *see also* ¶ 307.2). It shall recommend courses of reading and also provide advanced courses of study for preachers who have finished the above courses.

2. It shall co-operate with the Boards of Ministerial Training and Qualifications and other conference boards in organizing, financing, and conducting **pastors' schools,** which shall be of two kinds: (*a*) short-term schools to provide programs of inspiration and instruction for all ministers; (*b*) schools which offer work in the courses of study.

3. It shall, in co-operation with the Methodist schools of theology, administer **correspondence** work in the courses of study described in § 1.

4. All work in the courses of study for candidates for the traveling ministry (¶¶ 325.2, .3, 343) and for local preachers seeking renewal of license (¶ 307.2), including approved supply pastors qualifying for appointment (¶ 317.2, .3) and for authority to administer the Sacraments (¶ 318), shall be taken under the direction of the Department of Ministerial Education either in an approved course of study school or through correspondence.

¶ **1375.** The department shall develop and promote a program of selective enlistment and guidance of candidates for the ministry in co-operation with the Interboard Committee on Christian Vocations, the Methodist schools of theology, the Boards of Ministerial Training and Qualifications, and the bishops, district superintendents, counselors with preministerial students in the colleges and universities, and directors of Wesley Foundations. It shall also sponsor and promote conferences on the ministry in the Annual Conferences in co-operation with the Interboard Committee on Christian Vocations and the respective bishops, Conference Committees or Commissions on Christian Higher Education, Conference Boards of Education, and Boards of Ministerial Training and Qualifications.

¶ 1376. The department shall be responsible for a continuing study of the ministry, and a report of its findings shall be given to each General Conference.[10]

SEC. IV.   **Schools of Theology**

¶ 1378. 1. The **schools of theology** of the church are established and maintained for the education of ministers. They exist for the benefit of the whole church, and their support shall be provided by the church as a part of its general benevolent giving. (*See* ¶ 1354.2.)

2. For the purpose of providing for the better support of these schools, the Division of Higher Education, in consultation with their administrative officers, shall establish budget askings for their adequate support; and the amount necessary for such support shall be added as a separate item in the askings of the General Board

---

[10] The General Conference of 1960 directed that during the 1960-64 quadrennium this study be made of "the ministry of The Methodist Church in the light of historic Christianity for the purpose of clarifying the doctrine of the Church in relation to its ministry and as it bears on such questions as the proper use of the terms 'minister' and 'pastor,' ordination (including the ordination of local preachers and their status in Methodism), the administration of the Sacraments, the relation of supply pastors to the Annual Conference, the functions and responsibilities of the ministry, careers properly included in the ministerial office and positions to which episcopal appointment may be made, the structure of the Department of Ministerial Education, and problems of recruitment and the most effective use of our ministerial manpower"; that at least two representatives appointed by the Division of World Missions co-operate in the study; and that the findings be reported to the church three months before the General Conference of 1964. In another action the General Conference added to this study the new legislation limiting the authority of a local preacher to the bounds of his pastoral charge (¶¶ 304.2, 374, 392, 402).

of Education from the benevolence funds as determined by the authoritative body; *provided*, however, that the receiving of appropriations of such funds through the division shall not debar the schools from soliciting additional funds from the Annual and Jurisdictional Conferences as a part of the program of Christian higher education.

3. No school of theology or department of theology in a college or university shall be established without first submitting its proposed organization and classification to the University Senate for prior approval. (*See* ¶ 1391.)

¶ **1379.** It is expected that our schools of theology, in addition to preparing their students for effective service for Christ and the Church, shall acquaint them with the current programs of The Methodist Church, such as its educational, missionary, social, and other service programs, and with the organizations and the terminology of the the church, and shall provide such instruction in Methodist history, polity and doctrine as is required of candidates for membership in the Annual Conferences (¶ 344).

¶ **1380.** The Methodist schools of theology share with the Boards of Ministerial Training and Qualifications the responsibility for the selection and education of young people for admission to the Annual Conferences.

1. It is recommended therefore that these schools, before admitting a candidate for the Methodist ministry as a divinity student, shall (*a*) inquire into his personal character and promise of usefulness in the ministry, (*b*) require satisfactory evidence of his having been licensed to preach, and (*c*) require a letter of recommendation from the Board of Ministerial Training and Qualifications of the Annual Conference in which he resides.

2. It is further recommended that, when such a candidate has been admitted, the school shall give careful attention to his progress in studies and his personal and religious development, to determine whether he should be continued in his preparation for the ministry. When a candidate's progress is adjudged to be unsatisfactory, he should not be permitted to continue. Notification of the

termination of his relationship in the school shall be given by the school to the registrar of the Board of Ministerial Training and Qualifications where his Annual Conference relations are recorded.

SEC. V.   **University Senate**

¶ **1382.** The **University Senate** shall be the accrediting and standardizing agency for all the educational institutions related to The Methodist Church in the United States.

¶ **1383.** The University Senate shall be composed of twenty-one persons, not members of the General Board of Education, who are actively engaged in the work of education and are fitted by training and experience for the technical work of establishing standards and evaluating educational institutions in accordance with such standards. Eleven of these members shall be elected quadrennially by the General Board of Education, and ten shall be appointed by the Council of Bishops. Due regard shall be given to representation from the various types of institutions included in the University Senate's classification of educational institutions. If, in consequence of the retirement of a member from educational work or for any other cause, a vacancy occurs in the senate during the quadrennium, it shall be filled by the agency by which the retiring member was elected, at its next meeting.

¶ **1384.** The senate shall establish and assist in maintaining standards for the educational institutions related to The Methodist Church in the United States and shall sustain an advisory relation to the General Board of Education in matters of educational institutions. It shall prepare and publish annually a proper classification of all educational institutions in the United States which are related to The Methodist Church. Such classification shall comprise the official senate list of educational institutions related to the church, and on the basis of this list, the Division of Higher Education shall be governed in its work.

¶ **1385.** At its discretion the senate shall investigate, as conditions may warrant or require, the objectives, academic programs, educational standards, personnel, plant and equipment, business and management practices, financial program, public relations, student personnel services, religious life, and church relations of any designated educational institution claiming or adjudged to be related to The Methodist Church and shall report to the sponsoring board or agency through the Division of Higher Education decisions as to whether or not the institution is such as to justify its official recognition and continued financial support by the church.

¶ **1386.** The senate shall act as consultant and counselor on all educational matters to all educational institutions related to the church and as needed shall make to the sponsoring board or other agency of the church through the Division of Higher Education, to the Conference Boards of Education, or to other constituent bodies recommendations leading to their improvement or accreditation. Failure of any educational institution to make reasonable progress in complying with said recommendations of the senate may render the institution ineligible for further support by the Division of Higher Education, or by its related board or other agency, Annual Conference, or Conferences.

¶ **1387.** The senate as the accrediting agent for all educational institutions of the church may investigate, on its own initiative or at the written request of any general board of the church or Conference Board of Education or institutional board of trustees, the educational work of an institution related to said board, and shall report to the board concerned its recommendations as to what specific changes or improvements should be made.

¶ **1388.** The senate shall elect its own presiding officer and may appoint such committees and may delegate to them such powers as are incident to its work. The general secretary of the Division of Higher Education shall be the **executive secretary** of the senate. He shall convene the senate at the beginning of each quadrennium for organization. Thereafter the senate shall meet annually at such time and place as it may determine. Special meetings may be called on the written request of five members or at the discretion of the presiding officer and the executive secretary.

¶ **1389.** After consultation with the officers of the senate, the Division of Higher Education shall provide in its annual budget, as it may deem sufficient, for the expense of the senate, except that expenses incurred by the senate on behalf of any other board of the church shall be borne by that board.

¶ **1390.** Educational institutions in the United States related to The Methodist Church are classified as follows:

1. Universities
2. Colleges of liberal arts
3. Schools of theology
4. Junior colleges
5. Secondary schools
6. Training schools for religious workers
7. Other schools

It shall be the duty of the executive secretary of the senate to secure from each educational institution related to The Methodist Church such information as may be needed by the senate for an understanding of the status, work, and progress of the institution. This information shall be supplied on forms approved by the senate.

¶ **1391.** 1. The senate may, in co-operation with the Division of Higher Education, study population growth and trends and consider recommendations to the Annual Conferences concerning the need for new institutions of learning, and the discontinuance, relocation, and merger of existing institutions. (*See* ¶ 1355.1.)

2. No educational institution or foundation of The Methodist Church shall hereafter be established until its plans and organization shall have been approved by the senate and the division; and no Annual or Provisional Annual Conference in the United States shall acquire, or affiliate with, through any board or society, a school, college, university, or other educational institution unless the approval of the senate and the division shall have been previously obtained and unless, in the judgment of the division, there is reasonable assurance of financial support sufficient to equip and maintain the institution in the classification approved for it by the senate. In no case shall the division aid an institution which announces a change in its classification until the senate shall have approved the new classification. (*See* ¶ 1355.2.)

Sec. VI.   **Division of the Local Church**

¶ **1396.** The Division of the Local Church shall develop a comprehensive and unified program of Christian education which shall lead to commitment to Christ and membership in his Church and to a knowledge of the Holy Scriptures, the Christian religion, and the Christian Church. It shall provide for worship, fellowship, study, and service, including social, recreational, evangelistic, stewardship, and missionary activities, and education in the Christian way of life. It shall be responsible for forming standards and preparing programs for the organization and work of Christian education in the local church in accordance with provisions as set forth in ¶¶ 231-51, including standards for the offices of minister or director of Christian education and minister or director of music. It shall also seek ways and means of promoting the attendance of children, youth, and adults in all church-school organizations, and especially in the group known as the Sunday school, and shall establish standards defining membership and attendance in the church school and governing the maintenance of the membership roll. In co-operation with the Editorial Division it shall seek to inform the church on all phases of church-school work; shall establish and maintain standards; shall co-operate with the Curriculum Committee in determining the curriculum of the church school, including the courses of leadership education; and give direction to a comprehensive and unified program of Christian education in the local church. It shall provide for instruction concerning the significance and work of the church and the functions of its various officers and boards. In co-operation with the Television, Radio, and Film Commission it shall plan and provide education in the use of audio-visual materials.

¶ **1397.** The division shall organize such departments as may be necessary for the proper promotion of Christian education of children, youth, young adults, and other adults in local churches; and for leadership education, evangelism, and missionary education in the church schools.

¶ **1398.** 1. The division shall have supervision of all the training processes of the church for both lay and ministerial workers, except where these have been specifically delegated to other agencies.

2. The division shall provide programs for the training of pastors, parents, teachers, officials, and others in the work of the local church, and promote these programs through various types of training schools, correspondence work, and such other agencies as it may see fit to establish. It shall have authority also to promote and conduct educational conferences, councils, assemblies, and other meetings in the interest of church schools and Christian education of children, youth, and adults, and in the interest of an improved leadership.

¶ 1399. The division shall co-operate with other agencies in the promotion of brotherhoods, men's councils, and kindred organizations to the end that the different organizations of the church may be correlated under a unified program for aggressive Christian service.

¶ 1400. The division shall have authority to co-operate with the Jurisdictional and Annual Conference Boards of Education, the Editorial Division, and other agencies in the promotion and holding of a meeting to be known as the **Methodist Conference on Christian Education.**

¶ 1401. 1. The division shall provide guidance for local churches in equipment, arrangement, and design of church-school buildings or rooms.

2. The division shall develop, in consultation with the Department of Ministerial Education, standards governing the work of local-church ministers and directors of Christian education and concerning their certification as provided in ¶¶247, 1451.

3. The division shall develop standards governing the work of local-church ministers and directors of music and serve as may be possible in advancing this field of work in the church. It shall co-operate with the **National Fellowship of Methodist Musicians.**

4. The division shall prepare standards for all types of camping, including standards for camp sites and other physical aspects of camping and standards for the program, leadership, and curriculum for use in Methodist camps, including day camps.

¶ 1402. The division, with the co-operation of the

Division of Higher Education where its program is concerned, shall have authority to develop, within the church, organizations of youth, nationally and in jurisdictions, conferences, districts, and subdivisions of districts; *provided*, however, that such organizations shall include all groups within a given age range within the local church.

¶ **1403.** The youth of The Methodist Church between the ages of twelve and twenty-one inclusive, except as provided in ¶ 244.1, who belong to any group for or organizational unit of youth in the church shall be members of the Youth Division, and thereby members of the **Methodist Youth Fellowship.** These provisions shall include college students who are related to the local church through activities which the Commission on Education shall provide. In churches at college campuses these plans shall be worked out co-operatively with the campus-related Methodist student organizations.

¶ **1404.** 1. The Division of the Local Church, with the co-operation of the other agencies of The Methodist Church which have an interest in youth work, is authorized to sponsor the **National Conference of the Methodist Youth Fellowship,** whose functions shall include the following:

a) To participate in planning the program of the Methodist Youth Fellowship for senior high and older youth related to the local church, by expressing needs and interests and by contributing ideas for program content to meet their needs, particularly to the Youth Department of the Division of the Local Church and the Department of Youth Publications of the Editorial Division, General Board of Education.

b) To initiate and support special plans and projects at the national level which are of particular interest to youth.

c) To provide for the free expression of the convictions of Methodist youth on issues vital to them.

d) To counsel with and make recommendations to appropriate agencies of The Methodist Church, through their staff representatives and youth members, on the church's program, especially on matters of interest and concern to youth.

2. The membership of this conference shall consist of presidents of senior high and older youth organizations of Annual Conferences, or their duly elected representatives, the youth members of the boards and other agencies of the church, and six conference directors of youth work (one from each jurisdiction, elected by the conference directors of youth work of that jurisdiction for a two-year term, the election to take place during the Methodist Conference on Christian Education). In addition, the following shall be ex officio members: staff members of the Division of the Local Church responsible for youth work; staff members of the Department of Youth Publications of the Editorial Division; and one staff member from each of the following: the Woman's Section and the General Section of the Joint Section of Education and Cultivation of the Board of Missions, the three divisions of the Board of Christian Social Concerns, and the Board of Evangelism, Interboard Committee on Christian Vocations, Board of Lay Activities, and Commission on Chaplains.

3. The conference shall meet annually and shall elect from its membership its own officers, from among whom the Methodist representatives to the General Council of the United Christian Youth Movement shall be chosen. The treasurer of the General Board of Education shall be its treasurer. Its financial support shall be provided by the general agencies which co-operate in sponsoring it. It may adopt a constitution and bylaws governing its operations. It shall report annually on its meetings and activities to the Division of the Local Church.

4. For administrative purposes the conference shall be related to the Youth Department of the Division of the Local Church. Any staff employed shall be recommended by the conference to the general secretary of the division for nomination to and election by the General Board of Education. Such staff shall have membership on the Youth Department staff for administrative procedures and intrastaff work, and shall be responsible to the conference for carrying out its program.

¶ **1405.** 1. The Division of the Local Church shall be responsible for unifying youth work of The Methodist Church, and the Division of Higher Education shall be responsible for unifying student work of The Methodist Church. For the purpose of correlating youth and student work of the General Board of Education, the two divisions shall develop interstaff co-operation between their staff members responsible for youth work and for student work through a **Joint Staff on Youth and Student Work.** This joint staff shall correlate youth and student work of the board, giving particular emphasis to areas of mutual concern. At least once each year it shall meet with the council of officers and staff advisers of the National Conference of the Methodist Youth Fellowship (¶ 1404) and of the National Conference of the Methodist Student Movement (¶ 1370), meeting jointly to review the program and activities of these organizations, discuss needs and trends in youth and student work, correlate efforts of mutual interest and concern, and nominate youth and student members to the general boards of the church.

2. In making nominations to the boards, the joint staff shall select the youth nominees, all of whom (except those named ex officio) shall be twenty years of age or younger at the time of their election, from lists submitted by the National Conference of the Methodist Youth Fellowship and the student nominees from lists submitted by the National Conference of the Methodist Student Movement, and shall consider ability and experience, youth age range and student status, and jurisdictional representation.

¶ **1407.** 1. In order that church schools may be made available for those for whom The Methodist Church is responsible, the Division of the Local Church shall be authorized to project and promote plans for church-school extension throughout the church, and to contribute to the support of church schools requiring assistance in mission territory.

2. The division shall have authority to enter into agreements with Jurisdictional Boards of Education by which the jurisdictional board may promote a program of church-school extension in accordance with the policies

of the general board and employ extension secretaries for work in rural and neglected areas. As part of this agreement, the jurisdictional board shall make an annual budget for the extension program which shall be submitted, together with quarterly reports on the distribution of the funds herein provided for, to the general secretary of the division.

¶ **1408.** The division shall have the responsibility for working out, in co-operation with Jurisdictional Boards of Education, a general program and plan of organization for the furtherance within the Annual Conference of all the interests of Christian education with the supervision of which the division is charged. This shall include the holding within the conference territory of training schools, conferences, educational councils, federations, assemblies, and such other meetings in the interest of Christian education as the division may deem wise. It shall call together the officers and representatives of the jurisdictional boards for counsel regarding Annual Conference organization and program of work in the field of Christian education in the local church.

¶ **1409.** 1. The division shall have authority to receive and administer funds, gifts or bequests that may be committed to it for any portion of its work; and to solicit, establish, and administer any special funds that may be found necessary for the carrying out of its plans and policies.

2. The division may solicit special contributions in the church schools in its own area of work. Only such special solicitations as are approved by the Divisional Committee on the Local Church may be promoted in the church schools.

¶ **1410.** The division shall, in co-operation with the Division of Higher Education, discover and give guidance to volunteers for all forms of vocational religious work, offering training courses and all other aids designed to provide vocational guidance for all young people of the church.

SEC. VII. **Co-operation with Other Boards**

¶ **1412.** 1. There shall be an Interboard Committee on Town and Country work. (*See* ¶ 1230.)

2. There shall be a Joint Committee on Christian Education in Foreign Fields. (*See* ¶¶ 1283-85.)

3. There shall be a Joint Committee on Architecture. (*See* ¶ 1289.)

4. There shall be an Interboard Committee on Stewardship. (*See* ¶ 753.4.)

¶ **1413.** There shall be an Interboard Committee on Missionary Education for the purpose of promoting effective co-operation between the Board of Missions and the Board of Education. (*See* ¶ 1286-88.)

¶ **1414.** 1. In the discharge of its responsibility for supervising missionary education in the church school and for unifying youth work in The Methodist Church the Division of the Local Church shall provide for participation by the local-church, District, and Conference Methodist Youth Fellowships in the **Methodist Youth Fund.** Local treasurers shall send the full amount of the Methodist Youth Fund offerings to the treasurer of the Annual Conference, by whom it shall be sent monthly to the treasurer of the General Board of Education to be directed for missions and youth work as follows: 45 per cent for missions through the Woman's Division of Christian Service; 25 per cent for Christian education in mission fields to strengthen local-church work through the Annual Conference; 15 per cent returned to the Annual Conferences for youth work therein; 15 per cent for youth work through the Division of the Local Church. The Methodist Youth Fund shall be given recognition in a separate column in the pastor's report to the Annual Conference, but shall not receive benevolence credit.

2. There shall be an **Advisory Committee on the Methodist Youth Fund** consisting of the general secretaries of the Division of World Missions, Division of National Missions, Woman's Division of Christian Service, and Woman's Section of the Joint Section of Education and Cultivation of the Board of Missions; the director of the Youth Department and the general secretary of the Division of the Local Church of the Board of Education; the executive secretary of the Interboard Committee on Missionary Education; and the staff member responsible for the promotion of the Methodist Youth Fund. The com-

mittee shall meet at least once a year. It shall have responsibility for annual review of the promotion and distribution of the Methodist Youth Fund, and shall give special attention to creative and new developments in the use of the fund and to the requests of youth thereon. It shall review and recommend the annual budget to be used for promotion by the Methodist Youth Fund office, and shall nominate for election by the General Board of Education and confirmation by the Woman's Division of Christian Service such staff as may be necessary for adequate promotion. The office shall be administratively related to the Division of the Local Church. The committee shall report for information to the Interboard Committee on Missionary Education.

3. The policies under which the Methodist Youth Fund office operates shall be those agreed on by all the agencies related thereto. The promotion shall be done in harmony with the philosophy of missionary education expressed through the program and work of the Interboard Committee on Missionary Education and with the philosophy of unity in the total Methodist Youth Fellowship program. (*See* ¶¶ 1287, 1403.)

¶ **1415.** 1. There shall be an **Interboard Committee on Christian Vocations.** Its purpose shall be to develop plans and correlate efforts for the more effective enlistment and guidance of persons in vocations in the church and its agencies, and to seek to interpret to the church through its several agencies the total field of vocation in Christian terms. It shall give leadership in developing a philosophy of Christian vocation, always stressing the potential sacredness of all useful work. It shall lead in discovering and making known the various needs of the church at home and abroad, and seek to enlist youth for Christian service through all the appropriate agencies of the church. (*See* ¶¶ 146, 670, 675-77, 1184, 1364, 1375, 1564.)

2. The committee shall be composed of six bishops, one selected by the College of Bishops of each jurisdiction; four representatives from the Board of Missions, four from the Board of Education, two from the Board of Hospitals and Homes, and one each from the Association of Methodist Theological Schools, the Board of Lay Activities,

the Board of Christian Social Concerns, the Commission on Chaplains, and the Board of Evangelism, selected by their respective agencies; and the director of the Department of Ministerial Education.

3. It shall elect from its membership an **executive committee** of seven persons, consisting of one bishop, one representative from the Department of Ministerial Education, one from the Board of Hospitals and Homes, two from the Board of Education, and two—one a woman—from the Board of Missions.

4. There shall be an **executive secretary** for the committee, elected by the General Board of Education on nomination of the committee. He shall be responsible to the committee. He shall be administratively related to the Division of the Local Church and have such staff relationships with the other participating agencies as shall be necessary to the promotion of his work.

5. The expenses of the committee shall be met by the participating agencies on such ratio as they may decide.

¶ **1416.** In order to extend and strengthen temperance education in The Methodist Church there shall be a **Joint Committee on Temperance Education,** composed of the general secretary and two other representatives from the Division of the Local Church, the associate general secretary and two other representatives from the Division of Temperance and General Welfare of the Board of Christian Social Concerns, and two representatives from the Woman's Division of Christian Service. The duties of this committee shall be to plan for and correlate the program of The Methodist Church in temperance education, and to make recommendations to the Division of the Local Church and to the Division of Temperance and General Welfare.

¶ **1417.** 1. There shall be a **General Committee on Family Life,** which shall be related administratively to the Division of the Local Church and shall co-operate with its Department of the Christian Family to promote activities of a creative nature that can be most efficiently engaged in by the boards working together, including the planning of national, regional, and area conferences on family life. (*See* ¶¶ 234, 1453.)

2. The committee shall be composed of four bishops, one of whom shall be designated chairman, three ministers, and three laymen elected by the Council of Bishops, and staff members or other representatives elected by general agencies as follows: five from the Division of the Local Church and two from the Editorial Division of the Board of Education; two from the Board of Evangelism; one each from the Divisions of World Missions and of National Missions and one staff and one board member from the Woman's Division of Christian Service of the Board of Missions; one from each division of the Board of Christian Social Concerns; and one each from the Board of Lay Activities, the Television, Radio, and Film Commission, the Board of Hospitals and Homes, the Commission on Chaplains, and The Methodist Publishing House. In addition three ministers and three laymen at large shall be elected by the committee.

3. The program of the committee shall be financed by the General Administration Fund according to the budget adopted by the General Conference.

¶ 1418. A **Joint Committee on Materials for Training for Church Membership** shall be created by the Board of Education and the Board of Evangelism for the purpose of preparing materials for the training of persons for church membership. It shall be composed of two bishops, three pastors and three laymen (one from each jurisdiction), the general secretaries of the Division of the Local Church and of the Editorial Division of the Board of Education, the general secretary of the Board of Evangelism, the book editor, the director of the Department of Ministerial Education, and three qualified persons elected by the committee.

SEC. VIII.   **Education in the Local Church**

The program for education in the local church is described in ¶¶ 231-51, under Part II, The Local Church.

SEC. IX.   **Editorial Division**

¶ 1421. There shall be an **Editorial Division,** which shall have responsibility for development of the curriculum materials for use in Methodist church schools (see ¶ 243).

Materials shall be provided to guide in the development of a balanced, comprehensive, and unified curriculum in the local church. These materials shall be designed to provide opportunities for experience through which the influence of the Holy Spirit may lead children, youth, and adults into a maturing faith in God through commitment to Jesus Christ and his Church.

¶ **1422.** The division shall reflect through its publications and other materials the official positions of The Methodist Church and the policies of the General Board of Education. It shall give appropriate support through its publications and other materials to the world service causes and special emphases authorized by the General Conference.

¶ **1423.** The division may co-operate with the Curriculum Committee in the development for the Board of Education of theological and educational statements representative of Methodist life and thought to serve as a guide in curriculum construction. It may also formulate objectives for the curriculum of Christian education to provide for balance, sequence, and progression. The above shall be subject to the approval of the Board of Education.

¶ **1424.** The division shall issue a list of the curriculum materials that are approved by the Curriculum Committee for use in Methodist church schools. Such materials shall include the materials prepared through the Board of Education and may include materials prepared by other agencies.

¶ **1425.** The division may co-operate with other denominations through the National Council of Churches or in other ways in curriculum planning. It may develop patterns of co-operative publication wherever both the division and The Methodist Publishing House find this to be practicable and in harmony with editorial and publishing policies.

¶ **1426.** The division may co-operate in curriculum planning and construction for and by Methodist bodies overseas, through the Joint Committee on Christian Education in Foreign Fields and with such agencies as the National Council of Churches, the World Council of

Christian Education and Sunday School Association, and the World Council of Churches.

¶ **1427.** The division may co-operate with the Jurisdictional and Annual Conference Boards of Education, the Division of the Local Church, the Division of Higher Education, and other agencies in the holding of the meetings of the Methodist Conference on Christian Education. (*See* ¶ 1400.)

¶ **1428.** The division shall co-operate through its representatives in the work of the Interboard Committee on Missionary Education (¶ 1286), the Joint Committee on Christian Education in Foreign Fields (¶ 1283), the Interboard Committee on Christian Vocations (¶ 1415), the General Committee on Family Life (¶ 1417), the Joint Committee on Materials for Training in Church Membership (¶ 1418), the National Conference of the Methodist Youth Fellowship (¶ 1404), and the Television, Radio, and Film Commission (¶ 1581.2).

¶ **1429.** The **general secretary** of the division, who shall be the editor of church-school publications (¶¶ 1145-53), shall be elected quadrennially by the General Board of Education from nominations of a joint committee composed of the chairman and two other members of the Board of Publication and the president of the Board of Education and two members from the Editorial Division. The election of the editor shall be subject to confirmation by the Board of Publication. A vacancy in this office shall be filled by the same procedure.

¶ **1430.** The general secretary shall appoint his assistants. He shall be responsible for directing their activities and for establishing their relationships to the General Board of Education and to the Board of Publication.

¶ **1431.** The general secretary shall be responsible to the General Board of Education through the Editorial Division regarding editorial policies, content, and preparation of the church-school publications and other materials. In matters of publication and financing he shall be responsible to the Board of Publication. (*See* ¶¶ 1148-53.)

¶ **1432.** The division shall carry on its activities through a **Department of Children's Publications,** a **Department** of **Youth Publications,** a **Department of Adult Publications,** a **Department of General Publications,** and such other departments as it may determine.

¶ **1433.** 1. There shall be a **Curriculum Committee,** which shall determine the nature and content of the curriculum of the church school. Descriptions of this curriculum shall be recommended by the general secretary to the Editorial Division for final approval by the General Board of Education.

2. The Curriculum Committee shall consist of seventeen voting members. Ten shall be elected by the General Board of Education, on nomination by the Editorial Division after consultation with the general secretaries of the board, and shall be chosen on the basis of training and experience in the curriculum and program of Christian education in the local church and in the various aspects of the church's life and work. The other seven members shall be the general secretaries of the three divisions, the chairman of the Editorial Division, the book editor, the publisher, and the executive secretary of the Interboard Committee on Missionary Education.

3. Members of the staffs of the three divisions of the General Board of Education appointed by the respective general secretaries shall be consulting members of the Curriculum Committee. The executive committee of the board may elect on nomination of the general secretaries additional persons (especially from staffs of other boards and agencies) to serve as consulting members. Consulting members shall have full privileges of membership except for voting on final recommendations to the board.

¶ **1434.** In the development of formats and types of curriculum materials, the Editorial Division shall work co-operatively with the Board of Publication, which agency has final responsibility in relation to publishing and financial matters. The division shall authorize additions or changes in the list of publications to be produced, within the provisions of ¶ 1149. These materials may include a variety of formats, such as periodicals, books and booklets, graphic resources, recordings, and projected audio-visual resources.

¶ **1435.** The publications and materials of the Editorial

Division shall be published, manufactured, promoted, and distributed through The Methodist Publishing House as set forth in ¶¶ 1145-53. The interpretation and promotion of these materials shall be a responsibility of the General Board of Education and the Board of Publication.

¶ 1436. The publisher may sit with the General Board of Education for the consideration of matters pertaining to the joint interests of the Board of Education and the Board of Publication and shall have the privilege of the floor, without vote. (*See also* ¶ 1152.)

SECTION X.   **Jurisdictional Boards**

¶ 1440. In each jurisdiction there may be a **Jurisdictional Board of Education,** auxiliary to the general board, as the Jurisdictional Conference may determine. (*See* ¶¶ 15.3, 527.)

SEC. XI   **Annual Conference Boards**

¶ 1441. In each Annual Conference there shall be a **Conference Board of Education,** elected by the conference to promote church-school extension, the program of Christian education, and the use of church-school literature approved by the General Board of Education. Each conference shall set apart a portion of a session in which the interests of Christian education shall be adequately considered.

¶ 1442. 1. The board shall be auxiliary to the jurisdictional board, if there be any, and to the general board, and shall co-operate with them. It shall be responsible for developing and promoting a conference program of Christian education which will provide guidance and help for all the agencies of Christian education within the bounds of the conference, such as: the Commissions on Education in local churches and the related agencies of Christian education (*see* ¶¶ 241, 243), leadership training schools, Bible conferences, camps, assemblies, institutes, and other educational agencies. It shall encourage and give help in the use of Methodist curriculum materials. It shall promote and assist all institutions of higher education related to the conference, Wesley Foundations, and the Methodist

Student Movement, and shall give leadership and support to the Faculty Christian Movement.

2. The board may be incorporated under the laws of the state (or all of the states) within whose bounds the conference is located. The board may receive gifts for its work. It may hold title to property for use in its work and housing for its personnel. It shall report to each session of the conference on the legal and financial status and physical condition of all such property.

3. The board shall be responsible for developing and recommending to the Annual Conference long-range plans for the procurement of camp and conference properties in accordance with standards of camping developed by the General Board of Education (¶ 1401.4). The development and operational policies of all camp and conference properties shall be under the direction of the conference board or organizations delegated by it. (*See* ¶ 1454.)

¶ **1443.** The board shall be composed of: (1) an equal number of laymen and ministers elected quadrennially, the number and manner of election to be determined by the conference; (2) three representatives of the Conference Methodist Youth Fellowship, of whom one shall be its president, one shall be the president or duly elected representative of its Older Youth Council or Committee, and the third shall be chosen by the fellowship and shall be twenty years of age or younger at the time of his selection; and one student chosen by the state or regional student organization operating within the conference territory; (3) the president of the Conference Young Adult Fellowship; (4) one certified minister or director of Christian education employed in a local church within the conference; and (5) additional members, either clerical or lay, nominated at any time during the quadrennium by the board in such numbers as it may deem advisable, for election by the conference. Vacancies in the elected membership between conference sessions may be filled by the executive committee of the board pending the action of the next conference session. Care shall be taken to elect persons who, by training and experience, are qualified for the work of the board. No salaried officer or employee of the board shall be a member. A majority of the members shall constitute a quorum. The members shall continue in office until their successors have been elected and the successor board organized.

¶ **1444.** The officers of the board shall be a president, vice-president, recording secretary, and treasurer, all of whom shall be elected by the board for the quadrennium. There shall also be an executive secretary (who may serve two or more contiguous conferences), elected by the board after consultation with the bishop and his Cabinet and confirmed by the conference; *provided* that in the filling of a vacancy which occurs between conference sessions the approval of the conference shall not be required for the interim period. The retiring board shall complete the business and make its annual report to the conference, and shall make such recommendations as it may desire to the new board.

¶ **1445.** Organization of the new board shall be effected at the beginning of the quadrennium in the following way: The bishop shall appoint a convener, who shall assemble the board during the Annual Conference session or within thirty days after adjournment to effect a permanent organization. The new board shall take office upon the adjournment of the Annual Conference session at which it was elected.

¶ **1446.** The president shall be a presiding, not an administrative, officer. The treasurer, who shall be adequately bonded, shall receive, and receipt for, all funds of the board and disburse them by check as ordered by the board. All checks must be countersigned by the executive secretary or some other person duly authorized by the board.

¶ **1447.** There shall be an **executive committee** of the board, of which the president shall be a member. The executive committee shall meet on the call of the president or of one third of the members, and shall transact all necessary business of the board *ad interim*, under such regulations as the board may adopt. Its acts shall be reported to the annual meeting of the board. The executive committee shall act as the finance committee of the board, and shall prepare a statement of its financial needs for the next year.

1448. 1. The **executive secretary** shall have responsibility for the general oversight and promotion of all the work of the board and for the direction and supervision of its salaried and other workers, who shall report to him as may be required. He shall make a full report annually both to the board and to each of the three general secretaries of the General Board of Education.

2. The executive secretary shall give leadership and direction to the program of Christian education in the local churches, enlisting the co-operation of the district superintendents and the district directors.

3. The executive secretary shall give active co-operation to the Methodist schools, colleges, and universities within the conference; through the Interconference Commission on College and University Religious Work assist in supporting the Wesley Foundations and co-ordinating the intercollegiate program of the Methodist Student Movement within the state or region; and help to integrate the work of Christian education as undertaken by the local church and by the schools and colleges. He shall consult with this commission about the duties and relation to the conference staff of the state or regional director of student work.

4. On nomination of the executive secretary such additional salaried and other workers as the board may deem necessary shall be elected annually by the board. The executive secretary shall consult with the responsible officers of the Conference Methodist Youth Fellowship before nominating conference directors of youth work.

5. The executive secretary shall nominate annually, after consultation with each district superintendent, the district directors, as provided in ¶ 1460.

¶ **1449.** The board shall report its proceedings and policies to the Annual Conference, including the treasurer's report, showing all resources and liabilities of the board, its income and its expenditures. Immediately following the conference session it shall report to the Jurisdictional Board of Education, through its executive secretary, a summary of its acts and the names of its officers and salaried workers. It shall transmit to the jurisdictional board the names and addresses of church-school superintendents and the officers of the district and conference organizations operating under the conference board and of youth assemblies and other organizations.

¶ **1450.** The president, or someone designated by him, shall present to the Commission on World Service and Finance of the conference the financial needs of the colleges and Wesley Foundations related to the conference (as determined by the board on recommendation of its Committee or Commission on Christian Higher Education), of the work of the board in its field program of Christian education in the local churches of the conference, and of other work in which the board may be engaged. In accordance with the financial plan of the church, an apportionment shall be allotted to the churches within the conference for the work of the Conference Board of Education. Other sources of income shall be gifts, returns from special days, and receipts from missionary offerings in the church school. The board shall determine the distribution of the funds thus received to each of the general interests under the care of the board.

Note: For description of the program for Church School Rally Day, Methodist Student Day, and Race Relations Sunday *see* ¶ 250.2-.4.

¶ **1451.** 1. It shall be the duty of the board to determine whether applicants meet the standards of the General Board of Education for ministers and directors of Christian education (¶¶ 247.1, 1401.2) and ministers and directors of music (¶¶ 247.2, 1401.3), and to certify and keep a record of those who do. The board shall set up a committee or committees on these offices whose duties shall be: (*a*) to review the credentials of candidates and make recommendations to the board for certification in harmony with the said standards and (*b*) to recommend to the board plans for institutes, conferences, and other occasions for fellowship and training for ministers and directors of Christian education and educational assistants, and for ministers and directors of music and others responsible for music in the local church. Whenever possible one or more ministers or directors of Christian education and of music shall serve on this committee. All persons certified shall furnish to the board, on blanks provided by the general board, information for purposes of annual review and approval of status.

2. A roster of certified ministers and directors of Christian education and certified ministers and directors of music shall be included in the annual report of the board and published in the conference journal. A person so certified may move to another Annual Conference and be recorded there without re-establishing status.

3. Certified directors of Christian education may be consecrated and commissioned at a conference session or other suitable time. (*see* ¶ 1926.)

¶ 1452. 1. The board shall constitute a **Conference Committee on Christian Higher Education,** composed of not fewer than eight of its members selected in consultation with the bishop and the Cabinet. This committee shall have specific responsibility for developing knowledge of and support for the schools, colleges, universities, schools of theology, and Wesley Foundations related to The Methodist Church and particularly those related to the conference.

2. An Annual Conference, at its discretion, may enlarge the committee into a **Conference Commission on Christian Higher Education,** which shall include the members of the committee, the executive secretary of the board, the bishop and district superintendents, the conference lay leader, the president of the Conference Woman's Society of Christian Service, the state or regional director of student work, and up to twenty members at large elected by the committee because of their experience and ability in the field of education. The members shall be named as soon after the adjournment of the General Conference as feasible. They shall serve four years except that ex officio membership shall coincide with term of office. The commission shall elect its officers quadrennially, and they shall serve until their successors are duly elected and qualified. It may employ such staff members as are deemed necessary for its work. The Annual Conference shall make provision for its expense as the conference may determine.

3. Two or more Annual Conferences at their discretion may join in constituting an **Area** or **Regional Commission**

on Christian Higher Education, the membership of which shall be determined by the bishop or bishops and Cabinets of the conferences involved.

4. The committee or commission shall:

a) Co-operate with the Division of Higher Education in the achievement of its objectives (¶¶ 1351-52).

b) Make provision for such conferences, training courses, and study groups as will assist in meeting its responsibility.

c) Report annually to the board and the Annual Conference on the programs of those institutions of learning and Wesley Foundations related to the conference and supported by it, including a statement concerning the capital and current financial needs of each and their program of service to The Methodist Church. (*See* ¶ 1351.)

d) Recommend annually to the board, for presentation to the Annual Conference, a minimum goal for the support of educational institutions and Wesley Foundations; or, if none are related to the conference, recommend the method of distributing to Methodist educational institutions, either directly or through the Division of Higher Education, the funds raised for higher education.

¶ **1453.** The board may constitute a **Conference Committee on Family Life** composed of the executive secretary and two members of the board; the conference directors of children's, youth, and adult work; the president of the Conference Methodist Youth Fellowship; a representative of the Conference Young Adult Fellowship; the secretary of Christian social relations of the Conference Woman's Society of Christian Service; the conference lay leader; and one district superintendent elected by the Cabinet. Special resource persons may be added as the committee shall determine. Its duty shall be to study the forces which affect family life within the conference and recommend to the board program plans to strengthen family life. It shall be administratively related to the board and shall report to it annually. (*See* ¶¶ 234, 1417.)

¶ **1454.** 1. On recommendation of the board, in co-operation with other conference agencies, the Annual Conference may constitute a **Conference Committee on**

Camps and Conferences, composed of: the executive secretary and three or more members of the board, of whom one shall be a youth and one a young adult; the conference directors of camps and conferences, children's work, youth work, adult work, and general church-school work; one or more district superintendents elected by the Cabinet; the chairmen of District Committees on Camps and Conferences (¶ 1461); a representative of the trustees of any camp or conference properties of the board (¶ 1442.3); one representative each of the Conference Board of Trustees and any other incorporated trustees holding title to properties used extensively in the Christian education program of camping, conferences, and related enterprises of the Annual Conference or of the districts; and a representative each of the Conference Woman's Society of Christian Service and the Conference Board of Lay Activities. Other persons may be added on the basis of qualifications to meet specific needs.

2. The committee may select, develop, and operate properties as charged by the board and authorized by the Annual Conference; develop and recommend to the board policies and long-range plans for the selection, development, and operation of campsites and facilities to meet program needs; recommend fund-raising procedures for the purchase and development of sites and facilities; and work with District Committees on Camps and Conferences as directed by the board.

¶ **1455.** The board shall have authority, in co-operation with the Conference Television, Radio, and Film Commission, to provide training conferences for selected persons in the Annual Conference, district, and local church in the effective use of audio-visual materials. (*See* ¶ 1583.1.)

¶ **1456.** The board shall have authority to co-operate with other conference boards in matters of common interest. It shall also have authority to co-operate with the General and Jurisdictional Boards of Education and other agencies in the holding of the Methodist Conference on Christian Education. (*See* ¶ 1400.)

Note: For the constitution of the Commission on Town and Country Work *see* ¶ 1231.

1458. In each Annual Conference there shall be an official conference youth organization known as the **Conference Methodist Youth Fellowship.** Its purpose shall be to strengthen the youth program in the local churches of the conference. It shall be under the sponsorship and the responsibility of the Conference Board of Education, to which it shall report, and of the General Board of Education. It shall co-operate with other agencies with which youth are concerned within the conference and with the National Conference of the Methodist Youth Fellowship (¶ 1404). The executive secretary of the conference board and the conference director of youth work shall be advisers to its council.

SEC. XII.   **District Organizations**

¶ **1460.** In each district the Annual Conference shall elect annually a district director of adult work, of youth work, of children's work, and of general church-school work, and such others as may be desired, who with the district superintendent shall constitute the **district staff of Christian education.** They shall be nominated by the executive secretary of the Conference Board of Education, after consultation with the district superintendent, and the nominations shall be reported to the board for confirmation and transmittal to the Annual Conference. Interim vacancies shall be filled by the executive secretary in consultation with the district superintendent. Unless otherwise stipulated by the board, the district director of general church-school work shall serve as chairman and, in situations where separate statements are impractical, spokesman for the staff.

¶ **1461.** 1. The District or Annual Conference may constitute a **District Committee on Camps and Conferences** on recommendation of the district staff of Christian education, in co-operation with other district agencies. The chairman shall be nominated and confirmed in the same manner as the district directors (¶ 1460). The committee shall include the district superintendent and other members of the district staff, at least one camp director or institute dean representing each age group actively involved in camps and conferences and related enterprises in the district, and other persons to meet specific needs.

2. Its responsibilities shall be: to co-operate with the Conference Committee on Camps and Conferences (¶ 1454); to make available to pastors and church-school superintendents information as to suitable locations and recommended guidance materials relating to camping, conferences, and retreats; to encourage and initiate training for such enterprises; to interpret and assist the local church in implementing standards relating to program and leadership and to the use and care of any sites or facilities used for camping, planning conferences, and retreats; and to refer to the district staff, for confirmation by the District Conference, nominations by the age-group directors of persons to serve as directors or deans of summer camps, institutes, or conferences sponsored by the district.

3. If the committee is charged with the development and/or operation of camp or conference facilities held in trust by the Conference or District Board of Trustees, there shall be added to its membership a representative from such board. The selection, development, or improvement of any such properties, or of conference- or district-owned property the title to which is vested in other incorporated boards but which is used primarily for Christian education enterprises of the district, shall be in harmony with the policies and standards of the Conference and General Boards of Education.

4. District property may be acquired for use in the program of camps and conferences when authorized by the District or Annual Conference on recommendation of the district staff of Christian education, after consultation with the Conference Board of Education and in keeping with the standards of the general board.

CHAPTER IX

BOARD OF EVANGELISM

SECTION I.   The Aim of Evangelism

¶ 1464. The aim of evangelism is to bring all men into

living, active fellowship with God through Jesus Christ as divine Saviour and through the regenerating power of the Holy Spirit; to gather them into the fellowship of the Church; to lead them to express their Christian discipleship in every area of human life that the Kingdom of God may be realized.

SEC. II **Incorporation**

¶ **1465.** There shall be an incorporated **General Board of Evangelism** of The Methodist Church, hereinafter called the board. It shall be incorporated under the laws of the state in which its headquarters are established by the General Conference; or the present Tennessee charter of incorporation of the Commission on Evangelism may be amended.

SEC. III **Constitution**

¶ **1466.** *Article 1: Name and Object.*—The name of this organization shall be the General Board of Evangelism of The Methodist Church. Its objects are religious, evangelistic, designed to diffuse the blessings of the gospel of the Lord Jesus Christ by the promotion and support of all forms and phases of evangelism; to promote evangelistic intelligence, interest, and zeal throughout the membership of The Methodist Church; to promote the practice of intercession and of individual and family worship; and to stimulate the entire membership of the church in worship and in Christian service.

¶ **1467.** *Art. 2. Authority.*—The board shall have authority to regulate its own proceedings in accordance with its constitution and charter; to buy, acquire, receive by gift, devise, or bequest, property, real, personal, and mixed, and to hold, sell, and dispose of property; to secure, appropriate, and administer funds for its work; to sue and be sued; to elect the necessary officers and members of its staff, remove them for cause, and fill vacancies; to make by-laws in harmony with the Discipline of The Methodist Church and the charter of the board; and shall have the right to do any and all things which shall be authorized by its charter; *provided* that, in cases of devises or gifts of real estate to this board in states where such devises or gifts are not valid when made to religious corporations, the board shall be empowered to name trustees for the purpose of receiving and taking title to such gifts or devises for the benefit of the board.

¶ **1468.** *Art.* 3. *Membership.*—The membership of the board shall be composed of seven bishops elected by the Council of Bishops at the time of the General Conference, one of these elected from the church at large to be president of the board and one from each jurisdiction; two ministers, one lay man, and one lay woman from each jurisdiction, elected by the Jurisdictional Conferences; the secretary of spiritual life of the Woman's Division of Christian Service; the chairman of Christian witness of the National Conference of the Methodist Youth Fellowship; the national chairman of the Commission on Communication of the Gospel of the Methodist Student Movement; and twelve members from the church at large, elected by the board.

¶ **1469.** *Art.* 4. *President.*—The president of the board shall be the bishop selected by the Council of Bishops from the church at large and shall serve for the quadrennium. He shall make a report and present a program of work for the board to the Council of Bishops for their approval at each regular meeting of the council.

¶ **1470.** *Art.* 5. *Other Officers.*—The board shall elect from its membership a vice-president, a recording secretary, and an **executive committee** of seven members, including the president of the board, the other six members to be selected by the board, one from each jurisdiction of the church. A treasurer shall be elected by the board, and shall be a member of the staff.

¶ **1471.** *Art.* 6. *Executive Officers.*—The board shall elect a **general secretary** and, on nomination by the executive committee, shall elect such other secretaries, directors, and editors as may be needed.

¶ **1472.** *Art.* 7. *Financial Support.*—The financial support of the general work of the board shall be derived from the general benevolence funds of the church, and that of *The Upper Room* as provided for in ¶ 1485.

¶ **1473.** *Art.* 8. *Meetings.*—The board shall hold an annual meeting and such other meetings as it may deem necessary for the accomplishment of the work.

¶ **1474.** *Art.* 9. *Duties.*—1. The board shall give particular emphasis to the promotion of full, well-rounded, and practical programs of evangelism on the conference, district, and local-church levels. To this end it shall give guidance and help to the Jurisdictional Boards of Evangelism, the Conference Boards of Evangelism, the District Committees on Evangelism, and the Commissions on Membership and Evangelism in local churches. (*See* ¶ 119.) The board shall give guidance to the church in using the appropriate days and seasons of the Christian calendar for special evangelistic emphasis.

2. The board shall set up standards for **conference evangelists** and shall make these standards known to the church at large. It shall send copies of the standards annually to the bishops, the district superintendents, the Conference Boards of Evangelism, and the Association of Conference Evangelists. It shall provide uniform report blanks for use of the conference evangelist in reporting to the Annual Conference. It shall supervise the work of the Association of Conference Evangelists.

(For the responsibility of the board in producing and distributing literature for the cultivation of the devotional life *see* ¶ 1485.)

¶ **1475.** *Art.* 10. *Co-operation.*—The board shall co-operate with the various agencies of the church in the training of our ministers for leadership in the field of evangelism and in creating a literature to serve the cause of evangelism. (For interboard agencies on which the Board of Evangelism is represented *see* ¶¶ 1160, 1164, 1230, 1415, 1417, 1418.)

¶ **1476.** *Art.* 11. *Chaplains.*—The board and its staff shall co-operate closely with the Commission on Chaplains. It shall attempt to help Methodist chaplains in every possible way, informing them concerning all forms and phases of evangelism, including evangelistic and devotional literature.

SEC. IV.   **Jurisdictional Board of Evangelism**

¶ **1477.** In each jurisdiction there may be a **Jurisdictional Board of Evangelism,** auxiliary to the general board, as the Jurisdictional Conference may determine. (See ¶¶ 15.3, 527.)

SEC. V. **Annual Conference Board of Evangelism**

¶ **1478.** 1. Each Annual Conference shall elect for the quadrennium a **Conference Board of Evangelism,** which shall plan and promote a program of evangelism throughout the conference. It shall give guidance to the District Committees on Evangelism and to local-church Commissions on Membership and Evangelism in carrying out their purposes and responsibilities, as outlined in ¶ 222; and it shall co-operate with the general and jurisdictional boards in promoting evangelistic plans and programs.

2. The board shall include in its membership the district superintendents, the district secretaries of evangelism, the vice-chairmen of the District Committees on Evangelism, one pastor from each district, such members of the general and jurisdictional boards as reside within the bounds of the conference, the secretary of spiritual life of the Conference Woman's Society of Christian Service, a layman nominated by the Conference Board of Lay Activities, the conference secretary of evangelism, and the chairman of Christian witness of the Conference Methodist Youth fellowship, together with a representative from any other organization that the conference desires. If the conference desires, its nominating committee may nominate additional members, one half of whom shall be ministers and one half laymen; *provided* that no salaried officer, employee, or one receiving remuneration from the board shall be a member thereof.

3. The board shall elect its own chairman, vice chairman, recording secretary, and treasurer quadrennially, together with such other officers and executive committee members as desired, and shall fill vacancies throughout the quadrennium as they occur. At the end of the quadrennium the retiring board shall complete its business and make its report to the Annual Conference and its

recommendations to the new board. The new board shall organize immediately, formulate plans for an ongoing evangelism, and also make its report and recommendations to the Annual Conference.

4. The chairman shall be the presiding, not the administrative, officer of the board, and shall not be the conference secretary or director of evangelism. His duties shall be to preside over all board and executive committee meetings, to present the report of the board to the Annual Conference, and to support the evangelistic causes and programs of the conference. In co-operation with the secretary or director he shall annually present the askings of the board to the Commission on World Service and Finance (¶ 793).

¶ 1479. 1. Each Annual Conference, on nomination of its Board of Evangelism, shall elect annually a **conference secretary of evangelism** (except as provided in § 2), to be publicly assigned by the bishop, who shall promote the policies and program of the General, Jurisdictional, and Conference Boards of Evangelism in the Annual Conference. He shall be the administrative and executive officer of the board. It shall be his duty to lead in program planning, to implement and execute the plans and programs adopted, and to carry the leadership of evangelism throughout the conference, working closely with the board, the bishop, the district superintendents, and district secretaries of evangelism, and the District Committees on Evangelism. He shall direct the expenditure of the funds of the board, faithfully adhering to its program and financial policies.

2. The board may elect, after consultation with the bishop and his Cabinet, a full-time **conference director of evangelism,** who shall be subject to confirmation by the Annual Conference; *provided* that in filling a vacancy confirmation shall not be required for the interim period. He shall serve as the administrative and executive officer of the board, instead of a conference secretary of evangelism, and shall assume all the duties assigned to that office (*see* § 1). Additional duties shall be carefully outlined by the board, to which he shall be amenable.

¶ 1480. The board may recommend to the Annual

Conference and to the bishop in charge the appointment of certain effective members of the conference as **conference evangelists;** *provided* that such persons shall meet the standards set up by the general board and the conference board for conference evangelists (¶ 1474.2).

SEC. VI.   **District Committee on Evangelism**

¶ **1481.** Each district of each Annual Conference shall provide a **District Committee on Evangelism,** which shall promote the program of evangelism as outlined by the General Board and in co-operation with the Conference Board of Evangelism.

¶ **1482.** The committee shall include in its membership such members of the conference board as reside within the bounds of the district, the secretary of spiritual life of the District Woman's Society of Christian Service, the district superintendent, the conference evangelists whose Quarterly Conference membership is within the district, and also three pastors, three lay men, three lay women, and three youth members elected by the District Conference or, if no District Conference is held, appointed by the district superintendent.

¶ **1483.** There shall be a **district secretary of evangelism** in each district, nominated by the district superintendent and publicly assigned by the bishop. He shall be chairman of the committee, and a layman selected by the district superintendent shall be vice-chairman. The chairman and vice-chairman shall work in co-operation with the district superintendent, the conference board, and the conference secretary or director of evangelism.

SEC. VII.   **Local-Church Commission**

¶ **1484.** Each local church shall have a Commission on Membership and Evangelism. (*See* ¶¶ 219-22, under Part II, The Local Church.)

SEC. VIII.   *The Upper Room*

¶ **1485.** The General Board of Evangelism is hereby instructed to assume the management and publication of *The Upper Room* and to produce and distribute such literature as that now represented by *The Upper Room* for the cultivation of the devotional life; *provided*, however, that no funds either now in hand or hereafter accumulated by *The Upper Room* or other devotional and related literature hereafter produced shall be used for the support of other features of the board's work, but all net income from the sale of such publications shall be conserved by the board for the purpose of preparing and circulating such literature; *provided*, however, that this shall not prevent the setting up of a reserve fund out of such produce as a protection against unforeseen emergencies.

CHAPTER X

BOARD OF LAY ACTIVITIES

SECTION I. **The General Board**

¶ **1490.** The purpose of the **Board of Lay Activities** shall be to deepen the spiritual life of the lay members of the church and to cultivate among them an increasing loyalty and interest that they may become an active working force in each local church.

¶ **1491.** 1. The board shall be composed of three effective bishops, elected by the Council of Bishops; six effective ministers, one from each jurisdiction; and thirty-two lay members, twenty-seven of whom shall be distributed among the several jurisdictions on the basis of church membership; *provided* that no jurisdiction shall have fewer than two lay members. The six ministers and the twenty-seven lay members shall be elected by the Jurisdictional Conferences on nomination of their Committees on Lay Activities; *provided* that the lay members shall be selected from the conference lay leaders of the several Annual Conferences in the jurisdiction; and *provided*, further, that retirement from the office of conference lay leader shall automatically vacate jurisdictional lay membership on the board. There shall be five lay members at large elected by the board on nomination of the Council of Bishops.

2. The headquarters of the board shall be fixed by the General Conference.

3. The board shall be duly incorporated.

¶ **1492.** The board shall be charged with leadership for and development of the several major areas of the work of lay activities in The Methodist Church, and shall use suitable means to promote an effective general program, to co-operate with other agencies of the church in the interest of lay activities, and to assist Jurisdictional, Annual Conference, and District Boards of Lay Activities in their programs, to the end that every available resource may be provided to help each local church carry on an effective program of lay activities.

¶ **1493.** The program of lay activities shall include:

1. *Christian Stewardship.*—Christian stewardship recognizes God's ownership of all that we are, all that we have, and all that we can do, and man as trustee. It shall be the duty of the board to use all practicable means to promote this principle to the point where it will be accepted and practiced by all Methodists.

2. *Sound Finance in the Local Church.*—Since the success of every function of our church is dependent on adequate finances, it shall be the duty of the board to promote a program of sound finance for the local church. This shall include the annual every-member canvass program for local churches and the simultaneous every-member canvass program for Conference and District Boards of Lay Activities, with provisions for adequate training of personnel essential to guarantee their success. (*See* ¶ 1494.)

3. *Adequate Support of the Ministry.*—The board shall give careful attention to assuring adequate support for the ministry, taking into consideration such factors as cost of living, cost of education, travel, automobile expense, and an adequate standard of living.

4. *Benevolences.*—In view of the ever-growing need for increased world service and other benevolent giving by our Methodist membership, the board shall be alert to its responsibility for keeping all Methodists informed of the church's needs, and shall give all possible en-

couragement to increased giving for world service and other benevolent purposes.

5. *Men's Work; Methodist Men.*—The board shall give special consideration to men's work and its correlation with other lay activities. **Methodist Men** shall be the authorized organization for promoting and carrying on men's work; development of an effective and efficient organization and the formation and chartering of a local chapter of Methodist Men in every pastoral charge shall be a continuing objective. The board shall promote, by appropriate means, the full and active participation of men in all the programs and activities of the church; regular attendance at church services shall be given special emphasis and attention. Recognizing that individuals grow in Christian character not only through private study and devotion but also through the stimulus that arises from interchange of ideas, purposes, and interests among individuals and groups, the board shall promote the planning of opportunities for men to grow by sharing in the execution of challenging plans and projects designed to serve the Kingdom of God, by participating in workshops and similar activities for interchange of purposes and plans, and by active sharing through Christian social activities. The board shall emphasize the importance of and shall plan for participation of men in personal evangelism, especially among men and boys.

6. *Lay Leadership.*—The board shall have the duty to develop lay leadership for the promotion of all phases of lay activities. It shall co-operate with conference and district organizations in the training of the laity to work effectively in each phase. It shall enlist the co-operation of conference, district, and local-church leaders and organizations to make use of periodicals and materials furnished by the church to the laity, giving special attention to those referred to in ¶ 1494. It shall co-operate with other boards and agencies in finding the greatest possible service for every person who belongs to The Methodist Church.

7. *Lay Speaking.*—The board shall supervise the program of lay speaking, which shall include training courses and other materials for lay speakers, and other means

to encourage the development of an adequate number of qualified lay speakers, to the end that there may be no silent pulpits in Methodist churches.

8. *Training of Official Boards.*—The board shall provide a program of training for Official Boards, to help the officers and members become acquainted with their responsibilities, understand and appreciate the organization of the church, and co-ordinate the total program of the local church with the program of the church at large. (*See* ¶ 1494.)

¶ 1494. The board shall develop effective methods for the program of lay activities in the local church and provide instructional and promotional materials to encourage their use. In particular it shall develop a program of sound finance for the local church, including the continual development and improvement of the annual every-member canvass program, with methods and materials for its promotion, and also the simultaneous every-member canvass program. It shall produce training and program materials for conference, district, and local-church lay leaders, and training courses and other materials for lay speakers. For the training of Official Board officers and members it shall prepare the needed materials in accordance with policies and materials developed through the Interboard Commission on the Local Church.

¶ 1495. The board shall develop suggested standards and a program of in-service training for church business managers, and serve as may be possible in advancing this field of service in the church.

¶ 1496. The board shall solicit the co-operation of the Jurisdictional and Annual Conference Boards of Lay Activities and other agencies in the promotion and holding each quadrennium of a **National Conference of Methodist Men** and of a **Convocation on Christian Stewardship.**

¶ 1497. To further the work of lay activities, one Sunday each year shall be designated as **Laymen's Day,** the program to be under the direction of the General Board of Lay Activities. The official date for Laymen's Day shall be the date approved by the General Division of United Church Men of the National Council of the

Churches of Christ in the United States of America as a joint observance by the constituent denominations; *provided* that this designation of a date shall not apply to conferences outside the United States.

¶ **1498.** The board shall elect a **general secretary,** who shall have general supervision of the work under the direction of the board, and who shall be subject to the authority and control of the board. On nomination of the general secretary, such other staff members as the board deems necessary shall be elected by the board. The board shall have authority to fill vacancies in offices occurring *ad interim*, including that of the general secretary.

¶ **1499.** The board is authorized to solicit and create special funds, to receive gifts and bequests, to hold properties and securities in trust, and to administer all these financial affairs in accordance with its own rules and the provisions of the Discipline.

¶ **1500.** The work of the board shall be considered a benevolence interest of the church, and the Council on World Service and Finance shall include in the appropriations recommended for adoption by the General Conference such sum as may be necessary for the proper support of the board. The board shall report to the council its estimate of the amount needed annually for its work.

¶ **1501.** The board shall be organized by the election of a president, a vice-president, a recording secretary, and a treasurer. It shall have authority to regulate its own proceedings, including the fixing of the time for its annual sessions. All officers and members of the board shall remain in office until their successors are duly elected and qualified, following which the new board shall be organized. The new board shall elect its own officers, including the general secretary and other staff members. It shall report quadrennially to the General Conference and to the several Jurisdictional Conferences.

SEC. II.   **Jurisdictional Boards**

¶ **1502.** In each jurisdiction there may be a **Jurisdictional Board of Lay Activities,** auxiliary to the general board, as the Jurisdictional Conference may determine. (*See* ¶¶ 15.3, 527.)

Sec. III.   **Annual Conference Boards**

¶ **1503.** 1. There shall be in every Annual Conference a **Conference Board of Lay Activities,** composed of the conference lay leader (¶ 1505.1), who shall be chairman, the associate conference lay leaders and conference directors of program activities if any (¶ 1505.4), the district and associate district lay leaders (¶ 1508.1), the district superintendents, any members of the general and jurisdictional boards residing within the conference, and three members at large, if desired, nominated by the Cabinet in consultation with the conference lay leader and elected by the Annual Conference.

2. The board shall elect a vice-chairman, secretary, and treasurer.

3. The board may set up an **executive committee,** composed of the conference lay leader as chairman, the elected officers (§ 2), the associate conference lay leaders and conference directors of program activities if any, and the district superintendents and district lay leaders.

¶ **1504.** 1. Within the Annual Conference the board shall promote a program of lay activities as outlined in ¶ 1493, auxiliary to that of the general board. It shall be charged with leadership for and development of the several major areas of the work of lay activities in the conference, and shall use suitable means to promote an effective conference program, to co-operate with other conference agencies in the interest of lay activities, and to assist District Boards of Lay Activities in their programs, to the end that every available resource may be provided to help each local church carry on an effective program of lay activities.

2. The board shall use the training and program materials prepared by the general board for district and local-church lay leaders, and shall encourage the use of other training, instructional, and promotional materials developed and distributed by the general board. (*See* ¶ 1494).

3. The board shall co-operate with the General and Jurisdictional Boards of Lay Activities in promoting and encouraging attendance at the National Conference of Methodist Men and the Convocation on Christian Stewardship.

4. The board shall co-operate with the other conference boards in executing their plans for larger service in the work of the church.

5. The board shall report to the Annual Conference each year and shall hold an anniversary, or otherwise provide for an adequate representation of the work of lay activities during the session of the conference.

6. The board shall hold an annual meeting in connection with the Annual Conference session and such other meetings as may be deemed advisable by the board and on the call of the conference lay leader.

7. The board shall, during the latter part of the conference year, develop plans for carrying forward the work in the coming conference year. It shall estimate the necessary amount for the support of this work, and shall make provisions for the adequate presentation of this need to the Commission on World Service and Finance for its consideration and recommendation to the Annual Conference.

¶ 1505. 1. The **conference lay leader** shall be elected annually by the Annual Conference on nomination of the board, which nomination shall be by ballot.[11] An interim vacancy may be filled by the board.

2. The conference lay leader shall be seated in the Annual Conference, but without vote unless he is otherwise a member.

3. As executive officer of the board the conference lay leader shall: (*a*) take the initiative in developing quadrennial and/or annual objectives, in formulating plans, and in assigning responsibilities for carrying out the program of lay activities as outlined by the general board; (*b*) confer with the bishop and correlate the work of the board with all other activities within the conference; (*c*) make a written report to the board at its regular session and to the Annual Conference each year; and (*d*) make a comprehensive report to the general board, following the close of the conference year, which shall include the names and correct addresses of the district and associate district lay leaders of the several districts.

---

[11] *See* Judicial Council Decision 77.

4. If it appears advisable, the board may elect, on nomination of the conference lay leader, one or more associate conference lay leaders and/or conference directors of such program activities as stewardship, Methodist Men, lay speaking, etc.

SEC. IV.   **District Boards**

¶ **1506.** 1. There shall be in every district a **District Board of Lay Activities,** composed of the district lay leader, who shall be chairman, the associate district lay leaders, the district director of lay speaking and other district directors of program activities if any (¶ 1508.4), the group lay leaders if any (¶ 1508.5), the district superintendent, the church lay leader of each local church, and the president of each chartered Methodist Men club.

2. The board shall elect a secretary and, if desired, a treasurer and a vice-chairman, who shall be a representative Methodist Men president or church lay leader.

3. The board shall have an **executive committee,** composed of the district lay leader as chairman, the elected officers (§ 2), the associate district lay leaders, the district director of lay speaking and other district directors of program activities if any, and the district superintendent. It shall meet at least quarterly, and shall confer with the district superintendent regarding the promotion of lay activities and the correlation of the work with all other activities within the district.

¶ **1507.** The board shall co-operate with the conference board in promoting the program of lay activities outlined under the direction of the General, Jurisdictional, and Conference Boards of Lay Activities.

¶ **1508.** 1. The **district lay leader** and the associate district lay leaders shall be elected annually by the Annual Conference on nomination of the district superintendent and the conference lay leader; *provided* that, where the conference so determines, the nominations may be made by the board. The board shall have authority to fill interim vacancies; *provided* that, where the conference so determines, the conference lay leader and the district superintendent shall have authority to fill such vacancies.

2. As the executive officer of the board the district lay

leader shall: (a) call at least one meeting annually of all members of the board to give direction to its work; (b) take the initiative in developing quadrennial and/or annual objectives, in formulating plans, and in assigning responsibilities for carrying out the program of lay activities as outlined by the general and conference boards; (c) make a written report to each regular meeting of the board and to the District Conference; and (d) make a detailed report to the conference lay leader at the close of the conference year, which shall include the names and correct addresses of the associate district lay leaders.

3. The associate district lay leaders shall co-operate with the district lay leader in the work of lay activities as the board may direct. It is recommended that each one visit every Methodist Men club within his assigned section of the district annually, and make a written report to the district lay leader quarterly.

4. The board may elect, on nomination of the district lay leader, a **district director of lay speaking** and, if desired, other district directors of program activities such as stewardship, Methodist Men, etc.

5. If the large number of churches in the district makes it advisable to distribute the work load to meet organizational needs, the board may elect, on nomination of the district lay leader, **group lay leaders** who shall work with the associate lay leaders, and whose duty it shall be to guide the church lay leaders, preferably six in number, and chapters of Methodist Men assigned to them.

¶ 1509. There shall be a **District Committee on Lay Speaking,** composed of the district superintendent, district lay leader, and district director of lay speaking (¶ 1508.4), which shall recommend candidates for certification as lay speakers in accordance with ¶ 293.

SEC. V. **Methodist Men**

¶ 1511. The General Board of Lay Activities shall give special consideration to men's work, correlating it with the total program of lay activities. **Methodist Men** shall be the duly authorized organization for this purpose. The board shall have authority to promote and charter local units of Methodist Men and to affiliate with the movement other existing men's organizations in the local church. Larger units—such as county, subdistrict, metropolitan area, or district units—may be chartered by the board for the purpose of promoting units in the local churches and as a means of developing a wider fellowship of service, in co-operation with the district lay leader, district superintendent, and conference lay leader. The board shall develop such organizational and administrative procedures as are necessary to meet the needs of an expanding fellowship of Christian service. (For the program of Methodist Men in the local church *see* ¶¶ 291-92.)

SEC. VI.   **Christian Stewardship**

¶ **1512.** The General Board of Lay Activities is charged with the cultivation and promotion of Christian stewardship in The Methodist Church. It shall initiate plans, develop literature, and perfect organization to utilize effectively in the work of the church and in the development of Christian character this vital doctrine of Christian faith and practice.

¶ **1513.** The study, practice, and promotion of Christian stewardship are essential to the highest individual holiness as well as the fullest realization of the Church's mission. The individual Christian must know, love, and live the truth himself before he can lead others into the experience of "stewards of the manifold grace of God."

¶ **1514.** God is the owner of all things. Man is a steward. God's ownership and man's stewardship ought to be acknowledged.

Stewardship is the practical expression of one's experience of God. Therefore, all one's life, all personal abilities, and all material resources constitute a gift from God, which should be used for his glory and for the welfare of mankind. This is central in Christian faith and should control and direct all one's being.

Stewardship involves both motives and methods in the production and acquisition of wealth, the service ideal in vocation and avocation, and the conservation of natural resources. It also governs motives and methods in the investment and expenditure of one's total material gains.

Christian experience demonstrates that the acknowledgment of God's ownership and man's stewardship should result in systematic, proportionate, and abundant giving. Tithing is commended as a historic and workable method attested by many Christians throughout centuries of religious custom and joyful experience.

Stewardship likewise requires the offering of oneself and the sharing of one's abilities in the work of the organized agencies of the church and community which serve Kingdom interests.

Christian stewardship inevitably expresses itself in one's daily economic experiences and in all life and service.

Sec. VII. Lay Activities in Local Churches

For information on lay activities in local churches *see* Part II, The Local Church, especially the following: concerning the over-all program of lay activities, including the duties of church lay leaders and the program of Methodist Men, ¶¶ 286-93; concerning the promotion of Christian stewardship in the financial program of the local church, ¶¶ 262-64.

Chapter XI

BOARD OF CHRISTIAN SOCIAL CONCERNS

Section I. Purpose and Name

¶ 1516. Through all of its history Methodism has sought to relate the gospel which it has preached to the life of its members and to the communities in which they have lived. It has sought to follow Christ in bringing the whole of life, with its activities, possessions, and relationships, into conformity with the will of God. To lift up before the members of the church and also the secular world the Christian concern for personal, social, and civic righteousness, to analyze the issues which confront the nation and the world as well as the local community and the person, and to propose Christian lines of action, there shall be a **Board of Christian Social Concerns.** The board shall be incorporated.

Sec. II.   **Organization**

¶ **1518.** *Membership.*—The Board of Christian Social Concerns, hereinafter referred to as the board or the general board, shall be composed as follows: two bishops elected by the College of Bishops in each jurisdiction; one minister and one lay person for each 400,000 members or major fraction thereof, *provided* that there shall be no fewer than three ministers and three laymen from each jurisdiction, elected by the Jurisdictional Conference; three young people—two representing the Methodist Youth Fellowship, one of whom shall be the chairman of Christian citizenship of the National Conference thereof, and one representing the Methodist Student Movement— elected by the board on nomination of the Joint Staff of Youth and Student Work, which shall have selected the nominees as provided in ¶ 1405.2; the chairman of the Department of Christian Social Relations of the Woman's Division of Christian Service of the Board of Missions; and nine members at large elected by the board on nomination of its divisions, as provided in ¶ 1526.3. In addition, in order that there may be an established liaison relationship with certain other boards of the church, there shall be eight liaison members with privilege of the floor but without vote: two elected by the Board of Missions from its own membership, one each from the Divisions of World Missions and of National Missions; three by the Board of Education, one from each of its divisions; one by the Board of Evangelism; one by the Board of Lay Activities; and one by the Board of Hospitals and Homes. No member of the board shall be a salaried officer thereof.

¶ **1519.** *Vacancies.*—If a vacancy occurs in the board by death or resignation, it shall be filled as follows: in the case of a bishop, by the College of Bishops of the jurisdiction; in the case of a ministerial or lay representative from a jurisdiction, by the board on nomination of the College of Bishops of the jurisdiction, such member to serve until the next meeting of the Jurisdictional Conference; in the case of a youth or student member or a member at large, as provided in ¶ 1518.

¶ 1520. *Officers.*—The board shall elect a president, who shall be a bishop; three vice-presidents, each of whom shall serve as the chairman of one division; a recording secretary; a treasurer; and such other officers as it may determine.

¶ 1521. *Executive Committee.*—The board shall establish an **executive committee,** which shall consist of the officers of the board and four additional members from each of the three divisions of the board, one of whom shall be the recording secretary of the division. This committee shall have the power *ad interim* to fill any vacancies occurring in the field and office staff and to transact such business as is necessary between the meetings of the board. It shall report all of its actions for confirmation at the next meeting of the board.

¶ 1522. *Nominating Committee.*—A **nominating committee** of seven members shall be constituted. It shall be composed of one member, ministerial or lay, from each jurisdiction, chosen by the board members from that jurisdiction, and one bishop chosen by the bishops who are board members. The bishop shall serve as convener. This committee shall nominate the officers of the board (¶ 1520) and assign each member of the board, including the vice-presidents, to one of the three divisions (¶ 1526).

¶ 1523. *Meetings.*—1. The board shall meet for purposes of organization and other necessary actions quadrennially after the adjournment of the General Conference and not later than October 15 of that year. The organization meeting shall be convened by the bishop designated by the Council of Bishops for that purpose, and he shall fix the time and place.

2. The board shall hold an annual meeting, at a time and place to be determined by its executive committee, and such other meetings as its work may require, and shall enact suitable by-laws governing the activities of the board and its employees. A majority of the membership shall constitute a quorum.

¶ 1524. The members of the board shall constitute the membership of its predecessor boards, namely, the Board of Temperance of The Methodist Church and all of its legal predecessors, the Board of World Peace of The Methodist Church and all of its legal predecessors, and the Board of Social and Economic Relations of The Methodist Church.

¶ **1525.** *Financial Support.*—1. The work of the board shall be supported from the general benevolences of the church, the amount to be determined by the General Conference, on recommendation of the Council on World Service and Finance. The board shall present quadrennially to the council a statement of the amount required for its general expense and for the support of each of its divisions.

2. Either on behalf of its total work or on behalf of one or more of its divisions, the board may solicit and create special funds, receive gifts and bequests, hold properties and securities in trust, and administer all these financial affairs in accordance with its own rules and the provisions of the Discipline (*see* ¶¶ 743, 748). Funds vested in any of the predecessor boards shall be conserved for the exclusive use of the appropriate division of this board and for the specific purposes for which such funds have been given.

¶ **1526.** *Divisions.*—1. The board shall be organized into three divisions: the Division of Temperance and General Welfare, the Division of Peace and World Order, and the Division of Human Relations and Economic Affairs. The members of the board shall be assigned to divisions by the nominating committee (¶ 1522), subject to the approval of the board. It shall be the duty of this committee to assign the membership, other than members at large, to the three divisions so that the three shall as nearly as possible be of the same size, and shall have members from each jurisdiction and from ministerial and lay groups in as nearly as possible equal proportion. No member shall belong to more than one division, except that the president of the board shall be a member ex officio of each division.

2. Each division shall organize itself under the chairmanship of a vice-president of the board and shall elect a recording secretary. It shall also elect three of its own number by written ballot who, together with the chairman

and recording secretary, shall constitute the executive committee of that division. The members of the divisional executive committee shall be members of the executive committee of the board.

3. Each division shall nominate for election by the board three members at large, selected on the basis of their specialized skills and knowledge relevant to the work of the division, to be members of that division and of the board. (*See* ¶ 1518.)

¶ 1527. Each division shall meet at the same time and place as the board. A special meeting of the division may be held on the call of its chairman, or of three members of its executive committee, or of ten of its members. All such special meetings shall be chargeable to the budget of the division.

¶ 1528. 1. The members assigned to each division shall have the responsibility of establishing policies relating to the work of that division and the conduct of its staff, subject to the approval of the board.

2. The divisions shall co-operatively carry forward the total work of the board through the Annual Conferences and districts, in the local churches, and in such other places and by such means as they may have opportunity to present the witness of Christian social concern.[12]

¶ 1530. *Staff.*—The board shall elect quadrennially a general secretary, three associate general secretaries, and a staff treasurer on nomination of the executive committee. Other staff personnel shall be approved by the executive committee of the board on nomination of the president and the general secretary. The executive committee of the board may, at its discretion, assign this responsibility to the executive committee of a division. The salaries and duties of all employees of the board shall be fixed by the board.

¶ 1531. *General and Associate General Secretaries.*—1.

---

[12] In adopting these provisions the General Conference of 1960 directed as follows: "During the third year of the quadrennium, in 1962-63, the board shall review, in co-operation with the Co-ordinating Council, the above divisional structure to determine whether a threefold or other divisional organization of the board will be more effective in the performance of the total work assigned to the board, and shall make appropriate recommendations to the General Conference of 1964."

The **general secretary** shall be an ex officio member of the board, of its executive committee, and of the executive committee of each division, without vote. He shall be the chief administrative officer of the board, responsible for the co-ordination of the total program of the board and for the general administration of the headquarters office and of such facilities and functions as serve all three divisions of the board. Under his supervision there shall be a **director of organizational administration,** who shall have charge of the service bureau, finance, and purchasing; a **director of communication and publication,** who shall edit and prepare publicity, promotional, and audio-visual materials; a **director of educational liaison,** who shall maintain close relations with, and interpret the work of the board to, the several divisions of the Board of Education; a legislative officer if the board so orders; and such other staff persons as are deemed necessary by the board.

2. Each of the **associate general secretaries** shall have primary responsibility for those Christian social concerns which are assigned to his particular division. Within this area and under the direction of the division and its executive committee he with his staff shall develop a program of research, education, and action, bringing these concerns to the attention of the denomination and all its churches and of the communities they serve. He shall be responsible, under the direction of the division and its executive committee, for the administration of the budget, including the income from trust funds allocated to his division. The three associate general secretaries shall co-operate with one another and with the general secretary to prevent undue overlapping in the work of the divisions and to avoid conflicts in scheduling of meetings and conferences.

3. The general secretary and the associate general secretaries shall be members of the Council of Secretaries (¶ 1593).

SEC. III.   **Headquarters**

¶ **1534.** 1. The headquarters of the board and of its divisions shall be in Washington, D. C.

2. In addition to the general headquarters, there shall be a New York United Nations office conducted in co-opera-

tion with the Woman's Division of Christian Service of the Board of Missions. In the operation of this office the Division of Peace and World Order shall represent the board and shall carry the board's responsibility for staffing and budget.

SEC. IV. Division of Temperance and General Welfare

¶ **1535.** 1. It shall be the responsibility of the **Division of Temperance and General Welfare** to conduct a program of research, education, and action centering around the following Christian social concerns: alcohol problems; addiction to injurious habits such as use of tobacco and drugs; gambling; pornography; juvenile delinquency and crime; penal system and rehabilitation; mental health and medical care; problems associated with aging, population, and planned parenthood; traffic safety; and such other concerns as the board may specify; *provided* that the division shall have no jurisdiction to advise or administer work in connection with any hospital or home for children, youth, or the aged (*see* ¶ 1551), and shall not duplicate the research, educational, or action program of the Board of Hospitals and Homes relating to medical care and related problems associated with the aging. The general policies shall be established by the division, subject to the approval of the board.

2. The work assigned to the division shall be carried forward by the associate general secretary and such other staff members as the division shall determine, subject to budget allocations. The staff shall report to the division at the time of the annual board meeting concerning the work of the past year and plans proposed for further implementation of its assigned responsibilities.

¶ **1536.** To enlist Methodists and encourage others to commit themselves to personal abstinence from alcoholic beverages and to temperate living, and to challenge church members to creative action for a sober home and social life, the first Sunday in December shall be observed each year as **Commitment Day,** to be promoted in every church with assistance by the General Board of Christian Social Concerns for that purpose. Because of the particular

emphasis of the day it is suggested that no spec___
be received, unless it be for the propagation of ___
ist program of temperance.

SEC. V.   **Division of Peace and World Order**

¶ **1538.** 1. It shall be the responsibility of the _____ __
of Peace and World Order to conduct a pro___ ___ of
research, education, and action centering arou___ the
following Christian social concerns: American ___ eign
policy; United Nations and related international organizations; disarmament and nuclear weapon control; space
control; foreign aid, tariffs, and trade; immigration and
naturalization; military policy and conscription legislation; conscientious objectors and the draft; and such other
concerns as the board may specify. The general policies
shall be established by the division, subject to the approval
of the board.

2. The work assigned to the division shall be carried
forward by the associate general secretary and such other
staff members as the division shall determine, subject to
budget allocations. The staff shall report to the division at
the time of the annual board meeting concerning the work
of the past year and plans proposed for further implementation of its assigned responsibilities.

Note: For co-operation with the Board of Missions in
developing service projects for conscientious objectors
see ¶ 1291.

SEC. VI.   **Division of Human Relations**
and Economic Affairs

¶ **1541.** 1. It shall be the responsibility of the **Division
of Human Relations and Economic Affairs** to conduct a
program of research, education, and action centering
around the following Christian social concerns: race relations; civil liberties; public policy on education; church
and state relations; civic responsibility; labor-manage-
ment relations; agriculture; conservation; government
and private economic policy and practice; technological
change; unemployment; housing; and such other concerns as the board may specify. The general policies shall

be established by the division, subject to the approval of the board.

2. The work assigned to the division shall be carried forward by the associate general secretary and such other staff members as the division shall determine, subject to budget allocations. The staff shall report to the division at the time of the annual board meeting concerning the work of the past year and plans proposed for further implementation of its assigned responsibilities.

SEC. VII.   **Jurisdictional Boards**

¶ **1544.** In each jurisdiction there may be a **Jurisdictional Board of Christian Social Concerns,** auxiliary to the general board, as the Jurisdictional Conference may determine. (*See* ¶¶ 15.3, 527.)

SEC. VIII.   **Annual Conference Boards**

¶ **1545.** Each Annual Conference shall elect, on nomination of the nominating committee of the conference, or otherwise as the conference may direct, a **Conference Board of Christian Social Concerns.** It shall have no fewer than fifteen nor more than sixty members, with an approximately equal number of laymen and ministers. The lay members shall include the chairman of Christian citizenship of the Conference Methodist Youth Fellowship, a student nominated by the state or regional unit of the Methodist Student Movement, and the secretary of Christian social relations of the Conference Woman's Society of Christian Service. The remaining lay members shall consist of an equal number of men and women. All district directors of Christian social concerns and any members of the general and jurisdictional boards living within the bounds of the conference shall be ex officio members.

¶ **1546.** The conference board, in co-operation with the general board, shall develop and promote programs on Christian social concerns within the bounds of the conference. To this end it may divide its membership into three committees of approximately equal size, patterned after the divisions of the general board. They shall have re-

437

sponsibility to co-operate with one another to advance the concerns of their respective divisions.

¶ **1547.** The board shall estimate annually the amount necessary for the support of its work and report this amount to the Commission on World Service and Finance for its consideration and recommendation to the Annual Conference. The work of the board shall be considered a benevolence interest of the church within the conference.

¶ **1548.** The board may employ a person or persons to further its purposes. Two or more Annual Conferences may co-operate in developing their programs and in the employment of one or more persons.

SEC. IX.   **District Committees**

¶ **1549.** The district superintendent, after consultation with the conference board, shall appoint a **district director of Christian social concerns** and, if desired, a **District Committee on Christian Social Concerns** of laymen and ministers to work with him to further the purposes of the conference board. The secretary of Christian social relations of the District Woman's Society of Christian Service shall be an ex officio member. If the Annual Conference so orders, three district directors shall be appointed, each to represent the interests of one of the divisions within the general board.

SEC. X.   **Local-Church Commissions**

For the program of Christian social concerns in the local church *see* ¶¶ 274-75.

CHAPTER XII

BOARD OF HOSPITALS AND HOMES

SECTION I.   **Constitution**

¶ **1551.** *Name and Purpose.*—There shall be a **Board of Hospitals and Homes** of The Methodist Church, which shall have an advisory relationship to Methodist philanthropic interests and institutions, such as hospitals, homes for the aged, homes for children, and homes for youth, located in the United States, its territories, and dependencies. This advisory relationship shall apply also to a hospital or home which is owned or supervised by any agency of The Methodist Church in the United States, its territories, or dependencies.

¶ 1552. *Incorporation.*—The Board of Hospitals and Homes of The Methodist Church shall be duly incorporated according to the laws of Illinois. Its headquarters shall be located in the state of Illinois.

¶ 1553. *Management.*—The management of the board shall be vested in a Board of Managers of eighteen: two bishops, elected by the Council of Bishops; one minister and one lay member from each jurisdiction, elected by the Jurisdictional Conference, at least one of whom shall be an active administrator of an institution under the general supervision of the board; and four members at large, elected by the board. All of the Board of Managers shall be members of The Methodist Church. Should a vacancy occur among those elected by the jurisdictions, the College of Bishops where such vacancy occurs shall elect the person to fill the unexpired term. All other vacancies shall be filled by the electing body.

¶ 1554. *Officers.*—1. The officers of the Board of Managers shall be a president, elected by said board from among the bishops who are members; four vice-presidents, each of whom shall represent one of the four major interests of this board, namely, hospitals, child welfare, homes for aged, homes for youth; a recording secretary; and a treasurer. All of these officers shall be elected by the board for the quadrennium. In addition there shall be such other officers and agents as the board may from time to time determine.

2. The board may elect a **general secretary** and provide for his salary and necessary help. This secretary shall be subject to the authority and control of the board.

¶ 1555. *Meetings.*—1. An annual meeting of the board shall be held at such time and place as the board may determine.

2. An **executive committee** of twelve members shall be elected by the board, such committee to include the officers

of the board and five additional members to be elected by the board with the provision that each jurisdiction shall be represented on the committee by an elected member, the general secretary being a member of the executive committee ex officio without vote (¶ 1103). Seven members of the executive committee shall constitute a quorum.

¶ **1556.** *Affiliation.*—In order that Methodist philanthropic activities may be made scientific and Christian, hospitals or homes known as institutions of The Methodist Church and maintaining Christian standards or looking to Methodist constituency for support, and not affiliated with any other board of the church, shall be expected to affiliate with the Board of Hospitals and Homes.

¶ **1557.** *Financial Support.*—Since the Board of Hospitals and Homes is empowered to act only in an advisory, educational, and co-operative capacity, its support shall be derived as follows: (*a*) from gifts, devises, wills, bequests, and from administration of trust funds; and (*b*) from such share in the general benevolences of the church as the General Conference may determine.

¶ **1558.** *Powers.*—1. The board may make surveys, disseminate information, suggest plans for securing funds, maintain a bureau for the purpose of securing experts in all lines of work, provide architectural data, and render assistance, other than financial assistance, in the promotion and establishment of new institutions. It shall make appraisals and advise as to the validity and wisdom of accepting or rejecting institutions, such as hospitals or homes, to become beneficiaries in any way of the approval or support of The Methodist Church in any Annual Conference of the United States. It may suggest plans for Annual Conferences regarding their religious ministry to state and non-Methodist hospitals and homes needing such ministry.

2. The board shall formulate standards, spiritual, financial, and scientific, to protect the aims and ideals of The Methodist Church and shall encourage and assist institutions in attaining these standards.

3. The board is empowered to act as trustee for the administration of bequests or endowments for institutions

of the church and, as a result of said trusts, to assist designated Christian social welfare work anywhere throughout the church.

4. As an advisory, standardizing, and educational agency of The Methodist Church, the board is empowered to prepare interpretative literature which can be used in a practical manner throughout the church for Golden Cross or other appeals.

5. The Board of Managers is authorized to organize committees, set up financial accounts, assist institutions in efforts to secure funds, and perform such other functions as the normal work of the board may require.

6. The Board of Hospitals and Homes shall not be responsible, legally or morally, for the debts, contracts, or obligations, or for any other financial commitments of any character or description, created, undertaken, or assumed by any institution, agency, or interest of The Methodist Church, whether or not such institution, agency, or interest shall be approved, accepted, or recognized by the board, or shall be affiliated with the board, or whether or not the promotion or establishment of the same shall be approved, under any of the provisions of this constitution, or otherwise. No such institution, agency, or interest of The Methodist Church, and no officer or member of the Board of Managers of this board, shall have any authority whatsoever to take any action, directly or by implication, at variance with, or deviating from, the limitation contained in the preceding sentence hereof.

SEC. II.   **Golden Cross Society**

¶ 1559. 1. There shall be a **Golden Cross Society** of The Methodist Church, which shall promote the hospitals and homes work under the direction of the Board of Hospitals and Homes and shall collect moneys and afford other material assistance in providing care for the sick, older persons, children, and youth. The enrollment in the Methodist Golden Cross Society shall be held annually in order to secure interest in, and support of, hospitals and homes in every congregation in such manner and on such date as determined by the patronizing Annual Conference or Conferences. The week following **Golden Cross Enroll-ment Sunday** shall be known as **Hospitals and Homes Week.** Funds raised through said enrollment shall be used as directed by the Annual Conference through its Board of Hospitals and Homes, in keeping with the policies of said society.

2. The right of any Annual Conference to employ such methods for financing its philanthropic institutions as it may decide on is recognized, and the Board of Hospitals and Homes shall be available for advice and guidance.

SEC. III.   **Jurisdictional Boards**

¶ 1560. In each jurisdiction there may be a **Jurisdictional Board of Hospitals and Homes,** auxiliary to the general board, as the Jurisdictional Conference may determine. (*See* ¶¶ 15.3, 527.)

SEC. IV.   **Annual Conference Boards**

¶ 1561. 1. Each Annual Conference shall promote within its bounds a **Conference Board of Hospitals and Homes,** composed as follows: (*a*) At least one ministerial and one lay member shall be elected from each district of the conference; *provided* that there shall be a minimum of four ministers and four lay members. (*b*) Any member of the general board within the conference shall be an ex officio member. (*c*) Administrators of hospitals and homes related to the conference shall be ex officio members, without vote.

2. The board shall meet at least once before or during each regular conference session and shall act in co-operation with the general board to promote the interest of the hospitals and homes within the bounds of the conference. It may aid in planning and developing a religious ministry, wherever practicable, in state and non-Methodist hospitals and homes needing such ministry. Where civil law requires the election of boards of trustees or managers by the Annual Conference, it may nominate the persons for such election.

3. The board shall organize with a chairman, who may become a voting member of the National Association of

Methodist Hospitals and Homes under the payment of the personal membership dues of the association; and he shall be expected to take as much interest as possible in the program of Christian philanthropy in Methodism as represented by the association.

Sec. V.   **Local-Church Committees**

See ¶ 278.3 under Part II, The Local Church.

Sec. VI.   **Sundry Provisions**

¶ **1563. Women's Auxiliaries** connected with the various philanthropic institutions of Methodism may be organized under, or given approval on compliance with, established standard requirements and procedures, such as the adoption of a constitution and by-laws fixing the identity, responsibility, and relationship of such organization as an auxiliary of a Methodist institution. Such an auxiliary, when so organized, and when request is made by the board of trustees of the institution which it represents, shall be granted a certificate of recognition from the Board of Hospitals and Homes.

¶ **1564.** The board may organize a **Personnel Bureau,** under such rules and regulations as it may determine: (*a*) to help institutions of philanthropic service in The Methodist Church to find adequately trained Christian personnel to conduct the various types of work represented by Methodist hospitals and homes; (*b*) to encourage Methodist youth who are socially minded and who are desirous of investing their lives in some form of Christian institutional work; and (*c*) to co-operate in the work of the Interboard Committee on Christian Vocations (¶ 1415).

¶ **1565.** There shall be organized a **National Association of Methodist Hospitals and Homes,** to be composed of the representatives of institutions and the presidents of jurisdictional and conference boards who are connected with Methodist philanthropy. This association shall have its own constitution and by-laws, shall meet in convention once a year, and shall establish its requirements for membership and have such membership dues as it may require. It shall work under the general direction of the Board of Hospitals and Homes, whose general secretary shall be an ex officio member of the association's executive committee. The aim and purpose of this association, in co-operation with the board, shall be to help lift the spiritual, scientific, and financial standards of our church hospitals and homes.

¶ **1566.** The board shall cause to be established a **code of ethics** to serve as a standard and guide for service institutions of The Methodist Church in developing Christian and scientific characteristics.

¶ **1567.** 1. There shall be a consultive interboard staff committee between the Woman's Division of Christian Service and the Board of Hospitals and Homes, established by these agencies.

2. There may be in each Annual Conference an interboard committee of ten persons, composed of five representatives elected by the Conference Woman's Society of Christian Service and five representatives elected by the Conference Board of Hospitals and Homes, for co-operation in matters of mutual interest.

Chapter XIII

COMMISSIONS

Section I.   **Commission on Worship**

¶ **1568.** 1. There shall be a **Commission on Worship,** composed of the book editor ex officio and two bishops, one minister and one lay person from each jurisdiction, and three members from the church at large elected by the General Conference on nomination of the Council of Bishops. Vacancies during the quadrennium shall be filled by the Council of Bishops.

2. The officers of the commission shall be a chairman, a vice-chairman, and a secretary, elected quadrennially in such manner as it may determine.

3. The commission shall meet at least once a year, and at such other time as the commission and its officers shall determine.

4. The expense of the commission shall be borne by the General Administration Fund. The commission shall present a proposed budget to the Council on World Service and Finance for its consideration and action.

¶ **1569.** The functions of the commission shall be:

1. To cultivate beauty, dignity, and meaning in the worship experience of the church.

2. To encourage by means of manuals and other publications, and by seminars, workshops, and other media, good taste and practice in the conduct of worship, church music, church architecture, and the use of the arts in the church.

3. When need arises, to prepare forms of worship and to revise existing orders of worship for recommendation to the General Conference.

4. To supervise future editions of *The Book of Worship for Church and Home*, as may be authorized by the General Conference. (*See* ¶ 1901.)

5. To make recommendations to the General Conference concerning future editions of *The Methodist Hymnal*. (*See* ¶ 2014.)

6. To advise with any of the general agencies of the church in the publication and circulation of any orders of service and other liturgical materials bearing the imprint of The Methodist Church.

7. To advise with official publications of the church concerning material offered in the fields of worship and liturgical arts.

8. To consult with the Television, Radio, and Film Commission on matters of joint concern.

9. To encourage in our schools of theology and pastors' schools the best possible instruction in the meaning and conduct of worship.

10. To advise with those responsible for planning the program of the General Conference and other general assemblies of the church regarding the worship services on these occasions.

11. To offer suggestions and direction to the Commissions on Worship of the various conferences and of the local churches. (*See* ¶ 276.)

12. To relate The Methodist Church to the Department of Worship and the Arts of the National Council of

Churches and to the Interdenominational Bureau of Architecture.

¶ **1570.** It shall be the purpose of the commission to enrich and not to govern the devotional life of the church, recalling our dual heritage of liturgical and free worship, and that "it is not necessary that rites and ceremonies should in all places be the same" (¶ 82).

¶ **1571.** 1. Each Annual Conference may constitute a **Conference Commission on Worship,** which shall be auxiliary to the general and jurisdictional commissions, to report each year to the conference in such manner as the conference may direct. It shall be composed of at least one ministerial and one lay member from each district. Any member of the general commission within the conference shall be an ex officio member.

2. The commission shall meet at least once before each regular conference session. It shall organize with a chairman, vice-chairman, and secretary.

3. The duties of the commission shall be to act in co-operation with the general commission:

a) To promote the interests of worship within the bounds of the conference.

b) To foster the use of the best resources for worship at conference meetings, and in all the churches of the conference.

c) To promote the use of *The Book of Worship* and *The Methodist Hymnal* in all the churches of the conference.

d) To plan and promote seminars and demonstrations on ways of worship and the use of hymns within the bounds of the conference.

e) To provide exhibits at the conference sessions in such fields as architecture, church appointments, etc.

f) To co-operate with the Board of Education and the National Fellowship of Methodist Musicians in promoting seminars and all other conferences on church music.

Sec. II.   **Commission on Chaplains**

¶ **1572.** 1. There shall be a **Commission on Chaplains,** which shall represent The Methodist Church in the recruitment, endorsement, and general oversight of all Methodist ministers serving as chaplains in the Armed

Forces, Veterans Administration, and other federal agencies; in industry; and in state and local public and private institutions, other than those of The Methodist Church. The commission shall render such other services to these chaplains as may be referred to it by the Council of Bishops.

2. The commission shall be composed of six bishops, one from each jurisdiction, and five ministers and five laymen, elected by the General Conference on nomination of the Council of Bishops. Vacancies shall be filled by the Council of Bishops. A member bishop shall serve as chairman. The commission may elect advisory members, without vote, one from each department of the Armed Forces, from the Veterans Administration, and from other fields where Methodist chaplains are serving.

3. The commission is authorized to receive and disburse such share of the Fellowship of Suffering and Service offering as may be determined by the General Conference and such other funds and special gifts as are specifically given to the Commission on Chaplains.

SEC. III.   **Commission on Church Union**

¶ 1575. There shall be a **Commission on Church Union,** composed of one bishop, one minister, and one layman from each jurisdiction, nominated by the Council of Bishops for election by the General Conference. The duties of this commission shall be: (a) to consider specific overtures or proposals for organic union with other denominations and report to the General Conference, (b) to initiate studies looking toward organic union, (c) to confer with representatives of other denominations in any general discussion of church union, (d) to encourage interdenominational co-operation throughout the church and to have responsibility for any interdenominational activities not specifically cared for by other agencies. The expenses of this commission shall be paid from the General Administration Fund.

SEC. IV.   **Interagency Commission on
Cultivation, Promotion,
and Publication**

¶ 1576. There shall be an **Interagency Commission on**

Cultivation, Promotion, and Publication, whose function shall be to act as the co-ordinator of the policies and activities of the Commission on Promotion and Cultivation, the Television, Radio, and Film Commission, the Commission on Public Relations and Methodist Information, and the Board of Publication.

¶ **1577.** The membership of the commission shall be composed of the following representatives from its constituent agencies: four members from the Commission on Promotion and Cultivation, two from the Television, Radio, and Film Commission, one from the Commission on Public Relations and Methodist Information, and two from the Board of Publication.

¶ **1578.** The commission, in carrying out its function of co-ordinating the work of the agencies which it represents, shall see that plans and programs relating to cultivation, promotion, films, radio, television, public relations, Methodist information, and publishing do not overlap or duplicate. Any questions of overlapping or duplication which cannot be resolved by the commission shall be referred to the Co-ordinating Council. (*See* ¶ 1113.1.) When in the judgment of the commission such action would facilitate co-ordination among its agencies, it may authorize interboard staff committees.

¶ **1579.** Implementing the work of the commission there shall be a **secretarial council,** consisting of the general secretary, or other representative of each constituent agency. It shall be the function of this council to facilitate co-operation among the agencies in the creative planning of their respective programs and in avoiding overlapping of function or duplication of activity. The chairmanship of the secretarial council shall rotate annually among its members.

Sec. V.   **Commission on Promotion and Cultivation**

For the organization and functions of the Commission on Promotion and Cultivation *see* ¶¶ 750-64, under Part V, Temporal Economy.

Sec. VI.   **Television, Radio and Film Commission**

¶ **1581.** 1. There shall be an incorporated **Television,**

Radio, and Film Commission of The Methodist Church. Its headquarters shall be in Nashville, Tennessee.

2. The membership shall consist of three bishops elected by the Council of Bishops; one person from each jurisdiction elected by its College of Bishops; two representatives elected by the Joint Section of Education and Cultivation of the Board of Missions; three elected by the Board of Education; one each elected by the Boards of Publication, Evangelism, Hospitals and Homes, Pensions, Lay Activities, and Christian Social Concerns, and by the Commission on Public Relations and Methodist Information; and nine members at large elected by the commission.

3. Officers of the commission shall be a president, vice-president, secretary, and treasurer, elected quadrennially in such manner as the commission may determine.

4. The purpose and function of the commission shall be:

a) To unify and co-ordinate the audio-visual programs of all Methodist agencies dealing with projected pictures, recordings, transcriptions, radio and television programs, and other audio-visual materials.

b) To make the studies necessary for the development of a unified and comprehensive program of resources to serve all age groups in the home, church, and community, and to represent the great causes of the church.

c) To produce and distribute such programs and materials in the area of the work of member agencies as the agencies may request and finance, and such other resources as are needed to serve the great causes of the church. In so far as practical the rental or sale of materials for Methodist use shall be handled through The Methodist Publishing House.

d) To represent The Methodist Church in the Broadcasting and Film Commission of the National Council of Churches, and any other interdenominational agencies working in the area of mass communication.

e) To provide funds for scholarships, and other training opportunities, to prepare qualified persons for full-time Christian service in this field, and to work with other Methodist agencies in providing training opportunities for ministers and lay leaders so that resources provided may be effectively used.

5. The financial support of the commission shall be determined as follows: The General Conference shall determine and provide from world service funds, on the recommendation of the Council on World Service and Finance, the budget of the commission. The budget shall include provision for necessary staff and administrative cost and such funds as may be deemed necessary to enable the commission to fulfill its stated functions. Additional contributions may be accepted from member agencies which are not supported by world service funds. (*See* ¶ 762.)

6. The General Conference, on recommendation of the Council on World Service and Finance and of the commission, shall allot such funds as it deems wise to the Broadcasting and Film Commission of the National Council of Churches. If this apportionment is included in a total church budget for the National Council of Churches, it shall be paid only after annual approval by the commission.

¶ 1582. There may be in each jurisdiction a **Jurisdictional Television, Radio, and Film Commission** auxiliary to the general commission.

¶ 1583. 1. There shall be a **Conference Television, Radio, and Film Commission** in each Annual Conference, which, in co-operation with the program boards, and other agencies in the conference, shall have for its purpose serving the conference in the field of mass-communication media, including radio, television, and audio-visual materials, by:

a) Promotion of the principles of good communication.

b) Promotion of the use of mass-communication methods and materials by the local churches.

c) Promotion of the Methodist Television-Radio Ministry Fund.

d) Where necessary, establishment of audio-visual libraries.

e) Production and distribution of programs for conference-wide use.

f) In co-operation with the Conference Board of Education, provision of training conferences for selected persons from local churches for effective use of these materials.

g) Service to other agencies of the conference, and close co-operation with the conference or area public relations office.

2. The commission shall be composed of one district superintendent designated by the bishop; five persons whose experience and training qualify them for this service, elected by the conference; one representative of the Conference Commission on Promotion and Cultivation; three members of the Conference Commission on Public Relations and Methodist Information, or of such other agency as functions for the conference in this area; one representative each from the Conference Boards of Education, Missions, Evangelism, Lay Activities, and Christian Social Concerns, and from the Woman's Society of Christian Service, named by the agency; and at least three members at large, who may be elected by the commission. Any member of the general or jurisdictional commission residing within the bounds of the conference shall be an ex officio member.

3. The commission shall organize by electing a chairman, secretary, and treasurer, who may be the conference treasurer.

4. The commission may elect a **director,** whose duty shall be to execute the policies and program established by the commission.

5. The commission shall have a **Committee on Finance,** consisting of three members of the commission and two members at large, to promote the Methodist Television-Radio Ministry Fund in the conference, the districts, and the local churches. It shall co-operate with the General Television, Radio, and Film Commission and the Commission on Promotion and Cultivation.

6. The commission may request funds from the conference through the Commission on World Service and Finance.

7. Where desired, the officers of the conference commissions within an episcopal area may, at the request of the bishop, function as an **Area Television, Radio, and Film Commission.**

451

¶ **1584.** There may be in each district a **district tele-vision, radio, and film director,** who shall be responsible for implementing the work of the commission on the district level. He shall be appointed by the district super-intendent in consultation with the chairman of the con-ference commission. The several district directors may, on vote of the conference commission, be members of that commission.

¶ **1585.** The chairman of the Intercommission Audio-Visual Committee (¶ 235) shall be the liaison person be-tween the local church and the Conference and General Television, Radio, and Film Commissions.

SEC. VII.   **Commission on Public Relations and Methodist Information**

¶ **1586.** There shall be a **Commission on Public Rela-tions and Methodist Information,** which shall gather news of public interest concerning Methodist activities and opin-ion and disseminate it through the secular press, the religious press, radio, television, and other legitimate media of public information; *provided* that in its relations with the media it serves, and with the public generally, the commission may use such abbreviation of its name as it may deem appropriate. It shall be composed of nine persons, one of whom shall be a bishop, who shall act as chairman, elected by the General Conference on nomina-tion of the Council of Bishops. Care shall be taken to nominate persons whose experience in public relations, journalism, advertising, radio and television, business, or the church particularly qualifies them for this service. Vacancies occurring between sessions of the General Con-ference shall be filled by the commission. Members shall hold office until the next session of the General Confer-ence, or until their successors are elected.

¶ **1587.** The commission is authorized to employ a **general secretary,** who may be known as director, and such other persons as may be necessary to give effect to its purpose.

¶ **1588.** The expense of the commission shall be borne by the General Administration Fund. The commission shall present a proposed budget to the Council on World Service and Finance for its consideration and action.

¶ **1589.** 1. The commission shall be the official general news gathering and distributing agency for The Methodist Church and its general agencies. It may arrange with other general agencies for some persons in those organizations to represent the commission in direct release of Methodist news items to the religious and/or secular press; but agencies which supported news gathering and distribution services during the 1948-52 quadrennium shall continue to provide for their budgets.

2. The commission shall have general supervision over planning public relations and procedures for making releases throughout the church in the United States. It may encourage and work with area and conference directors of public relations, may assist in pastors' schools and conduct seminars in public relations, and may prepare instruction materials for local-church use concerning public relations.

3. The commission shall maintain co-operative relationship with the editors of all boards and other agencies and editors of area and conference periodicals.

¶ **1590.** There may be area, conference, district, and local-church Commissions or Committees on Public Relations and Methodist Information, to be constituted and organized as the respective governing bodies may determine. Such commissions or committees shall be related to the general commission.

CHAPTER XIV

ASSOCIATION OF
METHODIST HISTORICAL SOCIETIES

¶ **1591.** 1. *Organization and Purpose.*—a) The **Association of Methodist Historical Societies** shall be a federation of the Jurisdictional, Annual Conference, and other Historical Societies of The Methodist Church. It shall be affiliated with the International Methodist Historical Society.

b) Its purpose shall be to gather, preserve, and disseminate materials and facts on the history of Methodism, to co-operate with other bodies, especially the international society and the World Methodist Council, and to do any and all things necessary to the promotion and care of the historical interests of The Methodist Church. It shall maintain archives in which shall be preserved historical records and materials of every kind relating to The Methodist Church.

2. *Executive Committee.*—*a*) The activities of the association shall be directed by an **executive committee** designated quadrennially. It shall be composed of its own officers; the presidents or chairmen of the active jurisdictional societies recognized by Jurisdictional Conferences; the active officers of the International Methodist Historical Society and the World Methodist Council from The Methodist Church; the editor of *Christian Advocate;* and six additional persons appointed by the Council of Bishops because of their interest in and knowledge of Methodist history and their availability for meetings.

b) The executive committee shall meet on the call of the president and executive secretary. It shall hold an annual meeting, elect the officers, and exercise the authority usually incident to an executive body.

c) There shall be a subcommittee composed of the officers, which shall perform the duties and exercise the authority of the executive committee between meetings.

d) The executive committee and subcommittee may vote by mail on any matter. Mail polls shall be carried out by the executive secretary, who shall state clearly the propositions to be voted on and announce the results to all the members.

3. *Officers.*—*a*) There shall be a president, two or more vice-presidents, an executive secretary, and a treasurer, all elected quadrennially.

b) These officers shall perform the duties usually incident to the positions. The executive secretary shall be the executive and administrative officer and shall carry on all the work of the association, keep the records and minutes, and do the editorial work.

c) The executive committee may elect such other officers as may be needed and prescribe their duties.

4. *Finances.*—*a*) The association shall be financed by appropriations of the General Conference, the sale of literature and historical materials, and the gifts of interested individuals and groups.

b) The executive committee shall prepare an annual budget based on the expected income and shall prescribe the manner of its administration.

¶ **1592.** There may be a **Jurisdictional Historical Society** in each jurisdiction, auxiliary to the Association of Methodist Historical Societies, as the Jurisdictional Conference may determine.

Note: For description of the Historical Society in each Annual Conference *see* ¶ 663.

Chapter XV

COUNCIL OF SECRETARIES

¶ **1593.** 1. There shall be a **Council of Secretaries,** whose membership shall consist of the chief executives of the following agencies: one each from the Divisions of World Missions and of National Missions, the Woman's Division of Christian Service, and the Commission on Deaconess Work, and two, one man and one woman, from the Joint Section of Education and Cultivation of the Board of Missions; one from each division of the Board of Education; one from the Board of Christian Social Concerns and one from each of its divisions; one each from the Boards of Hospitals and Homes, Evangelism, Lay Activities, and Pensions; and one each from The Methodist Publishing House, the Council on World Service and Finance, the Commission on Chaplains, the Television, Radio, and Film Commission, the American Bible Society, the Interboard Committee on Missionary Education, the Interboard Committee on Christian Vocations, the Commission on Promotion and Cultivation, the Commission on Public Relations and Methodist Information, the Methodist Committee for Overseas Relief, the Commission on Camp Activities, and the Association of Methodist Historical Societies.

2. The council shall meet periodically to consider matters of common interest and co-operation among the several general agencies of the church. It shall consider existing and emerging conditions and needs where the co-operative services of two or more agencies are needed, and devise ways and means of meeting those needs when they fall within the Disciplinary functions of two or more general agencies. It shall seek to further co-operation between existing agencies in their regular work and in carrying out such additional responsibilities as the General Conference may place on them. It shall report annually to the Council of Bishops and to the Council on World Service and Finance, and quadrennially to the General Conference.

Chapter XVI

INTERDENOMINATIONAL AGENCIES

¶ **1594.** The Methodist Church is a charter member of the **World Methodist Council.** The members of the section representing The Methodist Church shall be nominated by the Council of Bishops, due regard being given to geographical representation. Financial support of the World Methodist Council shall be channeled through the central treasury, as shall be directed by the Council on World Service and Finance.

¶ **1595.** 1. The Methodist Church is a charter member of the **National Council of the Churches of Christ in the United States of America.** It has borne its proportionate share of financial support, and through the Interdenominational Co-operation Fund is authorized and directed to continue its support. (*See* ¶ 778.)

2. The representatives of The Methodist Church to the Assembly, the General Board, and other agencies of the National Council of Churches shall be nominated by the Council of Bishops and elected by the General Conference, due regard being given to geographical representation.

When representatives must be chosen or vacancies must be filled between sessions of the General Conference, the Council of Bishops is authorized and instructed to do so.

3. Methodist support of the National Council of Churches shall be channeled through the central treasury, as shall be directed by the Council on World Service and Finance, which shall give due credit for Methodist gifts and contributions to this cause, and shall include them in its annual financial report to the church. The sources of income shall include: (a) the National Council of Churches' share of the Interdenominational Co-operation Fund, as determined by the General Conference; and (b) such payments by the general agencies of the church as each agency may deem its responsibility and proportionate share in the co-operative program of the council. Personal, group, or local-church gifts shall be included as a part of the ratio distribution of the Interdenominational Co-operation Fund.

¶ 1596. 1. The Methodist Church is a charter member of the **World Council of Churches.** It has borne its proportionate share of financial support, and through the Interdenominational Co-operation Fund is authorized and directed to continue its support.

2. The representatives of The Methodist Church to the Assembly and other agencies of the World Council of Churches shall be nominated by the Council of Bishops and elected by the General Conference, due regard being given to geographical representation. When representatives must be chosen or vacancies must be filled between sessions of the General Conference, the Council of Bishops is authorized and instructed to do so.

4. Methodist support of the World Council of Churches shall be channeled through the central treasury, as shall be directed by the Council on World Service and Finance, which shall give due credit for Methodist gifts and contributions received by the World Council of Churches, and shall include them in its annual financial report to the church.

¶ 1597. 1. The Council of Bishops is authorized to create a **Commission on Ecumenical Consultation,** to co-operate in such ways as the council may require as it discharges its responsibility for the direction of relations of The

Methodist Church with the World Council of Churches and the ecumenical movement. The commission shall be composed of six bishops, a pastor and a layman from each jurisdiction, twelve representatives from the Methodist schools of theology, the secretary of the Association of Methodist Theological Schools, one representative each from the Boards of Missions and of Education and the World Methodist Council, and two members at large.

2. At the direction of the Council of Bishops the commission shall: (*a*) receive and respond to communications received from the World Council of Churches, the National Council of Churches, and duly appointed agencies of these bodies; (*b*) report to the Council of Bishops and to the General Conference on its deliberations and findings; and (*c*) inform the general church in regard to developments of the ecumenical movement through regular channels of communication.

3. The Council on World Service and Finance shall make provisions for the support of the work of this commission.

¶ **1598.** To encourage the wider circulation of the Holy Scriptures throughout the world, and to provide for the translation, printing, and distribution essential thereto, the **American Bible Society** shall be recognized as one of the general missionary agencies of The Methodist Church, and the Council on World Service and Finance shall make appropriate provision for participating in its support.

¶ **1599. Religion in American Life, Incorporated,** is recognized as an interdenominational and interfaith agency through which The Methodist Church may work to direct attention to church attendance and loyalty to the Christian faith. In endorsing this program the Council of Bishops shall nominate to its board of directors five members, to be elected by the General Conference. Further, the Council on World Service and Finance shall recommend to the General Conference, for its action and determination, the amount to be included in the General Administration Fund as the Methodist share in this participation.

Part VIII

PENSIONS AND PERMANENT FUNDS

Chapter I

GENERAL BOARD OF PENSIONS

Section I.   Organization

¶ 1601. 1. There shall be a **General Board of Pensions** of The Methodist Church (hereafter called the board in this chapter and the general board in the remainder of Part VIII) with its principal office and place of business in Cook County, Illinois, having the general supervision and administration of the support of conference claimants of The Methodist Church. The Board of Pensions of The Methodist Church, Incorporated in Illinois, which is incorporated under the laws of the state of Illinois in that name (formerly known as "The Board of Pensions and Relief of The Methodist Episcopal Church") and The Board of Pensions of The Methodist Church, Incorporated in Maryland, which is incorporated under the laws of the state of Maryland in that name (formerly known as "The General Fund for Superannuates of The Methodist Protestant Church"), and The Board of Pensions of The Methodist Church, Incorporated in Missouri, which is incorporated under the laws of the state of Missouri in that name (formerly known as "The Board of Finance of the Methodist Episcopal Church, South") shall be continued, subject to the direction, supervision, and control of the General Board of Pensions of The Methodist Church.

2. The general supervision and administration of the pension and relief systems and plans of The Methodist

Church, subject to the direction, supervision, and control of the board, shall be conducted by and through the office of the board in Cook County, Illinois.

3. The office at St. Louis, Missouri, of The Board of Pensions of The Methodist Church, Incorporated in Missouri, shall be continued under and subject to the direction, supervision, and control of the General Board of Pensions of The Methodist Church. The board shall have authority to establish, maintain, and discontinue from time to time such subordinate offices as it shall deem proper and advisable.

¶ **1602.** 1. The board shall be composed of one bishop, elected by the Council of Bishops, and two ministers and two laymen from each jurisdiction having three million members, or major fraction thereof, in the jurisdiction; *provided*, however, that there shall be at least one minister and one layman from each jurisdiction. The required number of members from each jurisdiction shall be elected quadrennially by the General Conference on nomination of the College of Bishops of that jurisdiction.

In addition there shall be six members at large, not more than two from the same jurisdiction, nominated and elected by the board in such manner as it shall provide in its by-laws.

The general secretary of the board shall be an ex officio member thereof without vote.

The terms of all members so elected shall be four years, to take effect at the annual meeting of the board following the General Conference; *provided*, however, that members elected in 1956 for eight years by the Jurisdictional Conferences shall continue in office until 1964. Members shall serve during the terms for which they are elected or until their successors shall have been elected and qualified.

2. A vacancy in the membership shall be filled for the unexpired term by the board.

3. The members of the board shall constitute the membership of the respective boards of directors of the aforesaid three constituent corporations. The general secretary shall be an ex officio member of each without vote.

4. In all matters not specifically covered by General Conference legislation, the board shall have authority

to adopt rules and policies for the administration of the support of conference claimants.

5. The annual meetings of the board and of the boards of directors of the constituent corporations shall be held at the same date and place, at which time the board shall review and consider responsibilities committed to its care and take such action as it deems advisable in the furtherance of the best interests of the pension program of The Methodist Church. Special meetings of the board may be called by any two of the officers named in ¶1603.1.

6. A majority of the members of the board shall constitute a quorum.

¶ **1603.** 1. The board shall elect quadrennially at its annual meeting following the General Conference a president, a vice-president, and a recording secretary, all of whom shall be members of the board, and shall also elect quadrennially a **general secretary** and one or more other secretaries for four-year terms. The treasurers of the respective corporations shall be elected by the board for terms of four years, and may be persons who are not members of the board. A vacancy in any of these offices shall be filled by the board for the remainder of the unexpired term.

2. An **executive committee** shall be elected by the board. The same committee shall also respectively be elected by, and serve as the executive committee of, each of the three constituent corporations, unless otherwise required by applicable laws of the said respective states of incorporation, in which case the board shall recognize such laws and the corporations shall have power to comply therewith.

SEC. II. **Authorizations**

¶ **1604.** 1. The General Board of Pensions is authorized to adopt and further any and all plans, to undertake any and all activities, and to create, obtain, accept, receive, and administer any and all trust or other funds or property for the purpose of increasing the revenues, and of providing for, aiding in, and contributing to the support, relief, assistance, and pensioning of Methodist ministers and their families, conference claimants of The Methodist Church, and other church workers and lay employees in The Methodist Church and its constituent boards, organizations, and institutions; and to do any and all acts and things necessary and convenient in connection therewith or incident thereto; and to perform any and all other duties and functions from time to time imposed or directed by the General Conference of The Methodist Church.

2. The board is authorized to receive, hold, manage, merge, consolidate, administer, invest, and reinvest, by and through its constituent corporations, all connectional pension funds, subject to the other provisions of the Discipline, and with due regard to any and all special contracts, agreements, and laws applicable thereto. (For rules and regulations of the Ministers Reserve Pension Fund, *see* ¶¶ 1642-57; for other pension funds, *see* ¶¶ 1658-59, 1666, 1671, 1676.)

3. The board is authorized to receive, hold, manage, administer, invest, and reinvest, by and through its constituent corporations, endowment funds belonging to Annual Conferences, or other funds for the support of conference claimants to be administered for the benefit of such Annual Conferences; *provided* that at no time shall any part of the principal of the endowment funds be appropriated by the board for any purpose. The net income of such endowment funds shall be accounted for annually to the board and paid over to the Annual Conferences concerned for the benefit of their conference claimants.

4. The board, by and through its constituent corporations, is authorized and empowered to receive any gift, devise, or bequest made or intended for the benefit of disabled, superannuated, or retired ministers, widows of ministers, and the dependent children of ministers, such persons being commonly called conference claimants, of The Methodist Church (being successor to the Methodist Episcopal Church, the Methodist Episcopal Church, South, and the Methodist Protestant Church); and if the language or terms of any gift, devise, or bequest be inexact or ambiguous, the board shall dispose of or administer the same in the manner deemed most equitable

according to the apparent intent of the donor as determined by the board, after careful inquiry into the circumstances in connection with the making of such gift, devise, or bequest.

5. The three constituent corporations shall, until otherwise determined by the board, continue to collect, receive, and administer such gifts, devises, and bequests and other funds as may be specifically designated to them by donors, subject to the rules and regulations of the board with respect thereto. All undesignated gifts, devises, bequests, and donations shall be collected, received, and administered under the direction of the board.

¶ **1605.** The board shall adopt ways and means to increase the endowment funds to be administered, either for the board or for the Annual Conferences, by obtaining gifts, annuities, and bequests, and also to increase the current contributions of the pastoral charges for conference claimants.

¶ **1606.** The board shall share in the funds raised for the world service budget of The Methodist Church, as provided for in ¶¶ 741-42 and enabling acts.

Chapter II

PERMANENT FUNDS

¶ **1607.** The **Chartered Fund** shall be administered by the General Board of Pensions for the benefit of all the Annual and Provisional Annual Conferences in The Methodist Church the boundaries of which are within the United States, its territorial and insular possessions, and Cuba, unless the General Conference shall order otherwise; and once a year the net earnings of the fund, after provision for depreciation, shall be divided equally among such Annual and Provisional Annual Conferences in accordance with the restrictive rule contained in ¶ 9.5.

¶ **1608.** The General Board of Pensions shall order and direct that the income from the **General Endowment Fund for Conference Claimants** (formerly known as the General Endowment Fund for Superannuates of The

Methodist Episcopal Church, South) now held by the Board of Pensions of The Methodist Church, Incorporated in Missouri, shall be distributed on account of service of conference claimants rendered in an Annual Conference of the former Methodist Episcopal Church, South, or service rendered in an Annual Conference of The Methodist Church; *provided*, however, that such distribution shall be restricted to Annual Conferences which, directly or through their predecessor Annual Conferences, participated in raising this fund, in proportion to the number of approved years of annuity responsibility of each such Annual Conference as shall be determined by the General Board of Pensions.

¶ **1609.** 1. Whenever two or more Annual Conferences or Provisional Annual Conferences are to be merged, in whole or in part, there shall be elected by each conference affected a Distributing Committee of three members, and three alternates, which shall act jointly with similar committees from the other conference or conferences. The **Joint Distributing Committee** thus formed shall have power and authority: (1) to allocate the pension responsibility involved; (2) to distribute equitably the permanent funds and other pension assets of the conference or conferences affected, taking into consideration in the division to the successor conference or conferences the number of churches, ministerial conference members, and pension responsibility involved. It shall be governed by the legal restrictions or limitations of any contract, pledge, deed, or other instrument.

2. The Joint Distributing Committee shall conduct a hearing thereon, after publication of notice thereof in two consecutive issues of *Christian Advocate* and *Together*, the last publication to be not less than thirty days preceding the hearing; and it shall have power to continue and adjourn such hearing from time to time until it is finally concluded and a final decision is rendered.

3. The committee shall be convened promptly by the general secretary of the General Board of Pensions, or by some other officer of that board appointed by him in writing, and shall elect a chairman, a vice-chairman, and

a secretary from its membership. It shall prescribe the time and place of the hearing, and the secretary of the committee shall give the notice aforesaid.

4. The committee shall determine the number of years of approved service rendered in the conferences which will lose their identity in the merging of conference territory, and the findings of the committee shall be final unless definite evidence to the contrary is discovered, and the annuity payments by the continuing conference or conferences shall be made accordingly.

5. The committee shall keep complete minutes of its transactions, and a copy thereof shall be filed with the secretary of each conference involved and with the General Board of Pensions.

6. Until the committee's work shall have been completed, the corporate organization of each conference in the process of merger shall be maintained. After the committee shall have completed its work, the officers of such corporation, subject to the completion of its business, shall dissolve or merge it, being authorized to do so by the conference involved.

CHAPTER III

ANNUAL CONFERENCE ORGANIZATIONS

SECTION I.   Authorization

¶ 1610. 1. Annual Conferences, hereafter in this chapter called conferences, are authorized to establish and maintain investment funds, preachers aid societies, and organizations and funds of similar character, under such names, plans, rules, and regulations as they may determine, the income from which shall be applied to the support of conference claimants. It is recommended that each conference provide a corporation to administer its permanent funds, under some other corporate name than that used by the General Board of Pensions, the directors of which shall be elected, or otherwise disignated, by the conference where permissible under the laws of the state of incorporation.

465

2. All distributable funds, unless otherwise ordered by the conference, shall be disbursed by the Conference Board of Pensions, excepting only such funds as are otherwise restricted by specific provisions or limitations in gifts, devises, bequests, trusts, pledges, deeds, or other similar instruments, which restrictions and limitations shall be observed.

3. On and after June 1, 1956, it shall not be permissible for any conference or permanent-fund organization thereof, to deprive its conference claimants who are conference claimants in other conferences of the privilege of sharing in the distribution of the earned income of such permanent funds through the clearinghouse operations as provided hereinafter in ¶ 1636; *provided*, however, that a lien may be filed on the annuity of any conference claimant on account of unpaid assessments, obligations, or pledges owed to such permanent funds, in accordance with ¶ 1634.

4. Provided that no laws of the state in which it is organized or incorporated prohibit its so doing, a conference shall have power to require from its ministerial members and approved supply pastors who are appointed with annuity claim on the conference an annual contribution to either its permanent or reserve fund or for current distribution or to a preachers aid society for the benefit of its annuitants, subject to the following provisions: (1) the annual payment may be made in installments as provided by the conference; (2) the conference may fix a financial penalty for failure of the member to pay; (3) in case his membership in the conference is terminated under the provisions of the Discipline, the conference may refund the amount so paid, in whole or in part, after hearing has been given to him in case such hearing is requested; (4) the making of such payment shall not be used as the ground of contractual obligations upon the part of the conference, or as the ground of any special or additional annuity claim of a member against the conference, neither shall it prevent disallowance of his annuity claim by conference action; (5) ministers entering a conference shall not be charged an initial entry fee by any organization mentioned in § 1 of this paragraph; furthermore, the annual contribution required from a

ministerial member of the conference or an approved supply pastor shall not exceed the equivalent of three per cent of his cash salary.

5. Each conference shall hold one service during its sessions, to be known as the **Conference Claimants Anniversary,** for the promotion of the interests of the conference claimants.

6. Each conference, on recommendation of its Conference Board of Pensions or one of the organizations mentioned in § 1 of this paragraph, shall select a Sunday in each year to be observed in the churches as **Retired Ministers Day,** in honor of the retired ministers, their wives, and the widows of ministers, and in recognition of the church's obligation for their support. The bishop shall request each conference in his area to insert Retired Ministers Day in its calendar, and he shall diligently promote the observance of it.

SEC. II.   Conference Board of Pensions

¶ **1611.** 1. There shall be organized in each Annual Conference a conference board, auxiliary to the General Board of Pensions, to be known as the **Conference Board of Pensions** (hereafter called the board in this section and the conference board in the remainder of Part VIII), which shall have charge of the interests and work of providing for the support of its conference claimants, except as otherwise provided for by the general board.

2. The board shall be composed of not less than twelve members, not indebted to or beneficiaries of conference claimants' funds of the conference, effective ministers and laymen in equal number, elected for a term of eight years and so arranged in two equal classes that one half shall be elected quadrennially; and in addition thereto any ministerial member of the conference or lay member of a church within the conference who is a member of the General Board of Pensions. A lay member of the board may or may not be a member of the Annual Conference. A vacancy in the membership of the board shall be filled by the board for the remainder of the conference year in which the vacancy occurs, and at its next session the

467

conference shall fill the vacancy for the remainder of the unexpired term.

3. The members shall assume their duties at the adjournment of the conference session at which they were elected.

4. The board shall organize by electing a chairman, vice-chairman, secretary, and treasurer, who shall serve during the ensuing quadrennium, or until their successors shall have been elected and qualified. These officers shall constitute an **executive committee;** *provided,* however, that three members may be added thereto by the board. The duty of the executive committee shall be to administer the work of the board during the conference year in the interim between regular or special meetings of the board. The office of secretary may be combined with that of treasurer. The treasurer may be a person who is not a member of the board, in which case he shall not be a member of the executive committee. Calls for special meetings of the board shall be issued by the secretary on request of the chairman, or the vice-chairman, when the chairman is unable to act.

5. The board shall report to the conference the names, addresses, and years of approved service of the conference claimants, the names of those who have died during the year, the names of the dependent children of deceased ministerial members of the conference, and any other useful information, and shall show separately the amount paid to each by the conference from the annuity and necessitous funds.

6. The appropriations to the conference claimants shall be subject to the approval of the conference.

7. The board shall make a report to the General Board of Pensions immediately following the session of the conference, on forms provided for that purpose by the general board.

8. The conference shall constitute the board a committee on proportional payment of ministerial support, for the purpose of comparing the records of amounts paid on support of pastors and conference claimants by each pastoral charge, computing the proportional distribution thereof, and keeping a permanent record of defaults; or

the conference may organize a special **Committee on Proportional Payment of Ministerial Support,** which shall keep permanent records and furnish necessary information to the board regarding adjustment of annuities. (*See* ¶ 1624.)

9. The board shall administer all annuities and relief provided for the benefit of special conference claimants. (*See* ¶ 1631.)

10. The board shall investigate carefully all cases in which applications have been made by conference claimants for relief or necessitous appropriation, so as to determine equitably the amount of relief to be granted in each case.

11. The conference, on recommendation of the board, shall designate a bank or other depository for deposit of the funds held by the board.

12. The board, through the Conference Commission on World Service and Finance, shall provide a fidelity bond in suitable amount for all persons handling its funds. (*See* ¶¶ 729, 804.)

13. The board may build up a stabilization fund from the income for conference claimants in order to stabilize the annuity rate. Such stabilization fund should be at least the equivalent of twenty-five per cent of the average annual income of the board for all purposes for the five years immediately preceding. Such stabilization fund shall be held as the conference shall direct and shall be subject to the requirements of § 11 of this paragraph.

SEC. III.   **Financial Policy**

¶ **1612.** The following rules shall apply to financial administration of Annual Conference pension and pension-related permanent funds:

1. Persons connected in any way with the securities, real estate, or other forms of investment sold to or purchased from such funds shall be ineligible to serve on the investment committee responsible therefor.

2. No officer or member of a conference agency handing such funds shall receive a personal commission, bonus, or remuneration in connection with the purchase or sale of securities or other properties for that agency, or shall be

eligible to obtain a loan in any amount from funds committed to the care of that agency.

3. No local church or organization thereof shall be eligible to obtain a loan in any amount from such funds.[1]

4. The principle of diversification of investments shall be observed, in order to obtain proper geographical and class distribution of investment commitments.

5. Real property may be accepted as consideration for gift annuity agreements only with the stipulation that the annuity shall not exceed the net income from the property until such property shall have been liquidated. Upon liquidation, the annuity shall be paid upon the net proceeds at the established annuity rate.

6. A conference agency handling such funds shall not offer higher rates of annuity than those listed in the annuity schedule approved by the Council on World Service and Finance. (*See* ¶ 737.10.)

7. On order of the conference, there shall be printed in its journal a list of the investments held by each agency handling such funds directly or indirectly under the control of the conference, or such list may be distributed directly to the members of the conference at their request. A copy of all such lists concerning conference claimants shall be filed annually with the General Board of Pensions.

8. The borrowing of money in any conference year by a conference corporation or organization to enable the Conference Board of Pensions to complete payment of annuities at a designated annuity rate shall be done only on authority of the conference granted by three-fourths vote of the members present and voting.

CHAPTER IV

PENSION CODE

¶ **1613.** The administration of the pensions and support of conference claimants within the Annual Conferences situated in the United States, hereafter in this

---

[1] *See* Judicial Council Decision 145.

chapter called conferences, shall be the responsibility of the General Board of Pensions, and shall be governed by the rules and regulations contained in the following **code,** and such amendments thereto as may hereafter be adopted.

¶ **1614.** *Definition of Conference Claimants.*—Retired ministers, the widows of ministers, and dependent children of deceased ministers are **conference claimants.**

¶ **1615.** *Nature of Ministerial Support.*—Assumption of the obligations of the ministry required to be made at the time of his admission to membership in an Annual Conference puts upon the church the inevitable counter-obligation of providing a comfortable support for the minister during the period of his conference membership and for his widow and dependent children after his death; but such counterobligation with reference to these benefits shall not be construed as contractual unless and until provision shall have been made therefor on an actuarial reserve basis. (*See* ¶ 821.)

¶ **1616.** *Approval of Claim.*—The Annual Conference shall be the sole judge of the admissibility and validity of annuity claims and shall be fully competent to determine all payments, disallowances, and deductions thereunder, subject to the specific regulations relating thereto contained in the Discipline.[2]

¶ **1617.** *Retirement.*—1. The Annual Conference may place any ministerial member thereof in the retired relation, with or without his consent and irrespective of his age, if such relation be recommended by the Committee on Conference Relations. (*See* ¶ 367.)

2. Every ministerial member of an Annual Conference who has attained age seventy-two prior to the first day of the session of the conference shall be placed in the retired relation. (*See* ¶ 368.)[3]

3. At his own request the Annual Conference may place any ministerial member thereof in the retired relation, with the privilege of making an annuity claim, if he has attained age sixty-five, or has completed forty years of full-time approved service, as defined in ¶ 1618, prior to

---

[2] *See* Judicial Council Decision 171.
[3] *See* Judicial Council Decisions 7, 15, 165.

the first day of the session of the conference to which said request is presented. (*See* ¶ 369.) [4]

4. Retirement with the privilege of making an annuity claim on the ground of personal disability shall be permitted only after a thorough investigation of the case by, and presentation of a medical certificate to, the Committee on Conference Relations. This certificate shall be made on a form approved by the General Board of Pensions, and shall be given by a regular medical doctor, other than the personal physician of the applicant, who has been approved by the Committee on Conference Relations. If such disability continue for more than one year, such medical certificate shall be required annually. [5]

5. If retirement take place for other reasons than personal disability, the right to make an annuity claim from the time of retirement until the ministerial member qualifies under § 3 shall be granted on recommendation of the Committee on Conference Relations and a three-fourths vote of those present and voting in the Annual Conference; *provided*, however, that in case of emergency occurring between sessions of the conference the Conference Board of Pensions shall have authority to grant relief at its discretion.

6. When because of physical or mental incapacity a minister is forced to give up his ministerial work during the conference year, upon recommendation of the Cabinet, accompanied by a medical certificate, as set forth in § 4 of this paragraph, the Conference Board of Pensions may grant him an appropriation from an emergency fund for the remaining part of the conference year.

7. The Conference Board of Pensions, on recommendation of the Cabinet, may grant aid to a minister in the effective relation who has attained the age of voluntary retirement and has been compelled because of an emergency to relinquish his ministerial work during the conference year.

¶ **1618.** *Definitions.*—1. The term **years of approved service** shall mean full-time service rendered in and to

---

[4] *See* Judicial Council Decision 150.
[5] *See* Judicial Council Decisions 149, 171.

any appointment mentioned in § 2 of this paragraph.[6] Part-time service can be counted for annuity claim only by a three-fourths vote of those present and voting in the Annual Conference on recommendation of the Conference Board of Pensions.

2. The following years of approved service on trial or in the effective relation in an Annual Conference of The Methodist Church, as defined in § 8 of this paragraph, are eligible to be counted for the purpose of determining the annuity claims payable thereon:

a) As pastor, associate or assistant pastor, or other minister in a pastoral charge.

b) As district superintendent, presiding elder, conference president, or other full-time salaried official of the conference.

c) Under special appointment to an institution, organization, or agency which in the judgment of the Annual Conference rendered to it some form of service, direct or indirect, sufficient to warrant granting an annuity from the conference funds therefor, or to a community church; *provided*, however, that such institution, organization, agency, or community church accepts and pays annually such apportionments as the conference may require in accordance with the provision set forth in ¶ 1623.7; and *provided*, furthermore, that any institution, organization, agency, or community church may arrange for a pension related to such service through the Joint Contributory Annuity Fund administered by the General Board of Pensions. (All service in special appointment as ministerial members of conferences of the Methodist Episcopal Church prior to May 29, 1924, shall be regarded as valid, irrespective of subsequent limitations enacted by the General Conference of the Methodist Episcopal Church; and, furthermore, nothing hereinbefore provided in this subsection shall prevent a conference from fulfilling any special arrangement which it may have entered into prior to January 1, 1946, whereby it agreed to assume the annuity responsibility for a minister while serving under special appointment to an institution or organization not under the control of the conference.)

---

[6] *See* Judicial Council Decision 150.

d) Under the special appointment as an evangelist; *provided*, however, that if annuity responsibility be accepted by the conference therefor, such conference may require the payment of an apportionment by such evangelist in accordance with the provision in ¶ 1623.7.

e) As a student appointed to attend school, not to exceed three years; *provided*, however, that all years of appointment to attend school prior to the General Conference of 1960 are eligible to be counted for the purpose of determining the annuity claim thereon.

f) As a minister on sabbatical leave. (*See* ¶ 364.)

g) As the wife of a minister during his years of approved service. (*See* ¶ 1620.)

h) As a chaplain on full-time duty prior to December 31, 1946, in case no pension is granted for such years of service by the employing organization, institution, or agency related to the Commission on Chaplains of The Methodist Church as set forth in ¶ 1572; *provided*, however, that provision for pension on account of service rendered after December 31, 1946, as a chaplain on full-time duty shall be made by the Chaplains Pension Fund in accordance with rules and regulations to be determined jointly by the General Board of Pensions and the Commission on Chaplains.

i) In calculating fractional years of service of a conference claimant the following formula shall be used in all cases, irrespective of the time when such service was rendered, including those involved in clearinghouse operations: Any period up to one month and fourteen days shall not be counted; one month and fifteen days to four months and fourteen days shall be counted as one quarter of a year; four months and fifteen days to seven months and fourteen days shall be counted as one half of a year; seven months and fifteen days to ten months and fourteen days shall be counted as three quarters of a year; ten months and fifteen days to eleven months and twenty-nine days shall be counted as one year. Each of the above-mentioned periods shall be inclusive of all days therein.

3. The following years of service on trial or in the effective relation shall not be approved as a basis of annuity claim:

a) Years for which a pension, or any other form of compensation or "deferred salary," is received from any source other than the Annual Conference.

b) A year of service rendered concurrently by a minister and his wife, whether on the same pastoral charge, or otherwise as members of an Annual Conference, or as approved supply pastors therein, shall be counted only as one year. A year of service rendered as an approved supply pastor by the wife of a ministerial member of the conference on a separate pastoral charge shall not be eligible for count as full-time pastoral service.

4. On recommendation of the Conference Board of Pensions and approval by the Annual Conference, special appointments shall be listed in the conference journal as follows: (1) with annuity claim (*a*) upon this Annual Conference, or (*b*) upon a general board, an institution, or an agency of The Methodist Church; (2) without annuity claim upon this Annual Conference.[7] If at any session the conference shall fail to make such listing, it may be done subsequently, whenever desirable, under the Disciplinary question, "What other personal notation should be made?" (¶ 651.46.)

5. The **annuity rate** shall mean the sum determined annually by the Annual Conference, payable as an annuity for each year of approved service of a retired minister rendered in The Methodist Church. The annuity rate shall be determined by the conference without restriction, but it is recommended that such rate be not less than one per cent of the average salary of the conference as hereinafter defined in § 6.

6. The **average salary** of the conference for the purposes of this annuity plan shall mean the average salary (including house rent at a valuation equivalent to twenty per cent of the cash salary in cases in which a parsonage is occupied or house rent is provided) of the ministers in the conference who are on trial or in the effective relation as pastors or district superintendents, and the full-time approved supply pastors named in answer to question 22 in the business of the Annual Conference (¶¶ 651, 1631.10), based on the salaries as published in the statisti-

---

[7] *See* Judicial Council Decision 95.

cal report of the conference; *provided*, however, that the
conference may request that its average salary be computed on the basis of the salaries paid all pastors and
district superintendents. In computing the average salary
no account shall be taken of salaries of ministers who have
served less than one year on a pastoral charge. The average salary shall be established by the General Board of
Pensions for each conference annually.

7. **Dependent child** shall mean a child of a deceased
minister or a child legally adopted before the minister's
retirement or death, under sixteen years of age, and dependent for his or her support. If the child be kept in a
standard school, the age limit may be extended not to
exceed six additional years by action of the Conference
Board of Pensions. (*See* ¶ 1621.)

8. **The Methodist Church** shall mean The Methodist
Church after the Uniting Conference of 1939, also any of
the churches united in 1939, as they were constituted prior
to 1939.

9. On recommendation of the Conference Board of
Pensions, the Annual Conference shall determine the
Methodist institutions and organizations related to it
service in which shall be approved for annuity responsibility of the conference; *provided*, however, that such list
may be revised at any session of the conference. Such list
shall be printed annually in the conference journal under
the Disciplinary question "What Methodist institutions
or organizations are approved by the conference for
annuity responsibility?" (¶ 651.15.)

¶ **1619.** *Claim of a Retired Minister.*—The annuity
claim of a retired minister shall be for an amount equivalent to the total of his years of approved service multiplied
by the annuity rate as defined above, irrespective of
breaks in the sequence of such service; *provided*, however,
that if the minister has been retired for reason of personal
disability and if the years of approved service be less than
ten, effective with the 1961 clearinghouse year, the pension
shall be based on ten years of service. The clearinghouse
shall allocate this additional obligation *pro rata* among
the conferences served.

¶ **1620.** *Claim of a Widow.*—1. The annuity claim of a widow shall be for an amount equivalent to the total of her years of approved service (¶ 1618.2*g*, .3*b*) multiplied by seventy per cent of the annuity rate. The seventy per cent may be raised to seventy-five per cent at the option of the Annual Conference. The fact that a widow served as the wife of a minister of The Methodist Church until his death and, after an intervening period of widowhood, served again as the wife of another minister of The Methodist Church shall not prevent the approval of all such years of service for the purpose of computing her annuity claim. If the total years of service upon which her annuity claim is based be less than ten, effective with the 1961 clearinghouse year, the pension shall be based on ten years of service. The clearinghouse shall allocate this additional obligation *pro rata* among the conferences charged with her annuity claim.

2. The annuity claim of a widow of a ministerial member or of an approved supply pastor shall become effective immediately upon the death of such husband; *provided*, however, that if he was himself a conference claimant or a special conference claimant at the time of his death, her annuity claim shall become effective with the date of the next payment which would have been scheduled for him if he had lived.

3. The widow of a deceased ministerial member of a conference or approved supply pastor who remarries shall have no annuity claim during such marriage until her attainment of age sixty-five, at which time her annuity claim may be reinstated; but if such subsequent marriage be dissolved by the husband's death or by legal process, the conference on recommendation of the Conference Board of Pensions may reinstate her annuity claim thereafter subject to the provisions of the pension code.

4. The widow of a deceased minister whose conference membership was terminated under the provisions of ¶¶ 374-82 or 935-37, 952 shall have the right to make an annuity claim on the conferences concerned based on her years of approved service; *provided*, however, that such claim must be approved, on recommendation of the Con-

ference Board of Pensions, by a two-thirds vote of those present and voting in the Annual Conference.

5. An Annual Conference, on recommendation of its Conference Board of Pensions, may by a two-thirds vote of those present and voting grant annuity and/or necessitous relief to a wife for her years of approved service without granting annuity to her husband if he has disqualified himself by some moral dereliction, mental illness, or other cause beyond the wife's control.

6. The Conference Board of Pensions shall obtain annually satisfactory evidence that a widow is living and is eligible to receive annuity payments in accordance with the provisions of the pension code.

7. The clearinghouse is hereby authorized to assign and transfer the obligation for the payment of the claims of the widow and minor children of a deceased conference member to such other conference as the widow may request in writing, subject to the consent of the Conference Board of Pensions of the conference thereby obligated; *provided*, however, that the requirements of divided annuity responsibility as set forth in ¶ 1636 shall be observed.

¶ **1621.** *Claim of a Dependent Child.*—1. The claim of an unmarried dependent child shall be determined by multiplying the equivalent of the deceased father's years of approved service by one fourth of the annuity rate to which the retired ministers are entitled. If the total years of service upon which the child's annuity claim is based be less than ten, effective with the 1961 clearinghouse year, the pension shall be based on ten years of service. The clearinghouse shall allocate this additional obligation pro rata among the conferences charged with the annuity claim.

2. The claim of an unmarried dependent child shall become effective immediately upon the death of the father and shall cease upon attainment of age sixteen. If the child be kept in a standard school, the age limit may be extended, not to exceed six additional years, by action of the Conference Board of Pensions. On recommendation of the board and approval by two thirds of those present and voting in the Annual Conference, renewed annually,

a claim may be validated for a child past sixteen years of age in case of evident mental or physical incapacity to provide self-support; *provided*, however, that such mental or physical incapacity shall have become apparent prior to the attainment of age twenty-one and shall have continued thereafter; and *provided*, furthermore, that before recommending such claim the board shall require a medical certificate and may require subsequent certificates certifying the continuance of such incapacity.

3. A certificate of attendance of a dependent child at a standard school shall be obtained annually between the ages of sixteen and twenty-two by the conference board, on a form to be provided by the general board.

¶ 1622. *Claim of a Missionary.*—1. A regularly commissioned missionary of the Board of Missions, holding membership in an Annual Conference or Provisional Annual Conference or connected with a Mission, shall be entitled to make an annuity claim upon the division of the Board of Missions which provides his support.

2. A retired missionary who has been granted the retired relation in an Annual Conference abroad shall be entitled to make an annuity claim upon a conference in the United States on account of years of approved service rendered therein. Such claim shall be presented to the General Board of Pensions, and payments due thereunder shall be collected from the conferences concerned and forwarded to the claimant by the general board in such manner as it may deem most expeditious and economical. In such cases the general board shall certify the years of approved service to each conference concerned.

¶ 1623. *Apportionments.*—1. The Annual Conference, on recommendation of the Conference Board of Pensions, shall determine the annuity rate payable. The recommended standard annuity rate is a sum equivalent to one per cent of the average salary of the conference. (*See* ¶ 1618.5, .6.)

2. The Conference Board of Pensions shall compute the total amount necessary to meet the prospective annuity disbursements according to the annuity rate determined. After all amounts which will be received from other sources for the support of conference claimants have been

subtracted from this total, the remaining amount necessary shall be apportioned to the several pastoral charges of the conference on such basis as the conference may from time to time determine. (*See* ¶ 822.) In case the basis of apportionment adopted is that of a percentage of the cash salaries of the ministers, where there is more than one minister serving a pastoral charge the apportionment thereto shall be on the basis of all cash salaries paid to such ministers.

3. The apportionment to the pastoral charges for both regular relief and emergency appropriations for conference claimants who are in distress, or because of other special circumstances, shall be estimated by the Conference Board of Pensions.[8]

4. The Conference Commission on World Service and Finance shall include in its recommendations to the Annual Conference the amounts computed by the Conference Board of Pensions as necessary to meet the needs for annuity payments and relief. (*See* ¶ 798.)

5. The apportionment for aged and disabled supply pastors, if any, shall be combined with the apportionment for regular conference claimants.

6. The apportionment to a federated church, if and when it is served by a ministerial member or an approved supply pastor of the Annual Conference, shall be made on the same basis as the apportionments to the pastoral charges of the conference; *provided*, however, that an annual apportionment may be made to a federated church in accordance with the terms of an agreement between the Conference Board of Pensions and such federated church.

7. *a*) An Annual Conference which accepts annuity responsibility in any conference year for service rendered by a member thereof under special appointment to an institution, organization, agency, or community church, as provided in ¶ 1618.2c, may make an apportionment to such institution, organization, agency, or community church served for such amount as the conference may determine; *provided*, however, that such apportionment shall not exceed an amount equivalent to twelve times

---

[8] Amended in 1944 following Judicial Council Decision 13.

the annuity rate which has been adopted for that conference year. (*See also* ¶ 1618.4, .9.)

b) Until the person concerned or his widow becomes a conference claimant, moneys collected on apportionments made under authority of this subsection may be conserved by the Conference Board of Pensions in a special fund.

c) Such moneys shall be released for general distribution when the parties concerned become conference claimants; one twelfth of the funds accumulated, in each case, to be released annually thereafter for distribution. Moneys so conserved and distributed shall be regarded as part of the general resources for distribution by the Conference Board of Pensions.

¶ **1624.** *Proportional Payment.*—1. When the apportionment to the pastoral charges for the support of conference claimants and for the Ministers Reserve Pension Fund has been determined as provided in ¶¶ 822 and 1645.4, payments made thereon by each pastoral charge shall be exactly proportionate to payments made on the salary or salaries of the minister or ministers serving it. (*See* ¶ 823.)

2. The amount apportioned to each pastoral charge for the support of conference claimants and for the Ministers Reserve Pension Fund shall be paid to the conference treasurer monthly or quarterly, and the conference treasurer shall remit monthly to the treasurer or treasurers of these respective funds.

3. The treasurer of the pastoral charge shall be primarily responsible for the application of § 1 of this paragraph; but in the event of his failure to apply it, the pastor shall adjust his cash salary and the payment according to the proper ratio, as provided above, before he enters the respective amounts in his statistical report to the Annual Conference. And, on retirement, amounts in default shall be deducted from his annuity as provided in ¶ 1634.1. If such pastor be a member of the Ministers Reserve Pension Fund, the annual contribution to the service annuity credit by the conference of such member shall be withheld in any conference year unless and until proportional payment, as required herein, has been observed.

4. The Conference Board of Pensions shall render a statement annually to all ministers of the conference who have failed to observe the provisions of this paragraph, indicating the amounts in default for that and all preceding conference years. Copies thereof shall be sent to the clearinghouse of the general board, and the information contained thereon shall be recorded upon the service records of the individual ministers concerned.

5. In the event of the failure of a retired minister to observe the provisions of this paragraph while serving as a supply pastor in any conference year, the amount of such default shall be deducted from such retired minister's annuity during the ensuing conference year.

6. It shall not be permissible for a pastor to receive a bonus or other supplementary compensation tending to defeat proportional payment. Failure to comply with this section shall be deemed disobedience to the order and discipline of The Methodist Church. The Conference Board of Pensions may recommend to the conference that the pastor's annuity claim be disallowed for the year during which such bonus or supplementary compensation was so received.[9]

¶ **1625.** *Distribution.*—1. Moneys designated for distribution to the claimants as annuities shall be distributed on the basis of years of approved service, and shall consist of:

a) The appropriation from The Methodist Publishing House.

b) The income from investments for annuity distribution held for this purpose.

c) Gifts and bequests for annuity distribution.

d) Money received from the apportionments to the pastoral charges for annuity distribution.

e) Money received from all special offerings for distribution to conference claimants.

2. Moneys designated for relief on the basis of special need and emergency relief shall consist of:

a) The appropriation from the Chartered Fund.

b) Money received from the apportionment to the pastoral charges; *provided* that each conference shall set

---

[9] *See* Judicial Council Decisions 51, 151.

aside for necessitous and emergency distribution such part of its fund as it may deem necessary, but not to exceed five per cent of the total amount collected on apportionment to the pastoral charges.

3. The Conference Board of Pensions may pay annuities in quarterly or monthly installments.

4. The amount received for the support of conference claimants each year from the pastoral charges in advance of the conference sessions shall be reserved for appropriation and expenditure during the ensuing conference year; *provided*, however, that the conferences now paying on a current income basis may continue to do so temporarily, but as quickly as feasible shall change to collection of income one year in advance of payment.

¶ **1626.** *Relinquishment.*—1. For a year at a time a conference claimant may voluntarily relinquish in writing his annuity claim and any amount payable thereunder; *provided* that the disposal of the relinquished amount shall be entirely under the control of the Conference Board of Pensions.

2. Any agreement made prior to retirement to relinquish at retirement a future annuity claim shall be null and void.

¶ **1627.** *Disallowance.*—1. Upon recommendation of a majority of the Conference Board of Pensions, after opportunity has been given for hearing the claimant's objections, which may be made in person, or by a ministerial member of an Annual Conference acting as the claimant's personal representative, the annuity claim of any conference claimant may be disallowed, in whole or in part, by three-fourths vote of the ministers of the Annual Conference, present and voting, for any of the following causes:

a) Receipt of a pension or other periodical income from an individual church, or from other sources, which may be presumed to cover and adequately compensate for certain years of service included in the claim.

b) Service in a special appointment which did not confer sufficient benefit on The Methodist Church to justify apportioning the annuity cost thereof to the pastoral charges of the conference.

c) Having been found guilty of unministerial or unchristian conduct by the Disciplinary processes.

2. The following rules and procedures shall be observed in all cases of disallowance of annuity claims:

a) The secretary of the Conference Board of Pensions shall notify the conference claimant, by registered mail, at the last address known to the conference secretary, concerning the proposed disallowance not less than three months in advance of the conference session at which his case will be adjudicated.

b) The notification of the claimant shall specify the cause or causes under which the case will be cited.

c) If he or she cannot be present, the claimant shall have the right to choose a ministerial member of any Annual Conference to present his or her objections to the proposed disallowance before the Conference Board of Pensions prior to action on the case.

d) The Conference Board of Pensions shall present to the conference the proposal for disallowance in written form with a full statement of the case and a record of its vote for and against recommendation.

e) Disallowance cannot be made by general rule of the Annual Conference; each case must be heard and adjudicated separately.

3. When an annuity claim shall have been disallowed, under § 1 of this paragraph, it may be reconsidered at any subsequent annual session of the conference, upon recommendation of the Conference Board of Pensions, or by two-thirds vote of the members of the conference present and voting.

4. Disallowance can be made only by the conference where membership is held or, in the case of a widow or minor dependent children, the conference with which the claimant is directly connected.

¶ **1629.** *Service Records.*—1. The General Board of Pensions shall maintain complete service records of ministerial members of the Annual Conferences compiled from the answers to the Disciplinary questions as published in the conference journals and in the General Minutes of The Methodist Church.

2. Power to revise, correct, or adjust a minister's service

record as it concerns his annuity lies with the Annual Conference solely. It is recommended that, prior to the revision of a member's service record, the General Board of Pensions be requested to review the relevant data and report its findings. Such revisions, corrections, and adjustments, after having been adopted by the conference concerned, shall be published in the conference journal as a personal notation in the answers to the Disciplinary questions (¶ 651.46), and notice thereof shall be sent to the general board by the conference secretary.

3. The secretary of each Annual Conference shall publish annually in the conference journal the chronological roll of ministerial members and approved supply pastors, indicating the total number of years of approved service of each; *provided*, however, that if the alphabetical roll printed in the conference journal contains the required information, a separate chronological roll shall not be mandatory. (*See* ¶ 632.) [10]

4. In the conference statistical tables there shall be provided a separate column with the caption "Conference Claimants," which shall show the amount apportioned to each charge and the amount paid.

5. The conference secretary shall have the power to require from each and every ministerial member of it a signed statement concerning the date of his birth, the date of birth of his wife, the date of their marriage, and the dates of birth of their dependent children, and to require similar data from approved supply pastors.

¶ **1630.** *General Regulations.*—1. A minister who refuses to prorate ministerial support may be brought to trial for violation of a law of the church.

2. Annuities are granted by the conference annually, including those granted on the ground of disability; the determination of what constitutes disability lies with the conference. If a member of the conference who is receiving an annuity on the ground of disability recovers sufficiently to resume ministerial work or to engage in a remunerative occupation, his annuity may be continued, reduced, or terminated by the Annual Conference on

---

[10] *See* Judicial Council Decision 165.

recommendation of the Conference Board of Pensions. (*See* ¶ 1617.4.)

3. The annuity claim of an effective minister cannot be recognized by the Conference Board of Pensions between annual sessions of the conference; he must be retired first. Provision for emergency cases may be made in accordance with ¶ 1617.5-.7.

4. A minor child of a living retired minister cannot be a conference claimant.

5. Although the conference has power to require a contribution to its funds and to fix a financial penalty for defaults, a minister cannot be brought to trial for failure to make such required contribution.

6. A conference may withhold money from a conference claimant in order to discharge his obligation for assessments voted by the conference for conference claimants.

7. A minister cannot be retired automatically by operation of a conference rule fixing an age of retirement other than that specified in the Discipline.

8. A minister cannot present his credentials to and be accepted into the ministry of another denomination and at the same time retain his standing in an Annual Conference of The Methodist Church. Such action constitutes withdrawal from our ministry. However, if a ministerial member while in good standing in an Annual Conference voluntarily withdraws from the ministry of The Methodist Church and enters the ministry of another church within one year from the date of withdrawal, upon the attainment of age sixty-five and retirement from the ministry of such other church or denomination, upon recommendation of the Conference Board of Pensions and a three-fourths vote of those present and voting in the Annual Conference in which ministerial membership was last held, he may be recognized as a conference claimant and allowed an annuity claim on account of approved service in The Methodist Church.

9. A conference member cannot relinquish his annuity claim at conference time and then ask for it, or a portion of it, during the conference year.

10. An Annual Conference may not make any arrangement with a life insurance company for the purchase of

annuities for the benefit of individual effective or retired ministers, or take any steps to nullify, in whole or in part, the annuity plan of The Methodist Church by making contracts with outside parties. However, group life insurance may be provided through the medium of a life insurance company.

11. Money received for the support of conference claimants shall be appropriated only for the payment of pension or relief benefits to conference claimants and the administrative costs of the pension program, except as provided in ¶ 1631.5.

12. A minister on trial or the widow and dependent children of a minister who was on trial at the time of his death may become conference claimants subject to the provisions of the pension code.

13. A widow of a retired minister who married him after his retirement or a child born of such marriage is not entitled to make an annuity claim, except as provided in the last sentence of ¶ 1620.1.

14. A minister in the supernumerary relation cannot make an annuity claim, but may be granted emergency relief by the Conference Board of Pensions.

15. a) If a located person, whether located voluntarily or involuntarily, remains a member in good standing of The Methodist Church until the attainment of age seventy-two, he shall retain the right to make an annuity claim based on his years of approved service; *provided*, however, that upon presentation of satisfactory evidence regarding his character during location he shall have been readmitted into the Annual Conference, or its legal successor, which granted him location. (*See* ¶¶ 374-79.)

b) If a located person becomes physically or mentally disabled so as to be unable to provide self-support, upon presentation of satisfactory evidence regarding his character during location, accompanied by a medical certificate in accordance with the provision in ¶ 1617.4, upon joint recommendation of the Committee on Conference Relations and the Conference Board of Pensions, he may be readmitted by a three-fourths vote of the Annual Conference, or its legal successor, which granted him location, and placed in the retired relation for the purpose of making an annuity claim; *provided*, however, that such certificate of disability shall be made on a form approved by the General Board of Pensions and shall be presented annually to the conference board during such disability prior to age seventy-two.

16. In determining the annuity claim of a regular conference claimant, the years of approved service as a full-time approved supply pastor rendered prior to admission on trial by a conference may be counted and payment made therefor at the rate for a special conference claimant. (*See* ¶ 1631.)

17. Full-time service rendered as pastor of a charge between the date of termination of membership in an Annual or Provisional Annual Conference and the date of readmission may be approved for an annuity claim on recommendation of the Conference Board of Pensions and vote of the conference.

18. If the conference provides a dwelling for the use of a conference claimant, an adjustment may be made in his annuity as determined by the conference, after recommendation by the Conference Board of Pensions.

19. Pension responsibility on account of appointment to attend school after May 7, 1960, by a member on trial or in full connection shall be allocated to the Annual Conference in which he shall thereafter first render a full year of approved service as a member in the effective relation under an appointment other than to attend school; *provided*, however, that if no such service is rendered, the responsibility shall be allocated to the conference in which membership was held at the time of appointment to attend school.

¶ **1631.** *Special Conference Claimants.*—1. An approved supply pastor who shall have qualified under ¶¶ 314-17, and who shall have rendered not less than four consecutive years of full-time approved service in one Annual Conference as pastor of a charge may upon retirement make an annuity claim as a **special conference claimant;** *provided*, however, that any period of less than one full year of service in any conference may not be counted; and *provided*, furthermore, that years of full-time service rendered to a board, institution, or other agency of The Methodist Church may be counted when determining eligibility, but the annuity as a special conference claimant shall be based only on full-time approved service as pastor of a charge. Full-time approved service for which pension credit may be given shall mean service under appointment as pastor of a charge for which the pastor's cash support per annum from all church sources shall be not less than the minimum salary established by the conference for full-time approved supply pastors.

2. On recommendation of the Committee on Conference Relations an approved supply pastor who has attained age sixty-five prior to the first day of the conference session, and who has rendered the minimum number of years of approved service may request retirement, and upon retirement shall be designated a special conference claimant.

3. Every approved supply pastor who has attained age seventy-two prior to the first day of the conference session shall be retired. (*See* ¶ 368.) [11]

4. A special conference claimant (§ 1) shall be entitled to make an annuity claim, for each year of approved service rendered as a regularly appointed pastor, the equivalent of one per cent of the average salary (including house rent at a valuation equivalent to twenty per cent of the cash salary) of the regularly appointed approved supply pastors of the conference as computed by the Conference Board of Pensions; *provided*, however, that any conference may apply the same annuity rate to the claims of special conference claimants as to the claims of the regular conference claimants.

5. In necessitous cases, the Conference Board of Pensions may grant relief to special conference claimants subject to the approval of the conference; *provided*, also, that relief may be granted to an approved supply pastor who has been retired by reason of age or disability prior to completion of the years of approved service required under § 1 of this paragraph for eligibility as a special conference claimant.

6. The list of special conference claimants showing their respective years of service and the payments to

[11] *See* Judicial Council Decision 165.

them shall be kept separately from the list of regular conference claimants, and shall be published in the conference journal.

7. The regulations of the general pension code, including those on proportional payment and the claims of widows and children, shall apply to the administration of funds for special conference claimants with the exceptions specified in this paragraph; *provided*, however, that all years of approved service of such claimants shall be the direct responsibility of the conference in which the service was rendered and shall not involve clearinghouse operations.

8. The sources of annuity and relief funds payable to special conference claimants shall be: (1) collections for that purpose from the pastoral charges; (2) any amounts specifically designated for that purpose coming from any source.

9. Missions within the United States may organize a Conference Board of Pensions to care for the special needs of special conference claimants with the help of the General Board of Pensions. In such cases the Mission shall establish the annuity rate to be paid annually.

10. The following questions shall be included in the business of the Annual Conference: (*a*) "What approved supply pastors are credited with annuity claim on account of full-time service during the past year? (To be answered after consultation of the Conference Board of Pensions with the district superintendents.)" (*b*) "What approved supply pastors have been retired: This year? Previously?" (*See* ¶ 651.22, .43.)

11. The widow of an approved supply pastor whose husband died prior to completion of the years of full-time approved service required under § 1 of this paragraph may, on recommendation of the Conference Board of Pensions and a two-thirds vote of those present and voting in the Annual Conference, be granted a pension based on the approved years of her husband's service during the time that she was his wife.

¶ **1633.** *Operation in Other Countries.*—The provisions in this pension code are to give guidance in the administration of pensions in the conferences of The Methodist

Church outside the United States. In so far as may be practicable, the general principles involved in the code shall be regarded and employed in such conferences until the General Conference shall order otherwise.

¶ 1634. *Liens on Annuities.*—1. Whenever a conference claimant shall be in debt to the conference or any of its organizations on account of unpaid assessments, obligations, or pledges for the benefit of conference claimants, such debt shall constitute a lien on the annuity of the person involved, and the conference shall have power to appropriate and apply his or her annuity, or any part thereof, to the payment of such debt; *provided*, however, that not more than one quarter of the annuity payable by the conference in which the debt was incurred, or one quarter of the total indebtedness, whichever is greater, shall be appropriated in any year for such purpose, and *provided*, furthermore, that such power shall not be interpreted as applying to the settlement of other debts of a conference claimant. (*See* ¶ 1624.)

2. *a*) A conference having a claim for unpaid assessments in connection with its funds for conference claimants against a ministerial member of another conference, through its Conference Board of Pensions, shall file such claim with the clearinghouse within two years following the date of transfer from the conference having the claim; *provided*, however, that this time limit shall not apply to any claim filed on or before December 31, 1957.

b) The clearinghouse shall file a copy of said claim with the Conference Board of Pensions of the conference to which the member has been transferred, shall send a copy thereof to the member concerned, and shall record the claim on his service record.

3. *a*) A conference which has filed a claim in accordance with § 2 of this paragraph may file a lien through the clearinghouse against the annuity of a conference claimant for the unpaid amount of the said claim; *provided*, however, that the said lien shall be filed within one year of the date of retirement or death of the minister concerned, whichever first occurred. Thereupon the clearinghouse shall request the conference concerned to deduct the unpaid amount of the claim from the annuity of the

conference claimant against whose annuity the said lien has been filed, and to remit to the clearinghouse as soon as practicable the amounts deducted.

b) The amount of any deduction made under this subsection shall be subject to the limitations provided in § 1 of this paragraph; and, furthermore, it is hereby stipulated that interest on liens of this character, if charged, shall be computed only at simple interest. The clearinghouse shall have no responsibility for transmission of moneys collected under this subsection until such moneys have been remitted to it. No "debtor" conference shall withhold or deduct a part of the money it is required to pay to the clearinghouse with the intent of satisfying in advance any claims which the conference may desire to make under this subsection.

¶ **1635.** *Operation Through the General Board.*— 1. When authorized by the Annual Conference, the Conference Board of Pensions may deposit all or any part of the funds under its control with the general board as set forth in ¶ 1604.3.

2. The Annual Conference may authorize the general board to make the periodical payments to the conference claimants; and in such case the conference board shall prepare annually a complete schedule of the plan of distribution for the guidance of the general board in making such payments, and shall co-operate fully with it, in order to ensure efficient and prompt service. Checks issued, as the general board may determine, under the provisions of this subsection, shall show plainly the name of the conference for which the disbursements are made.

3. The general board shall be entitled to collect an annual service fee, figured on a cost basis, for the work specified in the preceding subsection.

4. The general board shall furnish annually to the conference board a report showing full details of the transactions under § 2 of this paragraph.

¶ **1636.** *Divided Annuity Responsibility.*—1. The responsibility for annuity for years of approved service of a conference claimant shall rest with the Annual Conference in which the service was performed, or its legal successor.

2. The clearinghouse system of distribution of divided annuity responsibility shall be continued. The clearinghouse figures shall be determined by the General Board of Pensions, subject to such modifications as may be necessitated by the provisions of § 1 above. The general board shall have authority to fix annually in advance the clearinghouse rate of annuity for each Annual Conference. The clearinghouse rate shall be based on a conservative estimate of the prospective income available for distribution and need not coincide with the annuity rate fixed subsequently by the conference. In the event that the conference fixes a higher rate than the clearinghouse rate, the difference shall be paid directly to all claimants within and without the conference.

3. The general board is authorized and empowered to make all the rules concerning details that may be necessary to put this paragraph into effect, and shall determine the distribution of service responsibility for each conference claimant involved in the operation of the clearinghouse.

4. The fiscal year for clearinghouse operations shall be the calendar year.

¶ **1637.** *Annuity Responsibility in Missions or Provisional Annual Conferences.*—The responsibility for the annuity on account of years of approved service in a Mission or Provisional Annual Conference within the United States shall rest jointly with (*a*) the Mission or Provisional Annual Conference concerned, (*b*) the General Board of Pensions, and (*c*) the Division of National Missions. The revenue for annuity purposes covering such service shall be provided by the aforesaid parties in accordance with such plan or plans as may be mutually agreed to by them.

Chapter V

MINISTERS RESERVE PENSION FUND

¶ **1642.** *Establishment.*—1. A reserve pension system to be called the **Ministers Reserve Pension Fund** of The Methodist Church, hereinafter called the Fund, is hereby established. It shall be administered by the General Board of Pensions in accordance with and subject to the provisions that follow.

2. An Annual or Provisional Annual Conference, hereafter in this chapter called a conference, at any time, on its own determination, by a two-thirds vote of its membership present and voting, may enter the Fund and may actively participate therein when it accepts the conditions and fulfills the requirements herein set forth.

¶ 1643. *Definitions.*—The following definitions shall apply to the interpretation of the plan of the Fund, unless the context plainly indicates otherwise:

1. **Employer** shall mean any connectional board, organization, or institution which receives the services of a member of the Fund in either a pastoral or nonpastoral capacity, and which shall pay therefor any form of salary, compensation, or allowance.

2. **Support** of a member of the Fund shall mean:

a) The sum or sums annually received from a pastoral charge as compensation for his services, plus an amount equivalent to twenty per cent thereof, if the minister occupy a parsonage free of rent.

b) The salary of a district superintendent received from the district as compensation for his services, plus an amount equivalent to twenty per cent thereof if he occupy a district parsonage free of rent.

c) The salary or compensation received by a pastor from a federated or community church, or from a church of another denomination, plus an amount equivalent to twenty per cent thereof, if he occupy a parsonage free of rent.

d) The financial aid furnished by a missionary board, or other organization, or by the minimum salary fund of the conference.

e) The salary, compensation, or allowance received for services rendered under special episcopal appointment.

3. **Regular interest** shall mean interest, compounded annually, at a rate periodically determined by the general board on the basis of net earnings but not to exceed four per cent per annum.

4. **Service annuity** shall mean an annuity payable quar-

terly in advance during life, beginning at the date of retirement, to be provided by the Fund on the basis of allocated credits together with the regular interest accumulated thereon. (*See* ¶¶ 1645, 1653.1.)

5. Income annuity shall mean an annuity payable quarterly in advance during life, beginning at the date of retirement, to be provided by the Fund on the basis of personal contributions of the member together with the regular interest accumulated thereon.

6. Pension shall mean the total of the service annuity and the income annuity.

7. Widow's pension shall mean an annuity, payable quarterly in advance, to the widow of a member of the Fund who dies before attaining retirement, to be provided by the Fund on the basis of the personal contributions of the deceased member, together with the regular interest accumulated thereon, plus seventy per cent of the service annuity credits, together with the regular interest accumulated thereon.

8. Child's annuity shall mean an annuity payable quarterly in advance to a minor child of a deceased member of the Fund.

9. Minor child shall mean a child under twenty-two years of age.

10. The meaning of the word "child" shall be interpreted to include a child legally adopted.

11. New entrant shall mean a minister who shall be admitted on trial in an Annual or Provisional Annual Conference on or after the entry of such conference into the Fund, including a minister who on May 1, 1952, was on trial in a conference which prior to that date had entered the Fund. (Approved service on trial, as defined in ¶ 1618.2, rendered by a minister who became a member of the Fund prior to May 1, 1952, may be approved for annuity claim under the provision of the pension code, or under the Ministers Reserve Pension Fund as provided in ¶ 1644.5.)

12. Previous entrant shall mean a minister in good standing on trial or in full membership in an Annual or Provisional Annual Conference prior to the entry of such conference into the Fund.

13. **Pension code** shall mean the rules and regulations concerning pensions and relief contained in ¶¶ 1613-37 inclusive.

¶ **1644.** *Membership.*—1. The membership of the Fund shall consist of the new entrants in Annual or Provisional Annual Conferences in the United States of America, such previous entrants as are received under § 2 below, and qualified full-time approved supply pastors. Members of such conferences who have not been enrolled as members of the Fund, and who are serving under special appointment to a board, institution, organization, or a community church, without annuity claim on the conference, may be enrolled as members of the Fund for the purpose of arranging for pension coverage on account of such service with the agency covered, in accordance with the rules and regulations of the Fund, and with the consent of the General Board of Pensions.

2. Previous entrants who are members of conferences participating in the Fund may become members of the Fund by a two-thirds vote of the conference membership present and voting; *provided*, however, that accrued service obligations under the pension code shall be funded for or by such previous entrants, in such manner and amount as shall be satisfactory to the general board.

3. A minister received by transfer into a conference on or after the date of entry of the conference into the Fund shall be classed as a new entrant while serving in such conference; *provided*, however, that members received by transfer past forty years of age shall not be accepted as members of the Fund unless an initial provision for service annuity be made by or for them in such manner and amount as shall be satisfactory to the executive officers of the general board.

4. A member of the Fund shall be classed as a new entrant while serving in any conference participating in the Fund.

5. The accrued service obligation of a conference under the pension code for a member of the Fund may be funded by such conference upon entry into the Fund in such manner and amount as shall be satisfactory to the executive officers of the general board.

6. When a member of the Fund shall transfer to a conference not participating in the Fund, he shall be subject to the provisions of the pension code for years served in such conference; but upon subsequent entry into a conference participating in the Fund such member shall resume contribution and receive credits therefrom.

¶ **1645.** *Contributions by the Conference.*—1. Each conference that hereafter enters the Fund shall contribute annually thereto an amount equivalent to not less than nine per cent of the average salary of the conference (as defined in ¶ 1618.6 of the pension code) for each qualified member of the conference who is also a member of the Fund.

2. In case of the transfer of a member of the Fund into a conference participating in the Fund the contribution required on behalf of such member shall be proportional to the number of days of service rendered such conference during the fiscal year of the Fund in which the transfer shall have been effected.

3. In case of the transfer of a member of the Fund out of a conference participating in the Fund the contribution required on behalf of such member shall be proportional to the number of days of service rendered such conference during the fiscal year of the Fund in which the transfer shall have been effected.

4. Each conference shall determine the plan by which it shall secure the annual contribution to the Fund required in § 1 of this paragraph and shall make suitable and adequate provision therefor.

5. Each conference shall collect the contributions due the Fund, and shall have power to adjudicate all questions in connection therewith.

6. The contributions required in § 1 of this paragraph shall be made to the conference treasurer, or any other officer who may be designated by the conference, who shall transmit the same to the general board within thirty days after the conference session, together with a schedule of information showing the members covered by the payment transmitted.

7. A deficiency in the payment of the annual amount required of a conference shall reduce accordingly the

service annuity credits of the members of the Fund in such conference, and also any other benefits provided by the Fund for them, unless otherwise ordered by the conference as provided in § 8.

8. In the event of the failure of a pastoral charge, district, or employer to pay, in whole or in part, the amount apportioned in any year by a conference for the purposes of the Fund, such conferences shall reduce equitably the service annuity credit for such year of service of such member of the Fund serving said pastoral charge, district, or employer, and shall advise the general board and the member concerned of its action in the case.

9. It shall be the duty of the Conference Board of Pensions to instruct the newly enrolled members of the Fund concerning its rules and regulations, to cooperate with the general board in obtaining information from members as may be required by the Fund, to adjudicate matters pertaining to contributions to the Fund, and to recommend to the conference any apportionment for the Fund that may be levied on the pastoral charges.

10. When a member of a conference who is also a member of the Fund is under special appointment without annuity claim upon such conference, the organization he is serving shall contribute annually to the Fund the equivalent of the current contribution made on behalf of each qualified member of the Fund in good standing. Failure to make such contribution in any conference year shall deprive the appointee concerned of service annuity credit for that conference year.

¶ **1646.** *Contributions by Members.*—1. An annual contribution, the equivalent of three per cent of the average salary of the conference (as defined in ¶ 1618.6 of the pension code), shall be paid directly to the Fund by each qualified member thereof in monthly or quarterly installments, payable in advance in accordance with the schedule of payment dates as determined by the general board; *provided*, however, that if his support (as defined in ¶ 1643.2) be less than the average salary of the conference, a member may elect to contribute annually the equivalent of three per cent of such support; and *provided*, further-

---

12 Amended in 1956 following Judicial Council Decision 118.

more, that by vote of the conference, on recommendation of the conference board, the amounts of the annual contributions required of members of the Fund shall be withheld by the treasurers of the pastoral charges, or other organizations concerned, and remitted directly to the Fund in monthly or quarterly installments. Such contributions shall be applicable to income annuity credit only.[12]

2. In case a minister transfers into a conference participating in the Fund and, by reason of such transfer, becomes a member of the Fund, the first installment due from him shall be that which next falls due for the members of the Fund in that conference following the date of such transfer.

3. In case a member of the Fund transfers out of a conference participating in the Fund, the last installment due from him while he is a member of such conference shall be that which normally falls due before the date of such transfer.

4. In case the transfer of a member of the Fund is effected between conferences, both of which are participating in the Fund, the amounts of the quarterly installments and the dates upon which installments fall due shall be adjusted in accordance with the schedule of payment dates for such conferences as determined by the general board.

5. If a minister be required to make a contribution to the Fund, he shall not be required by the conference, or by any organization thereof related to the support of conference claimants, to make any other contribution for pension purposes. If he consents to make such other contribution, it shall be voluntary. (*See* ¶ 1610.4.)

6. In any case a minister who has previously obtained membership in the Fund, while he is a member of a conference not participating in the Fund, shall have the right to continue contributions toward the accumulations for providing income annuity.

7. *Additional Member Contributions.*—Subject to such limitations, regulations, and conditions as the general board may adopt, a member of the Fund may pay into the Fund, in addition to the required member contributions such amounts as he may elect for the purpose of providing an income annuity or other benefits additional

to the income annuity provided through his regular contributions.

¶ **1647.** *Pensions.*—1. *Service Annuity.*—A member of the Fund who shall have attained age sixty-five or completed forty years of full-time approved service and who shall have been granted the retired relation shall receive thereafter, during his lifetime, a service annuity. Upon the death of a member of the Fund while receiving a service annuity the equivalent of seventy per cent of such annuity shall be continued to his widow, if their marriage took place before the member entered into the service annuity.

The service annuity and the seventy per cent thereof to be continued to the widow shall be the actuarial equivalent of his allocated service annuity credits together with the regular interest accumulated thereon, determined on the basis of the actual ages of the member and his wife at the time of entry into the service annuity.

If at the time of his entry into the service annuity a member be unmarried or a widower, the calculation of the amount of such service annuity shall be made on the basis of assumed equal ages for man and wife.

The service annuity shall be determined according to the tables of annuity rates for such purpose in current use by the general board.

2. *Income Annuity.*—At the same time that a member of the Fund, whether married or single, is granted a service annuity, he shall be entitled to an income annuity of a type identical with his service annuity, the amount thereof to be the actuarial equivalent of his personal contributions to the Fund together with the regular interest accumulated thereon.

The income annuity shall be determined according to the tables of annuity rates for such purpose in current use by the general board.

3. *Income Annuity Credit Guarantee Option.*—At the time of entering upon his pension, a member of the Fund may elect an option under which he shall receive a reduced pension, but with the provision that if the pension payments received by him and his widow aggregate less than his income annuity credits at the time of retirement, there

shall be paid to his designated beneficiary or to his estate, as he shall have designated, an amount equivalent to the excess of such income annuity credits over such pension payments.

¶ **1648.** *Widow's Pension.*—1. If a member of the Fund die prior to retirement, his widow shall receive a pension consisting of an income annuity which shall be the actuarial equivalent of her deceased husband's income annuity credits and a service annuity which shall be the actuarial equivalent of seventy per cent of his service annuity credits.

2. If the service annuity of a widow be less than fifteen per cent of the average salary of the conference, it shall be supplemented by a grant from the Disability, Widows, and Children Fund sufficient to produce such an amount; *provided* that the total annual benefit from these sources shall not be less than $450. The income annuity payable under § 1 of this paragraph shall be in addition to said service annuity and grant.

¶ **1649.** *Child's Pension.*—1. Each unmarried minor child of a deceased member of the Fund shall be granted an annuity equal to five per cent of the average salary of the conference, but not less than $150, payable until attainment of age sixteen.

2. Upon presentation to it annually of a satisfactory certificate of enrollment, attendance, and work done in a standard school or college, the general board shall grant an unmarried child of a deceased member of the Fund an annuity equal to ten per cent of the average salary of the conference, but not less than $300, payable from age sixteen until attainment of age twenty-two.

¶ **1650.** *Limitation of Annual Payments.*—1. If a member of the Fund die prior to retirement, the total of the annual payments thereafter, in any year, to his widow and minor children shall not exceed seventy per cent of the average salary of the conference as defined in the pension code (¶ 1618.6).

2. If a member of the Fund die while receiving a pension, the total of the annual payments thereafter, in any year, to his widow and children shall not exceed the annual pension which he was receiving prior to his decease.

¶ **1651.** 1. *Disability Benefits.*—*a*) An annual disability benefit shall be given to a disabled member of the Fund under age sixty-five if disability shall have been evident for a period of not less than one hundred eighty days, and the member shall have submitted to such examinations as may be required by the general board, and it shall appear from the reports that his health has failed as a result of a disease or injury, and that presumably he is totally and permanently incapacitated for both ministerial work and the support of his family. This benefit shall not exceed one third of the average salary of the conference as defined in the pension code (¶ 1618.6). At the discretion of the general board, the initial payment of the benefit may be made to cover all or any part of the waiting period of one hundred eighty days, or only the period of disability following the termination of the waiting period.

b) During the continuance of his disability, a member of the Fund shall receive an annual allocation to be applied on his service annuity credit, equivalent to the current service annuity credit in the conference of which he is a member, said allocation to be provided from the disability fund.

c) When recommended by the general board, the continuation of the above disability benefits (§§ 1*a*, 1*b*) shall be subject to the yearly approval of the member's conference.

d) During the continuance of his disability, a member of the Fund shall be exempt from the requirement to contribute to the Fund, but when his disability has been terminated and he has entered into a salaried relationship with a pastoral charge, district, or employer, he shall resume contributions to the Fund.

e) If a disabled member of the Fund recover sufficiently to resume ministerial work or to engage in a remunerative occupation, his disability allowance may be reduced or terminated by the general board at its discretion.

f) During the continuance of his disability, the member may be required, at the discretion of the general board, while still under age sixty-five, to have a medical examination at any time by a physician appointed to act in behalf of the general board.

g) If disability continue until age sixty-five, the disability benefits shall terminate, and thereafter a disabled member of the Fund shall receive his pension, according to the provisions of ¶ 1647.

2. *Death Benefit.*—When a member of the Fund dies, a benefit may be paid in one sum out of the Contingent Fund to his widow, if any, in accordance with rules and regulations which shall be adopted by the general board.

¶ 1652. *Refunds.*—1. On ceasing to be a member of a conference prior to retirement, a member of the Fund shall receive as a refund, in lieu of all other benefits, a sum equivalent to the total of his own contributions to the Fund, together with the regular interest accumulated thereon; *provided*, however, that if such member enter the ministry of another church or denomination, and allow his accumulated income annuity credits to remain in the Fund, then his accumulated income annuity credits and service annuity credits shall be applied in accordance with the provisions set forth in ¶¶ 1647-48; and *provided*, furthermore, that the exercise of this privilege shall not confer any right to make a claim on the Fund for disability or other benefits not specifically provided for in this paragraph.

2. On his ceasing to be a member of a conference after retirement, the service annuity shall cease automatically and the income annuity shall be commuted in the form of a cash settlement to be actuarially determined and made by the general board.

3. If a member of the Fund die prior to receipt of any installment of his income annuity, and without leaving a widow òr minor child or children, there shall be refunded to his estate a sum equivalent to the total of his contributions to the Fund, together with the regular interest accumulated thereon.

4. If the widow of a member of the Fund remarry, the service annuity shall cease automatically, but may be reinstated upon her attainment of age sixty-five or upon the termination of her marital status by her husband's death or by legal process; and the income annuity shall be

commuted in the form of a cash settlement to be actuarially determined and made by the general board. This shall apply to a surviving widow of a member who dies while in the retired relation, as well as to a widow of a member who dies prior to retirement.

¶ **1653.** *Funds.*—1. The annual contributions required in ¶ 1645.1, up to and including nine per cent of the average salary of the conference, shall be appropriated for the purposes of the Fund according to the following percentages:

Service Annuity Fund 70%
Disability, Widows, and Children Fund 27%
Contingent Fund 3%

The amount of the contributions in excess of nine per cent of the average salary of the conference shall be allocated to the Service Annuity Fund.

2. The seventy per cent of the contributions of each conference for the Service Annuity Fund shall be apportioned equally among its members in the effective relation and probationers who shall be also members of the Fund, except as provided in ¶ 1645.7, .8, .10, and shall be allocated to each of them annually. The amounts so allocated together with the regular interest thereon shall be held by the general board for the service annuities described in ¶ 1647.1.

3. The twenty-seven per cent of the contributions of the conferences for the Disability, Widows, and Children Fund shall be administered by the general board as indicated in ¶¶ 1647-51.

4. The three per cent of the contributions of the conferences for the Contingent Fund shall be administered by the general board as hereinafter provided.

5. A Contingent Fund shall be created and administered by the general board to which shall be credited:

a) The three per cent of the conference contributions provided in §§ 1, 4 of this paragraph.

b) The excess interest earnings above regular interest in any of the other funds.

c) The service annuity credits released when a minister ceases to be a member of the Fund.

d) Any resources of the Ministers Reserve Pension Fund not otherwise designated or allocated.

6. The Contingent Fund shall be used at the discretion of the general board in such ways and for such purposes as in its judgment shall best serve the interests for which the Ministers Reserve Pension Fund is created.

¶ **1654.** *Initial Reserve Fund.*—1. Each conference entering the Fund shall be required to provide an initial reserve fund for the liabilities assumed on account of new entrants. The amount of such initial reserve fund, the conditions of its actuarial calculation, and the manner of financing its liabilities shall be determined by the general board on request of the conference concerned.

2. The initial reserve fund and the earnings therefrom shall be used exclusively for the financing of the aforesaid liabilities.

¶ **1655.** *Authorization.*—1. The general board is authorized, instructed, and empowered to put the Ministers Reserve Pension Fund plan as herein set forth into operation in any conference after such conference shall have decided to enter and shall have made provision for the requisite initial reserve fund specified herein.

2. The general board is hereby authorized to act as a reserve funding agency for such conferences as may desire to transfer to it any or all of their obligations for previous entrants under the pension code at a fixed rate of annuity per year of service.

3. The general board is hereby authorized to administer the Fund and to adopt such rules and regulations as may be necessary for its efficient operation, subject to the limitation that this power shall not be exercised so as to nullify any of the provisions of the plan.

¶ **1656.** *Partial Reserve Funding.*—The general board may make provision for partial reserve funding of annuities payable under the pension code as described in ¶¶ 1613-37.

1. An Annual or Provisional Annual Conference, at any time, on its own determination, by a two-thirds vote of its membership present and voting, may actively participate in the Partial Reserve Pension Fund, hereafter in this

paragraph referred to as the Fund, when it accepts the conditions and fulfills the requirements set forth.

2. *Membership.*—*a*) The membership of the Fund shall consist of the ministers who are on trial or in full connection in a conference which is actively participating in the Fund, and who are not members of the Ministers Reserve Pension Fund.

b) When a member of the Ministers Reserve Pension Fund is received by transfer into a conference participating in the Partial Reserve Pension Fund, but not in the Ministers Reserve Pension Fund, he shall be subject to the provisions of the Partial Reserve Pension Fund for the years served in such conference. (*See* ¶ 1644.3.)

3. *Contributions by the Conference.*—*a*) Each conference participating in the Fund shall contribute annually to the credit of each qualified member of the Fund such sum as it may designate, based on a percentage of the average salary of the conference (as defined in the pension code, ¶ 1618.6).

b) Each conference shall determine the plan by which it shall secure the amount necessary to make the contributions required in § 3*a* and shall make suitable and adequate provision therefor.

c) A deficiency in the payment of the annual amount required of a conference shall reduce accordingly the credits of the members of the Fund in such conference.

d) The provisions in ¶ 1645.2, .3 shall determine the amount of contribution to the credit of a member of the Fund transferring into or out of a conference actively participating in the Fund.

4. *Contributions by Members.*—*a*) An annual contribution, the equivalent of three per cent of the average salary of the conference (as defined in ¶ 1618.6 of the pension code), shall be paid directly to the Fund by each qualified member thereof in monthly or quarterly installments, payable in advance in accordance with the schedule of payment dates as determined by the general board; *provided*, however, that if his support (as defined in ¶ 1643.2) be less than the average salary of the conference, a member may elect to contribute annually the equivalent of three per cent of such support; and *provided*, further-

more, that by vote of the conference, on recommendation of the conference board, the amounts of the annual contributions required of members of the Fund shall be withheld by the treasurers of the pastoral charges, or other organizations concerned, and remitted directly to the Fund in monthly or quarterly installments. Such contributions shall be applicable to income annuity credit only.

b) The provisions of ¶ 1646.2-.4 shall determine the amount and the date of payment of the contribution required of a member who transfers into or out of a conference actively participating in the Fund.

c) A member of the Fund, while he is a member of a conference not participating in the Fund, shall have the right to continue contributions toward the accumulations for providing income annuity.

5. *Additional Member Contributions.*—Subject to such limitations, regulations and conditions as the general board may adopt, a member of the Fund may pay into the Fund, in addition to the required member contributions, such amounts as he may elect for the purpose of providing an income annuity or other benefits additional to the income annuity provided through his regular contributions.

6. It shall be the duty of the Conference Board of Pensions to instruct the newly enrolled members of the Fund concerning its rules and regulations, to co-operate with the general board in obtaining information from members as may be required by the Fund, to adjudicate matters pertaining to contributions to the Fund, and to recommend to the conference any apportionment for the Fund that may be levied on the pastoral charges.

7. *Initial Reserve Fund.*—*a*) A conference participating in the Fund may provide an **initial reserve fund** from which there shall be allocated the annual contributions to the credit of the members of the Fund as required in § 3*a*.

b) The amount of such initial reserve fund shall be determined by the general board on request of the conference concerned.

c) The initial reserve fund and the earnings therefrom

shall be used exclusively in financing the aforesaid annual contributions.

d) The general board shall determine the circumstances under which an initial reserve fund shall be required of a conference in order to participate in the Fund.

8. *Pensions.*—*a*) *Service Annuity.*—A member of the Fund who shall have attained age sixty-five and who shall have been granted the retired relation shall receive thereafter, during his lifetime, a service annuity. Upon the death of a member of the Fund while receiving a service annuity the equivalent of seventy per cent of such annuity shall be continued to his widow, if their marriage took place before the member entered into the service annuity.

The service annuity and the seventy per cent thereof to be continued to the widow shall be the actuarial equivalent of his allocated service annuity credits together with the regular interest accumulated thereon, determined on the basis of the actual ages of the member and his wife at the time of entry into the service annuity.

b) A conference participating in the Fund may regard the service annuity based on the contributions made by such conference as a part of the annuity provided for a conference claimant by such conference under the pension code (¶¶ 1619, 1620, 1631).

c) *Income Annuity.*—At the same time that a member of the Fund is granted a service annuity, he shall be entitled to an income annuity of a type identical with his service annuity, the amount thereof to be the actuarial equivalent of his personal contributions to the Fund together with the regular interest accumulated thereon. The income annuity payable under the provisions of this section shall be considered as an addition to the pension normally provided under the pension code.

d) The service annuity and the income annuity shall be determined according to the tables of annuity rates for such purpose in current use by the general board.

e) *Income Annuity Credit Guarantee Option.*—At the time of entering upon his pension, a member of the Fund may elect an option under which he shall receive a reduced pension, but with the provision that if the pension payments received by him and his widow aggregate less than his income annuity credits at the time of retirement, there shall be paid to his designated beneficiary or to his estate, as he shall have designated, an amount equivalent to the excess of such income annuity credits over such pension payments.

9. *Widow's Pension.*—If a member of the Fund die prior to retirement, a pension shall be paid to his widow, based on her age and provided by the total of her deceased husband's personal contributions together with the regular interest accumulated thereon, plus seventy per cent of his service annuity credits together with the regular interest accumulated thereon at the time of his death.

10. *Death Benefit.*—When a member of the Fund dies, a benefit may be paid in one sum out of the Contingent Fund to his widow, if any, in accordance with rules and regulations which shall be adopted by the general board.

11. *Refunds.*—The regulations concerning refunds as provided in ¶ 1652 shall apply in the Partial Reserve Pension Fund. Participation in this Fund does not imply any right of the participant to make a claim on the general board for disability or other benefits not specifically provided for in this paragraph.

12. A Contingent Fund shall be created and administered by the general board for the Partial Reserve Pension Fund, to which shall be credited:

a) The excess interest earnings above regular interest credited.

b) The service annuity credits released when a minister ceases to be a member of the Fund.

c) Any resources of the Partial Reserve Pension Fund not otherwise designated or allocated.

The Contingent Fund shall be used at the discretion of the general board in such ways and for such purposes as in its judgment shall best serve the interests of the Fund.

13. The general board is hereby authorized to administer the Fund and to adopt such rules and regulations as may be necessary for its efficient operation, subject to the limitation that this power shall not be exercised so as to nullify any of the Disciplinary provisions of the plan.

¶ 1657. The general board shall have authority to make special arrangements with conferences whereby partial reserve funding of the pensions for full-time approved supply pastors can be accomplished along lines similar to those hereinbefore described in ¶ 1656.

CHAPTER VI

LAY EMPLOYEES PENSION FUND

¶ **1658.** 1. A pension fund to be known and designated as the **Lay Employees Pension Fund** of The Methodist Church is hereby established. The Fund shall be held, administered, and disbursed by the General Board of Pensions of The Methodist Church in accordance with rules and regulations which shall be adopted from time to time by the board.

2. The purpose of the Fund shall be to provide annuities for lay employees of local churches, boards, commissions, agencies, institutions, and organizations in the United States of America listed in the book of Discipline of The Methodist Church or in the directory printed in the journal of any Annual Conference of The Methodist Church situated in the United States of America.

¶ **1659.** 1. Effective June 1, 1948, any person then resident within the United States who was then serving as a secretary of an effective bishop of The Methodist Church, or who had previously served as a secretary to an effective bishop or bishops of The Methodist Church and was then serving or thereafter shall serve in any form of employment connected with The Methodist Church, upon retirement or being no longer in the employ of a bishop, board, or agency of The Methodist Church and upon attainment of age sixty shall be entitled to make an annuity claim upon the Episcopal Fund for the secretarial service rendered an effective bishop or bishops prior to June 1, 1948.

2. The bishops or boards or agencies respectively shall be responsible for informing their employees concerning their pension rights under this paragraph and shall notify all who are involved in providing the pension.

3. Effective June 1, 1952, the full-time lay employees

of an effective bishop resident in the United States of America shall be enrolled as participating lay employees in the Lay Employees Pension Fund of The Methodist Church, in accordance with the rules and regulations of said Fund.

4. As the participating employer of such participating lay employees the bishop shall deduct the required contributions from the compensation of such participating lay employees and shall forward such amounts concurrently with the required employer's contributions to the Fund; *provided*, however, that the employer's contributions shall be paid from the allowances made by the Episcopal Fund or other sources for office expense of the bishop.

5. Effective June 1, 1952, the General Board of Pensions shall transfer the individual accounts held for secretaries, assistant secretaries, or other office employees of a bishop, together with accrued interest, to the Lay Employees Pension Fund, and thereafter such employees shall be enrolled as participating lay employees in the Lay Employees Pension Fund, as provided in § 3 of this paragraph.

Chapter VII

JOINT CONTRIBUTORY ANNUITY FUND

¶ **1666.** 1. A pension fund to be known and designated as the **Joint Contributory Annuity Fund** of The Methodist Church is hereby established. The Fund shall be held, administered, and disbursed by the General Board of Pensions of The Methodist Church in accordance with rules and regulations which shall be adopted from time to time by the board.

2. The purpose of the Fund shall be to provide pensions for ministerial members of Annual or Provisional Annual Conferences, their widows or dependent children, on account of service rendered under special appointment to an institution, organization, agency, or community church for which a pension is not otherwise provided.

Chapter VIII

CHAPLAINS PENSION FUND

¶ **1671.** A pension fund to be known and designated as the **Chaplains Pension Fund** of The Methodist Church is hereby established. The Fund shall be held, administered, and disbursed by the General Board of Pensions of The Methodist Church in accordance with rules and regulations to be determined jointly by the board and the Commission on Chaplains of The Methodist Church.

2. The purpose of the Fund shall be to provide pensions for ministerial members of Annual or Provisional Annual Conferences, their widows or dependent children, on account of approved service rendered under special appointment as chaplains on full-time duty with the Armed Forces of the United States, or with organizations, institutions, or agencies related to the Commission on Chaplains of The Methodist Church, for which a pension is not otherwise provided.

Chapter IX

STAFF PENSION FUND

¶ **1676.** 1. A pension fund to be known and designated as the **Staff Pension Fund** of The Methodist Church is hereby established. The Fund shall be held, administered, and disbursed by the General Board of Pensions of The Methodist Church in accordance with rules and regulations which shall be adopted from time to time by the board.

2. The purpose of the Fund shall be to provide annuities for ministerial members of Annual or Provisional Annual Conferences under appointment to, and lay employees of, boards, commissions, agencies, institutions, and organizations in the United States of America listed in the book of Discipline of The Methodist Church or in the directory printed in the journal of any Annual Conference of The Methodist Church situated in the United States of America.

Chapter X

HOSPITALIZATION AND MEDICAL EXPENSE PROGRAM

¶ **1681.**—The General Board of Pensions of The Methodist Church is hereby authorized to establish and administer, through the Board of Pensions of The Methodist Church, Incorporated in Illinois, in accordance with the authority vested in the general board under ¶ 1601, a **Hospitalization and Medical Expense Program** for ministers of The Methodist Church, and lay employees as defined in ¶ 1658.2, and their dependents, under rules and regulations which shall be adopted from time to time by the general board.

Chapter XI

EPISCOPAL PENSIONS

¶ **1686.** The provisions regarding pensions for retired bishops, and for the widows and minor children of deceased bishops, are set forth in ¶¶ 774-77 under Part V, Temporal Economy.

Chapter XII

COMMITTEE ON PENSION LEGISLATION

¶ **1699.** The General Board of Pensions shall appoint quadrennially from its membership a **Committee on Pension Legislation,** which shall consist of one bishop, and one minister and one layman from each jurisdiction, whose responsibility it shall be to study the operation of the various pension programs of The Methodist Church and to present recommendations to each succeeding General Conference.

513

PART IX

WORSHIP AND RITUAL

CHAPTER I

ORDERS OF WORSHIP

¶ **1901.** In recognition of the various needs of our several congregations, four orders of worship have been provided which may be used according to desire. But while liberty is given in the use of these orders of worship, it is urged that all ministers and congregations make use of some one of these orders.[1]

Let each service proceed without announcement, as far as possible.

Choral responses may be used as desired. See numbers 589-624 in *The Methodist Hymnal*.

For calls to worship, invocations and confessions, words of assurance, affirmations of faith, and prayers, see *The Book of Worship for Church and Home*.

Where there is a junior service or sermon, it should immediately precede or follow the offertory.

¶ **1902.** In commending the Sunday Service to "our societies in America," Mr. Wesley wrote: "I believe there is no Liturgy in the World, either in ancient or modern language, which breathes more of a solid, scriptural, rational piety than the Common Prayer of the Church of England. And though the main of it was compiled considerably more than two hundred years ago, yet is the

---

[1] The General Conference of 1944 authorized optional use of the orders of worship and other worship materials in *The Book of Worship for Church and Home*. The General Conference of 1960 authorized experimental use during the 1960-64 quadrennium of proposed material for a revision of this book, on the basis of which the General Commission on Worship might perfect the content and report a completed draft for adoption by the General Conference of 1964.

language of it not only pure, but strong and elegant in the highest degree."

¶ 1903.   ORDER OF WORSHIP I

Let the service of worship begin at the time appointed. Let the people kneel or bow in silent prayer upon entering the sanctuary.

PRELUDE *The people in devout meditation.*

CALL TO WORSHIP *Which may be said or sung.*

HYMN *If a processional, the hymn shall precede the call to worship, and the people shall then rise at the second stanza and join in singing.*

PRAYER OF CONFESSION *To be said by all, the people seated and bowed, or kneeling. The following, or other prayer of confession, may be said:*

Our heavenly Father, who by thy love hast made us, and through thy love hast kept us, and in thy love wouldest make us perfect; we humbly confess that we have not loved thee with all our heart and soul and mind and strength, and that we have not loved one another as Christ hath loved us. Thy life is within our souls, but our selfishness hath hindered thee. We have resisted thy Spirit. We have neglected thine inspirations. Forgive what we have been; help us to amend what we are; and in thy Spirit direct what we shall be; that thou mayest come into the full glory of thy creation, in us and in all men; through Jesus Christ our Lord. Amen.

SILENT MEDITATION *The people seated and bowed, or kneeling.*

WORDS OF ASSURANCE *The Minister.*

THE LORD'S PRAYER *Which may be said or sung.*

ANTHEM or CHANT *Which may be the* Venite *or the* Te Deum.

THE RESPONSIVE READING *The people to stand and remain standing until after the Affirmation of Faith.*

GLORIA PATRI

AFFIRMATION OF FAITH *To be said by the minister and people.*

THE LESSON FROM THE HOLY SCRIPTURES *The Old and New Testaments.*

PASTORAL PRAYER *The people seated and bowed, or kneeling.*

OFFERTORY *The dedication of offerings, with prayer or offertory sentences.*

HYMN *The people standing.*

THE SERMON

PRAYER *The people seated and bowed, or kneeling.*

AN INVITATION TO CHRISTIAN DISCIPLESHIP

HYMN or DOXOLOGY *The people standing. The closing hymn may be a recessional.*

BENEDICTION *The people seated and bowed, or kneeling.*

SILENT PRAYER

POSTLUDE

¶ 1904. ORDER OF WORSHIP II

Let the service of worship begin at the time appointed. Let the people kneel or bow in silent prayer upon entering the sanctuary.

PRELUDE

CALL TO WORSHIP

INVOCATION

HYMN

AFFIRMATION OF FAITH

I believe in God the Father Almighty, Maker of heaven and earth; and in Jesus Christ his only Son our Lord; who was conceived by the Holy Spirit, born of the Virgin Mary, suffered under Pontius Pilate, was crucified, dead, and buried; the third day he rose from the dead; he ascended into heaven, and sitteth at the right hand of God the Father Almighty; from thence he shall come to judge the quick and the dead. I believe in the Holy Spirit, the holy catholic Church, the communion of saints, the forgiveness of sins, the resurrection of the body, and the life everlasting. Amen.

ANTHEM

THE RESPONSIVE READING

GLORIA PATRI

516

THE LESSON FROM THE HOLY SCRIPTURES

SILENT MEDITATION

PASTORAL PRAYER

THE LORD'S PRAYER

OFFERTORY *The dedication of offerings, with prayer or offertory sentences.*

HYMN

THE SERMON

PRAYER

AN INVITATION TO CHRISTIAN DISCIPLESHIP

HYMN

BENEDICTION

POSTLUDE

¶ 1905.   ORDER OF WORSHIP III

Let the service of worship begin at the time appointed. Let the people kneel or bow in silent prayer upon entering the sanctuary.

PRELUDE *The people in devout meditation.*

CALL TO WORSHIP *Which may be said or sung.*

HYMN *If a processional, the hymn shall precede the call to worship, and the people shall then rise at the second stanza and join in singing.*

PRAYER OF CONFESSION *To be said by all, the people seated and bowed, or kneeling. The following, or other prayer of confession, may be said:*

Almighty God, from whom every good prayer cometh, and who pourest out, on all who desire it, the spirit of grace and supplication; deliver us, when we draw nigh to thee, from coldness of heart and wanderings of mind, that with steadfast thoughts, and kindled affections, we may worship thee in spirit and in truth; through Jesus Christ our Lord. Amen.

SILENT MEDITATION *The people seated and bowed, or kneeling.*

THE LORD'S PRAYER *Which may be said or sung.*

517

ANTHEM

THE LESSON FROM THE HOLY SCRIPTURES *If a responsive reading is used, it should be followed by the* Gloria Patri, *the people standing.*

PASTORAL PRAYER *The people seated and bowed, or kneeling.*

PRESENTATION OF OFFERINGS

HYMN *The people standing.*

THE SERMON

AN INVITATION TO CHRISTIAN DISCIPLESHIP

HYMN or DOXOLOGY *The people standing.*

SILENT PRAYER

BENEDICTION *The people seated and bowed, or kneeling.*

POSTLUDE

¶ 1906. AN ORDER FOR MORNING OR EVENING PRAYER, ADAPTED FROM THE SUNDAY SERVICE OF JOHN WESLEY

Suggested for Occasional Use

Let the service of worship begin at the time appointed. Let the people kneel or bow in silent prayer upon entering the sanctuary.

PRELUDE *The people in devout meditation.*

SCRIPTURE SENTENCES *One or more of them to be read by the minister, the people standing.*

The LORD is in his holy temple: let all the earth keep silence before him.

Let the words of my mouth, and the meditation of my heart, be acceptable in thy sight, O LORD, my strength and my redeemer.

This is the day which the LORD hath made, we will rejoice and be glad in it.

The hour cometh, and now is, when the true worshipers shall worship the Father in spirit and in truth.

518

The sacrifices of God are a broken spirit: a broken and a contrite heart, O God, thou wilt not despise.

HYMN *If a processional, the hymn shall precede the Scripture Sentences, and the people shall then rise at the second stanza and join in singing.*

CALL TO CONFESSION *By the minister, the people standing.*

Dearly beloved, the Scripture moveth us to acknowledge and confess our sins before Almighty God our Heavenly Father with a humble, lowly, penitent, and obedient heart, to the end that we may obtain forgiveness by his infinite goodness and mercy. Wherefore I pray and beseech you, as many as are here present, to accompany me with a pure heart and a humble voice unto the throne of the heavenly grace. Let us pray.

GENERAL CONFESSION *To be said by all, the people seated and bowed, or kneeling.*

Almighty and most merciful Father, we have erred and strayed from thy ways like lost sheep. We have followed too much the devices and desires of our own hearts. We have offended against thy holy laws. We have left undone those things which we ought to have done, and we have done those things which we ought not to have done. But thou, O Lord, have mercy upon us. Spare thou those, O God, who confess their faults. Restore thou those who are penitent, according to thy promises declared unto mankind in Christ Jesus our Lord. And grant, O most merciful Father, for his sake, that we may hereafter live a godly, righteous, and sober life; to the glory of thy holy name. Amen.

PRAYER FOR PARDON *The minister.*

O Lord, we beseech thee, absolve thy people from their offenses, that through thy bountiful goodness we may be delivered from the bonds of those sins which by our frailty we have committed. Grant this, O heavenly Father, for Jesus Christ's sake, our blessed Lord and Saviour. **Amen.**

The people shall answer here, and at the end of all other prayers, **Amen.**

THE LORD'S PRAYER *To be said by all.*

Minister: O Lord, open thou our lips.

People: **And our mouth shall show forth thy praise.**

Minister: Praise ye the Lord.

People: **The Lord's name be praised.**

VENITE *To be said or sung by all, the people standing.*

PSALTER *To be said by all, the people standing.*

GLORIA PATRI *To be said or sung by all, the people standing.*

THE LESSON FROM THE OLD TESTAMENT

TE DEUM *To be said or sung by all, the people standing.*

THE LESSON FROM THE NEW TESTAMENT

JUBILATE DEO *To be said or sung by all, the people standing.*

DECLARATION OF FAITH *Here shall be said the Apostles' Creed.*

Minister: The Lord be with you.

People: **And with thy spirit.**

Minister: Let us pray.

COLLECT FOR GRACE *To be said by all, the people seated and bowed, or kneeling.*

O Lord, our heavenly Father, almighty and everlasting God, who hast safely brought us to the beginning of this day; defend us in the same with thy mighty power; and grant that this day we fall into no sin, neither run into any kind of danger, but that all our doings may be ordered by thy governance, to do always that which is righteous in thy sight; through Jesus Christ our Lord. Amen.

PRAYER *Then may the minister offer a prayer, ending with:*

The grace of our Lord Jesus Christ, the love of God, and the fellowship of the Holy Spirit, be with us all evermore. **Amen.**

OFFERTORY *Then may be sung an anthem, and an offering may be received.*

THE SERMON *When the service is followed by a sermon or the Holy Communion, the minister shall make use of appropriate hymns and prayers. Otherwise the service may close with a hymn and the following benediction.*

BENEDICTION

The peace of God, which passeth all understanding, keep your hearts and minds in the knowledge and love of God, and of his Son Jesus Christ our Lord; and the blessing of God Almighty, the Father, the Son, and the Holy Spirit, be among you, and remain with you always. **Amen.**

When this service is to be used for Evening Prayer, the following changes shall be made:
The Magnificat shall be used in place of the Te Deum.
The Nunc Dimittis shall be used in place of the Jubilate Deo.
In place of the Collect for Grace shall be said the following Collects:

Lighten our darkness, we beseech thee, O Lord; and by thy great mercy defend us from all perils and dangers of this night; for the love of thine only Son, our Saviour, Jesus Christ. Amen.

Direct us, O Lord, in all our doings, with thy most gracious favor, and further us with thy continual help, that in all our works, begun, continued, and ended in thee, we may glorify thy holy name, and finally, by thy mercy, obtain everlasting life; through Jesus Christ our Lord. Amen.

CHAPTER II

THE RITUAL

¶ 1907. We call upon all our ministers to make faithful use of the forms and orders here provided, without other deviation than is here indicated.[2]

---

[2] The General Conference of 1960 authorized experimental use during the 1960-64 quadrennium of proposed revised orders for Baptism, Confirmation and Reception into the Church, the Lord's Supper, Marriage, and Burial of the Dead, on the basis of which the General Commission on Worship might perfect these and other contents of a revision of *The Book of Worship for Church and Home* and report a completed draft for adoption by the General Conference of 1964.

We urge all ministers to encourage and train the people to participate audibly in those portions of the service provided for this purpose, particularly in the celebration of the Lord's Supper. The portions to be used as responses are especially indicated by **bold-face type.**

¶ 1908. AN ORDER FOR THE ADMINISTRATION OF THE SACRAMENT OF THE LORD'S SUPPER OR HOLY COMMUNION I

The following is a complete order of public worship and is intended to replace the regular order of morning worship when the Sacrament of the Lord's Supper is administered. The responses may be sung if desired. See numbers 565-88 in *The Methodist Hymnal.*

The Lord's Table should have upon it a fair linen cloth.

Let the pure, unfermented juice of the grape be used.

It is our custom to receive the Sacrament of the Lord's Supper kneeling, but if persons so desire, they may receive the elements while seated or standing.

Upon entering the church let the communicants bow in prayer and in the spirit of prayer and meditation approach the blessed Sacrament.

The people shall stand and join in singing the hymn, "Holy, holy, holy, Lord God Almighty," or other suitable hymn, and remain standing until after the singing of the Gloria Patri.

God is a Spirit. They that worship him must worship him in spirit and in truth.

Glory be to God on high.

God is Light. If we walk in the light, as he is in the light, we have fellowship one with another; and truly our fellowship is with the Father, and with his Son Jesus Christ.

Glory be to God on high.

God is Power. They that wait upon the Lord shall renew their strength; they shall mount up with wings as eagles; they shall run, and not be weary; and they shall walk, and not faint.

Glory be to God on high.

God is Love. Behold, what manner of love the Father hath bestowed upon us, that we should be called the sons of God. Hereby perceive we the love of God, because he laid down his life for us.

Glory be to God on high.

Then the Gloria Patri *shall be said or sung:*

Glory be to the Father, and to the Son, and to the Holy Ghost; as it was in the beginning, is now, and ever shall be, world without end. Amen.

Then shall the minister say:

Let us pray.

Almighty God, unto whom all hearts are open, all desires known, and from whom no secrets are hid; cleanse the thoughts of our hearts by the inspiration of thy Holy Spirit, that we may perfectly love thee, and worthily magnify thy holy name; through Jesus Christ our Lord. Amen.

Our Father who art in heaven, hallowed be thy name; thy kingdom come; thy will be done on earth as it is in heaven. Give us this day our daily bread. And forgive us our trespasses, as we forgive those who trespass against us. And lead us not into temptation, but deliver us from evil. For thine is the kingdom, and the power, and the glory, forever. Amen.

Then may the minister read the Ten Commandments, and the people, still in the attitude of prayer, shall in response ask God's mercy for their transgressions in times past and grace to keep the law in time to come.

God spake these words and said: I am the LORD thy God:

Thou shalt have no other gods before me.

Thou shalt not make unto thee any graven image, or any likeness of any thing that is in heaven above, or that is in the earth beneath, or that is in the water under the earth: thou shalt not bow down thyself to them, nor serve them: for I the LORD thy God am a jealous God, visiting the iniquity of the fathers upon the children unto the third and fourth generation of them that hate me; and showing mercy unto thousands of them that love me, and keep my commandments.

Lord, have mercy upon us, and write all these thy laws in our hearts; we beseech thee.

Thou shalt not take the name of the LORD thy God in vain; for the LORD will not hold him guiltless that taketh his name in vain.

Remember the Sabbath day, to keep it holy. Six days shalt thou labor, and do all thy work: but the seventh day is the Sabbath of the LORD thy God: in it thou shalt not do any work, thou, nor thy son, nor thy daughter, thy manservant, nor thy maidservant, nor thy cattle, nor thy stranger that is within thy gates: for in six days the LORD made heaven and earth, the sea, and all that in them is, and rested the seventh day: wherefore the LORD blessed the Sabbath day, and hallowed it.

Lord, have mercy upon us, and write all these thy laws in our hearts, we beseech thee.

Honor thy father and thy mother: that thy days may be long upon the land which the LORD thy God giveth thee.

Thou shalt not kill.

Thou shalt not commit adultery.

Thou shalt not steal.

Thou shalt not bear false witness against thy neighbor.

Thou shalt not covet thy neighbor's house, thou shalt not covet thy neighbor's wife, nor his manservant, nor his maidservant, nor his ox, nor his ass, nor anything that is thy neighbor's.

Lord, have mercy upon us, and write all these thy laws in our hearts, we beseech thee.

In place of or in addition to the Ten Commandments the minister may read the summary of the divine law in the words of Jesus, and the people, in the attitude of prayer, shall ask God's mercy and gracious aid.

Hear what our Lord Jesus Christ saith:

Thou shalt love the Lord thy God with all thy heart, and with all thy soul, and with all thy mind. This is the first and great commandment. And the second is like unto it, Thou shalt love thy neighbor as thyself.

Lord, have mercy upon us, and write all these thy laws in our hearts, we beseech thee.

Then may the minister read the Beatitudes of the Lord Jesus, and the people, still in the attitude of prayer, shall humbly ask God that they may be fulfilled in their hearts. Or here Isaiah 53:1-10 may be used as a responsive scripture.

Hear the Beatitudes of our Lord Jesus Christ:

Blessed are the poor in spirit: for theirs is the kingdom of heaven.

Lord, be gracious unto us, and help us to obtain this blessing.

Blessed are they that mourn: for they shall be comforted.

Lord, be gracious unto us, and help us to obtain this blessing.

Blessed are the meek: for they shall inherit the earth.

Lord, be gracious unto us, and help us to obtain this blessing.

Blessed are they which do hunger and thirst after righteousness: for they shall be filled.

Lord, be gracious unto us, and help us to obtain this blessing.

Blessed are the merciful: for they shall obtain mercy.

Lord, be gracious unto us, and help us to obtain this blessing.

Blessed are the pure in heart: for they shall see God.

Lord, be gracious unto us, and help us to obtain this blessing.

Blessed are the peacemakers: for they shall be called the children of God.

Lord, be gracious unto us, and help us to obtain this blessing.

Blessed are they which are persecuted for righteousness' sake: for theirs is the kingdom of heaven.

Blessed are ye, when men shall revile you, and persecute you, and shall say all manner of evil against you falsely, for my sake.

Rejoice, and be exceeding glad: for great is your reward in heaven: for so persecuted they the prophets which were before you.

Grant unto us thy Holy Spirit, O God, and enable us to obtain all these blessings; through Jesus Christ our Lord. Amen.

If desired, the following form may be used:

Hear the Beatitudes of our Lord Jesus Christ:

Blessed are the poor in spirit: for theirs is the kingdom of heaven.

Blessed are they that mourn: for they shall be comforted.

Blessed are the meek: for they shall inherit the earth.

Lord, be gracious unto us, and help us to obtain these blessings.

Blessed are they which do hunger and thirst after righteousness: for they shall be filled.

Blessed are the merciful: for they shall obtain mercy.

Blessed are the pure in heart: for they shall see God.

Blessed are the peacemakers: for they shall be called the children of God.

Lord, be gracious unto us, and help us to obtain these blessings.

Blessed are they which are persecuted for righteousness' sake: for theirs is the kingdom of heaven.

Blessed are ye, when men shall revile you, and persecute you, and shall say all manner of evil against you falsely, for my sake.

Rejoice, and be exceeding glad: for great is your reward in heaven: for so persecuted they the prophets which were before you.

Grant unto us thy Holy Spirit, O God, and enable us to obtain all these blessings; through Jesus Christ our Lord. Amen.

The responsive scripture, Isaiah 53:1-10:

Who hath believed our report? and to whom is the arm of the LORD revealed?

For he shall grow up before him as a tender plant, and as a root out of a dry ground: he hath no form nor comeliness; and when we shall see him, there is no beauty that we should desire him.

He is despised and rejected of men; a man of sorrows, and acquainted with grief: and we hid as it were our faces from him; he was despised, and we esteemed him not.

Surely he hath borne our griefs, and carried our sor-

rows: yet we did esteem him stricken, smitten of God, and afflicted.

But he was wounded for our transgressions, he was bruised for our iniquities: the chastisement of our peace was upon him; and with his stripes we are healed.

All we like sheep have gone astray; we have turned every one to his own way; and the LORD hath laid on him the iniquity of us all.

He was oppressed, and he was afflicted, yet he opened not his mouth: he was brought as a lamb to the slaughter, and as a sheep before his shearers is dumb, so he openeth not his mouth.

He was taken from prison and from judgment: and who shall declare his generation? for he was cut off out of the land of the living: for the transgression of my people was he stricken.

And he made his grave with the wicked, and with the rich in his death; because he had done no violence, neither was any deceit in his mouth.

Yet it pleased the LORD to bruise him; he hath put him to grief: when thou shalt make his soul an offering for sin, he shall see his seed, he shall prolong his days, and the pleasure of the LORD shall prosper in his hand.

Then may the minister read the Epistle, to be followed by the Gospel.

Here may the minister and people repeat the Apostles' Creed or some other of the authorized affirmations of faith, the people standing.

Then may follow the sermon or communion meditation and a suitable hymn (see hymns 408-15). During the singing of this hymn the minister shall remove the linen cloth that covers the elements.

After the hymn has been sung, the minister, standing by the Lord's Table, shall announce the offering for the needy, using one or more of the following groups of sentences.

I

Remember the words of the Lord Jesus, how he said, It is more blessed to give than to receive.

Let your light so shine before men, that they may see your good works, and glorify your Father which is in heaven.

Not everyone that saith unto me, Lord, Lord, shall enter into the kingdom of heaven; but he that doeth the will of my Father which is in heaven.

And the King shall answer and say unto them, Verily I say unto you, Inasmuch as ye have done it unto one of the least of these my brethren, ye have done it unto me.

Therefore all things whatsoever ye would that men should do to you, do ye even so to them: for this is the law and the prophets.

II

They shall not appear before the LORD empty: every man shall give as he is able, according to the blessing of the LORD thy God which he hath given thee.

Blessed is he that considereth the poor: the LORD will deliver him in time of trouble.

Thou shalt open thine hand wide unto thy brother, to thy poor, and to thy needy, in thy land.

Be merciful after thy power. If thou hast much, give plenteously: if thou hast little, do thy diligence gladly to give of that little: for so gatherest thou thyself a good reward in the day of necessity.

He that hath pity upon the poor lendeth unto the LORD; and that which he hath given will he pay him again.

III

To do good and to communicate forget not: for with such sacrifices God is well pleased.

As we have therefore opportunity, let us do good unto all men, especially unto them who are of the household of faith.

He which soweth sparingly shall reap also sparingly; and he which soweth bountifully shall reap also bountifully. Every man according as he purposeth in his heart, so let him give; not grudgingly or of necessity: for God loveth a cheerful giver.

Whoso hath this world's good, and seeth his brother have need, and shutteth up his compassion from him, how dwelleth the love of God in him?

God is not unrighteous to forget your work and labor

of love, which ye have showed toward his name, in that ye have ministered to the saints, and do minister.

IV

Offer unto God thanksgiving; and pay thy vows unto the most High.

Lay not up for yourselves treasures upon earth, where moth and ruth doth corrupt, and where thieves break through and steal: but lay up for yourselves treasures in heaven, where neither moth nor rust doth corrupt, and where thieves do not break through nor steal: for where your treasure is, there will your heart be also.

Zacchaeus stood, and said unto the Lord; Behold, Lord, the half of my goods I give to the poor; and if I have taken anything from any man by false accusation, I restore him fourfold.

Charge them that are rich in this world, that they be rich in good works, ready to distribute, willing to communicate; laying up in store for themselves a good foundation against the time to come, that they may lay hold on eternal life.

Godliness with contentment is great gain. For we brought nothing into this world, and it is certain we can carry nothing out.

As the minister receives the offering, the people shall stand, and the following may be said or sung:

All things come of thee, O Lord, and of thine own have we given thee.

Then may the minister say:

Thine, O Lord, is the greatness, and the power, and the glory, and the victory, and the majesty: for all that is in the heaven and in the earth is thine; thine is the kingdom, O Lord, and thou art exalted as head above all.

The people shall remain standing while the minister reads the invitation.

Ye that do truly and earnestly repent of your sins, and are in love and charity with your neighbors, and intend to lead a new life, following the commandments of God, and walking from henceforth in his holy ways; draw near with faith, and take this holy Sacrament to your comfort; and devoutly kneeling make your humble confession to Almighty God.

Then shall this general confession be made by the minister and those who are minded to receive the Holy Communion, the minister kneeling, facing the Lord's Table, and all the people in the attitude of prayer.

Almighty God, Father of our Lord Jesus Christ, Maker of all things, Judge of all men; we acknowledge and bewail our manifold sins and wickedness, which we from time to time most grievously have committed, by thought, word, and deed, against thy divine majesty. We do earnestly repent and are heartily sorry for these our misdoings; the remembrance of them is grievous unto us. Have mercy upon us, have mercy upon us, most merciful Father; for thy Son our Lord Jesus Christ's sake, forgive us all that is past; and grant that we may ever hereafter serve and please thee in newness of life, to the honor and glory of thy name; through Jesus Christ our Lord. Amen.

Then shall the minister offer this prayer:

Almighty God, our heavenly Father, who of thy great mercy hast promised forgiveness of sins to all them that with hearty repentance and true faith turn unto thee; have mercy upon us; pardon and deliver us from all our sins; confirm and strengthen us in all goodness; and bring us to everlasting life; through Jesus Christ our Lord. **Amen.**

Then shall the minister say:

Hear what the Scripture saith to those of a humble and contrite heart:

If any man sin, we have an advocate with the Father, Jesus Christ the righteous: and he is the propitiation for our sins: and not for ours only, but also for the sins of the whole world.

This is a faithful saying, and worthy of all acceptation, that Christ Jesus came into the world to save sinners.

God so loved the world, that he gave his only-begotten Son, that whosoever believeth in him should not perish, but have everlasting life.

Come unto me, all ye that labor and are heavy laden, and I will give you rest.

After which the minister and people may say:

Lift up your hearts.

We lift them up unto the Lord.

Let us give thanks unto the Lord.

It is meet and right so to do.

Then the minister, still kneeling and facing the Lord's Table, shall say:

It is very meet, right, and our bounden duty that we should at all times and in all places give thanks unto thee, O Lord, holy Father, almighty, everlasting God.

Then shall be said or sung:

Therefore with angels and archangels, and with all the company of heaven, we laud and magnify thy glorious name, evermore praising thee, and saying: Holy, holy, holy, Lord God of hosts, heaven and earth are full of thy glory. Glory be to thee, O Lord most high! Amen.

Then shall the minister offer the prayer of consecration:

Almighty God, our heavenly Father, who of thy tender mercy didst give thine only Son Jesus Christ to suffer death upon the cross for our redemption; who made there, by the one offering of himself, a full, perfect, and sufficient sacrifice for the sins of the whole world; and did institute, and in his holy gospel command us to continue, this memorial of his precious death: hear us, O merciful Father, we most humbly beseech thee, and grant that we, receiving this bread and wine, according to thy Son our Saviour Jesus Christ's holy institution, in remembrance of his death and passion, may also be partakers of the divine nature through him, who in the same night that he was betrayed took bread; [3] and when he had given thanks, he brake it, and gave it to his disciples, saying, Take, eat; this is my body, which is given for you; do this in remembrance of me. Likewise

---

[3] Here may the minister take the plate in his hands.

after supper he took the cup; [4] and when he had given thanks, he gave it to them, saying, Drink ye all of this; for this is my blood of the new covenant which is shed for you, and for many, for the remission of sins; do this, as oft as ye shall drink it, in remembrance of me. **Amen.**

Then shall the minister, kneeling before the Lord's Table, unite with the people in this prayer:

We do not presume to come to this thy table, O merciful Lord, trusting in our own righteousness, but in thy manifold and great mercies. We are not worthy so much as to gather up the crumbs under thy table. But thou art the same Lord, whose mercy is unfailing. Grant us therefore, gracious Lord, so to partake of these memorials of thy Son Jesus Christ, that we may be filled with the fullness of his life, may grow into his likeness, and may evermore dwell in him, and he in us. Amen.

Then shall the minister first receive the Holy Communion in both kinds himself, after which he shall proceed to deliver the same to other ministers in like manner, if any be present. After this, the minister shall administer the Holy Communion to the people, while they are devoutly kneeling.

Before giving the bread, the minister shall say:

Jesus said, "This is my body, which is given for you." Take and eat this in remembrance that Christ died for you, and feed on him in your heart by faith, with thanksgiving.

Likewise before giving the cup he shall say:

Jesus said, "This cup is the new covenant in my blood, which is shed for you." Drink this in remembrance that Christ died for you, and be thankful.

When all have communed, the minister shall place upon the Lord's Table what remains of the consecrated elements, covering the same with the linen cloth.

Then shall the minister and people say:

O Lord, our heavenly Father, we, thy humble servants, desire thy fatherly goodness mercifully to accept this our sacrifice of praise and thanksgiving; most humbly beseeching thee to grant that, by the merits and death

---

[4] Here may the minister take the cup in his hands.

of thy Son Jesus Christ, and through faith in his blood, we and thy whole Church may obtain forgiveness of our sins, and all other benefits of his passion. And here we offer and present unto thee, O Lord, ourselves, our souls and bodies, to be a reasonable, holy, and living sacrifice unto thee; humbly beseeching thee that all we who are partakers of this Holy Communion may be filled with thy grace and heavenly benediction. And although we be unworthy, through our manifold sins, to offer unto thee any sacrifice, yet we beseech thee to accept this our bounden duty and service; not weighing our merits, but pardoning our offenses; through Jesus Christ our Lord, by whom, and with whom, in the unity of the Holy Spirit, all honor and glory be unto thee, O Father Almighty, world without end. Amen.

Then shall be said or sung the Gloria in Excelsis, *the people standing:*

Glory be to God on high, and on earth peace, good will toward men. We praise thee, we bless thee, we worship thee, we glorify thee, we give thanks to thee for thy great glory, O Lord God, heavenly King, God the Father Almighty!

O Lord, the only-begotten Son Jesus Christ; O Lord God, Lamb of God, Son of the Father, that takest away the sins of the world, have mercy upon us. Thou that takest away the sins of the world, have mercy upon us. Thou that takest away the sins of the world, receive our prayer. Thou that sittest at the right hand of God the Father, have mercy upon us. For thou only art holy; thou only art the Lord; thou only, O Christ, with the Holy Ghost, art most high in the glory of God the Father. Amen.

Then shall the minister let the people depart with this blessing:

The peace of God, which passeth all understanding, keep your hearts and minds in the knowledge and love of God, and of his Son Jesus Christ our Lord; and the blessing of God Almighty, the Father, the Son, and the Holy Spirit, be among you, and remain with you always. **Amen.**

¶ 1909. AN ORDER FOR THE ADMINISTRATION OF THE SACRAMENT OF THE LORD'S SUPPER OR HOLY COMMUNION II

The Lord's Table should have upon it a fair linen cloth.

Let the pure, unfermented juice of the grape be used.

It is our custom to receive the Sacrament of the Lord's Supper kneeling, but if persons so desire, they may receive the elements while seated or standing.

Upon entering the church let the communicants bow in prayer and in the spirit of prayer and meditation approach the blessed Sacrament.

The minister shall read one or more of these sentences, during the reading of which the stewards shall take up the offering for the needy.

Let your light so shine before men, that they may see your good works, and glorify your Father which is in heaven.

Lay not up for yourselves treasures upon earth, where moth and rust doth corrupt, and where thieves break through and steal: but lay up for yourselves treasures in heaven, where neither moth nor rust doth corrupt, and where thieves do not break through nor steal.

Whatsoever ye would that men should do to you, do ye even so to them: for this is the law and the prophets.

Not everyone that saith unto me, Lord, Lord, shall enter into the kingdom of heaven; but he that doeth the will of my Father which is in heaven.

Zacchaeus stood, and said unto the Lord; Behold, Lord, the half of my goods I give to the poor; and if I have taken anything from any man by false accusation, I restore him fourfold.

He which soweth sparingly shall reap also sparingly; and he which soweth bountifully shall reap also bountifully. Every man according as he purposeth in his heart, so let him give; not grudgingly, or of necessity: for God loveth a cheerful giver.

As we have therefore opportunity, let us do good unto all men, especially unto them who are of the household of faith.

Godliness with contentment is great gain. For we

brought nothing into this world, and it is certain we can carry nothing out.

Charge them that are rich in this world, that they be ready to distribute, willing to communicate; laying up in store for themselves a good foundation against the time to come, that they may lay hold on eternal life.

God is not unrighteous to forget your work and labor of love, which ye have showed toward his name, in that ye have ministered to the saints, and do minister.

To do good and to communicate forget not: for with such sacrifices God is well pleased.

Whoso hath this world's good, and seeth his brother have need, and shutteth up his bowels of compassion from him, how dwelleth the love of God in him?

He that hath pity upon the poor lendeth unto the LORD; and that which he hath given will he pay him again.

Blessed is he that considereth the poor: the LORD will deliver him in time of trouble.

Then shall the minister read this invitation:

Ye that do truly and earnestly repent of your sins, and are in love and charity with your neighbors, and intend to lead a new life, following the commandments of God, and walking from henceforth in his holy ways; draw near with faith, and take this holy Sacrament to your comfort; and make your humble confession to Almighty God, meekly kneeling upon your knees.

Then shall this general confession be made by the minister and all those who are minded to receive the Holy Communion, both he and they humbly kneeling, and saying:

Almighty God, Father of our Lord Jesus Christ, Maker of all things, Judge of all men; we acknowledge and bewail our manifold sins and wickedness, which we from time to time most grievously have committed, by thought, word, and deed, against thy divine majesty, provoking most justly thy wrath and indignation against us. We do earnestly repent, and are heartily sorry for these our misdoings; the remembrance of them is grievous unto us. Have mercy upon us, have mercy upon us, most merciful Father; for thy Son our Lord

Jesus Christ's sake, forgive us all that is past; and grant that we may ever hereafter serve and please thee in newness of life, to the honor and glory of thy name; through Jesus Christ our Lord. Amen.

Then shall the minister say:

O Almighty God, our heavenly Father, who of thy great mercy hast promised forgiveness of sins to all them that with hearty repentance and true faith turn to thee; have mercy upon us; pardon and deliver us from all our sins; confirm and strengthen us in all goodness; and bring us to everlasting life; through Jesus Christ our Lord. **Amen.**

The Collect

Almighty God, unto whom all hearts are open, all desires known, and from whom no secrets are hid; cleanse the thoughts of our hearts by the inspiration of thy Holy Spirit, that we may perfectly love thee, and worthily magnify thy holy name; through Christ our Lord. Amen.

Then shall the minister say:

It is very meet, right, and our bounden duty, that we should at all times and in all places give thanks unto thee, O Lord, holy Father, almighty, everlasting God.

Therefore with angels and archangels, and with all the company of heaven, we laud and magnify thy glorious name, evermore praising thee, and saying: Holy, holy, holy, Lord God of hosts, heaven and earth are full of thy glory. Glory be to thee, O Lord most high! Amen.

Then shall the minister say:

We do not presume to come to this thy table, O merciful Lord, trusting in our own righteousness, but in thy manifold and great mercies. We are not worthy so much as to gather up the crumbs under thy table. But thou art the same Lord whose property is always to have mercy. Grant us therefore, gracious Lord, so to eat the flesh of thy Son Jesus Christ, and to drink his blood, that our sinful souls and bodies may be made clean by his death, and washed through his most precious blood, and that we may evermore dwell in him, and he in us. **Amen.**

Then the minister shall say the prayer of consecration as followeth:

Almighty God, our heavenly Father, who of thy tender mercy didst give thine only Son Jesus Christ to suffer death upon the cross for our redemption; who made there (by his oblation of himself once offered) a full, perfect, and sufficient sacrifice, oblation, and satisfaction for the sins of the whole world; and did institute, and in his holy gospel command us to continue, a perpetual memory of his precious death until his coming again: hear us, O merciful Father, we most humbly beseech thee, and grant that we, receiving these thy creatures of bread and wine, according to thy Son our Saviour Jesus Christ's holy institution, in remembrance of his death and passion, may be partakers of his most blessed body and blood; who in the same night that he was betrayed took bread; and when he had given thanks, he brake it, and gave it to his disciples, saying, Take, eat; this is my body, which is given for you; do this in remembrance of me. Likewise after supper he took the cup; and when he had given thanks, he gave it to them, saying, Drink ye all of this; for this is my blood of the New Testament, which is shed for you, and for many, for the remission of sins; do this, as oft as ye shall drink it, in remembrance of me. **Amen.**

Then shall the minister first receive the Holy Communion in both kinds himself, and then proceed to deliver the same to the other ministers in like manner, if any be present.

Then shall he say the Lord's Prayer, the people still kneeling and repeating after him every petition:

Our Father who art in heaven, hallowed be thy name; thy kingdom come; thy will be done on earth as it is in heaven. Give us this day our daily bread. And forgive us our trespasses, as we forgive those who trespass against us. And lead us not into temptation, but deliver us from evil. For thine is the kingdom, and the power, and the glory, forever. Amen.

Then a hymn may be sung, and the communicants shall be invited to the Lord's Table. The minister shall deliver both kinds to the people into their hands.

When he delivereth the bread, he shall say:

The body of our Lord Jesus Christ, which was given for *thee*, preserve *thy soul* and *body* unto everlasting life. Take and eat this in remembrance that Christ died for *thee*, and feed on him in *thy heart* by faith with thanksgiving.

And the minister that delivereth the cup shall say:

The blood of our Lord Jesus Christ, which was shed for *thee*, preserve *thy soul* and *body* unto everlasting life. Drink this in remembrance that Christ's blood was shed for *thee*, and be thankful.

When all have communed, the minister shall return to the Lord's Table, and place upon it what remaineth of the consecrated elements, covering the same with a fair linen cloth.

Then shall the minister and people say:

O Lord, our heavenly Father, we, thy humble servants, desire thy fatherly goodness mercifully to accept this our sacrifice of praise and thanksgiving; most humbly beseeching thee to grant that, by the merits and death of thy Son Jesus Christ, and through faith in his blood, we and thy whole Church may obtain remission of our sins, and all other benefits of his passion. And here we offer and present unto thee, O Lord, ourselves, our souls and bodies, to be a reasonable, holy, and lively sacrifice unto thee; humbly beseeching thee that all we who are partakers of this Holy Communion may be filled with thy grace and heavenly benediction. And although we be unworthy, through our manifold sins, to offer unto thee any sacrifice, yet we beseech thee to accept this our bounden duty and service; not weighing our merits, but pardoning our offenses; through Jesus Christ our Lord; by whom, and with whom, in the unity of the Holy Spirit, all honor and glory be unto thee, O Father Almighty, world without end. Amen.

Then may be said or sung:

Glory be to God on high, and on earth peace, good will toward men. We praise thee, we bless thee, we worship thee, we glorify thee, we give thanks to thee for thy great glory, O Lord God, heavenly King, God the Father Almighty!

O Lord, the only-begotten Son Jesus Christ; O Lord God, Lamb of God, Son of the Father, that takest away the sins of the world, have mercy upon us. Thou that takest away the sins of the world, have mercy upon us. Thou that takest away the sins of the world, receive our prayer. Thou that sittest at the right hand of God the Father, have mercy upon us. For thou only art holy; thou only art the Lord; thou only, O Christ, with the Holy Ghost, art most high in the glory of God the Father. Amen.

Then the minister, if he see it expedient, may offer an extempore prayer; and afterward shall let the people depart with this blessing:

The peace of God, which passeth all understanding, keep your hearts and minds in the knowledge and love of God, and of his Son Jesus Christ our Lord; and the blessing of God Almighty, the Father, the Son, and the Holy Spirit, be among you, and remain with you always. **Amen.**

Baptism

Let every adult person, and the parents of every child to be baptized, have the choice of sprinkling, pouring, or immersion.

It is proper and desirable that this Sacrament should not only be accompanied by prayer, admonition, and the reading of Scripture, as herein provided, but that it should be administered in the presence of the people, and most suitably in the house of God.

¶ 1910. THE ORDER FOR THE BAPTISM OF INFANTS

Dearly beloved, forasmuch as all men are heirs of life eternal and subjects of the saving grace of the Holy Spirit; and that our Saviour Christ saith, Suffer the little children to come unto me, and forbid them not, for of such is the kingdom of God; I beseech you to call upon God the Father, through our Lord Jesus Christ, that of his bounteous goodness he will grant unto *this child*, now to be baptized, the continual replenishing of his grace that *he* become *a* worthy *member* of Christ's holy Church.

Then shall the minister say:

Let us pray.

Almighty and everliving God, we beseech thee that of thine infinite goodness thou wilt look upon *this child* and grant that by the aid of thy Holy Spirit *he* may be steadfast in faith, joyful through hope, and rooted in love, and that *he* may so live the life which now is, that *he* may enter triumphantly the life which is to come; through Jesus Christ our Lord. **Amen.**

Then shall the minister address the parents or sponsors as follows:

Dearly beloved, forasmuch as *this child is* now presented by you for Christian Baptism, and *is* thus consecrated to God and to his Church, it is your part and duty to see that *he* be taught, as soon as *he* shall be able to learn, the meaning and purpose of this holy Sacrament; that *he* be instructed in the principles of our holy faith and the nature of the Christian life; that *he* shall be trained to give reverent and regular attendance upon the public and private worship of God and the teaching of the Holy Scripture; and that in every way, by precept and example, you shall seek to lead *him* into the love of God and the service of our Lord Jesus Christ.

Do you solemnly promise to fulfill these duties so far as in you lies, the Lord being your helper?

We do.

Then shall the people stand, and the minister shall say:

Hear the words of the Gospel written by St. Mark:

And they brought young children to him, that he should touch them: and his disciples rebuked those that brought them. But when Jesus saw it, he was much displeased, and said unto them, Let the little children come unto me, and forbid them not: for of such is the kingdom of God. Verily I say unto you, Whosoever shall not receive the kingdom of God as a little child, he shall not enter therein. And he took them up in his arms, put his hands upon them, and blessed them.

Then shall the minister, who may here take the child in his arms, say to the parents or sponsors:

What name shall be given to this child?

And then, repeating the name, he shall baptize the child, saying:

N., I baptize thee in the name of the Father, and of the Son, and of the Holy Spirit. **Amen.**

Then shall the minister say:

Let us pray.

O God, our heavenly Father, grant that *this child*, as *he grows* in years, may also grow in grace and knowledge of the Lord Jesus Christ, and that by the restraining and renewing influence of thy Holy Spirit *he* may ever be *a true child of thine*, serving thee faithfully all *his* days, through Jesus Christ our Lord. **Amen.**

Almighty God, fount of all love and wisdom, source of all power; so guide and uphold the parents [or sponsors] of *this child* that, by loving care, wise counsel, and holy example, they may lead *him* into that life of faith whose strength is righteousness and whose fruit is everlasting joy and peace; through Jesus Christ our Lord. **Amen.**

Or the minister may offer extempore prayer.

Then may the minister and the people say:

Our Father who art in heaven, hallowed be thy name; thy kingdom come; thy will be done on earth as it is in heaven. Give us this day our daily bread. And forgive us our trespasses, as we forgive those who trespass against us. And lead us not into temptation, but deliver us from evil. For thine is the kingdom, and the power, and the glory, forever. Amen.

Then may be sung a hymn, such as:

406—"Friend of the home: as when in Galilee."
407—"See Israel's gentle Shepherd stand."
440—"I think when I read."

Then may the minister say:

Now unto him that is able to keep you from falling, and to present you faultless before the presence of his glory with exceeding joy, to the only wise God our Saviour, be glory and majesty, dominion and power, now and evermore. **Amen.**

¶ 1911. THE ORDER FOR THE BAPTISM OF CHILDREN AND YOUTH

The minister, coming to the font, shall say:

Hear the words of the gospel written by St. Matthew, in the twenty-eighth chapter, beginning at the sixteenth verse.

Then the eleven disciples went away into Galilee, into a mountain where Jesus had appointed them. And when they saw him, they worshiped him; but some doubted. And Jesus came and spake unto them, saying, All power is given unto me in heaven and in earth. Go ye therefore, and make disciples of all nations, baptizing them in the name of the Father, and of the Son, and of the Holy Spirit: teaching them to observe all things whatsoever I have commanded you: and lo, I am with you always, even unto the end of the world. **Amen.**

Then shall the minister say:

Let us pray.

Almighty and everliving God, whose most dearly beloved Son Jesus Christ gave himself for our salvation, and did command his disciples that they should go teach all nations, and baptize them in the name of the Father, and of the Son, and of the Holy Spirit; regard, we beseech thee, the supplications of thy congregation; and grant that *these persons* now to be baptized may so open *their hearts* to thee that *they* may receive the fullness of thy grace, and may ever remain in the number of thy faithful children; through Jesus Christ our Lord. **Amen.**

Then the minister shall say to the persons to be baptized:

Well beloved, who are come hither, desiring to receive holy Baptism, you have heard how the congregation hath

542

prayed that God would assist you to open your *hearts* to his love and direction, that you may be faithful *disciples* of our Lord.

Wherefore, for your part, it is needful that in the presence of Almighty God, and the hearing of this congregation, you should now make known your purpose to accept the obligations of this holy Sacrament by answering the following questions:

Will you faithfully put away from you every known sin, of thought, word, or deed, and accept and confess Jesus Christ as your Saviour and Lord?

God helping me, I will.

Will you diligently study the Bible as God's Holy Word, and in all things strive to make it the rule of your life?

God helping me, I will.

Having been taught how the Spirit of our Lord separates right from wrong, will you faithfully endeavor to live so as to be pleasing unto him?

God helping me, I will.

Will you be baptized in this faith?

This is my desire.

Then shall the minister ask each person his name, and shall baptize him, saying:

N., I baptize thee in the name of the Father, and of the Son, and of the Holy Spirit. **Amen.**

Here the minister shall offer an extempore prayer.

¶ 1912. THE ORDER FOR THE BAPTISM OF ADULTS

The minister, addressing the people, shall say:

Dearly beloved, forasmuch as our Saviour Jesus Christ sent forth his disciples to teach all nations and baptize them in the name of the Father, and of the Son, and of the Holy Spirit, and wherefore *these persons come* now to be baptized, I beseech you to call upon God the Father that of his bounteous goodness he will grant unto *them* the renewing power of the Holy Spirit and enable *them* by divine grace to attain unto the fullness of salvation in Jesus Christ our Lord.

Let us pray.

Almighty and immortal God, the aid of all that need, the helper of all that flee to thee for succor, the life of them that believe, and the resurrection of the dead; we call upon thee for *these persons* now to be baptized. May *they* be filled with thy Holy Spirit and may *they* find in thee *their* refuge, *their* strength, *their* wisdom, and *their* joy. May *they* be faithful to thee all the days of *their* life and finally come to the eternal kingdom which thou hast promised; through Jesus Christ our Lord. **Amen.**

Then may the minister read one or more of the following lessons:

Peter said unto them, Repent, and be baptized every one of you in the name of Jesus Christ for the remission of sins, and ye shall receive the gift of the Holy Spirit. For the promise is unto you, and to your children, and to all that are afar off, even as many as the Lord our God shall call. And with many other words did he testify and exhort, saying, Save yourselves from this untoward generation. Then they that gladly received his word were baptized: and the same day there were added unto them about three thousand souls. And they continued steadfastly in the apostles' doctrine and fellowship, and in the breaking of bread, and in prayers.

And it came to pass, that, while Apollos was at Corinth, Paul having passed through the upper coasts came to Ephesus: and finding certain disciples, he said unto them, Have ye received the Holy Spirit since ye believed? And they said unto him, We have not so much as heard whether there be any Holy Spirit. And he said unto them, Unto what then were ye baptized? And they said, Unto John's baptism. Then said Paul, John verily baptized with the baptism of repentance, saying unto the people that they should believe on him which should come after him, that is, on Christ Jesus. When they heard this, they were baptized in the name of the Lord Jesus. And when

Paul had laid his hands upon them, the Holy Spirit came on them.

There was a man of the Pharisees, named Nicodemus, a ruler of the Jews; the same came to Jesus by night, and said unto him, Rabbi, we know that thou art a teacher come from God: for no man can do these miracles that thou doest, except God be with him. Jesus answered and said unto him, Verily, verily, I say unto thee, Except a man be born again, he cannot see the kingdom of God. Nicodemus saith unto him, How can a man be born when he is old? can he enter the second time into his mother's womb, and be born? Jesus answered, Verily, verily, I say unto thee, Except a man be born of water and of the Spirit, he cannot enter into the kingdom of God. That which is born of the flesh is flesh; and that which is born of the Spirit is spirit. Marvel not that I said unto thee, Ye must be born again. The wind bloweth where it listeth, and thou hearest the sound thereof, but canst not tell whence it cometh, and whither it goeth: so is every one that is born of the Spirit.

For this cause I bow my knees unto the Father of our Lord Jesus Christ, of whom the whole family of heaven and earth is named, that he would grant you, according to the riches of his glory, to be strengthened with might by his Spirit in the inner man; that Christ may dwell in your hearts by faith; that ye, being rooted and grounded in love, may be able to comprehend with all saints what is the breadth, and length, and depth, and height; and to know the love of Christ, which passeth knowledge, that ye might be filled with all the fullness of God.

Then shall the minister say to the persons to be baptized:

Dearly beloved, who have come hither desiring to receive holy Baptism, the congregation gives thanks to God for your coming, and prays that the Holy Spirit may dwell within you, and that your faith may not fail. In the hearing of this congregation you should now make known your purpose to accept the obligations of this holy Sacrament.

Do you truly repent of your sins and accept and confess Jesus Christ as your Saviour and Lord?

I do.

Will you earnestly endeavor to keep God's holy will and commandments?

I will.

Do you desire to be baptized in this faith?

I do.

Then shall the minister say:

O merciful God, grant that all sinful affections may die in *these persons*, and that all things belonging to the Spirit may live and grow in *them*. **Amen.**

Almighty, everliving God; regard, we beseech thee, our supplications and grant that *these persons* may receive the fullness of thy grace, and ever remain in the number of thy faithful and beloved children; through Jesus Christ our Lord. **Amen.**

Then the minister, asking the name of each person, shall baptize him, repeating the name and saying:

N., I baptize thee in the name of the Father, and of the Son, and of the Holy Spirit. **Amen.**

Then may the minister offer extempore prayer. Then may the minister and the people say:

Our Father who art in heaven, hallowed be thy name; thy kingdom come; thy will be done on earth as it is in heaven. Give us this day our daily bread. And forgive us our trespasses, as we forgive those who trespass against us. And lead us not into temptation, but deliver us from evil. For thine is the kingdom, and the power, and the glory, forever. Amen.

Then may be sung one or more stanzas of a hymn, such as:
223—"Blessed Master, I have promised."
226—"O Jesus, I have promised."
257—"My gracious Lord, I own thy right."

Then may the minister say:

Now unto him that is able to keep you from falling, and to present you faultless before the presence of his glory with exceeding joy, to the only wise God our Saviour, be glory and majesty, dominion and power, now and evermore. **Amen.**

¶ 1913. THE ORDER FOR RECEIVING PERSONS AS PREPARATORY MEMBERS

[The use of this form is optional.]

Those who are to be received as preparatory members shall be called forward by name, and the minister, addressing the people, shall say:

Dearly beloved, that none may be admitted hastily into the Church, we receive persons who seek fellowship with us into a preparatory membership, in which they may be properly instructed, and also give proof, both to themselves and to the Church, of the sincerity and depth of their convictions and of the strength and purpose to lead a new life.

Then, addressing the persons seeking admission as preparatory members, the minister shall say:

Beloved in the Lord, you have by the grace of God made your decision to follow Christ and to serve him. Your confidence in so doing is not to be based on any notion of fitness or worthiness in *yourselves*, but on the gracious promise of God, through our Lord Jesus Christ, who loved us and gave himself for us.

That the Church may know your purpose, you will answer the following questions:

Have you an earnest desire to be saved from your sins?

I have.

Will you guard yourself against all things contrary to the teachings of God's Word, and endeavor to lead a holy life, following the commandments of God?

I will.

Will you give reverent attendance upon the private and public worship of God and the teaching of the Word?

I will.

Then shall the minister say:

On behalf of the Church, and in the hope that you will go forward to complete membership therein, I give you cordial welcome.

Then may the minister offer extempore prayer.

547

¶ 1914. THE ORDER FOR RECEIVING PERSONS INTO THE CHURCH

On the day appointed, all that are to be received into the Church shall be called forward, and the minister, addressing the people, shall say:

Dearly beloved, the Church is of God, and will be preserved to the end of time, for the promotion of his worship and the due administration of his word and ordinances, the maintenance of Christian fellowship and discipline, the edification of believers, and the conversion of the world. All, of every age and station, stand in need of the means of grace which it alone supplies.

Into this holy fellowship the *persons* before you, who *have* received the Sacrament of Baptism, who *have* learned the nature of these privileges and these duties, and who *have* also been instructed in the teachings and the aims of The Methodist Church, *come* seeking admission. We now propose in the fear of God to question *them* as to *their* faith and purpose, that you may know that *they are* proper *persons* to be admitted into this church.

Then, addressing those seeking admission, the minister shall say:

Beloved in the Lord, you are come hither seeking union with the Church of God. We rejoice that you are minded to undertake the privileges and the duties of membership in the Church. Before you are fully admitted thereto, you should here publicly renew your vows, confess your faith, and declare your purpose, by answering the following questions:

Do you here in the presence of God and this congregation renew the solemn promise and vow that was made at your baptism?

I do.

Do you confess Jesus Christ as your Saviour and Lord and pledge your allegiance to his Kingdom?

I do.

Do you receive and profess the Christian faith as contained in the New Testament of our Lord Jesus Christ?

I do.

Will you be loyal to The Methodist Church, and uphold it by your attendance, your prayers, your gifts, and your service?

I will.

Then those to be received shall kneel, and the minister, who may lay his hands upon the head of every one severally, shall say:

N., the Lord defend thee with his heavenly grace and by his Spirit confirm thee in the faith and fellowship of all true disciples of Jesus Christ. **Amen.**

Here the following form may be used:

Those being received shall rise, and the minister, addressing the people, shall say:

Brethren, I commend to your love and care *these persons* whom we this day recognize as members of the Church of Christ. What is your mind to them?

Whereupon the people shall say:

We rejoice to recognize you as *members* of the Church of Christ, and bid you welcome to all its privileges. Your peace, joy, and welfare are now our own. With you we renew our pledge to God and this church. The Lord bless *you*, and keep *you*: the Lord make his face shine upon *you*, and be gracious unto *you*: the Lord lift up his countenance upon *you*, and give *you* peace. Amen.

Or the following alternative form may be used:

The minister shall say to the candidates:

We rejoice to recognize you as *members* of the Church of Christ, and bid you welcome to all its privileges; and in token of our brotherly love we give you the right hand of fellowship, and pray that you may be numbered with his people here, and with his saints in glory everlasting.

And the minister shall say to the congregation:

Brethren, I commend to your love and care *these persons* whom we this day recognize as *members* of the

Church of Christ. Do all in your power to increase *their* faith, confirm *their* hope, and perfect *them* in love.

Then may be sung one or more stanzas of a hymn, such as:
    379—*"I love thy Kingdom, Lord."*
    380—*"Jesus, with thy Church abide."*
    383—*"How lovely is thy dwelling place."*

Then may the minister say:

The blessing of God Almighty, the Father, the Son, and the Holy Spirit, be among you, and remain with you always. **Amen.**

¶ 1915. THE ORDER FOR RECEIVING CHILDREN AND YOUTH INTO THE CHURCH

After the minister previously shall have formed the children into a class (baptizing any whose baptism may have been delayed or neglected), and shall have instructed them in the things necessary for them to know as to doctrines and rules of the Church, he shall cause them to be conveniently placed before the congregation, and after inviting their parents and teachers to stand with them on either hand, he shall say:

Brethren of the household of faith, let our hearts be lifted up in thanksgiving to Almighty God, who by the Holy Spirit hath inclined *these children*[5] to desire and ask for membership in the Church. As *they have* arrived at the years of discretion, and now of *their* own accord *appear* before this congregation to take upon *themselves* the vows and enter upon the privileges and duties of the Church, let us with one mind and heart most earnestly invoke in *their* behalf the blessings of Father, Son, and Holy Spirit.

Then shall the minister say:

Let us pray.

Almighty and everliving God, giver of every good and perfect gift; accept our hearty thanks for the *children* whom thou hast committed to our love and care. As thou

---

[5] The minister may use the words "youth" or "young people" at his discretion in place of the word "children" here and at other appropriate places in this order.

didst bring *them* into the world, now renew in thy servants, *their* parents, pastors, and teachers, wisdom to train *them* in the way *they* should go. Grant unto *these* thy *children* that from this day forth *they* may grow in grace, and wisdom, and in favor with God and man; through Jesus Christ our Lord. **Amen.**

Then shall the minister address the parents or sponsors:

Dearly beloved, let this be to you a day of peculiar joy and thanksgiving, in that *these* who *are* your own *have* also entered into a holier spiritual kinship with you in Jesus Christ. While the Church will continue to share with you the duty and privilege of bringing up *these children* in the nurture and admonition of the Lord, it renews its solemn injunction to you, by God's help, faithfully to continue both to teach and to train *them*, by example and precept, in the way of the Lord. Will you accept this duty, in the fear and favor of God, and here and now, in the presence of Almighty God and this congregation, renew the vows made by you in the baptism of *these children?*

With God's help, I will.

Then shall the minister address the children who are candidates and say:

Beloved *children*, our Lord Jesus, by his holy Word, hath expressly given to everyone who believes in him a place in his Kingdom and Church. Before you are admitted into the Church, it becomes my duty to inquire of you as to your purpose of mind and heart:

Do you, *each of you*, believe in God as your heavenly Father?

I do.

Do you accept Jesus Christ as your personal Saviour?

I do.

Do you believe in the Bible as God's holy Word?

I do.

Will you be loyal to The Methodist Church and uphold

it by your attendance, your prayers, your gifts, and your service?

I will.

Here the minister may offer an extempore prayer. Then those to be received shall kneel, and the minister, laying his hands upon every one of them severally, shall say:

I receive you into the Church of Christ and pray God to confirm you in the faith and fellowship of all true disciples of Jesus Christ. **Amen.**

Then shall the minister, the people, and the children say:

Our Father who art in heaven, hallowed be thy name; thy kingdom come; thy will be done on earth as it is in heaven. Give us this day our daily bread. And forgive us our trespasses, as we forgive those who trespass against us. And lead us not into temptation, but deliver us from evil. For thine is the kingdom, and the power, and the glory, forever. Amen.

¶ 1916. THE ORDER FOR RECEIVING MEMBERS BY TRANSFER OR ON REAFFIRMATION OF FAITH OR IN AFFILIATE MEMBERSHIP

The minister shall say:

The following *persons present certificates* of transfer commending *them* to the fellowship of this church: [names].

The following *persons* who *have* been *members* of the Church *desire* to present *themselves* for reaffirmation of *their* faith and reception into the fellowship of this church: [names].

The following *persons*, while retaining *their* membership in *other churches, are* to be welcomed as *affiliate members* in the fellowship of this church: [names].

The *persons* named will now present *themselves* for public reception into the fellowship of this church.

When they come forward, the minister shall say:

Dearly beloved, you have already confessed your faith in Christ, and given *yourselves* to the service of God. As

552

you come to join this church, will you renew your vows previously taken, and will you labor and pray for its up-building, and live with this people of God in Christian fellowship?

I will.

The members of this church bid you welcome, and on their behalf I give you the right hand of fellowship. We pray that, as all of us are united in faith and brotherhood, we may grow into the likeness of Christ, being fruitful in every good work and increasing in the knowledge of God; through Jesus Christ our Lord.

The LORD bless *you*, and keep *you:* the LORD make his face shine upon *you*, and be gracious unto *you:* the LORD lift up his countenance upon *you*, and give *you peace*. **Amen.**

¶ 1917. THE ORDER FOR THE SOLEMNIZATION OF MATRIMONY

At the time appointed, the persons to be married—having been qualified according to the law of the state and the standards of the church—standing together facing the minister, the man at the minister's left hand and the woman at the right, the minister shall say:

Dearly beloved, we are gathered here in the sight of God, and in the presence of these witnesses, to join together this man and this woman in holy matrimony; which is an honorable estate, instituted of God, and signifying unto us the mystical union which exists between Christ and his Church; which holy estate Christ adorned and beautified with his presence in Cana of Galilee. It is therefore not to be entered into unadvisedly, but reverently, discreetly, and in the fear of God. Into this holy estate these two persons come now to be joined.

Speaking to the persons to be married, the minister shall say:

I require and charge you both, as you stand in the presence of God, to remember that love and loyalty alone will avail as the foundation of a happy and enduring home. No other human ties are more tender, no other vows more sacred than those you now assume. If these solemn vows be kept inviolate, and if steadfastly you endeavor to do the will of your heavenly Father, your life will be full of joy, and the home which you are establishing will abide in peace.

Then shall the minister say to the man, using his Christian name:

N., wilt thou have this woman to be thy wedded wife, to live together in the holy estate of matrimony? Wilt thou love her, comfort her, honor and keep her, in sickness and in health; and forsaking all other keep thee only unto her, so long as ye both shall live?

The man shall answer:

I will.

Then shall the minister say to the woman, using her Christian name:

N., wilt thou have this man to be thy wedded husband, to live together in the holy estate of matrimony? Wilt thou love him, comfort him, honor and keep him, in sickness and in health; and forsaking all other keep thee only unto him, so long as ye both shall live?

The woman shall answer:

I will.

Then may the minister say:

Who giveth this woman to be married to this man?

The father of the woman, or whoever giveth her in marriage, shall answer:

I do.

Then the minister (receiving the hand of the woman from her father or other sponsor) shall cause the man with his right hand to take the woman by her right hand, and say after him:

I, N., take thee, N., to be my wedded wife, to have and to hold, from this day forward, for better, for worse, for richer, for poorer, in sickness and in health, to love and to cherish, till death us do part, according to God's holy ordinance; and thereto I plight thee my faith.

Then shall they loose their hands; and the woman, with her right hand taking the man by his right hand, shall say after the minister:

I, *N.*, take thee, *N.*, to be my wedded husband, to have and to hold, from this day forward, for better, for worse, for richer, for poorer, in sickness and in health, to love and to cherish, till death us do part, according to God's holy ordinance; and thereto I plight thee my faith.

Then shall they again loose their hands; and they may give unto each other rings, or the man may give unto the woman a ring, on this wise: The minister, taking the ring or rings, shall say:

The wedding ring is an outward and visible sign of an inward and spiritual grace, signifying unto all the uniting of this man and this woman in holy matrimony, through the Church of Jesus Christ our Lord.

Then the minister may say:

Let us pray.

Bless, O Lord, the giving of these rings, that they who wear them may abide forever in thy peace, and continue in thy favor; through Jesus Christ our Lord. **Amen.**

Or, if there be but one ring, the minister may say:

Bless, O Lord, the giving of this ring, that he who gives it and she who wears it may abide forever in thy peace, and continue in thy favor; through Jesus Christ our Lord. **Amen.**

The minister shall then deliver the proper ring to the man to put upon the third finger of the woman's left hand. The man, holding the ring there, shall say after the minister:

In token and pledge of the vow between us made, with this ring I thee wed; in the name of the Father, and of the Son, and of the Holy Spirit. Amen.

Then, if there be a second ring, the minister shall deliver it to the woman to put upon the third finger of the man's left hand; and the woman, holding the ring there, shall say after the minister:

In token and pledge of the vow between us made, with this ring I thee wed; in the name of the Father, and of the Son, and of the Holy Spirit. Amen.

Then shall the minister say:

Let us pray.

O eternal God, creator and preserver of all mankind, giver of all spiritual grace, the author of everlasting life; send thy blessing upon this man and this woman, whom we bless in thy name; that they may surely perform and keep the vow and covenant between them made, and may ever remain in perfect love and peace together, and live according to thy laws.

Look graciously upon them, that they may love, honor, and cherish each other, and so live together in faithfulness and patience, in wisdom and true godliness, that their home may be a haven of blessing and a place of peace; through Jesus Christ our Lord. **Amen.**

Then shall the minister join their right hands together and with his hand on their united hands shall say:

Forasmuch as *N.* and *N.* have consented together in holy wedlock, and have witnessed the same before God and this company, and thereto have pledged their faith each to the other, and have declared the same by joining hands (and by giving and receiving *rings*); I pronounce that they are husband and wife together, in the name of the Father, and of the Son, and of the Holy Spirit. Those whom God hath joined together, let not man put asunder. **Amen.**

Then, the husband and wife kneeling, the minister shall say:

Let us pray.

Our Father who art in heaven, hallowed be thy name; thy kingdom come; thy will be done on earth as it is in heaven. Give us this day our daily bread. And forgive us our trespasses, as we forgive those who trespass against us. And lead us not into temptation, but deliver us from evil. For thine is the kingdom, and the power, and the glory, forever. Amen.

Then shall the minister add this blessing:

God the Father, the Son, and the Holy Spirit, bless, preserve, and keep you; the Lord graciously with his favor look upon you, and so fill you with all spiritual benediction and love that you may so live together in this life that in the world to come you may have life everlasting. **Amen.**

¶ 1918. THE ORDER FOR THE BURIAL OF THE DEAD

The minister shall begin the service by reading one or more of the following sentences:

Jesus said, I am the resurrection, and the life: he that believeth in me, though he were dead, yet shall he live: and whosoever liveth and believeth in me shall never die.

The eternal God is thy refuge, and underneath are the everlasting arms.

The Lord is my light and my salvation; whom shall I fear? the Lord is the strength of my life; of whom shall I be afraid?

The righteous live forever, and the care of them is with the most High: with his right hand he shall cover them, and with his arm shall he shield them.

For we know that if our earthly house of this tabernacle were dissolved, we have a building of God, an house not made with hands, eternal in the heavens.

Then shall the minister say:

Let us pray.

Here may the minister offer one or both of the following prayers, ending with the Lord's Prayer.

Almighty God, fount of all life; thou art our refuge and strength; thou art our help in trouble. Enable us, we pray thee, to put our trust in thee, that we may obtain comfort, and find grace to help in this and every time of need; through Jesus Christ our Lord. **Amen.**

Almighty God, our Father, from whom we come, and unto whom our spirits return; thou hast been our dwelling place in all generations. Thou art our refuge and strength, a very present help in trouble. Grant us thy blessing in this hour, and enable us so to put our trust in thee that our spirits may grow calm and our hearts be comforted. Lift our eyes beyond the shadows of earth, and help us to see the light of eternity. So may we find grace and strength for this and every time of need; through Jesus Christ our Lord. **Amen.**

Our Father who art in heaven, hallowed be thy name; thy kingdom come; thy will be done on earth as it is in heaven. Give us this day our daily bread. And forgive us our trespasses, as we forgive those who trespass against us. And lead us not into temptation, but deliver us from evil. For thine is the kingdom, and the power, and the glory, forever. Amen.

Here may be read one or more of these lessons from the Old Testament:

The LORD is my shepherd; I shall not want.

He maketh me to lie down in green pastures: he leadeth me beside the still waters.

He restoreth my soul: he leadeth me in the paths of righteousness for his name's sake.

Yea, though I walk through the valley of the shadow of death, I will fear no evil: for thou art with me; thy rod and thy staff they comfort me.

Thou preparest a table before me in the presence of mine enemies: thou anointest my head with oil; my cup runneth over.

Surely goodness and mercy shall follow me all the days of my life: and I will dwell in the house of the LORD forever.

LORD, thou hast been our dwelling place in all generations.

Before the mountains were brought forth, or ever thou hadst formed the earth and the world, even from everlasting to everlasting, thou art God.

For a thousand years in thy sight are but as yesterday when it is past, and as a watch in the night.

Thou carriest them away as with a flood; they are as a sleep: in the morning they are like grass which groweth up.

In the morning it flourisheth, and groweth up; in the evening it is cut down, and withereth.

So teach us to number our days, that we may apply our hearts unto wisdom.

Let thy work appear unto thy servants, and thy glory unto their children.

And let the beauty of the LORD our God be upon us; and establish thou the work of our hands upon us; yea, the work of our hands establish thou it.

I will lift up mine eyes unto the hills, from whence cometh my help.

My help cometh from the LORD, who made heaven and earth.

He will not suffer thy foot to be moved: he that keepeth thee will not slumber.

Behold, he that keepeth Israel will neither slumber nor sleep.

The LORD is thy keeper: the LORD is thy shade upon thy right hand.

The LORD shall preserve thy going out and thy coming in from this time forth, and even for evermore.

The LORD is my light and my salvation; whom shall I fear? The LORD is the strength of my life; of whom shall I be afraid?

Though an host should encamp against me, my heart shall not fear; though war should rise against me, in this will I be confident.

For in the time of trouble he shall hide me in his pavilion: in the secret of his tabernacle shall he hide me; he shall set me up upon a rock.

Teach me thy way, O LORD, and lead me in a plain path.

I had fainted, unless I had believed to see the goodness of the LORD in the land of the living.

Wait on the LORD: be of good courage, and he shall strengthen thine heart: wait, I say, on the LORD.

Here may be said or sung the Gloria Patri:

Glory be to the Father, and to the Son, and to the Holy Ghost; as it was in the beginning, is now, and ever shall be, world without end. Amen.

Here shall be read one or more of these lessons from the New Testament:

Let not your heart be troubled: ye believe in God, believe also in me. In my Father's house are many mansions: if it were not so, I would have told you. I go to prepare a place for you. And if I go and prepare a place for you, I will come again, and receive you unto myself; that where I am, there ye may be also. I am the way, the truth, and the life. If ye love me, keep my commandments. And I will pray the Father, and he shall give you another Comforter, that he may abide with you forever; even the Spirit of truth; whom the world cannot receive, because it seeth him not, neither knoweth him; but ye know him; for he dwelleth with you, and shall be in you. I will not leave you comfortless: I will come to you. Because I live, ye shall live also.

Peace I leave with you, my peace I give unto you: not as the world giveth, give I unto you. Let not your heart be troubled, neither let it be afraid.

As many as are led by the Spirit of God, they are the sons of God. For ye have not received the spirit of bondage again to fear; but ye have received the Spirit of adoption, whereby we cry, Abba, Father. The Spirit itself beareth witness with our spirit, that we are the children of God: and if children, then heirs; heirs of God, and joint heirs with Christ; if so be that we suffer with him, that we may be also glorified together.

For I reckon that the sufferings of this present time are not worthy to be compared with the glory which shall be revealed in us.

And we know that all things work together for good to them that love God.

What shall we then say to these things? If God be for us, who can be against us? Who shall separate us from the love of Christ? shall tribulation, or distress, or persecution, or famine, or nakedness, or peril, or sword? Nay, in all these things we are more than conquerors through him that loved us. For I am persuaded, that neither death, nor life, nor angels, nor principalities, nor powers, nor things present, nor things to come, nor height, nor depth, nor any other creature, shall be able to separate us from the love of God, which is in Christ Jesus our Lord.

Now is Christ risen from the dead, and become the firstfruits of them that slept.

But some man will say, How are the dead raised up? and with what body do they come? Thou fool, that which thou sowest is not quickened, except it die: but God giveth it a body as it hath pleased him.

So also is the resurrection of the dead. It is sown in corruption; it is raised in incorruption.

It is sown in dishonor; it is raised in glory: it is sown in weakness; it is raised in power.

It is sown a natural body; it is raised a spiritual body. There is a natural body, and there is a spiritual body.

And as we have borne the image of the earthy, we shall also bear the image of the heavenly.

For this corruptible must put on incorruption, and this mortal must put on immortality. So when this corruptible shall have put on incorruption, and this mortal shall have put on immortality, then shall be brought to pass the saying that is written, Death is swallowed up in victory. O death, where is thy sting? O grave, where is thy victory? The sting of death is sin; and the strength of sin is the law. But thanks be to God, who giveth us the victory, through our Lord Jesus Christ. Therefore, my beloved brethren, be ye steadfast, unmovable, always abounding in the work of the Lord, forasmuch as ye know that your labor is not in vain in the Lord.

And I John saw the holy city, new Jerusalem, coming down from God out of heaven, prepared as a bride adorned for her husband. And I heard a great voice out of heaven saying, Behold, the tabernacle of God is with men, and he will dwell with them, and they shall be his people, and God himself shall be with them, and be their God. And God shall wipe away all tears from their eyes; and there shall be no more death, neither sorrow, nor crying; neither shall there be any more pain; for the former things are passed away.

And he showed me a pure river of water of life, clear as crystal, proceeding out of the throne of God and of the Lamb. In the midst of the street of it, and on either side of the river, was there the tree of life, which bare twelve manners of fruits, and yielded her fruit every month: and the leaves of the tree were for the healing of the nations. And there shall be no more curse: but the throne of God and of the Lamb shall be in it; and his servants shall serve him: and they shall see his face; and his name shall be in their foreheads. And there shall be no night there; and they need no candle, neither light of the sun; for the Lord God giveth them light: and they shall reign for ever and ever.

For this cause I bow my knees unto the Father of our Lord Jesus Christ, of whom the whole family in heaven and earth is named, that he would grant you, according to the riches of his glory, to be strengthened with might by his Spirit in the inner man; that Christ may dwell in your hearts by faith; that ye, being rooted and grounded in love, may be able to comprehend with all saints what is the breadth, and length, and depth, and height; and to know the love of Christ, which passeth knowledge, that ye might be filled with all the fullness of God. Now unto him that is able to do exceeding abundantly above all that we ask or think, according to the power that worketh in us, unto him be glory in the church by Christ Jesus throughout all ages, world without end. **Amen.**

Here may follow music and an address, closing with extempore prayer, or one of the following prayers:

Eternal God, who committest to us the swift and solemn trust of life; since we know not what a day may bring forth, but only that the hour for serving thee is always present, may we wake to the instant claims of thy holy will, not waiting for tomorrow, but yielding today. Consecrate with thy presence the way our feet may go; and the humblest work will shine, and the roughest places be made plain. Lift us above unrighteous anger and mistrust into faith and hope and love by a simple and steadfast reliance on thy sure will. In all things draw us to the mind of Christ, that thy lost image may be traced again, and that thou mayest own us as at one with him and thee. **Amen.**

O God, who art the strength of thy saints, and who redeemest the souls of thy servants; we bless thy name for all those who have died in the Lord, and who now rest from their labors, having received the end of their faith, even the salvation of their souls. Especially we call to remembrance thy lovingkindness and thy tender mercies to this thy servant. For all thy goodness that withheld not *his* portion in the joys of this earthly life, and for thy guiding hand along the way of *his* pilgrimage, we give thee thanks and praise. Especially we bless thee for thy grace that kindled in *his* heart the love of thy dear name, that enabled *him* to fight the good fight, to endure unto the end, and to obtain the victory, yea, to become more than conqueror, through him that loveth us. We magnify thy holy name that, *his* trials and temptations being ended, sickness and death being passed, with all the dangers and difficulties of this mortal life, *his* spirit is at home in thy presence, with whom dwelleth eternal peace. And grant, O Lord, we beseech thee, that we who rejoice in the triumph of thy saints may profit by their example, that, becoming followers of their faith and patience, we also may enter with them into an inheritance incorruptible and undefiled, and that fadeth not away; through Jesus Christ our Lord. **Amen.**

O God, the Lord of life, the Conqueror of death, our help in every time of trouble, who dost not willingly grieve or afflict the children of men; comfort us who mourn, and give us grace, in the presence of death, to worship thee, that we may have sure hope of eternal life and be enabled to put our whole trust in thy goodness and mercy; through Jesus Christ our Lord. **Amen.**

Father of spirits, we have joy at this time in all who have faithfully lived, and in all who have peacefully died. We thank thee for all fair memories and all living hopes; for the sacred ties that bind us to the unseen world; for the dear and holy dead who compass us as a cloud of witnesses, and make the distant heaven a home to our hearts. May we be followers of those who now inherit the promises; through Jesus Christ our Lord. **Amen.**

O Lord and Master, who thyself didst weep beside the grave, and art touched with the feeling of our sorrows; fulfill now thy promise that thou wilt not leave thy people comfortless, but wilt come to them. Reveal thyself unto thy sorrowing servants, and cause them to hear thee say, I am the resurrection, and the life. Help them, O Lord, to turn to thee with true discernment, and to abide in thee through living faith, that, finding now the comfort of thy presence, they may have also a sure confidence in thee for all that is to come; until the day break, and the shadows flee away. Hear us for thy great mercy's sake, O Jesus Christ our Lord. **Amen.**

O Thou who hast ordered this wondrous world, and who knowest all things in earth and heaven; so fill our hearts with trust in thee that, by night and by day, at all times and in all seasons, we may without fear commit those who are dear to us to thy never-failing love for this life and the life to come. **Amen.**

O Lord, we pray thee, give us thy strength, that we may live more bravely and faithfully for the sake of those who are no longer with us here upon earth; and grant us so to serve thee day by day that we may find eternal fellowship with them; through him who died and rose again for us all, Jesus Christ our Lord. **Amen.**

Almighty God, who art leading us through the changes of time to the rest and blessedness of eternity; be thou near to comfort and uphold. Make us to know and feel that thy children are precious in thy sight, that they live evermore with thee, and that thy mercy endureth forever. Thankful for the life which thou hast given us for these seasons, we pray thy help now to resign it obediently unto thee. Assist us to return to the scenes of our daily life, to obey thy will with patience, and to bear our trials with fortitude and hope. And when the peace of death falls upon us, may we find our perfect rest in thee; through Jesus Christ our Lord. **Amen.**

Then may the minister say:

The LORD bless you, and keep you: the LORD make his face shine upon you, and be gracious unto you: the LORD lift up his countenance upon you, and give you peace. **Amen.**

At the grave when the people are assembled, the minister shall say:

Our help is in the name of the LORD, who made heaven and earth.

Like as a father pitieth his children, so the LORD pietieth them that fear him.

Say to them that are of a fearful heart, Be strong, fear not: behold, your God will come and save you.

The mercy of the LORD is from everlasting to everlasting upon them that fear him, and his righteousness unto children's children.

Then the minister may say:

Forasmuch as the spirit of the departed has entered into the life immortal, we therefore commit *his* body to its resting place, but *his* spirit we commend to God, remembering how Jesus said upon the cross, "Father, into thy hands I commend my spirit."

Or the minister may say:

Forasmuch as Almighty God hath received unto himself the soul of our departed *brother*, we therefore tenderly commit *his* body to the ground, in the blessed hope that as *he* hath borne the image of the earthly so also *he* shall bear the image of the heavenly.

Or the minister may say:

Forasmuch as the spirit of the departed hath returned to God who gave it, we therefore commit *his* body to the ground, earth to earth, ashes to ashes, dust to dust; looking for the general resurrection in the last day, and the life of the world to come, through our Lord Jesus Christ; at whose coming in glorious majesty to judge the world, the earth and the sea shall give up their dead; and the corruptible bodies of those who sleep in him shall be changed and made like unto his own glorious body; according to the mighty working whereby he is able to subdue all things unto himself.

Then may be said:

I heard a voice from heaven, saying unto me:

Blessed are the dead who die in the Lord from henceforth: Yea, saith the Spirit, that they may rest from their labors; and their works do follow them.

> Lord, have mercy upon us.
> **Christ, have mercy upon us.**
> Lord, have mercy upon us.

Here may the minister and people unite in the Lord's Prayer:

Our Father who art in heaven, hallowed be thy name; thy kingdom come; thy will be done on earth as it is in heaven. Give us this day our daily bread. And forgive us our trespasses, as we forgive those who trespass against us. And lead us not into temptation, but deliver us from evil. For thine is the kingdom, and the power, and the glory, forever. Amen.

Then the minister may say one or more of the following prayers:

Almighty God, with whom do live the spirits of those who depart hence in the Lord, and with whom the souls of the faithful after death are in strength and gladness; we give thee hearty thanks for the good examples of all those thy servants who, having finished their course in faith, do now rest from their labor. And we beseech thee that we, with all those who have finished their course in faith, may have our perfect consummation and bliss in thy eternal and everlasting glory; through Jesus Christ our Lord. **Amen.**

O merciful God, the Father of our Lord Jesus Christ, who is the resurrection and the life, in whom whosoever believeth shall live, though he died, and whosoever liveth and believeth in him shall not die eternally; we meekly beseech thee, O Father, to raise us from the death of sin unto the life of righteousness, that when we shall depart this life we may rest in him, and may receive that blessing which thy well-beloved Son shall pronounce to all that love and fear thee, saying, Come, ye blessed of my Father, receive the kingdom prepared for you from the foundation of the world. Grant this, we beseech thee, O merciful Father, through Jesus Christ our Mediator and Redeemer. **Amen.**

O God of infinite compassion, who art the comforter of thy children; look down in thy tender love and pity, we beseech thee, upon thy servants. In the stillness of our hearts we entreat for them thy sustaining grace. Be thou their stay, their strength, and their shield, that trusting in thee they may know thy presence near, and in the assurance of thy love be delivered out of their distresses; through Jesus Christ our Lord. **Amen.**[6]

Then may the minister say:

The grace of the Lord Jesus Christ, and the love of God, and the communion of the Holy Spirit, be with you all. **Amen.**

¶ 1919. THE ORDER FOR THE BURIAL OF A CHILD

The minister shall begin the service by reading the following sentences:

Jesus said, I am the resurrection, and the life: he that believeth in me, though he were dead, yet shall he live: and whosoever liveth and believeth in me shall never die.

He shall feed his flock like a shepherd: he shall gather the lambs with his arm, and carry them in his bosom.

Blessed are the pure in heart: for they shall see God.

Then shall the minister say:

Let us pray.

Here may the minister offer one or both of the following prayers:

Our heavenly Father, look upon us in our sorrow, and abide with us in our loneliness. O thou who makest no

---

[6] Adapted by permission from *The Book of Common Order* (1932) of the United Church of Canada.

life in vain, and who lovest all that thou hast made, lift
upon us the light of thy countenance and give us peace;
through Jesus Christ our Lord. **Amen.**

O God our Father, we pray that thou wilt keep in
tender love the life which we shall hold in blessed memory. Help us who continue here to serve thee with con-
stancy, trusting in thy promise of eternal life, that hereafter we may be united with thy blessed children in
glory everlasting; through Jesus Christ our Lord. **Amen.**

Here may be read:

The LORD is my shepherd; I shall not want.

He maketh me to lie down in green pastures: he leadeth
me beside the still waters.

He restoreth my soul: he leadeth me in the paths of
righteousness for his name's sake.

Yea, though I walk through the valley of the shadow of
death, I will fear no evil: for thou art with me; thy rod
and thy staff, they comfort me.

Thou preparest a table before me in the presence of
mine enemies: thou anointest my head with oil; my cup
runneth over.

Surely goodness and mercy shall follow me all the
days of my life: and I will dwell in the house of the
LORD forever.

I will lift up mine eyes unto the hills; from whence
cometh my help.

My help cometh from the LORD, who made heaven
and earth.

He will not suffer thy foot to be moved: he that keepeth thee will not slumber.

Behold, he that keepeth Israel shall neither slumber
nor sleep.

The LORD is thy keeper: the LORD is thy shade upon
thy right hand.

The LORD shall preserve thy going out and thy coming
in from this time forth, and even for evermore.

Here shall be read these lessons from the Gospel:

At the same time came the disciples unto Jesus, saying, Who is the greatest in the kingdom of heaven? And Jesus called a little child unto him, and set him in the midst of them, and said, Verily I say unto you, Except ye be converted, and become as little children, ye shall not enter into the kingdom of heaven. Whosoever therefore shall humble himself as this little child, the same is the greatest in the kingdom of heaven. And whoso shall receive one such little child in my name receiveth me.

Take heed that ye despise not one of these little ones; for I say unto you, That in heaven their angels do always behold the face of my Father which is in heaven.

Let not your heart be troubled: ye believe in God, believe also in me. In my Father's house are many mansions: if it were not so, I would have told you. I go to prepare a place for you. And if I go and prepare a place for you, I will come again, and receive you unto myself; that where I am, there ye may be also. I am the way, the truth, and the life. If ye love me, keep my commandments. And I will pray the Father, and he shall give you another Comforter, that he may abide with you forever; even the Spirit of truth; whom the world cannot receive, because it seeth him not, neither knoweth him; but ye know him; for he dwelleth with you, and shall be in you. I will not leave you comfortless: I will come to you. Because I live, ye shall live also.

Peace I leave with you, my peace I give unto you: not as the world giveth, give I unto you. Let not your heart be troubled, neither let it be afraid.

Here may follow music and an address, after which the minister shall say:

Let us pray.

Here may the minister offer extempore prayer or one or more of the following prayers:

O God, who art the Father of the families of the earth; look with compassion upon this bereaved family, and pour thy heavenly comfort into their hearts. Help them by faith to see this child, over whom they grieve, safe in that home where sin and sorrow cannot enter. Enrich with thy presence those who mourn; abide in their home;

lift up their hearts; bless them with thy favor, which is better than life; and so guide them through the trials and temptations of this world that their reunited family may know fulness of joy in thy presence for evermore. Grant this through him who loved little children and blessed them, even thy Son Jesus Christ our Lord. **Amen.**

O merciful Father, whose face the angels of thy little ones do always behold in heaven; grant us steadfastly to believe that this thy child hath been taken into the safe keeping of thine eternal love; through Jesus Christ our Lord. **Amen.**

O God, who healest the broken in heart, and bindest up their wounds; look down in tender pity and compassion upon thy servants whose joy has been turned into mourning. Leave them not comfortless, but grant that they may be drawn closer to one another by their common sorrow. As thou hast given them this new tie to bind them to the world unseen, so grant unto them that where their treasure is, there may their hearts be also. Fill their souls with the light and comfort of thy presence. Grant unto them such a vision of that life wherein all mysteries shall be revealed, and all tears be wiped away, that they may be able to endure as seeing thee who art invisible. So dwell with them and be their God, until the day break and the shadows flee away; through Jesus Christ our Lord. **Amen.**

Then may the minister say:

The LORD bless you, and keep you; the LORD make his face shine upon you, and be gracious unto you: the LORD lift up his countenance upon you, and give you peace. **Amen.**

At the grave, when the people are assembled, the minister shall say:

Jesus saith to his disciples, Ye now therefore have sorrow: but I will see you again, and your heart shall rejoice, and your joy no man taketh from you.

Forasmuch as the departed has entered into the life immortal, we therefore commit *his* body to its resting place, but *his* spirit we commend to God, remembering how Jesus said upon the cross, "Father, into thy hands I commend my spirit."

Then shall the minister say:

Almighty God, Father of our Lord Jesus Christ, who gave his life for our redemption, and who promised the Holy Spirit, the Comforter; strengthen, we beseech thee, the faith of these bereaved ones, that they may contemplate with peace the blessedness of that eternal home which thou hast prepared for all who love and serve thee. Grant that they, and all others whose joy is turned into mourning, cleaving more closely unto him who is the resurrection and the life, may be led by thy spirit through this uncertain life, till the day break and the shadows flee away. **Amen.**

O God, whose most dear Son did take little children into his arms and bless them; give us grace, we beseech thee, to entrust the soul of this child to thy never-failing care and love, and bring us all to thy heavenly kingdom; through the same thy Son, Jesus Christ our Lord. **Amen.**

Almighty God, Father of mercies and giver of all comfort; deal graciously, we pray thee, with all those who mourn; that, casting every care on thee, they may know the consolation of thy love; through Jesus Christ our Lord. **Amen.**

Here the minister and the people may unite in the Lord's Prayer:

Our Father who art in heaven, hallowed be thy name; thy kingdom come; thy will be done on earth as it is in heaven. Give us this day our daily bread. And forgive us our trespasses, as we forgive those who trespass against us. And lead us not into temptation, but deliver us from evil. For thine is the kingdom, and the power, and the glory, forever. Amen.

Then may the minister say:

The grace of the Lord Jesus Christ, and the love of God, and the communion of the Holy Spirit, be with you all. **Amen.**

¶ 1920. THE ORDER FOR THE ORDINATION OF DEACONS

When the day appointed by the bishop is come, there shall be a sermon or exhortation declaring the duty and office of such as come to be admitted deacons, how necessary that order is in the Church of Christ, and also how the people ought to esteem them in their office; after which one of the elders shall present unto the bishop all who are to be ordained, and say:

I present unto you *these persons* **present to be ordained** *deacons:* [names].

Their names having been read aloud, the bishop shall say to the people:

Brethren, *these are they* whom we purpose, God willing, this day to ordain *deacons.* For, after due examination, we find that *they are* lawfully called to this office and ministry and that *they are persons* meet for the same. But if there be any of you who knoweth any valid reason for which *any one of them* ought not to be received into this holy ministry, let him come forth in the name of God, and disclose what the impediment is.

If any impediment be alleged, the bishop shall desist from ordaining that person until he shall be found to be innocent.

Then shall be read the Collect:

Almighty God, who by thy divine providence hast appointed divers orders of ministers in thy Church, and didst inspire thine apostles to choose into the order of deacons thy first martyr, St. Stephen, with others; mercifully behold *these thy servants*, now called to the like office and administration; so replenish *them* with the truth of thy doctrine, and adorn *them* with innocency of life, that by both word and good example *they* may faithfully serve thee in this office, to the glory of thy name and the edification of thy Church; through the merits of our Saviour Jesus Christ, who liveth and reigneth with thee and the Holy Spirit, now and forever. **Amen.**

Then shall be read the Epistle:

Likewise must the deacons be grave, holding the mystery of the faith in a pure conscience. They that have used the office of a deacon well purchase to themselves a good degree, and great boldness in the faith which is in Christ Jesus.

See then that ye walk circumspectly, not as fools, but as wise. Wherefore be ye not unwise, but understanding what the will of the Lord is. Giving thanks always for all things unto God and the Father in the name of our Lord Jesus Christ; submitting yourselves one to another in the fear of God. Finally, my brethren, be strong in the Lord, and in the power of his might. Put on the whole armor of God, that ye may be able to stand against the wiles of the devil. For we wrestle not against flesh and blood, but against principalities, against powers, against the rulers of the darkness of this world, against spiritual wickedness in high places. Wherefore take unto you the whole armor of God, that ye may be able to withstand in the evil day, and having done all, to stand. Stand therefore, having your loins girt about with truth, and having on the breastplate of righteousness; and your feet shod with the preparation of the gospel of peace; above all, taking the shield of faith, wherewith ye shall be able to quench all the fiery darts of the wicked. And take the helmet of salvation, and the sword of the Spirit, which is the word of God; praying always with all prayer and supplication in the Spirit, and watching thereunto with all perseverance and supplication for all saints.

Then shall the bishop, in the presence of the people, examine every one of those to be ordained, after this manner:

Do you trust that you are inwardly moved by the Holy Spirit to take upon you the office of the ministry in the Church of Christ, to serve God for the promoting of his glory and the edifying of his people?

I trust so.

Do you unfeignedly believe the Scriptures of the Old and New Testaments?

I do believe them.

Will you diligently read and expound the same unto the people whom you shall be appointed to serve?

I will.

573

It appertaineth to the office of a deacon to conduct divine worship and to assist the elder when he ministereth the Holy Communion, to help him in the distribution thereof; to read and expound the Holy Scriptures; to instruct the youth; and to baptize. And, furthermore, it is his office to search for the needy, that they may be visited and relieved. Will you do this gladly and willingly?

I will so do, by the help of God.

Will you apply all your diligence to frame and fashion your own *lives* and the lives of your *families* according to the teachings of Christ?

I will, the Lord being my helper.

Will you reverently heed them to whom the charge over you is committed, following with a glad mind and will their godly admonitions?

I will so do.

Then those to be ordained shall kneel, and the bishop, laying his hands severally upon the head of every one of them, shall say:

Take thou authority to execute the office of a deacon in the Church of God; in the name of the Father, and of the Son, and of the Holy Spirit. **Amen.**

Then shall the bishop deliver to every one of them the Bible, saying:

Take thou authority to read the Holy Scriptures in the Church of God, and to preach the Word. **Amen.**

Then shall the bishop, or one appointed by him, read the Gospel:

Let your loins be girded about, and your lights burning; and ye yourselves like unto men that wait for their lord, when he will return from the wedding; that when he cometh and knocketh, they may open unto him immediately. Blessed are those servants, whom the lord when he cometh shall find watching: verily I say unto you, that he shall gird himself, and make them to sit down to meat, and will come forth and serve them. And if he shall come in the second watch, or come in the third watch, and find them so, blessed are those servants.

Then shall the bishop pray:

Almighty God, giver of all good things, who of thy great goodness hast vouchsafed to accept *these* thy *servants* into the office of deacon in thy Church; make *them*, we beseech thee, O Lord, to be modest, humble, and constant in *their* ministration, and to have a ready will to observe all spiritual discipline; that *they*, continuing ever stable and strong in thy Son Jesus Christ, may so well behave *themselves* in this office that *they* may be found worthy to be called into the higher ministry in thy Church; through thy Son our Saviour Jesus Christ, to whom be glory and honor, world without end. **Amen.**

Direct us, O Lord, in all our doings, with thy most gracious favor, and further us with thy continual help, that in all our works, begun, continued, and ended in thee, we may glorify thy holy name, and finally, by thy mercy, obtain everlasting life; through Jesus Christ our Lord. **Amen.**

Then may the bishop say:

The peace of God, which passeth all understanding, keep your hearts and minds in the knowledge and love of God, and of his Son Jesus Christ our Lord; and the blessing of God Almighty, the Father, the Son, and the Holy Spirit, be among you, and remain with you always. **Amen.**

¶ 1921. THE ORDER FOR THE ORDINATION OF ELDERS

When the day appointed by the bishop is come, there shall be a sermon of exhortation declaring the duty and office of such as come to be admitted elders, how necessary that order is in the Church of Christ, and also how the people ought to esteem them in their office; after which one of the elders shall present unto the bishop all who are to be ordained, and say:

I present unto you *these persons* **present to be ordained** *elders:* [names].

Their names having been read aloud, the bishop shall say to the people:

Brethren, *these are they* whom we purpose, God willing, this day to ordain *elders.* For, after due inquiry, we find that *they are* lawfully called to this office and ministry, and that *they are persons* meet for the same. But if there be any of you who knoweth any valid reason for which *any one of them* ought not to be received into this holy ministry, let him come forth in the name of God, and disclose what the impediment is.

If any impediment be alleged, the bishop shall desist from ordaining that person until he shall be found to be innocent.

Then shall be read the Collect:

Almighty God, giver of all good things, who by thy Holy Spirit hast appointed divers orders of ministers in thy Church; mercifully behold *these* thy *servants*, now called to the office of elder, and so replenish *them* with the truth of thy doctrine, and adorn *them* with innocency of life, that by both word and good example *they* may faithfully serve thee in this office, to the glory of thy name and the advancement of thy Church; through the merits of our Saviour Jesus Christ, who liveth and reigneth with thee and the Holy Spirit, world without end. **Amen.**

Then shall be read the Epistle and the Gospel:

I was made a minister, according to the gift of the grace of God given unto me by the effectual working of his power. Unto me, who am less than the least of all saints, is this grace given, that I should preach the unsearchable riches of Christ; and to make all men see what is the fellowship of the mystery, which from the beginning of the world hath been hid in God, who created all things by Jesus Christ. And he gave some, apostles; and some, prophets; and some, evangelists; and some, pastors and teachers; for the perfecting of the saints, for the work of the ministry, for the edifying of the body of Christ: till we all come in the unity of the faith and of the knowledge of the Son of God, unto a perfect man, unto the measure of the stature of the fullness of Christ.

Jesus said, I am the door: by me if any man enter in, he shall be saved, and shall go in and out, and find pasture. The thief cometh not, but for to steal, and to kill, and to destroy: I am come that they might have life, and that they might have it more abundantly. I am the good shepherd: the good shepherd giveth his life for the sheep. But he that is an hireling, and not the shepherd, whose own the sheep are not, seeth the wolf coming, and leaveth the sheep, and fleeth; and the wolf catcheth them, and scattereth the sheep. The hireling fleeth, because he is an hireling, and careth not for the sheep. I am the good shepherd, and know my sheep, and am known of mine. As the Father knoweth me, even so know I the Father: and I lay down my life for the sheep. And other sheep I have, which are not of this fold: them also I must bring, and they shall hear my voice; and there shall be one fold, and one shepherd.

Then shall the bishop say unto the persons to be ordained elders:

Dearly beloved, you have heard of what dignity and of how great importance is this office whereunto you are called. And now again we exhort you, in the name of our Lord Jesus Christ, that you are to be *messengers*, *watchmen*, and *stewards* of the Lord; to teach and to admonish, to feed and provide for the Lord's family; to seek for Christ's sheep that are dispersed abroad, and for his children who are in the midst of this evil world, that they may be saved through Christ forever.

Have always, therefore, in your remembrance how great a treasure is committed to your charge. For they unto whom you are to minister are the sheep of Christ, for whom he gave his life. The Church which you must serve is his Bride and his Body. And if it shall happen the Church, or any member thereof, do take any hurt or hindrance by reason of your negligence, you know the greatness of the fault. Wherefore see that you never cease your labor, your care, and your diligence until you have done all that lieth in you, according to your bounden duty, to bring all such as shall be committed to your charge unto perfectness in Christ.

Forasmuch, then, as your office is both of so great excellency and of so great difficulty, consider how you ought to forsake, as much as you can, all worldly cares, and be studious in learning the Scriptures, and in acquiring such knowledge and skill as may help you to declare the living Word of God.

We hope that you have weighed and pondered these things with *yourselves* long before this time, and that you have clearly determined, by God's grace, to give *yourselves* wholly to this work whereunto it has pleased God to call you. Also that you will continually pray that the Holy Spirit may assist you to order the lives of you and yours after the rule and doctrine of Christ, that you may grow riper and stronger in ministry and be godly and wholesome *examples* for the people to follow.

And now, that this congregation of Christ here assembled may also understand your purpose in these things, and that this your promise may the more move you to perform your duties, you shall answer plainly to these things which we, in the name of God and his Church, shall ask of you touching the same:

Do you believe in your heart that you are truly called, according to the will of our Lord Jesus Christ, to the ministry of elders?

I do so believe.

Are you persuaded that the Holy Scriptures contain all truth required for eternal salvation through faith in Jesus Christ? And are you determined out of the same Holy Scriptures so to instruct the people committed to your charge that they may enter into eternal life?

I am so persuaded and determined, by God's grace.

Will you give faithful diligence duly to minister the doctrine of Christ, the Sacraments, and the discipline of the Church, and in the spirit of Christ to defend the Church against all doctrine contrary to God's Word?

I will so do, by the help of the Lord.

Will you be diligent in prayer, in the reading of the Holy Scriptures, and in such studies as help to the knowledge of God and of his Kingdom?

I will, the Lord being my helper.

Will you apply all your diligence to frame and fashion your own *lives* and the lives of your *families* according to the teachings of Christ?

I will, the Lord being my helper.

Will you maintain and set forward, as much as lieth in you, quietness, peace, and love among all Christian people, and especially among them that shall be committed to your charge?

I will so do, the Lord being my helper.

Will you reverently heed them to whom the charge over you is committed, following with a glad mind and will their godly admonitions?

I will so do.

Then shall the bishop say:

Almighty God, who hath given you this will to do all these things, grant also unto you power to perform the same, that he may accomplish his work which he hath begun in you; through Jesus Christ our Lord. **Amen.**

Then the people shall be requested to make their earnest supplications in silent prayer to God for those who are to be ordained as elders, and silence shall be kept for a space; after which shall be said the Veni, Creator Spiritus, *the bishop beginning, and all others answering as followeth, both the bishop and the people uniting in the final couplet.*

Come, Holy Ghost, our souls inspire,
And lighten with celestial fire.

**Thou the anointing Spirit art,
Who dost thy sevenfold gifts impart.**

Thy blessed unction from above
Is comfort, life, and fire of love.

**Enable with perpetual light
The dullness of our blinded sight.**

Anoint and cheer our soilèd face
With the abundance of thy grace.

**Keep far our foes; give peace at home;
Where thou art Guide, no ill can come.**

Teach us to know the Father, Son,
And thee, of both to be but One;

**That through the ages all along
This may be our endless song:**

Praise to thy eternal merit,
Father, Son, and Holy Spirit. Amen.

Then shall the bishop say:

Let us pray.

Almighty God, our heavenly Father, we bless and magnify thy holy name for the gift of thy most dearly beloved Son Jesus Christ our Redeemer, and for all his apostles, prophets, evangelists, teachers, and pastors, whom he hath sent abroad into the world. For these here present whom thou hast called to the same holy office and ministry, we render unto thee our most hearty thanks. And now, O Lord, we humbly beseech thee to grant that by *these* thy *ministers*, and by those over whom *they* shall be appointed, thy holy name may be forever glorified, and thy blessed Kingdom enlarged; through thy Son Jesus Christ our Lord, who liveth and reigneth with thee in the unity of the Holy Spirit, world without end. **Amen.**

Then shall the bishop and the elders present lay their hands severally upon the head of every one that receiveth the order of elder, the receivers kneeling, and the bishop saying:

The Lord pour upon thee the Holy Spirit for the office and work of an elder in the Church of God, now committed unto thee by the authority of the Church through the imposition of our hands. And be thou a faithful dispenser of the Word of God, and of his holy Sacraments; in the name of the Father, and of the Son, and of the Holy Spirit. **Amen.**

Then shall the bishop deliver to every one of them, kneeling, the Bible into his hands, saying:

Take thou authority as an elder in the Church to preach the Word of God, and to administer the holy Sacraments in the congregation. **Amen.**

Then shall the bishop pray:

Most merciful Father, we beseech thee to send upon *these* thy *servants* thy heavenly blessings, that *they* may be clothed with righteousness, and that thy Word spoken by *them* may never be spoken in vain. Grant also that we may have grace to receive what *they* shall deliver out of thy Word as the means of our salvation, and that in all our words and deeds we may seek thy glory, and the increase of thy Kingdom; through Jesus Christ our Lord. **Amen.**

Direct us, O Lord, in all our doings, with thy most gracious favor, and further us with thy continual help, that in all our works, begun, continued, and ended in thee, we may glorify thy holy name, and finally, by thy mercy, obtain everlasting life; through Jesus Christ our Lord. **Amen.**

Then may the bishop say:

The peace of God, which passeth all understanding, keep your hearts and minds in the knowledge and love of God, and of his Son Jesus Christ our Lord; and the blessing of God Almighty, the Father, the Son, and the Holy Spirit, be among you, and remain with you always. **Amen.**

If on the same day the order for deacon be given to some and that of elder to others, the deacons shall be first presented and then the elders. The Collect shall be said and the Epistle read, immediately after which they who are to be ordained deacons shall be examined and ordained as above described. Then, the Gospel having been read, they who are to be ordained elders shall likewise be examined and ordained, as in this office before appointed.

¶ 1922. THE ORDER FOR THE CONSECRATION OF BISHOPS

When the time appointed for the consecration of bishops is come, the service shall begin with a hymn, after which the Collect shall be read:

Almighty God, who by thy Son Jesus Christ didst give to thy holy apostles, elders, and evangelists many excellent gifts, and didst charge them to feed thy flock; give grace, we beseech thee, to all the ministers and pastors of thy Church, that they may diligently preach thy Word and duly administer the godly discipline thereof; and grant to the people that they may faithfully follow the same, that they may receive the crown of everlasting glory; through Jesus Christ our Lord. **Amen.**

581

Then shall one of the elders read the Epistle:

And from Miletus he sent to Ephesus, and called the elders of the church. And when they were come to him, he said unto them, Ye know, from the first day that I came into Asia, after what manner I have been with you at all seasons, serving the Lord with all humility of mind, and with many tears, and temptations, which befell me: how I kept back nothing that was profitable unto you, but have showed you, and have taught you publicly, and from house to house, testifying both to the Jews, and also to the Greeks, repentance toward God, and faith toward our Lord Jesus Christ. And now, behold, I go bound in the spirit unto Jerusalem, not knowing the things that shall befall me there: save that the Holy Spirit witnesseth in every city, saying that bonds and afflictions abide me. But none of these things move me, neither count I my life dear unto myself, so that I might finish my course with joy, and the ministry, which I have received of the Lord Jesus, to testify the gospel of the grace of God. Take heed therefore unto yourselves, and to all the flock, over which the Holy Spirit hath made you overseers, to feed the church of God, which he hath purchased with his own blood. For I know this, that after my departing shall grievous wolves enter in among you, not sparing the flock. Also of your own selves shall men arise, speaking perverse things, to draw away disciples after them. Therefore watch, and remember, that by the space of three years I ceased not to warn everyone night and day with tears. And now, brethren, I commend you to God, and to the word of his grace, which is able to build you up, and to give you an inheritance among all them which are sanctified.

Then shall another elder read the Gospel:

So when they had dined, Jesus saith to Simon Peter, Simon, son of Jonas, lovest thou me more than these? He saith unto him, Yea, Lord; thou knowest that I love thee. He saith unto him, Feed my lambs. He saith to him again the second time, Simon, son of Jonas, lovest thou me? He saith unto him, Yea, Lord; thou knowest that I love thee. He saith unto him, Feed my sheep. He saith unto him the third time, Simon, son of Jonas, lovest thou me? Peter was grieved because he said unto him the third time, Lovest thou me? And he said unto him, Lord, thou knowest all things; thou knowest that I love thee. Jesus said unto him, Feed my sheep.

And Jesus came and spake unto them, saying, All power is given unto me in heaven and in earth. Go ye therefore, and teach all nations, baptizing them in the name of the Father, and of the Son, and of the Holy Spirit: teaching them to observe all things whatsoever I have commanded you: and, lo, I am with you alway, even unto the end of the world. **Amen.**

Then shall the elected person be presented by two elders unto the bishop, the elders saying:

We present unto you this elder chosen to be consecrated a bishop.

Then shall the bishop call upon the people present to pray, saying:

Dearly beloved, it is written in the Gospel of St. Luke that our Saviour Christ continued the whole night in prayer before he chose and sent forth his twelve apostles. It is also written in the Acts of the Apostles that the disciples who were at Antioch did fast and pray before they laid hands on Paul and Barnabas and sent them forth on their first mission to the Gentiles. Let us therefore, following the example of our Saviour Christ and his apostles, give ourselves to prayer before we admit and send forth *this person* presented to us, to the work whereunto we trust the Holy Spirit hath called *him*.

Then shall the bishop pray:

Almighty God, giver of all good things, who by thy Holy Spirit hast appointed divers offices in thy Church; graciously behold *this* thy *servant* now called to the office and ministry of a bishop. So replenish *him* with the truth of thy doctrine, and so adorn *him* with innocency of life, that by both word and deed *he* may faithfully serve thee in this office, to the glory of thy name and the edifying and well governing of thy Church; through the merits of our Saviour Jesus Christ, who liveth and reigneth with thee and the Holy Spirit, world without end. **Amen.**

Then shall the bishop say to him that is to be consecrated:

Brother, forasmuch as the Holy Scriptures command that we should not be hasty in admitting any person to government in the Church of Christ, before you are admitted to this ministration, you will, in the fear of God, give answer to these questions:

Are you persuaded that you are truly called to this ministration, according to the will of our Lord Jesus Christ?

I am so persuaded.

Are you persuaded that the Holy Scriptures contain sufficiently all truth required for eternal salvation through faith in Jesus Christ? And are you determined out of the same Holy Scriptures so to instruct the people committed to your charge that they may enter into eternal life?

I am so persuaded and determined, by God's grace.

Will you then faithfully exercise *yourself* in the Holy Scriptures, and call upon God through study and prayer for the true understanding of the same?

I will so do, by the help of God.

Are you ready with all faithful diligence to seek and to promote the truth of Christ and to defend the Church against all doctrine contrary to God's Word?

I am ready, the Lord being my helper.

Will you live soberly, righteously, and devoutly in this present world, that you may show *yourself* in all things an example of good works unto others, to the honor and glory of God?

I will so do, the Lord being my helper.

Will you show *yourself* gentle, and be merciful for Christ's sake to poor and needy people, and to all strangers destitute of help?

I will, by the help of God.

Will you maintain and set forward, as much as lieth in you, quietness, love, and peace among all men; and faithfully exercise such discipline in the Church as shall be committed unto you?

I will so do, by the help of God.

Will you be faithful in ordaining and appointing others; and will you ever seek to deal justly and kindly with your brethren of the ministry over whom you are placed as chief pastor?

I will so do, by the help of God.

Then shall the bishop pray:

Almighty God, our heavenly Father, who hath given you a good will to do all these things, grant also unto you wisdom and power to perform the same, that he may accomplish in you the good work which he hath begun, that you may be found blameless; through Jesus Christ our Lord. **Amen.**

Then the people shall be requested to make their earnest supplications in silent prayer to God for those who are to be consecrated as bishops, and silence shall be kept for a space; after which shall be said the Veni, Creator Spiritus, *the bishop beginning, and all others answering as followeth, both the bishop and the people uniting in the final couplet.*

Come, Holy Ghost, our souls inspire,
And lighten with celestial fire.

**Thou the anointing Spirit art,
Who dost thy sevenfold gifts impart.**

Thy blessed unction from above
Is comfort, life, and fire of love.

**Enable with perpetual light
The dullness of our blinded sight.**

Anoint and cheer our soilèd face
With the abundance of thy grace.

**Keep far our foes; give peace at home;
Where thou art Guide, no ill can come.**

Teach us to know the Father, Son,
And thee, of both, to be but One;

**That through the ages all along
This may be our endless song:**

Praise to thy eternal merit,
Father, Son, and Holy Spirit. Amen.

Then shall the bishop say:

Let us pray.

Almighty and most merciful Father, who of thine infinite goodness hath given thine only and dearly beloved Son Jesus Christ to be our Redeemer, and hast made some apostles, some prophets, some evangelists, some pastors and teachers, to the edifying and making perfect of thy Church; grant, we beseech thee, to *this* thy *servant* such grace that *he* may evermore be ready to spread abroad thy gospel, the glad tidings of reconciliation with thee, and to use the authority given *him*, not to destruction, but to salvation; not to hurt, but to help; so that as *a* wise and faithful *servant*, giving to all their portion in due season, *he* may at last be received into everlasting joy; through Jesus Christ our Lord, who, with thee and the Holy Spirit, liveth and reigneth, one God, world without end. **Amen.**

Then the bishops and elders present shall lay their hands upon the head of the elected person kneeling before them, the consecrating bishop saying:

The Lord pour upon thee the Holy Spirit for the office and work of a bishop in the Church of God, now committed unto thee by the authority of the Church through the imposition of our hands, in the name of the Father, and of the Son, and of the Holy Spirit. And remember that thou stir up the grace of God which is in thee; for God hath not given us the spirit of fear, but of power, and of love, and of a sound mind. **Amen.**

Then shall the bishop deliver to him the Bible, saying:

Give heed unto reading, exhortation, and teaching. Think upon the things contained in this Book. Be diligent in them, that the increase coming thereby may be manifest unto all men. Take heed unto thyself and to thy teaching; for by so doing thou shalt save both thyself and them that hear thee. Be to the flock of Christ a shepherd. Hold up the weak, heal the sick, bind up the broken, bring again the outcast, seek the lost; faithfully minister discipline, but forget not mercy; that the Kingdom of God may come upon the earth and, when the Chief Shepherd shall appear, that you may receive the never-fading crown of glory; through Jesus Christ our Lord. **Amen.**

Then shall the bishop pray:

Most merciful Father, we beseech thee to send down upon *this* thy *servant* thy heavenly blessing, and so endue *him* with thy Holy Spirit that *he*, preaching thy word, not only may be earnest to reprove, beseech, and rebuke with all patience and doctrine, but also may be to such as believe a wholesome example in word, in conversation, in love, in faith, in chastity, and in purity; that, faithfully fulfilling *his* course, at the latter day *he* may receive the crown of righteousness laid up by the Lord, the righteous judge, who liveth and reigneth, one God with the Father and the Holy Spirit, world without end. **Amen.**

Direct us, O Lord, in all our doings, with thy most gracious favor, and further us with thy continual help, that in all our works, begun, continued, and ended in thee, we may glorify thy holy name, and finally, by thy mercy, obtain everlasting life; through Jesus Christ our Lord. **Amen.**

Then may the bishop say:

The peace of God, which passeth all understanding, keep your hearts and minds in the knowledge and love of God, and of his Son Jesus Christ our Lord; and the blessing of God Almighty, the Father, the Son, and the Holy Spirit, be among you, and remain with you always. **Amen.**

¶ 1923. AN ORDER FOR LICENSING PERSONS TO PREACH

At the time appointed, those to be licensed shall be presented by their respective pastors, one of whom shall say:

Brethren, *we* present unto you *these persons* to be licensed to preach the gospel of the Lord Jesus Christ: [names].

Their names having been read aloud, the district superintendent shall say:

Take heed that *these persons* whom you present unto us this day *are* fitted in character and skill for this sacred vocation.

Then shall the pastor say:

Their churches have inquired diligently concerning them and have examined them and found them so to be.

The district superintendent shall then say:

Brethren, you have heard the recommendation of *these persons* by *their pastors*. If there be any of you who knows any reason why *any one of them* should not be licensed to preach the gospel, let him arise now and declare the same.

If no impediment be alleged, the district superintendent shall say:

All vocations are sacred in the sight of the Lord, who created all things and sanctified them by the power of his Spirit. Especially precious in his sight is the preaching of his Word.

Then shall the Scripture be read:

Comfort ye, comfort ye my people, saith your God. Speak ye comfortably to Jerusalem, and cry unto her, that her warfare is accomplished, that her iniquity is pardoned: for she hath received of the LORD's hand double for all her sins.

The voice of him that crieth in the wilderness, Prepare ye the way of the LORD, make straight in the desert a highway for our God. Every valley shall be exalted, and every mountain and hill shall be made low: and the crooked shall be made straight, and the rough places plain: and the glory of the LORD shall be revealed, and all flesh shall see it together: for the mouth of the LORD hath spoken it.

The voice said, Cry. And he said, What shall I cry? All flesh is grass, and all the goodliness thereof is as the flower of the field: the grass withereth, the flower fadeth: because the Spirit of the LORD bloweth upon it: surely the people is grass. The grass withereth, the flower fadeth; but the word of our God shall stand for ever.

The district superintendent shall then ask of those being licensed:

Do you believe you are moved by the Holy Spirit to preach the Word of God?

I do.

Will you strive to live a life in keeping with what you preach?

I will.

Then shall the district superintendent say to every one severally:

N., take thou authority to preach the truths of the Old and New Testaments in the Church of God.

Then shall the district superintendent pray:

Almighty God, whose Word is truth, in the keeping of which is eternal life; we thank thee for *these persons* whom this day we set aside in thy name as *preachers* of thy gospel. Prepare *them* in body, mind, and spirit for *their* task, and continue *them* in thy grace, that *they* may increase and bless thy Church through *their* labors; through Jesus Christ our Lord. **Amen.**

Then may the district superintendent say:

The peace of God, which passeth all understanding, keep your hearts and minds in the knowledge and love of God, and of his Son Jesus Christ our Lord; and the blessing of God Almighty, the Father, the Son, and the Holy Spirit, be among you, and remain with you always. **Amen.**

¶ 1924. AN ORDER FOR THE ADMISSION OF CANDIDATES TO MEMBERSHIP IN AN ANNUAL CONFERENCE

This order provides a single service for admitting classes both on trial and into full connection. When it is to be used for only one class, the bishop, following his address or exhortation, may select the portion of the order which concerns this class, then conclude with the prayer of consecration and the benediction.

When the time appointed is come, the bishop shall have those to be admitted seated before him by classes.

HYMN *The people standing.*

CALL TO PRAYER

Bishop: The Lord is nigh unto all them that call upon him in truth.

People: **Our help is in the name of the Lord, who made heaven and earth. Amen.**

INVOCATION *The bishop.*

Let us pray.

Direct us, O Lord, in all our doings, with thy most gracious favor, and further us with thy continual help, that in all our works, begun, continued, and ended in thee, we may glorify thy holy name, and finally, by thy mercy, obtain everlasting life; through Jesus Christ our Lord. **Amen.**

PRAYER FOR UNITY IN FAITH *Here let the people unite with the bishop in prayer.*

O God, who hast joined together divers peoples in the confession of thy name; grant us both to will and to be able to do what thou commandest, that thy people, being called to an eternal inheritance, may hold the same faith in their hearts, and disclose the same godliness in their lives; through Jesus Christ our Lord. Amen.

WORDS OF ASSURANCE *The bishop.*

Who shall ascend into the hill of the LORD? or who shall stand in his holy place? He that hath clean hands and a pure heart; who hath not lifted up his soul unto vanity, nor sworn deceitfully. He shall receive the blessing from the LORD, and righteousness from the God of his salvation. **Amen.**

COLLECT *Here let all the people unite with the bishop in prayer*

Almighty and everlasting God, from whom cometh every good and perfect gift; send down upon all ministers, and upon the people committed to their charge, the inspiration of thy Holy Spirit, that they may give themselves with all their powers unto thee, and so bring forward thy Kingdom of righteousness, peace, and good will; through Jesus Christ our Lord. Amen.

DOXOLOGY

THE LESSON FROM THE OLD TESTAMENT *Joshua 1:5-9.*

GLORIA PATRI *Here let all the people arise and sing.*

THE LESSON FROM THE NEW TESTAMENT *John 10:9-16.*

HYMN OF PRAISE *Which may be followed by an address or exhortation by the bishop.*

THE ADMISSION ON TRIAL *Here the bishop shall cause to stand before him those who are to be admitted on trial, and shall address them as follows:*

Dearly beloved, this is a solemn hour in your life and also a high moment in the proceedings of this conference. You are entering into a glorious fellowship. You are following in the footsteps of those who have sought to spread scriptural holiness through the lands of the earth. There is no calling more sacred than that which you now enter, and there is no privilege more meaningful than that which comes to you through this holy ministry. Before this Annual Conference I ask you:

Is it your purpose, following the leadership of God's Spirit, to give faithful diligence to the work of the ministry?

It is my purpose, with God's help, to give myself fully to the work of the ministry, and to serve God faithfully all my days.

After this the formal vote on admitting the candidates to membership on trial shall be taken.[7] Then those received shall return to their seats.

THE ADMISSION INTO FULL CONNECTION *Here the bishop shall cause to stand before him those who are to be admitted into full connection, and shall address them as follows:*

According to the usage and Discipline of The Methodist Church, you have indicated that you are convinced that you should enter the ministry of Christ's holy Church. You have declared that you are willing to face any sacrifice that may be involved in the consecration of life. You have indicated that you are so situated in life that you can accept the obligations of the itinerant minister. You have affirmed that you will abstain for those

---

[7] *See* Judicial Council Decision 134.

acts which may injure your work and influence as a minister of Christ, and that you will keep before you as the one great objective of your life the advancement of the Kingdom of God. Give heed to the words of the gospel of Christ when he said: "If any man will come after me, let him deny himself, and take up his cross, and follow me."

In accordance with the Discipline of The Methodist Church and the historic usages of our communion, you will in the presence of this conference give answer to the following questions:

(1) Have you faith in Christ?

(2) Are you going on to perfection?

(3) Do you expect to be made perfect in love in this life?

(4) Are you earnestly striving after it?

(5) Are you resolved to devote yourself wholly to God and his work?

(6) Do you know the General Rules of our church?

(7) Will you keep them?

(8) Have you studied the doctrines of The Methodist Church?

(9) After full examination do you believe that our doctrines are in harmony with the Holy Scriptures?

(10) Will you preach and maintain them?

(11) Have you studied our form of church discipline and polity?

(12) Do you approve our church government and polity?

(13) Will you support and maintain them?

(14) Will you diligently instruct the children in every place?

(15) Will you visit from house to house?

(16) Will you recommend fasting or abstinence, by both precept and example?

(17) Are you determined to employ all your time in the work of God?

(18) Are you in debt so as to embarrass you in your work?

(19) Will you observe the following directions?

(*a*) Be diligent. Never be unemployed. Never be triflingly employed. Never trifle away time; neither spend any more time at any one place than is strictly necessary. (b) Be punctual. Do everything exactly at the time. And do not mend our rules; but keep them; not for wrath, but for conscience' sake.

After this the formal vote on admitting the candidates to membership shall be taken. Then shall the bishop say the following or some other prayer of consecration:

THE PRAYER OF CONSECRATION

O God, our heavenly Father, who didst manifest thy love in sending thine only-begotten Son into the world that all might have life through him; pour out thy Spirit upon thy Church, that it may fulfill thy command to preach the gospel to every creature. Send forth, we beseech thee, laborers into thy harvest; fill them with the Holy Spirit, and with faith; defend them in all dangers and temptations; and hasten the time when the fullness of the nations shall be gathered into thy Kingdom; through the grace of Jesus Christ our Lord. **Amen.**

BENEDICTION

¶ 1925. THE ORDER FOR THE CONSECRATION OF DEACONESSES

When the time appointed is come, a sermon or address may be given declaring what is the office and duty of a deaconess; after which one shall present those to be consecrated deaconesses, saying:

I present unto you *these persons* to be consecrated deaconesses.

Then shall the consecrator say to those present:

Dearly beloved, *these are they* whom we purpose this day to consecrate *deaconesses* in the Church of God. After inquiry and examination we discover that *they have* met the stated requirements of the Church, and believe *them* to be worthy and proper *persons* for this office.

Then shall the Scripture be read:

When the Son of man shall come in his glory, and all the holy angels with him, then shall he sit upon the throne of his glory and before him shall be gathered all nations: and he shall separate them one from another, as a shepherd divideth his sheep from the goats; and he shall set the sheep on his right hand, but the goats on the left.

Then shall the King say unto them on his right hand, Come, ye blessed of my Father, inherit the kingdom prepared for you from the foundation of the world; for I was an hungred, and ye gave me meat: I was thirsty, and ye gave me drink: I was a stranger, and ye took me in: naked, and clothed me: I was sick, and ye visited me: I was in prison, and ye came unto me.

Then shall the righteous answer him, saying, Lord, when saw we thee an hungered, and fed thee? or thirsty, and gave thee drink? When saw we thee a stranger, and took thee in? Or naked, and clothed thee? Or when saw we thee sick, or in prison, and came unto thee?

And the King shall answer and say unto them, Verily I say unto you, Inasmuch as ye have done it unto one of the least of these my brethren, ye have done it unto me.

Then shall the consecrator say to those to be deaconesses:

Dearly beloved, we rejoice that in the providence of God you have been led by the Holy Spirit to devote *yourselves* to Christlike service under the direction of the Church of Christ. You are to give *yourselves* to the service of the Lord, going about doing good. You are come as your Master to lead the sick and sinning world to the Saviour. Such service lays upon you solemn responsibility.

Do you believe that you are led of God to engage in this work and to assume the duties of this office?

I do.

Do you in the presence of God and of this congregation promise faithfully to perform the duties of a deaconess in the Church of God?

I do.

Will you be diligent in prayer, in the study of the Holy Scriptures, and in such other devotions as will help you to grow in the knowledge and love of God?

I will.

Will you be guided by the will and direction of those whom the Church may place over you in the doing of your work?

I will.

Then shall those to be consecrated kneel for a brief season of silent prayer, after which shall be said:

O eternal God, the Father of our Lord Jesus Christ, who didst call Phoebe and Dorcas into the service of thy Church; look upon *these* thy *servants* who *are* now to be set apart to the office of deaconess. Give to *them*, we pray thee, such understanding of thy holy gospel, such firmness of Christian purpose, such diligence in service, and such beauty of life in Christ, that *they* may be to all whom *they teach* or *serve* a worthy revelation of the meaning and power of the Christian life. May *they* so order *their* time and nourish *their minds* and *hearts* that *they* may constantly grow in grace and in the knowledge of our Lord Jesus Christ, and may steadily increase in power to lead others unto him.

Grant that *they* may have strength of body, mind, and soul for the fulfillment of thy will in the holy task to which thou hast called *them:* and grant *them* thy Holy Spirit, that *they* may worthily discharge the work committed to *them*, to the blessing of mankind and to the praise of Christ our Saviour. **Amen.**

Then the consecrator, laying his hands upon the head of every one severally, shall say:

I admit thee to the office of deaconess in the Church of God, in the name of the Father, and of the Son, and of the Holy Spirit. **Amen.**

Then may a hymn be sung, the deaconesses and the people standing; after which the people shall be dismissed with this blessing:

May Christ dwell in your hearts by faith; that ye, being rooted and grounded in love, may be able to comprehend with all saints what is the breadth, and length, and depth, and height; and to know the love of Christ, which passeth knowledge, that ye might be filled with all the fullness of God. Now unto him that is able to do exceeding abundantly above all that we ask or think, according to the power that worketh in us, unto him be glory in the church by Christ Jesus throughout all ages, world without end. **Amen.**

¶ 1926. THE ORDER FOR THE CONSECRATION OF DIRECTORS OF CHRISTIAN EDUCATION

It is recommended that this order be used at the time of the report of the Conference Board of Education, or other suitable time approved by the program committee of the Annual Conference, but that it not be used in connection with the conference ordination service.

At the time appointed, the bishop shall declare the office and duty of a director of Christian education, as follows:

Dearly beloved, we rejoice that there is a vocation within the Church for those persons who have been called to serve Christ in the field of Christian education. It is the office of a director of Christian education to assist the pastor in guiding the work of Christian education in the local church. It is the duty of a director of Christian education, through personal endeavor and through the service of others, to lead the people to Christ, to inform them of the way of Christ, and to guide their growing understanding of how to live as Christians.

Then the chairman of the Conference Board of Education shall present those to be consecrated, saying:

I present unto you *these persons,* having been duly certified, to be consecrated *directors* of Christian education: [names].

Their names having been read aloud, the bishop shall say to those to be consecrated:

Dearly beloved, we rejoice that you have purposed in your *hearts* to devote *yourselves* to this task. You are to be among those who serve and teach. Such a vocation confers a great privilege; it also lays upon you a solemn responsibility. What you have done alone with God in consecrating *yourselves* to this service, we now ask you to declare publicly in the presence of this congregation.

Do you believe in your heart that you have been led by the Spirit of God to engage in Christian education and to assume its responsibilities?

I do so believe.

Will you be diligent in prayer, in the reading of the Holy Scriptures, and in other studies necessary to the development of a program of Christian education?

I will, the Lord being my helper.

Will you strive so to live that the power of God may be manifest in your life, enabling you through a program of Christian education to bring others to an awareness of the presence of God and to become disciples of our Lord Jesus Christ?

I will, by God's grace.

Will you maintain and set forward, as much as lieth in you, quietness, peace, and love among all Christian people, and especially among those who shall be committed to your charge?

I will do so, the Lord being my helper.

Will you be loyal to the Church and accept the authority of those to whom the Church has committed the direction of your work?

I will, the Lord being my helper.

Then those being consecrated shall kneel while the bishop says the prayer of consecration:

O eternal God, the Father of our Lord Jesus Christ; look upon *these* thy *servants* whom we this day consecrate *directors* of Christian education. Grant that *they* may have strength of body, mind, and soul for the fulfillment of thy will, that *they* may worthily discharge the work committed to *them*, to the blessing of mankind and the glory of Christ our Saviour. **Amen.**

¶ 1927. AN ORDER FOR THE COMMISSIONING OF MISSIONARIES AND DEACONESSES

PRELUDE *The people in devout meditation.*

PROCESSIONAL HYMN *The people standing. If there be no processional, let the first hymn follow the Call to Worship.*

CALL TO WORSHIP

Minister: O magnify the Lord with me, and let us exalt his name together.

People: **With him is the fountain of life: in his light shall we see light.**

Minister: Light is sown for the righteous, and gladness for the upright in heart.

People: **From the rising of the sun unto the going down of the same the Lord's name is to be praised. Amen.**

Here let the people be seated.

INVOCATION *The minister.*

Let us pray.

Everlasting Father, the radiance of faithful souls, who didst bring the nations to thy light and kings to the brightness of thy rising; fill, we beseech thee, the world with thy glory, and show thyself unto all the nations; through him who is the true light and the bright and morning star, Jesus Christ thy Son our Lord. **Amen.**

COLLECT *Here let the people unite with the minister in prayer.*

Almighty God, our heavenly Father, who through thy Son Jesus Christ hast given commandment unto thy people to go into all the world and preach the gospel to every creature; grant us a ready will to obey thy word; and as we have entered into the labors of other men, help us to serve thee, that others may enter into our labors, and that we with them, and they with us, may attain unto everlasting life; through the same Jesus Christ thy Son our Lord. Amen.

Minister: O Lord, open thou our lips.

People: **And our mouth shall show forth thy praise.**

Minister: Praise ye the Lord.

People: **The Lord's name be praised.**

ANTHEM

RESPONSIVE READING *"The Christian Mission"; of which let the paragraphs be read in turn by the minister, those to be commissioned, and the people. Let all stand and remain standing for the Gloria Patri.*

Hear, all ye nations of the earth, the gospel of the unsearchable riches of Christ.

Jesus came, saying: The Spirit of the Lord is upon me, because he hath anointed me to preach the gospel to the poor; and recovering of sight to the blind, to set at liberty them that are bruised, to preach the acceptable year of the Lord.

He came forth and saw a great multitude, and he had compassion on them, for they were as sheep not having a shepherd; and he welcomed them and spoke to them of the kingdom of God, and them that had need of healing he cured.

God, who commanded the light to shine out of darkness, hath shined in our hearts, to give the light of the knowledge of the glory of God in the face of Jesus Christ.

God so loved the world, that he gave his only-begotten Son, that whosoever believeth in him should not perish, but have everlasting life.

For God sent not his Son into the world to condemn the world; but that the world through him might be saved.

Therefore if any man be in Christ, he is a new creature; old things are passed away; behold, all things are become new.

There is no difference between the Jew and the Greek: for the same Lord over all is rich unto all that call upon him.

For whosoever shall call upon the name of the Lord shall be saved.

How then shall they call on him in whom they have not believed? and how shall they believe in him of whom they have not heard? and how shall they hear without a preacher? and how shall they preach, except they be sent?

The gospel of the kingdom shall be preached in all the world, for a witness unto all nations.

The harvest truly is plenteous, but the laborers are

few; pray ye therefore the Lord of the harvest, that he will send forth laborers into his harvest.

Also I heard the voice of the Lord, saying, Whom shall I send, and who will go for us?

Then said I, Here am I; send me.

And the King shall say, Inasmuch as ye have done it unto one of the least of these my brethren, ye have done it unto me.

He that hath my word, let him speak my word faithfully, saith the LORD.

Let thy mercy, O LORD, be upon us, according as we hope in thee.

For all things are yours; whether Paul, or Apollos, or Cephas, or the world, or life, or death, or things present, or things to come; all are yours; and ye are Christ's; and Christ is God's.

GLORIA PATRI

THE LESSON FROM THE NEW TESTAMENT *Mark 3:13-15; Matthew 10:38-42.*

SILENT MEDITATION

PRAYER

THE LORD'S PRAYER

OFFERTORY *The dedication of gifts and tithes. An offertory sentence may be said or sung.*

HYMN OF PREPARATION

> With thee, our Master and our Lord,
> We greet this wondrous day;
> The gates swing open at thy word,
> The paths stretch far away.
> The way we take is known to thee,
> Thy footprints there we trace;
> Oh, grant us now that we may see
> The radiance of thy face.
>
> We little bring, our gift is small,
> Yet all we are is thine.

Ourselves we give, our life, our all;
  Thy life in ours enshrine.
Oh, lead us forth, with ardor bright
  Enkindled from above;
O Christ, reveal in heaven's own light
  The challenge of thy love.

O living Lord! with courage bless
  This loyal company,
They go to seek the comfortless,
  To find the lost for thee.
Within their hearts they bear thy word,
  They sing with joy thy praise,
Be ever near them, Jesus, Lord,
  Be with them all the days.

Together still! E'en though we part,
  Our life is one in prayer:
Our hearts are ever where thou art,
  And thou art everywhere.
About the world thy servants stand;
  With them one song we sing,
Thy conquering love in every land,
  Thy triumph, Christ, our King! Amen.

THE ADDRESS

THE PRESENTATION OF THE MISSIONARIES AND DEACONESSES TO BE COMMISSIONED

THE COMMISSIONING SERVICE

Those to be commissioned shall take their places at the chancel, facing the Bishop, who shall say to them:

Hear the words of our Master:

As the Father hath loved me, so have I loved you.

Ye have not chosen me, but I have chosen you, and ordained you, that ye should go and bring forth fruit, and that your fruit should remain: that whatsoever ye shall ask of the Father in my name, he may give it you.

Go ye therefore, and teach all nations, baptizing them in the name of the Father, and of the Son, and of the Holy Spirit: and lo, I am with you alway, even unto the end of the world.

Your church, in its endeavor to carry out this Great Commission, has declared, "The supreme aim of missions is to make the Lord Jesus Christ known to all people in all lands as their divine Saviour, to persuade them to become his disciples, and to gather these disciples into Christian churches; to enlist them in the building of the Kingdom of God; to co-operate with these churches, to promote world Christian fellowship; and to bring to bear on all human life the spirit and principles of Christ."

Dearly beloved, we rejoice that you have purposed in your *hearts* to devote your *lives* to this task. Your labors may take you to the mountains and to the plains, to isolated villages and teeming cities of this country, and to lands across the sea. You are to be among men as *those* who *serve*—teaching, preaching, and healing, ever testifying within the varied activities of our common life to the infinite love of God shed abroad in Christ Jesus. Such a vocation confers a great privilege; it also lays upon you a solemn responsibility. What you have done alone with God in consecrating your *lives* to this service, we now ask you to do formally and publicly in the presence of this congregation.

Do you believe in your heart that you have been led by the Spirit of God to engage in this work and to assume its responsibilities?

I do so believe.

Will you endeavor, as much as lieth in you, to perform faithfully the duties of *missionaries and deaconesses* in the Church of Christ?

I will endeavor so to do.

Will you be diligent in prayer, in the reading of the Holy Scriptures, and in such studies as help to the knowledge of God and his Kingdom?

I will, the Lord being my helper.

Will you strive so to live that the power of God may be manifest in your life, enabling you to convey the blessed sense of God's presence to those you would serve?

I will, by God's grace.

Will you be loyal to the Church, and accept the authority of those to whom the Church has committed the direction of your work?

I will, the Lord being my helper.

Then shall all bow for a brief period of silent prayer, after which the bishop shall say:

Almighty God, Father of all mercies; graciously behold *these* thy *servants* now to be commissioned as *deaconesses and missionaries* of thy Church. Endue *them* with thy Holy Spirit; enrich *them* with thy heavenly grace; and strengthen *them* for the tasks which lie ahead, that in all *their* works, begun, continued, and ended in thee, *they* may glorify thy holy name, and advance thy blessed Kingdom; through Jesus Christ our Lord. **Amen.**

Then the bishop, taking the right hand of each one, and repeating the name, shall say:

N., I commission you to take the gospel of our Lord Jesus Christ into all the world, in the name of the Father, and of the Son, and of the Holy Spirit. **Amen.**

To each deaconess the bishop shall say:

N., I commission you a deaconess to take the gospel of our Lord Jesus Christ into all the world, in the name of the Father, and of the Son, and of the Holy Spirit. **Amen.**

When all have been commissioned, the bishop shall turn to the missionaries and deaconesses in the congregation. They shall rise and the bishop, addressing them, shall say:

Beloved in the Lord, once you stood where *these* now *stand,* answering the call of God in your hearts. Obedient to this divine imperative, you have labored at home and abroad, ministering to the needs of men and bringing to them words of life. We are justly proud of your work and are continually thankful for the fullness of your devotion.

These younger *workers* will look to you for help and guidance as *they go* forth to serve with you. I commend *them* to your love and care.

Those who have just been commissioned shall then turn to face these missionaries and deaconesses, who, addressing them, shall say:

We welcome you into our fellowship, and into the

joyous service of Christ and his Kingdom. Your peace, joy, and welfare are now our own, and we pledge to you through the days ahead our unfailing support.

With you we renew our dedication to God and to the Church we delight to serve.

Now the God of peace make you perfect in every good work to do his will, working in you that which is well pleasing in his sight, through Jesus Christ; to whom be glory for ever and ever. Amen.

Then shall all the people stand, and the bishop, addressing them, shall say:

Members of this congregation, I commend to you *these men and women* whom we this day have commissioned to carry into all the world the sacred and imperishable message of eternal salvation.

In this holy moment we too are called to a renewed consecration of our lives to Christ and his Kingdom. As *these,* our fellow *workers, go* forth upon *their* mission, let us assure *them* that we are with *them* in spirit and are supporting *them* by word and gift and deed.

Then all the people, addressing those who have just been commissioned, shall say:

We rejoice to recognize you as *missionaries and deaconesses* of our church, and we thank God that you have dedicated your *lives* to his service throughout all the world.

We shall follow you with our prayers; we shall support your work with our gifts; and together we shall strive to minister to the needs of our fellow men and to bring to them the saving knowledge of our Lord Jesus Christ.

Then shall all the people and the newly commissioned missionaries and deaconesses join in saying:

We, being many, are one body in Christ, and every one members one of another.

United we pray: Thy kingdom come; thy will be done on earth as it is in heaven. And to this end we dedicate ourselves; in the name of the Father, and of the Son, and of the Holy Spirit. Amen.

SILENT PRAYER *Here let the people be seated and with heads bowed offer their personal intercessions for those who have just been commissioned and for the missionary enterprise.*

CLOSING PRAYER *The Bishop.*

For this cause I bow my knees unto the Father, of whom the whole family in heaven and earth is named, that he would grant you, according to the riches of his glory, to be strengthened with might by his Spirit in the inner man; that Christ may dwell in your hearts by faith; that ye, being rooted and grounded in love, may be able to comprehend with all saints what is the breadth, and length, and depth, and height; and to know the love of Christ, which passeth knowledge, that ye might be filled with all the fullness of God. Now unto him that is able to do exceeding abundantly above all that we ask or think, according to the power that worketh in us, unto him be glory in the church by Christ Jesus throughout all ages, world without end. **Amen.**

RECESSIONAL HYMN

BENEDICTION

POSTLUDE

¶ 1928. AN ORDER FOR THE RECOGNITION OF CHURCH-SCHOOL OFFICERS AND TEACHERS

This order may be used as a part of an order of worship when the work of Christian education is the theme of the day. After the sermon the minister may call the officers and teachers of the church school to stand before the chancel or altar.

The minister shall say:

Dearly beloved, we have here met in the presence of God that we may recognize his call, received and acknowledged by these of our fellowship, to the work of teaching and directing in our church school. As they come in a spirit of devotion to offer themselves to God for this service, it is our obligation to support them by our loyalty and prayers, seeking with them and for them the consecration which is from on high, that they may be enabled to discharge this responsible calling with reverence and faithfulness and to the glory of God.

Then the chairman of the Commission on Education or the minister may read the names of the officers and teachers of the church school. The officers and teachers shall then confess their faith in Christ, responding to the minister as follows:

There is one body, and one Spirit, even as ye are called in one hope of your calling; one Lord, one faith, one baptism, one God and Father of all, who is above all, and through all, and in all.

By grace are we saved through faith; and that not of ourselves: it is the gift of God.

There are diversities of gifts, but the same Spirit. And there are differences of administrations, but the same Lord.

One is our Master, even Christ.

Ye are laborers together with God: ye are God's husbandry, ye are God's building.

Other foundation can no man lay than that is laid, which is Jesus Christ.

I beseech you therefore, by the mercies of God, that ye present your bodies a living sacrifice, holy, acceptable unto God, which is your reasonable service.

The love of Christ constraineth us.

Study to show yourselves approved unto God, workmen that need not to be ashamed, rightly dividing the word of truth.

Who is sufficient for these things? Without him we can do nothing.

God is able to make all grace abound toward you; that ye may abound to every good work.

Faithful is he who calleth us, who also will do it.

Now unto him that is able to do exceeding abundantly above all that we ask or think, according to the power that worketh in us,

Unto him be glory in the church by Christ Jesus throughout all ages, world without end. Amen.

Romans 12:1-8 read responsively may be used alternatively.

Here let the people be seated and bow in prayer while the officers and teachers kneel at the altar. Then shall the minister say:

Ye are not your own; ye are bought with a price; therefore glorify God in your body, and in your spirit, which are God's.

Neglect not the gift that is in you. Give heed to reading, to exhortation, to teaching.

If any of you lack wisdom, let him ask of God, who giveth to all men liberally, and upbraideth not. But let him ask in faith, nothing wavering.

Then shall the minister and the officers and teachers unite in prayer.

Eternal and everliving Father, who dost call us to thy service, and dost promise grace and strength for the fulfilling of thy will; look with favor upon us, as we dedicate ourselves to the task of working in this school. Grant that we may grow in the knowledge and love of thy Word, that we may minister to the growing life of thy Church, and to the glory of thy holy name; through Jesus Christ our Lord. Amen.

Then may follow a short extempore prayer of dedication by the minister. Afterward a suitable hymn may be sung, which may be followed by the benediction.

¶ 1929. AN ORDER FOR THE RECOGNITION OF CHORISTERS

At an appointed time the choir director, with his choristers properly robed, shall stand before the minister, who shall say:

It is a good thing to give thanks unto the LORD, and to sing praises unto thy name, O most High:

To show forth thy lovingkindness in the morning, and thy faithfulness every night.

Then the choir director shall say:

I present these persons to be recognized as choristers in this church.

Then shall the minister say:

Are you convinced that these persons by their integrity of life, good behavior, and knowledge of music will exercise this office to the honor of God and the edifying of the Church?

Then shall the choir director say:

I have inquired of them and have also examined them and commend them for this service in the Church.

Then the minister, addressing the persons who are seeking admission as choristers, shall question them as follows:

Do you desire to become a member of this choir?

I do.

Do you promise obedience to its rules and officers?

I do.

Will you endeavor always to be reverent in the house of God?

I will, with the help of God.

Will you seek to hold your life to the high level that is in accordance with this high office?

I will, the Lord being my helper.

Then shall the choir director and candidates kneel, and the minister, calling each by name, shall say:

N., I admit thee into the choir of this church. What thou singest with thy mouth, believe in thy heart; what thou believest in thy heart, practice in thy life. And may our heavenly Father give thee grace to sing his praise and live to his glory, both in this world and in the world to come; through Jesus Christ our Lord. **Amen.**

Here let all the people unite in prayer.

Almighty God, unto whom all hearts are open, all desires known, and from whom no secrets are hid; cleanse the thoughts of our hearts by the inspiration of thy Holy Spirit, that we may perfectly love thee, and worthily magnify thy holy name; through Christ our Lord. Amen.

Our Father who art in heaven, hallowed be thy name; thy kingdom come; thy will be done on earth as it is in

heaven. Give us this day our daily bread. And forgive us
our trespasses, as we forgive those who trespass against
us. And lead us not into temptation, but deliver us from
evil. For thine is the kingdom, and the power, and the
glory, forever. Amen.

Then may the minister say:

The LORD bless you, and keep you: the LORD make his
face shine upon you, and be gracious unto you: the LORD
lift up his countenance upon you, and give you peace.
Amen.

¶ 1930. AN ORDER FOR THE ORGANIZING OF A CHURCH

PRELUDE *The people in devout meditation.*

DECLARATION OF PURPOSE *The district superintendent (or
pastor authorized by him).*

Dearly beloved, we are met on this occasion to establish
a new congregation of The Methodist Church, which is a
part of the body of Christ; and to that end we dedicate
ourselves and this hour.

The Church is of God, and will be preserved to the end
of time, for the promotion of his worship and the due
administration of his word and ordinances, the maintenance of Christian fellowship and discipline, the edification of believers, and the conversion of the world. All,
of every age and station, stand in need of the means of
grace which it alone supplies.

HYMN 379 *"I love thy kingdom, Lord,"* the people standing.

THE LESSON FROM THE OLD TESTAMENT

Behold, I will gather them out of all countries; and I
will bring them again unto this place: and they shall be my
people, and I will be their God. And I will give them one
heart, and one way, that they may fear me for ever, for
the good of them, and of their children after them: and
I will make an everlasting covenant with them, that I
will not turn away from them to do them good; but I
will put my fear in their hearts, that they shall not de-

part from me. Yea, I will rejoice over them to do them good, and I will plant them in this land assuredly with my whole heart, and with my whole soul.

LITANY

For the revelation of thy word to humankind as it has come through patriarchs, prophets, and sages,

We praise thy name, O Lord.

For salvation from sin, for redeeming love, and for all the ministry of the gospel as it has blessed the seeking souls of men,

We praise thy name, O Lord.

For the glorious hope of immortality, and the life of eternal fellowship,

We praise thy name, O Lord.

For the high and holy privilege of knowing our lives redeemed, of following the way and spirit of Jesus Christ, and of accepting responsibility in the Church of Christ,

We praise thy name, O Lord.

For the purpose of establishing this church, and in the full hope that it will render a complete ministry of redemption, education, worship, fellowship, and service,

We pledge ourselves, O God, to thee this day. Amen.

RECEPTION OF MEMBERS AND ORGANIZATION *The district superintendent shall give opportunity for those in attendance to present themselves for membership by certificates of transfer and on profession of faith and, when he is satisfied as to the genuineness of their faith and purpose, shall receive those who present themselves, using the regular forms in the Ritual. After this he shall complete the organization of the church as prescribed in the Discipline.*

DECLARATION OF ORGANIZATION

The district superintendent shall say:
By what name shall this church henceforth be known?

To which the pastor, chairman of the Official Board, or other official shall answer:

It shall be called the *N.* Methodist Church.

Then shall the district superintendent say:

In accordance with the laws and the Discipline of The Methodist Church, I hereby declare that the *N.* Methodist Church is duly constituted and organized for the glory of God, the proclamation of the gospel, and the service of humanity.

THE LESSON FROM THE NEW TESTAMENT

Grace and peace be multiplied unto you through the knowledge of God, and of Jesus our Lord, according as his divine power hath given unto us all things that pertain unto life and godliness, through the knowledge of him that hath called us to glory and virtue: whereby are given unto us exceeding great and precious promises; that by these ye might be partakers of the divine nature, having escaped the corruption that is in the world through lust. And beside this, giving all diligence, add to your faith virtue; and to virtue knowledge; and to knowledge temperance; and to temperance patience; and to patience godliness; and to godliness brotherly kindness; and to brotherly kindess charity. For if these things be in you, and abound, they make you that ye shall neither be barren nor unfruitful in the knowledge of our Lord Jesus Christ. But he that lacketh these things is blind, and cannot see afar off, and hath forgotten that he was purged from his old sins. Wherefore the rather, brethren, give diligence to make your calling and election sure: for if ye do these things, ye shall never fall.

HYMN 416 *"Blest be the tie that binds."*

THE ADDRESS

HYMN 381 *"The Church's one foundation,"* the people standing.

BENEDICTION

¶ 1931. AN ORDER FOR THE BREAKING OF GROUND FOR A CHURCH

At the time appointed let the congregation assemble at the site set apart for the new church building.

HYMN 18 *"For the beauty of the earth,"* or other suitable hymn, the people standing.

CALL TO WORSHIP

Minister: Give unto the Lord the glory due unto his
name: bring an offering, and come into his
courts.

People: **Praise waiteth for thee, O God, and unto thee
shall the vow be performed.**

Minister: Our help is in the name of the Lord, who made
heaven and earth.

People: **Except the Lord build the house, they labor in
vain that build it. Amen.**

INVOCATION *The minister.*

Let us pray.

O Lord God, almighty and most merciful, whom the
heaven, even the heaven of heavens, cannot contain, much
less temples built with hands, but who also dwellest with
men, and delightest thyself in the fellowship of thy people; cleanse our hearts, we beseech thee, from all evil
thought and desire, and vouchsafe thy divine presence
and blessing, both that those things may please thee which
we do at this present, and also that we may at length
obtain thy favor with life everlasting in thy heavenly
kingdom; through Jesus Christ our Lord. **Amen.**

COLLECT *Here let the people unite with the minister in prayer.*

**Almighty and everlasting God, who art ever exalted
yet always nigh; grant that we may worthily offer unto
thee, the Father, the Son, and the Holy Spirit, this
ground upon which we stand, to be made holy with
sacred aspiration and divine purpose, as a place upon
which to build a temple and a sanctuary where thy glory
shall be manifest among us, and where all people shall
come to call upon thy name; through Jesus Christ our
Lord. Amen.**

PRAYER *The Minister.*

O eternal God, our heavenly Father, who hast committed to us the work of building a temple to thy blessed
name; grant that when thy gospel is preached in this

place, it may be in demonstration of thy Spirit and with power; and that when thy holy Sacraments are here administered, those spiritual graces which the outward signs do but represent may flow into the hearts of thy people. Here let men worship thee in spirit and in truth. Here, when they come to offer their gifts upon thine altar, let them consider thy Son, who though he was rich for their sakes became poor, that they through his poverty might become rich. Let the fullness of thy love fill all who shall seek thy presence in this place. Upon the church to be builded here let thy Spirit, O God, descend; and within this sanctuary let thy glory dwell; through Jesus Christ our Lord. **Amen.**

THE LORD'S PRAYER

Our Father who art in heaven, hallowed be thy name; thy kingdom come; thy will be done on earth as it is in heaven. Give us this day our daily bread. And forgive us our trespasses, as we forgive those who trespass against us. And lead us not into temptation, but deliver us from evil. For thine is the kingdom, and the power, and the glory, forever. Amen.

RESPONSIVE PSALM

The earth is the LORD's and the fullness thereof; the world, and they that dwell therein.

For he hath founded it upon the seas, and established it upon the floods.

Who shall ascend into the hill of the LORD? or who shall stand in his holy place?

He that hath clean hands, and a pure heart; who hath not lifted up his soul unto vanity, nor sworn deceitfully.

He shall receive the blessing from the LORD, and righteousness from the God of his salvation.

This is the generation of them that seek him, that seek thy face.

Lift up your heads, O ye gates; and be ye lift up, ye everlasting doors.

And the King of glory shall come in.

Who is this King of glory?

The LORD strong and mighty, the LORD mighty in battle.

Lift up your heads, O ye gates; even lift them up, ye everlasting doors.

And the King of glory shall come in.

Who is this King of glory?

The LORD of hosts, he is the King of glory.

GLORIA PATRI

THE SCRIPTURE LESSON

I therefore, the prisoner of the Lord, beseech you that ye walk worthy of the vocation wherewith ye are called, with all lowliness and meekness, with longsuffering, forbearing one another in love; endeavoring to keep the unity of the Spirit in the bond of peace. There is one body, and one Spirit, even as ye are called in one hope of your calling; one Lord, one faith, one baptism, one God and Father of all, who is above all, and through all, and in all. But unto every one of us is given grace according to the measure of the gift of Christ.

And he gave some, apostles; and some, prophets; and some, evangelists; and some, pastors and teachers; for the perfecting of the saints, for the work of the ministry, for the edifying of the body of Christ: till we all come in the unity of the faith, and of the knowledge of the Son of God, unto a perfect man, unto the measure of the stature of the fullness of Christ: that we may grow up into him in all things, which is the head, even Christ: from whom the whole body fitly joined together, and compacted by that which every joint supplieth, according to the effectual working in the measure of every part, maketh increase of the body unto the edifying of itself in love.

Here let the minister offer an extempore prayer, which may be followed by an address.

DECLARATION *The Minister*

To the glory of God, in the presence of this congregation, I now request that ground be broken for N. Methodist Church. Upon you as members of this congregation rests the responsibility and privilege to cause a church to rise here which shall be devoted to the honor and worship of Almighty God our Father, and to the glory of his blessed Son and our Saviour, Jesus Christ.

THE BREAKING OF GROUND *Here let those selected come forward; and as each turns a spadeful of earth, let him repeat one of the following sentences, to which the people shall respond.*

That a church may rise here in which the ancient gospel of her Lord shall be proclaimed,

We break this ground today.

That a church may rise here where little children shall learn to love God and grow in the beauty of Christian grace and character,

We break this ground today.

That a church may rise here where through the years countless youth shall come to worship, pause to pray, and rise to serve,

We break this ground today.

That a church may rise here where the weary and heavy laden shall find that inner peace which the world can neither give nor take away,

We break this ground today.

That a church may rise here where the Word of God shall be so read and preached that it shall become the Living Word, and the Sacraments so adminstered that all life shall become a sacrament,

We break this ground today.

That a church may rise here where moments of meditation and hours of worship shall be touched with life-giving reality,

We break this ground today.

That a church may rise here where those who seek first the kingdom of God shall dedicate themselves to the unfinished tasks of evangelizing the whole of life,

We break this ground today.

That a church may rise here where multitudes shall be refreshed in spirit, relieved from pain, released from bondage, redeemed from sin,

We break this ground today.

That a church may rise here where the unsearchable riches of Christ shall bear fruit in making our human loves constant, our homes Christlike, and our families creative centers of Christian influence,

We break this ground today.

That a church may rise here where all who bow in sorrow shall rise in faith in him in whom to believe is life eternal,

We break this ground today.

RESPONSIVE PRAYER *Here let the people bow.*

Almighty and everlasting God, in communion with the saints in all the ages, and remembering the heritage that has been given us, we offer thee our praise and thanksgiving.

O Lord, hear our prayer.

Help us to accept the privilege and responsibility of this thy fellowship of faith; here may we keep the unity of the spirit in the bond of peace.

So may we fulfill the law of love.

Enable us, by thy grace, to dedicate ourselves this day to the great task which thou dost lay upon our hearts and consciences.

In all that we do, be thou, O Lord, our strength and help.

Reveal to us the beauty of thy perfect law, the joy of our living Lord, so that with glad hearts we may move forward in paths of high devotion and great achievement.

Be thou, O Lord, our guide and help for evermore. Amen.

BENEDICTION

¶ 1932. AN ORDER FOR THE LAYING OF THE CORNERSTONE OF A CHURCH

At the time appointed the hymn "The Church's one foundation is Jesus Christ her Lord" may be sung, all the people standing, after which the minister shall say:

Our help is in the name of the LORD, who made heaven and earth.

Except the LORD build the house, they labor in vain that build it.

Dearly beloved, we are assembled to lay the cornerstone of a new house for the worship of the God of our fathers. Let us not doubt that he will favorably approve our godly purpose, and let us now devoutly invoke his blessing on this our undertaking.

Then shall the minister offer an extempore prayer.

Then the following lesson from the Old Testament may be read responsively by the minister and the people, the people standing:

The earth is the LORD's, and the fullness thereof; the world and they that dwell therein.

For he hath founded it upon the seas, and established it upon the floods.

Who shall ascend into the hill of the LORD? or who shall stand in his holy place?

He that hath clean hands, and a pure heart; who hath not lifted up his soul unto vanity, nor sworn deceitfully.

He shall receive the blessing from the LORD, and righteousness from the God of his salvation.

This is the generation of them that seek him, that seek thy face.

Lift up your heads, O ye gates; and be ye lift up, ye everlasting doors.

And the King of glory shall come in.

Who is this King of glory?

The LORD strong and mighty, the LORD mighty in battle.

Lift up your heads, O ye gates; even lift them up, ye everlasting doors.

And the King of glory shall come in.

Who is this King of glory?

The LORD of hosts, he is the King of glory.

Then may the Gloria Patri *be said or sung:*

Glory be to the Father, and to the Son, and to the Holy Ghost. As it was in the beginning, is now, and ever shall be, world without end. Amen.

Then shall be read the lesson from the New Testament, the people being seated:

For we are laborers together with God: ye are God's husbandry, ye are God's building. According to the grace of God which is given unto me, as a wise master builder, I have laid the foundation, and another buildeth thereon. But let every man take heed how he buildeth thereon. For other foundation can no man lay than that is laid, which is Jesus Christ. Now if any man build upon this foundation, gold, silver, precious stones, wood, hay, stubble; every man's work shall be made manifest: for the day shall declare it, because it shall be revealed by fire; and the fire shall try every man's work of what sort it is. If any man's work abide which he hath built thereupon, he shall receive a reward. If any man's work shall be burned, he shall suffer loss: but he himself shall be saved; yet so as by fire. Know ye not that ye are the temple of God, and that the Spirit of God dwelleth in you?

Here may follow a prayer, offering, anthem, address, and hymn.

Then, standing at the side of the cornerstone, the minister may read the following scripture sentences:

The LORD hath chosen thee to build a house for the sanctuary: be strong, and do it. Fear not, nor be dismayed: for the LORD God, even my God, will be with thee; he will not fail thee, nor forsake thee, until thou hast finished all the work for the service of the house of the LORD.

Therefore thus saith the Lord GOD, Behold, I lay in Zion for a foundation a stone, a tried stone, a precious cornerstone, a sure foundation.

According to the grace of God which is given unto me, as a wise master builder, I have laid the foundation.

Other foundation can no man lay than that is laid, which is Jesus Christ.

Then shall the minister offer the prayer of consecration:

Almighty God, the Rock of Ages; on thee we build all our hopes for this life and that which is to come. Other foundation we would not seek to lay than that is laid, which is Jesus Christ; and we are to build upon this cornerstone a holy temple to the living God. Accept the act by which we lay this cornerstone. Bless those whose offerings enable us to build this house of worship. Graciously guard and direct those who labor in erecting it, shielding them from accident and peril. May the walls of this building rise in security and in beauty; and may the hearts of these thy people be fitly joined together into a living temple, builded upon the foundation of the apostles and prophets, Jesus Christ being the chief cornerstone. **Amen.**

Then may the minister and the people recite the Litany for the Laying of a Cornerstone:

To the glory of God our Father, to the service of our dear Master and his Church, and to the abiding presence of the Holy Spirit,

We lay the cornerstone of this church.

For a building of which Jesus Christ is the chief cornerstone, the pillar and ground of the truth,

We lay this cornerstone.

For a building that shall stand as a symbol of the Church Universal, the cornerstone of which is truth, the creed of which is love, and its towers eternal hope,

We lay this cornerstone.

For a church that shall exalt, not a religion of creed or of authority, but a religion of saving grace, of personal experience, and of spiritual power,

We lay this cornerstone.

For a church that shall exalt the ministry of the open Bible, with its faithful record of human life, its unfolding of the redeeming grace of God through Jesus Christ, its message of warning, inspiration, comfort, and hope,

We lay this cornerstone.

For a church that shall teach and incarnate the doctrine of the fatherhood of God and the brotherhood of man,

We lay this cornerstone.

For a church that shall fulfill a ministry of social service and be a blessing unto men,

We lay this cornerstone.

For a church that shall be a renewing and cleansing power in the community, and that loves every other communion that exalts Christ in the service of man,

We lay this cornerstone.

For a church with an open door for all people, rich or poor, homeless or desolate, who need the help of God through us,

We lay this cornerstone.

For a church that shall gather the children in its arms and hold them close to Christ, that they may grow up in the Church and never be lost from the fold,

We lay this cornerstone.

For a church which stands for the sacramental truth: "It is more blessed to give than to receive,"

We lay this cornerstone.

For a church which takes hold on two worlds, and stands for the unseen and eternal, and which offers to men the abundant life which now is and which is to come,

We lay this cornerstone in the name of Almighty God.

In loving memory of those who have gone from us, whose hearts and hands have served this church; with gratitude for all whose faith and consecrated gifts make this house possible, for all who may share this spiritual adventure; and with hope for all who shall worship in this house in years to come,

We lay this cornerstone in the name of Almighty God, Father, Son, and Holy Spirit, unto the ages of ages, world without end. Amen.

Then shall the minister, standing by the stone, exhibit to the people a box to be placed in the stone. It may contain such articles as a Bible, The Methodist Hymnal, *the latest* Discipline, *church periodicals, names of the pastor, Official Board, the building committee of the church, with such other documents as may be desired. The minister may read the list of articles so deposited in the box. Then with the aid of the builder, the minister shall lay the stone in its place.*

Then shall the people sing the following hymn:

On this stone now laid with prayer
Let thy church rise, strong and fair;
Ever, Lord, thy name be known,
Where we lay this cornerstone.

May thy Spirit here give rest
To the heart by sin oppressed,
And the seeds of truth be sown,
Where we lay this cornerstone.

Open wide, O God, thy door
For the outcast and the poor;
May they know this house their own,
Where we lay this cornerstone.

By wise master builders squared,
Here be living stones prepared
For the temple near thy throne,
Jesus Christ its Cornerstone.

Then shall the minister say:

Now unto him that is able to keep you from falling,
and to present you faultless before the presence of his
glory with exceeding joy, to the only wise God our
Saviour, be glory and majesty, dominion and power, both
now and evermore. **Amen.**

This order may be abridged according to the needs of the occasion.

¶ 1933. AN ORDER FOR THE DEDICATION OF A CHURCH

*Let the service of worship begin at the time appointed. Let the
people kneel or bow in silent prayer upon entering the sanctuary.*

PRELUDE *The people in devout meditation.*

HYMN *The people standing.*

CALL TO WORSHIP

Minister: Serve the Lord with gladness.

People: **Enter into his gates with thanksgiving, and
into his courts with praise.**

Minister: O come, let us worship and bow down: let us kneel before the Lord our Maker.

People: **He is our God; and we are the people of his pasture, and the sheep of his hand. Amen**

Here let the people be seated.

INVOCATION *The Minister.*

Let us pray.

O God, eternal and ever blessed, who delightest in the assembling of thy people in the sanctuary; receive us graciously as we come into thy house, and grant, we entreat thee, that peace and prosperity may be found within its walls, that the glory of God may be the light thereof, and that we may be satisfied with the goodness of thy house; through Jesus Christ our Lord. **Amen.**

COLLECT FOR DEDICATION DAY *Here let the people unite with the minister in prayer.*

Direct us, O Lord, in all our doings, with thy most gracious favor, and further us with thy continual help, that in all our works, begun, continued, and ended in thee, we may glorify thy holy name, and finally, by thy mercy, obtain everlasting life; through Jesus Christ our Lord. Amen.

ANTHEM

CANTICLE OF THE CHURCH *To be said responsively by the minister and the people. Here let the people stand and remain standing until after the Affirmation of Faith.*

Arise, shine; for thy light is come, and the glory of the LORD is risen upon thee.

For behold, darkness shall cover the earth, and gross darkness the people.

But the LORD shall rise upon thee, and his glory shall be seen upon thee.

And the nations shall come to thy light, and kings to the brightness of thy rising.

The abundance of the sea shall be turned unto thee; the wealth of the nations shall come unto thee.

Thy gates shall stand always open; they shall not be shut day nor night,

That men may bring unto thee the wealth of the nations, and their kings led with them.

For the nation and kingdom that will not serve thee shall perish; yea, it shall be utterly wasted.

Violence shall no more be heard in thy land, wasting nor destruction within thy borders.

But thou shalt call thy walls Salvation, and thy gates thou shalt call Praise.

The sun shall be no more thy light by day; neither for brightness shall the moon give light unto thee.

But the LORD shall be unto thee an everlasting light, and thy God thy glory.

Thy sun shall no more go down; neither shall thy moon withdraw itself.

For the LORD shall be thine everlasting light, and the days of thy mourning shall be ended.

GLORIA PATRI

AFFIRMATION OF FAITH *The minister and the people.*
I believe in God the Father Almighty, Maker of heaven and earth; and in Jesus Christ his only Son our Lord; who was conceived by the Holy Spirit, born of the Virgin Mary, suffered under Pontius Pilate, was crucified, dead, and buried; the third day he rose from the dead; he ascended into heaven, and sitteth at the right hand of God the Father Almighty; from thence he shall come to judge the quick and the dead. I believe in the Holy Spirit, the holy catholic Church, the communion of saints, the forgiveness of sins, the resurrection of the body, and the life everlasting. Amen.

THE SCRIPTURE LESSON

PRAYER

HYMN

THE SERMON *Which may be followed by prayer.*

THE DEDICATION OF GIFTS AND TITHES

OFFERTORY RESPONSE *The people standing.*

> **Praise God, from whom all blessings flow;**
> **Praise him, all creatures here below;**
> **Praise him above, ye heavenly host;**
> **Praise Father, Son, and Holy Ghost. Amen.**

Here let the people be seated.

THE ACT OF DEDICATION

Some person authorized shall say to the officiating minister:

We present this building to be dedicated to the glory of God and the service of men.

Then shall the minister say:

By what name shall this church henceforth be known?

To which shall be answered:

It shall be called the *N.* Methodist Church.

Then shall the minister say to all the people:

Beloved in the Lord, we rejoice that God put it into the hearts of his people to build this house to the glory of his name. I now accept this building to be known as *N.* Methodist Church, to dedicate it, and to set it apart for the worship of Almighty God and the service of all men. Let us therefore, as we are assembled, solemnly dedicate this place to its proper and sacred uses.

Then, all standing, the minister shall say, the people responding:

To the glory of God the Father, who has called us by his grace;

To the honor of his Son, who loved us and gave himself for us;

To the praise of the Holy Spirit, who illumines and sanctifies us;

We dedicate this house.

For the worship of God in prayer and praise;

For the preaching of the everlasting gospel;

For the celebration of the holy Sacraments;

We dedicate this house.

For the comfort of all who mourn;

For strength to those who are tempted;

For light to those who seek the way;

We dedicate this house.

For the hallowing of family life;
For teaching and guiding the young;
For the perfecting of the saints;

We dedicate this house.

For the conversion of sinners;
For the promotion of righteousness;
For the extension of the Kingdom of God;

We dedicate this house.

In the unity of the faith;
In the bond of Christian brotherhood;
In charity and good will to all;

We dedicate this house.

In gratitude for the labors of all who love and serve this church;
In loving remembrance of those who have finished their course;
In the hope of a blessed immortality through Jesus Christ, our Lord;

We dedicate this house.

Then shall the minister and people together say:

We now, the people of this church and congregation, compassed about with a great cloud of witnesses, grateful for our heritage, sensible of the sacrifice of our fathers in the faith, confessing that apart from us their work cannot be made perfect, do dedicate ourselves anew to the worship and service of Almighty God; through Jesus Christ our Lord. Amen.

Then shall the minister say:

Accept, O God our Father, this service at our hands, and bless it to the end that this congregation of faithful people may make manifest the Church of the living God, the pillar and ground of truth, and so may this house be the place where thine honor dwelleth and the whole earth be filled with thy glory; through Jesus Christ our Lord.

THE SANCTUS *To be sung or said responsively by the minister and the people.*

Therefore with angels and archangels, and with all the company of heaven, we laud and magnify thy glorious name, evermore praising thee, and saying:

Holy, holy, holy, Lord God of hosts, heaven and earth are full of thy glory. Glory be to thee, O Lord most high! Amen.

PRAYER *Here the minister may offer an extempore prayer or one or more of the following prayers:*

O eternal God, whom the heaven of heavens cannot contain, much less the walls of temples made with hands; graciously accept the dedication of this house to thy honor and glory. **Amen.**

Grant, O Lord, that all who here share in the Sacraments, the ministry of the Word, and the fellowship of praise and prayer may know that God is in this place, may hear thy voice within their hearts, and may go forth to extend to the uttermost bounds of life the Lord Christ's Kingdom. **Amen.**

Now therefore, O Lord, let thine eyes be open toward this house day and night; and let thine ears be ready toward the prayers of thy children, which they shall make unto thee in this place. And whensoever thy servants shall make to thee their petitions, do thou hear them, and when thou hearest, forgive. Grant, O Lord, we beseech thee, that here and elsewhere thy ministers may be clothed with righteousness, and thy saints rejoice in thy salvation. And may we all, with thy people everywhere, grow up into a holy temple in the Lord, and be at last received into the glorious temple above, the house not made with hands, eternal in the heavens. And to the Father, and the Son, and the Holy Spirit, be glory and praise, world without end. *Amen.*

HYMN

SILENT PRAYER

BENEDICTION

POSTLUDE

¶ 1934. AN ORDER FOR THE OPENING OF A CHURCH FOR WORSHIP

According to the Discipline of The Methodist Church a church cannot be dedicated until it is free of debt. This is not a service of dedication. It is an opening of a church for worship with the expectancy that the congregation of faithful people will make every sacrifice to remove all encumbrance from the House of God.

Let the service of worship begin at the time appointed. Let the people kneel or bow in silent prayer upon entering the sanctuary.

PRELUDE *The people in devout meditation.*

HYMN *The people standing.*

CALL TO WORSHIP

Minister: Our help is in the name of the LORD, who made heaven and earth.

People: **Except the Lord build the house, they labor in vain that build it.**

Minister: Give unto the Lord the glory due unto his name: bring an offering, and come into his courts.

People: **Praise waiteth for thee, O God, and unto thee shall the vow be performed. Amen.**

Here let the people be seated and bow in prayer.

INVOCATION *The minister*

Let us pray.

O Lord God, almighty and most merciful, whom the heaven, even the heaven of heavens, cannot contain, much less temples built with hands, but who also dwellest with men, and delightest thyself in the fellowship of thy people; cleanse our hearts, we beseech thee, from all evil thought and desire, and vouchsafe thy divine presence and blessing, both that those things may please thee which we do at this present, and also that we may at length obtain thy favor with life everlasting in thy heavenly kingdom; through Jesus Christ our Lord. **Amen.**

COLLECT *Here let the people unite with the minister in prayer.*

Direct us, O Lord, in all our doings with thy most gracious favor, and further us with thy continual help, that in all our works, begun, continued, and ended in thee, we may glorify thy holy name, and finally, by thy mercy, obtain everlasting life; through Jesus Christ our Lord. Amen.

THE LORD'S PRAYER

Our Father who art in heaven, hallowed be thy name; thy kingdom come; thy will be done on earth as it is in heaven. Give us this day our daily bread. And forgive us our trespasses, as we forgive those who trespass against us. And lead us not into temptation, but deliver us from evil. For thine is the kingdom, and the power, and the glory, forever. Amen.

ANTHEM

RESPONSIVE PSALM *Here let the people stand and remain standing until after the* Gloria Patri.

The earth is the Lord's, and the fullness thereof; the world, and they that dwell therein.

For he hath founded it upon the seas, and established it upon the floods.

Who shall ascend into the hill of the Lord? or who shall stand in his holy place?

He that hath clean hands, and a pure heart; who hath not lifted up his soul unto vanity, nor sworn deceitfully.

He shall receive the blessing from the Lord, and righteousness from the God of his salvation.

This is the generation of them that seek him, that seek thy face.

Lift up your heads, O ye gates; and be ye lift up, ye everlasting doors.

And the King of glory shall come in.

Who is this King of glory?

The Lord strong and mighty, the Lord mighty in battle.

Lift up your heads, O ye gates; even lift them up, ye everlasting doors.

And the King of glory shall come in.

Who is this King of glory?

The LORD of hosts, he is the King of glory.

GLORIA PATRI

THE SCRIPTURE LESSON

DECLARATION *The Minister.*

In the name of God and in the presence of this congregation I now declare this church to be open for the worship of God and the service of men. May it be a house of prayer for all people. Upon you as a congregation there rests the solemn responsibility to see to it that all liability of a financial character resting upon this property be speedily lifted so that this church may be dedicated to God in the name of the Father, and the Son, and the Holy Spirit. Let us join in the act of consecration to God and his Church.

RESPONSIVE PRAYER *Here let the people bow.*

Almighty and everlasting God, in communion with the saints in all the ages, and remembering the heritage that has been given us, we offer thee our praise and thanksgiving.

O Lord, hear our prayer.

Help us to accept the privilege and responsibility of this thy fellowship of faith; here may we keep the unity of the spirit in the bond of peace.

So may we fulfill the law of love.

Enable us, by thy grace, to dedicate ourselves this day to the great task which thou dost lay upon our hearts and consciences.

In all that we do, be thou, O Lord, our strength and help.

Reveal to us the beauty of thy perfect law, the joy of our living Lord, so that with glad hearts we may move forward in paths of high devotion and great achievement.

Be thou, O Lord, our guide and help for evermore. Amen.

PRAYER OF THANKSGIVING *The minister.*

Most glorious God, accept through thy beloved Son our thanksgivings for thine unspeakable love and goodness. Thou art the Father of mercies, and God of all comfort, full of compassion, forgiving iniquity, transgression, and sin. We thank thee that thou hast founded thy Church upon the apostles and prophets, Jesus Christ himself being the chief cornerstone. We thank thee that thou hast committed to thy ministers the word of reconciliation. Continue thy lovingkindness unto us, that we may rejoice and be glad in thee all our days. Guide us by thy counsel, and afterward receive us to thy glory; where, with all the blessed host of heaven, we may behold, adore, and perfectly and joyfully praise thee, our most glorious creator, redeemer, and sanctifier, for ever and ever. **Amen.**[8]

ANTHEM

OFFERTORY *The dedication of gifts and tithes. An offertory sentence may be said or sung.*

HYMN

THE SERMON *Which may be followed by prayer.*

AN INVITATION TO CHRISTIAN DISCIPLESHIP

HYMN or DOXOLOGY *The people standing.*

SILENT PRAYER

BENEDICTION

POSTLUDE

¶ 1935. AN ORDER FOR THE DEDICATION OF AN ORGAN

DOXOLOGY *The people standing.*

[8] From *The Book of Common Worship* (revised, 1932), by permission of the Presbyterian Board of Christian Education.

CALL TO WORSHIP

Minister: Surely the Lord is in this place.

People: **This is none other but the house of God, and this is the gate of heaven.**

Minister: Enter into his gates with thanksgiving, and into his courts with praise.

People: **O magnify the Lord with me, and let us exalt his name together. Amen.**

Here let the people be seated.

INVOCATION *The minister.*

Let us pray.

Almighty God, who hast made the heart of man to respond to the touch of thy Spirit as a harp to the hand of a master; give to us the vision of thy glory as we worship thee. We laud thee, we bless thee, we give thanks unto thy great name for thy lovingkindness and thy truth. Unto thee we bring the obedience of our thanksgiving and the praise of our devotion; through Jesus Christ our Lord. **Amen.**

COLLECT *Here let the people unite with the minister in prayer.*

Almighty God, unto whom all hearts are open, all desires known, and from whom no secrets are hid; cleanse the thoughts of our hearts by the inspiration of thy Holy Spirit, that we may perfectly love thee, and worthily magnify thy holy name; through Christ our Lord. Amen.

ACT OF PRESENTATION *The people standing. The organ may be presented for dedication by one of the trustees, or someone designated for that purpose, in some such words as:*

We present this organ for dedication, [the gift of *N*. for the glory of God, and in loving memory of *N*.]

ACT OF DEDICATION *To be said responsively by the minister and the people.*

In the name of the Father, and of the Son, and of the Holy Spirit, we dedicate this organ to the praise of Almighty God.

631

Praise God in his sanctuary: praise him in the firmament of his power. Praise him with the sound of the trumpet: praise him with psaltery and harp.

We dedicate this organ to the cultivation of a high art: to the interpretation of the message of the masters of music, to an appreciation of the great doxologies of the Church, and to the development of the language of praise which belongeth both to earth and to heaven.

Praise him with stringed instruments and organs. Let everything that hath breath praise the LORD. Praise ye the LORD

We dedicate this organ to the wedding march, to thanksgiving on festal occasions, and to such inspiration in the service of song that all people may praise the Lord.

O sing unto the LORD a new song: sing unto the LORD all the earth, in psalms and hymns and spiritual songs, singing and making melody in your heart to the Lord.

We dedicate this organ to the healing of life's discords, and the revealing of the hidden soul of harmony; to the lifting of the depressed and the comforting of the sorrowing; to the humbling of the heart before the eternal mysteries, and the lifting of the soul to abiding beauty and joy, by the gospel of infinite love and good will.

That at the name of Jesus every knee should bow, of things in heaven, and things in earth, and things under the earth; and that every tongue should confess that Jesus Christ is Lord, to the glory of the Father.

PRAYER OF DEDICATION *The minister.*

Let us pray.

Our God and Father, whom the generations have worshiped with concord of sweet sound; be pleased to accept this organ as a song of praise unto thee. **Amen.**

Grant that its music, with accompanying song, may come as a blessed benediction upon all who worship here. **Amen.**

May this organ become undying music in the world as its notes of cheer, comfort, communion, and courage are modulated into human lives for daily task and noble service. **Amen.**

To all organists who shall sound its notes, and to all worshipers who shall be lifted Godward by its voice, may there come at times the sweep of hallelujahs from the throne of the redeemed, until earth below shall be attuned to heaven above, singing hallelujah to him who reigneth, Lord of hosts, the King of kings. Hallelujah! **Amen.**

Here may be sung a suitable hymn or anthem, after which may follow a recital or sermon. An offering may then be received, followed by the singing of a hymn.

BENEDICTION

POSTLUDE

¶ 1936. AN ORDER FOR THE DEDICATION OF A CHURCH-SCHOOL BUILDING OR PARISH HOUSE

PRELUDE *The people in devout meditation.*

HYMN *The people standing.*

CALL TO WORSHIP

Minister: Our help is in the name of the Lord, who made heaven and earth.

People: **Except the Lord build the house, they labor in vain that build it.**

Minister: Establish thou the work of our hands upon us; yea, the work of our hands establish thou it.

People: **Blessed be the name of the Lord from this time forth, and for evermore. Amen.**

Here let the people be seated.

INVOCATION *The minister.*

Let us pray.

Almighty and eternal God, whose lovingkindness never faileth, who rulest both in heaven and in earth, keeping mercy for thy people who walk before the presence of thy glory; graciously vouchsafe thy presence as we dedicate this building to thy service; mercifully illumine and brighten it with thine own glory, and pour down thy blessing upon it; through Jesus Christ our Lord. **Amen.**

THE LORD'S PRAYER

Our Father who art in heaven, hallowed be thy name; thy kingdom come; thy will be done on earth as it is in heaven. Give us this day our daily bread. And forgive us our trespasses, as we forgive those who trespass against us. And lead us not into temptation, but deliver us from evil. For thine is the kingdom, and the power, and the glory, forever. Amen.

HYMN

THE SCRIPTURE LESSON

Hear, O Israel: the LORD our God is one LORD: and thou shalt love the LORD thy God with all thy heart, and with all thy soul, and with all thy might. And these words, which I command thee this day, shall be in thine heart: and thou shalt teach them diligently unto thy children, and shalt talk of them when thou sittest in thine house, and when thou walkest by the way, and when thou liest down, and when thou risest up. And thou shalt bind them for a sign upon thine hand, and they shall be as frontlets between thine eyes. And thou shalt write them upon the posts of thy house, and on thy gates.

The heart of him that hath understanding asketh knowledge.

In the morning sow thy seed, and in the evening withhold not thine hand.

It is written in the prophets, And they shall be all taught of God. Every man therefore that hath heard, and hath learned of the Father, cometh unto me.

Who hath known the mind of the Lord, that he may instruct him? But we have the mind of Christ. That we may grow up into him in all things, which is the head, even Christ.

Master, we know that thou art true, and teachest the way of God in truth.

And the servant of the Lord must not strive; but be gentle unto all men, apt to teach, patient, in meekness instructing those that oppose themselves; if God peradventure will give them repentance to the acknowledging of the truth.

Go ye therefore, and teach all nations, . . . teaching them to observe all things whatsoever I have commanded you: and lo, I am with you alway, even unto the end of the world.

ANTHEM or HYMN

THE ADDRESS

OFFERTORY *Followed by an offertory response, which may be the Doxology.*

ACT OF PRESENTATION *Here let the Commission on Education stand up before the people, and let the chairman of the commission say to the minister:*

We present unto you this building to be dedicated to the glory of Almighty God and to the purposes of worship, fellowship, study, and service.

ACT OF DEDICATION *Here let the people stand and unite in the responses to the words of the minister.*

Dearly beloved, it is right and proper that buildings erected for such service in the name of our Lord and Saviour Jesus Christ should be formally and devoutly set apart for their special uses. For such a dedication we are now assembled. And, as the dedication of this building is vain without the solemn consecration of those whose gifts and labors it represents, let us now give ourselves anew to the service of God: our souls, that they may be renewed after the image of Christ; our bodies, that they may be fit temples for the indwelling of the Holy Spirit; and our labors and business, that they may be according to God's holy will, and that their fruit may tend to the glory of his name and the advancement of his Kingdom.

In the name of the Father, and of the Son, and of the Holy Spirit, we dedicate this building to the worship of God.

God is a Spirit: and they that worship him must worship him in spirit and in truth.

We dedicate this building to the purpose of Christian education: to the work of the church school, to the study of the Scriptures, and to the development of Christian character.

Whatsoever things were written aforetime were written for our learning. Blessed are they that hear the word of God, and keep it.

We dedicate this building to the broadening of mental horizons and the deepening of knowledge, that young and old may be awakened and informed.

Thy word is a lamp unto my feet, and a light unto my path.

We dedicate this building to Christian fellowship and to recreation of mind and body.

Thou wilt show me the path of life; in thy presence is fullness of joy; at thy right hand there are pleasures for evermore.

We dedicate this building to those tasks and aims in which the Christian serves his place and time: to the causes of missions, of Christian citizenship, and the broad field of social relations.

The kingdoms of this world are become the kingdoms of our Lord, and of his Christ; and he shall reign for ever and ever.

The minister and the people:

We dedicate ourselves anew to that service of our fellow men wherein can best be performed our true service of God, in obedience to the spirit of the Master when he said: Thou shalt love the Lord thy God with all thy heart, and thy neighbor as thyself.

PRAYER OF DEDICATION *The minister.*

Almighty God, our heavenly Father, whose eyes are ever toward the righteous, and whose ears are ever open unto their cry; graciously accept, we pray thee, this building which we now dedicate to thee, to thy service, and to thy glory, that in it love and wisdom may unite to bring joy and strength to those who gather here; and we beseech thee, receive us thy servants who here dedicate ourselves anew to thee and to those offices of fellowship and good will in which thou art well pleased. Grant that those who come here may be cheered and quickened in mind and body, and that they may be stirred in spirit to serve thee wisely and steadfastly; and the praise shall be thine forever; through Jesus Christ our Lord. **Amen.**

Blessed Lord, who hast caused all holy Scriptures to be written for our learning; grant that we may in such wise hear them, read, mark, learn, and inwardly digest them, that by patience, and comfort of thy holy Word, we may embrace and ever hold fast the blessed hope of everlasting life, which thou hast given us in our Saviour Jesus Christ. **Amen.**

O God, by whom the meek are guided in judgment, and light riseth up in darkness for the godly; grant us, in all doubts and uncertainties, the grace to ask what thou wouldest have us to do, that the spirit of wisdom may save us from all false choices, and that in thy light we may see light, and in thy straight path may not stumble; through Jesus Christ our Lord. **Amen.**

BENEDICTION

POSTLUDE

¶ 1937. AN ORDER FOR THE DEDICATION OF A HOSPITAL

SENTENCES OF PRAISE

Minister: Our help is in the name of the Lord,

People: **Who made heaven and earth.**

Minister: O give thanks unto the Lord; for he is good.

People: **For his mercy endureth forever. Amen.**

Here let the people be seated.

DECLARATION *The minister.*

Dearly beloved, this building, which by the favor of God and the labor of man has been so far completed, is a symbol of that care for the sick and the suffering which was supremely exemplified in the Lord Jesus, and which has always inspired those who follow him. We believe that the heavenly Father not only desires, but gladly accepts, the service of comfort and healing for which this building is to provide, and that he looks with favor upon the dedication of the building to himself and to the welfare of his children.

Let us therefore bring to him our praises for his guidance and aid in this undertaking, and our prayers on behalf of those who by their gifts or their services shall unite in fulfilling those purposes of love and skill for which this building is prepared.

HYMN OF PRAISE

THE SCRIPTURE LESSON

The Spirit of the Lord God is upon me; because the Lord hath anointed me to preach good tidings unto the meek; he hath sent me to bind up the broken-hearted, to proclaim liberty to the captives, and the opening of the prison to them that are bound; to proclaim the acceptable year of the Lord; to comfort all that mourn; to appoint unto them that mourn in Zion, to give unto them beauty for ashes, the oil of joy for mourning, the garment of praise for the spirit of heaviness.

The wilderness and the solitary place shall be glad for them; and the desert shall rejoice, and blossom as the rose. Strengthen ye the weak hands, and confirm the feeble knees. Say to them that are of a fearful heart, Be strong, fear not: behold, your God will come and save you. Then the eyes of the blind shall be opened, and the ears of the deaf shall be unstopped. Then shall the lame man leap as an hart, and the tongue of the dumb sing.

And the disciples of John showed him of all these things. And John calling unto him two of his disciples sent them to Jesus, saying, Art thou he that should come? or look we for another? And in that same hour he cured many of their infirmities and plagues, and of evil spirits; and unto many that were blind he gave sight. Then Jesus answering said unto them, Go your way, and tell John what things ye have seen and heard; how that the blind see, the lame walk, the lepers are cleansed, the deaf hear, the dead are raised, to the poor the gospel is preached. And blessed is he, whosoever shall not be offended in me.

HYMN OF DEDICATION

ADDRESS

OFFERTORY *Followed by an offertory response, which may be the Doxology.*

RESPONSIVE READING *The minister and the people.*

Bless the LORD, O my soul: and all that is within me, bless his holy name.

Bless the LORD, O my soul, and forget not all his benefits:

Who forgiveth all thine iniquities; who healeth all thy diseases;

Who redeemeth thy life from destruction; who crowneth thee with lovingkindness and tender mercies.

Like as a father pitieth his children, so the LORD pitieth them that fear him.

For he knoweth our frame; he remembereth that we are dust.

As for man, his days are as grass: as a flower of the field, so he flourisheth.

For the wind passeth over it, and it is gone; and the place thereof shall know it no more.

But the mercy of the LORD is from everlasting to everlasting upon them that fear him, and his righteousness unto children's children;

To such as keep his covenant, and to those that remember his commandments to do them.

Bless the LORD, ye his angels, that excel in strength, that do his commandments, hearkening unto the voice of his word.

Bless ye the LORD, all ye his hosts; ye ministers of his, that do his pleasure.

Bless the LORD, all his works in all places of his dominion.

Bless the LORD, O my soul.

GLORIA PATRI

Glory be to the Father, and to the Son, and to the Holy Ghost; as it was in the beginning, is now, and ever shall be, world without end. Amen.

ACT OF PRESENTATION *Here let the Board of Trustees or the proper committee stand up before the people, and let the chairman of the board or some properly designated person say to the minister:*

We present unto you this building, to be dedicated to the service of Almighty God in the relief of the sick and the suffering, [the gift of N. for the glory of God, and in loving memory of N.]

ACT OF DEDICATION *Here let the people stand and unite in the responses.*

Dearly beloved, it is right and proper that buildings erected for such service in the name of our Lord and Saviour Jesus Christ should be formally and devoutly set apart for their special uses. For such a dedication we are now assembled. And, as the dedication of this building is vain without the solemn consecration of those whose gifts and labors it represents, let us now give ourselves anew to the service of God: our souls, that they may be renewed after the image of Christ; our bodies, that they may be fit temples for the indwelling of the Holy Spirit; and our labors and business, that they may be according to God's holy will, and that their fruit may tend to the glory of his name and the advancement of his Kingdom.

In the name of the Father, and of the Son, and of the Holy Spirit, we dedicate this building as a hospital to the holy ministry of healing.

Blessed are the merciful: for they shall obtain mercy.

We dedicate this building to Christian helpfulness.

Whosoever shall give to drink unto one of these little ones a cup of cold water only, shall in no wise lose his reward.

We dedicate this building to sustaining power of the Holy Spirit in time of pain and suffering.

In all their afflictions he was afflicted, and the angel of his presence saved them.

We dedicate this building to the skill and wisdom that bring relief and cure, and to the patient research that uncovers fresh resources with which to serve the public health.

Happy is the man that findeth wisdom. Length of days is in her right hand. She is a tree of life to them that lay hold upon her.

The minister and the people.

We dedicate ourselves anew to that service of our fellow men wherein can best be performed our true service of God, in obedience to the spirit of the Master when he said: Thou shalt love the Lord thy God with all thy heart, and thy neighbor as thyself.

PRAYER OF DEDICATION *The Minister.*

Let us pray.

Almighty God, our heavenly Father, whose eyes are ever toward the righteous, and whose ears are ever open unto their cry; graciously accept, we pray thee, this building which we now dedicate to thee, to thy service, and to thy glory, that in it skill and tenderness may unite to bring health and cure to those who come for aid; and we beseech thee, receive us thy servants who here dedicate ourselves anew to thee and to those offices of love and good will in which thou art well pleased. Grant that those who come here in weakness may be made strong, that those who come in pain may find relief, and that those who come in sorrow may find joy and gladness; and the praise shall be thine forever; through Jesus Christ our Lord. **Amen.**

O blessed Lord, who hast power of life and death, of health and sickness; give wisdom and gentleness to all thy ministering servants, to physicians and surgeons, nurses and watchers by the sick, that, always bearing thy presence with them, they may not only heal but bless, and shine as lamps of hope in the darkest hours of distress and fear; through Christ our Lord. **Amen.**

O most merciful Father, we look to thee for thy grace on behalf of those who, coming here in grievous illness, may not return to earthly joys and sorrows, but pass from here into that life immortal where thou dost receive all who put their trust in thee. Thou hast said that as the heavens are higher than the earth, so are thy ways higher than our ways, but we know that all thy children are in thy tender and unfailing love which passeth our understanding, and we pray that the blessed ministry of thy Holy Spirit may sustain them, and that light eternal may shine upon them. **Amen.**

And now, O loving Father, we bow before thee, of whom the whole family in heaven and earth is named, praying that thou wouldest grant us, according to the richest of thy glory, to be strengthened with might by thy Spirit in the inner man; that Christ may dwell in our hearts by faith; that we, being rooted and grounded in love, may be able to comprehend with all saints what is the breadth, and length, and depth, and height; and to know the love of Christ, which passeth knowledge, that we might be filled with the fullness of God. **Amen.**

BENEDICTION

¶ 1938. AN ORDER FOR THE DEDICATION OF A SCHOOL, COLLEGE, OR UNIVERSITY BUILDING

PRELUDE *The people in devout meditation.*

SENTENCES OF PRAISE

Minister: O worship the Lord in the beauty of holiness: fear before him, all the earth.

People: **They that worship him must worship him in spirit and in truth. Amen.**

DECLARATION *The minister.*

Dearly beloved, this building, which by the favor of God and the labor of man has been so far completed, embodies the obligation of each generation to impart its treasures of wisdom and knowledge to the generation following. For the fulfillment of this task we need, not only the best that men can do, but above all the blessing of Almighty God. Let us therefore bring to him our praises for his aid in this undertaking, and our prayers on behalf of those who by their gifts or their service shall unite in fulfilling the purpose for which this building is prepared.

HYMN OF PRAISE

THE SCRIPTURE LESSON

Happy is the man that findeth wisdom, and the man that getteth understanding. For the merchandise of it is better than the merchandise of silver, and the gain thereof than fine gold. She is more precious than rubies: and all the things thou canst desire are not to be compared unto her. Length of days is in her right hand; and in her left hand riches and honor. Her ways are ways of pleasantness, and all her paths are peace. She is a tree of life to them that lay hold upon her: and happy is everyone that retaineth her. The Lord by wisdom hath founded the earth; by understanding hath he established the heavens. By his knowledge the depths are broken up, and the clouds drop down the dew. My son, let not them depart from thine eyes: keep sound wisdom and discretion: so shall they be life unto thy soul, and grace to thy neck, Then shalt thou walk in thy way, safely, and thy foot shall not stumble.

Enter ye in at the strait gate: for wide is the gate, and broad is the way, that leadeth to destruction, and many there be which go in thereat: because strait is the gate, and narrow is the way, which leadeth unto life, and few there be that find it. Therefore whosoever heareth these sayings of mine, and doeth them, I will liken him unto a wise man, which built his house upon a rock: and the rain descended, and the floods came, and the winds blew, and beat upon that house; and it fell not: for it was founded upon a rock. And everyone that heareth these sayings of mine, and doeth them not, shall be likened unto a foolish man, which built his house upon the sand: and the rain descended, and the floods came, and the winds blew, and beat upon that house; and it fell: and great was the fall of it.

HYMN OF DEDICATION

THE ADDRESS

OFFERTORY *Followed by an offertory response, which may be the Doxology.*

RESPONSIVE READING

Wisdom hath builded her house, she hath hewn out her seven pillars.

Doth not wisdom cry? and understanding put forth her voice?

She standeth in the top of high places, by the way in the places of the paths.

She crieth at the gates, at the entry of the city, at the coming in at the doors.

Unto you, O men, I call; and my voice is to the sons of man.

O ye simple, understand wisdom: and ye fools, be ye of an understanding heart.

Hear; for I will speak of excellent things; and the opening of my lips shall be right things.

For my mouth shall speak truth; and wickedness is an abomination to my lips.

Receive my instruction, and not silver; and knowledge rather than choice gold.

For wisdom is better than rubies; and all the things that may be desired are not to be compared to it.

But where shall wisdom be found? and where is the place of understanding?

Behold, the fear of the Lord, that is wisdom; and to depart from evil is understanding.

GLORIA PATRI

Glory be to the Father, and to the Son, and to the Holy Ghost; as it was in the beginning, is now, and ever shall be, world without end. Amen.

ACT OF PRESENTATION *Then let the Board of Trustees or the proper committee stand up before the people, and let one of them say unto the minister:*

We present unto you this building to be dedicated to the service of Almighty God in the enlightenment of his children, [the gift of *N.* for the glory of God, and in loving memory of *N.*]

ACT OF DEDICATION *The minister, the people uniting in the responses.*

Dearly beloved, it is right and proper that buildings erected for such service in the name of our Lord and Saviour Jesus Christ should be formally and devoutly set apart for their special uses. For such a dedication we are now assembled. And, as the dedication of this building is vain without the solemn consecration of those whose gifts and labors it represents, let us now give ourselves anew to the service of God: our souls, that they may be renewed after the image of Christ; our bodies, that they may be fit temples for the indwelling of the Holy Spirit; and our labors and business, that they may be according to God's holy will, and that their fruit may tend to the glory of his name and the advancement of his kingdom.

In the name of the Father, and of the Son, and of the Holy Spirit, we dedicate this building to the holy ministry of education.

Take fast hold of instruction; let her not go: keep her; for she is thy life.

We dedicate this building to the spiritual enrichment of all who shall come here in pursuit of knowledge.

Happy is the man that findeth wisdom, and the man that getteth understanding.

We dedicate this building to the loyal service of those whose training and devotion have prepared them to lead students toward the truth.

The Lord God hath given me the tongue of the learned, that I should know how to speak a word in season to him that is weary.

We dedicate this building to that ministry of administration upon whose ability and fruitfulness depends the wise conduct of its affairs.

Who then is that faithful and wise steward, whom his lord shall make ruler over his household? Blessed is that servant, whom his lord when he cometh shall find so doing.

The minister and the people.

We dedicate ourselves anew to that service of our fellow men wherein can best be performed our true service of God, in obedience to the spirit of the Master when he said: Thou shalt love the Lord thy God with all thy heart, and thy neighbor as thyself.

PRAYER OF DEDICATION *The minister.*

Let us pray.

Almighty God, our heavenly Father, whose eyes are ever toward the righteous, and whose ears are ever open unto their cry; graciously accept, we pray thee, this building which we now dedicate to thee, to thy service, and to thy glory, that in it love and wisdom may unite to make plain the path of knowledge to those who gather here, and we beseech thee, receive us thy servants who here dedicate ourselves anew to thee and to those offices of fellowship and good will in which thou art well pleased. Grant that those who come here, whether as administrators, teachers, or students, may come with pure minds, upright purpose, and steadfast endeavor to learn and to do thy holy will; through Jesus Christ our Lord. **Amen.**

God of our Fathers, we offer thee our heartfelt thanks for all thy servants, the parents and teachers, the benefactors and friends, by whose love and devotion we have come into our great inheritance of health, truth, and piety. Help us to guard faithfully this great boon, to profit by it, to augment it, and loyally to pass it on to the coming generation, that they through us may rise up to serve thee; in the name of Jesus Christ our Lord. **Amen.**

POSTLUDE

BENEDICTION

¶ 1939. AN ORDER FOR THE DEDICATION OF A HOME

SENTENCES OF PRAISE *The minister.*

Peace be to this house.

Beloved, let us love one another; for love is of God; and everyone that loveth is born of God, and knoweth God.

INVOCATION *The minister.*

Let us pray.

Almighty God, who hast mercifully promised to hear the prayers of thy people who call upon thee; we beseech thee graciously to bless this home which we dedicate to thy honor and service, and make it the abode of purity and peace and truth. Watch over thy people in their going out and their coming in, and direct their footsteps ever in the way of thy commandments; through Jesus Christ our Lord. **Amen.**

THE LORD'S PRAYER *Here let the people unite with the minister in prayer.*

Our Father who art in heaven, hallowed be thy name; thy kingdom come; thy will be done on earth as it is in heaven. Give us this day our daily bread. And forgive us our trespasses, as we forgive those who trespass against us. And lead us not into temptation, but deliver us from evil. For thine is the kingdom, and the power, and the glory, forever. Amen.

HYMN

ACT OF DEDICATION *To be said responsively by the minister and the people.*

In the name of the Father, and of the Son, and of the Holy Spirit, we dedicate this home to the glory of God, committing to his loving care this house and all who dwell in it.

Have thou respect unto the prayer of thy servant, O LORD my God, which thy servant prayeth before thee today; that thine eyes may be opened toward this house night and day.

647

We dedicate this home to the deep affections of the family circle, and to all friendly hospitalities.

Now God himself and our Father, and our Lord Jesus Christ, make you to increase and abound in love.

We dedicate this home to the courage, patience, and self-control which make life cheerful and serene.

Let patience have her perfect work, that ye may be perfect and entire, wanting nothing.

We dedicate this home to all beautiful things of heart and mind that lead the soul to wider vision and to higher aims.

> **Whene'er a noble deed is wrought,**
> **Whene'er is spoken a noble thought,**
> **Our hearts in glad surprise**
> **To higher levels rise.**

We dedicate this home to happiness, to hopefulness, and to health, that it may ever be, to those whose home it is, a dear haven of peace and joy.

> **Serene will be our days and bright,**
> **And happy will our nature be,**
> **When love is an unerring light,**
> **And joy its own security.**

PRAYER OF DEDICATION *The minister.*

Let us pray.

O God, our heavenly Father, giver of life; we pray thee, make this home an abode of light and love. May all that is pure, tender, and true grow up under its shelter. May all that hinders godly union and concord be driven far from it. Make it the center of fresh, sweet, and holy influence. Give wisdom for life, and discretion in the guidance of affairs.

Let thy work appear unto thy servants and thy glory unto their children. And let the beauty of the LORD our God be upon us: and establish thou the work of our hands upon us; yea, the work of our hands establish thou it. And the praise shall be thine forever. **Amen.**

HYMN

BENEDICTION *The minister.*

The LORD bless us, and keep us: the LORD make his face shine upon us, and be gracious unto us: the LORD lift up his countenance upon us, and give us peace, now and forevermore. **Amen.**

¶ 1940. AN ORDER FOR THE DEDICATION OF A MEMORIAL

The service shall be conducted in the customary way, and, when the sermon is ended, an appropriate hymn shall be sung; after which the minister, accompanied by those who are to takes part with him in the servoce, shall proceed to that part of the church where the act of dedication is to take place; and when the music ends, the people still standing, he shall say:

SENTENCES OF PRAISE

Minister: Our help is in the name of the Lord, who made heaven and earth.

People: **Give unto the Lord, O ye kindreds of the people, give unto the Lord glory and strength.**

Minister: Honor and majesty are before him: strength and beauty are in his sanctuary.

People: **Blessed be the name of the Lord from this time forth and forevermore. Amen.**

Here let the people be seated.

INVOCATION *The minister.*

Let us pray.

Blessed and glorious Lord God Almighty, by whose power, wisdom, and love all things are sanctified, enlightened, and made perfect; be merciful unto us and bless us, we beseech thee, and cause thy face to shine upon us, that what we now do may please thee, and show forth the honor of thy name. Let thy work appear unto thy servants, and thy glory unto their children. And let the beauty of the LORD our God be upon us: and establish thou the work of our hands upon us; yea, the work of our hands establish thou it; through Jesus Christ our Lord. **Amen.**

PRESENTATION AND DEDICATION *When that which is to be dedicated is a memorial, the minister shall then call upon the person appointed to perform the presentation of the memorial.*

We ask N. now to present the memorial.

The person making the presentation shall say:

In the name of [*or,* In memory of] **N.** we present to this church this memorial, to be dedicated to the glory and praise of God.

To which the properly designated official shall respond:

We accept this gift as a sacred trust, and shall guard it reverently, in honor of the faithful and devoted life to whose memory it is erected.

Then the minister shall pronounce the words of dedication:

In the faith of our Lord Jesus Christ, I dedicate this memorial to the glory of God, and in memory of his servant N.; in the name of the Father, and of the Son, and of the Holy Spirit. **Amen.**

DEDICATORY PRAYER *Let the people unite in the response.*

Give unto the LORD the glory due unto his name: worship the LORD in the beauty of holiness.

We see Jesus, because of the suffering of death, crowned with glory and honor.

Let us pray.

Almighty God our heavenly Father, without whom no words or works of ours have meaning, but who dost accept the gifts of our hands as the tokens of our devotion; grant thy blessing upon us as we dedicate this gift to thy glory. May this memorial which we now dedicate be an enduring witness before all thy people of the faithful service of thy servant. May our lives, being consecrated unto thy service, be joined with thy faithful ones into that building which groweth unto a holy temple in the Lord. **Amen.**

HYMN

BENEDICTION

POSTLUDE

APPENDIX

CHAPTER I

JUDICIAL COUNCIL: RULES AND DIGESTS OF DECISIONS

¶ 2001.   Rules of Practice and Procedure

1. *Officers.*—The officers of the Judicial Council shall be a president, a vice-president, and a secretary, to be elected quadrennially by a majority vote of the council; *provided* that no officer shall be elected to succeed himself in any particular office.

2. *Duties of President.*—The president shall perform all the duties incident to the office of a presiding officer of a judicial body, including the right to call the Judicial Council into session, as provided by the Discipline.

3. *Duties of the Vice-President.*—In case of absence or inability of the president, or at the request of the president, the vice-president shall preside over part or all of any session of the Judicial Council and perform all duties devolving upon the presiding officer while so presiding at such session.

4. *Duties of the Secretary.*—The secretary shall perform all duties incident to the position of secretary or clerk of a judicial body, and such other duties as shall be requested of him by the Judicial Council, among which shall be:

a) To keep a correct and complete record of all proceedings of the Judicial Council, including discussions, opinions, and all other actions taken by the council.

b) To keep the docket and perform the duties incident thereto, as hereinafter provided.

c) To furnish certified copy or copies of the record of the action of the Judicial Council, or any matter determined by it, to the party or parties interested and to such others as may have a right thereto.

d) To send to the secretary of the Council of Bishops certified copies of all decisions of the Judicial Council on questions of law, as provided in ¶ 909.

e) To notify the president of the Judicial Council immediately upon the filing of any matter submitted to the Judicial Council for determination, giving him a full and complete statement of the matter involved, together with such additional data as he may deem necessary.

5. *Docket.*—All matters of whatsoever kind and character which may be brought before the Judicial Council for determination shall be filed in consecutive order by the secretary and shall be reported fully to the council. At the conclusion of any annual session or General Conference session of the Judicial Council, all papers, documents, and exhibits in all matters finally disposed of shall be sent by the secretary for safekeeping to the library of Drew University.

6. *Proceedings Preparatory for Hearing.*—*a*) When any matter is appealed to the Judicial Council for determination, the document or documents and exhibits setting forth the same shall be filed with the secretary of the Judicial Council, and entered by him upon the docket of the council.

b) When a cause has been placed on the docket of the Judicial Council, the secretary thereof shall, within thirty (30) days from said date, furnish to each member of the council a copy of the document or documents and exhibits setting forth such appeal, or a careful and accurate digest thereof.

7. *Arguments.*—Interested parties may be heard in person or by others appearing for them, or both, but not more than two on the same side shall be heard except by consent of the council. Arguments shall be limited to one hour for each side; but upon request before the argument is begun, the council may allow such additional time as it may deem necessary for an adequate presentation of the issues involved.

8. *Interested Persons Not Parties May Be Heard.*—Any person or persons not parties to the record, but interested in a question of law pending before the Judicial Council may, with the consent of the council, be heard thereon before the council in session.

9. *Decisions.*—All decisions by the council shall be in writing and shall be accompanied by an opinion in which the reasons upon which it is based shall be stated with a citation of the pertinent authorities, and shall show whether or not all members of the council concur in the decision, giving the names of such members as do not concur. Any member of the council who dissents may give in writing the reasons for his dissent, which shall be entered of record.

10. *Approval and Signing of the Record.*—The record of all sessions of the Judicial Council shall be approved by the council in session and signed by the president and attested by the secretary.

11. *No Discussions Outside Council Meetings.*—The members of the Judicial Council will not permit discussion with them on matters pending before them, or that may be referred to them for determination, save and except before the Judicial Council in session.

12. *Rules May Be Amended.*—These rules may be amended, repealed, or extended at any session of the Judicial Council by a majority vote thereof.

¶ 2002.   Digests of Decisions

[These digests reproduce the official summaries prepared by the Judicial Council except that references to Disciplinary paragraphs have been edited for the convenience of readers of the present edition. Each paragraph number, if the number or the legislation itself has been changed since the date of the decision, is followed by an editorial note enclosed in square brackets, like those enclosing this explanation. The note gives the date of the edition of the Discipline used in the decision and the corresponding paragraph number in the present edition, with an indication if there has been any significant amendment. Other bracketed notes bring terminology up to date. For complete texts of the decisions see the Journals of the General Conferences of 1952 (1-87) and 1956 (88-130) and the General Minutes of 1960 (131-75), or see the volume *Decisions of the Judicial Council* (Methodist Publishing House, 1960).—EDITORS.]

1. Lay missionaries as defined in ¶ 974 [1939; now ¶ 1187.2, amended] are not eligible to vote in an Annual Conference for ministerial delegates to General Conference. April 26, 1940.

2. An appeal was taken from a bishop's rulings in an Annual Conference before Unification, which appeal passed to the Judicial Council under ¶ 1624 [1939; an interim enabling act]. This appeal involved a request for rulings asking interpretations of prior pension laws of the Methodist Episcopal Church. As the record did not show that any vested rights of the appellant were affected, the appeal was dismissed, and the bishop's rulings affirmed. April 26, 1940.

3. A member of an Annual Conference located under the provisions of the 1932 Discipline (Methodist Episcopal Church), although he may have been improperly deprived of his right to be heard when his Annual Conference was considering the report of the Conference Relations Committee on his case, but who thereafter defied the action of the conference by continuing to preach in a charge where previously appointed, thereby forfeits his right of appeal. A member may forfeit his right of appeal by contumacious treatment of the church and its authority. April 27, 1940.

4. ¶ 462 [1939; now ¶ 558], providing for election by Central Conferences of bishops for a limited term, is constitutional. April 30, 1940.

5. That part of ¶ 492 [1939; now ¶ 607, amended] which attempts to grant to members of a Mission Conference [Provisional Annual Conference] the right to elect delegates to Jurisdictional Conferences is unconstitutional. May 2, 1940. [*See* ¶ 45 iv.]

6. That part of ¶ 452 [1939; now ¶ 543, amended] which attempts to grant to Mission Conferences [Provisional Annual Conferences] the right to elect delegates to Central Conferences is unconstitutional. May 3, 1940. [*See* ¶ 45 ii.]

7. The legislation enacted by the 1940 General Conference providing for automatic retirement of clerical members of Annual Conferences whose seventy-second birthday precedes the first day of the regular session of the Annual Conference (¶ 231 [1940; now ¶ 368]) is constitutional, as it is a general principle of constitutional construction that legislation must be upheld unless it is clearly in conflict with the Constitution interpreted as a whole. The matter of uniform regulations for retirement of ministers is a connectional matter, and as such it is a subject over which the General Conference under the Constitution has legislative power. May 5, 1940.

8. An "unstationed" minister under the provisions of the Methodist Protestant Church Discipline of 1936 is in the same relation to an Annual Conference as "located" ministers under the provisions of ¶¶ 235-39 [1940; now ¶¶ 374-79]. April 15, 1941.

9. A general rule by action of an Annual Conference as to retired ministers receiving a pension and also receiving pay as supply pastor is in conflict with the provisions of ¶ 1329 [1940; now ¶ 1627, amended] as to disallowance of claims in whole or in part, as it denies the claimant the right to make an oral or written statement to the Board of Conference Claimants [Conference Board of Pensions], and denies him the protection of the two-thirds vote of the conference prescribed in said paragraph. April 15, 1941.

10. Members of an Annual Conference Board of Lay Activities, being a board that asks for appropriations from the Annual Conference Commission on World Service and Finance, are ineligible for membership on the commission, under the provisions of ¶ 1224 and ¶ 1228 [1940; now ¶¶ 1503.1, 1504.7]. April 28, 1942.

11. In view of the inhibition by the Missouri state constitution of religious corporations except to hold title to real estate for church edifices, parsonages, and cemeteries, the trustees of an Annual Conference in Missouri may not be incorporated, but the trustees duly elected as an unincorpo-

rated board are the proper parties to recover possession of property of abandoned churches under the provisions of ¶ 782 [1940; now ¶ 188]. April 29, 1942.

12. The decisions of a Joint Distributing Committee duly constituted under the provisions of ¶ 1312 [1939; now ¶ 1609, amended], having acted in accordance with such provisions, are binding upon the several conferences affected by merger. April 29, 1942.

13. An Annual Conference Board of Conference Claimants [Conference Board of Pensions] is not required to submit its askings for appropriations to the Annual Conference Commission on World Service and Finance under the provisions of ¶¶ 832, 834, and 835 [1940; now ¶¶ 791, 793, 794, amended] but reports its recommendations directly to the Annual Conference in accordance with ¶ 1323.2 [1940; now ¶ 1623 .3-.4, amended]. To reconcile conflicting provisions in legislative enactment, the entire legislation must be considered, and the legislative intent is to be drawn from the act as a whole. April 29, 1942.

14. Under the provisions of ¶ 1330 [1940; now ¶ 1636, amended], no liability rests on the Annual Conference of which the claimant was a member on retirement for the years of service of such claimant which he served in a Mission Conference. December 8, 1943.

15. Action of an Annual Conference in retiring ministers on age limit, under the provisions of ¶ 231 [1940; now ¶ 368], is legal, as said paragraph has been heretofore held to be constitutional. December 8, 1943.

16. An Annual Conference Committee on Conference Relations and Ministerial Qualifications [Board of Ministerial Training and Qualifications] may, under the provisions of ¶¶ 463 and 466 [1940; now ¶¶ 669-71, amended], recommend for admission a minister claiming to come from another evangelical church (¶ 311 [1940; now ¶ 411, amended, but see ¶¶ 412-13]), even though such minister had previously been a member of the same conference from which he had withdrawn; but final action thereon rests with the Annual Conference, which may accept or reject the recommendations for admission submitted by the committee. December 8, 1943.

17. The expenses which may be paid from the General Administration Fund are strictly limited by the provisions of ¶ 848 [1940; now ¶ 765, amended], and therefore the General Commission [Council] on World Service and Finance is not thereby authorized to pay expenses incurred by a Jurisdictional Committee of Appeals acting under the provisions of ¶ 694 [1940; now ¶ 1045]. April 27, 1944.

18. The procedure for restoration of credentials of a traveling deacon or elder which have been surrendered, under ¶ 707 [1940; now ¶ 993, amended], requires that the steps therein outlined shall be strictly followed. April 26, 1944.

19. Under the provisions of ¶ 1309 [1940; now ¶ 1608], ministers who at time of retirement may have been members of an Annual Conference within the territory assigned to the Illinois Corporation are nevertheless entitled to annuities from the Endowment Fund for Superannuates held by the Missouri Corporation on account of the years of service formerly rendered in an Annual Conference of the Methodist Episcopal Church, South, or in an Annual Conference of the Methodist Episcopal Church in territory assigned to the Missouri Corporation. However, no claimant has any vested right or equity in such General Endowment Fund nor the income derived therefrom. April 26, 1944.

20. The widow of a former member of a conference of the Methodist Episcopal Church, who voluntarily located under the then provisions of the Discipline of that church, may not invoke the provision of that Discipline applying to involuntary locations, and therefore has no claim for a pension which the deceased located minister himself did not have. May 2, 1944.

21. As the only provision in the Constitution relating to election of bishops is that they shall be elected by the respective Jurisdictional and Central Conferences, it would be unconstitutional for the General Conference to elect missionary bishops. May 1, 1944.

22. A bishop, effective or retired, is not a member of an Annual Conference, and should not be counted in reporting total membership of the conference for voting or other purposes. May 2, 1944.

23. The provisions of the Discipline as to declaratory decisions by the Judicial Council do not confer upon the council any legislative power, and whenever there is doubt as to the meaning of any General Conference legislation, it is the duty of the General Conference itself to clarify its own enactment. May 2, 1944.

24. That part of ¶ 934 [1940; now ¶ 1187.2, amended], which provides that outside the United States of America lay missionaries may be seated in an Annual Conference "with the right to vote on all questions not ministerial or constitutional, etc.," is unconstitutional, as ¶ 21 of the Constitution strictly defines the composition and qualifications of the members of an Annual Conference. May 2, 1944.

25. ¶ 1716 [1940], under heading "Statement on Peace and War," and ¶ 1712 [1940; now ¶ 2020, amended], under the

heading "Our Social Creed," contained identical provisions as to claims for exemption from military service by conscientious objectors who may be members of The Methodist Church, and although the Statement on Peace and War adopted by the 1944 General Conference is somewhat at variance with the "Statement on Peace and War," ¶ 1716, yet it did not repeal ¶ 1712; and accordingly conscientious objectors who are members of The Methodist Church still have the same protection as heretofore. May 4, 1944.

26. The determination of the meaning of the words "church members" as used in ¶ 871 [1940; now ¶ 1129, amended] is a legislative matter within the province of the General Conference, and is not a judicial matter to be settled by the Judicial Council, unless the question arises in some case legally pending before the council. May 3, 1944.

27. Under the provisions of ¶ 1619 and ¶ 1618.8 a retired minister of the Mississippi Conference, formerly a member of the Methodist Protestant Church, who originally entered the ministry of the Methodist Episcopal Church, South, but was involuntarily located, and who was subsequently received into the ministry of the Methodist Protestant Church, is entitled to have the years of service in the Methodist Episcopal Church, South, included in the number of years on which his annuity claim is based. December 4, 1944.

28. The Constitution of The Methodist Church provides that boundaries of Annual Conferences shall be determined by the respective Jurisdictional Conference, and this power may not be delegated to the Annual Conferences themselves. December 4, 1944.

29. The Board of Trustees of a local church is not such a body as would have the right to appeal directly to the Judicial Council, so that it may petition for a declaratory decision under the provisions of ¶ 914; but the questions of law involved in any such request for a declaratory decision may be acted upon by the Quarterly Conference under ¶ 362 .14 and may thus eventually become subject to review by the Judicial Council. December 4, 1944.

30. The action of the General Conference of 1944 in asking for contributions to world service determined by a percentage in excess of contributions during a particular fiscal year is within the constitutional powers of the General Conference as prescribed by ¶ 8.9, even though in a particular case it may seem to result in an unfair apportionment. December 5, 1944.

31. Ministers coming from other evangelical churches, whether proceeding under § 1, 2, or 3 of ¶ 411 [1944; now §§ 1-

4, amended], are in all cases subject to the requirement of meeting "the educational standards required of Methodist ministers." December 5, 1944.

32. Under the constitutional provisions contained in ¶ 8 .12 the General Conference may change boundaries of Jurisdictional Conferences only by consent of the Annual Conferences in each Jurisdictional Conference involved. Accordingly the action of the 1944 General Conference granting permission to the Central Jurisdiction only to change boundaries of the Delaware Annual Conference, which proposed changes involved also changes in boundaries of certain Annual Conferences in the Northeastern Jurisdiction, did not grant any power to the Northeastern Jurisdictional Conference to initiate any such boundary changes. December 5, 1944.

33. The provision of ¶ 914 limits the jurisdiction of the Judicial Council as to declaratory decisions so that they do not include moot or hypothetical questions; and the same principle applies to requests for rulings by a bishop in an Annual Conference, which requests should be based upon some action taken or proposed to be taken, wherein under the specific facts in each case some doubt may have arisen as to the legality of the action taken or proposed. May 8, 1946.

34. District Conferences may license proper persons to preach and other orders under the provisions of ¶ 670 et seq. [1944]; but "all votes to license shall be by ballot," and the casting of a ballot by the secretary pursuant to a vote authorizing him to do so is illegal. May 8, 1946.

35. The provision of ¶ 437, in connection with retired bishops of Jurisdictional Conferences, stating that "he may participate in the Council of Bishops, but without vote," is not in conflict with the Constitution, ¶ 34, as the Constitution by ¶ 8.5 granted unto the General Conference the power to "define and fix the powers, duties, and privileges of the episcopacy." May 8, 1946.

36. As an Annual Conference has no quorum, a session of conference held in wartime abbreviated to one day, and ostensibly restricted in attendance to officers and certain committees (although it was stated that all members of the conference were entitled to be present), although irregular, was nevertheless a legal session. May 9, 1946.

37. The jurisdiction of the Judicial Council to pass on the constitutionality of an act of the General Conference is limited by ¶ 43.1, and its jurisdiction as to declaratory decisions is limited by ¶ 914 [1944; later amended], in neither one of which paragraphs is provision made for initiating any such procedure by an Annual Conference. Accordingly the

Judicial Council may not render any decision involving the constitutionality of ¶ 646 on the request, petition, or other action of an Annual Conference only. May 9, 1946.

38. In a case where an Annual Conference (as permitted by the Discipline) has been incorporated under the provisions of the statutes of the state of Kansas, and the corporation has adopted by-laws in statutory form, the corporate sessions must be called in the manner provided by the by-laws; but when the conference is once in such corporate session, it may exercise all the powers it ever possessed, including the right to amend its by-laws and its charter. May 9, 1946.

39. A resolution of the General Conference of 1944 "that in all official literature and pronouncements of The Methodist Church respecting the date of its origin, it shall date from 1784" does not involve a constitutional question, and accordingly the Judicial Council will not take jurisdiction; but at the same time the council holds that under Art. V of the Declaration of Union the present organization of The Methodist Church began in 1939. May 9, 1946.

40. The decision of the Judicial Council upholding the constitutionality of ¶ 437 as to voting by retired bishops affirmed. (See Judicial Council Decision 35.) April 23, 1947.

41. The footnote to Art. XXIII, Articles of Religion [¶ 83], held to be not a constitutional part of the Articles of Religion. It was made a footnote by legislative act only. April 24, 1947.

42. The provisions of ¶ 646 permitting an Annual Conference to "order an executive session of the ministerial members to consider questions relating to matters of ordination, character, and conference relations," held to be constitutional. April 24, 1947.

43. A standing rule of an Annual Conference, adopted according to ¶ 631 [1944; now ¶ 634], which provides that "a retired minister may not serve on a quadrennial board or commission" is not contrary to the Constitution. April 23, 1947.

44. In Annual Conferences which provide for support of district superintendents according to ¶ 788 [1944; now ¶ 801] the amount of such support (including salary and allowances) and the apportionments thereof must be recommended annually by the Annual Conference Commission on World Service and Finance, and may not be regulated by a standing rule of the conference. April 23, 1947.

45. An Annual Conference may by proper action make appropriations from conference funds to institutions or organizations on the governing boards of which the Annual

Conference is not represented by trustees, directors, or other officials. April 23, 1947.

46. The provision of ¶ 1618.2*i* as to calculating years of service of a conference claimant covers "all cases" and refers to all service of retired ministers, irrespective of whether before or after the year 1944. April 24, 1947.

47. A minister tried in the year 1941, in accordance with the provisions of the 1940 Discipline, and the judgment of the trial court affirmed by the Jurisdictional Committee of Appeals in 1942, which judgment became final under the provisions of the Discipline, may not appeal to the Judicial Council to review the case for alleged errors of law under the provisions of ¶¶ 1033 and 1045, which legislation was enacted in 1944 to cover cases decided after said paragraphs became effective; and therefore such an attempted appeal was dismissed. April 24, 1947.

48. A Jurisdictional Conference has the right under ¶ 440 to assign a bishop to the supervision of Mission Conferences and Provisional Annual Conferences, even though the geographical territory covered by such Mission and Provisional Conferences may overlap the geographical territory assigned to other bishops, as there is nothing in the Discipline that would limit the phrase "episcopal area" as used in ¶ 440 to a geographical definition. April 24, 1947.

49. The proviso in ¶ 341 [1944; later amended] as to admission into full connection in the Annual Conference of one who while a student has been regularly appointed as pastor does not eliminate the two-year trial period as required by the first part of this paragraph. May 3, 1948.

50. None of the provisions of the Pension Code, with particular reference to ¶¶ 1618, 1623, and 1624, limit an Annual Conference, in making an apportionment for conference claimants, to an amount exactly necessary to meet the disbursements for that particular year; but under the provisions of ¶ 1613.10 [1944; now ¶ 1611.13] any excess amount raised by such an apportionment may be used to create a reserve fund for future years. May 3, 1948.

51. An allowance for "travel expenses" to pastors is not to be regarded as supplementary compensation tending to defeat proportional payment under the terms of ¶ 1624, provided always that such item represents an actual expense for the purpose stated, and is not a cover-up for additional salary paid to the pastor. May 4, 1948.

52. The Quarterly Conference of a local church may not appeal to the Judicial Council, nor petition for a declaratory decision, as it is not an "authority in the church that would

have the right of appeal" under the provisions of ¶ 914. May 5, 1948.

53. The provision of ¶ 555 [1944; now ¶ 444; see ¶ 45 vi] giving a Central Conference bishop the right to vote in the Council of Bishops "whenever the interest of his Central Conference or the interests common to all Central Conferences are involved" is constitutional. May 6, 1948.

54. Enabling acts, adopted in 1940 and 1944, as to continuing the corporate life or operation of various corporations, boards, and other agencies of the church, where the incomplete status still continues, do not need to be re-enacted in 1948, as this legislation, unless specifically limited as to time, is in effect until repealed or amended. May 6, 1948.

55. When the procedure provided by the Constitution for making changes in Jurisdictional Conference boundaries has been complied with, the enactment of legislation by the General Conference making such boundary changes is constitutional. May 6, 1948.

56. Under the constitutional provisions contained in ¶ 8 .12 the General Conference may change the boundaries of Jurisdictional Conferences only by consent of a majority of the Annual Conferences in each jurisdiction as therein prescribed. Accordingly any legislation attempted by General Conference without complying with these provisions is invalid. May 6, 1948.

57. An amendment to ¶ 440 which would require the consent of the Jurisdictional Committee on Episcopacy for fixing boundaries of episcopal areas is unconstitutional, as this power is reserved to the bishops as a part of episcopal administration under the Constitution. May 6, 1948.

58. Under the Constitution, the General Conference has unlimited authority, *inter alia*, to define and fix the qualifications of elders and deacons; and accordingly a special act of the General Conference prescribing that in the Germany Central Conference the ordination of an elder may take the place of ordination as a deacon, and that the ordination as a deacon may be omitted, is constitutional. May 6, 1948.

59. The Judicial Council has no jurisdiction to determine constitutionality of affirmations of faith. May 7, 1948.

60. That portion of ¶ 607 [1944; later amended; see ¶ 45 iv, vii, viii] reading "and they (Provisional Annual Conferences) may elect one ministerial and one lay delegate to the Jurisdictional Conference" is unconstitutional. May 7, 1948.

61. A Central Conference bishop whose term of office expires and he is not re-elected is returned to membership in the Annual Conference of which he ceased to be a member when

elected bishop. His term of office expires at the close of the Central Conference at which his successor is elected; hence he would be entitled to participate as a bishop in the consecration of his successor. April 29, 1949.

62. The act of the 1948 General Conference adding to ¶ 901 Art. 1 the following clause: "*Provided*, however, that as a result of the election each jurisdiction shall be represented on the council," is constitutional. The decision is based on the interpretation that same refers to the manner of election and does not constitute any member of the Judicial Council as the representative of any particular group, section, area, or jurisdiction. The Judicial Council is a judicial tribunal, and not a representative body as such. The members are to be free from any sectional interests and to serve the entire church. Any other interpretation of the act in question would render it wholly unconstitutional. April 29, 1949.

63. Designated gifts under ¶ 775 of the 1944 Discipline (¶ 745 of the 1948 Discipline) [deleted in 1952] are subject to the settled and established plan that contributions for the cause of world service and conference benevolences by a charge shall first be divided on the ratio prescribed by the Annual Conference. Only that portion of such contributions allocated under the conference ratio to world service can be designated to world service projects; and only that portion of such contributions allocated under the conference ratio to conference benevolences can be designated to conference benevolence projects. April 29, 1949.

64. An Annual Conference can dispose of by gift to a non-denominational body a college owned and controlled by it even though same has been built by private donations; *provided* that, if there should be assets belonging to the college made in consideration of its remaining a Methodist college under the control and management of the Annual Conference, the disposition of such particular assets would be a matter of property rights and controlled by civil law, over which property rights the Judicial Council would probably have no jurisdiction. April 29, 1949.

65. Terms and provisions set out in ¶ 807 [1948; now ¶ 827] are defined or interpreted as follows: (1) "At any regular session" means any session of an Annual Conference at which business is transacted. (2) "Regular active itinerants," as used in said paragraph, includes only effective members of the Annual Conference serving as pastors, and does not include district superintendents and members of the conference serving under special appointments. (3) By "basic" is meant the schedule of salaries to be paid pastors and

supply pastors from a common treasury under any basic salary plan adopted by an Annual Conference; such salaries to be uniform, subject only to the variants allowed under said ¶ 807. Such salaries may be augmented by pastoral charges as provided in ¶ 807.3. (*See also* Judicial Council Decision 70.) April 29, 1949.

66. The Judicial Council does not have jurisdiction to review the decision of a bishop not requested or made in open session of an Annual or District Conference. April 29, 1949.

67. Under the Constitution, ¶ 15, the Jurisdictional Conference has authority "to make rules and regulations for the administration of the work of the church within the jurisdiction." The act of the South Central Jurisdictional Conference recommending that "no Annual Conference establish a conference encampment without consideration by the Conference Board of Education" is constitutional. April 29, 1949.

68. When a minister is elected and consecrated as a bishop in The Methodist Church, he ceases to be a member of an Annual Conference and is no longer subject to the Ministers Reserve Pension Plan. April 29, 1949.

69. Under the grant of powers to Central Conferences by General Conference legislation within the provisions of the Constitution, the Germany Central Conference had authority to create an administrative committee to have charge of current matters of business, and to represent that conference in legal matters arising between conference sessions. Such committee, however, shall be responsible to the Central Conference. April 26, 1950.

70. Although by the general terms of ¶ 807 [1948; now ¶ 827] district superintendents are not included in the classification of "regular active itinerants" (*see* Judicial Council Decision 65), yet in an Annual Conference which provides for support of district superintendents on recommendation of the Conference Commission on World Service and Finance (¶ 788 [1948; now ¶ 801]), if it also adopts the basic salary plan, there should be included therein the support of district superintendents. April 27, 1950.

71. Enabling acts, adopted in 1940 and in 1944, as to continuing the corporate life or operation of various corporations, boards, and other agencies of the church, where the incomplete status still continues, do not need to be re-enacted, as this legislation, unless specifically limited as to time, is in effect until repealed or amended. April 28, 1950.

72. ¶ 327 [1948; now ¶ 330, amended] applies only to the four-year course of study and does not apply to the two years' graduate study required of members of the conference ad-

mitted by the three-fourths vote rule under ¶ 323 [1948; now ¶ 325.3]. The Annual Conference under ¶ 22 has authority to prescribe time in which these two years of graduate study must be completed. For dereliction of a member in this respect the Annual Conference could, under other provisions of the Discipline, take appropriate action. April 29, 1950.

73. An Annual Conference has the authority to instruct its Board of Conference Claimants [Conference Board of Pensions] to include supply years in computing the annuity years of a member of the conference. January 3, 1951.

74. A business session of the lay delegates to an Annual Conference would be illegal if not called for the purpose of electing lay delegates to the General and Jurisdictional Conferences. January 3, 1951.

75. The Ohio Annual Conference of The Methodist Church, now being the White Cross Hospital Association of Ohio, is the source of ultimate control of the White Cross Hospital and has the right and power at its discretion to change or amend the method of electing the trustees of the corporation; but, until the Annual Conference changes the method set forth in Art. VI of the present constitution of said White Cross Hospital Association, it is bound thereby. January 3, 1951.

76. § 2 of ¶ 502 [1948; now ¶ 504] is not unconstitutional. The following sentence in § 3 of ¶ 502, "A spring Annual Conference may elect the delegates to the General and Jurisdictional Conferences at its third regular session following the adjournment of the General Conference," is unconstitutional. November 28, 1951.

77. (1) A report to an Annual Conference, containing a financial statement which the Discipline requires to be audited, should not be approved until the audit is made and the financial statement is shown to be correct. Other parts of the report may be approved pending such audit.

(2) The Discipline does not specify the manner of presenting nominations for conference lay leader to the Annual Conference; hence oral nominations are permissible unless the Annual Conference has provided otherwise.

(3) In the Kentucky Annual Conference the nomination of the conference lay leader, to be valid, must be made by the Annual Conference Board of Lay Activities by ballot at a meeting of such board at which a majority of the members of the board are present and voting, and by a majority vote of the members of the board present and voting.

(4) The Discipline does not require that a certificate reciting the process by which the nomination was determined shall be presented with the nomination. When the nomination of a

conference lay leader is presented to the Annual Conference by a representative of the Board of Lay Activities, the regularity of same will be presumed in the absence of a showing to the contrary. November 27, 1951.

78. The Annual Conference has no authority to delegate its responsibilities and powers to Quarterly Conferences except as explicitly given that authority by the General Conference. Therefore the Pittsburgh Annual Conference had no authority to delegate to the Quarterly Conferences the power to determine whether or not the Annual Conference would adopt the [Ministers] Reserve Pension Plan. November 28, 1951.

79. The Annual Conference has no authority to delegate its responsibilities and powers to Quarterly Conferences except as explicitly given that authority by the General Conference. Therefore the Illinois Annual Conference had no authority to delegate to the Quarterly Conferences the power to determine whether or not the Annual Conference would adopt the [Ministers] Reserve Pension Plan. November 28, 1951.

80. A Central Conference bishop whose term of office expires or is terminated is returned to membership in the Annual Conference of which he was a member when elected bishop. D. D. Alejandro is bound by the 1946 action of the Central Conference under which he was elected, consecrated, and served as bishop. At the close of the 1948 session of the Philippines Central Conference he automatically became an effective member of the Philippines Annual Conference. November 27, 1951.

81. A retired minister whose pension payments from the Annual Conference were reduced during the quadrennium 1944-48 in accordance with the provisions of ¶ 1630.1, Discipline of 1944 [deleted in 1948], has no right to claim from the Board of Conference Claimants [Conference Board of Pensions] the amount of such reductions. November 28, 1951.

82. It is not necessary to adopt a fixed rule to determine the applicability of the term "full-time ministry" (¶ 343 Question 17 [1948; now ¶ 345]), as each case must be considered by the Committee on Conference Relations on the facts applicable thereto. November 28, 1951.

83. Under present provisions of the Discipline no age limit has been made for the retirement of Central Conference bishops. ¶ 436 applies only to bishops assigned to jurisdictions under the Plan of Union and those elected by Jurisdictional Conferences since Union. Under ¶ 8 the General Conference has the right to prescribe a uniform rule for the superannua-

tion of all bishops, but to date it has not exercised that power. April 26, 1952.

84. All bishops elected by a Jurisdictional Conference under ¶ 439 have the same status as any bishop assigned to a jurisdiction under the Plan of Union or who has been elected by a Jurisdictional Conference; and any bishop assigned to or elected by any Jurisdictional Conference may be assigned to any area over which the jurisdiction has been given episcopal supervision, including missions outside the territory of such jurisdiction. April 30, 1952.

85. The transfer of a local church of the Central Jurisdiction to an Annual Conference of another jurisdiction can be done only in accordance with appropriate action of the General Conference, Jurisdictional Conferences, and Annual Conferences, as provided in the Constitution. This method of making such a change can only be changed by a constitutional amendment. May 1, 1952.

86. (1) The sentence: "Such a society of believers, being within The Methodist Church and subject to its Discipline, is also an inherent part of the Church Universal, which is composed of all who accept Jesus Christ as Lord and Saviour, and which in the Apostles' Creed we declare to be the holy catholic Church," is not so clearly in violation of the First Restrictive Rule as to constitute its insertion in the proposed legislation of which it forms a part a legal matter of such a nature as to authorize the Judicial Council to take jurisdiction and render a decision as to its constitutionality.

(2) The proposal to add by legislation the words "is the creation of God and" to ¶ 101 of the report under consideration, same being Art. XIII of the Articles of Religion, does alter and change said article. It is therefore in violation of the First Restrictive Rule, and is unconstitutional. May 3, 1952.

87. There is nothing in either the Constitution or the general legislation of The Methodist Church that would deprive a retired traveling preacher of his right to vote as a full member of the Annual Conference. May 5, 1952.

88. A retired member of an Annual Conference may be elected to membership in a Central Conference if he meets the conditions required by law of all those who represent their Annual Conferences in the General or Central Conference. November 25, 1952.

89. A Committee of Investigation has authority only to inquire whether or not the accused person is guilty of committing one of the offenses enumerated in ¶ 921. Its findings must be certified and declared to the Annual Conference by

the district superintendent. If in the judgment of the committee the evidence does seem to substantiate the accusation, the committee has no alternative but to prepare and file the proper charges and specifications. November 25, 1952.

90. The provisions of ¶ 806.4 [1948; now ¶ 826.3, amended] are mandatory.

91. An unordained student pastor, who is a candidate for the traveling ministry, while serving as a regularly appointed pastor of a charge, may be authorized to administer the Sacraments of Baptism and the Lord's Supper, and, if the laws of the state permit, to perform the marriage ceremony within the bounds of his pastoral charge, provided he has passed the course of study for admission on trial; but he may be excused from advancing in the conference course of study while attending a college or seminary "approved by the authorized standardizing agency." November 25, 1952.

92. An Annual Conference may authorize a subsidiary hospital corporation to borrow up to a certain percentage of the value of its property for the purpose of its expansion program. When appraised as provided in the resolution under consideration, it cannot be held that such resolution authorized an unlimited incurring of indebtedness. November 25, 1952.

93. No quorum is necessary for a session of the Quarterly Conference, and it is legal to reduce the number of the trustees in a church from nine to three to comply with the state law. November 25, 1952.

94. Dr. L. Dorsey Spaugy, being the first in order of election of the ministerial alternates to membership upon the Judicial Council, is the lawful successor of Dr. Chas. B. Ketcham, deceased. June 25, 1953. [From the decision: "The expressions 'of each class' or 'respective classes' as used in the articles of ¶ 901 quoted above refer to ministerial and lay members or ministerial alternates or lay alternates, and not to the class or classes of any particular year or years."]

95. Special appointments listed in the Annual Conference journal in compliance with ¶ 1618.4, showing annuity responsibility, must be the special appointments of the current conference and not those of the previous conference. June 26, 1953.

96. The Discipline of The Methodist Church is a book of law, and the only official and authoritative book of law of The Methodist Church—"a body of laws pertaining to church government," regulating every phase of the life and work of The Methodist Church, including regulations relating to its temporal economy and to the ownership, use, and disposition of church property. June 26, 1953.

97. All "approved full-time supply pastors" except those who have already been ordained elders are required to obey the provisions of ¶ 320 [1952; now ¶ 317.2, amended]. June 26, 1953.

98. An Annual Conference may create a commission or "council" for the purpose of correlating and promoting the work of the various agencies of the conference but without authority over those boards, commissions, and committees whose powers and duties are defined in certain paragraphs of the Discipline. July 19, 1954.

99. General legislation giving the Division of National Missions of the Board of Missions control over the work of the Board of Church Extension of the Methodist Episcopal Church, South (a Kentucky corporation) did not give it the authority to change the residence of the secretary from Louisville, Kentucky, where it was fixed by basic law under the facts in this case. The General Conference is the only body which has power to make the change contemplated. July 19, 1954.

100. Where there is no District Conference, the District Committee on Ministerial Qualifications has sole and final authority to license local preachers, and to renew their licenses. Where there is a District Conference, the final authority for licensing local preachers and for renewing their licenses is vested in the District Conference. In either case, for the securing of a license that applicant must comply with the provisions of ¶ 304 [1952; now ¶ 306, amended]. In the matter of renewal of a license, where there is a District Conference, it is the duty of the District Committee on Ministerial Qualifications to examine the applicant and report to the District Conference whether in its opinion the "gifts, graces, and usefulness" of the applicant warrant a renewal; but the final action for such renewal shall be taken by the District Conference. July 20, 1954.

101. The word "consult" in ¶ 432.1 means an exchange of ideas between the district superintendent and the pastor concerning his appointment before the final announcement. Simultaneous releasing of the appointments before the final reading does not constitute consultation as required in ¶ 432.1. July 20, 1954.

102. (1) A second Quarterly Conference held on May 13, 1953, on a call announced to the congregation at its prayer service April 29, 1953, was regular and had the right to consider and act upon the matter of proceedings to recover from the ex-treasurer the treasurer's books and records for the previous year; and the courts will entertain suits between mem-

bers of the church as between members of society and other groups.

(2) The action of the Quarterly Conference of Inglenook First Methodist Church adding to its Board of Trustees three new members at its second Quarterly Conference was null and void.

(3) The resolution of the Quarterly Conference authorizing the trustees to employ attorneys without the fee being stipulated was within the authority of the Quarterly Conference and was legal.

(4) The meeting of the Board of Trustees not called by the chairman and participated in by three illegally elected trustees was illegal and void. July 20, 1954.

103. A steward and trustee having been church treasurer for years and having failed of re-election, and then withholding the church records and account books from his successor and from the Commission on Finance and Auditing Committee, was acting at variance to his duties as a steward and trustee, and was subject to being removed from the offices of steward and trustee by the Quarterly Conference to which he was amenable without having been previously notified of such proposed action, and without charges being preferred against him under ¶¶ 1001-5. The Board of Stewards [Official Board] and the Board of Trustees are subject to the Quarterly Conference, and so are the individual stewards and trustees; and when a steward or trustee acts contrary to his duties as such the Quarterly Conference has the inherent right and authority to vacate his offices as steward and trustee. July 20, 1954.

104. After a lapse of two years since the charges were lodged by the Investigating Committee, and when the application is accompanied by the proper recommendations, and other requirements of the Discipline have been met, no trial is necessary on the old charges in order to have a preacher's credentials restored according to ¶ 993. The Annual Conference determines for itself whether there has been complete amendment of life on the part of the applicant and what committee shall present the recommendation to the Annual Conference. July 20, 1954.

105. The words "upon recommendation of the Committee on Conference Relations" [¶ 365] do not mean that an Annual Conference cannot act contrary to its committee's recommendation if it wishes to do so. July 20, 1954.

106. There is no legislation in the 1952 Discipline of The Methodist Church dealing with pension for a resigned bishop or his widow and therefore no basis for a declaratory decision on such legislation by the Judicial Council as requested

by the executive committee of the Council on World Service and Finance. The Judicial Council therefore declines to accept jurisdiction in this instance. July 20, 1954. [*See* ¶ 435 .2 as amended in 1956.]

107. The words "or subdivisions" as they appear in the second line of ¶ 174 mean subdivisions of governmental agencies and not subdivisions of private real estate projects. July 20, 1954.

108. If the Board of Trustees of the Annual Conference are the directors of the incorporated Annual Conference and are performing the same functions and duties as those assigned to an incorporated Board of Trustees in ¶ 709 [1952; now ¶ 711, amended], that constitutes a substantial compliance with the provisions of ¶ 709, and the separate incorporation of the Board of Trustees of the Annual Conference is not necessary. July 21, 1954.

109. An Official Board or a Quarterly Conference has no authority in the law of The Methodist Church to order or instruct lay or reserve lay members to vote in any prescribed manner on issues expected to come before an Annual Conference. July 21, 1954.

110. A minister who locates voluntarily retains his relationship as a local preacher in the Quarterly Conference where he resides. His license is not subject to renewal annually. He is held amenable for his conduct and the continuance of his ordination rights to the Annual Conference in which his Quarterly Conference membership is held. He continues as a local preacher in the Quarterly Conference until such time as he voluntarily surrenders his credentials or is deprived of such by due process of trial. July 21, 1954.

111. The answer of a candidate for the traveling ministry to the question set out in ¶ 321 Question 4 [1952; now ¶ 322 .5 Question 5] as to abstinence from the use of tobacco in order to be satisfactory must be in the affirmative and without qualification. July 21, 1954.

112. An approved supply pastor represents his charge as a pastor in every respect except the right to vote. Therefore he cannot represent the charge in the dual capacity of pastor and lay member at the same time. July 29, 1955.

113. A pastoral charge consists of all the churches of a circuit, and they are entitled to elect only one lay member to an Annual Conference. July 29, 1955.

114. That part of ¶ 431.7 which requires the consent of a ministerial member of an Annual Conference before he can be transferred to another Annual Conference is constitutional. July 29, 1955.

115. While an Annual Conference has the right to fix the dates of the fiscal year on which it operates, from the legal point of view the conference year begins with the adjournment of an Annual Conference session and ends with the adjournment of the next regular session of the conference. July 29, 1955.

116. The Judicial Council has jurisdiction only on questions of law. The charges against appellant, though meager, are sufficient to inform him of the offense with which he is charged. The charges having been made during the session of the Annual Conference, the accused was triable under ¶¶ 936 and 937, and not under ¶ 935. Five days were given the accused to prepare for trial. As a matter of law that cannot be held to be insufficient time. ¶ 1006 establishes a policy that the council for the accused must be a traveling preacher. By inference the assistant counsel provided in ¶ 1007 must be a traveling preacher. The trial having been conducted substantially in accordance with the provisions of the Discipline, the judgments of the Trial Court and of the Court of Appeals are in all things affirmed. July 29, 1955.

117. A retired bishop of a Central Conference is authorized to attend meetings of the Council of Bishops with expenses paid. July 29, 1955.

118. Church treasurers cannot withhold the three per cent pension fund assessments on salaries of ministers and remit them to the pension board. Such assessments must be sent in by the ministers themselves. If the ministers should agree to such withholding and authorize the church treasurer to send same to the fund in quarterly installments, that would constitute compliance with ¶ 1646 [1952; amended in 1956]. July 29, 1955.

119. When an Annual Conference adopts a standing rule, it is bound by such rule unless same is suspended or rescinded and some other action taken. Any action in conflict with the standing rule taken without suspending or rescinding the rule is void. Therefore, the proceeds of the sale of Grace Methodist Church belong to the Conference Claimants Endowment Fund as determined by the standing rule of the Oregon Annual Conference. July 29, 1955.

120. Fred B. Noble being automatically retired from membership upon the Judicial Council at the 1956 General Conference, he would be in all respects eligible to serve as a delegate to the 1956 Jurisdictional Conference of the Southeastern Jurisdiction of The Methodist Church, which meets after the 1956 General Conference closes. The time of his election as such a delegate is immaterial, his eligibility to serve as such

delegate at the time the Jurisdictional Conference meets being the determining factor as to the validity of his election. July 30, 1955.

121. Since the Philippines Central Conference has failed to take action regarding the ordination of women, the Northwest Philippines Annual Conference has the right to ordain a woman as a local deacon. July 30, 1955.

122. The phrase "who has been appointed in the regular itinerant work on circuits or stations" in ¶ 341 [1952; amended in 1956] must be interpreted as applying only to pastoral appointments to circuits or stations. April 26, 1956.

123. An Annual Conference has the power to hear, discuss, amend, adopt, or reject reports from conference boards even though they contain material referring to persons or organizations in a derogatory manner without their having prior notice. April 26, 1956.

124. A preacher on trial in an Annual Conference cannot serve as lay delegate in a Central Conference. April 26, 1956.

125. The Tennessee Annual Conference of the Central Jurisdiction with forty-one ministerial members is entitled to only one ministerial and one lay delegate to the Jurisdictional Conference. These two are the delegates elected to the General Conference. April 26, 1956.

126. A Central Conference bishop may preside over the General Conference. April 27, 1956.

127. The General Conference has authority to authorize a Jurisdictional Conference to elect a missionary bishop. April 30, 1956.

128. The Liberia Annual Conference cannot be a part of the Central Jurisdiction. May 1, 1956.

129. An Annual Conference may grant the privileges of the floor to a minister in a sister church, but cannot grant to such minister the right to vote. May 3, 1956.

130. A Quarterly Conference may adopt a policy for the election of trustees which is subject at all times to suspension or rejection by a majority vote of the Quarterly Conference. May 5, 1956.

131. A missionary minister serving on the field shall be counted in the Annual Conference of which he is a member for General Conference representation. October 24, 1956.

132. A Provisional Annual Conference may not vote on the constitutional amendments handed down to the Annual Conferences by the 1956 General Conference. October 24, 1956.

133. The effective date of the retirement of a minister who voluntarily retires is the date of the adjournment of the

Annual Conference which approved his retirement. October 24, 1956.

134. The words "formal vote of the conference" as used in ¶ 1924, and in the amendment thereto made by the General Conference of 1956, were intended to mean the formal vote of the ministers of the conference entitled to vote under the Constitution on the question before the conference. October 24, 1956.

135. Annual Conference Boards of Trustees or other Annual Conference organizations may legally receive title to real estate which does not contain the "trust clause" as contained in ¶ 174. October 24, 1956.

136. An Annual Conference may not extend voting privileges to full-time approved supply pastors who are ordained elders and who have served charges during the past year. October 24, 1956.

137. The General Conference acted within its constitutional powers in directing the Board of Education of The Methodist Church through its Division of Educational Institutions [Division of Higher Education] to appoint a Commission on Standards for Wesley Foundations to establish standards and evaluate the educational, religious, and financial program of Wesley Foundations and report to the division the Wesley Foundations which meet the standards established by the commission and therefore qualify for financial support from the General Board of Education and the Annual Conferences. October 18, 1957.

138. The trustees of an Annual Conference can dispose of funds belonging to the Woman's Society of Christian Service of a discontinued church as directed by the Annual Conference. October 18, 1957.

139. The general provisions of ¶¶ 1101-8 are applicable only to the general administrative agencies of The Methodist Church and cannot be held to apply to a Board of Directors or Trustees of a children's home which is the property of an Annual Conference or of Annual Conferences of The Methodist Church. October 18, 1957.

140. The report of the Joint Committee on Distribution of Responsibility for Conference Claimants submitted to the 1955 session of the California-Nevada Annual Conference did not change the report of the Joint Distributing Committee of 1940. Therefore, the ruling of Bishop Tippett on this question is affirmed. October 18, 1957.

141. An Annual Conference may adopt a rule establishing a quorum for the transaction of business. October 18, 1957.

142. The enactments of the Latin America Central Confer-

ence revising ¶ 127 are contrary to the Constitution of The Methodist Church and may not be included in the Discipline of said conference under the provisions of ¶ 562. October 18, 1957.

143. The sale of property of an abandoned church should and must be authorized by action of an Annual Conference in session as an ecclesiastical body. October 18, 1957.

144. When an appellant fails to comply with the provision of ¶ 1025 which requires that a written statement of the grounds of appeal be furnished at the same time notice of appeal is given, the appeal must be dismissed. February 8, 1958.

145. ¶ 1612.3 is constitutional and is binding on the West Texas Conference Endowment Association, charged with the administration of the pension-related funds in its hands. February 8, 1958.

146. ¶ 362.10 is not in violation of the Constitution of The Methodist Church, and its provision for the publication of the names of local-church lay leaders in the journals of Annual Conferences is mandatory. February 8, 1958.

147. A Central Conference cannot adopt legislation which would have the effect of changing, modifying, or altering ¶ 207, relating to the qualification for membership on the Official Board of the local church. February 8, 1958.

148. An Interboard Council may serve as a budget review committee for the Annual Conference Commission on World Service and Finance.

An Annual Conference Commission on World Service and Finance may utilize the services of an Interboard Council in the preparation of its report to the Annual Conference, provided the right is reserved to every conference agency to appear before the Conference Commission on World Service and Finance for the purpose of presenting its cause to said commission. October 17, 1958.

149. A ministerial member of an Annual Conference who has been placed in the retired relation with the privilege of making an annuity claim on the ground of personal disability may not serve a church in a ministerial capacity and receive compensation for such service and at the same time draw an annuity from the Board of Pensions of an Annual Conference. October 17, 1958.

150. Full-time years of service as an approved supply pastor, prior to admission on trial by an Annual Conference, may be counted as a part of the forty years of service as a basis for the request of any ministerial member of an Annual Conference for the retired relation. October 17, 1958.

151. The adoption of a rule by an Annual Conference authorizing Official Boards to pay in whole or in part such parsonage utilities as heat, light, gas, telephone, and water, the amount paid not to exceed the actual cost of such utilities and requiring that the amounts paid shall be reported in an appropriate column in the statistical records of the minutes is not in conflict with the provisions of ¶ 1624.6, or any other provision of the 1956 Discipline. October 17, 1958.

152. Appointment to attend school as provided for in ¶ 432.7 does not meet the requirements of ¶ 341 (*a*) relating to qualifications for admission into full connection in an Annual Conference. October 17, 1958.

153. When the provisions of the Discipline concerning appeals from episcopal decisions on questions of law (¶¶ 43.2 and 908), or concerning episcopal decisions of law made in response to questions properly submitted (¶¶ 40, 43.3, and 909), are not followed, the Judicial Council must decline to take jurisdiction. October 17, 1958.

154. Amendments VII and VIII to the Constitution of The Methodist Church were constitutionally adopted. October 17, 1958.

155. A Central Conference may not change General Conference legislation regarding the granting of full clergy rights for women.

A Central Conference may not refuse to accept a woman who has been given full clergy rights by an Annual Conference.

A bishop has the power to transfer a woman ministerial member of an Annual Conference to any other Annual Conference provided he has the consent of the bishop of the receiving conference, and provided the ministerial member agrees to said transfer. October 17, 1958.

156. The determination of the meaning of the words "part-time approved supply pastor" and "full-time approved supply pastor" as used in ¶¶ 317.2-.3 [amended in 1960] is a legislative matter within the province of the General Conference and is not a judicial matter to be determined by the Judicial Council. October 17, 1958.

157. An Annual Conference Board of Ministerial Training and Qualifications may withhold recommendation for ordination or full connection in the Annual Conference of a candidate who, in its judgment, has been unfaithful to his ministerial vows. October 17, 1959.

158. On the basis of factual data supplied him, Bishop Valencia ruled that Lingkod A. Juane had been a member of The Methodist Church for four years prior to election as a lay member of the Philippines Annual Conference and was there-

fore eligible to sit as a lay member of the Philippines Annual Conference in its 1959 session. His ruling is hereby affirmed. October 17, 1959.

159. A pastoral charge served by three ministers or traveling preachers, only one of whom is in full connection with the Annual Conference within the territorial boundaries of which the pastoral charge is situated, is entitled to elect only one of its lay members to represent it as a member of such Annual Conference. October 17, 1959.

160. Funds in the Permanent Fund of an Annual Conference are disposable by that Annual Conference. October 17, 1959.

161. No decision. ["In view of (a later development) we consider the matter moot and now deem no further action on our part necessary."] October 17, 1959.

162. In determining the eligibility of a ministerial member of an Annual Conference for election as ministerial delegate to the General Conference or Central Conference under ¶ 24 of the Constitution, his years as a traveling preacher may be counted from the date of his admission on trial. October 17, 1959.

163. The petition of the Council of Bishops for a rehearing of Case No. 114 is denied. October 17, 1959.

164. Central Conference bishops have been granted full rights of membership and participation in the Council of Bishops and are entitled to attend all meetings of the Council of Bishops with expenses paid. April 30, 1960.

165. (1) A ministerial member or approved supply pastor retired under the provisions of the Discipline at age seventy-two is then automatically subject to the provisions of the Discipline relating to annuity claims.

(2) The Conference Board of Pensions may determine the number of years of service for which a minister is eligible for annuity, without formal action of the Annual Conference session. April 30, 1960.

166. (1) Southern Methodist University (including the Perkins School of Theology) is an integral agency of The Methodist Church.

(2) An effective Methodist minister who has been appointed by a bishop to the Perkins School of Theology of Southern Methodist University is performing his services in such post on an assignment or designation by the church.

(3) Effective Methodist ministers appointed by bishops to the faculty of the Perkins School of Theology of Southern Methodist University are in the exercise of their ministry. May 2, 1960.

167. (1) An effective Methodist minister who has been ap-

pointed by a bishop to the faculty of a Methodist theological school is performing his services in such post on an assignment or designation of The Methodist Church.

(2) An effective Methodist minister who has been appointed by a bishop to the faculty of a Methodist theological school is in the exercise of his ministry in the services rendered by him at said institution. May 2, 1960.

168. Unmeritorious and untimely resubmission of appeal [of Case No. 116] declined. May 2, 1960.

169. An Annual Conference may be transferred from one jurisdiction into another under Amendment IX [without regard to the geographical boundaries of the jurisdictions involved (from the decision)]. May 2, 1960.

170. The ruling of Bishop José L. Valencia that the Northwest Philippines Annual Conference could accept the report of its Credentials Committee in unseating Benjamin Casiano, a lay member, is affirmed. May 5, 1960.

171. A ministerial member of an Annual Conference who h s been placed in the retired relation with the privilege of making an annuity claim on the ground of personal disability can receive payment for "full-time" or "nearly full-time" secular employment and at the same time draw an annuity from the Conference Board of Pensions. May 5, 1960.

172. (1) A request for an explanation, or for a statement of the implications or effect of decisions of the Judicial Council, does not constitute a request for a declaratory decision under the provisions of ¶ 914 of the Discipline.

(2) The powers and duties of the General Conference and the Judicial Council are totally different and separate and apart and cannot be jointly exercised. May 5, 1960.

173. The ruling of Bishop Valencia that Ezekias G. Gacutan, a former minister who had voluntarily located, thereupon became a layman, is affirmed. May 6, 1960.

174. (1) A former minister who is now under voluntary location can be elected lay delegate to the General or Central Conference by an Annual Conference.

(2) A reserve lay member of an Annual Conference or anyone who meets the requirements set forth in ¶ 45 iii of the Constitution can be elected lay delegate to the General or Central Conference. May 6, 1960.

175. (1) Direct and final responsibility for the supervision of a local Wesley Foundation rests with a local board of directors subject only to prior authority vested in Annual Conference Boards of Education, Interconference Commissions on Student [College and University] Religious Work, and the General Board of Education, and subject in regard to employed

personnel who may be effective ministerial members of an Annual Conference to prior obligations inherent in the Methodist appointive system.

(2) Likewise direct and final responsibility for the supervision of programs of religious work (Methodist Student Movement) for Methodist students on the campuses of Methodist institutions of higher education rests solely with the Boards of Trustees of such institutions, subject only to prior and final authority vested in Annual Conferences and other constitutional bodies, and subject in regard to employed personnel who may be effective ministerial members of an Annual Conference to prior obligations inherent in the Methodist appointive system. May 6, 1960.

Chapter II

ENABLING ACTS

¶ 2003. Past Enabling Acts

The enabling acts adopted by the General Conference of 1956 appear in the 1956 Discipline. Those adopted by the General Conferences of 1940, 1944, 1948, and 1952 may be found in the journals of those conferences.[1]

¶ 2004. Numbers of Bishops in Central Conferences

1. The Africa Central Conference is authorized, subject to the provisions of ¶ 2005.2, to elect one bishop for that Central Conference, provided that by such election there shall not be more than three effective bishops resident in that field at any one time during the quadrennium.

2. The China Central Conference is authorized to elect one or more bishops for China, provided that by such election there shall not be more than four effective bishops resident in that field at any one time during the quadrennium.

3. The Latin America Central Conference is authorized to elect two bishops for Latin America, provided that by such election there shall not be more than two effective bishops in that field at any one time during the quadrennium.

4. The Southern Asia Central Conference is authorized to elect one or more bishops for that Central Conference, provided that by such election there shall not be more than four effective bishops resident in that field at any one time during the quadrennium.

---

[1] See Judicial Council Decisions 54, 71.

5. The Philippines Central Conference is authorized to elect two bishops for that Central Conference, provided that by such election there shall not be more than two effective bishops resident in the field at any one time during the quadrennium.

6. Any episcopal vacancy in a Central Conference occurring during the quadrennium shall be filled as set forth in ¶ 557; *provided*, however, that the number of bishops holding residential supervision within the bounds of the respective Central Conferences shall at no time during the quadrennium exceed the numbers specified above in §§ 1-5, and one each in Central and Southern Europe, Germany, Northern Europe, and Southeastern Asia.

¶ 2005. Special Provisions for Episcopal Supervision

Presidential, visitational, and residential episcopal supervision of fields outside the United States not included in Central Conferences, and in emergency situations in Central Conferences, shall be provided during the 1960-64 quadrennium as follows:

1. The Central Jurisdictional Conference shall provide residential and presidential supervision for the work in Liberia and is hereby authorized according to the provisions of ¶¶ 8.4, 439 to have one bishop in addition to its membership quota in order to provide for this supervision.

2. The Northeastern Jurisdictional Conference shall provide residential and presidential supervision within the Africa Central Conference, and is hereby authorized according to the provisions of ¶¶ 8.4, 439 to have one bishop in addition to its membership quota in order to provide for this supervision. The Northeastern Jurisdictional Conference shall have power to delegate to a commission or committee of the Jurisdictional Conference authority during the 1960-64 quadrennium at any time to grant authorization to the Africa Central Conference to elect another bishop, bringing their total to three.

3. The South Central Jurisdictional Conference shall provide for episcopal visitation to the Latin America Central Conference and to the affiliated autonomous churches in Latin America.

4. The Council of Bishops shall provide episcopal supervision for the work in Pakistan and for the Pakistan Provisional Central Conference (¶ 2006.2) when it is organized.

5. The Council of Bishops shall provide episcopal supervision for the Taiwan–Hong Kong Provisional Annual Conference, which shall be administered outside the China Central Conference for the 1960-64 quadrennium.

Inasmuch as the territory in which is located the work for which the foregoing provides the episcopal supervision is not in any case included in the geographical boundaries of the Jurisdictional Conference which elects the bishop or bishops involved, therefore the said bishops are directed to report on the supervision of their fields to the Council of Bishops as well as to the Central Conferences to which they are related.

If during the ensuing quadrennium any emergency in episcopal supervision should arise in any of the fields covered by the foregoing provisions, the Council of Bishops shall provide the necessary episcopal supervision.

¶ 2006. Central and Provisional Central Conferences

1. On full compliance with all the provisions of the Discipline of 1960 relating thereto the Latin America Central Conference is authorized to conduct a Central Conference with privileges and powers as provided under Central Conference legislation, provided that it shall have at least a total of twenty ministerial delegates and twenty lay delegates on the regular basis of representation.

2. On full compliance with all the provisions of the Discipline of 1960 pertaining thereto (see ¶¶ 586-93), the Indus River Annual Conference and the Karachi Provisional Annual Conference are authorized to separate from the Southern Asia Central Conference and to establish a Provisional Central Conference in Pakistan.

3. Any Central Conference already provided for in the enabling acts of this General Conference hereby is authorized to continue during the quadrennium ending in 1964 even though it may fall below the Disciplinary membership.

¶ 2007. Organization of Annual and Provisional Annual Conferences

1. On full compliance with all the provisions of the Discipline of 1960 relating thereto, authority is hereby given for the Bolivia, Mindanao, Peru, Poland, Sumatra, and Uruguay Provisional Annual Conferences to become organized into Annual Conferences during the quadrennium ending in 1964, provided that they shall have a minimum of twenty-five ministerial members.

2. On full compliance with all the provisions of the Discipline of 1960 relating thereto, the work in Patagonia is hereby authorized to become organized into a Provisional Annual Conference during the quadrennium ending in 1964, provided it shall have a minimum of six ministerial members.

3. On full compliance with all the provisions of the Discipline of 1960 relating thereto, the Taiwan–Hong Kong Provisional Annual Conference is hereby authorized to become organized into the Taiwan Provisional Annual Conference and the Hong Kong Provisional Annual Conference during the quadrennium ending in 1964, provided each shall have a minimum of six ministerial members.

4. On full compliance with all the provisions of the Discipline of 1960 relating thereto, the Central America Provisional Annual Conference is hereby authorized to become organized into the Costa Rica Provisional Annual Conference, provided that it shall have a minimum of ten ministerial members, and the Panama Provisional Annual Conference, provided that it shall have a minimum of six ministerial members.

5. On full compliance with all the provisions of the Discipline of 1960 relating thereto, authority is hereby given for the Sarawak Iban Provisional Annual Conference to become organized during the quadrennium ending in 1964.

6. On full compliance with all the provisions of the Discipline of 1960 relating thereto, the Philippines Annual Conference is authorized to divide into two Annual Conferences during the quadrennium ending in 1964.

¶ 2008. Continuation of Annual and Provisional Annual Conferences

1. Authority is hereby given the Belgium, Cuba, Czechoslovakia, Denmark, Idaho, and Northeast Germany Annual Conferences to continue as Annual Conferences during the quadrennium ending in 1964.

2. Authority is hereby given the Baltic and Slavic and the Kalgan Provisional Annual Conferences to continue as Provisional Annual Conferences during the quadrennium ending in 1964.

3. The Northeast Germany Annual Conference may change its boundaries if necessary during the quadrennium ending in 1964.

4. Any Annual or Provisional Annual Conference already provided for in the enabling acts of this General Conference hereby is authorized to continue during the quadrennium ending in 1964 even though it may fall below the Disciplinary membership.

¶ 2009. Merger of Mission

Authority is hereby given to the Hawaii Mission to become

a district of the Southern California-Arizona Annual Conference during the quadrennium ending in 1964, when requested by the Mission and approved by the Southern California-Arizona Annual Conference.

CHAPTER III

QUADRENNIAL COMMISSIONS

¶ 2012. Commission on the Structure of Methodism Overseas

1. There shall be a Commission on the Structure of Methodism Overseas for the quadrennium 1960-64. Recognizing the difference in conditions that exist in various fields of the world, and the changes taking place in those fields, this commission shall continue to study the structure and supervision of The Methodist Church in its work outside of the United States and its territories, and its relationship to other church bodies, and in particular shall review the historical development, structure, and operation of Central Conferences and the legislation pertaining thereto, and shall prepare such recommendations as it considers necessary for presentation to the General Conference of 1964. All memorials, resolutions, and petitions related to Central Conferences presented to the General Conference shall be referred to this commission for consideration, action, and report to the General Conference.

2. The commission shall be constituted as follows: four bishops administering in Jurisdictional Conferences, four bishops administering in Central Conferences, one minister and one layman from each Jurisdictional Conference, and one person from each Central Conference; *provided* that a Central Conference having a church membership of 200,000 or more shall have two representatives; and *provided*, further, that at the meeting immediately before and during the General Conference of 1964 there shall be one minister and one layman from each Central Conference, the additional persons to be named from the delegates elected to the General Conference. All of these shall be nominated by the Council of Bishops and approved by the General Conference. There shall be added to the commission by the Board of Missions four persons: two from the Division of World Missions, and two from the Department of Work in Foreign Fields of the Woman's Division of Christian Service. Bishops having super-

vision of work outside the United States and its territories and bishops of affiliated autonomous churches shall be considered consultive members of the commission and shall be called in, when available, at the time of meeting of the commission. When a representative of a Central Conference cannot be present to represent his field, the bishop or bishops of that field shall designate someone to represent it. Those members of the commission representing Central Conferences who are not delegates to the General Conference or who are not in the United States at the time the commission will meet shall be replaced by persons who are in the United States on nomination of the bishops of the Central Conferences they represent.

3. The commission shall meet immediately following election for organization, annually at the time and place of the meeting of the Board of Missions, and immediately before the General Conference of 1964.

4. The expenses of this commission shall be paid from the General Conference Expense Fund.

¶ 2013. Commission on Interjurisdictional Relations

1. The continuing program of The Methodist Church to abolish the Central Jurisdiction, promote interracial brotherhood through Christian love, and achieve a more inclusive church shall be entrusted to a quadrennial Commission on Interjurisdictional Relations. The General Conference of 1960 shall elect on nomination of the College of Bishops of each jurisdiction a commission composed of the following representatives of each jurisdiction: one bishop, two ministers, and three laymen. Officers shall be elected from the ministerial or lay membership.

2. The responsibilities and authority of this commission shall be as follows:

a) To study and recommend courses of action which shall implement the use of Amendment IX on all levels of church structure.

b) To study the possibilities and problems inherent in the transfer of local churches, districts, Annual Conferences, and areas as provided in Amendment IX, and to give such information, guidance, and other assistance as may be possible and proper to those considering such transfer.

c) To make an immediate study of the reasons for reluctance to make use of Amendment IX, where such reluctance exists, and to bring together responsible churchmen, ministerial and lay, to expedite action.

d) Where such transfers cannot be made in either direction at present, to recommend the immediate development of a long-range program designed to create better understanding of mutual problems.

e) To give special attention and study to such matters as may impede the speedy implementation of Amendment IX, including the adjustment of ministerial requirements, pension and apportionment differentials, minimum support, church extension, and ministerial itinerancy.

f) To make progress reports to the Council of Bishops, and to the church through the church press.

g) To present an inclusive report to the General Conference of 1964 containing findings and recommendations which shall be printed and distributed to the delegates at least three months prior to the convening of the conference.

h) To work closely with the General, Jurisdictional, and Annual Conference Boards of Christian Social Concerns, with the Department of Christian Social Relations of the Woman's Division of Christian Service, and with all other agencies having information and facilities for expediting the use of Amendment IX and for promoting interracial brotherhood and Christian love.

3. The commission shall consider the duly elected representatives of each jurisdiction on its membership as jurisdictional commissions, and delegate to them such responsibilities as may properly and expeditiously be fulfilled by them.

4. The general commission shall make specific delegation of responsibilities, wherever possible, on local, district, conference, and area levels of church structure:

a) In co-operation with existing agencies to formulate and promote programs of education and courses of action to develop greater interracial understanding and brotherhood on all levels of church life.

b) To study the policies, programs, and activities of the church, its agencies, and related institutions with respect to the practice of interracial brotherhood.

c) To assist church extension through the establishment, wherever possible, of preaching places, and the organization of new congregations characterized by interracial brotherhood.

5. The commission shall be given adequate financing to carry out fully and efficiently the responsibilities assigned to it.

6. The commission shall meet before the conclusion of the 1960 General Conference.

¶ 2014. Commission to Revise the Hymnal

The Commission on Worship is authorized and directed to revise *The Methodist Hymnal*, including the Responsive

Readings, and to complete the work so that its report may be ready for the 1964 General Conference, The Methodist Publishing House to publish the hymnal as soon thereafter as feasible.

The following shall be consultants to the commission with voting rights: one bishop elected by the College of Bishops of each jurisdiction, the president and the director of church music of The Methodist Publishing House, and one representative from each division of the Board of Education. The commission may seek advice and counsel from other recognized authorities on hymnody and sacred music, and from other agencies of the church as it may deem wise. It shall recommend what rituals and other aids to worship, developed in its studies and authorized by the General Conference, shall be included in the revised hymnal. The expenses of the commission in carrying out this editorial assignment shall be financed from the General Administration Fund. The Methodist Publishing House shall bear all publishing costs of the hymnal as revised.

¶ 2015.   Commission to Study the Christian Faith and War in the Nuclear Age

There shall be a special Commission to Study the Christian Faith and War in the Nuclear Age, which shall be composed of theologians, natural and political scientists, and church leaders. There shall be twelve members, six named by the Council of Bishops and six by the Board of Christian Social Concerns, all chosen with respect to competence. Its findings shall be reported to these two bodies, if possible by January 1, 1962, and when approved by them shall be used in appropriate study programs throughout the church. The expenses of the commission, the amount not to exceed $10,000, shall come from the budget of the Division of Peace and World Order.

CHAPTER IV

THE METHODIST SOCIAL CREED

"We instruct those in charge of publishing the Discipline to include the Social Creed, with such revisions as may be adopted from time to time, in all future editions unless other directions are received from the General Conference."—Discipline, 1940.

¶ 2020.

I. OUR HERITAGE.—The interest of The Methodist Church

in social welfare springs from the gospel, and from the labors of John Wesley, who ministered to the physical, intellectual, and social needs of the people to whom he preached the gospel of personal redemption.

In our historic position we have sought to follow Christ in bringing the whole of life, with its activities, possessions, and relationships, into conformity with the will of God.

As Methodists we have an obligation to affirm our position on social and economic questions.

II. Our Theological Basis.—The Methodist Church must view the perplexing times and problems which we face today in the light of the teachings of Jesus. Jesus taught us to love our neighbors and seek justice for them. To be silent in the face of need, injustice, and exploitation is to deny him.

We believe that God is Father of all peoples and races, that Jesus Christ is his Son, that all men are brothers, and that man is of infinite worth as a child of God.

We believe that "the earth is the Lord's, and the fulness thereof." Our own capacities and all we possess are gifts of the Creator, and should be held and used in stewardship to him.

We believe that a Christian society is essential to the full nurture of a Christian person.

We believe that sin, both individual and social, stands under the judgment of God, and that the grace of God in Christ is available for redemption in all areas of life as we seek in penitence and obedience to do his holy will.

We believe that all persons have supreme value in the sight of God, and ought to be so regarded by us. We test all institutions and practices by their effect upon persons. Personality is oppressed in many parts of the world, and we seek its emancipation and those things which will enrich and redeem it. Since Jesus died for the redemption of human life, we believe we should live to help save man from sin and from every influence which would harm or destroy him.

III. Our Declaration of Social Concern.—Applying the foregoing principles, The Methodist Church declares itself as follows:

A. *The Family.*—We seek equal rights and justice for all men; protection of the individual and the family by high standards of morality; Christian education for marriage, parenthood, and the home; adequate housing, proper regulation of marriage, and uniform divorce laws.

We believe that the church must be vitally concerned with the health and welfare needs of all people, first within the family, and where necessary in institutional care with high standards of scientific service and Christian dedication.

We believe in planned parenthood, practiced in Christian conscience.

We stand for regulation of working conditions for women, especially mothers, and safeguards for their physical and moral environment; for the abolition of injurious child labor; for the protection, education, spiritual nurture, and wholesome recreation of every child; and for religious and educational programs which will secure these ends.

B. *Economic Life.*—1. *Christianity and the Economic Order.*—With full acknowledgment of stewardship under God and accountability to him, we stand for the acquisition of property by Christian processes and the right of private ownership thereof. We refuse to identify Christianity with any economic system. We test every economic order by the commands of our Christ and judge its practices by the Christian gospel. We believe that it is our duty not only to bring Christ to the individual, but also to bring the society within which we live more nearly into conformity with the teachings of Christ. We believe that the free democratic way of life ruled by Christian principles can bring to mankind a society in which liberty is preserved, justice established, and brotherhood achieved. We therefore pledge ourselves to sustain these values and to implement the teachings of Christ by voting our Christian convictions in all elections, by participating in political action as party members or independents, and by offering and supporting candidates who will translate our social ideas into social reality.

2. *Responsible Use of Power.*—The Christian point of view demands that concentrations of power in government, labor, business, and religious organizations be used responsibly. The task of the church in this regard is to help people in positions of power and the organizations which they serve to achieve and exercise a high level of social responsibility.

3. *Poverty and Unemployment.*—We believe that the economic development which makes possible material plenty for all imposes upon us great moral responsibility, in that the physical and spiritual development of millions of persons throughout the world is now needlessly hindered by poverty. We therefore stand for the abatement and prevention of poverty everywhere.

We believe that it is our Christian duty to provide for all men opportunity to earn an adequate livelihood for themselves and their dependents. Since lack of significant employment tends to destroy human self-respect, we believe that workers must be safeguarded from enforced unemployment.

4. *Wealth.*—We recognize the perils of prosperity. Our Lord

has told us that we cannot serve God and mammon. As Christians we must examine earnestly before God both our personal and our business practices, lest we unwittingly adopt the standards and assumptions of a materialistic society to the exclusion of our Christian stewardship.

Since churches and their institutions as well as individuals own property, invest funds, and employ labor, care must be exercised that all such relationships conform to the highest Christian standards. Any judgment upon society must "begin at the house of God."

5. *Working Conditions.*—We oppose all forms of social, economic, and moral waste. We urge the protection of the worker from dangerous and unsanitary working conditions, and from occupational diseases.

We stand for reasonable hours of labor, for just wages, for a fair day's work for a fair day's wage, for fair working conditions, for periods of leisure, and for an equitable division of the product of industry.

6. *Social Benefits for Workers.*—We stand for security for old age, for insurance against sickness and injury to the worker, and for increased protection against those preventable conditions which produce want.

7. *The Right to Organize for Collective Bargaining.*—We stand for the right of employees and employers alike to organize for collective bargaining, protection of both in the exercise of their right, the responsibility of both to bargain in good faith, and the obligation of both to work for the public good.

8. *Town and Country Life.*—We recognize the basic significance of town and country areas in relation to population supply, natural resources, community life, and Christian culture. We believe the farmer and all other agriculture workers should have opportunity to earn a fair income.

Methodism, because of its large town and country membership and world-wide impact, must lead in developing an adequate Christian program in rural areas everywhere. This should pertain to people in their relationship to God, to the stewardship of the soil and the conservation of all natural resources, and to family, church, and community welfare.

We recognize that in many rural sections a new type of community is emerging, due to an increase of nonfarm rural dwellers. To this the church must give its attention.

9. *Urban Life.*—Our society is becoming increasingly urban. The city is a center of power for good or ill, and its shifting multitudes desperately need the guiding and healing power of

religion. The church must recognize that the city exhibits great needs and offers amazing opportunities for Kingdom building.

10. *Christian Vocation.*—We believe that every adult should be engaged, so far as possible, in some vocation productive of common good. Every such vocation should be viewed as a Christian calling, and our daily work as a sphere of service to God for the advancement of his Kingdom.

C. *Temperance.*—We believe that the disciplined life in Christ is a temperate life. Total abstinence from the use of alcoholic beverages is the historic position of The Methodist Church. We seek to aid the individual, the home, and society to overcome the social, economic, and moral wastes which accompany the traffic in intoxicants and narcotics, gambling in any form, and the distribution of pornographic materials. We would protect the home and society from degrading and salacious materials so prevalent in the mass media. The church should also seek to understand the causes of alcoholism and drug addiction, and to give help to their victims in a healing and redemptive ministry and fellowship.

D. *Treatment of Crime.*—We stand for the application of the redemptive principle to the treatment of offenders against the law, to reform of penal and correctional methods, and to criminal court procedure. For this reason we deplore the use of capital punishment.

We recognize that crime, and in particular juvenile delinquency leading to crime, is often a result of family failure and bad social conditions. Christian citizens and churches have a special opportunity and responsibility for creating those conditions of family life and social surroundings, wholesome recreation, vocational training, personal counseling, and social adjustment by which crime may be reduced and the offender rehabilitated.

E. *Freedom from Discrimination.*—We stand for the equal rights of racial, cultural, and religious groups and insist that the social, economic, and spiritual principles set forth in this creed apply to all alike. The right to choose a home, enter a school, secure employment, vote, or join a church should not be limited by a person's race, culture, or religion.

F. *Peace and World Order.*—1. *Principles.*—Christianity cannot be nationalistic; it must be universal in its outlook and appeal. War makes its appeal to force and hate, Christianity to reason and love. The methods of Jesus and the methods of war move in different directions. The influence of the church must therefore always be on the side of every effort seeking to remove those conditions of heart and mind, of social and international injustice, in which wars begin, and which are contrary to the spirit and teaching of Christ.

It is not enough to declare the evil of war; we must actively and constantly create the will to peace, the conditions of peace, and the organization for peace. These tasks include the promotion of understanding, reconciliation, and good will; the relief of suffering; the lifting of living standards around the world; concern for the freedom and welfare of dependent and subject peoples; the removal of racial tensions; the taking of all available steps toward disarmament; the giving of encouragement and support to patient negotiation by our leaders. These efforts must be viewed as a personal Christian responsibility and steadfastly undergirded with prayer.

2. *International Organization.*—We believe that the United Nations is a working center of international co-operation which provides our most hopeful avenue leading to peace and world order. The prayers and efforts of churches helped to shape it at birth, and through many of its programs opportunities for the expression of Christian concern arise. We believe that the United Nations, with its related agencies, should be sustained, upheld, undergirded, and strengthened by all informed and conscientious churchmen. We further believe that the missionary enterprise of the church makes an important contribution to the development of world order.

3. *The Christian and Military Service.*—The Methodist Church, true to the principles of the New Testament, teaches respect for properly constituted civil authority. It encourages both love of country and love of all men. Believing that government rests upon the support of its conscientious citizens, it holds within its fellowship those who sincerely differ as to the Christian's duty in regard to war. We ask and claim exemption by legal processes from all forms of military preparation or service for all religious conscientious objectors, as for those of the historic peace churches. We recognize the right of the individual to answer the call of his government according to the dictates of his Christian conscience. We also recognize that non-violent resistance can be a valid form of Christian witness. In all of these situations members of The Methodist Church have the authority and support of their church.[2]

G. *Civil Liberties and Civil Rights.*—We stand for the recognition and maintenance of the rights and responsibilities of free speech, free assembly, and a free press, and for the encouragement of free communication of ideas essential to the discovery of truth.

[2] *See* Judicial Council Decision 25.

We stand for the right of all individuals and groups to advocate any peaceful and constitutional method for the solution of problems that may confront society.

We stand upon the principle of testing every such proposal in the light of the teachings of Jesus.

IV. OUR MANDATE: READ, STUDY, APPLY.—We recommend that this Social Creed be presented to our congregations orally or in printed form at least once a year, and that frequent references be made to it. We further recommend that in every local church a committee shall encourage the study of our Social Creed and seek in every possible way to apply its principles.

CHAPTER VI

MISCELLANEOUS RESOLUTIONS

[The General Conference of 1960 adopted more than thirty resolutions of the type included in this chapter, but ordered the printing here of only those which replace resolutions printed in the 1956 Discipline. The remaining resolutions may be found in the Journal of the General Conference of 1960. In many cases an individual resolution is available in leaflet form from the Board of Christian Social Concerns or other agency responsible for action thereon.—EDITORS.]

¶ 2021.   The Christian Family

The modern family is struggling against great difficulties: the tensions created by the world situation, uncertainties due to the present military demands on youth, inadequate housing, uprooting of families due to unprecedented population shifts, and the coarsening influence of many mass media on the lives of children. The end result of these difficulties is evidenced by the high rate of divorce, juvenile delinquency, broken lives, and a general laxity of moral standards. It is only when the family fulfills its highest functions and is truly Christian that its members rise above these difficulties and thus aid in halting the trends threatening the home.

The home is the place where emotional weaknesses of the members of the family come to light, where children express their innate hunger to be secure, to belong, to be needed, to be recognized.

Religion and the family naturally belong together. What religion is to accomplish it can do best in the family. What the family must do, it cannot do without religion. Religion and the family are natural allies. Religion is inseparable from the family. Family life at its best is a matter of living life at the deepest level, which is a level of relationship to God.

1. *What Is a Christian Family?*—A Christian family is one in which parents so live the Christian life and practice the presence of God that children come to accept God as the greatest reality of life.

A Christian family is one in which each member is accepted and respected as a person having sacred worth.

A Christian family is one that seeks to bring every member into the Christian way of living.

A Christian family is one that accepts the responsibility of worship and instruction to the end of developing the spiritual life of each person.

A Christian family is one that manifests a faith in God, observes daily prayer and grace at meals, is committed to behavior in keeping with Christian ideals for family relations, community life, and national and world citizenship.

2. *Religion and the Family.*—The undergirding love of God, as taught by Christian parents, by word and example, is one of the greatest sources of emotional and spiritual security for the growing life. Where the awareness of God is present, families will find opportunities for informal experience of prayer in many situations of life. The beauties of nature, the joys of comradeship, the tragedies of bereavement, the elation that comes with good fortune, the facing of common problems—all these can be shared with God in the simple words of prayer.

In addition to these moments of informal religious expression, the Christian family will provide for planned periods of worship. This will include the participation in leadership by children as well as by adults. There is no substitute for the Bible as a central aid to worship when parents read it with appreciation for the growing needs of children. We recommend the use of such resources for worship as *The Christian Home, The Upper Room,* and the devotional materials in the church-school literature.

3. *Marriage Relations.*—Marriage is an achievement. It doesn't just happen. It comprises a growing oneness in which emotional adjustments from time to time are affected by an understanding of right ways of living together.

a) Preparation.—It is increasingly obvious that if marriage is to succeed, there must be adequate preparation. Therefore, it is recommended that a regular course of instruction for youth on the Christian ideals of friendship, courtship, and marriage be given in each local church, using the available materials. In our youth assemblies, camps, and institutes qualified persons should give counsel on personal problems, social relations, and the duties and privileges of Christian marriage. Suitable books, pamphlets, and audio-visual resources should be made available for young people. It is further recommended that courses of instruction for young married couples on home building, income budgeting, child training, life adjustments, and personality problems be given by each local church.

The time has come when every person planning marriage should have the opportunity for skilled and careful counseling by ministers or staff workers who are prepared in this field. If this is to be done, pastors must be trained to guide young people through premarital and postmarital counseling.

b) Mixed Marriages.—Religious convictions should be a strong tie in marriage. Recent research has emphasized the importance of common cultural and religious backgrounds as the foundations of successful marriage. It is therefore strongly urged that each young person consider carefully before becoming engaged to anyone who does not have a similar religious background. It is important that Protestant youth discuss this problem with their ministers before it is too late. Ministers are urged to discuss with both youth and parents the likelihood of failure in mixed marriages.

c) Planned Parenthood.—Parenthood is a Christian privilege and responsibility ; and the highest ideals of the Christian family can be achieved when children are wanted, anticipated, and welcomed into the home. We believe that planned parenthood, practiced in Christian conscience, fulfills rather than violates the will of God.

d) Divorce.—Divorce is not the answer to the problems that cause it. It is symptomatic of deeper difficulties. The church must stand ready to point out these basic problems to couples contemplating divorce, and help them to discover and, if possible, to overcome such difficulties. In addition, the church must stand ready to depict the unhappy circumstances that are to await the divorced person. As a Christian church, and as ministers, we are obligated to aid, by counsel, persons who have experienced broken marriage, and to guide them so that they may make satisfactory adjustments.

4. *Relationships in the Home.*—It is living together within the family that is the final test of religious living. The highest qualities are found in the life and character of Jesus Christ ; these must be manifest in daily family living.

If we want to help the children in our homes develop, there must be an inner acceptance of each child. He must be loved for himself with all the limitations he may possess. In each instance he must be treated as an individual.

a) Parent-Child Relations.—We recognize that parents are constantly teaching in the home in unrecognized ways as well as in their conscious efforts. Parents, in co-operation with the church-school teachers, should make possible the Christian education of their children throughout the week. There is great need for parents to interpret to their children in a Christian way the present world issues and needs, the politics of national and international relationships, the efforts of the people of the world through the United Nations to do those things which make for peace and more abundant life, the complex problems created by the use of beverage alcohol and narcotics, the need for adhering to Christian moral standards amid the tensions and pressures of our present-day living. There is also need for parents to guide their children in learning how to evaluate the propaganda to which they are constantly subjected through newspapers, magazines, radio, television, and movies. At these points the church and the family can support and strengthen each other in their ideals of personal conduct and social righteousness.

b) Co-operation.—We recommend that our churches co-operate with other agencies in the community that are working for the improvement of family life and for the strengthening of Christian character. The National Conference on Family Life has demonstrated one way in which the boards and agencies of the church can work together for the promotion of Christian family living.

c) Sex Education.—Parents must assume the responsibility of interpreting to each child, before his adolescence, the facts regarding the origin of life. If properly instructed, parents are best fitted to educate their children in regard to sex; but if they have been negligent, then qualified persons in the church should reverently teach the beautiful truths of life. We recognize that sex education is not mere information. It includes also the formation of attitudes and habits.

d) Mass Media.—Parents must also help their children evaluate literature and radio and television programs which come into the home and counteract the undesirable publicity brought into the home through these mass media in terms of Christian and wholesome attitudes, to the end that their children will develop a taste for the best.

e) Three-Generation Families.—In the family there must be a recognition of the older adult. Medical science is making life increasingly longer. Older adults need and should have a significant place of recognition as members of the family circle.

5. *The Church and the Family.*—The church and the family need each other. Through their support of the church, parents teach by example the importance of the church in the life of the nation. When they neglect the church, they teach their children that the church is of little importance in the lives of people.

To help parents understand the importance of teaching in the home, and the best methods for guiding their children, it is recommended that local churches make provision for study classes and discussion groups on child development, family relationships, and the teaching of religion in the home, using the helpful materials provided through the regular publications of the church.

There is value in all the members of the family worshiping together both in the home and in the church. It is expected that local churches will provide resources and help for the family worship experiences. Churches are encouraged to hold occasional special services at which the entire family can worship together, with the service planned for the participation of all age groups.

It is important for the churches to focus attention on the family at frequent intervals during the year. Especially do we recommend the observance of National Family Week, as provided in ¶ 250.5, and participation in the Family Life Conference.

Parents and teachers are urged to meet together frequently to discuss the Christian nurture of children and ways in which they can work together for better teaching. Parents are urged to read together with their children the lesson materials provided by the church. Teachers are urged to keep parents informed regarding the objectives of the lesson materials and to point out ways in which parents can further these objectives through home participation.

6. *Legislation.*—To protect both the individual and society from hasty marriages we favor legislation requiring a period of days or weeks between the application for a marriage license and the granting of it. This will allow sufficient time for consideration on the part of the two persons concerned. We also favor a longer interval between application for and granting of divorce.

We recommend laws requiring a medical examination of both contracting parties, and the refusal of a license to those unfitted physically or mentally by heredity or otherwise for the responsible state of matrimony.

We look with favor upon the increasing development of family life courts, and urge that when such courts are estab-

lished they employ among their staff counselors persons who
are prepared to give spiritual guidance to families in trouble.

We further favor uniform marriage and divorce laws, and
request that a study of the marriage and divorce laws be made
by the General Committee on Family Life.

¶ 2022.   Temperance and Public Morals

1. *Beverage Alcohol.*—The Methodist Church reasserts its
long-established conviction that the legalization of intoxicants
as beverages violates the Christian standards of morality and
social concern which this nation claims to accept. Alcoholic
indulgence inflicts serious loss to the community in damage to
health and efficiency, death through traffic accidents, the creation and intensification of poverty and economic waste. It
contributes to the public disorder, crime, and moral deviation
now threatening the welfare of the nation and the life of the
church. It keeps alive the alcohol industry, with its insidious
influence on social life and public affairs.

The Methodist Church is militant in opposition to the liquor
traffic also because its product assails the highest centers of
personality and its procedures contribute greatly to the sickness and degradation of people, leading to deterioration of
character, discord in family life, neglect and suffering of children. The use of alcoholic beverages adds serious and avoidable
hindrance to our fellowship with God and creative helpfulness
to men. Therefore, the church continues its unceasing battle
against intoxicating liquors.

Because the church seeks to lead believing souls into fullness
of life in Christ, our appeal is for total abstinence from all
uses of intoxicants. Methodists, in refusing alcoholic beverages,
should regard this as an essential part of their witness to the
faith they profess and as evidence of loyalty to the highest.
The practice of total abstinence should also be thought of by
Methodists as a matter of stewardship concern for our brothers,
for the inevitable influence of personal life imposes a solemn
responsibility on each one.

Since successful personal and social reforms stem from
convictions that must be based on broad and accurate knowledge, we give hearty endorsement to the program of our Board
of Christian Social Concerns, Division of Temperance and
General Welfare, and its special emphases on freedom from
alcohol:

a) Positive education for a life free from beverage alcohol.
This is the heart of the division's total effort. It is a broad
and comprehensive educational program designed to reach all

Methodists. Without it there can be no consistent and effective action for abstinence.

b) Commitment to abstinence is a natural and logical outgrowth of commitment to Christ. The division encourages sobriety as an essential manifestation of the Christian faith.

c) Rehabilitation of those who suffer because of beverage alcohol is clearly the obligation of all Christians. The division gives guidance to thousands of pastors and laymen who deal person-to-person with individuals and families seeking their help.

d) Legislation as an effective means to outlaw beverage alcohol is a natural outgrowth of the concern of informed citizens. The division stimulates local, state, and national legislation to protect individuals, families, and communities from the pressures of the organized traffic in beverage alcohol.

We denounce the continued invasion of the American home by liquor advertisers who seek through magazines, radio, television, and other media to indoctrinate even our children in the use of alcoholic beverages. We deplore governmental toleration of this practice and call on the Congress of the United States to enact legislation to prevent the use of radio, television, and other interstate means of advertising for such purposes.

We are deeply concerned over the growing practice of permitting the sale of alcoholic beverages through drug and grocery stores in a deliberate attempt to win the housewife as a customer.

We call upon all denominations to co-operate in a vigorous program of research and proclamation that the truth concerning the damage of social drinking and the benefits of personal abstinence may become known and accepted by all Christians.

We re-emphasize our concern for protective alcohol education in the public schools and call upon good citizens to inspire and support legislation that will effectively control and prohibit the traffic in alcohol.

2. *Gambling.*—The passion to acquire wealth without honest labor, inflamed by widely publicized giveaway programs and the growing movement to legalize gambling in state after state, is a serious concern for Christians. The practice of gambling undermines basic moral law as well as established economic laws. Gambling is a menace to business integrity, breeds crime, and is destructive of the interests of good government.

The dubious gains of petty gambling are not acceptable in financing the work of the church. All Methodist churches shall abstain from the use of raffles, lotteries, and games of chance for church support or church-related projects. Methodists should protest all forms of gambling practices carried on by secular organizations in their communities.

3. *Narcotics.*—Narcotic addiction and the traffic in narcotics are major problems in the United States and around the world. The indiscriminate use of barbiturates, tranquilizers, and other dangerous drugs is an increasing menace. We call upon our people to support all wise plans for the most effective control of narcotic distribution and use. We urge the development of more adequate facilities for the rehabilitation of narcotic addicts and proper education regarding the dangers in self-prescribed narcotics and tranquilizers.

4. *Tobacco.*—In the interest of a larger Christian influence and service we urge our people to abstain from the use of tobacco in all its forms. The American Cancer Society and the United States Public Health Service warn that a smoking-cancer relationship is definite.

We remind our membership that the principle of right example must be considered in regard to the use of tobacco. Organizations and institutions related to The Methodist Church should refrain from accepting and printing advertisements for tobacco in their periodicals.

5. *Exploitation of Sex.*—The recent deluge of "glamor" magazines and motion pictures which overemphasize sex to pornographic extremes reveals a growing and dangerous sickness in society. We urge our churches to institute courses of study for young people regarding Christian attitudes toward sex and personality growth. We call upon our members to encourage and participate in community action to eliminate the distribution and sale of pornographic literature, films, and amusements through voluntary and, where necessary, legislative means.

6. *Sunday Observance.*—We are concerned with the growing tendency toward the commercialization of Sunday. Some places of business need to be open on Sunday to serve the general welfare. But this is not true of many others. Sunday is a hallowed day commemorating our Lord's resurrection. By prayer and thanksgiving we glorify the risen Lord, who calls for the stewardship of our leisure, talents, and gifts to extend his Kingdom everywhere. We urge the voluntary closing of all nonessential commercial enterprises on Sunday. We encourage all Methodists to observe Sunday as a day of worship in our churches, rest, and family fellowship.

¶ 2023.　Abstinence Among Church Leaders

The Methodist Church advocates total abstinence for all its members. Those accepting nomination or appointment for any official leadership in the church are expected to refrain from all uses of intoxicating beverages.

¶ 2024. World Order and International Peace

The role of the Church in today's world situation is clear. Its task is to help mankind attain freedom, human rights, justice, adequate living standards, self-government, and the co-operation of all nations for the maintenance of peace.

With the development of increasingly horrible weapons of mass destruction, mankind stands at the threshold of possible extinction. In the face of this situation, Christians everywhere are confronted with a definite challenge.

Motivated and mobilized by the spirit of Christ and challenged by world conditions, Christians are in a strategic position to make the gospel articulate in world affairs to the end that peace may become real and dynamic.

We commend the National Council of Churches for its sponsorship of five conferences on world order in the last twenty years. These have added significantly to our understanding of world affairs and have provoked us to profound study and concerned Christian action. We urge the National Council of Churches to continue its fruitful work in the areas of peace education and action, and we urge all Methodists to participate actively in these efforts.

We call upon individual Methodists to hold fast to the gospel of the Christ of peace. One of the foundations of a warless world finds its origin within the thinking of the individual Christian. Hatred and prejudice must be overcome by love as the cementing bond of brotherhood. When the teachings of Jesus are fully accepted and implemented by virile, vigorous action, war as a means of settling international disputes will die. As war disappears, thereby setting the world free from the tyranny of destruction, man will be able to build anew, within a more Christian structure, an environment of lasting freedom and peace.

1. *Moral and Spiritual Aspects of Peace.*—The primary conditons of peace lie in the attitudes of men. Since it holds in its keeping the moral and spiritual forces for a peaceful world, the Church has a unique and God-given responsibility. Certainly the Church can be an agency of great power for the establishment of a world community, as has been demonstrated by the missionary and ecumenical movements. That the bonds of brotherhood among Christians have held so firm during years of war and international tension is occasion for humble thanksgiving to God. From the beginnings already made, a

wider world community must be fashioned through co-operation with persons of all religious faiths. To this ideal we dedicate ourselves unflinchingly.

2. *Man's Struggle Toward Self-Government.*—Since World War II there has been a surge toward self-government and self-determination on the part of subject peoples. Old imperialisms are breaking up. Colonial and dependent territories are seeking freedom and political independence. These affected peoples are struggling for the knowledge, the tools, and the skills necessary to provide themselves with a standard of living designed to alleviate hunger, disease, exposure, and ignorance. They are seeking, and many have already gained, a new status in the family of nations.

We reaffirm the Christian's unceasing interest in freedom and self-government for all people. We urge all governments to aid non-self-governing peoples through such educational, medical, and technical aid as may assist them to gain independence and to set up stable democratic governments and Christian social practices.

3. *Opposition to Materialistic Ideologies.*—The Christian religion stands in direct opposition to materialistic ideologies prevalent in many places in the world. These ideologies, with their disregard for human rights, their scorn for the dignity of the individual, and their failure to acknowledge the fatherhood of God and the brotherhood of man, are abhorrent to basic Christian principles.

We believe the best defense against these materialistic ideologies is found in the preservation and growth of democratic institutions and in the daily practice of the Christian way of life. We believe that such growth and practice provide powerful stimulus to the elimination, as rapidly as possible, of: (*a*) racial and class distinctions; (*b*) economic conditions which cause hunger, disease, and ignorance for large segments of the human race; and (*c*) the political suppression of human rights.

We believe that Christian concern for the physical and spiritual welfare of all people will promote unselfish sharing of essential goods and the value of life which God has so lavishly provided. Such sharing will give great impetus to the elimination of the basic causes of war.

4. *Implementing World Peace.*—Peace is the gift of God, but it is appropriated by man only through the practice of love and co-operation. The peace of God cannot be contained within any one nation, economic system, or religion. To be a stable and lasting reality it must become universal. While the ultimate aim of the Christian mission is the conversion of

the world, the urgent need to establish the conditions of peace calls for the immediate and unremitting efforts of Christians and non-Christians alike.

No one nation or group of nations, pitted against other nations, can initiate or maintain world peace. It can only be the result of understanding, forbearance, and co-operation on the part of all nations.

We give thanks to God for the United Nations and its agencies, and their continued efforts to create peace in the world. Particularly do we commend the United Nations for its direct approach, exploration, and action on crucial problems that arise periodically throughout the world and pose a direct threat to the peace of the world. We are extremely grateful, too, for the enlightened political leaders and representatives of various individual nations who so courageously share their part of the responsibility for world peace.

We believe there is continuing and urgent need to use more fully the various agencies of international understanding and co-operation which are presently available in the United Nations. We believe the United Nations and its agencies should be supported, strengthened, and improved. Moreover, if these facilities are to become most effective, the United Nations, with membership open to all nations, must be given sufficient authority to enact, interpret, and enforce world law against aggression and war.

We call upon the government of the United States to expand its leadership in an effort to bring about such charter revisions as are necessary to facilitate the work of the United Nations in maintaining international order and in preventing the outbreak of war.

We support the greater use of the International Court of Justice and urge the United States to lead the way in removing restrictions which impair the court's effectiveness.

5. *Universal Disarmament.*—From the Episcopal Address of the General Conference of 1960 we read: "Because of the technology which is our pride, this General Conference convenes under the most ominous circumstances in the long history of the Church. For the human race has within its hands for the first time the power of its own annihilation. In a sense, the tool has become the enemy of its maker. The nuclear power that might be our weal has become a weapon. The same technology which has shortened the distances has produced the intercontinental missile. Man has dominated the forces of nature, conquered the seas and the air, organized his commerce and combatted disease. Yet, the lord of the earth cannot enjoy his conquest, but for fear of his life must hide

underground, haunted by anxieties and the companion of uncertainties. The evils implicit in applied science are compounded by the residue of problems growing out of World War II and an armament race which, unless terminated early, can have but one result.

"We commend the international situation to the thoughtful, prayerful concern of the church and urge that the General Conference take the leadership in mobilizing Christian opinion within our connection in behalf of mutual disarmament, the prohibition of nuclear testing, and the peaceful use of atomic energy."

To meet this high challenge our objective must be nothing less than the abolition of the use of war by nations. Mere arms reductions or limitations are inadequate. Only complete disarmament, involving both nuclear and conventional weapons, down to the levels required for internal policing will deprive nations of the tools of war.

Such complete disarmament must be universal to be acceptable to all nations. It must be enforced by a competent international agency, preferably a strengthened United Nations. Complete, universal disarmament needs to be based upon confidence in the enforcement system.

Moreover, such disarmament requires international means for the peaceful settlement of disputes and controversies between nations. Extension of law and use of courts on the world level may well be a condition precedent to complete, universal, enforceable disarmament.

Disarmament is no simple goal, for its accomplishment requires agreement of all major powers, not only on the principles of disarmament, but also upon the delegation to the United Nations of the necessary authority and power to control, inspect, and enforce disarmament. In the face of national prejudices, suspicions, and fears this is a stupendous task. Its difficulty is exceeded only by its necessity and urgency. Negotiations must be pressed with all major powers to find an acceptable path to disarmament.

We commend the President, the Congress, and the State Department of the United States on their attention to disarmament; but we call for an expansion of effort and staff to develop a comprehensive, safeguarded disarmament plan upon which to focus negotiations.

We call upon the United States and all other governments to declare complete, universal, and enforceable disarmament to be their goal and to move in this direction.

We further call upon the United States and all other governments to exert forceful, imaginative, patient, and dedicated leadership toward the achievement of such disarmament.

We deplore the tendency of governments and individuals to discredit any proposal for disarmament not made by themselves. Such cynicism is not conducive to successful negotiations.

We encourage a number of immediate steps in addition to our continuing efforts to achieve complete, universal, enforceable disarmament.

a) *Nuclear Tests.*—We urge permanent cessation of all nuclear tests by all nuclear powers, present and future, in order that present and future generations may be protected from the dangers of nuclear radiation.

b) *Outer Space.*—We call for an international agreement establishing a United Nations agency for co-operative exploration of outer space and a control system to assure the use of outer space for peaceful purposes only.

c) *Peaceful Uses.*—We support the activities of the International Atomic Energy Agency to expand peaceful uses of nuclear energy and seek the establishment of an effective inspection system which may furnish the pattern for supervising world-wide cessation of the production of nuclear weapons.

d) *Safeguards.*—We support all reasonable steps which reduce the chances of war by miscalculation, accident, or inadvertent action, such as mutual aerial and ground inspection against surprise attack and the establishment and use of a United Nations permanent force.

e) *Economic Benefits.*—We call upon the United States to offer to devote a substantial percentage of the savings which will result from complete disarmament to the development of underdeveloped countries, using the United Nations as far as feasible. We urge study and planning of measures needed to cope with the domestic economic adjustments, largely localized to industry and labor, resulting from elimination of huge expenditures for armaments.

6. *The Individual and Military Training.*—*a*) For two decades the United States of America has had on its statute books legislation providing for military conscription. Many persons have come to regard this as an established and permanent policy. The same is true in varying degrees of a large number of other countries as well.

We are deeply troubled by the general indifference to the infringement of individual rights and freedom involved in compulsory military service. We urge that voluntary methods of recruiting military manpower be developed that accord the individual the freedom of choice which should characterize peacetime civilian life.

We reaffirm traditional Methodist opposition to any system of peacetime universal military training. We appeal to the United States to give bold leadership looking toward the universal abolition of peacetime conscription by or through the United Nations.

b) Christians cannot complacently accept rights or privileges accorded to them because of their religious views but denied to others equally sincere who do not meet a religious test. So long as draft legislation remains in effect, we believe that all sincere conscientious objectors should be granted recognition and assigned to appropriate service regardless of whether or not they profess religious grounds as the basis of their stand.

c) Regarding the duty of the individual Christian, opinions sincerely differ. Faced by the dilemma of participation in war, he must decide prayerfully before God what is to be his course of action in relation thereto. What the Christian citizen may not do is to obey men rather than God, or overlook the degree of compromise in our best acts, or gloss over the sinfulness of war. The Church must hold within its fellowship persons who sincerely differ at this point of critical decision, call all to repentance, mediate to all God's mercy, minister to all in Christ's name.

We believe it is our obligation to render every assistance to the individual who conscientiously objects to service in the military forces. He should receive counsel concerning his rights in this respect, assistance in bringing his claim before the proper authorities, and support in securing recognition thereof.

Thousands of our sons and daughters have, with sincere Christian conscience, responded to the call for service in the military forces. We are obligated to provide pre-induction counseling and educational material prepared by the related agencies of the church, such as the Board of Education, the Methodist Youth Fellowship, etc. This material should be directed toward the wise use of leisure time and the challenge to Christlike living during their military service. We believe particular emphasis should be directed to the serviceman's bearing a good witness for Christ, the Church, and the nation while on duty outside his country.

In meeting these obligations we reiterate our unswerving opposition to the principle of militarism and any dependence for security upon the sword alone.

We call upon local Methodist churches to enlist the interest of, and to offer hospitality to, the men and women of the armed services who are stationed in or near their communities.

We further recommend that the home pastors of those young people who have entered military service urge them to continue their active church affiliation and participation in the Methodist churches nearest the points they may be assigned, and to maintain contacts with their chaplains and chapel programs.

d) In public institutions where all male students are required to take ROTC in order to graduate, provision should be made for the exemption of those conscientiously opposed to participation in war and military training. The regulations of educational institutions in this matter should reflect as much respect for conscience as the Selective Service Law.

We urge our church-related colleges and universities to play a role distinct from that of secular educational institutions. We urge them to study seriously the implications of military training in a church-related institution, one of whose objectives is to train young people for world Christian community.

¶ 2026.   The Methodist Church and Race

Our Lord Jesus Christ teaches that all men are brothers. He permits no discrimination because of race, color, or creed. "In Christ Jesus you are all sons of God, through faith. . . . There is neither Jew nor Greek, . . . there is neither male nor female; for you are all one in Christ Jesus." (Gal. 3:26, 28.)

The position of The Methodist Church, long held and frequently declared, is an amplification of our Lord's teaching:

"To discriminate against a person solely upon the basis of his race is both unfair and unchristian. Every child of God is entitled to that place in society which he has won by his industry and his character. To deny him that position of honor because of the accident of his birth is neither honest democracy nor good religion." (The Episcopal Address, 1952 and 1956.)

"We believe that God is Father of all peoples and races, that Jesus Christ is his Son, that all men are brothers, and that man is of infinite worth as a child of God." (The Social Creed, ¶ 2020.)

"The Church is the instrument of God's purpose. This is his Church. It is ours only as stewards under his lordship. The requirements for its membership and the nature of its mission are set by God. The House of God must be open to the whole family of God. If we discriminate against any persons, we deny the essential nature of the Church as a fellowship in Christ." (Message of the Dallas Conference on Human Relations, August, 1959.)

The failure of our church to live up to its own pronouncements is a fault that must be shared by every section of the church. Our failure to achieve the aims of Christian brotherhood is grievous since Methodism is a world church. The problems of race relations must be approached in love lest the cause of Christ suffer at our hands. In the midst of the wide divergence of social customs and conscience affecting the complex issue of race relations, we must carry out the teachings of our Lord in order to attain the true nature of the Church as a complete fellowship in Christ.

The decisions of the Supreme Court of the United States relative to segregation have made necessary far-reaching and often difficult community readjustments throughout the nation. The period of stress and strain continues for many communities. On the whole very considerable progress has been made.

We must have compassion and understanding for those whose basic social concepts, customs, and traditions throughout the world may differ from those of our own. We call upon our people to go forward in all good faith, with brotherliness and patience seeking in all these areas to find the mind of Christ.

It is our desire to accomplish the realization of Christian brotherhood and full participation by all in every aspect of the Church's life. We join other people of good will around the world in moving toward the day when all races shall share richly without discrimination or enforced segregation in the good things of life. Therefore, we resolutely go forward with the work begun with respect to race relations in our church and in our world, following these principles of action:

Let us re-examine all our attitudes toward other persons in the light of the teaching of Jesus and God's demonstrated love for us.

Let us seek to create within our church, as within families, a climate of love and understanding, wherein freedom of expression and study are encouraged, especially in areas of disagreement and tension.

Let us endeavor to know each other better across dividing lines by working together toward the solution of common problems, such as housing, education, employment, health, recreation, and juvenile delinquency.

In this spirit we recommend:

1. That a co-operative study be made by the general boards of the church of our institutions—including local churches, colleges, universities, theological schools, publishing agencies, hospitals, and homes—as to their admission and employment

policies and practices and availability of services. It is the responsibility of these institutions that their policies and practices be in accord with the teachings of Jesus.

2. That Methodists in their homes, in their work, in their churches, and in their communities actively work to eliminate discrimination and enforced segregation on the basis of race, color, or national origin; that as a church we pursue a program of education and action to bring about Christian practices with respect to housing, open occupancy, schools, opportunity of employment, and community acceptance which, in the spirit of Christ, create a sense of belonging.

3. That as basic steps toward the removal of racial barriers in the organizational structure of the church are taken, consistent planning shall be undertaken by every jurisdiction and conference to implement the procedures duly authorized in Amendment IX of the Constitution of The Methodist Church. In realization of this goal bishops, district superintendents, pastors, and laymen are urged to use with greater Christian courage all available channels, including the local churches, to create a climate of understanding and acceptance of this responsibility.

4. That our pastors, upon whom rests the responsibility of receiving individuals into church membership discharge that responsibility without regard to race, color, or national origin.

5. That Methodists at national and international meetings of the church make provision for equality of accommodations for all races, without discrimination or segregation.

6. That the many racial and national groups which make up our Methodist world fellowship be afforded the opportunity without discrimination to enjoy full participation in all the activities of the church.

¶ 2028. Religion and the Public Schools in the United States

The Methodist Church is committed to the public school as the most effective means of providing common education for all our children. We hold that it is an institution essential to the preservation and development of our true democracy. But our public schools are hard pressed. Public tax funds, in increasing sums, are diverted to sectarian schools. Opponents of the public schools call the schools "Godless" while at the same time legal restrictions are placed upon the recognition of religion in the schools. It is time for the friends of the public schools to be alert to this situation and to be active in their support.

We desire to co-operate with educational leaders in achieving the highest functioning of the American public school system in terms of the intellectual and moral development of the pupils and the enrichment of the national life. We therefore call upon our people: (1) to acquaint themselves with the program and problems of the public school and to do all they can to encourage and strengthen the work of teachers and administrators, and (2) to present to our ablest youth the spiritual and public-service opportunities of public school teaching as a vocation.

We are unalterably opposed to the diversion of tax funds to the support of private and sectarian schools. In a short time this scattering process can destroy our American public school system and weaken the foundations of national unity.

We believe that religion has a rightful place in the public school program, and that it is possible for public school teachers, without violating the traditional American principle of separation of church and state, to teach moral principles and spiritual values. We hold that it is possible, within this same principle of separation of church and state, to integrate religious instruction with the regular curriculum—for example, teaching religious classics in courses in literature, and in social studies showing the influence of religion upon our society. Such teaching would afford a background for further and more specific instruction on the part of home and church. The home and church must carry the chief responsibility for nurturing vital faith which motivates life, but the home and church must have the support of our public schools. Our society must discover the techniques within the principle of separation of church and state by which that support can be achieved.

¶ 2029.   Methodists and Evangelism

Evangelism is the effort of persons and groups to witness to the new life that comes through the acceptance of Jesus Christ as Lord. Although evangelism expresses itself in many ways, it is basically a declaration of what, through Christ, has become experience and conviction. Evangelism, then, becomes the natural and normal activity of a Christian person. Every Christian is an evangelist, a bearer of the good news of God's care for all his children.

Furthermore, evangelism is an inevitable expression of personal relationship with Jesus Christ. Our experience is that of two of his first disciples: "We cannot but speak of what we have seen and heard." We are compelled by his spirit within us to say by word, act, and attitude what we have seen of God's love, power, and purpose through Jesus Christ our Lord.

In the Episcopal Address the bishops lifted up the need for evangelism: "The finally inescapable truth is that at the heart of all the problems that beset us, deeper than our social, economic, political, and cultural perplexities, the basic one is religion. It is the question as to what we know of God, what his will and purpose for us are, and what we are to do in right response and consequence."

Methodism must face adequately, creatively, and effectively the ever-present foes of the good life—secularism, nationalism, militarism, materialism, and sin in all its enticing forms.

Christ calls The Methodist Church to dynamic discipleship. On Methodism's response to Christ's call rests, in some measure, the future of our civilization and the spiritual renewal of the Church as the redemptive body of Christ.

Can Methodism recover for our decade the explosive sense of spiritual power which has been its heritage? Can we move beyond organization to become a living organism of the body of Christ? The major threat facing the Church today does not come from the enemies of the Church. It is the spiritual deadness of the witness of the Church, the lack of evangelistic initiative.

The Christian witness is a compulsion born of a personal discovery. The evangelistic task of Methodism is: A Mission to the Church and a Mission to the World. We must see the task! We must be obedient in our response to God!

In the total evangelistic enterprise there is definite place for program, professional leadership, meetings, and methods. There is also need for fully committed persons whose compelling concern is that Jesus Christ may become a living reality in the lives of all. To that end each Christian must witness in word and deed. The vitality of each person's witness is dependent upon his commitment to Christ.

The Church's evangelistic effort is to be neither seasonal nor sporadic. Nor should evangelism be reserved for the labors of specialists only. It must be made the continuing activity of all members of the Church. Only as dedicated Christians see evangelism in this light, and obey Christ's call for witnesses, will the cause of Christ make its redemptive way across the community and the world.

The General Conference, in approving the report of the Co-ordinating Council, has affirmed that "Jesus Christ is Lord." In the new quadrennium Methodists will be remembering this affirmation. Methodists are called upon to try to bring all of life under the leadership of the Lord of life.

Every activity in the local church ought to become an affirmation of the truth that Jesus Christ is Lord. If we have left evangelism to the local-church Commission on Membership and Evangelism, now is the time for every organization in the local church to be aware of its evangelistic privileges and responsibilities. The church school, Methodist Men, the Woman's Society of Christian Service, the Young Adult Fellowship, the Methodist Youth Fellowship—each group has its peculiar place as a group witnessing to the Christian faith and life. Let each group ask itself these questions: "What is our task?" "What are we doing to fulfill it?" "How can we make our Christian witness more effective?" Ingenious and consecrated men and women, for whom Jesus Christ is Lord, will find ways of persuading others to make Christ their Lord and Master.

There are many millions in the United States and across the world who have not yet accepted Christ. For these persons Methodists have a responsibility. We are called to be living witnesses to Christ's faith in God, his compassionate interest in persons, and his sacrificial self-giving. It is ours to do the truth and speak the truth in love. We are to live as Christians in a world whose ways do not always reflect the mind and will of God. Great forces of evil are asking for men's allegiance. Christ, too, lays claim to the whole of man, all men. As many as accept him, to them he gives life eternal. Methodists, alive to Christ and obedient to his spirit, can be the means of bringing many unchurched and nonprofessing Christians into the company of Christ's followers. There are growing evidences that Methodists want to be faithful witnesses to Jesus Christ, the Lord of life.

CHAPTER VI

TERRITORIES OF THE ANNUAL CONFERENCES

[Under the Constitution (¶ 29) the boundaries of Annual Conferences are determined by their respective Jurisdictional and Central Conferences, and accordingly their official delineations are recorded in the archives of the determining conferences. By order of the General Conference of 1960, unofficial condensed descriptions of the conference territories as they existed at the time of adjournment of the General Conference are presented here for information. So that each territory may be quickly identified, the descriptions are expressed in terms of the features shown on any good map, without attempt to trace the lines across counties and around deviations and exceptions. To verify that a particular church or circuit is within a certain conference, the reader should consult the lists of appointments in the General Minutes.—EDITORS.]

¶ 2036. Conferences of the Northeastern Jurisdiction

1. This jurisdiction comprises the states of Maine, New Hampshire, Vermont, Massachusetts, Rhode Island, Connecticut, New York, New Jersey, Pennsylvania, Delaware, Maryland, West Virginia; the District of Columbia; Puerto Rico.

2. BALTIMORE: The District of Columbia; the western shore of Maryland through part of Garrett County; in West Virginia the counties of Jefferson, Berkeley, Morgan.

3. CENTRAL NEW YORK: In New York the counties of Madison, Onondaga, Cortland (most), Cayuga, Tompkins, Chemung, Schuyler, Seneca, Yates, Ontario (part), Wayne (part); in Pennsylvania parts of Tioga and Bradford Counties.

4. CENTRAL PENNSYLVANIA: The part bounded by and included in the counties of Bedford, Cambria (part), Clearfield (most), Elk (part), Cameron (part), Clinton, Lycoming, Sullivan, Luzerne (part), Columbia, Northumberland, Perry, Cumberland, York; also the city of Harrisburg.

5. ERIE: Northwestern Pennsylvania through the counties of Lawrence, Butler (part), Armstrong (part), Jefferson, Clearfield (part), Elk (part), McKean (part); in New York the counties of Chautauqua and Cattaraugus (part).

6. GENESEE: In New York the counties of Wayne (part), Ontario (part), Steuben, and westward through Niagara, Erie, Cattaraugus (part); in Pennsylvania parts of Tioga and McKean Counties.

7. MAINE: All Maine; part of Coos County, New Hampshire.

8. NEW ENGLAND: Massachusetts except Berkshire County, the part north of the Merrimack River, and the part southeast from southeastern Norfolk County.

9. NEW ENGLAND SOUTHERN: Connecticut east of the Connecticut River; all Rhode Island; the part of Massachusetts southeast from southeastern Norfolk County.

10. NEW HAMPSHIRE: All New Hampshire except part of Coos County; the part of Massachusetts north of the Merrimack River.

11. NEW JERSEY: Southern New Jersey through the counties of Monmouth, Middesex (part), Somerset (part), Mercer.

12. NEW YORK: In New York the western part of New York

City and the counties of Westchester, Putnam, Duchess, Columbia, Greene, Delaware, Ulster, Sullivan (most), Orange (most), Rockland (part); parts of Litchfield County, Connecticut, and Berkshire County, Massachusetts.

13. NEW YORK EAST: The eastern part of New York City; Long Island; Connecticut west of the Connecticut River except part of Litchfield County.

14. NEWARK: Northern New Jersey through the counties of Hunterdon (most), Somerset (most), Middlesex (part); in New York the counties of Rockland (most), Orange (part), Sullivan (part).

15. NORTHERN NEW YORK: The counties of Franklin, St. Lawrence, Jefferson, Lewis, Oneida, Herkimer, Oswego, Madison (part), Otsego (part).

16. PENINSULA: All Delaware; the eastern shore of Maryland.

17. PHILADELPHIA: Southeastern Pennsylvania through the counties of Lancaster, Dauphin (excluding Harrisburg), Schuylkill, Carbon, Monroe.

18. PITTSBURGH: Southwestern Pennsylvania through the counties of Beaver, Butler (part), Armstrong (part), Indiana, Cambria (part), Somerset; in West Virginia the counties of Hancock and Brooke.

19. TROY: All Vermont; part of Berkshire County, Massachusetts; northeastern New York through the counties of Rensselaer, Albany, Schoharie, Montgomery, Fulton, Hamilton, Essex, Clinton.

20. WEST VIRGINIA: All West Virginia except the counties of Jefferson, Berkeley, Morgan, Brooke, Hancock; part of Garrett County, Maryland.

21. WYOMING: In New York the counties of Otsego, Chenango, Broome, Tioga, Cortland (part); in Pennsylvania the counties of Pike, Wayne, Lackawanna, Luzerne (part), Wyoming, Bradford (part), Susquehanna.

22. PUERTO RICO PROVISIONAL: Puerto Rico and the adjacent islands belonging to its civil jurisdiction, together with any work which may be established by The Methodist Church or come under its care in any of the islands known as the West Indies, except in the Republic of Cuba.

¶ 2037. Conferences of the Southeastern Jurisdiction

1. This jurisdiction comprises the states of Virginia, North Carolina, South Carolina, Georgia, Florida, Alabama, Mississippi, Tennessee, Kentucky; the Republic of Cuba.

2. ALABAMA–WEST FLORIDA: Southern Alabama through

the counties of Lee, Tallapoosa (part), Elmore, Chilton (most), Bibb (part), Hale, Greene, Sumter (most); the part of Florida west of the Apalachicola River.

3. CUBA: The entire republic.

4. FLORIDA: All east of the Apalachicola River.

5. HOLSTON: Southwestern Virginia through the counties of Giles (part), Pulaski, Carroll; Dade County, Georgia; East Tennessee through the counties of Scott, Morgan, Roane, Rhea, Bledsoe, Sequatchie, Marion.

6. KENTUCKY: Eastern Kentucky through the counties of Trimble, Oldham (part), Shelby, Spencer, Nelson (part), Washington (most), Marion (part), Casey (part), Pulaski, McCreary (part).

7. LOUISVILLE: Central Kentucky from the Tennessee River eastward through the counties of Oldham (part), Jefferson, Bullitt, Nelson (part), Washington (part), Marion (most), Casey (part), Russell, Wayne, McCreary (part).

8. MEMPHIS: The parts of Tennessee and Kentucky west of the Tennessee River.

9. MISSISSIPPI: Southern Mississippi through the counties of Issaquena, Sharkey, Humphreys (part), Yazoo, Madison, Leake, Neshoba, Kemper.

10. NORTH ALABAMA: Through the counties of Sumter (part), Pickens, Tuscaloosa, Bibb (part), Chilton (part), Coosa, Tallapoosa (part), Chambers.

11. NORTH CAROLINA: Eastern North Carolina through the counties of Caswell, Alamance, Chatham, Montgomery (most), Richmond.

12. NORTH GEORGIA: Northern Georgia, except Dade County, through the counties of Troup, Merriwether, Upson, Monroe, Jones, Baldwin, Hancock, Warren, McDuffie, Richmond.

13. NORTH MISSISSIPPI: Through the counties of Washington, Humphreys (part), Holmes, Attala, Winston, Noxubee.

14. SOUTH CAROLINA: The entire state.

15. SOUTH GEORGIA: Through the counties of Harris, Talbot, Taylor, Crawford, Bibb, Twiggs, Wilkinson, Washington, Glascock, Jefferson, Burke.

16. TENNESSEE: Middle Tennessee from the Tennessee River eastward through the counties of Pickett, Fentress, Cumberland, Van Buren, Grundy, Franklin.

17. VIRGINIA: All east of and including the counties of Giles (part), Montgomery, Floyd, Patrick.

18. WESTERN NORTH CAROLINA: Through the counties of Rockingham, Guilford, Randolph, Montgomery (part), Stanly, Anson.

¶ 2038. Conferences of the Central Jurisdiction

1. This jurisdiction comprises the Negro Annual Conferences and the Negro Provisional Annual Conferences and Missions in the United States of America.

2. CENTRAL ALABAMA: All Alabama; the part of Florida west of the Apalachicola River.

3. CENTRAL WEST: All Colorado, Montana, North Dakota, South Dakota, Nebraska, Kansas, Missouri, Iowa; western Illinois to U.S. Highway 51 (including towns thereon).

4. DELAWARE: All Delaware and New Jersey; the eastern shores of Virginia and Maryland; all New York except Manhattan and the Bronx in New York City and the city of Buffalo; eastern Pennsylvania to the Susquehanna River (excluding towns thereon).

5. EAST TENNESSEE: Eastern Tennessee through the counties of Scott, Fentress, Cumberland, Van Buren, Grundy, Marion; southwestern Virginia, through the counties of Giles, Montgomery, Floyd, Carroll; in West Virginia the counties of Mercer, Raleigh, Wyoming, McDowell, Logan, Mingo; in Kentucky the counties of Whitley, Knox, Bell, Harlan.

6. FLORIDA: All east of the Apalachicola River.

7. GEORGIA: The entire state.

8. LEXINGTON: All Ohio, Michigan, Indiana, Wisconsin, Minnesota; eastern Illinois to U.S. Highway 51 (excluding towns thereon); all Kentucky except the counties of Whitley, Knox, Bell, Harlan.

9. LOUISIANA: The entire state.

10. MISSISSIPPI: Southern Mississippi through the counties of Issaquena, Sharkey, Humphreys (part), Yazoo, Madison, Leake, Neshoba, Kemper.

11. NORTH CAROLINA: All North Carolina; southern Virginia through the counties of Patrick, Franklin, Pittsylvania (part), Halifax, Charlotte, Prince Edward, Nottoway, Dinwiddie, Prince George, Surry, Isle of Wight, Nansemond, Norfolk, Princess Anne.

12. SOUTH CAROLINA: The entire state.

13. SOUTHWEST: All Arkansas and Oklahoma.

14. TENNESSEE: Western Tennessee through the counties of Pickett, Overton, Putnam, White, Warren, Coffee, Franklin.

15. TEXAS: Eastern Texas through the counties of Brazoria, Ft. Bend, Austin, and parts of Washington, Burleson, Robertson, Limestone, Freestone, Navarro, Ellis, Dallas, Collin, Grayson.

16. UPPER MISSISSIPPI: Northern Mississippi through the counties of Washington, Humphreys (part), Holmes, Attala, Winston, Noxubee.

17. WASHINGTON: Northern West Virginia through the counties of Monroe, Summers, Fayette, Kanawha, Boone, Lincoln, Wayne; northern Virginia through the counties of Elizabeth City, Warwick, James City, Charles City, Henrico, Chesterfield, Amelia, Cumberland, Buckingham, Appomattox, Pittsylvania (part), Bedford, Roanoke, Craig; the District of Columbia; the western shore of Maryland.

18. WEST TEXAS: Through the counties of Matagorda, Wharton, Colorado, Washington (part), Burleson (part), Robertson (part), Limestone (part), Freestone (part), Navarro (part), Ellis (part), Dallas (part), Collin (part), Grayson (part).

¶ 2039. Conferences of the North Central Jurisdiction

1. This jurisdiction comprises the states of Ohio, Indiana, Illinois, Michigan, Wisconsin, Minnesota, Iowa, North Dakota, South Dakota.

2. DETROIT: In Michigan the eastern part of the Lower Peninsula through the counties of Lenawee, Jackson (part), Ingham (part), Shiawassee, Saginaw, Midland (part), Gladwin (part), Roscommon, Crawford, Otsego, Cheboygan; all the Upper Peninsula.

3. ILLINOIS: Central Illinois between and including, on the north, the counties of Whiteside (part), Bureau (part), Putnam, LaSalle (part), Grundy (part), Will (part), Kankakee and, on the south, the counties of Pike, Green (most), Macoupin (part), Montgomery (part), Shelby, Cumberland, Clark.

4. INDIANA: Southern Indiana to U.S. Highway 40 (excluding Terre Haute, Richmond, and the northern part of Indianapolis).

5. MICHIGAN: The western part of the Lower Peninsula through the counties of Hillsdale, Jackson (part), Ingham (part), Clinton, Gratiot, Midland (part), Gladwin (part), Clare, Missaukee, Kalkaska, Antrim, Charlevoix, Emmet.

6. MINNESOTA: The entire state.

7. NORTH DAKOTA: The entire state.

8. NORTH INDIANA: North from U.S. Highway 40 and east from U.S. Highway 421, State Highways 29 and 25, U.S. Highway 31 (including Richmond and the northeastern part of Indianapolis and excluding South Bend).

9. NORTH IOWA: Through the counties of Monona, Crawford (part), Sac, Calhoun, Webster, Hamilton, Hardin, Marshall, Tama, Benton, Johnson (part), Muscatine (part), Scott (most).

10. NORTH-EAST OHIO: Through parts of the counties of Ottawa, Sandusky, Seneca, Wyandot, Marion, Delaware, Licking, Muskingum, Morgan, Washington.

11. NORTHWEST INDIANA: North from U.S. Highway 40 and west from U.S. Highway 421, State Highways 29 and 25, U.S. Highway 31 (including South Bend, Terre Haute, and the northwestern part of Indianapolis).

12. OHIO: Southwestern Ohio through parts of the counties of Ottawa, Sandusky, Seneca, Delaware, Licking, Muskingum, Morgan, Washington.

13. ROCK RIVER: Northern Illinois through parts of the counties of Whiteside, Bureau, LaSalle, Grundy, Will.

14. SOUTH DAKOTA: The entire state.

15. SOUTH IOWA: Through the counties of Harrison, Crawford (part), Carroll, Greene, Boone, Story, Jasper, Poweshiek, Iowa, Johnson (part), Muscatine (most), Scott (part).

16. SOUTHERN ILLINOIS: Through the counties of Calhoun, Greene (part), Macoupin (part), Montgomery (part), Fayette, Effingham, Jasper, Crawford.

17. WEST WISCONSIN: Through the counties of Green, Dane (part), Columbia (part), Marquette (most), Waushara (part), Wood (part), Marathon (part), Taylor, Price, Iron (most).

18. WISCONSIN: Eastern Wisconsin through the counties of Rock, Dane (part), Columbia (part), Marquette (part), Waushara (part), Wood (part), Marathon (most), Lincoln, Oneida, Vilas, Iron (part).

¶ 2040. Conferences of the South Central Jurisdiction

1. This jurisdiction comprises the states of Missouri, Arkansas, Louisiana, Nebraska, Kansas, Oklahoma, Texas, New Mexico.

2. CENTRAL KANSAS: Western Kansas through the counties of Cowley, Butler, Marion, Dickinson, Clay, Washington.

3. CENTRAL TEXAS: The part bounded by and included in the counties of Williamson (most), Bell, Coryell, Hamilton, Milus, Brown, Coleman, Runnels (part), Eastland, Stephens, Young, Palo Pinto, Parker, Tarrant, Ellis, Navarro, Freestone (part), Limestone (part), McLennan.

4. KANSAS: Eastern Kansas through the counties of Chautauqua, Elk, Greenwood, Chase, Morris, Geary, Riley, Marshall.

5. LITTLE ROCK: Southern Arkansas through the counties of Polk, Montgomery, Garland, Saline, Pulaski (part), Lonoke (most), Prairie (most), Monroe (part), Arkansas.

6. LOUISIANA: The entire state.

7. MISSOURI: All north of the Missouri River except the counties of Montgomery, Warren, Lincoln, St. Charles.

8. NEBRASKA: The entire state.

9. NEW MEXICO: All New Mexico; southwestern Texas through the counties of Winkler, Ector, Crane, Pecos, Terrell, Val Verde (part).

10. NORTH ARKANSAS: Through the counties of Scott, Yell, Perry, Pulaski (part), Lonoke (part), White, Prairie (part), Monroe (most), Phillips, Desha (part).

11. NORTH TEXAS: Through the counties of Wichita, Archer, Jack, Wise, Denton, Dallas, Kaufman, Hunt, Hopkins, Franklin, Titus (part), Red River.

12. NORTHWEST TEXAS: Through the counties of Wilbarger, Baylor, Throckmorton, Shackleford, Callahan, Taylor, Nolan, Mitchell, Glasscock, Midland, Andrews.

13. OKLAHOMA: The entire state (excluding the Indian Mission).

14. RIO GRANDE: All Spanish-language work in Texas and New Mexico.

15. ST. LOUIS: Southeastern Missouri through the counties of Lincoln, Montgomery, Osage, Cole, Moniteau (part), Miller, Pulaski, Texas, Howell.

16. SOUTHWEST MISSOURI: Through the counties of Jackson, Lafayette, Saline, Cooper, Moniteau (part), Morgan, Camden, Laclede, Wright, Douglas, Ozark.

17. SOUTHWEST TEXAS: Southern Texas through the counties of Matagorda (part), Wharton (part), Colorado, Fayette, Bastrop, Travis, Williamson (part), Burnet, Lampasas, San Saba, McCulloch, Concho, Runnels (part), Coke, Sterling, Reagan, Upton, Crockett, Val Verde (most).

18. TEXAS: Eastern Texas through the counties of Matagorda (part), Wharton (part), Austin, Washington, Lee, Milam, Falls, Limestone (part), Freestone (most), Henderson, Van Zandt, Rains, Camp, Titus, Bowie.

19. INDIAN MISSION: The Indian pastoral charges and missions in Oklahoma.

¶ 2041. Conferences of the Western Jurisdiction

1. This jurisdiction comprises the states of Washington, Idaho, Oregon, California, Nevada, Utah, Arizona, Montana, Wyoming, Colorado, Alaska, Hawaii.

2. CALIFORNIA-NEVADA: Northern California through the counties of Monterey, Kern (most), Tulare, Fresno, Mono; northwest Nevada through the counties of Elko, Eureka, Nye (most).

3. IDAHO: Southern Idaho through the counties of Adams, Valley, Lemhi; eastern Oregon through the counties of Harney, Grant, Union, Wallowa.

4. MONTANA: The entire state.

5. OREGON: Western Oregon through the counties of Lake, Deschutes, Crook, Wheeler, Umatilla.

6. PACIFIC NORTHWEST: All Washington; northern Idaho through Idaho County.

7. ROCKY MOUNTAIN: All Colorado, Utah, Wyoming; White Pine County, Nevada.

8. SOUTHERN CALIFORNIA–ARIZONA: All Arizona; in Nevada the counties of Lincoln, Clark, Nye (part); southern California through the counties of Inyo, Kern (part), San Bernardino, Los Angeles, Ventura, San Luis Obispo.

9. ALASKA MISSION: The entire state.

10. HAWAII MISSION: The entire state.

11. PACIFIC JAPANESE PROVISIONAL: The work among the Japanese people in the Western Jurisdiction excepting that in the Hawaii Mission.

¶ 2042. Conferences of Africa

AFRICA CENTRAL CONFERENCE comprises:

1. Angola Annual Conference.

2. Central Congo Annual Conference—Sankuru-Lomani region.

3. Rhodesia Annual Conference—Southern Rhodesia.

4. Southeast Africa Annual Conference—Portuguese East Africa (Mozambique); in the Transvaal work among people coming from Portuguese territories.

5. Southern Congo Annual Conference—Katanga region.

¶ 2043. Conferences of Central and Southern Europe

CENTRAL AND SOUTHERN EUROPE CENTRAL CONFERENCE comprises:

1. Belgium Annual Conference—including Dunkirk, France.

2. Czechoslovakia Annual Conference.

3. Switzerland Annual Conference—including German-speaking churches of France.

4. Austria Provisional Annual Conference.

5. Bulgaria Provisional Annual Conference.

6. Hungary Provisional Annual Conference.

7. North Africa Provisional Annual Conference—Algeria, Tunisia, and adjacent territory.

8. Poland Provisional Annual Conference. (*See* ¶ 2007.1.)

9. Madeira Mission—Madeira Islands.
10. Yugoslavia Mission.

¶ 2044.   Conferences of China

CHINA CENTRAL CONFERENCE comprises:

1. East China (formerly China) Annual Conference—the territory of the Wu dialects and Manchuria.

2. Foochow Annual Conference—Foochow Municipality, Futsing, Kutien, Linseng, Mintsing, Pintang Counties, except such portions as are included in the Hinghwa and Yenping Conferences.

3. Hinghwa Annual Conference—the counties of Putien and Sienyu and the adjoining territory where the Hinghwa dialect is spoken.

4. Kiangsi Annual Conference—the province of Kiangsi and that portion of Anhwei Province west of a line drawn north and south through the west wall of the city of Anking, the capital of the province, and also Hwangmei County in Hupeh Province.

5. Mid-China (formerly Central China) Annual Conference —Central China, with its central station at the city of Nanking, on the Yangtze River, excluding the Kiangsi Annual Conference.

6. North China Annual Conference—the northern part of the province of Hopei; the southern part of the province of Chahar.

7. Shantung Annual Conference—the counties of Tsinan, Taian, Szushui, Yenchow, Ningyang, Wensang, Chufu, Tsouhsien, Feicheng, Laiwu, Tungping, Tsining, Tunge in the central part of Shantung Province.

8. West China Annual Conference—the counties of Chengtu, Whayang, Gintang, Jienyang, Tsiyang, Tschung, Meikang, Lochi, Anyoh, Chungkiang, Bahsien, Kiangpeh, Pishan, Yungchwan, Jungchang, Hochwan, Wusheng, Tunknan, Suining.

9. Yenping Annual Conference—in Fukien the counties of Nanping, Sha, Yungan, Mingchi, Shunchang, Sanyuan, Yuki; Kaotan of Chianglo County; Hsia-Shuan-keng of Kutien County.

10. Kalgan Provisional Annual Conference—the city of Kalgan and contiguous territory of the Hopei Province and Inner Mongolia.

11. Taiwan–Hong Kong Provisional Annual Conference—Taiwan (Formosa) and Hong Kong; but see ¶ 2005.5. (See also ¶ 2007.3.)

¶ 2045. Conferences of Germany

GERMANY CENTRAL CONFERENCE comprises:

1. Central Germany Annual Conference—Saxony and Thuringia, including the towns of Halle and Dessau.

2. Northeast Germany Annual Conference—bounded in the west by the Northwest Germany Conference, in the south by the Central Germany Conference, in the east by the boundary of Germany as of 1945. (*See* ¶ 2008.3.)

3. Northwest Germany Annual Conference—bounded in the east by the eleventh degree of longitude, in the south by the fifty-second degree of latitude to the boundary of the Southwest Germany Conference, in the west by the boundary of Germany as of 1945.

4. South Germany Annual Conference—Bavaria, except the Palatinate and Wuerttemberg.

5. Southwest Germany Annual Conference—bounded in the north by a line south of Lippe from Wesel to Hamm; in the east by a line from Hamm to Marburg, Geinhausen, Mosbach, Pforzheim to Lahr.

¶ 2046. Conferences of Latin America

LATIN AMERICA CENTRAL CONFERENCE comprises:

1. Argentina Annual Conference. (*See* ¶ 2007.2.)
2. Chile Annual Conference.
3. Bolivia Provisional Annual Conference. (*See* ¶ 2007.1.)
4. Central America Provisional Annual Conference—Costa Rica, Panama. (*See* ¶ 2007.4.)
5. Peru Provisional Annual Conference. (*See* ¶ 2007.1.)
6. Uruguay Provisional Annual Conference. (*See* ¶ 2007.1.)

¶ 2047. Conferences of Northern Europe

NORTHERN EUROPE CENTRAL CONFERENCE comprises:

1. Denmark Annual Conference.
2. Norway Annual Conference.
3. Sweden Annual Conference.
4. Baltic and Slavic Provisional Annual Conference—Estonia, Latvia, Lithuania.
5. Finland Provisional Annual Conference—Finland except as in § 6.
6. Finland-Swedish Provisional Annual Conference—the Swedish-speaking work in Finland.

¶ 2048. Conferences of the Philippines

PHILIPPINES CENTRAL CONFERENCE comprises:

1. Northern Philippines Annual Conference—the provinces

of Cagayan, Isabela, Nueva Vizcaya, Batanes; the sub-provinces Apayao, Kalinga, Ifugao of Mountain Province.

2. Northwest Philippines Annual Conference—the provinces of Pangasinan, La Union, Ilocos Sur, Ilocos Norte, Abra; northern Nueva Ecija and Tarlac Provinces; the sub-provinces Benguet and Bontoc of Mountain Province; the city of Baguio.

3. Philippines Annual Conference—southern Nueva Ecija and Tarlac Provinces; the provinces of Zambales, Bataan, Pampanga, Bulacan, Rizal, Tayabas; the city of Manila and Quezon City; all provinces south of Manila, including Mindoro, the Bicol provinces, Catanduanes, Visayas, Palawan. (*See* ¶ 2007.6.)

4. Mindanao Provisional Annual Conference—the island of Mindanao and the Sulu Archipelago. (*See* ¶ 2007.1).

¶ 2049. Conferences of Southeastern Asia

SOUTHEASTERN ASIA CENTRAL CONFERENCE comprises:

1. Burma Annual Conference—including the Andaman Islands.

2. Malaya Annual Conference—the Federation of Malaya and Singapore, except as in § 3.

3. Malaysia Chinese Annual Conference—vernacular Chinese work in Malaya, Singapore, and adjacent islands or portions thereof under British or Indonesian government or protection.

4. Sarawak Annual Conference—Sarawak (on the island of Borneo), except as in § 5.

5. Sarawak Iban Provisional Annual Conference—work among the Ibans of Sarawak. (*See* ¶ 2007.5.)

6. Sumatra Provisional Annual Conference. (*See* ¶ 2007.1.)

¶ 2050. Conferences of Southern Asia

SOUTHERN ASIA CENTRAL CONFERENCE comprises:

1. Agra Annual Conference—in Uttar Pradesh the Agra and Meerut Divisions.

2. Bengal Annual Conference—West Bengal; in Bihar the Bhagalpur and Chota Nagpur Divisions.

3. Bombay Annual Conference—all Bombay State.

4. Delhi Annual Conference—Delhi, Punjab (India), Himachal Pradesh, Rajasthan.

5. Gujarat Annual Conference—the state of Gujarat.

6. Hyderabad Annual Conference—Andhra Pradesh.

7. Indus River Annual Conference—in West Pakistan the Punjab and Bahawalpur Divisions. (*See* ¶ 2006.2.)

8. Lucknow Annual Conference—the part of Uttar Pradesh eastward from the civil districts of Bahraich, Gonda, Barabanki, Lucknow, Unnao, Farrukhabad, Etawah; in Bihar the Tirhut and Patna Divisions.

9. Madhya Pradesh Annual Conference—all Madhya Pradesh.

10. Moradabad Annual Conference—in Uttar Pradesh the civil districts of Bijnor, Garwhal, Moradabad, and parts of Rampur, Bareilly, Budaun.

11. North India Annual Conference—in Uttar Pradesh the civil districts of Kumaun, Shahjahanpur, Sitapur, and parts of Rampur, Bareilly, Budaun.

12. South India Annual Conference—Mysore State; Madras City.

13. Karachi Provisional Annual Conference—in West Pakistan the Karachi, Sind, and Baluchistan Divisions. (*See* ¶ 2006.2.)

14. Nepal Mission—the work of The Methodist Church with the United Christian Mission in Nepal.

¶ 2051. Other Work Outside the United States

1. Liberia Annual Conference. (*See* ¶ 2005.1.)

2. Affiliated autonomous churches: The Methodist Church of Mexico, The Methodist Church of Brazil, Korean Methodist Church, United Church of Christ in Japan, United Church of Christ of Okinawa.

GLOSSARY

This glossary, like the Index, is not part of the law of the church, but rather a guide to that law, arranged in alphabetical order for the convenience of readers. So far as possible the definitions are based on the Constitution and legislation, and use the Disciplinary language. Where there is no specific legislation, they are based on historical usage and accepted practice. For terms not defined here, see the Index, where paragraphs containing definitions or definitive information are indicated by boldface type.

Advance. The program for promoting special gifts to missionary causes over and above apportioned world service and conference benevolences. (¶¶ 756-614.)

Affiliate member. A person residing away from home for an extended period who is enrolled in a near-by church for fellowship, pastoral care, and participation in activities, but is still counted as a member of his home church. (¶ 116.)

Affiliated autonomous church. A self-governing church in whose establishment The Methodist Church has assisted and with which it is co-operating through its Board of Missions. (¶¶ 600-5.)

Agency. A council, board, division, commission, committee, or other body established to carry out the connectional work of the church. (¶¶ 1101-1599.)

Appointment. The pastoral charge or other position in the church to which a preacher is assigned by a bishop or, between sessions of the Annual Conference, by a district superintendent. (¶¶ 362 .3, 431-33.)

Apportionment. An amount assigned to a local church or other Methodist body by proper church authority to be raised by that body for some connectional purpose.

Approved supply pastor. A local preacher who on recommendation of the Board of Ministerial Training and Qualifications has been approved by the Annual Conference as eligible for appointment during the ensuing year as a supply pastor of a charge. (¶¶ 314-20.) See Supply pastor.

Area, episcopal. The Annual Conference or Conferences assigned to a bishop for residential and presidential supervision. (¶¶ 37-38, 440.)

Bishop. A general superintendent of The Methodist Church. He is an elder who has been set apart after the manner prescribed in the Discipline for that office. (¶¶ 34-41, 45 i.)

Cabinet. The district superintendents of an Annual Conference acting together as a body under the presidency of the bishop.

Charge, pastoral. One or more churches which are organized under, and subject to, the Discipline, with a single pastoral-charge Quarterly Conference, and to which a minister is or may be duly appointed or appointable as preacher in charge. (¶ 104.)

Church, local. A connectional society of persons who have professed their faith in Christ, have been baptized, have assumed the vows of membership in The Methodist Church, and are associated in fellowship as a local Methodist church in order that they may hear the Word of God, receive the Sacraments, and carry forward the work which Christ has committed to his Church. Such a society of believers, being within The Methodist Church and subject to its Discipline, is also an inherent part of the Church Universal, which is composed of all who accept Jesus Christ as Lord and Saviour, and which in the Apostles' Creed we declare to be the holy catholic Church. (¶ 102.)

Church school. The program of the local church for instructing and guiding its entire constituency in Christian faith and living. It includes Sunday school, the Methodist Sunday Evening Fellowship, weekday activities, and home and extension service. (¶¶ 241-45.)

Circuit. Two or more local churches which are joined together for pastoral supervision, constituting one pastoral charge. (¶ 104.)

College of Bishops. All the bishops assigned to or elected by a Jurisdictional or Central Conference.

Conference, Annual. The basic administrative body in The Methodist Church, having supervision over the affairs of the church in a specific territory, as established by the Jurisdictional or Central Conference. (¶¶ 21-25, 45 x, 621-79.) Also, the territory administered by such a body.

Conference, Central. A representative body outside the United States of America comparable to a Jurisdictional Conference within the United States. (¶¶ 16-19, 45 ii, 541-81.)

Conference, Church. An assembly of the members of a charge or church for review and planning of the church's work, for action on matters requiring a vote of the church membership, and, when so authorized by the Quarterly Conference, for election of church officers. (¶¶ 33, 196-200.)

Conference, District. An assembly held annually in each district where authorized by the Annual Conference. It includes lay and ministerial representatives from each local church (¶ 687) and performs the duties assigned to it. (¶¶ 689-91, 695.)

Conference, General. The legislative body for the entire church, meeting every four years, and having full legislative powers over all connectional matters. It is composed of elected representatives, ministerial and lay, from all the Annual Conferences. (¶¶ 5-10, 45 vii, xi, 501-12.)

Conference, Jurisdictional. The representative body in the United States, established by the Plan of Union, composed of ministerial and lay delegates from the several Annual Conferences of a jurisdiction, and meeting every four years. It elects the bishops and certain members of the general boards of the church. (¶¶ 11-15, 45 iv, 516-35.)

Conference, Provisional Annual. A body similar to an Annual Conference but with powers limited because of insufficient membership. (¶¶ 606-12.)

Conference, Provisional Central. A body similar to a Central Conference but with powers limited because of insufficient membership. (¶¶ 586-92.)

Conference, Quarterly. The governing body of the pastoral charge. (¶¶ 31-32, 137-50.) A Church Quarterly Conference is a body similarly constituted in each local church of a circuit, with authority limited to control of the property of the local church. (¶¶ 152-54, 158.)

Connectional. Of or pertaining to the organization or functioning of The Methodist Church other than on a local-church basis.

Council of Bishops. All the bishops of all the Jurisdictional and Central Conferences of the church. (¶ 36.)

Credentials. The official documents certifying to ministerial ordination.

Deacon. A preacher who, having fulfilled the requirements, has been elected to the order of deacon by an Annual Conference, has taken the vows prescribed, and has been duly ordained by the laying on of the hands of a bishop. (¶¶ 391-93.) A deacon may be either "local" or "traveling." *See* Preacher.

Deaconess. A woman who has been led by the Holy Spirit to devote herself to Christlike service under the direction of the Church, and who, having met the requirements, has been duly licensed, consecrated, and commissioned by a bishop. (¶ 1252.)

Disciplinary. In accordance with the Constitution and laws of The Methodist Church, as set forth in the Discipline.

Discipline. The official and published statement of the Constitution and laws of The Methodist Church, its rules of organization and procedure, the description of administrative agencies and their functions, and the Ritual.

District. The major administrative subdivision of an Annual Conference, established by the Annual Conference and formed by the bishop. It comprises a number of pastoral charges and is under the supervision of a district superintendent. (¶ 431.3.)

District superintendent. A minister appointed by the bishop to travel through a district in order to preach and to oversee the spiritual and temporal affairs of the church. (¶¶ 361-62.)

Elder. A preacher who, having fulfilled the requirements, has been elected to the order of elder by an Annual Conference, has taken the vows prescribed, and has been duly ordained by the laying on of the hands of a bishop and other elders. (¶¶ 401-3.)

Elder, *cont'd:*
This is the second and higher ministerial order in the church. An elder may be either "local" or "traveling." *See* Preacher.

Itinerancy. The system by which The Methodist Church moves its ministers from church to church so that every preacher has a church and every church has a preacher.

Judicial Council. The final court of appeal in The Methodist Church, elected by the General Conference. It determines, on appeal, the constitutionality of any act of a General, Jurisdictional, or Central Conference, and exercises other judicial functions as set forth in the Discipline. (¶¶ 42-44, 901-18.)

Jurisdiction. A major division of The Methodist Church in the United States as established by the Plan of Union, composed of several Annual Conferences, and under the administration of a Jurisdictional Conference. (¶¶ 26, 28, 45 ix.) *See* Conference, Jurisdictional.
NOTE: When the organization into jurisdictions was introduced at the time of Unification in 1939, there was uncertainty whether such a division should be called a "jurisdiction" or a "Jurisdictional Conference." Some of the resulting inconsistencies are still found in the Constitution; but in 1944 all legislation was edited to conform to the popular usage which had by that time become established, to use the word "jurisdiction" except for the administrative body.

Lay speaker. A member of a local church certified by his Quarterly Conference as qualified to conduct services of worship and hold meetings for prayer and exhortation under the direction of his pastor or district superintendent. (¶ 293.)

Layman. A member of a local church. This term applies to a local preacher, even though ordained.

Location. The voluntary or involuntary termination of a minister's membership in an Annual Conference and return to the status of a local preacher. (¶¶ 374-79.)

Member, church. A person who has been baptized and has accepted the baptismal and membership vows, entering into solemn covenant with the members of the church, as provided in the Ritual. (¶¶ 105-16, 1910-16.) *See also* Affiliate member.

Minister. Properly, an ordained traveling preacher. (*See* Order, ministerial; Preacher, traveling.) The term "minister" is generally used in place of "traveling preacher" as the alternative to "layman." It is sometimes loosely used of any ordained preacher, or of any pastor.

Minister on trial. One who, after meeting the conditions prescribed in the Discipline, has been received by vote of an Annual Conference as a probationary member of that body. (¶¶ 321-31.)

Minister in full connection. One who, having satisfactorily completed all the Disciplinary requirements, including the probationary period (except for those received on credentials), has been elected to full membership by an Annual Conference. (¶¶ 341-45.)

Minister in effective relation. One in full connection in an Annual Conference who is under appointment of a bishop.

Minister under special appointment (in detached service). One who has been appointed by a bishop to serve in some capacity other than as pastor or district superintendent. (¶ 432.4-.6.)

Minister, supernumerary. One who because of impaired health or other equally sufficient reason is temporarily unable to perform full work and has been granted this relation by vote of the Annual Conference. (¶ 365.)

Minister, retired (superannuated). One who has been placed in the retired relation by action of his Annual Conference or who has reached the age of seventy-two and therefore has automatically been placed in the retired relation. (¶¶ 367-71.)

Mission. The administrative body of a field of work outside any Annual Conference which is under the care of the Board of Missions and has not yet met the requirements of a Provisional Annual Conference. It exercises in a general way the functions of a District Conference. (¶¶ 1206, 1238.)

Missionary. A minister or layman who, on recommendation of the Joint Committee on Missionary Personnel, has been commissioned by the Board of Missions and assigned to some definite home or foreign field. (¶¶ 1184-86.)

Official Board. The adminstrative body of the local church, responsible to the Quarterly Conference. (¶¶ 206-16.)

Order, ministerial. The rank or status of a person in the Christian ministry. In The Methodist Church ministerial orders are of two classes: deacon's and elder's.

Ordination. The act of conferring ministerial orders. The ritual for ordination is set forth in the Discipline. (¶¶ 1920-21.)

Pastor. A preacher who, by appointment of the bishop or the district superintendent, is in charge of a station or circuit. (¶¶ 351-52.)

Preacher, local. A layman licensed to preach, or ordained, according to the laws of the church. He continues to be a lay member of a local church. (¶¶ 304-20.) *See note under* Preacher, traveling.

Preacher, traveling. One who is on trial or in full connection in an Annual Conference. (¶¶ 321-85.)

NOTE: This term has an interesting historical background. The minister, in early Methodism, who devoted his full time to the work of the ministry and was therefore subject to appointment in first one place, then another, was called a "traveling preacher," in distinction from the "local preacher," who, because he served only part time and earned his livelihood by other means, was tied to a local community and was unable to "travel" or "itinerate."

Reception on credentials. The process by which a minister coming from some other evangelical church is received into mem-

Reception on credentials, *cont'd:*
bership by an Annual Conference, on trial or in full connection, on presentation of his ministerial credentials. (¶¶ 411-13.)

Ritual. The rites and ceremonies which have been authorized for use in the administration of the Sacraments of the Lord's Supper and Baptism, in marriage, burial of the dead, ordination, and other offices for the conduct of public and private worship.

Special. A special gift to a specific benevolence cause, pledged and paid by a local church in addition to its apportioned benevolences. (¶¶ 745, 756-64.)

Steward. A layman charged with certain responsibilities; specifically, an elected or ex officio member of the Quarterly Conference and the Official Board in a local church. (¶¶ 208-11.)

Supply pastor. A preacher appointed to a pastoral charge as a substitute, either because of an emergency between sessions of the Annual Conference or because of a shortage of ministerial members of the conference.

World service. The basic general benevolences of The Methodist Church, approved by the General Conference and apportioned through the Annual Conferences to the local churches. The general agencies supported by world service funds are: the Board of Missions, the Board of Education, the schools of theology, the Board of Evangelism, the Board of Lay Activities, the Board of Christian Social Concerns, the Board of Hospitals and Homes, the Board of Pensions, the Television, Radio, and Film Commission, and the American Bible Society. (¶¶ 741-55.)

INDEX

The numbers refer to paragraphs (¶¶) and to subsections of paragraphs, the subsections being indicated by the figures following decimal points. The paragraphs are arranged according to the following plan:

Numbers in **bold-faced** type indicate main references or definitions.

Admission of preachers, *cont'd:*

On trial, **321-31,** 393, 651.25, 671, 695.3, 1374.1, 1924

Readmission, 362.3, 376, 379, 432.8, 651.34, 993, 1630.15

Ritual, 1924

Adult:

Baptism, 107, 1912

Classes, officers and teachers of, 246.2

Conference director of adult work, 1453, 1454.1

Department of Adult Publications, 1432

District director of adult work, 687, 1460

Division (church school), 235, 243-44, 246.2, 352.5, .7, .22c

Educational program, 1396-98

Funeral service, 1918

Home members, 243

Missionary education, 1287

Reception into church membership, 107-9, 1914

Young adults, 209, 234, 244.1, 352.7, .20, 1397, 1443, 1453, 2029

Advance, 756-61

Committee, General, 757-58

Conference Committee, 755.3

Conference specials, 759

District specials, 759.4

Emergency change, 761.6

Expenses 761.3

One Great Hour of Sharing, 760. *For details see* One Great Hour of Sharing

Promotion, 750.1, 761

Quotas not to be set, 761.1

Remittance of receipts, 758.3, 760.4

Reports, 758.1, .4, 759.5

Special-gift voucher, 746, 758.3, 760.5

Specials, 149.3, 257.5, 266.2, 735, 738, 745-46, 750.1, **756-61,** 805

Treasurer, 761.2

Week of Dedication. *See* One Great Hour of Sharing

Advisory Committee:

Board of Education, 1329.2, 1330.1

Methodist Youth Fund, 1414.2

Advisory members:

Commission on Chaplains, 1572

Advisory members, *cont'd:*

Department of Ministerial Education, 1372.1

Advocate. *See Central Christian Advocate; Christian Advocate*

Affiliate member, 116, 132, 1916

Affiliated autonomous churches, 427, **600-605,** 1205, 1207, 2005.3, 2012.2, 2051.2

Africa:

Annual Conferences, etc., 2042, 2043.7, 2051.1

Central Conference, 2004.1, 2005 .2, 2042

Age:

Church Conference members, 155.5, 160, 186.2, 196-97

Church school, divisions, 244.1, 1402-3

Methodist Youth Fellowship members, 244.5, 1403

Problems of aging, 1535.1

Quarterly Conference members, 138.3, 153.3

Retirement, 368-69, 436, 438, 1617

Stewards, 208, 211

Trustees, 159, 183, 711.1, 728

Youth members of agencies, 1295, 1405, 1443

Aged, home for. *See* Home

Agencies, administrative, 8.8, 15.3, 19.3, 556, 666, 781-84, 1101-8

Accounting, 737.6

Annual Conference, 651.4, .14, **666-79,** 711, 755, 762.2, 793, 804, 807-8, 812, 826, 923, 931, 1158, 1231, 1254, 1256, 1295, 1305, 1371, 1441, 1452-54, 1458, 1478, 1503, 1545, 1561, 1571, 1583, 1590, 1609, 1611

Annuity rates, 737.10

Appeals for funds, 743, 748, 810-11

Appointment, episcopal, of staff, 432.4

Auditing, 737.6, 1180.3

Bishop as member of, 773, 1102, 1105-6

Budgets, 737.2, .3

B

Baccalaureate addresses, 773

Ballot, vote by, 146.1, 501, 504, 518, 628, 695.2-.4, 901, 973, 1238.4, 1505.1

Baltic and Slavic Provisional Annual Conference, 2008.2, 2047.4

Baltimore Annual Conference, 2036.2

Bank account, 267.4, 1611.11. *See also* Depository for funds

Baptism:
Authority to administer, 318, 329, 392, 402
Certificate, 114.2
Children, 114, 1910-11
Church membership, 102, 107, 111, 114, 1910-12
Pastor's duty, 352.2, .24
Register of names, 114.3, 132, 352.24
Report of, 312, 365, 370
Ritual, 1907 note, 1910-12
Significance of, 76-77

Basic salary plan, 801, **827**

Belgium Annual Conference, 2008.1, 2043.1

Beneficiary of trust fund, 708, 711.5

Benevolences, 147, 261, 741-64, 793-97
Advance specials. *See* Advance
Apportionments. *See* Apportionments
Board of Lay Activities program, 1493.4
Conference, 732, **759**, 761, 791, **793-97**, 804, 808
District Conference, 215.3, 689
District superintendent's duties, 147, 362.15g, 689, 762.4, 797
Fellowship of Suffering and Service, 763
Local church, 142.7, 145.8, 147, 215.3, 250.1, 257.5-.7, 261, 266, 268, 288, 1226
Methodist Committee for Overseas Relief, 1312-14
Methodist Television-Radio Ministry Fund, 762
One Great Hour of Sharing, 760

Benevolences, *cont'd:*
Pastor's duties, 352.15, .22h, .27-.28, 762.4, 1226
Promotion, 743-48, 750.64
Special gifts and offerings, 744-47, 758-64, 1312-13. *See also* Advance
Week of Dedication. *See* One Great Hour of Sharing
World service and conference, **804.** *See also* Benevolences: Local church; World service

Bengal Annual Conference, 2050.2

Bequests:
Agencies, administrative, 737.11, 745, 746.5, 1170, 1183.2, 1235.8, 1328, 1354.5, 1409, 1467, 1525.2, 1557, 1605
Annual Conference, 711.2-.4, 1610.2
Committee on Wills and Legacies (local church), 145.10
Committee on Wills, Bequests, and Gifts (general), 737.11
Council on World Service and Finance, 737.11, 785
Institutions, 1352.6, 1558.3
Local church, 145.10, 157.3, 165, 188.3, 362.11
Property in District of Columbia, 710.2
Special gifts, 744-46
Trustees of The Methodist Church, 705-7

Bible:
Church school, 241, 1396
Conference, 1442.1
Minister's use of, 345.9, 352.21, 1920-24
Reading, 97, 222.12, 293.2
Society, 432.4. *See also* American: Bible Society
Sunday, Universal, 278.8, 296.2f
Women, 573

Bishop, 34-41, 45 i, 46.5, .6, 421-46
Addresses of bishops, 1120.8
Administration. *See* Episcopal administration
Agency membership, 750.2, 755.2, 757.1, 1102, 1104-6, 1111, 1113.1, 1116, 1129, 1158.1, 1172.1, 1195, 1210, 1220, 1230.1, 1231.1, 1240.3,

Bishop, *cont'd:*

1252.3, 1255.3, 1256.3, 1268, 1326, 1327.2, 1372, 1415.2-.3, 1417.2, 1418, 1452.2, 1468, 1491.1, 1518-20, 1522, 1553, 1568.1, 1572.2, 1581.2 1586, 1597.1, 2013.1, 2014

Amenability, 435-36, 446.2, 525, 775-76, 922

Appeal to Judicial Council, 525, 910, 925, 927, 930, **1022-43**

Appointments by, 145.2, 351, 393.5-.6, 403.5-.6, 431.4-.6, **432-33,** 437.1, 826.2, 1643.2*e*

Area system, 37-38, 46.6, 440, 526, 560

Assignment of, 20.5, 37-38, 46.6, 435.3, 436.4, 437.1, 439-41, 446, 526, 546, 560.1, 604, 775-76, 2005

Baccalaureate addresses, 773

Central Conference, 8.10, **20,** 34-37, 45 i, vi, 46.5, 422-24, 427, 431, 438, **441-45,** 446.3, 544-47, 557-61, 570, 930, 2004, 2012. *See also* Bishop: Overseas

College. *See* College of Bishops

Committee on Episcopacy, 526

Conference of Methodist Bishops, 427

Consecration of, 35, 45 i, 46.5, 423, 431.9, 442, 445, 1922

Council. *See* Council of Bishops

Credentials, 435.2, 445

Decisions on questions of law, 40, 43, 362.14, 547, 908-9, 918, 1034, 1036.1

Disability, 424, 435.3, 775

Discontinuance, 8.5

Duties, 37-38, 40-41, 188-89, 293.3*c*, 318.1, 352.13, 362.2, 363, 364, 374, 391, 393.5-.6, 401, **431-434,** 602.2, 716.3, 762.1, 803, 924, 931, 933-37, 939, 949, 996, 1009, 1021, 1206.3, 1219.1, 1220, 1224, 1231.1, 1238.4, 1302, 1375, 1444, 1452.1-.3, 1479. *See also* Bishop: Agency membership

Election of, 8.10, 15.2, 19.2, 20.1, 35, 422-23, 441-42, 445, 557-58

Expenses, 769-70, 772-73, 776

Health, 435.3, 775

Honoraria, acceptance of, 773

Jurisdictional Conference, 38, 435-36, 439-40, 524-26, 1105

Lectures, 773

Legal counsel, 1120.4

Bishop, *cont'd:*

Mission administration, 1206, 1238.3-.5

Missionary, **446,** 773

Number of bishops, 439, 441, 557, 2004-5

Office addresses of bishops, 1120.8

Ordination by, 391, 401, 431.9, 1920-21

Overseas, 1172.1. *See also* Bishop: Central Conference

Pensions, 435.2, 769-70, 772, 774-77

Preaching missions, 773

Presiding over conferences, 8.11, 20.3, 41, 431.2, 437.1, 524

Provisional Central Conference, 446.3

Questions of law. *See* Decisions on questions of law

Residence, 440, 526, 560, 712, 770, 772

Resignation of, 435.2

Retired, 8.5, 435-38, 770, 772, 774-76

Salary, 769-70, 772, 774.2, 775-76

Secretary, 1659

Support, 8.5, 15.2, 19.2, 261, 435.3, 559, 769-77, 821-23

Tenure, 526

Term episcopacy, 445, 558, 559.2

Transfer of, 38, 46.6

Travel, official, 427, 770, 773

Trial of, 9.3, 570, 910, **921-30,** 950-52, 1022-43

Widow and orphans of, 769-70, 772, 774, 777

Blanks. *See* Forms

Board:

Annual Conference, 651.4, .14, 666, 679, 711.2, 1120.8, 1643.1, .2*d*, 1658.1*b*. *See also* Agencies, administrative: Annual Conference. *For individual boards see* Conference Board of Christian Social Concerns, etc.

Central Conference, 19.3, 43.4, 556, 580, 906-7, 914

Definition, **783.1***a*

Directors. *See below* Board of Directors

District, 1120.8. *See* District

General, 8.8, 15.3, 43.4, 502, 533, 781-84, 902, 906-7, 914, 1065, 1101-8, 1111, 1113,

Building, *cont'd:*

Insurance, 165.7

Lot, 167-70, 174, 180.8, 722

Maintenance, 145.7, 165, 278.5-.6, 712, 716.2

Memorial, dedication of, ritual, 1940

Methodist Publishing House, 1107, 1156-57

Metropolitan Area Planning Commission, 722.2, 1220

Mortgage, 157.2, **171-73**, 1235.6-.7

Opening for worship, ritual, 1934

Organ, dedication of, ritual, 1935

Parish house, dedication of, ritual, 1936

Parking facilities, 722

Parsonage, 145.7, 180-81, 183, 278.5, 723, 1235.4, .6, 1236.1, .5

Purchase, 157.2, **167-70**, 174, 180, 723-24, 1221, 1235-37

Quarterly Conference authority, 157.2

Remodeling, 157.2, 164.5, 180, 723-24, 1235.4, 1236.1

Rituals for dedication, etc., 1931-40

Sale, 157.2, **171-73**, 175

School, dedication of, ritual, 1938

Section of Church Extension, 1235-37

Site, 180.8, 722, 1237.5

Use of, 165, 233.6*h*

See also Property

Bulgaria Provisional Annual Conference, 2043.5

Bulletin, weekly church, 160, 168, 170, 171.1, 172.1, 180.3, .6, 196

Bureau, 783.1*d*

Bureau of Architecture, Interdenominational, 1569.12

Burial of the dead:

Duty of pastor, 352.2

Report of, 312, 352.22*b*, 374

Ritual, 1907 note, 1918-19

Burma Annual Conference, 2049.1

Business manager, church, 143.11, 209, 212.2, 262.2, 269, 1495

C

Cabinet:

Agency membership, 675, 679, 755.2, 1231.1, 1254.3

Appointment of preachers, 314, 432.1-.2, .5

Called session of Annual Conference, 627

Consultation with, for nominations, 1231.4, 1302.1, 1305.1, 1479.2, 1452.1

District boundaries, 431.3

Election by, 675, 1299, 1453, 1454.1

Emergency financial appeal, 810

Location of minister, 378

Missions and church extension, 1303.2, .3, 1305

Nominations, 669.1, 791, 1231.1, 1444, 1503.1

Recommendation of preachers, 325.3, 393.5-.6

California-Nevada Annual Conference, 2041.2

Call to Evangelism (resolution), 2029

Call to preach, 301-3, 322.5, 352.20, 362.15*g*, 671

Camp Activities, Commission on, 763, 1102, 1593.1

Campaign, financial. *See* Appeal, financial; Canvass, every-member; Fund-raising agent

Camps and conferences:

Conference Committee on, **1454**, 1461.2

Directors, 1461.2

District Committee on, 1454, **1461**

Local church, 233.7*j*, 243

Property, 1442.2-.3, 1454.2, 1461.3-.4

Standards, 1401.4, 1442.1, .3, 1454.2, 1461.2-.4

Campus-Church Relations Committee, 1365.2-.3

Campus Religious Life, Committee on, 1365.2

Church school, *cont'd:*

National Family Week, 250.5, 296.2*b*

New, organizing, 233.6, 251, 257.8, 1407, 1441

Nursery school, 243, 245

Officers and teachers, 231, 233.3, .7, 246, 248-49, 1398.2, 1928

Organization, 243-48

Parent study groups, 243, 2021 .5

Pastor's authority and responsibility, 248.2, 352.5-.7, .17-.20, .22*c-f, i*

Policies, 233.1

Publications, 1132, 1143, **1145-53, 1421-36.** *See also* Church school: Literature

Race Relations Sunday, 250.3, 296.1*b*

Rally Day, 250.2, 296.1*f*

Recognition of officers and teachers, ritual, 1928

Records, 233.4, 243, 362.15*e*

Removal of unsatisfactory officers and teachers, 233.7*b*

Reports, 243, 352.22*c*, 689

Roll, 233.4, 243, 352.22*f*, 1396

Rooms, 233.7*h*, 1401.1

Secretary, 232.1

Special days, 233.7*d*, 250, 296. *See also* Special days

Students, college, 244.5, 1403

Study groups, 243

Sunday school, 243, 244.4, 1396

Superintendents, 143.7-.8, 145.9, 209, 221.1, 232-33, **246-49,** 256, 362.10, .15*e,* 687, 1449, 1461.2

Supervision, 233, 242, 246-48, 251

Vacation and weekday schools, 243

Wesley Foundation, co-operation with, 244.5, 1403

Workers' Conference, 231, 249

World Service Sunday, 215.3, 250.1, 257.5, 296.1*a*

Year, 246

Young Adult Fellowship, 209, 234, 244.1, 352.7, 1397, 1443, 1453

Youth Council, 138.3, 153.3, 209

Youth Division, 145.9, 236, 244-46, 352.5, .7, 1403. *See also* Methodist Youth Fellowship

Circuit, 104, 433

Apportionments, 145.8, 147-48

Circuit, *cont'd:*

Annual Church Conference, 197-99

Charge Board of Lay Activities, 289

Church Quarterly Conferences, 152-54, 158

Commission on Membership and Evangelism, 221.5

Division of, 184

Elections, 143-45

Membership roll, 352.25

Organizing a new church, 155.7

Parish organization, 362.15*i,* 1229.4

Parsonage, 145.7, 183-84

Trustees, 183-84

Citizenship:

Chairman of Christian, Methodist Youth Fellowship, 274 .1, 1518, 1545

Responsibility, 1541.1, 2020 III B.2

City (metropolitan) or district missionary societies, 155.1, 173.2, 432.4, 759.4, **1218-27,** 1295, 1303

City work. *See* Department of City Work

Civil liberties and rights, 1541 .1, 2020 III G

Claim:

Annuity. *See* Annuity: Claim

Pastor's salary, 825

Supernumerary minister's, 365

Class leader, 93, 352.10

Classes:

Church school, 243, 244.4, 246.2

Training in church membership, 114.5, 222.15, 352.22*e*

Classification of educational institutions, 1378.3, 1383-84, **1390,** 1391.2

Clearinghouse (pensions), 431.7, 1619, 1620.1, .7, 1621.1, 1631 .7, 1634.2-.3, 1636

Code of ethics (hospitals and homes), 1566

College:

Appointment to attend, 432.7

College, *cont'd:*

Building, ritual for dedication of, 1938

Campus-Church Relations Committee, 1365.2-.3

Classification, 1383-84, **1390,** 1391.2

Committee on Campus Religious Life, 1365.2

Department of College and University Religious Life, 1351.4, **1363,** 1369-71

Educational requirements for ministry, 307.1, 309.2, 318.1, 323-25, 669-70, 673

Faculty Christian Movement, 1442.1

Financial support, 651.12*f*, 689 .5, 810, 1352.6-.9, 1354-55, 1385-86, 1391.2, 1450, 1452.1, .4

Interconference Commission on College and University Religious Work, 1371, 1448.3

Loan Fund, Student, 250.4, 1358

Methodist Student Movement, **1369-71.** *For details see* Methodist Student Movement

Missionary education, 1287

Promotion of enrollment, 149.1, 233.7*f*, 352.17, 362.15*e,* 689.5

ROTC, 2024.6

Racial policies, 2026.1

Research studies, 1233

Scholarships. *See* Scholarships

Student religious work, 244.5, 1324, **1363-71,** 1403, 1405, 1442.1, 1448.3

Trustees, 711.2, 728

Wesley Foundation, **1364-68.** *For details see* Wesley Foundation

See also Educational institutions; School of theology

College of Bishops:

Called session, Jurisdictional or Central Conference, 523, 544-45

Disability of bishop, 775

Elections by, 1415.2, 1518-19, 1581.2, 2014

Nominations by, 750.2, 1045, 1172.2, 1311, 1519, 1602.1

President, 775, 923-24

Vacancies, filled by, 750.3, **1105,** 1111, 1311, 1553

Colored Methodist Episcopal Church. *See* Christian: Methodist Episcopal Church

Comity agreement, 189.2, 578

Commission:

Annual Conference, 651.4, .14, 666, 679, 1120.8, 1658. *See also* Agencies, administrative: Annual conference. *For individual commissions see* Conference Commission on Christian Higher Education, etc.

Chairman, local church, 143.6, 144, 209, 219.4, 221.1-.2, 232, 256, 262, 274.2, 352.16, 362.10, 1120.8

General, 783.2*a,* 1104, 1120.8, 1658. *See also* Agencies, administrative. *For individual commissions see below* Commission on Camp Activities, etc.

Local church, 142-44, 155.7, 209, 219-76. *For individual commissions see below* Commission on Christian Social Concerns (local church), etc.

Optional, 219.1, 276

Quadrennial, 2012-15

Commission on Camp Activities, 763, 1102, 1593.1

Commission on Chaplains, 393.6, 403.6, 763, 1102, 1404.2, 1415.2, 1417.2, 1476, **1572,** 1593.1, 1618.2*h,* 1671

Commission on Christian Higher Education, (Conference, Area, or Regional) 1375, 1378.2, 1450, **1452.2-.4**

Commission on Christian Social Concerns (local church), 219, 274-75

Commission on Christian Vocations, Conference, 651.4*q,* .14*d,* 670, **675-77**

Commission on Church Union, 765, 1575

Commission on College and University Religious Work, Interconference, 1371, 1448.3

Commission on Communication of the Gospel (Meth-

Committee on Research and Survey, Conference, 1304, 1305.1

Committee on Stewardship:
Interboard, 753.4
Local church, 262.5, 263

Committee on Temperance and General Welfare:
Annual Conference, 1546
Local church, 274.3

Committee on Temperance Education, Joint, 1416

Committee on Town and Country Work:
Annual Conference, 1306. See also Conference Commission on Town and Country work
Interboard, 1230. For details see Interboard Committee on Town and Country Work

Committee on Urban Work, Conference, 1220, 1295, **1305**

Committee on Wills and Legacies (local church), 145.10, 737.11

Committee on Wills, Bequests, and Gifts (general), 737.11

Committee on Woman's Work (Central Conference), 568-69

Committee to re-enlist inactive members, 127.1, 222.9

Communication and publication, director of, 1531.1

Communication of the Gospel, Commission on (Methodist Student Movement), 1468

Communion, Holy:
Ritual, 1908-9
Steward, 143.13
World-wide Communion Sunday, 296.1e, 763
See also Lord's Supper; Sacrament

Community:
Church, 189, 432.4, 1643.2c
Co-operation, 248.4
Service, 248.4, 278.3, 282.2, 1229.1

Complaints. See Judicial administration

Comptroller, Council on World Service and Finance, 737.6

Conference:
Advance specials, 759
Agencies, 651.4, .14, **666-79**, 793, 804, 807-8, 812. For individual agencies see below Conference Board of Christial Social Concerns, etc.
Annual, 21-25, 45 iii, viii, x, 46.4, 621-79. For details see Annual Conference
Annual Church, 32, 197-200. See also Church Conference
Benevolences, **732**, 761, 793-95. For details see Benevolences: Conference
Boards. See Board: Annual Conference; also Conference Board of Christian Social Concerns, etc., below
Central, 16-20, 45 ii, vi, 46.3, 541-82. For details see Central Conference
Christian Education, Methodist, 1400, 1427, 1456
Church, 33, 196-200. For details see Church Conference
Church Quarterly, 152-54, 158
Claimants, 821-23, 1601-57. For details see Pension regulations
Commissions. See Commission: Annual Conference; also Conference Commission on Christian Higher Education, etc., below
Committees. See Committee: Annual Conference; also Conference Committee of Investigation, etc., below
Council, 679
Director. See Director
District, 30, 686-95. For details see District Conference
Evangelist, 353, 363, 432.6, 1474.2, 1480, 1482
Family Life, 1417.1
General, 5-10, 45 vii, xi, 46.1, 501-12. For details see General Conference
Jurisdictional, 11-15, 26, 45 iv, ix, 46.2, 516-35. For details see Jurisdictional Conference
Lay leader, 1505. For details see Lay leader

771

Department of Christian Social Relations, *cont'd:*

Executive secretary, 1244.4, 1248.3, 1280

Standing committee, 1248.3

Department of City Work, 1215, **1217-28**

City (metropolitan) or district missionary societies, 155.1, 173.2, 432.4, 759.4, **1218-27,** 1295, 1303

Conference Committee on Urban Work, 1305

Convocation on Urban Work, 1228, 1305.3

Duties, 1217-18, 1228

Metropolitan Area Planning Commission, 722.2, 1220

Department of College and University Religious Life, 1351.4, **1363,** 1369-71

Department of Educational Institutions, 1351.4, **1353**

Department of Finance and Field Service, 1235.10, **1236**

Department of General Publications, 1432

Department of Goodwill Industries, 432.4, 1215, **1232**

Department of Ministerial Education, 1351.3, **1372-76**

Advisory members, 1372.1

Co-operation with other agencies, 326, 669-70, 1372, 1374-75, 1415

Correspondence courses, 1374.3-.4

Courses of study, 306.4, 307.2, 317.2-.3, 327, 1372.4, 1374. *See further* Courses of study

Director of ministerial education, 1372.2, 1415.2-.3, 1418

Duties, 326, 1372.4, 1374-76

Evaluation of academic credits, 326-27

Organization, 1372, 1376 note

Pastors' schools, 674.2, 1372.4, 1374.2

Reports to, 362.4, .10, 672

Support, 1373

Department of the Ministry, National Council of Churches, 1372.4

Department of Research and Statistics, 657, 765, 1115.1, **1120.5.** *See also* General Minutes; Statistical blanks

Department of Research and Surveys, 1115.1, 1215, **1233,** 1304

Department of Town and Country Work, 1215, **1229-31**

Annual Conference commission, 1231, 1306

Interboard Committee on Town and Country Work, 1230

National Conference on Town and Country Work, 1229.7

Department of Work in Foreign Fields, 1244, **1245**

Administration of a Mission, 1206. *See also* Administration: Mission

Chairman, 1244.3, 1245.1

Committees on Co-ordination, 1202-4

Executive secretaries, 1244.4, 1245.1, 1280

Interdivision Committee on Foreign Work, 1199.2

Methodist Committee for Overseas Relief, 1311-15

Missionaries, 1184-87, 1205-7, 1241. *See also* Missionary

Representatives on other agencies, 1283, 1290.2

Staff chairman, 1283

Standing committee, 1245.1

Department of Work in Home Fields, 1244, **1247,** 1280

Administration of a Mission, 1238. *See also* Administration: Mission

Chairman, 1244.3, 1247.1

Commission on Deaconess Work, 1247.5, 1252-54, 1593.1. *For details see* Commission on Deaconess Work; *also* Deaconess

Committee on Co-operation and Counsel, 1247.4, 1360

Executive secretaries, 1244.4, 1247.1, 1280, 1593.1

Interboard staff committee, Board of Hospitals and Homes, 1247.3, 1567

Interdivision Committee on Work in Home Fields, 1239, 1247.2

772

Executive secretary, *cont'd:*

Deaconess Work, 1252.1*c*, .3
Town and Country Work
(Annual Conference), 1231
.4
Conference Board of:
Education, 362.15*e*, 432.4,
675, 755.2, 1231.1, 1371,
1444, 1446, 1448-49, 1452.2,
1453, 1454.1, 1458, 1460,
1583.2
Missions, 1302.1
Interboard Committee on:
Christian Vocations, 1252.3,
1415.4
Missionary Education, 1288,
1414.2, 1433.2
Preachers' aid society, 432.4
Section of Church Extension,
1289
University Senate, 1388, 1390
Woman's Division of Christian
Service, 1244.4, 1245.1, 1247
.1, 1248.3, 1280
*See further under names of
above agencies*

**Executive session of minister-
ial members,** 646

Exhorter. *See* Lay speaker

Expenses:

Automobile, pastor's, 829
Bishop, 769-70, 772-73, 776
Conference agencies, 812
Current (local church), 148,
173.1, 184, 261, 266-68
District superintendent, 801-2
General Conference, 765, 2012
.4
Hospital and medical, 1681
Jurisdictional Court of Appeals,
1049
Moving to new pastoral charge,
148
Pastor's, 829

Expulsion:

Bishop, 951
Church member, 974-77
Minister, 362.3, 432.8, 651.38*d*,
991-95

**Extension members, church
school,** 233.4, 243

**Extension secretary, church-
school,** 432.4, 1407.2

F

Fact Book, 1120.5

Faculty Christian Movement,
1442.1

Family, Christian:

Christian Home, The, 2021.2
Committee on Family Life:
Annual Conference, 1453
General, 1417
Local church, 234
Conferences on family life, 1417
.1, 2021.5
Courts, family life, 2021.6
Department of the Christian
Family, 1417.1
Director of family life program,
234
Local-church program, 145.11,
233.7*e*, 234, 250.5-.6 2021.5
National Family Week, 250.5,
296.2*b*
Periodical for, 1144. *See also
Together*
Resolutions of General Confer-
ence, 2020 III A, 2021
Upper Room, The, 222.12, 1472,
1485, 2021.2
Woman's Division of Christian
Service, 1242
Worship, 97, 222.12, 1466,
2021.1, .5

Farm and Home, Committee on
(local church), 145.11

Federated church, 189.1, 432.4,
1230.3*d*, 1623.6, 1643.2*c*

**Federation of Methodist Wo-
men, World,** 568

Fellowship:

Committee on Fellowship and
Recreational Life, 236
Evangelism, 222.14
Methodist Men, promotion of,
291.4
Methodist Musicians, National,
1401.3
Methodist Sunday Evening, 243
Methodist Youth. *See* Method-
ist Youth Fellowship
Suffering and Service, 732, 735,
738, 746.2, **763**, 785, 805,
1313, 1572.3
Young Adult, 209, 234, 244.1,
352.7, 1443, 1453

Higher Education, *cont'd:*
Christian, Annual Conference, Area, or Regional, 1375, 1378, 1450, 1452
Committee on Christian, local church, 233.7f
Division of, 1351-75. *For details see* Division of Higher Education
See also Educational institutions

Hinghwa Annual Conference, 2044.3

Historical Societies:
Annual Conference, 663, 1591.1a
Association of Methodist, 1591-92
International Methodist, 1591 .1a, .2a
Jurisdictional, 1591.1a, 1592

Historical statement, *pages 3-6*

History, Committee on Records and, 145.4, 689

Holston Annual Conference, 2037.5

Holy Communion. *See* Lord's Supper

Home:
Farm and, Committee, 145.11
Fields, Department of Work in, 1247. *For details see* Department of Work in Home Fields
Fields, Interdivision Committee on Work in, 1239
For aged, children, or youth, 278.3, 362.15d, 432.4-.5, 689.8, 1535.1, 1551, 1554.1, 1556, 1558-66, 2026.1. *See also* Board of Hospitals and Homes; Institutions
Missions, Section of, 1214-33. *For details see* Section of Home Missions
Ritual for dedication of, 1939
The Christian, 2021.2
See also Family

Hong Kong, 2005.5, 2007.3, 2044.11

Honoraria, bishop's acceptance of, 773

Honorary steward, 211

Hospital:
Appeal for funds, special, 810-11. *See also* Golden Cross
Appointment to serve in, episcopal, 432.4-.5
Board of Hospitals and Homes, 1551-67. *For details see* Board of Hospitals and Homes
Chaplain, 432.4, 1572. *See also* Chaplain
Committee on Hospitals and Homes (local church), 278.3
District superintendent's duty, 362.15d, 689.8
Golden Cross, 278.3, 296.3a, 651.16, 1558.4, 1559
Racial policies, 2026.1
Ritual for dedication of, 1937
See also Institutions

Hospitalization and Medical Expense Program, 1681

Hospitals and homes steward, 143.14, 256, 274.1, 278.3

Housing:
Christian social concern, 1541.1, 2020 III A
Project, chaplain in, 432.4

Hungary Provisional Annual Conference, 2043.6

Hyderabad Annual Conference, 2050.6

Hymnal, The Methodist, 8.6, 1569.5, 1571.3c, 2014

Hymnbooks, church-school, 233.3

I

Iban. *See* Sarawak Iban Provisional Annual Conference

Idaho Annual Conference, 2008.1, 2041.3

Ill, visitation of, 215.5, 222.8. *See also* Visitation

Illinois Annual Conference, 2039.3

Immigration, 1538.1

Inactive church member, 127, 220, 222.9

Local preacher, *cont'd:*

Student, pretheological, 307.1, 309.2

Termination, 304, 311, 994

Transfer, 308-9

Trial of, 945, **957-65,** 981, 1051-52

Withdrawal under complaints or charges, 981

Location of minister, 310, 362.3, **374-79,** 412, 432.8, 636-37, 651.38, 1630.15*a*

Lord's Supper:

Authority to administer, 318, 329, 392, 402, 1376 note

Communion steward, 143.13

Fellowship of Suffering and Service offerings, 763

Pastor's duty, 352.2, 1907

Ritual for, 1908-9

Significance of, 76, 78

World-wide Communion Sunday, 296.1*e*, 763

Lotteries, 272, 2022.2

Louisiana Annual Conference (C), 2038.8

Louisiana Annual Conference (SC), 2040.6

Louisville Annual Conference, 2037.7

Love feasts, 352.8

Lucknow Annual Conference, 2050.8

M

Madeira Mission, 2043.9

Madhya Pradesh Annual Conference, 2050.9

Maine Annual Conference, 2036.7

Maladministration, 356, 947-49

Malaya Annual Conference, 2049.2

Malaysia Chinese Annual Conference, 2049.3

Manuals:

Church-school, 242, 244.3, 248.1

Worship, 1569.2

Manuscripts for publication, 1143

Marriage:

Authority to solemnize, 318, 329, 352.2, 392, 402

Counseling, 352.6, 355-56, 2020 III A, 2021.3*ab*

Divorce, 356, 2020 III A, 2021.3*d*

Mixed, 352.6, 2021.3*b*

Planned parenthood, 1535.1, 2020 III A, 2021.3*c*

Register of, 352.24

Report of, 312, 365, 370

Pronouncements on, 2020 III A, 2021

Ritual for, 1907 note, 1917

Study groups, 233.7*e*, 2021.3*a*

Materials for Training for Church Membership, Joint Committee on, 1418

Medical care, 1535.1

Medical Expense Program, Hospitalization and, 1681

Membership:

Agencies, administrative, 1101-4, 1111. *See also under individual agencies*

Annual Conference. *See* Annual Conference: Membership

Church. *See below* Membership, church

Church school, 132, 233.4, 243, 1396

Commission on. *See* Commission on Membership and Evangelism

Commissions, local church, 143.6, 144, 219, 221.1, 232.1, 256, 262.2, 274, 276

Conferences: General, Jurisdictional, Central, District. *See* Delegates

Cultivation superintendent (church school), 143.8, 232, 246.1

Methodist Youth Fellowship, 244.5, 1403

Ministerial. *See* Ministry

Official Board, 207

Quarterly Conference, 138, 153

Rolls:

Church. *See below* Membership, church: Rolls

Neglected Areas, Interboard Committee on Ministry to, 1164.1

Negro education, 250.3, 1335, 1352.7, 1357

Nepal Mission, 2050.14

New church. *See* Organization: New local church

New England Annual Conference, 2036.8

New England Southern Annual Conference, 2036.9

New Hampshire Annual Conference, 2036.10

New Jersey Annual Conference, 2036.11

New Mexico Annual Conference, 2040.9

New York Annual Conference, ence, 2036.13

New York East Annual Conference, 2036.13

Newark Annual Conference, 2036.14

News of Methodism. *See* Commission on Public Relations and Methodist Information

Nominating Committee:
Annual Conference, 755.2, 791, 1231.1, 1295, 1478.2, 1545
Board of Education, 1327.2-.3
See also Nominations: Committee on

Nominations:
Committee on (local church), **143-45**, 155.6, 160-61, 183, 208, 212.1, **278.1**, 352.16
From the floor, 143-44, 145.1, 160-61, 212.1, 278.1
Judicial Council candidates, 901
See also Nominating Committee *and under name of nominating body*

Non-violent resistance, 2020 III F.3

North Africa Provisional Annual Conference, 2043.7

North Alabama Annual Conference, 2037.10

North Arkansas Annual Conference, 2040.10

North Carolina Annual Conference (C), 2038.10

North Carolina Annual Conference (SE), 2037.11

North Central Jurisdiction, 26, 2039

North China Annual Conference, 2044.6

North Dakota Annual Conference, 2039.7

North Georgia Annual Conference, 2037.12

North India Annual Conference, 2050.11

North Indiana Annual Conference, 2039.8

North Iowa Annual Conference, 2039.9

North Mississippi Annual Conference, 2037.13

North Texas Annual Conference, 2040.11

Northeast Germany Annual Conference, 2008.1, .3, 2045 .2

North-East Ohio Annual Conference, 2039.10

Northeastern Jurisdiction, 26, 2036

Northern Europe Central Conference, 2047

Northern New York Annual Conference, 2036.15

Northern Philippines Annual Conference, 2048.1

817

Ritual, *cont'd:*

Licensing persons to preach, 1923
Lord's Supper, 1908-9
Matrimony, 1917
Methodist Hymnal, The, inclusion in, 2014
Opening of a church for worship, 1934
Ordination:
Deacon, 1920
Elder, 1921
Organizing a church, 1930
Reception of members:
Adults, 1914
Affiliate, 1916
By transfer, 1916
Children, youth, 1915
Preparatory, 1913
Recognition:
Choristers, 1929
Church-school officers and teachers, 1928
Revision of, 1901 note, 1907 note

Rock River Annual Conference, 2039.13

Rocky Mountain Annual Conference, 2041.7

Roll call, 506, 521, 645

Rolls (local church):
Affiliate membership, 116, **132**
Constituency, 114.4, 132
Membership, 114.5, 121-27, 130-33, 155.5, 222.18
Preparatory membership, 114, 132

Rotation in office, 210, 1104, 1326

Rules. *See* General Rules; Restrictive Rules

Rural work. *See* Town and country work

Ryukyu Islands (Okinawa), mission work, 2051.2

S

Sabbatical leave, 364, 432.9, 647, 651.41, 668, 1252.8, 1618.2*f*

Sacraments, 76-78, 101-2
Administration of, 352.2, 362 .15*h*, 1376 note, 1907

Sacraments, *cont'd:*

Authority to administer, **318,** 329, 392, 402, 1374.4
Ritual for, 1908-12
See also Baptism; Lord's Supper

Safety, traffic, 1535.1

St. Louis Annual Conference, 2040.15

Salary:
Approved supply pastor, 317.2- .3, 1631.1
Basic plan, 801, **827**
Bishop, 769-70, 772, 774.2, 775-76. *See also* Bishop: Support
Board staff, 1120.2
Christian Social Concerns, 1530
Education, 1148, 1327.8
Missions, 1179.2, 1181.2, 1201, 1212, 1243, 1269
Publication. *See* Salary: Methodist Publishing House
Claim of pastor, 365, 825
Conference agency personnel, 812
Deaconess, 1252.4*b*
District superintendent, 801-2. *See also* District Superintendent: Support
Editor of church-school publications and assistants, 1148
Methodist Publishing House editors and executives, 1132
Minimum, 317.2-.3, 826, 1252 .4*b*, 1295, 1631.1
Minister in special appointment, 812, 830
Pastor. *See* Pastor: Salary
Withholding from, 774.3, 1646 .1, 1656.4*a*
World service agency personnel, 1120.2
See also Ministerial support

Sarawak Annual Conference, 2049.4

Sarawak Iban Provisional Annual Conference, 2007.5, 2049.5

Scholarships:
Crusade, 257.11, 760.1, .3, **1290**
National Methodist, 250.4, 1358
Television, Radio, and Film Commission, 1581.4*e*